Masaaki Kurosu (Ed.)

Human-Computer Interaction

Technological Innovation

Thematic Area, HCI 2022
Held as Part of the 24th HCI International Conference, HCII 2022
Virtual Event, June 26 – July 1, 2022
Proceedings, Part II

Springer

Editor
Masaaki Kurosu
The Open University of Japan
Chiba, Japan

ISSN 0302-9743   ISSN 1611-3349 (electronic)
Lecture Notes in Computer Science
ISBN 978-3-031-05408-2   ISBN 978-3-031-05409-9 (eBook)
https://doi.org/10.1007/978-3-031-05409-9

This Springer imprint is published by the registered company Springer Nature Switzerland AG
The registered company address is: Gewerbestrasse 11, 6330 Cham, Switzerland

Foreword

Human-computer interaction (HCI) is acquiring an ever-increasing scientific and industrial importance, as well as having more impact on people's everyday life, as an ever-growing number of human activities are progressively moving from the physical to the digital world. This process, which has been ongoing for some time now, has been dramatically accelerated by the COVID-19 pandemic. The HCI International (HCII) conference series, held yearly, aims to respond to the compelling need to advance the exchange of knowledge and research and development efforts on the human aspects of design and use of computing systems.

The 24th International Conference on Human-Computer Interaction, HCI International 2022 (HCII 2022), was planned to be held at the Gothia Towers Hotel and Swedish Exhibition & Congress Centre, Göteborg, Sweden, during June 26 to July 1, 2022. Due to the COVID-19 pandemic and with everyone's health and safety in mind, HCII 2022 was organized and run as a virtual conference. It incorporated the 21 thematic areas and affiliated conferences listed on the following page.

A total of 5583 individuals from academia, research institutes, industry, and governmental agencies from 88 countries submitted contributions, and 1276 papers and 275 posters were included in the proceedings to appear just before the start of the conference. The contributions thoroughly cover the entire field of human-computer interaction, addressing major advances in knowledge and effective use of computers in a variety of application areas. These papers provide academics, researchers, engineers, scientists, practitioners, and students with state-of-the-art information on the most recent advances in HCI. The volumes constituting the set of proceedings to appear before the start of the conference are listed in the following pages.

The HCI International (HCII) conference also offers the option of 'Late Breaking Work' which applies both for papers and posters, and the corresponding volume(s) of the proceedings will appear after the conference. Full papers will be included in the 'HCII 2022 - Late Breaking Papers' volumes of the proceedings to be published in the Springer LNCS series, while 'Poster Extended Abstracts' will be included as short research papers in the 'HCII 2022 - Late Breaking Posters' volumes to be published in the Springer CCIS series.

I would like to thank the Program Board Chairs and the members of the Program Boards of all thematic areas and affiliated conferences for their contribution and support towards the highest scientific quality and overall success of the HCI International 2022 conference; they have helped in so many ways, including session organization, paper reviewing (single-blind review process, with a minimum of two reviews per submission) and, more generally, acting as goodwill ambassadors for the HCII conference.

This conference would not have been possible without the continuous and unwavering support and advice of Gavriel Salvendy, founder, General Chair Emeritus, and Scientific Advisor. For his outstanding efforts, I would like to express my appreciation to Abbas Moallem, Communications Chair and Editor of HCI International News.

June 2022   Constantine Stephanidis

HCI International 2022 Thematic Areas and Affiliated Conferences

Thematic Areas

- HCI: Human-Computer Interaction
- HIMI: Human Interface and the Management of Information

Affiliated Conferences

- EPCE: 19th International Conference on Engineering Psychology and Cognitive Ergonomics
- AC: 16th International Conference on Augmented Cognition
- UAHCI: 16th International Conference on Universal Access in Human-Computer Interaction
- CCD: 14th International Conference on Cross-Cultural Design
- SCSM: 14th International Conference on Social Computing and Social Media
- VAMR: 14th International Conference on Virtual, Augmented and Mixed Reality
- DHM: 13th International Conference on Digital Human Modeling and Applications in Health, Safety, Ergonomics and Risk Management
- DUXU: 11th International Conference on Design, User Experience and Usability
- C&C: 10th International Conference on Culture and Computing
- DAPI: 10th International Conference on Distributed, Ambient and Pervasive Interactions
- HCIBGO: 9th International Conference on HCI in Business, Government and Organizations
- LCT: 9th International Conference on Learning and Collaboration Technologies
- ITAP: 8th International Conference on Human Aspects of IT for the Aged Population
- AIS: 4th International Conference on Adaptive Instructional Systems
- HCI-CPT: 4th International Conference on HCI for Cybersecurity, Privacy and Trust
- HCI-Games: 4th International Conference on HCI in Games
- MobiTAS: 4th International Conference on HCI in Mobility, Transport and Automotive Systems
- AI-HCI: 3rd International Conference on Artificial Intelligence in HCI
- MOBILE: 3rd International Conference on Design, Operation and Evaluation of Mobile Communications

List of Conference Proceedings Volumes Appearing Before the Conference

http://2022.hci.international/proceedings

Preface

Human-Computer Interaction is a Thematic Area of the International Conference on Human-Computer Interaction (HCII). The HCI field is today undergoing a wave of significant innovation and breakthroughs towards radically new future forms of interaction. The HCI Thematic Area constitutes a forum for scientific research and innovation in human-computer interaction, addressing challenging and innovative topics in human-computer interaction theory, methodology, and practice, including, for example, novel theoretical approaches to interaction, novel user interface concepts and technologies, novel interaction devices, UI development methods, environments and tools, multimodal user interfaces, human-robot interaction, emotions in HCI, aesthetic issues, HCI and children, evaluation methods and tools, and many others.

The HCI Thematic Area covers three major dimensions, namely theory, technology, and human beings. The following three volumes of the HCII 2022 proceedings reflect these dimensions:

- Human-Computer Interaction: Theoretical Approaches and Design Methods (Part I), addressing topics related to theoretical and multidisciplinary approaches in HCI, design and evaluation methods, techniques and tools, emotions and design, and children-computer interaction
- Human-Computer Interaction: Technological Innovation (Part II), addressing topics related to novel interaction devices, methods and techniques, text, speech and image processing in HCI, emotion and physiological reactions recognition, and human-robot interaction.
- Human-Computer Interaction: User Experience and Behavior (Part III), addressing topics related to design and user experience case studies, persuasive design and behavioral change, and interacting with chatbots and virtual agents.

Papers of these volumes are included for publication after a minimum of two single-blind reviews from the members of the HCI Program Board or, in some cases, from members of the Program Boards of other affiliated conferences. I would like to thank all of them for their invaluable contribution, support, and efforts.

June 2022   Masaaki Kurosu

Human-Computer Interaction Thematic Area (HCI 2022)

Program Board Chair: **Masaaki Kurosu,** The Open University of Japan, Japan

- Salah Ahmed, University of South-Eastern Norway, Norway
- Valdecir Becker, Federal University of Paraiba, Brazil
- Nimish Biloria, University of Technology Sydney, Australia
- Zhigang Chen, Shanghai University, China
- Yu-Hsiu Hung, National Cheng Kung University, Taiwan
- Yi Ji, Guangdong University of Technology, China
- Tsuneo Jozen, Osaka Electro-Communication University, Shijonawate, Japan
- Masanao Koeda, Okayama Prefectural University, Japan
- Hiroshi Noborio, Osaka Electro-Communication University, Neyagawa-shi, Japan
- Michiko Ohkura, Shibaura Institute of Technology, Japan
- Katsuhiko Onishi, Osaka Electro-Communication University, Shijonawate, Japan
- Vinícius Segura, IBM Research, Rio de Janeiro, Brazil
- Mohammad Shidujaman, American International University-Bangladesh, Bangladesh

The full list with the Program Board Chairs and the members of the Program Boards of all thematic areas and affiliated conferences is available online at

http://www.hci.international/board-members-2022.php

HCI International 2023

The 25th International Conference on Human-Computer Interaction, HCI International 2023, will be held jointly with the affiliated conferences at the AC Bella Sky Hotel and Bella Center, Copenhagen, Denmark, 23–28 July 2023. It will cover a broad spectrum of themes related to human-computer interaction, including theoretical issues, methods, tools, processes, and case studies in HCI design, as well as novel interaction techniques, interfaces, and applications. The proceedings will be published by Springer. More information will be available on the conference website: http://2023.hci.international/.

General Chair
Constantine Stephanidis
University of Crete and ICS-FORTH
Heraklion, Crete, Greece
Email: general_chair@hcii2023.org

http://2023.hci.international/

Contents – Part II

Text, Speech and Image Processing in HCI

Human-Robot Interaction

Novel Interaction Devices, Methods and Techniques

VR Interface for Accumulation and Sharing of Knowledge Database in Neurosurgery

Ryuichiro Akehasu[1], Takahiro Fuchi[1], Ayuki Joto[2], Masahiro Nonaka[3], Katsuhiko Onishi[1], and Tsuneo Jozen[1(✉)]

[1] Osaka Electro -Communication University, Neyagawa, Japan
jozen@osakac.ac.jp
[2] Feature Architecture Software Technology, Osaka, Japan
[3] Kansai Medical University, Hirakata, Japan

Abstract. In the field of neurosurgery, a variety of knowledge has been accumulated through a lot of surgery experiences. Due to the difficulty of expression, not all of the points that skilled neurosurgeons pay attention to during neurosurgery and the detailed precautions and procedures obtained from experience have been clearly stated and shared. Postoperative reports, incident reports, and accident reports are effective means of recording and sharing empirical knowledge, but they are costly to analyze. So, new methods of knowledge sharing are needed. In this study, we propose an interface based on Virtual Reality as a new interface. In order to construct a virtual reality interface, we utilize the VR Head Mounted Display. By projecting a model of a human head made by 3D Computer Graphics technology in a virtual reality space, we can grasp the structure more accurately. It is also possible to see at the same time the empirical knowledge that neurosurgeons accumulate through surgery while confirming the surgical procedure. The VR Head Mounted Display makes the experience more immersive. In addition, Head Mounted Display has been put into practical use, and its operating functions have been improved. Therefore, it is easy to operate and can be used as an interface for recording according to neural medical ontology. In order to accumulate and share the empirical knowledge of neurosurgeons, we investigated a 3D brain model interface using Virtual Reality.

Keywords: Virtual reality · Head mounted display · Neurosurgery

1 Introduction

1.1 Research Background

In the field of neurosurgery, a variety of knowledge has been accumulated through surgery. For example, in the resection of brain tumors, it is necessary to make an

Supported by JSPS Grant-in-Aid for Scientific Research JP20K12086.

incision while avoiding the normal brain, important cranial nerves, and cerebral blood vessels in order to reach the diseased part, and there are a wide variety of things that must be taken into account during surgery. If the tumor has invaded the cerebral nerves or cerebral blood vessels, the operation should be performed just in time to avoid affecting the cerebral nerves or cerebral blood vessels, and if the tumor has invaded a particularly important part of the brain, the tumor may be left in place and the head closed. If too much of the tumor is left, the risk of recurrence is higher, but the risk of damaging important parts of the brain is lower. On the other hand, if the resection area is widened and the tumor is removed almost to the nerves and blood vessels of the brain, the nerves and blood vessels of the brain are cut open, which increases the risk of causing a medical accident, but lowers the risk of recurrence. This decision is based on the experience of the physician. The sharing of such empirical knowledge is done in various ways.

In October 2002, all hospitals and clinics with beds were required to establish an accident reporting system [1]. This has made it necessary for hospitals and bedside clinics to take measures for improvement to ensure safety in medical care, such as accident reporting in medical institutions. A reporting mechanism has been introduced. This has made it necessary for hospitals and bedside clinics to take measures for improvement to ensure safety in medical care, such as accident reporting in medical institutions, and many hospitals have now introduced a reporting system using incident[1] reports and accident[2] reports. Incident reports and accident reports often contain the empirical knowledge of physicians, and their analysis and sharing are said to be useful in preventing medical accidents. In large medical institutions, conferences are held on a regular basis to share empirical knowledge by utilizing electronic medical records, postoperative reports, and the aforementioned incident reports and accident reports.

However, it cannot be said that these reports are being used to the fullest extent due to problems such as the busyness of doctors and nurses. Doctors and nurses need to devote time to analysis while performing their normal daily duties, and the time they can devote to analysis is extremely limited for doctors and nurses who are busy with their normal duties alone. This analysis is highly dependent on the person in charge, with accuracy and efficiency varying greatly depending on the individual, and the empirical knowledge gained from the reports varies from analyst to analyst. Research has been conducted on dig-

---

[1] Refers to cases that have been experienced as near misses or surprises in daily practice, and are potential cases that have the potential to develop into adverse medical events, although they did not actually cause injury to the patient in most cases [2].

[2] An event, whether preventable or caused by negligence, in which an inappropriate medical act (including a failure to perform a necessary medical act) in the course of medical treatment results in an unintended injury to a patient and the course of the injury is affected to a certain degree. An event in which an inappropriate medical act (including a failure to perform a necessary medical act) in the course of medical care results in unintentional injury to a patient, whether preventable or due to negligence, and the course of the injury has a certain degree of impact [2].

itization of these reports and automation of the analysis, for example, research on text mining methods for incident report analysis [3].

In addition to the use of these reports, new methods have also been studied. In their study, Fujita et al. [4]. examined the ability of non-experts to accurately identify adverse events in a prospective survey of medical records using a simple questionnaire, and examined methods to reduce review costs. In this study, the effectiveness of the questionnaire was confirmed by the improvement in the detection rate of adverse events even by non-experts in medical record review.

These results indicate that existing reports are highly effective in sharing physicians' empirical knowledge, but at the same time, there is a problem in terms of analysis cost, and a new method of sharing empirical knowledge is required.

In neurosurgery, DICOM data, including MRI and CT, and 3DCG technology using them are used for surgical planning and medical treatment, and 3DCG technology has become indispensable during surgery, such as intraoperative navigation systems and research on superimposed displays using AR technology [5].

For example, StealthStation [9], an intraoperative navigation system used for surgical planning before and during surgery, integrates medical images such as CT^3, MRI^4, CTA^5, MRA^6, $fMRI^7$, PET^8, $SPECT^9$ and other medical images, and provides an interface that allows detailed data and subtle expressions to be represented by 3D models. The interface using 3D models can easily grasp relative positions in physical space, and can be used by physicians with specialized knowledge to obtain more information intuitively.

However, even with preoperative surgical planning and simulation using 3DCG technology, the preoperative condition may change at the time of surgery due to disease progression and brain shift associated with craniotomy. Under these conditions, neurosurgeons use their empirical knowledge to remove tumors while avoiding cranial nerves and large blood vessels that are difficult to identify with the naked eye.

We have therefore developed a knowledge base (hereinafter referred to as "BrainCGpedia") that utilizes 3DCG technology as a method for sharing the empirical knowledge of neurosurgeons in order to efficiently obtain empirical knowledge about surgical procedures and surgical sites. We have been conducting research on neurosurgical support that focuses on the empirical knowledge of doctors [6–8].

---

[3] Computed Tomography.
[4] Magnetic Resonance Imaging.
[5] CT Angiography.
[6] MR Angiography.
[7] functional MRI.
[8] Positron Emission Tomography.
[9] Single Photon Emission Computed Tomography.

1.2   The Purpose of This Research

In our previous research, we have studied interfaces for sharing empirical knowledge and proposed ontologies for storing and sharing empirical knowledge. As an interface, we proposed a display interface for empirical knowledge using a 3D brain model, and a non-contact interface that considers hygiene for operation during surgery. As an ontology, we defined nodes for disease parts, cases, and surgical procedures, and defined arrows to show the relationship between them and labels to add other detailed information, referring to medical ontology (see Fig. 1).

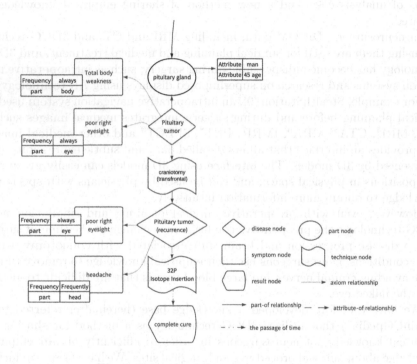

Fig. 1. Example of the proposed ontology

For the proposed ontology, we evaluated whether the proposed ontology can be used to represent cases based on past cases. It was shown that the proposed ontology could be used to represent some past cases.

In this paper, we report on the interface of BrainCGpedia using HMD[10], which can be operated and viewed more intuitively when handling 3D models, in addition to the usual interface on the web.

---

[10] Head Mounted Display.

1.3   Structure of this Paper

Sect. 2 describes the contents of this study, and Sect. 3 summarizes and discusses future issues.

2   Research Content

2.1   Consideration of Usage Model

In this study, we considered the use of a 3D brain model because it is necessary to accurately represent the positional relationships of the brain and brain blood vessels, which are composed of complex structures. This 3D brain model should be a standard brain model, not a specific model created from DICOM data such as CT and MRI of actual patients. Therefore, in this study, we examined the use of the brain model (see Fig. 2) and cerebrovascular model (see Fig. 3) of BodyParts3D, which is based on TARO [10], a numerical human model database.

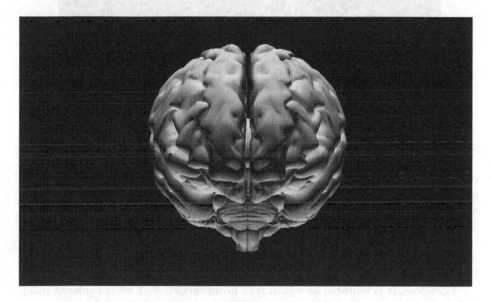

Fig. 2. BodyParts3D brain model

In particular, the cerebrovascular model included a large number of blood vessels, such as those in the eye and face. However, when representing the diseased part of the brain and cerebral blood vessels, these models were not used in this study because the relationship between the brain and cerebral blood vessels would be difficult to understand due to information overload.

In addition, in the representation of diseases in which the brain blood vessels are the diseased part, such as aneurysms, the representation was divided into

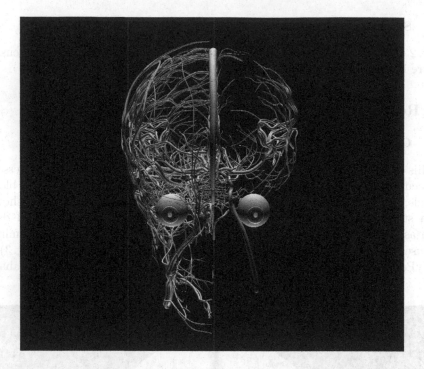

Fig. 3. BodyParts3D cerebrovascular model

arteries and veins in order to add diversity to the representation of the intricately intertwined brain blood vessels.

We also examined the use of the 3DCG database of the Department of Neurosurgery, Faculty of Medicine, University of Tokyo [11] (hereinafter referred to as the Head 3DCG Database). The 3DCG models published in this database can be used free of charge for non-commercial research or educational purposes. The 3DCG model of the head in the database is used as a basic blueprint for bionic humanoids[11]. The 3DCG model of the head is an anatomical polygon model of the head of a healthy Asian male adult, which was created based on the specimen data and the findings of several textbooks and doctors.

Therefore, it is suitable as a standard brain model, and we considered using it, but decided not to use it because 3DCG is not currently available.

2.2 Consideration of HMD

BrainCGpedia is a system that uses 3D models. Therefore, in order to enable more intuitive operation when viewing 3D models, we investigated the use of HMDs and their controllers. Learning and work support using HMDs in VR and AR spaces are considered to be useful [12–14].

---

[11] An elaborate human body model with sensors that can be used as a substitute for humans or laboratory animals.

In addition, in recent years, a place for interaction using VR space has been created VRChat is a social VR platform that was released in 2017. It does not necessarily require the use of a VR device such as an HMD; it can be used on a desktop PC. It also allows users to create their own avatar models in the VR space. horizon Workrooms is a VR workspace that was released in 2021. The PC and keyboard in the real space can be reflected in the VR space, and the PC screen can be displayed in the VR space. It can also be used as an online conference room by inviting other users, and it has a whiteboard function, which can be used like a real whiteboard by using the VR controller as a pen.

This kind of interaction platform using VR space is one of the sharing places that BrainCGpedia aims to create, and the construction of the interface using VR devices is the first step.

VRHMD include the Oculus Quest 2 released by Meta, the VIVE Pro 2 released by HTC, and the VALVE INDEX released by Valve. PlayStation VR released by Sony is also one of them, but it requires PlayStation4 or PlayStation5 to use, so it is excluded from this comparison.

The performance of Oculus Quest 2, VIVE Pro 2, and VALVE INDEX is shown in the table.

Table 1. Performance of Oculus Quest 2.

Screen resolution	One eye : 1832 × 1920
Refresh rate	60 Hz, 72 Hz, 90 Hz
Tracking system	Inside out
External sensor	Unnecessary

Table 2. Performance of VIVE Pro 2.

Screen resolution	One eye : 2448 × 2448
Refresh rate	90 Hz, 120 Hz
Tracking system	Outside in
External sensor	SteamVR base station 2.0

Table 3. Performance of VALVE INDEX.

Screen resolution	One eye : 1440 × 16000
Refresh rate	80 Hz, 90 Hz, 120 Hz, 144 Hz
Tracking system	Inside out
External sensor	Unnecessary

There are several types of tracking methods for HMD, and the tracking methods for the VRHMD that we have studied are inside-out and outside-in. In their research, Ishii et al. [15]. studied the tracking method using a camera and a marker, and the attempt and application of the tracking method in the plant maintenance field among the tracking methods to realize the augmented reality. In the inside-out method, a camera is attached to the user, and by capturing a set of feature points in the environment, the position and direction of the camera in the environment are obtained, and the position and direction of the user are recognized. In HMD, the position is estimated from the built-in camera and sensors, and no external terminal is required. In the outside-in method, a camera is fixed in an environment where the position and direction are known in advance, and the camera takes a picture of the user wearing the feature point group to recognize the position and direction of the user as the relative position from the camera. In the case of HMD, the position is estimated by recognizing the HMD with an external camera or sensor, and an external camera or sensor needs to be installed separately from the HMD. In this study, we decided to use Oculus Quest 2, which is an inside-out system with few spatial limitations, because it is intended to be used in a hospital.

2.3 Consideration of Interface

As mentioned above, we considered the use of 3D models in BrainCGpedia. In order to do so, we considered the use of HMD, and studied an interface that would allow us to access 3D models more intuitively, and constructed an interface(see Fig. 4) assuming the use of Oculus Quest 2 as the HMD. First, we implemented the VR space in Three.js to support VRHMD.

By viewing the brain model in the VR space, we can understand the brain structure in more detail. Since the viewing in the VR space is a virtual space, it is possible to select the part of the brain to be displayed, to make it transparent, and to enlarge the diseased part to simplify and observe the complex brain structure.

In order to represent empirical knowledge, we investigated an interface that allows cutting the model. Figure (see Fig. 5) shows a prototype of the cutting function created on a trial basis using Unity [16].

In this prototype, a rod-shaped object is used as a scalpel, and when the rod-shaped object intersects the brain model, the model is cut at the intersection point. The model used in this study is a surface model, and this new prototype implements a mechanism to generate a new surface by joining the vertices at the cut points and stretching the mesh.

By changing the angle of this bar-shaped object, you can cut not only vertically but also horizontally and diagonally (see Fig. 6). A high degree of freedom in interface is possible by linking the stick-like object to the HMD controller and moving it.

This makes it possible to record the actual surgical procedure and reproduce it, as well as to simulate the surgery by using the model generated from DICOM, which facilitates the understanding of the internal structure.

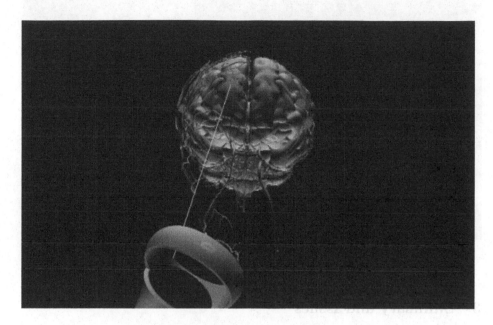

Fig. 4. Interface using HMD

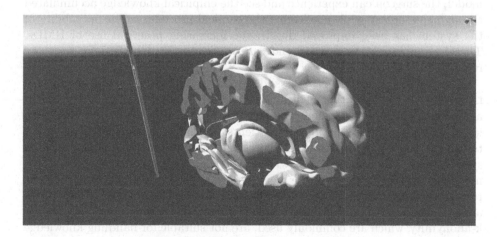

Fig. 5. A brain model cut vertically.

Fig. 6. A brain model cut horizontally.

3   Summary and Issues

In this paper, we investigated a 3D brain model interface using VR to accumulate and share the empirical knowledge of neurosurgeons. We propose a VR interface as a new interface. In order to construct the VR interface, HMD is utilized. In addition, by projecting a model of a human head made by 3DCG technology in the VR space, we can grasp the structure more accurately. Also, by cutting the model, the surgeon can experience and see the empirical knowledge accumulated through the surgery while confirming the surgical procedure. The operability of the system has been improved due to the increasing practical use of HMDs. Therefore, it is easy to operate and can be used as an interface for ontology recording.

The interface in this report is designed to be viewed only by doctors themselves. Therefore, the medical information handled in this study is not anonymized. However, the medical information handled in this study contains a lot of information that can identify patients. In the future, it will be necessary to carefully consider the handling of personal information when constructing a system for sharing empirical knowledge. For example, the rarer the case, the more easily the individual can be identified, but the empirical knowledge of the rare case is more important and should be shared widely, making it difficult to anonymize. In our current study, we believe that anonymization methods such as k-anonymity, which are commonly used, are not suitable for handling knowledge about rare cases. Therefore, as a first step of anonymization, we are considering to set some sharing levels and anonymize the data according to the disclosure range. For example, the data should be disclosed to the physician in charge including the medical team, the physician's office, the physician's hospital, the outside of the hospital, and the entire medical staff, and the information to be disclosed should be restricted and anonymized according to the scope.

References

1. Partial Revision of the Ordinance for Enforcement of the Medical Service Act for Medical Safety Measures. https://www.mhlw.go.jp/topics/bukyoku/isei/i-anzen/2/kaisei/index.html. Accessed 25 Jan 2022
2. Guidelines for the Management of Medical Proposals. https://www.jcho.go.jp/wp-content/uploads/2017/07/20170728anzenshishin.pdf. Accessed 29 Jan 2022
3. Okabe, T., Yoshikawa, T., Furuhash, T., Takesii, F.: Proposal of multi-connection hierarchical text mining method for incident report analysis. In: Proceedings of the Fuzzy System Symposium of the Japan Intelligent Information Fuzzy Society, vol. 22, pp. 54–54 (2006)
4. Fujita, S., Hirao, T., Ikeda, S., Kaneko, T., Hasegawa, T., Tomonori Hasegawa, F.: Research to accurately and efficiently grasp adverse events by reviewing medical records. J. Jpn. Soc. Med. Manag. **10**(4), 563–569 (2010)
5. Nishimoto, W., Kitazono, Y.: Proposal of 3D user interface using hand gestures. In: Proceedings of the Kyushu Chapter Joint Conference of the Electrical Society of Japan, pp. 189–190 (2017)
6. Fuchi, T., Joto, A., Onishi, K., Tsuneo, J.: 3D brain model interface for neurosurgery support database. In: IEICE Conference Proceedings (CD-ROM) (Institute of Electronics, Information and Communication Engineers Society Conference Proceedings (CD-ROM)) (2021)
7. Joto, A., Fuchi, T., Onishi, K., Tsuneo, J.: Examining interfaces for accumulating and utilizing knowledge to support neurosurgery. In: Proceedings of the 25th Annual Meeting of the Virtual Reality Society of Japan (2020)
8. Joto, A., Fuchi, T., Noborio, H., Onishi, K., Nonaka, M., Tsuneo, J.: Construction of a knowledge base for empirical knowledge in neurosurgery. In: International Conference on Human-Computer Interaction, pp. 521–537 (2021)
9. Jesus, M., et al.: Neuronavigation software to visualize and surgically approach brain structures. In: Proceedings of the Sixth International Conference on Technological Ecosystems for Enhancing Multiculturality, vol. 5, pp. 405–409 (2018)
10. Information on providing numerical human model data. https://emc.nict.go.jp/bio/data/index.html. Accessed 22 Jan 2022
11. The University of Tokyo Neurosurgery Head 3DCG Database. https://brain-3dcg.org. Accessed 29 Jan 2022
12. Tainaka, K.: Issues related to work support using augmented reality technology. In: The 25th Annual Meeting of the Virtual Reality Society of Japan (Mixed Reality Study Group Doctoral Consortium) 1B2-2 (2020)
13. Shibata, T., Harada, M.: Proposal of first aid learning using an optical transmissive head-mounted display. Educ. Media Stud. **23**(2), 35–45 (2017)
14. Oda, J., Mitoma, H.: Attempt of active tour training by feedback video teaching materials using VR/AR technology. Med. Educ. **52**(3), 253–258 (2021)
15. Ishii, H.: Plant maintenance work support using augmented reality. Image Lab **22**(2), 1–7 (2011)
16. Unity. https://unity.com/ja. Accessed 10 Feb 2022

BubbleBoard: A Zoom-Based Text Entry Method on Smartwatches

Gennaro Costagliola[1], Mattia De Rosa[1]([⊠]), Vittorio Fuccella[1],
and Benoît Martin[2]

[1] Department of Informatics, University of Salerno,
Via Giovanni Paolo II, 84084 Fisciano, SA, Italy
{gencos,matderosa,vfuccella}@unisa.it
[2] LCOMS, University of Lorraine, Metz, France
benoit.martin@univ-lorraine.fr

Abstract. We present a novel text entry method for smartwatches named *BubbleBoard*. It is based on a soft keyboard with a QWERTY layout in which some characters are in a big font and can be entered with a single touch, while other characters are in a small font and a touch enlarges the pressed character and its neighbors, so that they can be entered with a second touch.

Different variants of the method, regarding the use of a static or dynamic layout and the input of space/backspace with keys or gestures were evaluated through a user study, with the one with a dynamic layout and space/backspace keys resulting as the fastest.

This variant was then compared to *ZoomBoard*, an existing text entry method for smartwatches based on key magnification. The experiment showed a 33% advantage in text entry speed in favor of *BubbleBoard*. In particular, participants typed at 10.7 wpm with *BubbleBoard* and at 8.0 wpm with *ZoomBoard*.

Keywords: Text entry · Wearables · Smartwatches · User study

1 Introduction

Text entry on smartwatches is challenging, primarily due to the small size of their touchscreen. As the popularity of this kind of devices is increasing, a lot of research is being carried out on their input methods, from both industry and academia, to improve them. Despite these efforts, there is still a gap in comfort and efficiency between small touchscreens and bigger devices (smartphones, tablets, etc.). More generally, a common problem for touch-based text entry methods is the reluctance of the users to learn new keyboard layouts [20].

Since a full keyboard layout does not fit well a small screen, researchers adopted two common actions already used for maps: zoom and pan. *ZoomBoard* [15] is a zoom-based soft keyboard. Zoom is performed through a first touch to enlarge a part of the keyboard. Then, a character from the enlarged area is

© The Author(s), under exclusive license to Springer Nature Switzerland AG 2022
M. Kurosu (Ed.): HCII 2022, LNCS 13303, pp. 14–27, 2022.
https://doi.org/10.1007/978-3-031-05409-9_2

entered through a second touch. This additional zooming step, however, increases the time required to select each key. In fact, the recorded average number of keystrokes needed to enter a single a character is 2.15, i.e. a user needs more than two interactions to input a character.

Popular pan-based methods are Splitboard [12] and Driftboard [17]. In the former, the QWERTY layout is split into two (partially overlapping) parts along the vertical axis. The user can only visualize one part at a time and move between them with a swipe gesture. The advantage of this technique is that swipes are not so frequent, thus keeping low the key stroke per character. In the latter, the QWERTY layout can be *dragged* across the display. There is a cursor (a circle) fixed on the left side of the display, and the user can enter a character by dragging the keyboard until the corresponding key is placed under the cursor.

Different approaches include: DualKey [11], in which each key contains two characters and the selection depends on which finger (index/middle) touches the screen; SwipeBoard [2], an eyes-free text entry method in which two swipes are used to enter each character; WatchWriter [10], where the user can input by tapping on a key or by *swiping* through keys to write a whole word with a single gesture; C-QWERTY [3, 4] an adaptation of the classic layout in which the keys are arranged along the edge of a circular screen. It supports both tapping and gesture interaction modes. The *Optimal-T9* [16] and *T18* [6] soft keyboard are QWERTY-based variation of the original *T9* method; other methods also exploit handwriting [5].

The purpose of this paper is to introduce and evaluate a soft-keyboard for smartwatches, which is an improvement of the zoom-based methods. *Bubble-Board* is a soft keyboard for smartwatches with a QWERTY layout enhanced for small screens. In particular, some characters on the keyboard are in a big font and allow entering the corresponding character with a single touch, while other characters are in a small font and a touch enlarges the pressed character and its neighbors, so that they can be entered with a second touch.

In order to evaluate the extent of the improvement over previous zoom-based methods, we compared *BubbleBoard* with *ZoomBoard* [15] in a user study. In a previous user study, we compared different competing variants of the method in order to choose the best one.

The paper is organized as follows: Sect. 2 describes *BubbleBoard* and its design choices, Sects. 3 and 4 show its experimental evaluation. Finally, Sect. 5 concludes the paper with a discussion on future work.

2   BubbleBoard

While designing the method, we choose the QWERTY layout as a basis so that users would not be required to learn a new layout. We also decided to show a maximum of four large characters in the first two lines of the keyboard, and a maximum of five in the last line (since it has only seven characters) so that we can assign to the large characters a width (including left and right padding) equal to one-sixth of the screen. This is supported by two factors: firstly, six keys per line are already used in the literature (in SplitBoard [12]); secondly, in a short informal test [6] of layouts with 4–8 keys per line, tapping keys became difficult with 7 or more keys.

We also made the following design choices:

- small characters should always be grouped in at least two consecutive characters, otherwise their size would be too small to allow easy selection;
- the first and last characters of each line should always be large because otherwise in case the user would tap on the second (small) character of the line, there would not be enough space to allow the magnifying (at the exact point where the user touched) of that character without making the next one disappear.

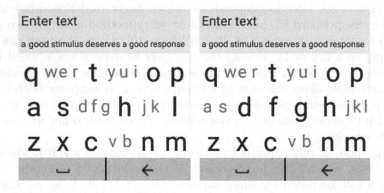

Fig. 1. *BubbleBoard* static layout (left) and example expansion of the *f* character (right).

Once these constraints were fixed, it was then necessary to choose the best layout regarding which characters are shown in large font and which in small font. To this end we used an English corpora [8,9] to choose, among all the possible layouts that respect the above constraints, the layout minimizing the number of touches. Figure 1 shows the selected layout and an example character expansion.

Although the user causes the layout to change when s/he taps on one of the small characters, the initial layout is restored immediately after a character is entered (with a second tap). For this reason we call this variant of the method "the static mode".

We also designed a dynamic mode, in which after a character is entered, the user is shown a new layout in which, based on the written text, the next key is most likely to be among the big ones. To this end, we built a simple predictive model on an English corpora [8,9], based on the last three typed characters. Although the dynamic mode theoretically has a lower key stroke per character (1.16 versus 1.38 of the static layout), it might be difficult to use because the continuous layout changes while typing can confuse the user.

Lastly, regarding the space and backspace keys, in addition to the use of dedicated keys as an additional last keyboard row, we also introduced the possibility to replace these keys with a swipe gesture to the right and to the left, respectively.

3 First User Study

In order to select the most promising *BubbleBoard* variant, we conducted a user study to compare the modes (static/dynamic) and the space/backspace entry methods (key/gesture).

3.1 Methods

Participants. For the experiment, we recruited 20 participants (5 female). They were all university students in Computer Science, between 22 and 28 years old ($M = 23.75$, $SD = 1.83$), who agreed to participate for free. Two of them were left-handed, but everyone decided to use the right hand to perform the experiment. All declared medium or high proficiency with English and a high level of experience with smartphones, and most of them at least a basic experience with smartwatches.

Apparatus. The experiment was conducted on a ASUS ZenWatch 2 equipped with a Snapdragon Wear 2100 Quad Core 1.2 GHz processor and running the Wear OS operating system (see Fig. 2). The device weighs 60 g and has a square display with a 1.63" diagonal and a resolution of 320×320 pixels.

Fig. 2. The ASUS ZenWatch 2 running the BubbleBoard application *(Dynamic Key)*.

The experimental software was a Wear OS application implementing the four variants of *BubbleBoard* (*Static Key, Static Gesture, Dynamic Key, Dynamic Gesture*). At startup, the application asked the participant to choose the desired variant. After that, the application showed the chosen keyboard and the sentence to transcribe. After entering the sentence, the participant can confirm the entered text by performing a long press over the transcribed text placed at the top of the screen. Once confirmed, the application showed the next sentence (or asked the participant to transcribe the same sentence again, if the threshold of 15% of non-corrected errors was exceeded).

Procedure. Before starting the experiment, participants were instructed on the aims and procedures of the experiment; they were then asked to complete a brief survey asking age, gender, dominant hand, level of proficiency with English and with the use of smartphones and smartwatches.

The experiment was conducted in a well-lit laboratory. Participants were asked to wear the device on the non-dominant arm and to perform the tasks while remaining seated, possibly placing the arm on a desk. They had a short practice session to get familiar with the keyboards and the experiment settings before starting the recorded tasks. Participants were given all the recommendations related to the experiment, and in particular to:

- read and memorize the sentence before starting to transcribe it;
- balance speed and accuracy while typing;
- correct mistakes made while entering text. Since the only way to correct errors is by using the backspace key, they were also told to avoid correcting errors noticed only after having already entered other words.

Each participant had to transcribe 7 short sentences for each of the four *BubbleBoard* variant (the first 2 sentences were used as practice and not recorded). For each participant, the sentences were chosen at random from the set by MacKenzie and Soukoreff [14], which includes English sentences without punctuation or numbers. At the end of each 7 sentence block, participants were allowed to rest for a few minutes.

After completing this phase, participants were asked to fill a System Usability Scale (SUS) [1] questionnaire for each of the two modes they tried (Static and Dynamic). SUS includes ten statements, that alternate between positive and negative, to which respondents have to specify their level of agreement using a five-point Likert scale. Each SUS questionnaire has a score between 0 and 100, which was averaged on all participants. Finally, they were asked to fill a questionnaire, in which they where asked their preferred *BubbleBoard* mode and their feedback in open form.

Design. The experiment was a two-factor within-subjects design. The two factors were the keyboard mode and the space/backspace entry method. The keyboard mode included two levels: the *Static* mode and the *Dynamic* mode, while the space/backspace entry method included two levels: *Key* and *Gesture*. Our dependent variables were text entry speed, accuracy and the keystrokes per character (KSPC). In particular, the text entry speed was measured in words per minute (wpm) as specified in [13] and the accuracy was measured in terms of *total error rate* (TER) and *non corrected error rate* (NCER) [19]. Moreover, to counterbalance keyboard mode and space/backspace entry method, we arranged the experiments according to the order shown in Table 1.

Table 1. Counterbalancing scheme used in the first user study.

Participants	Order
1, 5, 9, 13, 17	Static Key, Static Gesture, Dynamic Key, Dynamic Gesture
2, 6, 10, 14, 18	Dynamic Key, Dynamic Gesture, Static Key, Static Gesture
3, 7, 11, 15, 19	Static Gesture, Static Key, Dynamic Gesture, Dynamic Key
4, 8, 12, 16, 20	Dynamic Gesture, Dynamic Key, Static Gesture, Static Key

3.2   Results

All participants completed the experiment. For each participant, the experiment lasted about 25 min. We tested significance using an analysis of repeated variance measures (ANOVA) [7].

Speed. The text entry speeds (in wpm) are shown in Fig. 3. The grand mean was 10.6 wpm. Participant were fastest with *Dynamic Key* (11.4 wpm), followed by *Dynamic Gesture* (10.9 wpm), *Static Key* (10.0 wpm), and *Static Gesture* (9.8 wpm). This is probably due to the fact that in Dynamic mode participants were successfully helped by the layout predictive model.

From the ANOVA resulted that the effect of the keyboard mode on speed was statistically significant ($F_{1,19} = 13.619$, $p < .005$). However, there was no significant effect for space/backspace entry method ($F_{1,19} = 0.659$, ns) and for the interaction between keyboard mode and space/backspace entry method ($F_{1,19} = 0.466$, ns).

Accuracy. Average values for TER and NCER are shown in Fig. 4.

For TER the grand mean was 9.2%. *Dynamic Gesture* was the most accurate variant with a mean TER of 7.0%, followed by *Static Gesture* (9.3%), *Static Key* (9.9%), and *Dynamic Key* (10.5%). This is probably due to the fact that in Dynamic mode it was more likely for participants to make errors when the system changes the layout. However, from the ANOVA no statistically significant effect resulted neither for keyboard mode ($F_{1,19} = 1.034$, $p > .05$), nor for space/backspace entry method ($F_{1,19} = 2.965$, $p > .05$) nor for the interaction between keyboard mode and space/backspace entry method ($F_{1,19} = 2.532$, $p > .05$).

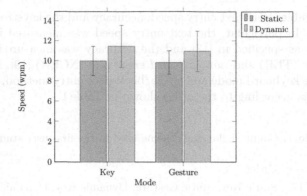

Fig. 3. First user study: text entry speed of *BubbleBoard*. Error bars show the standard deviation.

For NCER the grand mean was 0.6%. All variants achieved an NCER of less than 1%, and also in this case the *Dynamic Gesture* was the most accurate variant with a mean NCER of 0.4%. In fact, from the ANOVA no statistically significant effect resulted neither for keyboard mode ($F_{1,19} = 2.938, p > .05$), nor for space/backspace entry method ($F_{1,19} = 3.854, p > .05$) nor for the interaction between keyboard mode and space/backspace entry method ($F_{1,19} = 1.998, p > .05$).

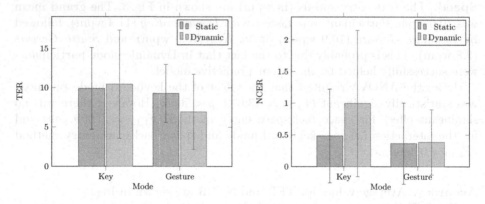

Fig. 4. First user study: total error rate (left) and non corrected error rate (right). Error bars show the standard deviation.

KSPC. Average values for keystrokes per character are presented in Fig. 5. The grand mean was 1.540. As expected the Dynamic mode had a lower KSPC at 1.419, with Static mode at 1.662.

From the ANOVA resulted that the effect of the keyboard mode on KSPC was statistically significant ($F_{1,19} = 77.259, p < .0001$), while the effect of space/backspace entry method ($F_{1,19} = 4.010$, $p > .05$) and interaction between between keyboard mode and space/backspace entry method ($F_{1,19} = 2.461$, $p > .05$) were not statistically significant.

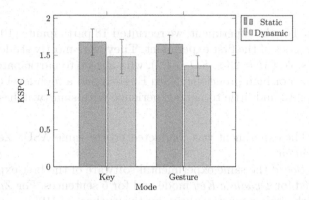

Fig. 5. First user study: keystrokes per character of *BubbleBoard*. Error bars show the standard deviation.

User Satisfaction and Free-form Comments. As regards user satisfaction, the mean SUS score was 86.38 ($SD = 10.18$) for the Static mode and 84.75 ($SD = 14.09$) for the Dynamic mode. A Wilcoxon matched-pairs signed-ranks test [18] performed on SUS scores revealed no statistical significant difference between the two techniques ($Z = -0.2831$, $p > .05$). This trend was not confirmed by the final questionnaire, where 13 participants preferred the *Dynamic* mode and 7 preferred the *Static* mode.

From the open-feedback questionnaire we noticed that, most of the participants who chose the *Dynamic* mode appreciated it for allowing faster typing. On the other hand, most of the participants that preferred the *Static* mode appreciated the fact that they could easily remember the size (small/large font) and position of characters on the keyboard. Finally, some participants complained about the fact that text correction is only possible through backspace, and asked to be able to freely position the text cursor to make corrections.

3.3 Discussion

Given these results, we could conclude that the dynamic mode showed the most promising performance, with the reduced number of required taps compensating for the higher difficulty and likelihood of errors. The use of gestures for space and backspace doesn't seem instead to bring benefits over the classic keys.

4 Second User Study

After selecting the most promising variant of *BubbleBoard* (*Dynamic Key*), we decided to compare it with *ZoomBoard* [15], an existing text entry method for smartwatches based on key magnification. As described in Sect. 1, however, *ZoomBoard* requires two touches for each character entry. To this end we conducted a second user study, in which we compared *BubbleBoard* with *ZoomBoard* over multiple text entry sessions.

Participants. For the experiment, we recruited 18 participants (10 female), different from the ones of the first experiment. They were mostly students, between 18 and 32 years old ($M = 23.8$, $SD = 4.2$), who agreed to participate for free. All declared medium or high proficiency with English and a high level of experience with smartphones, and little to none experience with smartwatches.

Apparatus. The experiment was conducted on the same ASUS ZenWatch 2 of the first experiment.

For *BubbleBoard* the same experimental software of the first experiment was used, configured for *Dynamic Key* mode and for 5 sentences. For *ZoomBoard* an application with similar functionalities by the authors of [12] was used.

Procedure. The procedure was similar to the one of the first experiment.

In this case, however, each participant had to perform a total of three sessions, where the task of each session was to transcribe 5 short text sentences (from the set by MacKenzie and Soukoreff [14]) for each of the two keyboard (*BubbleBoard* a *ZoomBoard*). At the end of each session, participants were allowed to rest for a few minutes.

After completing the three sessions, participants were asked to fill a System Usability Scale (SUS) questionnaire for each of the two keyboards, their preferred keyboard (for speed, accuracy, and overall) and their feedback in open form.

Design. The experiment was a two-factor within-subjects design. The two factors were the keyboard and the session. The keyboard included two levels: *BubbleBoard*, and *ZoomBoard*. The dependent variables were the same as in the first experiment. Moreover, to counterbalance the two keyboard layouts, we arranged the sessions according to the order shown in Table 2.

Table 2. Counterbalancing scheme used in the second user study.

Participants	Session 1	Session 2	Session 3
1, 3, 5, ..., 17	*BubbleBoard-ZoomBoard*	*ZoomBoard-BubbleBoard*	*BubbleBoard-ZoomBoard*
2, 4, 6, ..., 18	*ZoomBoard-BubbleBoard*	*BubbleBoard-ZoomBoard*	*ZoomBoard-BubbleBoard*

4.1   Results

All participants completed the experiment. For each participant, the experiment lasted about one hour. We tested significance using an analysis of repeated variance measures (ANOVA).

Speed. The text entry speeds (in wpm) are shown in Fig. 6. The grand mean was 9.4 wpm. *BubbleBoard* was the fastest keyboard layout with a mean of 10.7 wpm, outperforming *ZoomBoard* at 8.1 wpm. In fact, as can be seen from the Figure, *BubbleBoard* significantly outperforms *ZoomBoard* in every session. Moreover for both keyboards there is a slight speed increase between sessions. On the third (last) session *BubbleBoard* reached 11.2 wpm, while *ZoomBoard* 8.4 wpm.

From the ANOVA resulted that the effect of the keyboard on speed was statistically significant ($F_{1,17} = 75.417$, $p < .0001$). The effect of the session on the speed was also statistically significant ($F_{2,34} = 4.206$, $p < .05$), while the interaction between keyboard and session was not statistically significant ($F_{2,34} = 0.195$, ns).

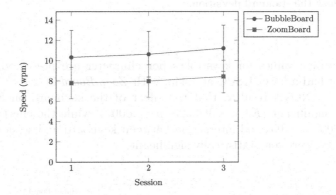

Fig. 6. Second user study: text entry speed of *BubbleBoard* and *ZoomBoard*. Error bars show the standard deviation.

Accuracy. Average values for TER and NCER are shown in Fig. 7.

For TER the grand mean was 6.6%. *ZoomBoard* was the more accurate keyboard with a mean TER of 4.0%, while *BubbleBoard* reached 9.3%.

From the ANOVA resulted that the effect of the keyboard on TER was statistically significant ($F_{1,17} = 26.882$, $p < .0001$), while the effect of session ($F_{2,34} = 2.126$, $p > .05$) and interaction between keyboard and session ($F_{2,34} = 0.661$, ns) were not statistically significant.

For NCER the grand mean was 1.5%. There was little difference between *ZoomBoard* at 1.7% and *BubbleBoard* at 1.4%. In fact, from the ANOVA no statistically significant effect resulted neither for keyboard ($F_{1,17} = 1.366$, $p > .05$), session ($F_{2,34} = 0.216$, ns) and the interaction between keyboard and session ($F_{2,34} = 0.028$, ns).

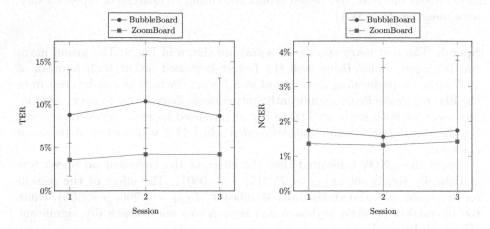

Fig. 7. Second user study: total error rate (left) and non corrected error rate (right). Error bars show the standard deviation.

KSPC. Average values for keystrokes per character are presented in Fig. 8. *BubbleBoard* had a lower KSPC at 1.443, with *ZoomBoard* at 2.168.

From the ANOVA resulted that the effect of the keyboard on KSPC was statistically significant ($F_{1,17} = 366.325$, $p < .0001$), while the effect of session ($F_{2,34} = 3.200$, $p > .05$) and interaction between keyboard and session ($F_{2,34} = 1.888$, $p > .05$) were not statistically significant.

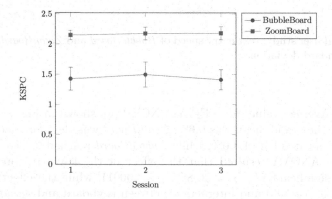

Fig. 8. Second user study: keystrokes per character of *BubbleBoard* and *ZoomBoard*. Error bars show the standard deviation.

User Satisfaction and Free-form Comments. As regards user satisfaction, the mean SUS score was 70.7 (SD = 12.5) for *ZoomBoard* and 66.1 (SD = 15.0) for *BubbleBoard*. A Wilcoxon matched-pairs signed-ranks test performed on SUS scores revealed no statistical significance between the two techniques (Z = −1.1361, p > .05). In the final questionnaire we obtained mixed results, with 61.1% of the participants preferred *BubbleBoard* regarding speed, 77.8% who preferred *ZoomBoard* regarding Accuracy, and 55.6% who preferred *BubbleBoard* overall. Given the differences in performance between the two keyboards, we expected a stronger preference for *BubbleBoard* by the participants, but we believe that the greater possibility of making errors in *BubbleBoard* influenced this result.

Through the open-feedback questionnaire some participants asked to further improve the dynamic layout prediction, while one lamented its presence.

4.2 Discussion

In this second experiment, slower speeds were detected for *BubbleBoard* than in the first experiment. This can likely be attributed to the greater experience with smartwatches and technology in general for the first experiment's participants (all Computer Science students).

Participants had significantly higher error totals with *BubbleBoard* than *ZoomBoard*, although in terms of non-corrected errors the difference was not significant. This may indicate a greater difficulty in using *BubbleBoard* that negatively affects text entry speeds, although they still remain significantly higher than *ZoomBoard*. The introduction of dictionary-based auto-correction functionality could, however, reduce the need for corrections and significantly increase the speed achievable with *BubbleBoard*, while *ZoomBoard* would likely benefit less from such functionality given the lower total errors.

5 Conclusions and Further Works

In this paper, we presented *BubbleBoard*, a new soft keyboard for smartwatches, that uses a QWERTY layout in which some characters are in a big font and can be entered with a single touch, while other characters are in a small font and a touch enlarges the pressed character and its neighbors, so that they can be entered with a second touch. The method may use a static or dynamic layout and space/backspace input with either keys or gestures, these variants were evaluated through a user study with the dynamic mode and keys for space/backspace being the most promising variant. The method was then compared to *ZoomBoard* in a second user study, which showed a 33% advantage in text input speed in favor of *BubbleBoard* with 10.7 wpm compared to *ZoomBoard* with 8.0 wpm.

Future work will focus on integrating auto-correction and prediction capabilities in order to enable lower error rates and faster speeds, and then further comparisons with other text entry methods for smartwatches, including those not based on magnification.

Acknowledgement. This work was partially supported by grants from the University of Salerno (grant numbers: 300392FRB20COSTA, 300392FRB21COSTA). The authors thank Filippo Avagliano, Roberto Contaldo, Gianluca De Luca Fiscone, Simone Monaco, Angela Nappo, Carmine Vincenzo Russo, and Sara Zaino for their support in carrying out the experiments.

References

1. Brooke, J.: Sus: a quick and dirty usability scale. Usability Eval. Ind. 189–194 (1996)
2. Chen, X.A., Grossman, T., Fitzmaurice, G.: Swipeboard: a text entry technique for ultra-small interfaces that supports novice to expert transitions. In: Proceedings of the 27th Annual ACM Symposium on User Interface Software and Technology UIST 2014, pp. 615–620. ACM, New York (2014). https://doi.org/10.1145/2642918.2647354
3. Costagliola, G., D'Arco, R., De Gregorio, S., De Rosa, M., Fuccella, V., Lupo, D.: Text entry on circular smartwatches: the C-QWERTY layout. J. Vis. Lang. Comput. **2019**(2), 127–133 (2019). Doi: https://doi.org/10.18293/JVLC2019-N2-014
4. Costagliola, G., De Rosa, M., D'Arco, R., De Gregorio, S., Fuccella, V., Lupo, D.: C-QWERTY: a text entry method for circular smartwatches. In: The 25th International DMS Conference on Visualization and Visual Languages, pp. 51–57 (2019). https://doi.org/10.18293/DMSVIVA2019-014
5. Costagliola, G., De Rosa, M., Fuccella, V.: Handwriting on smartwatches: an empirical investigation. IEEE Trans. Hum.-Mach. Syst. **47**(6), 1100–1109 (2017). https://doi.org/10.1109/THMS.2017.2754938
6. De Rosa, M., et al.: T18: an ambiguous keyboard layout for smartwatches. In: 2020 IEEE International Conference on Human-Machine Systems (ICHMS), pp. 1–4 (2020). https://doi.org/10.1109/ICHMS49158.2020.9209483
7. Girden, E.: ANOVA: Repeated Measures. No. No. 84 in ANOVA: Repeated Measures, SAGE Publications (1992). https://books.google.it/books?id=pCw3jwEACAAJ
8. Goldhahn, D., Eckart, T., Quasthoff, U.: Leizpig corpora News-typical 1M sentences (2016). https://wortschatz.uni-leipzig.de/en/download/English. Accessed 23 Dec 2021
9. Goldhahn, D., Eckart, T., Quasthoff, U.: Building large monolingual dictionaries at the Leipzig corpora collection: from 100 to 200 languages. In: Proceedings of the Eighth International Conference on Language Resources and Evaluation (LREC 2012), pp. 759–765. European Language Resources Association (ELRA), Istanbul, Turkey, May 2012
10. Gordon, M., Ouyang, T., Zhai, S.: WatchWriter: tap and gesture typing on a smartwatch miniature keyboard with statistical decoding. In: Proceedings of the 2016 CHI Conference on Human Factors in Computing Systems CHI 2016, pp. 3817–3821. ACM, New York (2016). https://doi.org/10.1145/2858036.2858242
11. Gupta, A., Balakrishnan, R.: DualKey: miniature screen text entry via finger identification. In: Proceedings of the 2016 CHI Conference on Human Factors in Computing Systems CHI 2016, pp. 59–70. ACM, New York (2016). https://doi.org/10.1145/2858036.2858052

12. Hong, J., Heo, S., Isokoski, P., Lee, G.: Splitboard: a simple split soft keyboard for wristwatch-sized touch screens. In: Proceedings of the 33rd Annual ACM Conference on Human Factors in Computing Systems CHI 2015, pp. 1233–1236. Association for Computing Machinery, New York (2015). https://doi.org/10.1145/2702123.2702273
13. MacKenzie, I.S.: A note on calculating text entry speed. http://www.yorku.ca/mack/RN-TextEntrySpeed.html (2015)
14. MacKenzie, I.S., Soukoreff, R.W.: Phrase sets for evaluating text entry techniques. In: CHI 2003 Extended Abstracts on Human Factors in Computing Systems. CHI EA 2003, pp. 754–755. Association for Computing Machinery, New York (2003). https://doi.org/10.1145/765891.765971
15. Oney, S., Harrison, C., Ogan, A., Wiese, J.: Zoomboard: a diminutive qwerty soft keyboard using iterative zooming for ultra-small devices. In: Proceedings of the SIGCHI Conference on Human Factors in Computing Systems. CHI 2013, pp. 2799–2802. Association for Computing Machinery, New York (2013). https://doi.org/10.1145/2470654.2481387
16. Qin, R., Zhu, S., Lin, Y.H., Ko, Y.J., Bi, X.: Optimal-T9: an optimized T9-like keyboard for small touchscreen devices. In: Proceedings of the 2018 ACM International Conference on Interactive Surfaces and Spaces ISS 2018, pp. 137–146. ACM, New York (2018). https://doi.org/10.1145/3279778.3279786
17. Shibata, T., Afergan, D., Kong, D., Yuksel, B.F., MacKenzie, I.S., Jacob, R.J.: DriftBoard: a panning-based text entry technique for ultra-small touchscreens. In: Proceedings of the 29th Annual Symposium on User Interface Software and Technology UIST 2016, pp. 575–582. ACM, New York (2016). https://doi.org/10.1145/2984511.2984591
18. Siegel, S.: Nonparametric Statistics for the Behavioral Sciences. McGraw-Hill, New York (1956)
19. Soukoreff, R.W., MacKenzie, I.S.: Metrics for text entry research: an evaluation of MSD and KSPC, and a new unified error metric. In: Proceedings of the SIGCHI Conference on Human Factors in Computing Systems CHI 2003, pp. 113–120. Association for Computing Machinery, New York (2003). https://doi.org/10.1145/642611.642632
20. Zhai, S., Hunter, M., Smith, B.A.: The metropolis keyboard - an exploration of quantitative techniques for virtual keyboard design. In: Proceedings of the 13th Annual ACM Symposium on User Interface Software and Technology UIST 2000, pp. 119–128. ACM, New York (2000). https://doi.org/10.1145/354401.354424

Trackable and Personalized Shortcut Menu Supporting Multi-user Collaboration

Xiaoxi Du[1], Lesong Jia[1], Xiaozhou Zhou[1], Xinyue Miao[2], Weiye Xiao[1], and Chengqi Xue[1(✉)]

[1] Southeast University, Nanjing 211189, China
ipd_xcq@seu.edu.cn
[2] Jiangsu Automation Research Institute, Lianyungang 222000, China

Abstract. Large interactive displays play an important role in multi-user collaboration scenarios, such as scheme discussion, situation plotting and brainstorming. Users in multi-user collaboration scenarios may have diverse task allocations and usage preferences. Moreover, users' positions in the interaction process is not fixed and they may move back and forth, because of the larger display and interactive areas. In order to promote the working efficiency and interactive experience of multi-user collaboration for large interactive displays, we have designed and added trackable and personalized shortcut menus to the large multi-touch desktop system——consultation platform. We use a Kinect to capture the skeletal information of different people to achieve multi-user recognition and real-time motion tracking. "Trackable" means that the shortcut menu could track the hand positions of different users, and the users could wake up the shortcut menu with touch gestures from anywhere on the screen. "Personalized" means that the users can set their shortcut menu content according to their usage frequency and preference of common functions. After testing, the shortcut menu received good feedback, and users said that this design could well balance the "shareability" and "independence" of large desktop systems. Our attempt to combine motion tracking with touch interaction in the consultation platform can provide ideas for human-computer interaction design for multi-user collaboration.

Keywords: Multi-user collaboration · Shortcut menu · Hand-tracking · Multi-touch

1 Introduction

With the development of display technology and multi-touch technology, large interactive displays are becoming more and more common in public and semi-public places. These displays can visualize complex problems and information in new ways. Most importantly, they make it possible for multiple users to simultaneously operate on the same device. They can provide a larger work space and support users to share ideas and achieve common goals, which can enhance the collaboration ability among team members. Besides, they can arouse people's interest and stimulate people's participation in various environments. Large interactive displays play an increasingly important role

© The Author(s), under exclusive license to Springer Nature Switzerland AG 2022
M. Kurosu (Ed.): HCII 2022, LNCS 13303, pp. 28–41, 2022.
https://doi.org/10.1007/978-3-031-05409-9_3

in multi-user collaboration scenarios, such as scheme discussion, situation plotting and brainstorming. People use these devices to share fresh ideas and discuss solutions, significantly improving work efficiency and increasing collective intelligence [1]. But at the same time, these multi-user collaboration tasks also bring new interactive requirements. How to improve the work efficiency and user experience of multi-user collaboration has attracted our attention.

Consultation platform is a large desktop system, which can be used for group discussion, plan formulation, GIS viewing and plotting, remote monitoring and other functions. The consultation system adopts operation authority management and concurrency control technologies to realize multi-user collaborative information analysis and program discussion [2]. At present, it is mainly used in flood prevention and relief, earthquake monitoring, communication management and other fields. In this research, through analyzing typical multi-user collaboration tasks, we dug out the problems that affect the work efficiency and user experience of multi-user collaboration, and carried out interactive optimization design for the consultation platform.

2 Related Work

Large shared displays have been proved to be very beneficial to group cooperation [1]. Especially for complex tasks, compared with distributed collaboration, face-to-face collaboration using shared displays has unique advantages in workspace setting, team member communication and allowing team members to identify themselves in meaningful and useful ways [3].

Large interactive displays are mainly divided into vertical and horizontal categories. The vertical display is better at providing a sharing interface, allowing a group of people to view information and discuss together, while the horizontal display can better support collaborative activities, and it can closely combine the resources used and/or created in various activities [1]. In particular, the large interactive display system represented by the desktop system allows multiple users in the team to share tools and information face to face easily [4, 5]. However, most related research is focused on the visual analysis tasks of multi-user collaboration. Under the premise of visual sharing, the research on optimizing the interaction input modality to make more people play their specialities to contribute to team tasks is not deep enough. Therefore, compared with other studies, this study focuses on enhancing the ability of multi-user collaboration by optimizing interaction design.

The primary interactive input modalities are: (1) interaction with external devices, such as keyboard and mouse; (2) interaction with physical objects; (3) multi-touch interaction; (4) voice interaction; (5) using air gestures or body movements to interact. These interaction modalities have different advantages and disadvantages in terms of economic cost, interaction range and interaction accuracy. For large shared displays, multi-touch technology is the mainstream. It not only enables users to select and operate digital content in a direct and natural way [4], but also supports multiple users to operate in parallel. However, in most large-screen touch devices, the system can't recognize the touch of specific users. With the development of sensing technology, using air gestures and body movements to interact with large interactive displays is becoming more and more popular in recent years. It allows users to input information without being close to the screens or wearing auxiliary devices [6]. Besides, the sensor devices based on computer vision are relatively low in cost, and can achieve good interaction effects. In addition, some studies also consider combining other interactive input modalities with multi-touch to enhance the user experience. Yoshiki et al. designed a interactive table combining air gestures with multi-touch, which could sense the approximate postures of fingers or hands in the proximity of the tabletop's surface, which enhanced the possibilities of existing user interfaces for tabletop computing [7]. Ken et al. found that gaze had the potential to complement multi-touch for interaction on the same surface, and they present gaze-touch, a technique that combined the two modalities based on the principle of "gaze selects, touch manipulates" [8]. These explorations compensated for the limitations of touch interaction by adding other interactive modalities, but they were only designed for individual user. Therefore, our study hopes to consider more about multi-user collaboration scenarios and optimize the touch interaction of the consultation platform based on the concept of multimodal interaction.

3   Analysis and Consideration

At the beginning of the research, we mainly analyzed the typical multi-user collaboration tasks on the consultation platform. By observing the operation process, we found out the main problems affecting multi-user collaboration and made some optimization considerations based on these problems.

3.1 Demand Analysis

The consultation platform in our study is a piece of horizontal large-screen equipment (see Fig. 1), which can support 1–6 people to analyze real-time situation information. At present, multi-touch is the primary interactive input modality for the platform. In addition, voice and keyboard can also assist operation.

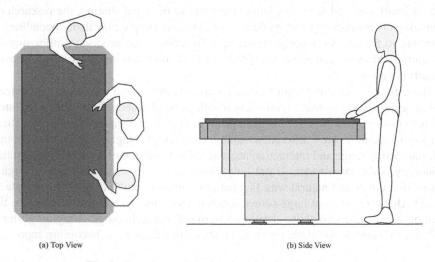

(a) Top View   (b) Side View

Fig. 1. Top view and side view of consultation platform

Typical tasks on the consultation platform mainly include map viewing, situation plotting, command sending and receiving, etc. We analyzed the operation process of these specific tasks and listened to users' use feelings, and then summarized the existing problems according to the observation and feedback (see Table 1).

Table 1. Typical task analysis on consultation platform

Task name	Task description	Operation	Existing problems
Map viewing	View global or local map information	Move, zoom and rotate the map through touch gestures	Because of the large display area, when users need to perform specific operations on map information outside the reachable region, users need to walk around or operate in an uncomfortable posture
Situation plotting	Take the map or scheme as the base drawing, and mark, annotate and modify the existing pattern with points, lines, planes and other vector symbols and characters	Select the plotting tool in the toolbar at the bottom of the screen to measure, calculate, plot and eliminate through touch gestures	Because the whole toolbar is set at the bottom of the screen and its position is fixed, some tool buttons are beyond users' reachable domain, and users' demand for functions will constantly change in the interaction process. Hence, users have to move to the position close to the toolbar to select the target tool
Command sending and receiving	Receive and send information, commands or messages	Edit, send, receive and view information through touch gestures	The task allocation among users in the team is different. Still, the location of tool buttons for information receiving and dispatching is fixed, so users who are mainly responsible for information receiving and dispatching have to stop near the relevant interaction areas all the time

For the existing problems, we summarized them into the following two main problems (see Fig. 2):

Problem 1. Different users may have diverse task allocation or usage preferences in multi-user collaboration tasks. At present, the toolbar position is fixed at the bottom of the screen, which is the same as the toolbar position setting in the single-user interactive displays. It does not fully consider the use needs of different users. It weakens users' sense of participation in collaboration tasks and makes them unable to contribute their value fully.

Problem 2. The display area of the consultation platform is large, and users' positions in the collaboration process is not fixed. When users want to use tools, they have to approach the toolbar at the bottom of the screen for specific operations. It hinders the flexibility advantage of the working range of large displays and reduces the efficiency of cooperation.

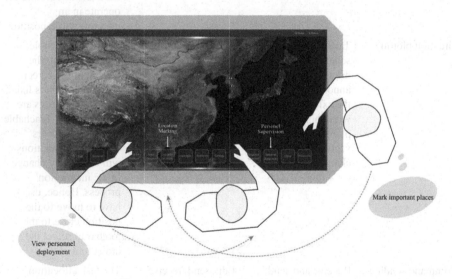

Fig. 2. Major problems in collaborative tasks

3.2 Optimal Consideration

In the scenes of multi-user collaboration, it is necessary to consider the balance between "shareability" and "independence" to make more people contribute to team tasks. In other words, we should try to enhance the sense of individual participation and allow them to play their independent value simultaneously. Under the premise of giving full play to the advantages of large interactive displays with wide sharing areas and flexible working areas, it is not appropriate to apply the single-user interactive paradigm on personal interactive devices directly to multi-user collaboration on large interactive displays. We should consider the individual need of different users. Given the above problems, we found that the location setting of the overall toolbar is the root of hindering multi-user collaboration. At the same time, the shortcut menu caught our attention. The shortcut menu is a menu that displays a list of commands related to a specific item, which can often be waked up by a shortcut instruction. We usually open the shortcut menu anywhere on the screen with the right mouse button on personal computers; we constantly look for common tools through drop-down pages on mobile phones. Commands in shortcut menus are often the most commonly used and primary tools, and the most significant point is that they can be operated quickly. In the multi-user collaboration scenes, if each user can have his/her own shortcut menu, users don't have to rely on the overall toolbar fixed at the bottom of the screen.

To sum up, we considered setting up multiple customized shortcut menus to meet the operation needs of different users and allowing users to wake up their own exclusive shortcut menus in any area of the consultation platform. The above two problems could be translated into the following two critical requirements:

Requirement 1. The shortcut menu can be personalized. While retaining the overall toolbar at the bottom of the screen, users can set their own shortcut menus according to their task allocation and usage preferences in the team.

Requirement 2. The shortcut menu can identify and trace the specific user. The system can identify the corresponding users of different shortcut menus, and they can move with the users, so that users can wake up the dedicated shortcut menus to operate in different areas of the consultation platform.

The realization of requirement 1 is relatively easy, and the engineers can realize it by adding new programs to the consultation system. The key problem is the realization of requirement 2: how to make the system quickly identify the owner of the shortcut menu. We thought of detecting and tracking users' limbs through sensing devices to identify users' positions. Adding motion recognition equipment to the consultation platform could solve this problem well. According to different sensing principles, body motion recognition technologies can be divided into body sensing interaction based on MEMS inertial sensor [9] and body sensing interaction based on optical sensor represented by Kinect [10]. Body sensing interactive devices based on inertial sensors can use inertial measurement units to solve the recognition problem of human postures in three-dimensional space, but the disadvantage is that users need to wear devices, which will cause physical burden and affect users' natural and comfortable interactive experience. The optical sensing device based on image analysis has the advantages of non-contact and non-destructive measurement. The realization of human motion detection and tracking by body sensing interaction technology based on optical sensing mainly includes two essential links: depth image acquisition and bone motion data acquisition. Users can be identified as long as they are within the detection range of the equipment, and it does not impose any additional burden on users. After the device captures the depth image, though preprocessing, contour extraction, key parts identification, and so on, the data information of human bones' key parts, including elbow joints and knee joints, is finally output. We can use this information to determine users' body postures and determine their positions. Therefore, we finally chose Kinect to distinguish and track different users in the detection range.

4 Design and Implementation

Based on the above analysis and consideration, we determined the detailed optimization design scheme, and implemented it technically according to the design scheme.

4.1 Design Scheme

A Kinect is set in front of the consultation platform to capture the position coordinates of each important node of different users' limbs and the direction information of each joint. A plurality of translucent floating balls are arranged on the consultation system. Each floating ball has a different color, and one color can correspond to one user.

The initial default positions of the floating balls are all at the bottom of the screen. When the user moves within the detection range of the Kinect, and the hand appears above the screen, the floating ball will be awakened and follow the user's hand movement accordingly. The color transparency of inactive floating balls is 30%; the color transparency of activated balls is 60% (see Fig. 3). The color transparency of the floating ball after being awakened is set to 60% instead of 100%, in order to avoid covering other contents on the screen during its movement. The floating ball returns to the default position when the user is entirely out of the Kinect detection range.

When the user wants to start a specific operation, he/she can touch the floating ball under his/her hand. The floating ball will expand and pop up the shortcut menu so that the user can select tools for specific operations (see Fig. 4). Different users have different task allocation and usage preferences, so each shortcut menu has different functions.

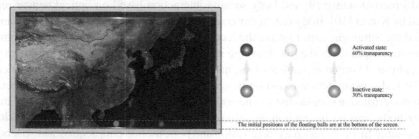

Fig. 3. The initial positions of the floating balls and the transparency difference between the activated and inactive states

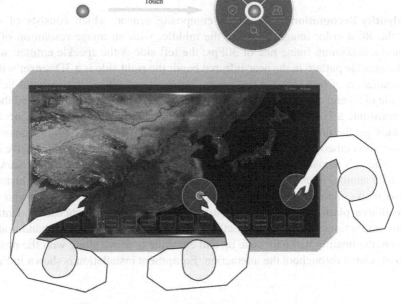

Fig. 4. The process of poping up the shortcut menu

4.2 Technology Implementation

Menu Function Setting. According to the previous research, we found that in the multi-user collaboration tasks on the consultation platform, the task allocation of each member is different. Generally, three users are required to cooperate to complete a collaboration task. They are respectively responsible for the overall command, situation plotting, and information collection. Therefore, we selected and combined three groups of shortcut menus according to the frequency of using common tools in this standard division of labor, and each set of shortcut menus contains four functions. The corresponding tool functions are as follows (see Fig. 5): (1) scheme determination, instruction issuing, all clearing, task selection. (2) location marking, area estimation, distance measurement, revocation; (3) regional regulatory, personnel supervision, retrieval and inquiry, message

(a) Functions related overall command   (b) Functions related situation plotting   (c) Functions related information collection

Fig. 5. Three sets of shortcut menus and their main functions

sending and receiving. The functions in a shortcut menu were written directly into the consultation platform system by engineers in code.

User Identity Recognition. Kinect is a composite sensor, which consists of three lenses: the RGB color image sensor in the middle, with an image resolution of 640 * 480 and a maximum frame rate of 30Fps; the left side is the speckle emitter, which emits the speckle pattern in the near-infrared band; the right side is a 3D sensor with an image resolution of 640 * 480, a maximum frame rate of 30Fps, a horizontal field of view angle of 58 and a vertical field of view angle of 45. The speckle emitter and the 3D sensor constitute a 3D depth sensor system. Through the SDK provided by Kinect, we can quickly get the node data of users' limbs. Kinect can detect the limb movements of six people simultaneously in the distance of 0.8 –4 m, and return a comprehensive node data set. Kinect's somatosensory algorithm [11] can identify different users: mark and track the ID number of users, and record the actions of different users in their historical operation tracks. Therefore, we used Kinect to identify and track the users who used the consultation platform, which could distinguish and record different users' identities, locations, and actions. When the user enters the recognition range and the hand is above the screen, the floating ball will wake up and continue to move along with the position of the user's hand throughout the interaction. Equipment installation is shown in Fig. 6.

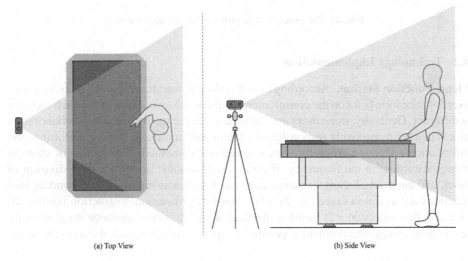

(a) Top View   (b) Side View

Fig. 6. The setting position of the Kinect

User Location Mapping. After obtaining the depth image of the captured object, Kinect will convert the coordinates of each frame depth image with the actual X, Y and Z coordinate units. In order to avoid the image noise caused by the environment, it is necessary to create a segmentation mask to filter out the background environment of the human body in the depth map. A large training database is established to store different human behaviors. After capturing the target object, Kinect evaluates each pixel and marks the identified human body parts with different colors. Kinect judges the specific joint point by evaluating each pixel obtained from the example. Finally, a pointed skeleton composed of 20 bone points is extracted from the skeleton stream. The tasks on the consultation platform are mainly completed by the motion of the upper part of the user's limbs, and there is no strict requirement for hand movements. Therefore, we simplified 20 bone nodes to 10 upper limb bone nodes, among which three nodes of the hand can be simplified to one node. According to the above node model, a characteristic sequence of cosine values of each angle was established for each frame of somatosensory data, as shown in Fig. 7(a). The joints of bones can be expressed by spatial coordinates (x, y, z) (unit: m). The coordinates took the Kinect' position as the spatial origin, the X-axis coordinates were the lateral distance difference from each joint point of human bone to the Kinect' horizontal position, the Y-axis coordinates were the longitudinal distance difference from each joint point of human bone to the Kinect' horizontal position, and the Z-axis coordinates were the distance from the Kinect' position to each joint of human bone. The user's hand was always on the screen during the task completion, so we took the wrist joint as the tracking point (X, Y, Z). The tracking point was projected vertically onto the screen of the consultation platform to obtain the coordinate position (X1, Y1) so that the activated floating ball was displayed in this position accordingly (see Fig. 7(b)).

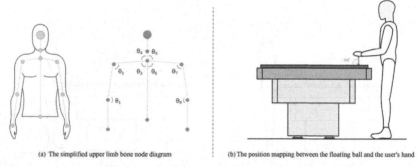

(a) The simplified upper limb bone node diagram   (b) The position mapping between the floating ball and the user's hand

Fig. 7. The simplified upper limb bone node diagram and the position mapping between the floating ball and the user's hand

Transition Design Between Hand Tracking and Touch Interaction. We found that when users wanted to click the floating ball with their hands to open the shortcut menu, the floating balls still slid forward in the direction of users' hand movement, which made it impossible for users to trigger the floating ball accurately and quickly (see Fig. 8(a)). This phenomenon might be caused by the limited recognition accuracy of the Kinect and the natural shaking of the human hand. In order to make the transition between hand tracking and touch click more smooth and natural, we proposed the following solution: when the tracked wrist node was less than 10 cm away from the screen, the position of the floating ball would be locked——the floating ball would no longer follow the user's hand movement (see Fig. 8(b)). After testing, this method could solve the transition problem between hand tracking and touch click, and users did not feel uncomfortable.

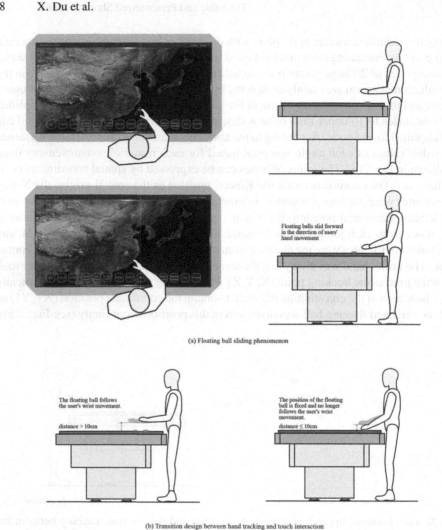

(a) Floating ball sliding phenomenon

The floating ball follows the user's wrist movement.

distance > 10cm

The position of the floating ball is fixed and no longer follows the user's wrist movement.

distance ≤ 10cm

(b) Transition design between hand tracking and touch interaction

Fig. 8. Floating ball sliding phenomenon and the solution to this problem

5 Discussion

We conducted an application evaluation after completing the technical implementation. We selected three users of the consultation platform to collaborate on the optimized platform, observed their operation process, and interviewed them after completing the task. We found that Kinect can realize good identity recognition and hand tracking for users——even if users walk around the consultation platform or three people exchange positions, floating balls could still accurately track users' hand positions. This gives full play to the advantages of large interactive displays with wide working areas and flexible operating areas and can make users' operation process more natural and comfortable. At the same time, this shortcut menu designed according to the task allocation also allows different users in the team to operate more conveniently and quickly, and give full play to their role in the group. Users also said that this interaction design attracted their interest and enabled them to give full play to their individual advantages in the process of completing teamwork tasks. However, we also found that there are still some limitations in the current design, and we are considering further improvement and optimization in our future research.

(1) The personalized shortcut menu was set directly by the engineers in the system backstage according to task allocation content and tool use frequency. It did not realize users' manually set. For novice users of the platform, default initial shortcut menus could give some guidance and reference. But for users who are familiar with tasks and systems, they may have some other clearer functional requirements. Therefore, we will consider adding related programs so that users can still modify and edit their own shortcut menu at the beginning or midway of the interactive process.

(2) The tracking range did not cover the entire consultation platform completely. Since the Kinect device was placed in front of the consultation platform, the actual traceable area was mainly the area directly opposite the Kinect. We will consider adding multiple Kinect devices in other locations to achieve a broader user tracking and positioning range.

In addition to the above shortcomings that need improvement, we also added air gesture interaction on the consultation platform, and thought about further providing personalized services on the consultation platform.

Mid-air gesture interaction. We found that not every user had a moving habit during the operation. The display area of the consultation platform was very large, and when some users needed to operate outside the reachable region, they often interacted with the platform in an uncomfortable posture. Given this, we added leap motion to the consultation platform to realize air gesture recognition. In this way, in areas outside the reachable domain, users could realize simple operations such as zooming, panning and rotating through gesture interaction. However, due to the limitation of the recognition range of leap motion, the current gesture interaction was mainly aimed at single-person operation, which couldn't play a good role in multi-user collaboration scenes.

Interactive intention recognition and prediction. Because Kinect can record the actions in users' historical operation track and store the actions in the database. We can associate these somatosensory motion data with the interactive operation data in the consultation platform, then identify and predict the target object and the degree of willingness that users want to interact with through logical judgment and machine learning algorithm. The time series can be introduced into the prediction algorithm through machine learning models such as Long Short Term Memory Network. And users' interactive behaviors on the consultation platform can be predicted using contextual information. Therefore, personalized active service can be provided in the interactive process to improve the intelligence of the interactive system and make the interactive process of multi-user collaboration more convenient and comfortable.

6 Conclusion

The large desktop system based on multi-touch technology is beneficial for multi-user collaboration tasks. But most systems can't recognize the touch of specific users. In some collaborative tasks, this is not conducive to the flexibility and independence of individual users, and limits the work efficiency and user experience of multi-user collaboration. In this study, the body sensing recognition equipment——Kinect was added to the consultation platform to capture the bone information of different users to realize multi-user recognition and real-time position tracking. On this basis, we designed trackable and personalized shortcut menus to support multi-user collaboration. "Trackable" means that the shortcut menu can identify different users and track their hand positions, and users can wake up the shortcut menu anywhere on the screen; "Personalization" means that users can set their own shortcut menu content according to their frequency and preference of common functions. Tests showed that the combination of gesture and body movement recognition technology and multi-touch technology reasonably could increase the flexibility and convenience of multi-user collaboration. However, due to sensing equipment's limited recognition range and accuracy, there is still much room for improvement in integrating the two technologies. On the whole, the exploration of this study could balance the "shareability" and "independence" of large interactive displays to a certain extent. In the future, we will continue to carry out more research on the consultation platform from the point of multimodal interaction to serve multi-user collaboration.

Acknowledgments. This work was supported jointly by National Natural Science Foundation of China (No. 71901061).

References

1. McGill, M., Williamson, J.H., Brewster, S.A.: A review of collocated multi-user TV. Pers. Ubiquit. Comput. **19**(5–6), 743–759 (2015). https://doi.org/10.1007/s00779-015-0860-1
2. Miao, X., Xue, C., Guo, C., Zhou, X., Yang, L., Jia, L.: Method and realization of multiplayer collaborative control oriented to the consultation platform. In: Proceedings of the 2021 5th International Conference on Electronic Information Technology and Computer Engineering, pp. 850–855 (2021)
3. Isenberg, P., Fisher, D., Paul, S.A., Morris, M.R., Inkpen, K., Czerwinski, M.: Co-located collaborative visual analytics around a tabletop display. IEEE Trans. Visual Comput. Graphics **18**(5), 689–702 (2011)
4. Madni, T.M., Nayan, Y.B., Sulaiman, S., Abro, A., Tahir, M.: Usability evaluation of orientation techniques for medical image analysis using tabletop system. In: 2016 3rd International Conference on Computer and Information Sciences (ICCOINS), pp. 477–482 (2016)
5. Forlines, C., Shen, C.: DTLens: multi-user tabletop spatial data exploration. In: Proceedings of the 18th annual ACM symposium on User interface software and technology, pp. 119–122 (2005)
6. Ardito, C., Buono, P., Costabile, M.F., Desolda, G.: Interaction with large displays: a survey. ACM Comput. Surv. (CSUR) **47**(3), 1–38 (2015)

7. Takeoka, Y., Miyaki, T., Rekimoto, J.: Z-touch: an infrastructure for 3D gesture interaction in the proximity of tabletop surfaces. In: ACM International Conference on Interactive Tabletops and Surfaces, pp. 91–94 (2010)
8. Pfeuffer, K., Alexander, J., Chong, M.K., Gellersen, H.: Gaze-touch: combining gaze with multi-touch for interaction on the same surface. In: Proceedings of the 27th Annual ACM Symposium on User Interface Software and Technology, pp. 509–518 (2014)
9. Shaeffer, D.K.: MEMS inertial sensors: a tutorial overview. IEEE Commun. Mag. **51**(4), 100–109 (2013)
10. Lv, W.: Gesture recognition in somatosensory game via Kinect sensor. Internet Technol. Lett. **e311** (2021)
11. Song, Y., Gu, Y., Wang, P., Liu, Y., Li, A.: A Kinect based gesture recognition algorithm using GMM and HMM. In: 2013 6th International Conference on Biomedical Engineering and Informatics, pp. 750–754 (2013)

Linear Arrangement of Spherical Markers for Absolute Position Tracking of a Passive Stylus

Ammar Hattab(✉) [ID]

Brown University, 02420 Providence, RI, USA
ammar_hattab@alumni.brown.edu

Abstract. We present a simple and novel method for the absolute position tracking of a passive stylus tip -or any hand-held tool. We use a linear arrangement of two or more spherical markers on the back of the stylus, and a stereo camera to track the positions of the two markers to find the stylus tip location by extending the line connecting the markers. Our compact design allows the stylus to be simple, light-weighted, and easy to hold. We show that our method can provide accurate position tracking across a range of distances and orientations.

Keywords: Stylus tracking · Spherical markers · Passive pen

1 Introduction

Tracking the tip of a stylus, a pen, or a tool, in general, is important for many applications, like digital writing, 3D modeling, reverse engineering, measurement, surgery simulation, and architectural applications. The current methods are complicated or limited. First, the industry-standard coordinate measurement machine (CMM) uses a mechanical arm to track the position of the stylus tip. But, these devices are expensive, limited in space, and still need the mechanical arm to be attached to the stylus.

Optical methods provide a simpler solution, the stylus is portable and doesn't have to be connected mechanically to an arm, and the workspace could be larger. Optical CMM devices use a non-linear arrangement of markers that are tracked with a stereo camera, but still, the current 3D arrangements make these devices bulky and cumbersome to use, since they need to be facing one direction -toward the camera- all the time, refer to Fig. 1 for some examples.

In this paper, we propose using a linear arrangement of spherical markers to ensure we have a simple and easy-to-use tracking method. The use of spherical markers centered and aligned along a linear axis allows the stylus to be symmetrical along its axis, thus, it doesn't need to be facing the camera from a certain direction all the time. A minimum of two spherical markers -attached to the back of the stylus- are required to form a line that could be extended to track the position of the stylus tip, thus allowing the stylus to be simple, light-weighted,

M. Kurosu (Ed.): HCII 2022, LNCS 13303, pp. 42–51, 2022.
https://doi.org/10.1007/978-3-031-05409-9_4

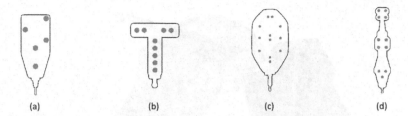

Fig. 1. Some examples of optical commercial CMMs -shown facing the camera- with their active or passive markers. (a) Polyga MeasureXL (b) Karbon Optical CMM (c) Keyence XM-2000 (d) handyProbe.

and easy to hold. The spherical markers could be active spherical light sources or passive retro-reflective markers that require no power on the stylus itself. See Fig. 2 to see an example of the proposed design.

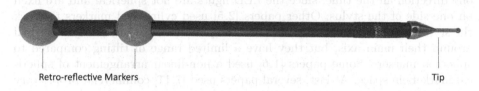

Retro-reflective Markers   Tip

Fig. 2. Our proposed passive stylus with two spherical markers at the back.

For these reasons the tracked stylus could be held and used as a regular pen, refer to Fig. 3 for example use of the suggested stylus to reverse engineer a mechanical component.

2 Related Work

To solve the need for a simple tracking method of a pen or a stylus, several research papers proposed novel tracking methods. Figure 4 shows some examples of these previous works.

ARpen [9] and DodecaPen [10] used binary square markers hand-glued on a cube and dodecahedron respectively, while [4] used a different patterns marker. Their method allows for passive tracking of a pen from all directions, but it requires the pen to be close enough to the camera to be able to recognize the pattern on the square markers. This limits the tracking distance range and requires bigger markers for larger distances which makes the stylus larger and cumbersome. In comparison, we propose the use of spherical markers which could be detected as circular blobs on the camera image from larger distances. Another paper [8] used a linear arrangement of four LED lights as active markers to track the stylus, but, it also requires the stylus to be facing the camera from

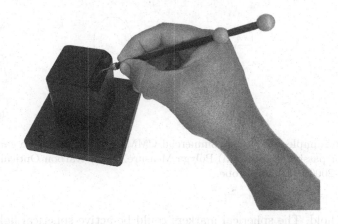

Fig. 3. An example application of the suggested stylus in reverse engineering.

one direction all the time, since the LED lights are not spherical and are fixed on one side of the stylus. Other papers [2,5] used cylindrical markers to track the stylus from any direction given that the cylindrical markers are symmetrical around their main axis, but they have a limited range of tilting compared to spherical markers. Some papers [1,6] used a non-linear arrangement of spherical markers in space. At last, several papers used [7,11] commercial proprietary tracking devices.

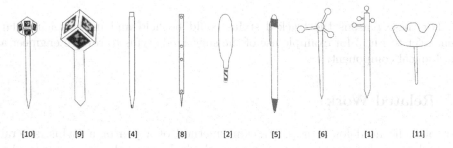

| [10] | [9] | [4] | [8] | [2] | [5] | [6] | [1] | [11] |

Fig. 4. Some examples of previous research papers with different stylus tracking methods.

3   Method

3.1   Stylus Design

The goal of position tracking is to detect and follow a 3D point over time. It's possible to achieve this goal using a stereo camera and one optical marker -for example a sphere or a circle- that can be detected on both sides of the stereo camera. In the case of tracking a stylus, the marker could be attached to tip of the stylus. But, for many applications, the tip could be hidden from the camera. For example, in 3D reverse engineering a physical object, the stylus tip could be obstructed by the physical object itself. For this reason, we need to attach the markers to the back of the stylus where it could be visible in the stereo camera all the time.

Spherical markers have many advantages; first, they allow tracking for a longer range, since they can be detected in the camera from a long distance, compared to markers with patterns. Second, they are symmetrical, which allows tracking from any direction. But, using spherical markers in a non-linear arrangement could limit the range of directions. Aligning the spherical markers along a linear axis extends their symmetry feature and allows tracking from any direction. At least two spherical markers should be used and aligned on the same linear axis with the stylus tip (or the point on the stylus that needs to be tracked)

Figure 5 shows the system components in one example application.

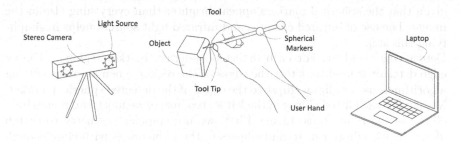

Fig. 5. Tracking system components.

The spherical markers could be retro-reflective passive markers, active spherical markers with light sources, special colored spherical markers, or any spherical object that could be easily distinguished in the camera images from the background. The size of the markers and the distance between them could vary depending on the stylus size and the required tracking range. The markers could be attached to the stylus body, or it could be machined/manufactured as one part of the whole stylus body.

A light source from the same camera direction is required in the case of using retro-reflective passive markers. The light source could be infrared or visible light depending on the type of filter used on the camera or vision sensor. An infrared light source with an infrared camera is preferred for hiding the implementation details of the system from the user and to prevent interference from other light sources in the environment. Figure 5 shows a circular arrangement of LED lights around the camera, but different shapes and types of lights could be used.

The stylus head could also vary depending on the application. For example, for reverse engineering applications, we could use a small spherical tip on the head to capture 3D points positions on the surface of the physical object. For digital writing, the head tip could be a writing stylus tip.

3.2 Algorithm

The tracking algorithm works -in general- by capturing images of the spherical markers, sending them to the computing device, detecting the markers in the images, computing the 3D position for each marker, then shooting a ray along the linear axis -formed by these 3D positions- to reach the stylus tip. Here we describe one example of a step by step algorithm in the case when we use a calibrated stereo-camera system:

- Capture: Capture two synchronized images -at the same time- of the stylus, the important part of the two images are the spherical markers, they should appear in the images, while the other components do not necessarily need to appear in the images.
- Rectify: In the computing device, the two images could be rectified to simplify the stereo search and matching of the markers in the two images.
- Threshold: After rectification, a thresholding algorithm is used to detect and separate the spherical markers from the background in each stereo image, given that the spherical markers appear brighter than everything else in the image. The use of infrared cameras and infrared light sources helps in simplifying this step.
- Detect edges and fit: For each detected spherical marker region, a Canny edge detector is used to detect the edges of the region. Then an ellipse fitting algorithm is used to fit an ellipse to the edges of the detected spherical marker.
- Match: For each fitted ellipse in the left stereo image, we must find a matching ellipse in the right stereo image. First, we use epipolar geometry to search along the left ellipse row to find ellipses in the right image with close enough rows. If only one ellipse is found in the right image, then a match is found. Otherwise, we select the ellipse in the right image with a similar column order to the order of the ellipse in the left image.
- Triangulate: After matching, for each matched ellipses pair, we use the two centers of the ellipses pair to triangulate and compute a 3D position for the center of the spherical marker represented by this pair. Note that the two rays from the centers of the ellipses will intersect at the center of sphere from any direction.
- Find the tip: The 3D positions of the spherical markers fall on a linear axis, we detect this axis and shoot a ray along the axis -starting from a base marker- for a certain distance (pre-calibrated) to find the 3D location of the stylus tip. The base marker is selected based on the application, for example, it could be selected to be the marker at the top (if the stylus is expected to be facing down all the time).

The output of this method is the 3D position of one point (the stylus tip), which is tracked over time.

3.3 Calibration

The algorithm computes the position of the stylus tip by shooting a ray starting from the base marker along the axis of the detected markers for a certain distance. This distance could be pre-calibrated and measured using a measurement tool. Another option is to measure it optically. We could do that by anchoring the stylus on a fixed point and capturing multiple stereo images while tilting the stylus in different directions. Then, we could detect the markers in each image and find the average intersection point of all the rays from all the captured images to get the stylus tip point. And, from that point, we could compute the distance to the base marker and then use this distance afterward.

3.4   Example Application

In 3D reverse engineering, we need to capture the shape and the surfaces of an object, although some of these surfaces might be hidden from the camera. We could capture the shape of these hidden surfaces by capturing 3D points on them by using this tracking method. We do that by moving the stylus tip to touch the hidden surface of the object in multiple locations, and for each location, we capture an image and use the described algorithm to compute the 3D location of the hidden stylus tip. Then depending on the chosen reverse engineering algorithm, we could reconstruct a 3D profile of the surface, or fit a geometric shape -for example, a cylinder- to the hidden surface to fully reconstruct a 3D CAD model of the object.

4   Results and Discussion

Our tracking method provides a simple, light-weighted, and easy to hold stylus design. But, optical tracking requires the spherical markers to be visible on the stereo camera -at least two of them. Thus we need to determine the range of distances and orientations where we can get accurate tracking of the stylus head.

To measure the accuracy of the stylus tracking across these ranges, we could replace the stylus tip with another spherical marker. Then, we capture many stereo images of the stylus with the three spherical markers. For each image, we detect and reconstruct the position of the three markers. We find the two markers at the back of the stylus and compute the orthogonal distance from the third marker to the line connecting the first two markers, see Fig. 6 for an example of this deviation distance. This distance indicates the total accuracy of the system optically (the accuracy of the stereo camera system) and mechanically (how straight is the stylus).

The optical accuracy of a stereo vision system depends on several factors according to [3]:

$$dZ_c = \frac{Z^2}{fb} dp_x$$

where f is focal length, b is baseline, and dp_x is disparity accuracy. In our experiments we used a synchronized USB stereo camera module ($80) with a baseline of 7cm and a focal length of 1.135 mm. Given these fixed values, the accuracy of the system inversely depends on the stylus distance to the camera. For this setup, We found that our tracking method gives an accurate result -with a deviation

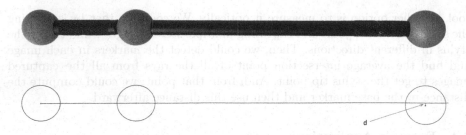

Fig. 6. Tracking accuracy measure, using the orthogonal distance d from the third marker to the line connecting the first two markers.

distance of less than a millimeter- between 20–80 cm to the camera, see Fig. 7(a). This range could be enhanced by increasing the baseline distance, by increasing the focal length of the lenses, or by enhancing the pixel size of the camera.

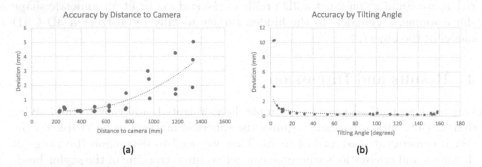

Fig. 7. (a) Tracking accuracy across a range of distances, in the range of 20–80 cm the accuracy is less than a millimeter. (b) Tracking accuracy with different tilting rotations in a plane orthogonal to the stereo camera plane.

There are three types of possible rotations of the stylus with respect to the stereo camera, see Fig. 8:

- Rotation in a plane parallel to the stereo camera plane.
- Tilting rotation: Rotation in a plane orthogonal to the stereo camera plane.
- Axis rotation: Rotation around the center axis of the stylus.

In the case of tilting the stylus in a plane orthogonal to the stereo camera plane, the accuracy is affected by the tilting angle, since the spherical markers appear at a different distance, see Fig. 7(b).

For angles less than 15°C or larger than 160, one of the spherical markers starts to cover the other which makes it harder for the algorithm to distinguish between the two markers. This creates two blind spots on the unit sphere of stylus orientations. See Fig. 9.

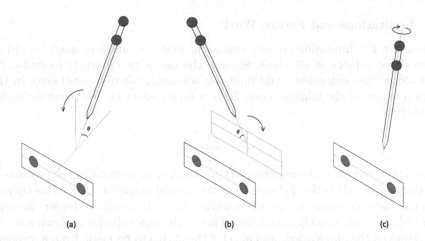

Fig. 8. Stylus rotation types. (a) Rotation parallel to the stereo camera plane. (b) Rotation in a plane orthogonal to the stereo camera plane. (c) Rotation around the center axis of the stylus.

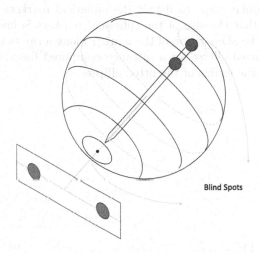

Blind Spots

Fig. 9. The user is free to move the stylus in any orientation in the unit sphere except the two blind spots shown here, where the stylus is perpendicular to the stereo camera.

In the case of the rotation around the center axis of the stylus, we don't expect any changes to the accuracy since the stylus is symmetrical around its axis. Our experiments confirmed that, see Fig. 10(a). Similarly, for rotations in a plane parallel to the stereo camera plane, we also didn't get a significant change in the accuracy, see Fig. 10(b).

4.1   Limitations and Future Work

There are a few limitations to our approach, first, the markers must be visible in the stereo camera at all times. Second, the use of two markers to find a 3D point along their extension could limit the accuracy, where a small error in the position of one of the markers could have a larger effect on the resulting stylus tip position.

$$e_o = \frac{d1}{d2}e_i$$

where e_o is the error in the resulting 3D position, e_i is the error in the position of the base marker, d1 is the distance from the second marker to the stylus tip and d2 is the distance between the two markers. Since d1 usually is larger than d2, the resulting error quickly multiplies. This limitation calls for a shorter stylus depending on the application, and also for the stylus to be made from a stronger material that reduces bending.

The new method could be used in many applications. In the future, it might be possible to use a single calibrated camera for the tracking, we could -for example- follow similar steps to detect the spherical markers in the captured image, then given that the size of the spherical markers is known beforehand, we could compute the 3D position of the marker along a ray that passes through the center of the fitted ellipse for a distance computed based on the spherical marker radius and the radius of the fitted ellipse.

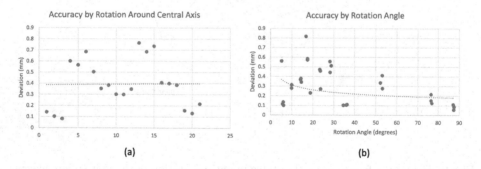

(a)   (b)

Fig. 10. (a) Tracking accuracy with different rotations around the stylus center axis. (b) Tracking accuracy with different rotations parallel to the stereo plane. In both cases, there's no significant difference between rotations, and the accuracy is less than a millimeter.

4.2   Conclusion

We have demonstrated a new method for optical tracking of a stylus using spherical markers aligned on the stylus axis and attached to the back of the stylus. We have introduced a new measure for tracking accuracy. We have found that our new design allows for accurate tracking across a wide range of distances and angles.

References

1. Bi, X., Moscovich, T., Ramos, G., Balakrishnan, R., Hinckley, K.: An exploration of pen rolling for pen-based interaction. In: Proceedings of the 21st Annual ACM Symposium on User Interface Software and Technology, pp. 191–200 (2008)
2. Bubník, V., Havran, V.: Light chisel: 6dof pen tracking. In: Computer Graphics Forum, vol. 34, pp. 325–336. Wiley Online Library (2015)
3. Chang, C., Chatterjee, S.: Quantization error analysis in stereo vision. In: Conference Record of the Twenty-Sixth Asilomar Conference on Signals, Systems & Computers, pp. 1037–1038. IEEE Computer Society (1992)
4. Gozen, E.: A framework for a five-axis stylus for design fabrication (2019)
5. Imad, F., Ahmad, S.M.S., Hashim, S., Samsudin, K., Ali, M.: Real-time pen input system for writing utilizing stereo vision. System 2(3), 1000–1009 (2018)
6. Joolee, J.B., Raza, A., Abdullah, M., Jeon, S.: Tracking of flexible brush tip on real canvas: silhouette-based and deep ensemble network-based approaches. IEEE Access 8, 115778–115788 (2020)
7. Kern, F., et al.: Off-the-shelf stylus: Using XR devices for handwriting and sketching on physically aligned virtual surfaces. Front. Virtual Real. 2, 684498 (2021). https://doi.org/10.3389/frvir
8. Milosevic, B., Bertini, F., Farella, E., Morigi, S.: A smartpen for 3D interaction and sketch-based surface modeling. Int. J. Adv. Manufact. Technol. 84(5–8), 1625–1645 (2016)
9. Wacker, P., Nowak, O., Voelker, S., Borchers, J.: Arpen: mid-air object manipulation techniques for a bimanual AR system with pen & smartphone. In: Proceedings of the 2019 CHI Conference on Human Factors in Computing Systems, pp. 1–12 (2019)
10. Wu, P.C., et al.: Dodecapen: accurate 6dof tracking of a passive stylus. In: Proceedings of the 30th Annual ACM Symposium on User Interface Software and Technology, pp. 365–374 (2017)
11. Yokokubo, A., Kato, Y., Siio, I.: TracKenzan: digital flower arrangement using trackpad and stylus pen. In: Stephanidis, C., Kurosu, M., Degen, H., Reinerman-Jones, L. (eds.) HCII 2020. LNCS, vol. 12424, pp. 332–343. Springer, Cham (2020). https://doi.org/10.1007/978-3-030-60117-1_25

Position and Orientation Registration of Intra-abdominal Point Cloud Generated from Stereo Endoscopic Images and Organ 3D Model Using Open3D

Masanao Koeda[1(✉)], Naoya Maeda[1], Akihiro Hamada[2], Atsuro Sawada[2], Toshihiro Magaribuchi[2], Osamu Ogawa[2], Katsuhiko Onishi[3], and Hiroshi Noborio[3]

[1] Faculty of Computer Science and Systems Engineering, Okayama Prefectural University, 111 Kuboki, Soja-shi, Okayama 719-1197, Japan
koeda@ss.oka-pu.ac.jp

[2] Department of Urology, Graduate School of Medicine, Kyoto University, Yoshida-Konoe-cho, Sakyo-ku, Kyoto 606-8501, Japan

[3] Department of Computer Science, Osaka Electro-Communication University, Kiyotaki 1130-70 Shijonawate-shi, Osaka 575-0063, Japan

Abstract. In endoscopic surgery, it is important to search for organs, tumors and blood vessels, recognize their locations, and perform the surgery safely and quickly. Robot-assisted surgery has made it possible to perform precise operations. However, it is still difficult to perform surgery in a narrow surgical field with a narrow view. Several surgical support systems using augmented reality (AR) have been studied, in which three-dimensional computer graphics (3DCG) models of organs, tumors and blood vessels are superimposed on the endoscope camera image. We have developed an AR surgical support system based on SLAM (Simultaneous Localization and Mapping) technology. The SLAM can estimate the camera position and orientation in global coordinates using only the camera image. However, it is difficult to achieve robust AR because of the errors in camera position and orientation estimation and the failure of SLAM due to camera shake, heavy movement and the reflection of surgical instruments. To solve this problem, we have attempted to perform local position and orientation estimation using ICP on the 3DCG model of the organ and the intra-abdominal point cloud.

Keywords: Augmented reality · Position and orientation registration · Intra-abdominal point cloud · 3DCG model · Point-to-plane ICP

1 Introduction

Robot-assisted laparoscopic partial nephrectomy (RAPN) is a technique that can preserve kidney function while removing the cancer. The surgeons are required to

© The Author(s), under exclusive license to Springer Nature Switzerland AG 2022
M. Kurosu (Ed.): HCII 2022, LNCS 13303, pp. 52–65, 2022.
https://doi.org/10.1007/978-3-031-05409-9_5

identify the borders between the tumor and the healthy tissue and rapidly decide on the area for partial resection. If the tumor is partially exposed, an ultrasound probe is used to assess the volume of the tumor area. However, if the tumor is completely internalized or is relatively isoechoic, this is not an appropriate method. Endoscopic images with proper guidance can help in identifying and resecting the tumor, allowing for a safe and quick surgical procedure.

To solve this problem, support systems using augmented reality (AR), which superimpose three-dimensional computer graphics (3DCG) models of organs and blood vessels on endoscope camera images, have been studied. Su et al. [1] investigated an AR overlay system for robot-assisted laparoscopic partial nephrectomy. The organ surfaces was observed by a stereo endoscope. Some fixed reference points on the kidney surface which manually selected by an operator were needed for ICP (Iterative Closest Point) and image-based registration. Edgcumbe et al. [2] introduced a AR surgical navigation system using a marker called the Dynamic Augmented Reality Tracker (DART). The DART is inserted into a kidney and tracked by the system to display the position of tumors during the surgery. Wang et al. [3] proposed an AR-guided system for oral and maxillofacial surgery. The patient's teeth model was created using 3D scanner and registered by ICP algorithm. Bertrand et al. [4] developed a AR surgical support system which can overlay a deformable model onto a laparoscopic image semi-automatically with a software called Hepataug. This system was used in hepatectomy surgery in 17 patients and feasiblity was confirmed.

Our goal is to build an AR support system with a non-invasive, markerless and robust AR display and an intuitive user interface that is easy-to-use for doctors. We have been developing a surgical support system for RAPN using augmented reality (AR) and virtual reality (VR) technology [5–7]. In our system, a three-dimensional computer graphics (3DCG) models including kidneys, arteries, veins, tumors and Ureters are generated from tomographic images (DICOM) acquired from CT and/or MRI using the commercial software preoperatively. The 3DCG models are superimposed on the endoscopic images and projected onto the operator's console and the operating room monitor. The transparency of the 3DCG can be manually changed at any time for each site according to the surgical situation. The position and orientation of the 3DCG models are automatically controlled in real time according to the movement of the endoscope camera image, and the display position and transparency of the 3DCG models can be changed manually by the surgical assistant if necessary. The display position and orientation of the 3DCG model is controlled by the estimated camera motion using the endoscope camera images.

We will achieve a robust AR display in the following three steps.

- Step 1. Automatic Control of the 3DCG position/orientation based on the estimated position/orientation of the endoscope camera
- Step 2. Automatic control of the 3DCG position/orientation by point cloud matching
- Step 3. Manual Adjustment of the 3DCG position/orientation

The first step is implemented and realized by a feature point-based markerless SLAM (ORB-SLAM2) using images from a stereo endoscope camera. The details of this system are described in [8]. In step 3, we have implemented and realized a system using an HMD with head tracking function and a 3D controller in order to provide an intuitive user interface. The details of this system are presented in [9].

We are currently working on the implementation of step 2. In this paper, we describe the registration experiments between the organ 3DCG model and the point cloud of intra-abdominal space using the point-to-plane ICP algorithm. The registration process is impremented using Open3D [10] and Python. The intra-abdominal point cloud is generated from stereo endoscopic images captured from daVinci Xi using OpenCV [11].

2   Generating Intra-abdominal Point Cloud from Stereo Endoscopic Image Pair

3D coordinate of the target point in real world $(XYZ)^T$ is calculated with

$$\begin{bmatrix} X \\ Y \\ Z \end{bmatrix} = \frac{1}{W'} \begin{bmatrix} X' \\ Y' \\ Z' \end{bmatrix} \tag{1}$$

$$\begin{bmatrix} 1 & 0 & 0 & -c_x \\ 0 & 1 & 0 & -c_y \\ 0 & 0 & 0 & f \\ 0 & 0 & 1/B & 0 \end{bmatrix} \begin{bmatrix} u \\ v \\ d \\ 1 \end{bmatrix} = \begin{bmatrix} X' \\ Y' \\ Z' \\ W' \end{bmatrix} \tag{2}$$

where $(uv)^T, d$ is the coordinate of the disparity image, d is the disparity, c_x, c_y are the coordinates of the principal point in the left camera (the left camera dominant when stereo matching), f is the focal length and B is the baseline length of the stereo camera pair.

Consequently, the following equation can be derived.

$$\begin{bmatrix} X \\ Y \\ Z \end{bmatrix} = \frac{1}{d/B} \begin{bmatrix} u - c_x \\ u - c_y \\ f \end{bmatrix} \tag{3}$$

The disparity image generated from the endoscopic stereo images is shown in Fig. 1. The point cloud of intra-abdominal space generated from this disparity image is shown in Fig. 2 and the circled area is the kidney region.

3   Point-to-plane ICP Algorithm

The general computational steps of the ICP algorithm are as follows

1. Compute nearest neighbor points
2. Compute the translation vector t and rotation matrix $\mathbf{R}$.
3. Transform p using the calculation result

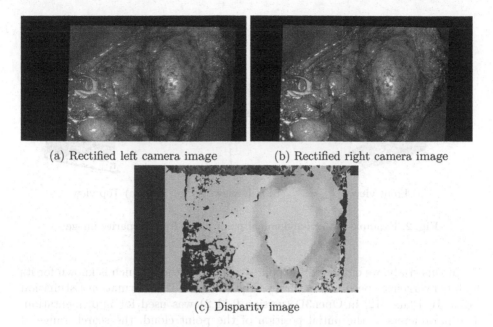

(a) Rectified left camera image   (b) Rectified right camera image

(c) Disparity image

Fig. 1. Disparity image generated from stereo endoscopic camera image pair

Iterate until the difference between the $k + 1$th and kth times of the objective function E becomes lower than the threshold γ.

Typical ICP algorithms are the point to point method and the point to plane method. The method requires only the coordinate information of each point for position and orientation registration. The objective function E in the point to point method is expressed by the following equation.

$$argminE = \sum_{i=1}^{N} \|\boldsymbol{p}_i - \boldsymbol{q}_i\|^2 \tag{4}$$

$$\boldsymbol{q}_i = \mathbf{R}\boldsymbol{p}_i + \boldsymbol{t} \tag{5}$$

where $\boldsymbol{p}_i, \boldsymbol{q}_i$ are the input point clouds and N is the number of point clouds.

The point to plane method uses point normal information in addition to each point's information. The point normal is the normal vector of the plane created from the interest point and its neighboring points. The objective function E in the point to plane method is expressed by the following equation.

$$argminE = \sum_{i=1}^{N} |\boldsymbol{n}_i \cdot (\boldsymbol{p}_i - \boldsymbol{q}_i)|^2 \tag{6}$$

$$\boldsymbol{p}_i = \mathbf{R}\boldsymbol{p}_i + \boldsymbol{t} \tag{7}$$

where $\boldsymbol{n}_i$ means the normal vector of point $\boldsymbol{p}_i$. It estimates $\mathbf{R}$ and $\boldsymbol{t}$ to minimize the inner product of the position vector and normal vector of the corresponding point.

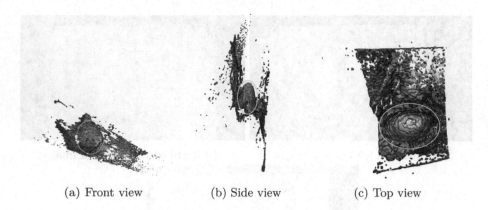

(a) Front view　　　　　(b) Side view　　　　　(c) Top view

Fig. 2. Example of Intra-abdominal point cloud from disparity image

In this study, we employed the point to plane method, which is known for its high convergence speed and accuracy. The function Transformation Estimation Point To Plane [12] in Open3D (version 0.11.2) was used for implementation. The parameters of the initial position of the point cloud, the search range of the corresponding points and the reduction of the point cloud were changed to verify the feasibility of position and orientation estimation.

4　Experiment 1: Verification of Position and Orientation Registration Between Organ Models

The point cloud PC_{origin} (Fig. 3) of the 3D polygon model of the organ generated from DICOM using 3D Slicer [13] is registered to the point cloud $PC_{partial}$ (Fig. 4) of a part of the model. In addition, the point cloud $PC_{partial}$ with Gaussian noise $\sigma = 0.5$ and $\sigma = 1.0$ is used to adjust the position of $PC_{partial}^{\sigma=0.5}$.

The number of points in PC_{origin} and $PC_{partial}$ are

$$N_{origin} = 57228 \tag{8}$$
$$N_{partial} = 14445 \tag{9}$$

4.1　Method

We examine the position and orientation matching when changing the maximum correspondence points-pair distance (denoted by th in the following), which specifies the search range of neighboring points in ICP. The experiments were conducted by changing th from 0.5 to 20 at 0.5 intervals. The PC_{origin} is moved 10 [mm] in the x, y, z axes and rotated 10 [deg] around the z axis from its initial position, and then the registration process with $PC_{partial}$ is performed.

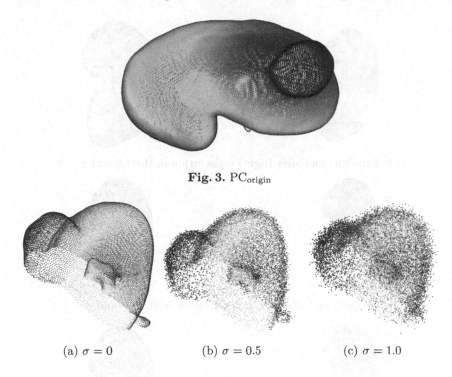

Fig. 3. PC$_{\text{origin}}$

(a) $\sigma = 0$ (b) $\sigma = 0.5$ (c) $\sigma = 1.0$

Fig. 4. PC$_{\text{partial}}$

The root mean square error (RMSE) is used for evaluation. In this experiment, we performed the process 10 times for each th and calculated the averaged RMSE. In addition, a time limit of 10 s was set for the registration process.

4.2   Result

Figure 5 shows an example of the estimation result for th $= 1.5$ and $\sigma = 0, 0.5, 1.0$. Figure 6 shows the averaged RMSE and the standard deviation. For $\sigma = 0$, the minimum RMSE is 0.014 [mm] at th $= 1.0$, for $\sigma = 0.5$, the minimum RMSE is 0.39 [mm] at th $= 1.0$, and for $\sigma = 1.5$, the minimum RMSE is 1.1 [mm] at th $= 1.5$. In both cases, the standard deviation was almost zero.

For all σ, the RMSE increased at th $= 0.5$. This may be because the amount of movement in each iteration was too small to converge within the time limit. Moreover, for all σ, the RMSE tended to increase at th ≥ 1.0. This is because, on the contrary, the movement was too large and could not converge.

(a) before (left) and after (right) registration in th=1.5 and $\sigma = 0$

(b) before (left) and after (right) registration in th=1.5 and $\sigma = 0.5$

(c) before (left) and after (right) registration in th=1.5 and $\sigma = 1.0$

Fig. 5. Registration results between PC_{origin} with rainbow color and $PC_{partial}$ with red color. (Color figure online)

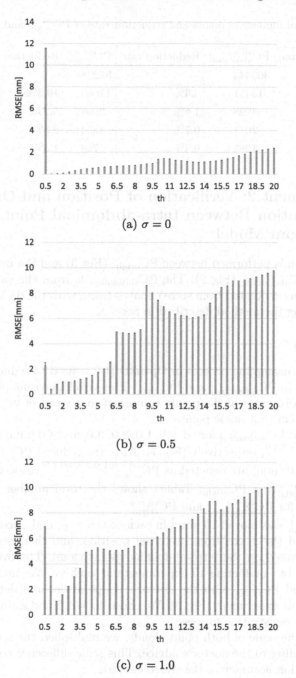

(a) $\sigma = 0$

(b) $\sigma = 0.5$

(c) $\sigma = 1.0$

Fig. 6. Averaged RMSE and standard deviation in Experiment 1

Table 1. Total number of points and reduction rate of $PC_{origin}^{vd=x}$ and $PC_{abdominal}^{vd=x}$

vd [mm]	$PC_{abdominal}^{vd=x}$	Reduction rate	$PC_{origin}^{vd=x}$	Reduction rate
0	303443	–	57228	–
1.0	13451	4.4%	11065	19.3%
2.0	4098	1.6%	2968	5.2%
3.0	2071	0.7%	1354	2.3%
4.0	1285	0.4%	768	1.3%

5 Experiment 2: Verification of Position and Orientation Registration Between Intra-abdominal Point Cloud and Organ Model

The registration is performed between PC_{origin} (Fig. 3) and the intra-abdominal point cloud $PC_{abdominal}$ (Fig. 2). The $PC_{abdominal}$ is from the same patient as PC_{origin} and was generated from stereo images taken with the da Vinci Xi stereo endoscope using the method described in Sect. 2.

5.1 Method

The Voxel Downsampling process in Open3D [14] is used to reduce the number of point clouds in $PC_{abdominal}$ and PC_{origin}. The Voxel Downsampling calculates the average coordinates of the points contained in a voxel of vd [mm] per side and reduces them to a single point.

The reduced $PC_{abdominal}$ for vd = 0, 1.0, 2.0, 3.0, and 4.0 [mm] are denoted as $PC_{abdominal}^{vd=0,1.0,2.0,3.0,4.0}$, respectively (Fig. 7). Also, the reduced PC_{origin} for vd = 0, 1.0, 2.0, 3.0, 4.0 [mm] are denoted as $PC_{origin}^{vd=0,1.0,2.0,3.0,4.0}$ respectively (Fig. 8). Note that $PC_{origin}^{vd=0} = PC_{origin}$. Table 1 shows the total number of points and reduction rate for $PC_{abdominal}^{vd=x}$ and $PC_{origin}^{vd=x}$.

The $PC_{origin}^{vd=x}$ was moved 10 [mm] in each of the x, y, and z axes and rotated 10 [deg] around the z axis from its initial position, and then registration process was performed on the intra-abdominal point cloud. The averaged RMSE was calculated by conducting 10 experiments at each vd. We manually aligned $PC_{abdominal}$ and PC_{origin} with the doctor's cooperation, and defined it as the true value of this experiment (Fig. 9). We chose th = 1.5 and a time limit of 10 s was set for the registration process.

To adjust the scale of both point clouds, we multiplied the scale of PC_{origin} by 0.585 according to the doctor's advice. This scale difference could be caused by the calibration accuracy of the stereo camera.

5.2 Result

Figure 10 shows the position and orientation estimation results for vd = 0, 1.0, 2.0, 3.0 and 4.0 [mm]. Figure 11 shows the comparison between the true value

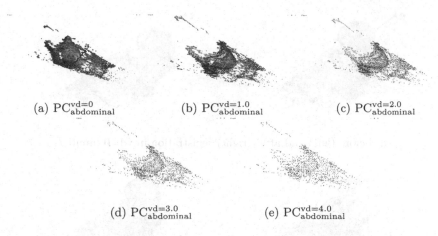

(a) $PC_{abdominal}^{vd=0}$ (b) $PC_{abdominal}^{vd=1.0}$ (c) $PC_{abdominal}^{vd=2.0}$

(d) $PC_{abdominal}^{vd=3.0}$ (e) $PC_{abdominal}^{vd=4.0}$

Fig. 7. Reduced $PC_{abdominal}$ by Voxel Downsampling

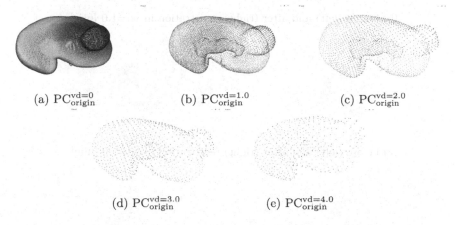

(a) $PC_{origin}^{vd=0}$ (b) $PC_{origin}^{vd=1.0}$ (c) $PC_{origin}^{vd=2.0}$

(d) $PC_{origin}^{vd=3.0}$ (e) $PC_{origin}^{vd=4.0}$

Fig. 8. Reduced PC_{origin} by Voxel Downsampling

Fig. 9. Manual registration result of $PC_{abdominal}$ and PC_{origin}

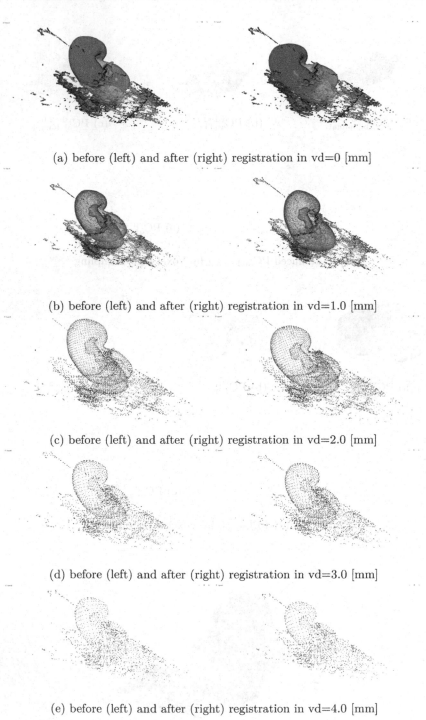

(a) before (left) and after (right) registration in vd=0 [mm]

(b) before (left) and after (right) registration in vd=1.0 [mm]

(c) before (left) and after (right) registration in vd=2.0 [mm]

(d) before (left) and after (right) registration in vd=3.0 [mm]

(e) before (left) and after (right) registration in vd=4.0 [mm]

Fig. 10. Registration results between $PC_{origin}^{vd\,=\,0,1.0,2.0,3.0,4.0}$ and $PC_{abdominal}^{vd\,=\,0,1.0,2.0,3.0,4.0}$

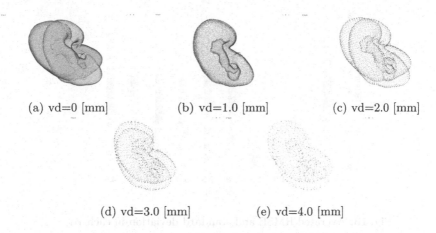

(a) vd=0 [mm]   (b) vd=1.0 [mm]   (c) vd=2.0 [mm]

(d) vd=3.0 [mm]   (e) vd=4.0 [mm]

Fig. 11. True position (yellow points) and estimated position (blue points). (Color figure online)

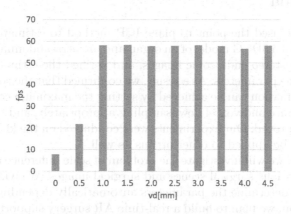

Fig. 12. Processing speed in each vd

and the estimated value at each vd. The position and orientation are estimated successfully for vd = 1.0 [mm], and failed at the other vds. Figure 12 indicates the processing speed [fps] at each vd. The speed for vd = 0 [mm] is 7.8 [fps], for vd = 0.5 [mm] is 21 [fps], and for vd ≥ 1.0 [mm] is approximately 58 [fps].

Figure 13 shows the averaged RMSE and the standard deviation in Experiment 2. The averaged RMSE is lower at vd = 0.5–1.5 [mm] and the lowest RMSE value of 0.61 [mm] was obtained at vd = 1.0 [mm], and the standard deviation was nearly zero. This can be considered to be the result of reduction, which improves the processing speed and removes noise to a reasonable level. The reason for the large RMSE at vd = 0 [mm] is that the point cloud of the non-organ region became a noise and the processing speed dropped due to the large number of points. vd ≥ 2.0 tended to increase the RMSE. This could be explained by the excessively large number of points that were deleted.

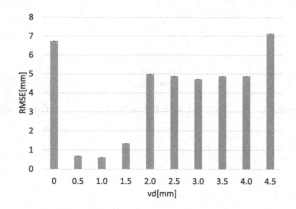

Fig. 13. Averated RMSE and standard deviation in each vd

6 Conclusion

In this study, we used the point to plane ICP method to estimate the position and orientation of a 3DCG model of an organ and an intra-abdominal point cloud obtained from a stereo endoscopic images, and verified the estimation accuracy by adjusting some parameters. As a result, we confirmed that the correct position and posture estimation can be achieved by setting the maximum correspondence points-pair distance and voxel downsampling appropriately, and the estimation speed can be improved. Our experiments were conducted on the kidney, however, the method can be applied to other organs as well.

In the future, we will investigate the problem of scale difference and verify our method using various surgical scenes and surgical images. We will also develop an algorithm to determine the parameters automatically depending on the situation. In addition, we plan to build a real-time AR surgery support system using GPGPU (General-purpose computing on graphics processing units) to speed up the processing.

Acknowledgement. This study was supported by the 2021 Grants-in-Aid for Scientific Research (No.21K03967) from the Ministry of Education, Culture, Sports, Science and Technology, Japan.

References

1. Li-Ming, S., Vagvolgyi, B.P., Agarwal, R., Reiley, C.E., Taylor, R.H., Hager, G.D.: Augmented reality during robot-assisted laparoscopic partial nephrectomy: toward real-time 3D-CT to stereoscopic video registration. Urology **73**(4), 896–900 (2009)
2. Edgcumbe, P., Singla, R., Pratt, P., Schneider, C., Nguan, C., Rohling, R.: Augmented reality imaging for robot-assisted partial nephrectomy surgery. In: Zheng, G., Liao, H., Jannin, P., Cattin, P., Lee, S.-L. (eds.) MIAR 2016. LNCS, vol. 9805, pp. 139–150. Springer, Cham (2016). https://doi.org/10.1007/978-3-319-43775-0_13

3. Wang, J., Shen, Yu., Yang, S.: A practical marker-less image registration method for augmented reality oral and maxillofacial surgery. Int. J. Comput. Assist. Radiol. Surg. **14**(5), 763–773 (2019). https://doi.org/10.1007/s11548-019-01921-5
4. Bertrand, L.R., et al.: A case series study of augmented reality in laparoscopic liver resection with a deformable preoperative model. Surg. Endosc. **34**(12), 5642–5648 (2020). https://doi.org/10.1007/s00464-020-07815-x
5. Koeda, M., et al.: Image overlay support with 3DCG organ model for robot-assisted laparoscopic partial nephrectomy. In: Stephanidis, C. (ed.) HCI 2016. CCIS, vol. 617, pp. 508–513. Springer, Cham (2016). https://doi.org/10.1007/978-3-319-40548-3_84
6. Sawada, A., Hamada, A., Sengiku, A., Koeda, M., Onishi, K., Ogawa., O.: The development of a 3D navigation system for robot-assisted partial nephrectomy using augmented reality technology. In: Proceedings of The 2019 Annual EAU Congress, vol. 18, no. 1 (2019)
7. Sengiku, A., et al.: Augmented reality navigation system for robot-assisted laparoscopic partial nephrectomy. In: Marcus, A., Wang, W. (eds.) DUXU 2017. LNCS, vol. 10289, pp. 575–584. Springer, Cham (2017). https://doi.org/10.1007/978-3-319-58637-3_45
8. Hamada, A., et al.: The current status and challenges in augmented-reality navigation system for robot-assisted laparoscopic partial nephrectomy. In: Kurosu, M. (ed.) HCII 2020. LNCS, vol. 12182, pp. 620–629. Springer, Cham (2020). https://doi.org/10.1007/978-3-030-49062-1_42
9. Koeda, M., Hamada, A., Sawada, A., Onishi, K., Noborio, H., Ogawa, O.: VR-based surgery navigation system with 3D user interface for robot-assisted laparoscopic partial nephrectomy. In: Kurosu, M. (ed.) HCII 2021. LNCS, vol. 12763, pp. 538–550. Springer, Cham (2021). https://doi.org/10.1007/978-3-030-78465-2_39
10. Open3D. http://www.open3d.org/
11. OpenCV. https://opencv.org/
12. ICP registration - Open3D 0.11.0 documentation. http://www.open3d.org/docs/0.11.0/tutorial/pipelines/icp_registration.html
13. 3D Slicer. https://www.slicer.org/
14. Voxel downsampling - Open3D 0.11.0 documentation. http://www.open3d.org/docs/0.11.0/tutorial/geometry/pointcloud.html#Voxel-downsampling

High-Speed Thermochromism Control Method Integrating Water Cooling Circuits and Electric Heating Circuits Printed with Conductive Silver Nanoparticle Ink

Motoyasu Masui[1], Yoshinari Takegawa[1(✉)], Yutaka Tokuda[2], Yuta Sugiura[3],
Katsutoshi Masai[3,4], and Keiji Hirata[1]

[1] Future University, Hakodate, Japan
{g2120045,yoshi,b1017177,hirata}@fun.ac.jp
[2] City University of Hong Kong, Hong Kong, China
[3] Keio University, Tokyo, Japan
{sugiura,masai}@imlac.ics.keio.com
[4] NTT Communication Science Laboratories, Kyoto, Japan

Abstract. With the widespread use of inkjet-printable conductive silver nanoparticle inks, lightweight, thin, and portable wearable displays that combine electrothermal circuit patterns and thermochromic inks have attracted much attention in recent years. Thermochromic displays, which undergo reversible color change according to temperature change, have the problem of low responsiveness due to the delay of heating and cooling. In this study, we propose a high-speed thermochromism control method that integrates a water-cooling circuit and an electric heating circuit using silver nanoparticle ink printing. As an evaluation experiment, we compared the cooling time of an electro-thermal pattern with and without the water-cooling circuit and verified the usefulness of the proposed method. In addition, we have developed applications such as PerformEyebrow, an artificial eyebrow device that extends facial expressions, and dynamic masks and questionnaires based on thermochromism, which demonstrate the potential of our high-speed color control method as a new media technology.

Keywords: Human extension · Communication · Cognitive psychology

This work was supported by JSPS KAKENHI Grant Number JP19H04157.

M. Kurosu (Ed.): HCII 2022, LNCS 13303, pp. 66–80, 2022.
https://doi.org/10.1007/978-3-031-05409-9_6

1 Problem

With the popularization of silver nanoparticle ink[1], sold by Mitsubishi Paper Mills, etc., it has become easier to create thin and flexible electronic circuits by printing conductive patterns using a general household inkjet printer.

In addition, new portable information presentation technologies that combine thermochromic ink with electric heating circuit patterns printed with silver nanoparticle ink, such as Inkantatory Paper [10] and ChromoSkin [1,2], are attracting attention. Thermochromic ink is a thermosensitive color-changing liquid that can visualize a predetermined temperature change as a change in color tone. There are several types of color-change temperature range for thermochromic ink. For example, SFXC Inc. offers thermochromic inks that change color in four different temperature ranges (15 °C, 21 °C, 31 °C, and 47 °C). Furthermore, Recording Materials Research Institute, Inc. sells thermochromic inks of differing color-change temperatures, beginning at –20 °C and increasing in 5 °C increments up to 60 °C[2] . There are two types of thermochromic ink: powder type and solution type. The solution type can be handled as easily as paint. By drawing figures on paper or silicon with thermochromic ink, and dynamically controlling the temperature of each region of the figure with an electric heating circuit, it is possible to design thin and soft analog displays. However, one of the major problems in presenting information using conventional thermochromic inks is the delay in colorization temperature control due to the bottleneck of natural cooling after heating.

In this study, we propose a high-speed thermochromism control method that integrates a water-cooling circuit and an electric heating circuit using silver nanoparticle ink printing. As an evaluation experiment, we compare the natural cooling time of an electro-thermal pattern with the cooling time when using a water cooling circuit, and verify the usefulness of the proposed method. In addition, we create applications such as PerformEyebrow, an artificial eyebrow device that extends facial expressions, dynamic masks based on thermochromism, and questionnaires that apply our high-speed color control method, and demonstrate its potential as a new media technology.

The contributions of this research are as follows.

- Proposal of a fast thermochromism control method using a water cooling circuit
- Evaluation of water cooling performance using water flow rate, water temperature and room temperature as parameters
- Construction of applications using fast thermochromism control methods

2 Related Research

2.1 Flexible Device Using Silver Nanoparticle Ink

A variety of flexible devices have been proposed using electronic circuit printing with silver nanoparticle ink [3]. Qi et al. proposed Electronic Popables, in which

---

[1] https://www.mpm.co.jp/electronic/gin-nano/index.html.
[2] https://www.kirokusozai.com/.

electrostatic sensors are printed onto picture books using silver nanoparticle ink, enabling interactive control of light and sound [9]. Olberding et al.'s A Cuttable Multi-Touch Sensor realized a capacitive touch sensor matrix, the shape of which a person can freely change by the intuitive operation of cutting paper [7]. In addition, Olberding et al.'s PrintScreen demonstrated the ability to create an EL display on paper by screen-printing a layer of silver nanoparticle ink and a thin-film EL [8].

In this study, we control the coloration of thermochromic ink by using an electric heating circuit with silver nanoparticle ink, which is inkjet printable and easy to prototype.

2.2 Thermochromism Control by Electrothermal Circuits

Maas et al. proposed a system that draws a heat-generating pattern on a printed circuit board and controls the color of thermochromic ink applied to the back of the board by generating heat. Tsuji et al. [1,2] have proposed an application of powdered thermochromics to change the color of eye shadow as an extendable cosmetic. In addition to the above, there are many other applications. Tsujii et al. proposed Inkantory Paper, a paper surface interface using silver nanoparticle inks, in which it is possible to control thermal feedback by a heat sensor [10]. By measuring the heat generation performance of the created heater, the constraints on the power supply, heat generation area, and response time were clarified.

In existing research, the electric heating circuit is naturally cooled after heat generation, and other cooling methods have not been verified. In this study, we propose a high-speed color control method that combines the conventional heat generation control method of silver nanoparticle ink with a water-cooling circuit to speed up the response of thermochromic displays.

2.3 Media Using Microfluidics and Soft Silicon

Venous Materials is a new tangible media representation technology using microfluidic channels and soft silicon. Venous Materials present interactive analog media by deforming the fluid in microfluidic channels in response to user interactions such as pushing and bending. Kobayashi et al. have developed a microfluidic-based flexible display, constructed using dyed water droplets and air gaps as pixel elements [4]. Inoue et al.'s TuVe uses as a display device a soft tube, into which a fluid such as a colored liquid is poured. Various kinds of information can be presented by precisely controlling the position and area of the fluid. Morin et al. developed a silicon-based soft four-legged robot that is 13 cm long and moves like an octopus or squid when compressed air is pumped through it [6]. The robot incorporates an ultra-thin sheet of special silicone that changes the color and pattern of the robot's skin as colored liquid passes through tiny microfluidic channels in the sheet.

In our study, we aim to realize a thin and soft analog display by using microfluidic channels to implement a thermochromism-control water-cooling circuit.

3   Design

In the design of the high-speed thermochromism control technology, this study assumes use on a flat surface such as a paper surface and on a curved surface such as a human skin surface. For the cooling of the electric heating circuit, the optimum cooling material is investigated from the viewpoint of cooling speed and thin and flexible design, and its performance is evaluated through preliminary experiments.

3.1   Consideration of Cooling Materials

The advantages and disadvantages of water-cooled microtubes, cooling fans, and cooling sheets were analyzed and the cooling material to be used was examined from the viewpoint of the ease of thin and flexible design, to enable use on flat surfaces such as paper and curved surfaces such as the surface of human skin.

Water-cooled Microtubes. The coloration of the thermochromic ink can be controlled by laying out microtubes across the back of the electric heating circuit to which the thermochromic ink is applied, and running cooling water through the tubes. For example, if we use Cole-Parmer's Microbore Tubing (inner diameter × outer diameter = 0.020 in. × 0.060 in.), we can realize a lightweight cooling mechanism. In addition, the microtubing is easy to bend, allowing for a variety of water-cooling circuit designs. In addition, a pump can be used to run cooling water through the tubing whenever the system user intends.

Cooling Sheets. Here, we describe the case of cooling an electric heating circuit by attaching a cooling sheet, such as Sanwa Supply's TK-CLNP12SV[3], to the back of the electric heating circuit. A cooling sheet is thin, lightweight, easy to fit to paper or skin, and its size can be freely changed. However, unlike other cooling materials, it is difficult to turn the cooling on and off whenever the user wishes.

Cooling Fans. A cooling fan could be used to cool the electric heating circuit. With a cooling fan, the user can decide the timing of circuit cooling. However, as is the case with Sanyo Denki Co., Ltd[4], cooling fan manufacturers generally only produce fans in circular or rectangular shapes, and thus this option lacks diversity of design. In addition, the thickness of the cooling fan itself makes it difficult to fit to a paper surface or human skin.

3.2   Preliminary Experiments with Cooling Materials

In order to compare and verify the cooling efficacy and cooling speed of the cooling materials, we measured the temperature change of the electric heating circuit during water cooling using microtubes, air cooling using a cooling fan,

---

[3] https://www.sanwa.co.jp/product/syohin.asp?code=TK-CLNP12SV.
[4] https://www.sanyodenki.co.jp/products/index.html.

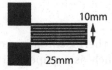

Fig. 1. Electric heating circuit pattern

and cooling using a cooling sheet. The microtubes, cooling fans, and cooling sheets were attached to the electric heating circuit with double-sided tape. The double-sided tape used was Nichiban Corporation's Nice Tack NW-15. For the pattern of the electric heating circuit, we used a printout of the pattern shown in Fig. 1, which consists of eight U-shaped line segments of 1 mm width and 25 mm length, spaced out at intervals of 0.25 mm. Silver nanoparticle ink (NBSIJ-FD02) and specialized media (NB-TP-3GU100) from Mitsubishi Paper Mills, Inc. were used for the printout. The procedure of the preliminary experiment is as follows.

1. Apply voltage to an electric heating circuit that has been left in a natural state.
2. After the electric heating circuit has reached the specified temperature, stop applying voltage.
3. Using each cooling material laid under the electric heating circuit, cool the circuit for 180 s.

The temperature of the cooling water used for water cooling was 2 °C, and the room temperature was 20 °C. A digital thermometer was used to measure the temperature of the surface of the electric heating circuit. The temperature change was captured by a video camera, and the temperature of the electric heating circuit was recorded every 5 s and calculated on a graph.

Figure 2 shows the results of preliminary experiments. The cooling rates immediately after the start of cooling were the highest for air cooling (0.88 °C/s), cooling sheet (0.74 °C/s), and water cooling (0.64 °C/s), indicating a large difference in cooling efficacy immediately after the start of cooling compared to natural cooling (0.26 °C/s). A similar decrease in cooling rate over time was observed for all materials, but the decrease for water cooling was the lowest, indicating that water cooling is the best method for cooling to temperatures below 30 °C.

For the stability and controllability of the cooling rate, as well as the flexibility and thinness of the structure, it was decided to use water cooling with microtubes to cool the electric heating circuit.

4   Implementation

4.1   Thermochromic Ink Layer

We used thermochromic ink (water-based screen ink) from Recording Material Research Institute, Inc. that changes color from black to transparent, with 35 °C

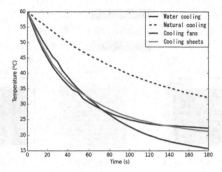

Fig. 2. Temperature change when using each cooling material (room temperature: 20, water temperature: 2)

as the discoloration temperature. As shown in Fig. 3-(a), thermochromic ink was applied to the electric heating circuit layer to form a square with an area of 50 mm × 50 mm.

4.2   Electric Heating Circuit Layer

As shown in Fig. 3-(b), we implemented a prototype electric heating circuit consisting of 11 U-shaped lines of 3 mm width and 50 mm length spaced 1.7 mm apart. A voltage is applied to the circuit to generate heat. The electric heating circuit was printed out using silver nanoparticle ink (NBSIJ-FD02) and specialized media (NB-TP-3GU100) from Mitsubishi Paper Mills Co.

4.3   Cooling Layer

The residual heat of the heated circuit layer is cooled by running cooling water through the tube. We used Cole-Parmer's Microbore Tubing (inner diameter × outer diameter = 0.0020 in. × 0.060 in.) as the tube. The MicroTubing was used only for the electric heating circuit, and the E-3603 Non-DEHP Lab Tubing (inner diameter × outer diameter = 1/16 in. × 1/8 in.) was used for the pump attached to the waist. These tubes were connected with a glue gun to prevent water leakage. In addition, a Dosing Pump Peristaltic Head (12 V 5000 RPM) was used as a pump to circulate the cooling water. The operating voltage of the pump is 5 V. The tubing on the pump and the tubing of the E-3603 Non-DEHP Lab Tubing were connected via Cole-Parmer's Barbed fittings.

4.4   Integration Method of Water Cooling Circuit and Electric Heating Circuit

The integration method of the water cooling circuit and the electric heating circuit is shown in Fig. 4. The method used is as follows.

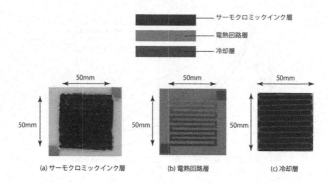

Fig. 3. Structure of the proposed method

1. The tube is inserted into the base made of filament resin. (Figure 4 upper left)
2. Double-sided tape is attached to the four corners of the electric heating circuit. (Figure 4 upper left) The double-sided tape used was Nichiban Corporation's Nice Tack NW-15, as in Sect. 3.2.
3. (1) and (2) are adhered using the double-sided tape attached in (2). (Figure 4 Bottom Left)
4. The filament resin is removed. The water cooling circuit and electric heating circuit are now integrated. (Figure 4 bottom right)

Using the method in Fig. 4, water cooling and electric heating circuits can be integrated and attached to curved surfaces such as paper and skin.

4.5   Preliminary Verification of Cooling Performance Using the Proposed Method

Preliminary experiments were carried out to verify the cooling performance of the proposed method. We compared the temperature change in the case of water cooling, and natural cooling without water cooling. For the experiments, we used the same configuration and integration method of the electric heating and water cooling circuits as in Fig. 3 and Fig. 4. The experiments were carried out using 2C cooling water.

The experiment was filmed with a FLIR ONE Pro LT thermal camera for smartphones[5]. The thermochromic inks used change color from 32 °C to 38 °C. Therefore, we filmed the cooling process from 35 °C in this experiment.

Figure 5 shows the electric heating circuit and water cooling circuit at 5-s intervals, as captured by the thermal camera. In the case without water cooling, the temperature of the electric heating circuit remained at 32.1 °C after 15 s. In contrast, the temperature of the circuit with water cooling dropped to 29.8 °C after 5 s. Therefore, it was found that the proposed method can improve the cooling performance of the electric heating circuit.

---

[5] https://www.flir.jp/products/flir-one-pro-lt/.

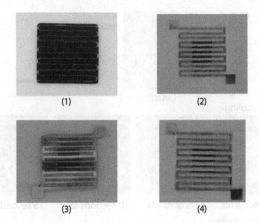

(1)   (2)

(3)   (4)

Fig. 4. Integration method of water cooling circuit and electric heating circuit

5 Measurement of Cooling Performance

An evaluation experiment was conducted to measure the cooling performance with and without the water cooling circuit. In this experiment, three different experimental conditions were set as shown below. The temperature change of the electric heating circuit was measured when cooling water flowed through the tubes after the circuit was heated to a certain temperature.

Experimental Conditions
To verify the effect of water cooling, the following experimental conditions were set.

– Water flow rate: Measure the temperature change when the cooling water is pumped at different rates to cool an electric heating circuit with a temperature of 40 °C. The electric heating circuit with a temperature of 40 °C is cooled. The temperature is compared when a voltage of 5 V or 10 V is applied to the pump for cooling. The initial temperature of the electric heating circuit is 40 °C. The temperature of the cooling water is 19.5 °C and the room temperature is 20 °C.
– Water temperature: The temperature change is measured when cooling water of different water temperatures is pumped. The temperature used for comparison are 19.5, 11.5, and 2 a. The initial temperature of the electric heating circuit is set at 40 °C. A voltage of 5 V is applied to the pump for cooling, and the room temperature is 20 °C.
– Room temperature: To measure the temperature change when cooling water is pumped at different room temperatures, two different room temperatures, 20 °C and 5 °C, are compared. The initial temperature of the electric heating circuit is set at 60 °C , to verify the cooling performance of the electric heating circuit at high temperature. 5 V voltage is applied to the cooling pump, and cooling water of 2 °C is used.

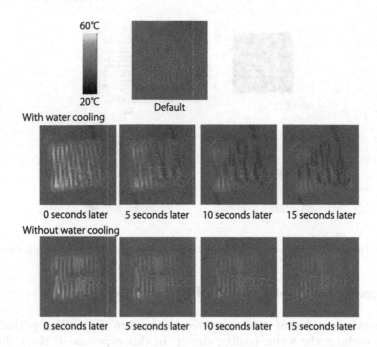

Fig. 5. Results of experiments

Experimental Devices

The experimental setup consists of water cooling tubes, a pump, a thermometer, an electric heating circuit, cooling water and a container for drainage as shown in Fig. 6. The water cooling tubes and pump used in the experiment are the same as in Figure 4.3. The electric heating circuit is the one in Fig. 1. A breadboard with a tube wrapped around it, shown in Fig. 7, was placed under the electric heating circuit. Double-sided tape was used to fix the tube to the electric heating circuit. The cooling water used for water cooling is sent to the drainage container through the pump and tubes. During natural cooling, the electric heating circuit was left to cool down from the specified temperature without using a pump, cooling water, or drainage.

Experimental Procedure

The experimental procedure is as follows.

1. Apply a voltage to an electric heating circuit that has been left in a natural state.
2. After the electric heating circuit has reached the specified temperature, stop applying voltage.
3. After applying each experimental condition, cool the electric heating circuit for 180 s.

5.1 Experimental Results

Water Flow Rate. The experimental results for different water flow rates are shown in Fig. 8. The horizontal axis of Fig. 8 is the time elapsed since the start of cooling of the electric heating circuit (sec), and the vertical axis is the temperature of the electric heating circuit at each time (C). Water was pumped at a rate of 0.03 mL/sec when a voltage of 5 V was applied to the pump, and 0.19 mL/sec when a voltage of 10 V was applied to the pump. No difference was observed in the temperature change of the electric heating circuit when the water flow rate was changed. This may be due to the fact that the temperature of the tube surface does not change even when the water flow rate is changed, and the cooling of the electric heating circuit is not directly affected.

Water Temperature. The results of the experiments using cooling water of 9.5 °C, 11.5 °C, and 2 °C and natural cooling without water cooling are shown in Fig. 9. The cooling rate immediately after cooling began was 0.34 °C/s when using cooling water of 19.5 °C, 11.5 °C, and 2 °C, and 0.12 °C/s during natural cooling. Thus, in this experiment, it can be seen that the use of water cooling enables faster cooling of the electric heating circuit than natural cooling. As shown in Fig. 9, between the cases of using each of the three types of cooling water there was no significant difference in the temperature change of the electric heating circuit immediately after cooling began. However, after 40 s, it was observed that the lower the water temperature was, the more easily the temperature of the electric heating circuit tended to decrease. In terms of cooling time, it took 75 s to cool the circuit from 40 °C to 25 °C when using 19.5 °C cooling water, while it took 55 s when using 2 °C cooling water, a difference of 20 s. Therefore, water temperature is considered to be an important parameter that affects the cooling time of the electric heating circuit.

The experimental results for the cases of cooling at room temperature of 20 °C and 3 °C are shown in Fig. 10. The most effective cooling was achieved with water cooling at 3 °C room temperature, followed by natural cooling at 3 °C room temperature and water cooling at 20 °C room temperature, while the longest cooling time was observed in water cooling at 20 °C room temperature. It was observed that the temperature of the electric heating circuit tended to decrease easily when the room temperature was lowered. Therefore, room temperature is considered to be an important parameter that affects the cooling time of the electric heating circuit, as well as the water temperature. The change in cooling was almost the same for the case of natural cooling at 3 °C room temperature and the case of water cooling at 20 °C room temperature. This indicates that water cooling has the same effect as lowering the room temperature by almost 20 °C. Furthermore, when the cooling rates of the water-cooled circuit at room temperature of 20 °C were compared, the cooling rate was 0.34 °C/s when the

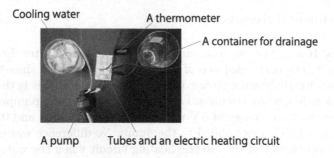

Cooling water   A thermometer
A container for drainage
A pump   Tubes and an electric heating circuit

Fig. 6. Scene of the experiment

Fig. 7. Tubes and electric heating circuits

circuit was at around 40 °C and 0.64 °C/s at around 60 °C. This demonstrates that the electric heating circuit cooled faster at a higher temperature.

6   Construction of Applications

Augmentation Towards PerformEyebrow

As an application of the high-speed color control method in this study, we verified the response speed improvement of PerformEyebrow [5] developed by the authors.

PerformEyebrow uses artificial eyebrows drawn with thermochromic ink to enable the user dynamically to change the eyebrow shape. An electrothermal circuit printed out with conductive ink is placed directly under the eyebrows to change the color of the thermochromic ink on the eyebrows.

In PerformEyebrow, the problem with natural cooling after heating the electric heating circuit is the delay in colorization temperature control. To solve this problem, we implemented a new cooling layer in PerformEyebrow in addition to the conventional thermochromic ink layer and electric heating circuit layer. In order to implement the cooling layer, tubes similar to those in the Sect. 4.3 were laid over the contours of the artificial eyebrows.

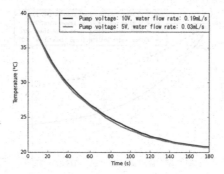

Fig. 8. Temperature change when different voltages are applied to the pump (Room Temperature: 20, Water Temperature: 19.5)

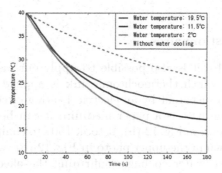

Fig. 9. Temperature change when using cooling water of different water temperatures (room temperature: 20, pump voltage: 5 V)

Figure 11 shows the electric heating circuit heated for one minute and then cooled. In the conventional natural cooling method without water cooling, it takes about 90 s to restore the shape of the artificial eyebrows, as shown in Fig. 11. By adding a cooling layer, the time required to restore the shape of the artificial eyebrows was reduced to about 15 s, which is a significant reduction in the cooling time.

6.1 Dynamic Masks

As shown in Fig. 12-(a), a dynamic mask was created, using thermochromic ink and an electric heating circuit to display and erase symbols of emotion, such as tears and blushing. It can be seen that, as with PerformEyebrow, the proposed method is valid for application to thermochromic facial expression augmentation displays.

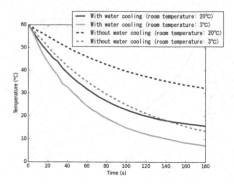

Fig. 10. Temperature change at different room temperatures (water temperature: 2, pump voltage: 5 V)

6.2 Dynamic Questionnaires

As shown in Fig. 12-(b), it is also possible to apply our method to a dynamic questionnaire [10], in which thermochromic ink is applied to a paper surface and the ink is made transparent by an electric heating circuit laid on the back of the paper. Since the base is a paper medium, it can be wrapped around a columnar object as shown in Fig. 12-(b). It took 150 s to completely return to the original shape (as shown in the upper photo in Fig. 12-(b)) with natural cooling, while it took 20 s with water cooling, confirming the effect of water cooling. This demonstrates that the proposed method is also effective in improving the response of thermochromic displays in analog media such as paper.

As described above, the use of water-cooling tubes enables us to realize a thin and flexible cooling method. As size and shape can be customized, the method can be applied to both flat and curved surfaces, such as paper and human skin. Other possible applications include to fabric products such as stuffed toys and flexible materials such as silicon.

7 Summary

In this study, we proposed a high-speed thermochromism control method that integrates a water cooling circuit and an electrothermal circuit created with silver nanoparticle ink printing. The proposed method enables faster cooling of the electric heating circuit than natural cooling. The cooling performance of the circuit was verified in terms of the amount of water supplied, the temperature of the cooling water, and the room temperature. As a result, it was found that the cooling time of the electric heating circuit is not affected by the amount of water supplied, with the temperature of the cooling water and the room temperature being the parameters that constitute the cooling time. We have also proposed applications of the proposed method, including the artificial eyebrow device PerformEyebrow.

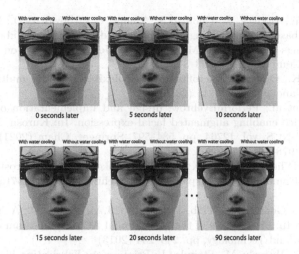

Fig. 11. A cooled PerformEyebrow

Fig. 12. Applications

Future work includes detailed cooling performance evaluation experiments with different geometries, construction of a mathematical model for the proposed fast thermochromism control method, and evaluation of the developed applications.

References

1. Kao, C.H.L., Nguyen, B., Roseway, A., Dickey, M.: Earthtones: Chemical sensing powders to detect and display environmental hazards through color variation. In: Proceedings of the 2017 CHI Conference Extended Abstracts on Human Factors in Computing Systems CHI EA 2017, pp. 872–883. Association for Computing Machinery, New York (2017). https://doi.org/10.1145/3027063.3052754
2. Kao, H.L.C., Mohan, M., Schmandt, C., Paradiso, J.A., Vega, K.: Chromoskin: towards interactive cosmetics using thermochromic pigments. In: Proceedings of the 2016 CHI Conference Extended Abstracts on Human Factors in Computing Systems CHI EA 2016, pp. 3703–3706. Association for Computing Machinery, New York (2016). https://doi.org/10.1145/2851581.2890270

3. Kawahara, Y., Hodges, S., Cook, B.S., Zhang, C., Abowd, G.D.: Instant inkjet circuits: lab-based inkjet printing to support rapid prototyping of ubicomp devices. In: Proceedings of the 2013 ACM International Joint Conference on Pervasive and Ubiquitous Computing, pp. 363–372 (2013)
4. Kobayashi, K., Onoe, H.: Microfluidic-based flexible reflective multicolor display. Microsyst. Nanoeng. 4(1), 1–11 (2018)
5. Masui, M., et al.: PerformEyebrow: design and implementation of an artificial eyebrow device enabling augmented facial expression. In: Kurosu, Masaaki (ed.) HCII 2021. LNCS, vol. 12764, pp. 584–597. Springer, Cham (2021). https://doi.org/10.1007/978-3-030-78468-3_40
6. Morin, S.A., Shepherd, R.F., Kwok, S.W., Stokes, A.A., Nemiroski, A., Whitesides, G.M.: Camouflage and display for soft machines. Science 337(6096), 828–832 (2012)
7. Olberding, S., Gong, N.W., Tiab, J., Paradiso, J.A., Steimle, J.: A cuttable multi-touch sensor. In: Proceedings of the 26th Annual ACM Symposium on User Interface Software and Technology, pp. 245–254 (2013)
8. Olberding, S., Wessely, M., Steimle, J.: Printscreen: Fabricating highly customizable thin-film touch-displays. In: Proceedings of the 27th Annual ACM Symposium on User Interface Software and Technology UIST 2014, pp. 281–290. Association for Computing Machinery, New York (2014). https://doi.org/10.1145/2642918.2647413
9. Qi, J., Buechley, L.: Electronic popables: exploring paper-based computing through an interactive pop-up book. In: Proceedings of the Fourth International Conference on Tangible, Embedded, and Embodied Interaction, pp. 121–128 (2010)
10. Tsujii, T., Koizumi, N., Naemura, T.: Inkantatory paper: dynamically color-changing prints with multiple functional inks. In: Proceedings of the Adjunct Publication of the 27th Annual ACM Symposium on User Interface Software and Technology, pp. 39–40 (2014)

A Self Learning Yoga Monitoring System Based on Pose Estimation

Prahitha Movva, Hemanth Pasupuleti, and Himangshu Sarma(✉)

Computer Vision Group, Department of Computer Science and Engineering,
Indian Institute of Information Technology, Sri City, Chittoor, India
{prahitha.m18,satyasaihemanth.p18,himangshu.sarma}@iiits.in

Abstract. Modern life is stressful - long working hours, poor diets, inactivity, and increasing social isolation in the digital age have all contributed to rising rates of anxiety and depression. The COVID-19 pandemic escalated this situation with a series of quarantines. Without physical interaction, learning a new skill can be frustrating and stressful, especially a skill like Yoga that requires balance and physical coordination. On the one hand, many people cannot afford a personal trainer, but on the other, books and video tutorials do not offer personalized feedback. These limitations make learning Yoga on our own an overwhelming task. We propose a minimal investment model that will help people learn and practice correct Yoga forms from the comfort of their homes in an easy, stress-free manner - just by using their camera. A deep learning model is proposed based on PoseNet which gives an accuracy of 96.77% on the test dataset. We also conducted a survey to measure the satisfaction, efficiency and effectiveness of our system. Overall, 81.8% of the participants felt that our system helped them learn and perform the exercises better and 52.2% of them rated it as being "very good".

Keywords: Yoga · Physical activity · Motion

1 Introduction

Sports and physical fitness activities have always been an attraction to people around the world. In the recent events of the pandemic, studies show that physical activity (PA) has decreased and the amount of sleep and sedentary lifestyle increased very drastically [20,29,33]. The rapid increase of self-isolation, socio-economic disputes, and decrease in physical activity can lead to many physical disorders [23] and mental health issues among various groups of people [5,14,17]. Mind-body exercises like yoga as demonstrated in its numerous studies have proven to have an effect on decreasing stress, anxiety, and depression [16,26].

The concept of using video games that involve PAs that are not sedentary is called Exergaming [12,21]. Physical activity includes anything from dancing to aerobics, martial arts, and a variety of sports moves. Even though there is no universal definition for exergames [3,6] we stick with the above-mentioned definition for this current paper. Exergames have been around us since the 1980 s [10] but an increasing interest and progress has been shown in the recent ten years. In the past, technology has been a hindrance to exercise. However, with exergaming, technology is now facilitating exercise, and it's growing in popularity. Games are fun and engaging - as exergaming combines both games and exercises, they motivate the users to exercise more frequently.

Usually performing yoga requires a tutor or an instructor in order to maintain a correct posture. But due to quarantine, people are stuck in homes and it is hard to go out and find a yoga trainer. Other methods of guidance which include but are not limited to personal fitness books, videos, mobile apps, etc., do not provide real-time monitoring and feedback which can lead to a wrong or even a harmful exercise performance [27,28]. With the uprising advancements in computer vision and deep learning techniques, researchers started to focus on intelligent fitness training systems since it is one of the most flexible options for people involved in this fast-moving world. In this paper, we wanted to address the above issues with the help of deep learning by focusing on an approach that would help to build self yoga training systems for people to learn and practice yoga.

2   Related Work

There has been an extensive amount of research done on exergames over the past few years. GrabApple [11] is a casual exergame that uses Microsoft Kinect to capture motion from the users and the user has to move in order to catch the falling apple. In this game, they have managed to burn 91.8 cal reaching up to an average of 72% of maximum heart rate with just 10 min of gameplay. PaperDude [7] is a virtual reality cycling-based exergame, they have used a Trek FX bicycle attached to a Kickr Power trainer. The gesture based controls for the player to grab and throw the paper was also implemented using Microsoft Kinect. Medical Interactive Rehabilitation Assistant (MIRA) [19] is a software platform that uses motion tracking with Kinect to design exergames that involve physiotherapy. ExerCube [18] is an immersive game setup that enables a full user experience. However, all of these exergames require some kind of setup or depth camera which might be hard for everyone to afford.

OpenPose [8] is a widely used human pose estimation model in various applications. It uses a multi-stage CNN pipeline to generate Part Affinity Fields (PAFs) and Part Confidence Fields (PCFs). PAFs are a set of 2D vector fields that encode the location and orientation of limbs over the image domain. These PAFs are utilized in the network for part associations which helps the model with multi-person parsing problems. PoseNet[1] is an another open-source pose estimation model developed by TensorFlow.js. It uses CNN regression to output the heatmaps and offset vectors for a given image. The heatmaps give the likelihood of each keypoint in each grid square while offset vectors give the location of each keypoint. PoseNet then uses these heatmaps and offset vectors to

---

[1] https://blog.tensorflow.org/2018/05/real-time-human-pose-estimation-in.html.

output a dictionary of poses, pose confidence, keypoints coordinates, and keypoints confidence scores. For multi-person pose estimation, they have used the fast greedy search algorithm [22] to group the keypoints into poses by following displacement vectors along a part-based graph.

"Real-time Yoga recognition using deep learning" [32] have used OpenPose [8] to extract the keypoints from a given frame of a video. The extracted keypoints are then sent into the LSTM layer in batches of 45 sequential frames to further classify the yoga pose in the given video. They tested the system in real time on 12 human subjects (five males and seven females) and achieved 98.92% accuracy. In "A Proposal of Yoga Pose Assessment Method Using Pose Detection for Self-Learning" [30], they use the OpenPose predicted keypoints to calculate angles between joints and give feedback if the angle is not good. However, they do not do any yoga pose recognition, instead, they just compare the angles and classify the posture among "perfect", "good", "not good" and "bad". There are many other works done [2,4,13,25] that use OpenPose to extract keypoints and create a yoga monitoring system. Even though OpenPose is one of the best performing human pose estimation models, it is still very computationally expensive to deploy on mobile applications since it requires NVIDIA GeForce GTX-1080 Ti GPU and an i7-6850K CPU to run smoothly at 22 fps. "AI-Based Yoga Pose Estimation for Android Application" [9] surveyed different pose estimation models such as OpenPose, PoseNet and DeepPose and concluded that the PoseNet is the most suitable for deploying yoga based applications on android. "Neuropose: Geriatric rehabilitation in the home using a webcam and pose estimation."[24] emphasised on the real-time feedback for the monitoring of the patients. They have also used PoseNet to compute the pose information and give scoring at the end of the exercise while utilizing the local GPU resources with TensorFlow.js and make it a real-time experience for fall prevention rehabilitation.

3   Methodology

3.1   Dataset Preparation

To start with the yoga poses dataset, we have selected three poses namely Mountain, Triangle, and Warrior-1. Most of the images were scraped from the internet and images with no good view of the person were deleted. We have merged the scraped images with images taken from the Yoga-82 dataset [31] and made sure that there are no duplicate images present in the dataset. To increase the number of images we have used Horizontal flipping as data augmentation.

These images are further sent into PoseNet[2] to extract the skeleton keypoints from the given image. PoseNet gives 17 keypoints with their x and y coordinates. These keypoints are further flattened to get a vector of length 34. Thus, having N images will give a feature matrix of dimensions Nx34.

The final dataset consists of 461 images (187 mountain poses, 153 triangle poses, and 121 warrior poses). In order to evaluate the model, we have made a

---

[2] https://blog.tensorflow.org/2018/05/real-time-human-pose-estimation-in.html.

stratified split retaining 60% of the entire data for training and 20% each for validation and test datasets.

Fig. 1. Sample images from the dataset (https://gethealthyu.com/exercise/mountain-pose/), (https://www.verywellfit.com/extended-triangle-pose-utthita-trikonasana-3567129.) [31]

3.2 Angle Calculation

In order to make the pose estimation accurate, the angle measurements have to be taken care. To address this, weformulated a method to calculate the angles when a pose is being identified. This is done by using the *arctan* function for the trainer and the user keypoints. The trainer angles are calculated using the keypoints from the pose with the most accuracy.

If we have 3 points $(x1, y1), (x2, y2), (x3, y3)$ and $(x2, y2)$ is the joint then the angle of each vector with respect to x-axis can be calculated as:

$$\theta_1 = atan2(y_1 - y_2, x_1 - x_2) \tag{1}$$

$$\theta_2 = atan2(y_3 - y_2, x_3 - x_2) \tag{2}$$

Finally, from Eq. 1 and Eq. 2 we can calculate the joint angle θ as:

$$\theta = \theta_1 - \theta_2 \tag{3}$$

Similarly, the same method has been used to calculate the angle for the user pose and are compared with each joint angle from the trainer poses. If the difference of these two angles is greater than 30° then we highlight that joint in red color and give text feedback where it went wrong. This will alert the users if they are in a wrong posture and make it easier for user to interact while exercising. The poses are classified using the neural Network.classify function provided by ml5js[3] library with a confidence threshold of 75%. On identifying the correct pose, an audio alert is made to intimate the user that the desired pose has been achieved. The timer then ticks down from 10 to 0 and then progresses to the next pose. If the user breaks out of the pose, the timer stops counting down.

3.3 Using p5.js and ml5.js

We take the keypoints predicted by the PoseNet and then send them to train a small neural network to predict the pose from the given keypoints. We have used Adam optimizer [15] to minimize cross entropy loss.

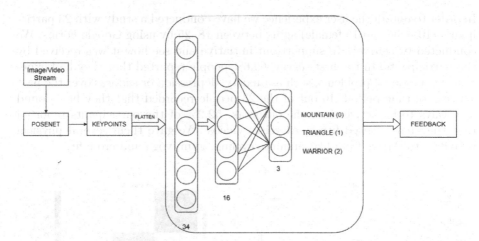

Fig. 2. Pipeline for the proposed system. The extracted keypoints by the Posenet will be flattened and sent into a Neural Network. This further predicts the pose and based on the classification, the joint angles are calculated to provide feedback.

We have trained the model in Tensorflow [1] for a total of 200 epochs with batch size 10, which was converted into TensorFlow.js [1]. The model achieves an accuracy of 96.77% on the test dataset. We have then loaded the model using ml5.js (see footnote 3) and deployed the model in browser using p5js[4] .

---

[3] https://ml5js.org/.
[4] https://p5js.org/.

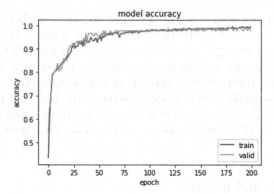

Fig. 3. Accuracy obtained by the model

4   Experiments and Study

In order to obtain the user experience we have conducted a study with 23 participants (10 male and 13 female) aging between 18–25 by using Google Forms. We conducted two surveys to support our initiative and see how it was received by the participants. In the first survey, 69.6% people reported that they had experienced emotional problems, such as anxiety, depression or sadness over the past 4 weeks of time period. 10 out of the 23 people recorded that they have found new ways to be active since the outbreak. 52.2% of the participants reported that they have viewed fitness exercises videos. We gave them several physical activities to choose from like running, cycling, gym, yoga and cross-fit.

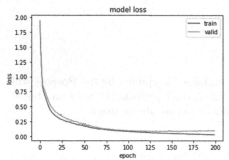

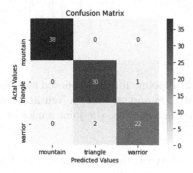

Fig. 4. Loss curve for the model

Fig. 5. Confusion matrix for the three poses

A strong 56.5% responded that they preferred yoga over the other options and also logged that they mainly looked for stress relief and flexibility while exercising or doing any physical activity. Based on the first survey results, we chose yoga for our application. After building the application, we conducted another survey with the same participants. The questionnaire was divided into three parts: (1) learning experience with only the images of the yoga poses, (2) learning experience with our application and questions about how they thought of it as compared to the previous system, (3) feedback on the overall application.

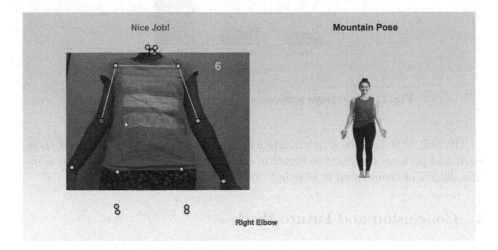

Fig. 6. Using the system. The user imitates the displayed yoga pose and if the pose is correctly classified, the timer starts to countdown and a text saying "Nice Job" appears. Any suggestible changes will be indicated in red color. (Color figure online)

We chose three poses namely - mountain (basic), warrior-1 (medium), triangle (hard) with varying difficulty levels to capture the effectiveness of the system. We will illustrate the results obtained from the survey consecutively. For the mountain pose, 22 out of the 23 recorded their ability to perform it accurately as "good" and "very good" with both the systems. With the first system, only 34.8% of the participants rated their concentration as "very good" whereas with the second system, we saw an increase of 8.7%. A whopping 69.6% rated the second system being better than the first one. Moving on to the warrior-1 pose, we again had 22 participants recording their ability to perform it accurately as "good" and "very good" with the first system in comparison to only 19 with the second system. The results for concentration level were also similar to those that of the previous pose - with the second system performing better by 8.7%. 65.2% said that they preferred the second system over the first one. Finally for the triangle pose, we see a slight decline in the number of participants recording their ability to perform it accurately as "good" and "very good" with the first system, i.e., 20 in comparison to a steady 19 with the second system. Coming to the concentration level, both the systems had 7 people reporting that their concentration level as "very good". Here too, 56.5% of the participants chose the second system with personalised feedback over the first one with only images.

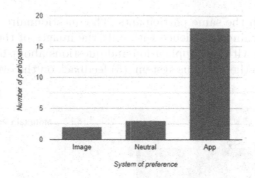

Fig. 7. Participants preference between Image and the app

Overall, 81.8% of the participants felt that the second system helped them learn and perform the exercise better in comparison to the first system. In addition, 52.2% of them rated it as being "very good".

5   Conclusion and Future Work

With the current situation requiring us to spend more time indoors, learning a new skill, especially one like yoga can be frustrating and stressful. While personal trainers are not affordable to everyone, books or video guides have their own drawbacks by not providing personalized feedback. All of this makes yoga really difficult to learn on our own. The objective of our research was to build a classification model that would recognize various yoga postures or asanas from a small set of images using Deep Learning. This involves a virtual trainer who will take us through a series of postures, demonstrating each pose and then instructing us to do it together. The poses are typically held for 10 s. There will be different levels and categories to choose from ranging from beginner to advanced and classic to modern yoga forms. While performing each pose, users get feedback on their posture and possible improvements by the pose estimation model.

In this article, a survey was conducted with a group of people about their physical activity and mental problems during the pandemic. In the survey, 56.5% of people chose yoga as their preference for physical activity. After the survey, a self yoga trainer is developed and introduced it to the same group of people in an another survey. The system consists of PoseNet as the pose extractor and then the poses are sent into a classifier to classify the pose. Once the pose is classified we calculate the angle between the joints and give the user real time feedback. A solid number of 81.8% of people agreed that the trainer offered them to achieve better posture and confidence when compared to traditional images.

To make this trainer a fully-functional intelligent fitness-training system, we should also introduce a plot or story around which the exergame revolves. Currently, we use PoseNet which estimates the human pose 2D space. Estimating pose only in 2D space is limited to only few selected yoga poses. In order to make this a robust system we should introduce pose estimation in 3D space. In the future work, the system will consists of some music and an interactive voice assistant to assist them during the training thus making it more wholesome experience. Further, including a progress chart and reward system will be beneficial for the users as they increase accountability and a sense of achievement. Finally, we conclude by pointing out that the current approach is limited to only a set of yoga postures and have to be improved in-order to accurately train for a diverse amount of poses.

References

1. Abadi, M., et al.: TensorFlow: large-scale machine learning on heterogeneous systems (2015). Software available from tensorflow.org
2. Anilkumar, A., Athulya, K.T., Sajan, S., Sreeja K.A.: Pose estimated yoga monitoring system. SSRN Electron. J. (2021)
3. Best, J.: Exergaming in youth. Zeitschrift für Psychol. **221**, 72 (2013)
4. Bhambure, S., Lawande, S., Upasani, R., Kundargi, J.: YOG-assist. Miss Yoga: a yoga assistant mobile application based on keypoint detection. In: Huang, R., Wang, J., Lou, H., Lu, H., Wang, B (eds.) 2@inproceedingsHuang2020 2020 Digital Image Computing: Techniques and Applications (DICTA) 021 4th Biennial International Conference on Nascent Technologies in Engineering (ICNTE). IEEE, January 2021. https://doi.org/10.1109/dicta51227.2020.9363384
5. Bhattacharyya, R., Chatterjee, S.S., Bhattacharyya, S., Gupta, S., Das, S., Banerjee, B.B.: Attitude, practice, behavior, and mental health impact of COVID-19 on doctors. Indian J. Psychiatry **62**(3), 257 (2020)
6. Bogost, I.: Persuasive Games: The Expressive Power of Videogames, MIT Press, Cambridge (2007)
7. Bolton, J., Lambert, M., Lirette, D., Unsworth, B.: Paperdude: a virtual reality cycling exergame. In CHI 2014 Extended Abstracts on Human Factors in Computing Systems, CHI EA 2014, pp. 475–478, New York. Association for Computing Machinery (2014)
8. Cao, Z., Hidalgo, G., Simon, T., Wei, S.-E., Sheikh, Y.: OpenPose: Realtime Multi-Person 2D Pose Estimation using Part Affinity Fields. arXiv e-prints, arXiv:1812.08008, December 2018
9. Chiddarwar, G.G., Ranjane, A., Chindhe, M., Deodhar, R., Gangamwar, P.: AI-based yoga pose estimation for android application. Int. J. Inn. Sci. Res. Tech. **5**(9) 1070–1073 (2020)
10. Finco, M.D., Maass, R.W.: The history of exergames: promotion of exercise and active living through body interaction. In 2014 IEEE 3nd International Conference on Serious Games and Applications for Health (SeGAH), pp. 1–6 (2014)
11. Gao, Y., Mandryk, R.L.: GrabApple: the design of a casual exergame. In: Anacleto, J.C., Fels, S., Graham, N., Kapralos, B., Saif El-Nasr, M., Stanley, K. (eds.) ICEC 2011. LNCS, vol. 6972, pp. 35–46. Springer, Heidelberg (2011). https://doi.org/10. 1007/978-3-642-24500-8_5
12. Gao, Z., Lee, J.E., Pope, Z., Zhang, D.: Effect of active videogames on underserved children's classroom behaviors, effort, and fitness. Games Health J. **5**(5), 318–324 (2016)

13. Huang, R., Wang, J., Lou, H., Lu, H., Wang, B.: Miss yoga: a yoga assistant mobile application based on keypoint detection. In: 2020 Digital Image Computing: Techniques and Applications (DICTA). IEEE, November 2020
14. Khan, K.S., Mamun, M.A., Griffiths, M.D., Ullah, I.: The mental health impact of the COVID-19 pandemic across different cohorts. Int. J. Ment. Health Add. 1–7 (2020)
15. Kingma, D.P., Ba, J.: Adam: A Method for Stochastic Optimization. arXiv e-prints, page arXiv:1412.6980, December 2014
16. Kwok, J.J.Y.Y., Choi, K.C., Chan, H.Y.L.: Effects of mind–body exercises on the physiological and psychosocial well-being of individuals with Parkinson's disease: a systematic review and meta-analysis. Complement. Ther. Med. **29**, 121–131 (2016)
17. Lai, J., et al.: Factors associated with mental health outcomes among health care workers exposed to coronavirus disease 2019. JAMA Netw. Open **3**(3), e203976 (2020)
18. Martin-Niedecken, A.L., Rogers, K., Turmo Vidal, L., Mekler, E.D., Márquez Segura, E.: ExerCube vs. personal trainer: evaluating a holistic, immersive, and adaptive fitness game setup. In: Proceedings of the 2019 CHI Conference on Human Factors in Computing Systems, pp. 1–15. Association for Computing Machinery, New York (2019)
19. Moldovan, I., et al.: Development of a new scoring system for bilateral upper limb function and performance in children with cerebral palsy using the mira interactive video games and the kinect sensor. In: Proceedings of the International Conference on Disability, Virtual Reality and Associated Technologies, pp. 2–4 (2014)
20. Sarah, A., et al.: Tremblay impact of the COVID-19 virus outbreak on movement and play behaviours of Canadian children and youth: a national survey. Int. J. Behav. Nutr. Phys. Act. **17**(1), 1–11 (2020)
21. Oh, Y., Yang, S.: Defining Exergames & Exergaming (2010)
22. Papandreou, G., Zhu, T., Chen, L.-C., Gidaris, S., Tompson, J., Murphy, K.: PersonLab: Person Pose Estimation and Instance Segmentation with a Bottom-Up, Part-Based, Geometric Embedding Model. arXiv e-prints, page arXiv:1803.08225, March 2018
23. Park, J.H., Moon, J.H., Kim, H.J., Kong, M.H., Oh, Y.H.: Sedentary lifestyle: overview of updated evidence of potential health risks. Korean J. Fam. Med. **41**(6), 365–373 (2020)
24. Rick, S.R., Bhaskaran, S., Sun, Y., McEwen, S., Weibel, N.: Neuropose: geriatric rehabilitation in the home using a webcam and pose estimation. In: Proceedings of the 24th International Conference on Intelligent User Interfaces: Companion, IUI 2019, pp. 105–106. Association for Computing Machinery, New York (2019)
25. Rishan, F., De Silva, B., Alawathugoda, S., Nijabdeen, S., Rupasinghe, L., Liyanapathirana, C.: Infinity yoga tutor: yoga posture detection and correction system. In: 2020 5th International Conference on Information Technology Research (ICITR). IEEE, December 2020
26. Ross, A., Thomas, S.: The health benefits of yoga and exercise: a review of comparison studies. J. Altern. Complement. Med. **16**(1), 3–12 (2010)
27. Sarma, H.: Virtual Movement from Natural Language Text. PhD thesis, Universität Bremen (2019)
28. Sarma, H., Porzel, R., Smeddinck, J.D., Malaka, R., Samaddar, A.B.: A text to animation system for physical exercises. Comput. J. **61**(11), 1589–1604 (2018)
29. Stanton, R., et al.: Depression, anxiety and stress during COVID-19: associations with changes in physical activity, sleep, tobacco and alcohol use in Australian adults. Int. J. Environ. Res. Publ. Health **17**(11), 4065 (2020)

30. Thar, M.C., Winn, K.Z.N., Funabiki, N.: A proposal of yoga pose assessment method using pose detection for self-learning. In 2019 International Conference on Advanced Information Technologies (ICAIT), pp. 137–142 (2019)
31. Verma, M., Kumawat, S., Nakashima, Y., Raman, S.: Yoga-82: A New Dataset for Fine-grained Classification of Human Poses. arXiv e-prints, page arXiv:2004.10362, April 2020
32. Yadav, S.K., Singh, A., Gupta, A., Raheja, J.L: Real-time Yoga recognition using deep learning. Neural Comput. Appl. **31**(12), 9349–9361 (2019). https://doi.org/10.1007/s00521-019-04232-7
33. Zheng, C., Huang, W.Y., Sheridan, S., Sit, C.H.-P., Chen, X.-K., Wong, S.H.-S.: COVID-19 pandemic brings a sedentary lifestyle in young adults: a cross-sectional and longitudinal study. Int. J. Environ. Res. Publ. Health **17**(17), 6035 (2020)

Statistical Evaluation of Orientation Correction Algorithms in a Real-Time Hand Tracking Application for Computer Interaction

Neeranut Ratchatanantakit, Nonnarit O-larnnithipong[(⊠)], Pontakorn Sonchan[(⊠)], Malek Adjouadi[(⊠)], and Armando Barreto[(⊠)]

Department of Electrical and Computer Engineering, Florida International University, Miami, FL, USA

{nratc001,nolarnni,psonc001,adjouadi,barretoa}@fiu.edu

Abstract. A new approach to correct the orientation estimate for a miniature Magnetic-Angular Rate-Gravity (MARG) module is statistically evaluated in a hand motion tracking system. Thirty human subjects performed an experiment to validate the performance of the proposed orientation correction algorithm in both non-magnetically distorted (MN) and magnetically distorted (MD) areas. The Kruskal-Wallis tests show that the orientation correction algorithm using Gravity and Magnetic Vectors with Double SLERP (GMV-D), the correction using Gravity and Magnetic Vectors with Single SLERP (GMV-S) and the on-board Kalman-Filter (KF) performed similarly in non-magnetically distorted areas. However, the statistical tests show that, when operating in the magnetically distorted region, the level of error in the orientation estimates produced by the three methods is significantly different, with the proposed GMV-D method yielding lower levels of error in the three Euler Angles Phi, Theta and Psi. This indicates that the GMV-D method was better able to provide orientation estimates that are more robust against local disturbances of the magnetic field that might exist in the operating space of the MARG module.

Keywords: MARG · Inertial measurement unit · Gyroscope drift · Drift correction algorithm · Quaternion correction · Magnetic distortion · Hand motion tracking

1 Introduction

Over the past decade, the popularity of Virtual Reality (VR) and Augmented Reality (AR) has dramatically increased in many applications [1–5]. Computers are part of many aspects of human activity and users seek to interact with computers in ways that are natural and intuitive [6–8]. The available input devices like mice, game pads, joysticks and wands are commonly used to interact with computers but may require the user to perform highly artificial sequences of actions. Therefore, the ability for computer systems to have the real-time capability to capture user hand movement or hand motion tracking is an interesting option for users to interact more naturally with 3D interfaces and may be a crucial step towards the improvement of the next generation of human-computer interaction systems.

An emerging approach for capturing the orientation of the hand is the use of Micro-Electro-Mechanical Systems (MEMS) Magnetic-Angular Rate-Gravity modules (MARGs). These miniature modules can be attached to multiple segments of an instrumented glove to monitor the different moving segments of the user's hand. In this initial development we have studied the use of a single MARG module (YEI 3-space Sensor) attached to the dorsal surface of a glove [9]. Simultaneously, a 3-camera IR-video tracking system (OptiTrack V120 Trio) is used in conjunction with the MARG module to provide position coordinates of the sensor. The 3D gyroscope in the MARG module measures its angular velocity and makes it possible to calculate the module's 3D orientation by quaternion (q) accumulation.

While this angle accumulation is the fundamental concept for orientation estimation using Inertial Measurement Units (IMUs), different types of gyroscopes are used in many industries and have a wide range of accuracy levels that tend to be in proportion to their price [10], from navigation systems in aviation to the MEMS gyroscopes used in portable devices (e.g., mobile phones). The different grades of gyroscopes have significantly different error and noise characteristics. MEMS gyroscopes may have significant offset levels in their outputs, which, furthermore, may not be exactly constant, but instead they may be slowly varying. This "bias offset error" can result in high levels of orientation tracking error, as the angular velocity readings have to be integrated over time to obtain orientation estimates. The resulting type of orientation error, called "drift," is a common effect that continues to grow through time as the sensor operates and keeps integrating the rotational speed measurements. Left uncorrected, the orientation drift is likely to result in orientation estimate errors that could soon render those estimates useless. In traditional inertial navigation systems, the inertial estimates of orientation and position are usually corrected periodically using information from external sources (e.g., GPS for outdoor position estimation). For our indoor, human-computer interaction application we sought to correct the gyroscope-based orientation estimates, expressed as a quaternion $\hat{q}_G$ using the 2 other sensor modalities available in MARG modules: 3-axis accelerometer and 3-axis magnetometer.

For both, the accelerometer and the magnetometer, instantaneous readings in each of the 3 axes will evolve as the module changes orientation. We can rely on the assumption that the gravity vector will always be perpendicular to the floor of the environment where the MARG module is used. Therefore, the 3 currently measured accelerometer components should match the transformation of the gravity vector sensed initially (when the sensor is considered aligned with the inertial frame of reference), by application of the total orientation change estimated by the gyroscope operation, $\hat{q}_G$, from the initial orientation. If a difference exists, it may be hypothesized that it is due to error that has developed in $\hat{q}_G$ (e.g., due to drift), and the 3 current accelerometer readings will offer a means to apply an accelerometer-based correction to $\hat{q}_G$. However, this reasoning is correct, and the accelerometer-based correction is adequate if, at the current time, the accelerometers are only recording the acceleration of gravity. This requires that the MARG module be, at this time, static, or very close to it, so that there is not a "linear acceleration" component in the accelerometer measurements (in addition to the measurement of gravity). Therefore, an initial version of our orientation correction algorithm defined a parameter $0 \leq \alpha \leq 1$, that is derived from the "stillness" parameter ("confidence value") provided by the MARG module, and would apply the accelerometer-based correction only in proportion to α, This correction is achieved by changing the corrected orientation from the original $\hat{q}_G$ orientation (if $\alpha = 0$) to the orientation that would be predicted by the accelerometer readings alone (if α were 1), using Spherical Linear Quaternion Interpolation (SLERP) [11]. In general, the SLERP interpolation between 2 quaternions $\hat{q}_0$ and $\hat{q}_1$ will be controlled by the scalar interpolating parameter h:

$$[SLERP(q_0, q_1, h)] = \frac{q_0 \sin((1 - h)\Omega) + q_1 \sin(h\Omega)}{\sin(\Omega)} \tag{1}$$

$$\text{where,} \quad \Omega = cos^{-1}(\hat{q}_0 \cdot \hat{q}_1) \tag{2}$$

So, for example, accelerometer-based correction could be interpolated under the control of α from $\hat{q}_G$ to $\hat{q}_{GA}$ to define a partially corrected $\hat{q}_{\text{partial}}$:

$$\hat{q}_{\text{partial}} = [SLERP(\hat{q}_G, \hat{q}_{GA}, a)] \tag{3}$$

Since the MARG module also has a 3-axis magnetometer, a completely similar correction mechanism could be attempted on the basis of the current readings of the magnetometer. However, while the gravity acceleration vector can be properly approximated as constant throughout the working environment of the MARG module, the constant orientation of the magnetic vector in a given working environment cannot usually be assumed. This is because the magnetic field lines produced by the Earth's magnetic field will be bent, perhaps significantly, in some regions within the space in which the MARG sensor operates by the presence of ferromagnetic objects located nearby [12, 13]. The combined MARG orientation correction process we propose accepts the possibility of these magnetically distorted areas in the working space of the sensor. However, it will only apply magnetometer-based corrections when the "trustworthiness" of the magnetic field orientation currently acting on the MARG module is deemed high, as encoded in a parameter $0 \leq \mu \leq 1$, that will act in the same way α acted for the accelerometer-correction.

2 Methodology and Materials

Previously, an initial Gravity-Magnetic Vector Compensation (GMV) approach was introduced by O-larnnithipong [14]. That algorithm involves signals from both accelerometer and magnetometer, but under exclusive control of a single parameter, α, and does not attempt to detect magnetically distorted regions in the working space of the sensor. An accelerometer-based corrected orientation $\hat{q}_{GA}$ is calculated and, similarly, a magnetometer-based corrected orientation, $\hat{q}_{GM}$ is also defined. Then, GMV uses SLERP to define the final orientation quaternion between $\hat{q}_{GA}$ and $\hat{q}_{GM}$, solely on the basis of α, bringing the final result closer to $\hat{q}_{GA}$ for α closer to 1. This followed the logic that, if the MARG module is very close to a static condition, the accelerometer-based correction is trustworthy. However, if the sensor operates in a magnetically distorted region, when simultaneously α is low, the previous method may still give $\hat{q}_{GM}$ a large weight in the definition of the final corrected orientation estimate. This could lead to orientation estimate errors, in those particular circumstances. Our new proposed method prevents those performance shortcomings by assessing the magnetic trustworthiness, encoded in μ, and using this parameter for the quaternion interpolation also.

2.1 Double SLERP (GMV-D)

The proposed method refines the previous approach by calculating a magnetic trustworthiness parameter, μ, which is then used to control the strength of the contribution from the magnetometer-based correction into the final corrected estimate. This μ parameter has to be different for different locations around the working space of the MARG module, and it is not known for any location at the beginning of the operation of the MARG module. To keep track of the μ values at different locations, the working space is considered divided into small (e.g., 2 cm per side) cubic regions, or "voxels". Initially, all voxels are assigned a μ value of 0, since it is not known that they are magnetically trustworthy.

As the computer user proceeds to operate the system, the processing of the data from the MARG module will approximately fall into one of 4 cases at every sampling time, which are summarized in Table 1. At every sampling instant, the position of the sensor will be retrieved from the OptiTrack system and, with this and the readings from the MARG module, the control parameters α and μ will be managed and used to determine the contribution of the accelerometer-based correction and the magnetometer-based correction to the final orientation estimate.

The final orientation estimate will be calculated form 2 preliminary results, $\hat{q}_{SA}$ and $\hat{q}_{SM}$, which represent the partial accelerometer-based and magnetometer-based corrections to $\hat{q}_G$, via corresponding SLERP operations:

$$\hat{q}_{SA} = SLERP(\hat{q}_G, \hat{q}_{GA}, \alpha) \tag{4}$$

$$\hat{q}_{SM} = SLERP(\hat{q}_G, \hat{q}_{GM}, \mu) \tag{5}$$

It must be noticed that, if α is low, $\hat{q}_{SA}$ will not be much different from $\hat{q}_G$. Similarly, if μ is low, $\hat{q}_{SM}$ will not be much different from $\hat{q}_G$.

The final orientation estimate will be obtained from a second SLERP operation on both of the preliminary results, and controlled by α:

$$\hat{q}_{OUT} = SLERP(\hat{q}_{SM}, \hat{q}_{SA}, \alpha) \tag{6}$$

Table 1. Summarizes the differential emphasis that are given to the accelerometer-based and magnetometer-based contributions to the final orientation estimate.

Case	μ close to:	α close to:	$\hat{q}_{SM} \approx$	$\hat{q}_{SA} \approx$	$\hat{q}_{OUT} \approx$
Case 0	0	0	$\hat{q}_G$	$\hat{q}_G$	$\hat{q}_G$
Case 1	0	1	$\hat{q}_G$	$\hat{q}_{GA}$	$\hat{q}_{GA}$
Case 2	1	0	$\hat{q}_{GM}$	$\hat{q}_G$	$\hat{q}_{GM}$
Case 3	1	1	$\hat{q}_{GM}$	$\hat{q}_{GA}$	$\hat{q}_{GA}$

2.2 The Control Parameters (α and μ)

Parameter α

Prior to being used to determine the value of the control parameter α, the average of recent stillness ("confidence") values read from the MARG module are processed by a first-order Gamma filter to smoothen the signal. The Gamma filter uses a weight parameter (W), which ranges from 0 to 1, to control the filtering characteristics of the low pass filter it implements on the signal. (We selected $W_\alpha = 0.25$.) The first-order Gamma filter has the difference equation derived in Eqs. 7 to 10.

$$H(z) = \frac{Y(z)}{X(z)} = \frac{W}{z - (1 - W)} \tag{7}$$

$$Y(z) = (W)z^{-1}X(z) + (1 - W)z^{-1}Y(z) \tag{8}$$

$$y[n] = (W)x[n - 1] + (1 - W)y[n - 1] \tag{9}$$

$$\alpha_g = W_\alpha(Stillness(n - 1)^2) + (1 - W_\alpha)\alpha_g(n - 1) \tag{10}$$

Then a linear equation was applied to accelerate the drop of the α parameter when the sensor begins departing from a static status. This equation is characterized by the value of its slope (m_α). The final value of the control parameter for quaternion interpolation of gravity vector correction (α) is calculated from Eqs. 11 and 12.

$$\alpha' = m_\alpha\alpha_g + (1 - m_\alpha) \tag{11}$$

$$\alpha = \alpha' + \frac{|\alpha'|}{2} \tag{12}$$

Magnetic Correction Trustworthiness (μ)

To define this Magnetic Correction Trustworthiness parameter (μ) the current position data from the OptiTrack system is used to identify in which voxel the MARG module is presently located, applying Eq. 13 for all three axes

$$Location\ of\ MARG\ module\ (index\ of\ voxel) = floor(\frac{current\ Coordinate}{Voxel\ Size}) + 1 \tag{13}$$

The μ parameter will be used for the definition of the final orientation estimate, as indicated in Eqs. 4, 5, and 6. However, before every iteration (sampling instant) is ended, the current value of α is compared against a threshold, α_{TH}. If $\alpha > \alpha_{TH}$, we can expect that the correction suggested by the accelerometer, here identified as $\hat{q}_G = \hat{q}_{Gpost}$, is correct. This will provide an opportunity to update the value of μ for the current voxel.

It is possible that the μ value retrieved from memory may simply be the zero-value assigned during initialization. To update this value, we will assess the difference between the orientation estimate that would be suggested from the current magnetometer readings, m_0 and the one calculated by rotating the initial magnetic field vector, M_{int}, with the recently computed $\hat{q}_{Gpost}$, which we trust to be correct. To do this we compute the angle γ, whose cosine ranges from -1 to 1.

The parameter μ is computed from cosine of γ by rescaling and application of a linear equation to severely penalize departures from perfect agreement (which would yield $\mu = 1$):

$$\vec{\mu}(q_{Gpost}) = q_{Gpost}^* \otimes M_{int} \otimes q_{Gpost} \tag{14}$$

$$cos(\gamma) = \frac{\vec{m}_0 \vec{\mu}(q_{Gpost})}{|\vec{m}_0||\vec{\mu}(q_{Gpost})|} \tag{15}$$

$$\mu' = m_m(acos(cos(\gamma))) + 1 \tag{16}$$

$$\mu = \frac{(1 + \mu')}{2} \tag{17}$$

It is expected that, as the user moves his/her hand through the working space of the system the initial $\mu = 0$ values assigned at initialization will be updated by μ values that really reflect the magnetic trustworthiness of the regions visited by the module.

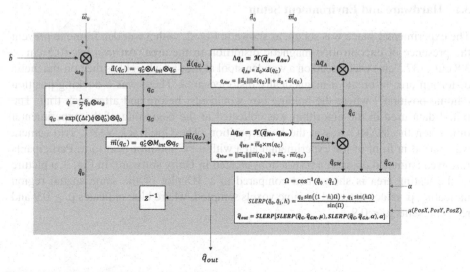

Fig. 1. Block diagram of the orientation correction algorithm using the gravity vector and magnetic North vector with Double SLERP (GMV-D).

This will enable the effective consideration of magnetometer-based correction in more instances but will prevent allowing magnetometer readings to introduce large errors where the magnetic field is distorted. The overall proposed algorithm is outlined in the block diagram shown in Fig. 1.

3 Implementation

To quantify the performance of the proposed algorithm, thirty human subjects (22 males and 8 females, all right-handed) participated in an experiment. Their ages ranged from 18 to 60 years old. None of the subjects reported any motion impediments which could affect the performance of the evaluation task. The MARG module was attached to a wooden holding box (prism) for ease of manipulation. During the performance, the locations of the holding box were recorded using the marker coordinates from the OptiTrack V120: Trio system, and the data from a Magnetic, Angular-rate, Gravity (MARG) module attached to the holding box was recorded. The orientations estimated by the methods implemented while the subjects were sustaining specific instructed poses were analyzed statistically. In the area without magnetic distortion, each subject held 9 poses (First, pose 1, then poses 2, 3, 4 and 5, with a return to Pose 1 after each). Similarly, each subject held 9 poses in the magnetically distorted area (Pose 6 and then 7, 8, 9 and 10 with returns to 6).

The proposed algorithm was implemented to calculate the estimated orientation. The calculated results obtained from the Gravity Vector and Magnetometer with Double SLERP (GMV-D) were compared with the orientation estimates obtained from the Gravity Vector and Magnetometer with Single SLERP (GMV-S), and the Kalman-based filter quaternion output that was provided directly from the Yost Labs 3-Space MARG sensor module.

3.1 Hardware and Environment Setup

The experimental space was set up, as shown in Fig. 2, with a wooden frame to prevent the presence of uncontrolled magnetic distortion in the area. An iron bar (0.5 cm × 3.8 cm × 37.5 cm) was placed on a wooden stool at the same height as the non-magnetic distortion area to create a magnetically distorted area. There was a docking position ("home position") where the holding box would rest before and after each trial. The initial data used in the algorithm was collected at the beginning of the experimental run, when the MARG was at the home position. The OptiTrack V120: Trio camera was placed in front of the experimental area with a PC monitor next to it. Participants followed animated on-screen instructions created in Unity software. In Fig. 3, a picture of the testing area is shown and compared to a 3D plot of the same spatial region indicating μ values detected in some voxels sampled, where blue indicates $\mu \geq 0.9$ and red represents $\mu < 0.9$.

Fig. 2. The subject performs the experiment at the testing area.

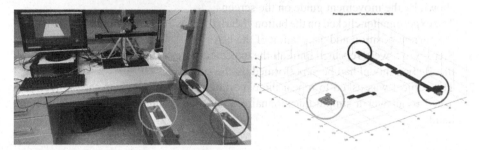

Fig. 3. The experiment station compared to a MU plot for some 3D voxels visited by the MARG. Red cubes indicate significant magnetic distortion (MU < 0.9) (Color figure online)

3.2 Software Setting

A virtual 3D environment was also created in the same project with Unity. A 3D rectangle shape was created to represent the wooden holding box. A C# script was written to pre-define the movements of the sensor box that the subject had to perform. They consisted of an initial position at the dock area, nine specific orientations (or "poses") at the

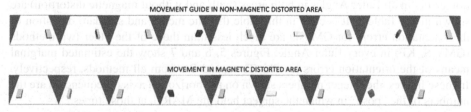

Fig. 4. The movement guide animation in non-magnetically distorted (top) and magnetically distorted (bottom) areas showing the identical rotations performed.

non-magnetic distorted area, nine poses at the magnetic distorted area, and the ending position at the dock area. The 3D box model was displayed as the movement guide for the subjects to follow and perform the experiment. The nine poses at both the non-magnetically distorted area and the magnetically distorted area are identical, as shown in Fig. 4.

3.3 Experiment Procedure

1. Firstly, the subject was asked to stand in the testing area, facing toward the IR camera and a desktop monitor with the holding box placed in front of him/her. Then, the experimenter started the program.
2. The experimenter clicked on the button "Mark this position and orientation" to record the initial position and orientation of the sensor.
3. The experimenter clicked on the button "Show next movement" to show the animation of the 3D box model. The 3D box model rotated and/or translated to the next state (pose) of the box movement sequence.
4. The subject grasped the box and moved it to match the position and orientation as shown by the movement guide on the screen.
5. The experimenter clicked on the button "Mark this position and orientation" to record the current position and orientation of the box.
6. Steps 3 to 5 were repeated until all the expected states or poses of the movement of the 3D box model had been performed by the subject.
7. The subject was asked to repeat the experiment two times. Then, the subject was asked to answer a simple questionnaire about age, gender, and his/her dominant hand.

4 Results and Discussion

The statistical analysis compares the performance of 3 algorithms: Kalman Filter (KF), GMV-S, and GMV-D. A total of 1620 rows of data (30 subjects x 18 orientations x 3 algorithms) were recorded and statistically analyzed using the SPSS statistical package. The recorded data represent the difference between the reference orientation (instructed to the subjects) and the output from the algorithms, measured in terms of the corresponding Euler Angles (Phi, Theta and Psi, which represent the value of the angles rotated about the x, y and z axes). If the orientation algorithm worked correctly, these differences were expected to be 'zero'. The estimated means and standard deviation of the orientation errors in all Euler Angles in both areas (with and without magnetic distortion) are shown in the Table 2. It is clear in this table that the means and standard deviation of the orientation errors for GMV-D are much less than those of the other two methods (GMV-S, KF) in every Euler Angle. Figures 5, 6 and 7 show the estimated marginal means of the orientation errors for Phi, Theta and Psi from all methods, respectively. In these figures, the integer numbers shown on the horizontal axis ("Sequence") are the numbers of the "pose" in which the subject held the MARG, at those times.

Table 2. Estimated means and standard deviation of the orientation output. (in degree)

Algorithm	Dependent variable	Phi	Theta	Psi
GMV-D	Mean	1.858	8.231	3.992
	Std. deviation	2.658	10.818	8.554
GMV-S	Mean	5.053	38.318	16.104
	Std. deviation	14.769	52.557	37.527
KF	Mean	11.065	53.452	17.887
	Std. deviation	17.071	65.382	40.489
Total	Mean	5.992	33.334	12.661
	Std. deviation	13.659	52.302	32.821
	N	1800	1800	1800

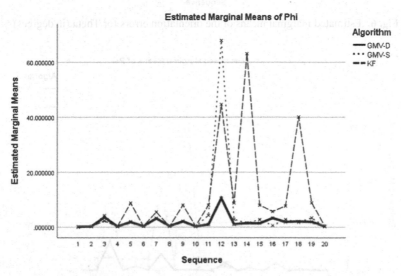

Fig. 5. Estimated marginal means of the orientation errors for Phi (in degrees)

The multivariate analysis of variance (MANOVA) was originally chosen to test for the effects of the three algorithms on the orientation output errors. However, the appropriate application of MANOVA analysis requires verification of two key assumptions in the data, which are normality of the error and equal variances across treatments. The null hypothesis for normality test is that the data are normally distributed within each treatment group. The results from the tests of normality (Kolmogorov-Smirnov and Shapiro-Wilk) are shown in Table 3 having the p-values of 0.000 for all angles and all methods. These results provided strong evidence that the orientation output errors are not normally distributed.

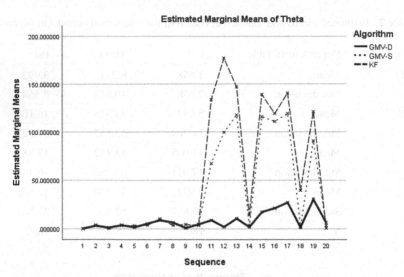

Fig. 6. Estimated marginal means of the orientation errors for Theta (in degrees)

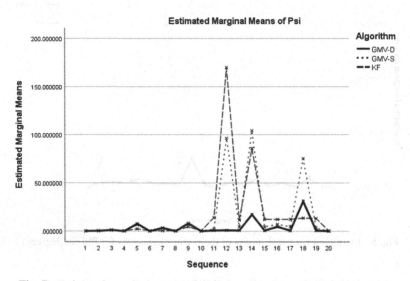

Fig. 7. Estimated marginal means of the orientation errors for Psi (in degrees)

Next, the homogeneity of variances was tested with the null hypothesis that the error variance of the dependent variable is equal across treatment groups, yielding the results shown in the Table 4. The p-values $= 0.000$ from all three dependent variables of the test of homogeneity of variances, provide strong evidence that the error variances are not equal among three treatment groups (GMV-D, GMV-S and KF) which, therefore, results in rejection of the null hypothesis.

Table 3. Tests of normality: Kolmogorov-Smirnov and Shapiro-Wilk

	Algorithm	Kolmogorov-Smirnov*			Shapiro-Wilk		
		Statistic	df	Sig.	Statistic	df	Sig.
Phi	GMV-D	.243	600	.000	.591	600	.000
	GMV-S	.424	600	.000	.314	600	.000
	KF	.319	600	.000	.643	600	.000
Theta	GMV-D	.224	600	.000	.692	600	.000
	GMV-S	.348	600	.000	.707	600	.000
	KF	.302	600	.000	.733	600	.000
Psi	GMV-D	.321	600	.000	.498	600	.000
	GMV-S	.412	600	.000	.462	600	.000
	KF	.377	600	.000	.446	600	.000

a. Lilliefors Significance Correction

Table 4. Levene's test of equality of error variances.

		Levene			
		Statistic	df1	df2	Sig.
Phi	Based on Mean	24.062	59	1740	.000
	Based on Median	21.110	59	1740	.000
	Based on Median and with adjusted df	21.110	59	131.746	.000
	Based on trimmed mean	22.299	59	1740	.000
Theta	Based on Mean	61.970	59	1740	.000
	Based on Median	37.068	59	1740	.000
	Based on Median and with adjusted df	37.068	59	193.641	.000
	Based on trimmed mean	58.456	59	1740	.000
Psi	Based on Mean	105.361	59	1740	.000
	Based on Median	64.094	59	1740	.000
	Based on Median and with adjusted df	64.094	59	96.072	.000
	Based on trimmed mean	103.864	59	1740	.000

Dependent variable: Phi, Theta, Psi

Design: Intercept + Algorithm + Sequence + Algorithm * Sequence

As the MANOVA analysis was found not to be appropriate for the data, the non-parametric Kruskal-Wallis H test was chosen to perform the analysis, since it does not require the assumptions of variance homogeneity and normality of errors [15]. The Kruskal-Wallis is a rank-based nonparametric test, commonly used for determining the statistical significance of the differences of a dependent variable across two or more treatment groups [16]. Each dependent variable (Phi, Theta and Psi) was tested with the

Kruskal-Wallis approach at a level of significance of 0.05 to determine if there are differences in means across the three algorithms (treatments). The analysis was performed separately for the poses held in the area that was not magnetically disturbed (Sequence number 2 to 10) and the area that was magnetically disturbed (Sequence number 11 to 19).

For the area, which was not magnetically distorted, Table 5 shows that the distributions of both Phi and Theta were not significantly different across the three algorithms, with H = 5.478, p = 0.065 and H = 2.439, p = 0.295, respectively. The null hypothesis that the distribution of orientation errors is the same across algorithms was rejected only for the Psi angle, for which H(2) = 14.586, p = 0.001, with a mean rank of 381.70 for GMV-S, 384.93 for GMV-D and 449.86 for KF. Through pairwise[1] comparisons, as shown in Table 6, the results indicate that there are no statistically significant differences of the orientation errors in Psi between GMV-S and GMV-D (p = 1.000) while KF shows statistically significant differences of the orientation errors with GMV-S (p = 0.002) and GMV-D (p = 0.004).

Table 5. Kruskal-Wallis test statistics results for the orientation errors in the Euler angle Phi, Theta and Psi across three different methods in the non-magnetically distorted area with N = 810

Dependent variable	Algorithm	Mean rank	Test statistic	Df	Asymp. Sig.
Phi	GMV-D	–	5.478	2	0.065
	GMV-S	–			
	KF	–			
Theta	GMV-D	–	2.439	2	0.295
	GMV-S	–			
	KF	–			
Psi	GMV-D	384.93	14.586	2	0.001
	GMV-S	381.70			
	KF	449.86			

Table 6. Pairwise comparison among three algorithms for orientation errors in the Euler angles Psi in the non-magnetically distorted area.

Algor 1–Algor 2	Test statistic	Std. error	Std. test statistic	Sig.	Adj. sig.
GMV-S-GMVD	3.230	20.137	0.160	0.873	1.000
GMV-S-KF	−68.159	20.137	−3.385	0.001	0.002
GMV-D-KF	−64.930	20.137	−3.224	0.001	0.004

---

[1] Each row tests the null hypothesis that the Sample 1 and Sample 2 distributions are the same. Asymptotic significance (2-sided tests) is displayed. The significance level is .05.

For the area affected by magnetic distortion, Table 7 shows the test summary, which leads to rejection of the null hypothesis that the distribution of orientation errors for all the angles (Phi, Theta and Psi) is the same across algorithms. Table 8 supplements the information by showing the statistics for pairwise comparisons among algorithms, regarding their error levels on Phi, Theta and Psi.

With respect to Phi, Table 7 shows results that lead to the rejection of the null hypothesis (that the distribution of Phi errors is the same across the algorithms). The results from the test indicate that there is a statistically significant difference between the orientation errors in Phi produced by different algorithms ($H(2) = 365.929$, $p = 0.000$), with a mean rank of 252.20 for GMV-D, 342.62 for GMV-S and 621.69 for KF. Through pairwise comparisons among the three algorithms, it was found that there are statistically significant differences of the orientation errors in Phi between GMV-D and GMV-S ($p = 0.000$), between GMV-D and KF ($p = 0.000$), and between GMV-S and KF ($p = 0.000$). GMV-D shows the best performance, which is 4.490 less than GMV-S and 18.349 less than KF, in standard test statistic value. With respect to Theta, Table 7 shows results that lead to the rejection of the null hypothesis (that the distribution of Theta errors is the same across the algorithms). The results from the test indicate that there is a statistically significant difference between the orientation errors in Theta produced by the different algorithms ($H(2) = 377.616$, $p = 0.000$), with a mean rank of 197.76 for GMV-D, 432.47 for GMV-S and 586.27 for KF. Through pairwise comparisons among the three algorithms, it was found that there are statistically significant differences of the orientation errors in Theta between GMV-D and GMV-S ($p = 0.000$), between GMV-D and KF ($p = 0.000$), and between GMV-S and KF ($p = 0.000$). GMV-D shows the best performance, which is 11.656 less than GMV-S and 19.293 less than KF in standard test statistic value. Lastly, with respect to Psi, Table 7 shows results that lead to the rejection of the null hypothesis (that the distribution of Psi errors is the same across the algorithms). The results from the test indicate that there is a statistically significant difference between the orientation errors in Psi for different algorithms ($H(2) = 278.583$, $p = 0.000$), with a mean rank of 229.84 for GMV-D, 421.93 for GMV-S and 564.73 for KF. Through pairwise comparisons among the three algorithms, it was found that there are statistically significant differences of the orientation errors in Psi between GMV-D and GMV-S ($p = 0.000$), between GMV-D and KF ($p = 0.000$), and between GMV-S and KF ($p = 0.000$). GMV-D shows the best performance, which is 9.539 less than GMV-S and 16.631 less than KF in standard test statistic value.

The preceding sections, overall, have shown results that match the key intent of the development of the newly proposed algorithm, GMV-D, which was to make the orientation estimation derived from signals of the MARG module more robust in circumstances where distortion of the geomagnetic field exist. The evaluation procedure was defined in such a way that its first half would take place within a region of space where the geomagnetic field was not distorted (non-magnetically distorted area), whereas the second half took place in the immediate neighborhood of the iron bar, which was known to introduce significant distortion of the magnetic field (magnetically distorted area).

Table 7. Kruskal-Wallis test statistics results for the orientation errors in the Euler angle Phi, Theta and Psi across three different methods in the magnetically distorted area with N = 810.

Dependent variable	Algorithm	Mean rank	Test statistic	Df	Asymp. Sig.
Phi	GMV-D	252.20	365.929	2	0.000
	GMV-S	342.62			
	KF	621.69			
Theta	GMV-D	197.76	377.616	2	0. 000
	GMV-S	432.47			
	KF	586.27			
Psi	GMV-D	229.84	278.583	2	0. 000
	GMV-S	421.93			
	KF	564.73			

Table 8. Pairwise comparison among three algorithms for orientation errors in the Euler angles in the magnetically distorted area.

Dependent variable	Algor 1–Algor 2	Test statistic	Std. error	Std. test statistic	Sig.	Adj. sig.
Phi	GMV-D-GMV-S	−90.422	20.137	−4.490	.000	.000
	GMV-D-KF	−369.489	20.137	−18.349	.000	.000
	GMV-S-KF	−279.067	20.137	−13.858	.000	.000
Theta	GMV-D-GMV-S	−234.711	20.137	−11.656	.000	.000
	GMV-D-KF	−388.511	20.137	−19.293	.000	.000
	GMV-S-KF	−153.800	20.137	−7.638	.000	.000
Psi	GMV-D-GMV-S	−192.093	20.137	−9.539	.000	.000
	GMV-D-KF	−334.896	20.137	−16.631	.000	.000
	GMV-S-KF	−142.804	20.137	−7.092	.000	.000

For a human-computer interface purpose, it was necessary to evaluate the results accounting for the diversity of trajectories, movement speed, etc. that various human subjects would use in completing the experimental task. To investigate the deviations of those recorded orientations from the "instructed orientations" ("ground truth") and in order to report the results in a more intuitive way, the orientation errors were expressed as Euler Angles, which are the errors around the 3 orthogonal axes of the "body frame" of the MARG module. These angles (Phi, Theta and Psi) are the angles rotated about the x, y, and z axes, and can, therefore, be more readily interpreted than the 4 numerical components of a quaternion [17]. Since the analysis was performed on angular errors, a lower mean value found for a given method than for another implies that the former performed better that the latter.

5 Conclusion

The statistical analyses show that the new algorithm (GMV-D) performance was similar to the performance of the previous algorithm (GMV-S) and both were slightly better than the on-board Kalman Filtering in the non-magnetically distorted area. However, the GMV-D algorithm can significantly reduce the errors in orientation tracking when compared to the GMV-S correction and Kalman filtering correction in the magnetically distorted area.

The advancement of hand motion tracking systems using MARG modules and infrared cameras can be a valuable contribution to the improvement in the realism of natural human-computer interactions within a 3D virtual environment.

Acknowledgments. This research was supported by National Sciences Foundation grants CNS-1532061 and CNS-1920182, and the FIU University Graduate School Dissertation Year Fellowship awarded to Dr. Neeranut Ratchatanantakit.

References

1. Kim, S.J.J.: A user study trends in augmented reality and virtual reality research: a qualitative study with the past three years of the ISMAR and IEEE VR conference papers. In: 2012 International Symposium on Ubiquitous Virtual Reality, pp. 1–5. IEEE, August 2012
2. Heeter, C.: Being there: the subjective experience of presence. Teleoper. Virtual Environ. **1**(2), 262–271 (1992). https://doi.org/10.1162/pres.1992.1.2.262
3. Mccall, R., O'Neil, S., Carroll, F.: Measuring presence in virtual environments. ACM (2004). ID: acm985934; ACM Digital Library; ACM Digital Library (Association for Computing Machinery); KESLI (ACM Digital Library)
4. Slater, M., Usoh, M., Steed, A.: Depth of presence in virtual environments. Teleoper. Virtual Environ. **3**(2), 130–144 (1994)
5. Slater, M., Wilbur, S.: A framework for immersive virtual environments (five). Teleoper. Virtual Environ. **6**(6), 603 (1997)
6. Pavlovic, V.I., Sharma, R., Huang, T.S.: Visual interpretation of hand gestures for human-computer interaction: a review. IEEE Trans. Pattern Anal. Mach. Intell. **19**(7), 677–695 (1997)
7. Roh, M.-C., Kang, D., Huh, S., Lee, S.-W.: A virtual mouse interface with a two-layered Bayesian network. Multimedia Tools Appl. **76**(2), 1615–1638 (2017). ID: Roh 2017
8. Zhang, X., Liu, X., Yuan, S.-M., Lin, S.-F.: Eye tracking based control system for natural human-computer interaction. Comput. Intell. Neurosci. (2017)
9. Ratchatanantakit, N., O-larnnithipong, N., Sonchan, P., Adjouadi, M., Barreto, A.: Live demonstration: double SLERP gravity-magnetic vector (GMV-D) orientation correction in a MARG sensor. In: 2021 IEEE Sensors, p. 1. IEEE (2021)
10. Foxlin, E.: Motion tracking requirements and technologies (Chapter 8). In: Stanney, K. (ed.) Handbook of Virtual Environments: Design, Implementation, and Applications, pp. 163–201. Lawrence Erlbaum Associates, New York (2002)
11. Shoemake, K.: Animating rotation with quaternion curves. In: Proceedings of the 12th Annual Conference on Computer Graphics and Interactive Techniques, pp. 245–254, July 1985

12. Bachmann, E.R., Yun, X., Peterson, C.W.: An investigation of the effects of magnetic variations on inertial/magnetic orientation sensors. In: IEEE International Conference on Robotics and Automation, Proceedings. ICRA 2004, vol. 2, pp. 1115–1122. IEEE, April 2004

13. Ratchatanantakit, N., O-larnnithipong, N., Barreto, A., Tangnimitchok, S.: Consistency study of 3D magnetic vectors in an office environment for IMU-based hand tracking input development. In: Kurosu, M. (ed.) HCII 2019. Lecture Notes in Computer Science, vol. 11567, pp. 377–387. Springer, Cham (2019). https://doi.org/10.1007/978-3-030-22643-5_29

14. O-larnnithipong, N., Barreto, A., Tangnimitchok, S., Ratchatanantakit, N.: Orientation correction for a 3D hand motion tracking interface using inertial measurement units. In: Kurosu, M. (ed.) HCI 2018. Lecture Notes in Computer Science, vol. 10903, pp. 321–333. Springer, Cham (2018). https://doi.org/10.1007/978-3-319-91250-9_25

15. Montgomery, D.C.: Design and Analysis of Experiments. Wiley, New York (2017)

16. Field, A.: Discovering Statistics Using SPSS. Sage Publications, Upper Saddle River (2009)

17. Kuipers, J.B.: Quaternions and Rotation Sequences: A Primer with Applications to Orbits, Aerospace, and Virtual Reality. Princeton University Press, Princeton (1999)

DESSK: Description Space for Soft Keyboards

Mathieu Raynal[1](✉), Georges Badr[2], and I. Scott MacKenzie[3]

[1] ELIPSE Team, IRIT Lab, University of Toulouse, Toulouse, France
mathieu.raynal@irit.fr
[2] TICKET LAB, Antonine University, Baabda, Lebanon
georges.badr@ua.edu.lb
[3] Electrical Engineering and Computer Science, York University, Toronto, Canada
mack@cse.yorku.ca

Abstract. We present DESSK, a description space for soft keyboards. DESSK provides a framework for any soft keyboard to be graphically described along four dimensions – context, representation, interaction, and linguistic system – each with multiple criteria. DESSK begins with a blank working template which is populated with labels and symbols to characterize the dynamics and interactions of the keyboard. The goal is to provide a framework within which any soft keyboard can be placed and to serve as a theoretical basis to situate soft keyboards in relation to proposed or existing systems.

Keywords: Soft keyboards · Description space · Interaction models · Descriptive model

1 Introduction

Early soft keyboards were identical representations of physical keyboards: The character layout was similar and each soft button corresponded to a physical key. These keyboards were originally created to allow people with motor disabilities to enter text. The keyboards were "soft" or "virtual", meaning they were rendered in graphics on a display. Interaction proceeded either through single-switch scanning [9] or using eye gaze [12].

Soft keyboards are also standard on virtually all desktop systems. Interaction can use any pointing device, such as a mouse, trackball, joystick, or even an eye tracking system. With the emergence of pen-based computing, smartphones, and tablets, these text entry systems are more common as they replace physical keyboards. And new interaction devices, such as smartwatches, joysticks, or virtual reality headsets, also support text entry. Moreover, because these systems are created in software, they offer more possibilities for interaction than a physical keyboard. Thus, they are able to evolve dynamically, adjusting to the user's input, and they often interact with other software components or use several interaction modalities.

M. Kurosu (Ed.): HCII 2022, LNCS 13303, pp. 109–125, 2022.
https://doi.org/10.1007/978-3-031-05409-9_9

These possibilities result in a wide variety of text entry systems using soft or virtual keyboards. Although contexts of use are diverse, the goal is the same: supporting and improving text entry speed and accuracy. Nevertheless, there is no theoretical framework to situate this work in relation to proposed or existing systems. Several reviews and workshops reflect on text input [18,23,27,44,50]; however, given the diversity of systems, interaction contexts, or interaction modalities, these reviews focus on one or a few specific criteria - e.g., accessibility according to a motor impairment [45] or visual impairment [46,55], mobile use [24], or 3D virtual environments [10] - and compare the systems according to this prism.

The purpose of this paper is to describe soft keyboards generally, whatever the intended context and constraints. We present different types of soft keyboards according to the elements that characterize them, including their context of use, the interaction modalities, and the software components coupled to the keyboard. For this, we present a DEscription Space for Soft Keyboards, called DESSK, which encompasses the criteria to describe any type of soft keyboard.

The goal of DESSK is to describe each soft keyboard from a system point of view: that is, to represent the way the user interacts with the keyboard, to describe the internal functioning of the keyboard, and how it evolves as the user types. Moreover, beyond functional aspects, we contextualize soft keyboards by including the intended environment.

DESSK only concerns soft keyboards. We define soft keyboards as any text entry system composed of several interactive zones to produce text strings. On a soft keyboard, the interactive zones appear on a display and are generally materialized by buttons or edges to which one or several characters (or codes) are linked. DESSK does not take into account gesture recognition or handwriting recognition systems or voice dictation systems used for text entry.

2   DESSK: A Descriptive Model

In the space of modeling, DESSK is an example of a *descriptive model* [20]. Descriptive models are tools for thinking. They breakdown a problem space into constituent parts and offer a visual depiction of the problem space. With this, they empower researchers to understand and think in different ways about the problem space and, importantly, to develop a deeper understanding of current phenomenon and to inspire new possibilities. This is in contrast to *predictive models* or *analytic models*, which are tools for predicting or quantifying [19].

Descriptive models are everywhere. Often, researchers describe the components of a problem space without framing their efforts as a model. That's what we do! The process is natural and unconscious, and usually just serves to present current practice as prelude to a new idea for empirical study. However, it is also the case that "describing the components of a problem space" is a contribution in itself, if done in a thorough, constructive, and illustrative manner. And the HCI literature is replete is with descriptive models presented in this way. Examples include Johansen's quadrant model for groupware [15], Buxton's three-state model for graphical input [6], MacKenzie and Castellucci's frame model for visual attention [21], or Card et al.'s model human processor [7].

The problem space of DESSK is soft keyboards. What are the interaction and contextual parts of soft keyboards? Can these be organized in a comprehensive framework that encompasses all soft keyboards? Is there an appropriate visual organization for this framework? These are the sort of questions we considered in developing our description space for soft keyboards, or DESSK for short. The components in DESSK are presented in the following sections.

3   Description Criteria

Our description space is defined along four dimensions. These are now described with reference to the blank working template shown in Fig. 1. The template will be populated with additional details later using specific examples of soft keyboards.

Context	User	
	Display	
	Device	
Representation	Visibility	
	Language	
	Cardinality	
	Layout	
Interaction	Navigation	
	Validation	
Linguistic system		

Fig. 1. Working template for description space of soft keyboards (DESSK)

Briefly, the first dimension, **Context**, concerns the context of use of the soft keyboard; that is, characteristics of the user and environment for which the system has been designed. The second dimension, **Representation**, describes the visual appearance of the soft keyboard - the way the keyboard is structured and its graphic representation. The third dimension, **Interaction**, focuses on how the user interacts with the system, both to navigate on the keyboard, and to validate desired zones. Finally, the last dimension, **Linguistic system**, defines the language components used to facilitate the input with soft keyboards. Each of these dimensions is broken into criteria presented as follows.

3.1   Context of Use

Soft keyboards were initially designed for people who cannot use a physical keyboard to enter text on their computer. However, since the emergence of smartphones and more generally touch screens, the soft keyboard has become an essential tool for most users. The design of a soft keyboard generally responds to a specific problem, often related either to the user's abilities or to the characteristics of the device on which the keyboard is used. Context of use therefore includes at least three criteria: User, Display, and Device.

User. This indicates whether the keyboard is designed for a particular profile of people. This can include the abilities of the user (due to a disability or the context of interaction), but also the expertise of the user (novice vs. expert).

For users' abilities, we distinguish soft keyboards intended for people without major constraints, those designed for motor-disabled people [36], and those studied for people with a visual impairment [4,43].

On the other hand, user performance evolves when using a soft keyboard [25]. Users are initially "novices", but with time learn the new layout and gradually become "experts". Some keyboards have been designed more specifically to help users get started with this new keyboard [26]. Conversely, other keyboards provide additional interactions or shortcuts to increase the text entry speed when users gain expertise with the keyboard [8,13].

Display. The first text input systems were mainly used on a traditional desktop computer where the soft keyboard was displayed on the screen. But the uses have greatly diversified over the last twenty years with the democratization of new display surfaces such as smartphones, smartwatches, interactive TVs, head-mounted displays, etc. The diversity of these display surfaces shows the importance of this criterion when designing a text entry system. For example, the layout may differ if displayed on a watch screen compared to a mixed-reality headset.

For the different possible values of this criterion, we have chosen to distinguish between soft keyboards displayed on traditional screens coupled to a computer, and those presented on touch screens. Usually the keyboards displayed on a computer screen are those used by motor-challenged people who use the keyboard to enter text on the computer.

With touch screens, we group together those on devices such as smartphones, tablets, or even interactive tables that are used with the finger or a stylus. On the other hand, we distinguish the very small touch screens used, for example, by smartwatches because the very small display surface brings about a specific problems of keyboard display and interaction.

Device. Beyond the display surface, the other important criterion when designing the system is the interaction modality available to the user to interact with the soft keyboard. An interaction modality, as defined by Nigay and Coutaz

[32], combines the physical device with the interaction language. This criterion determines which physical device (mouse, joystick, Wii Remote, touch screen, etc.) is used to interact with the soft keyboard. As we will see in the "interaction" dimension, input generally includes subtasks: navigation and validation. The interaction language used can be different for these two subtasks. This is why the interaction language is described in the "navigation" and "validation" criteria of the "interaction" dimension.

Many devices have been used to interact with a soft keyboard. The most widely used are certainly the touch screens that can be found in many situations: interactive terminals, interactive tables, or personal devices such as smartphones, tablets, or smartwatches. These screens have the particularity of being both the input device and the display surface. We distinguish two types of touch screens: those of smartwatches which are very small, and others with a larger footprint.

Some soft keyboards are also designed for entertainment systems. In this context, devices are varied: gamepad [14], joystick [52], or remote controller (like Wii [16]).

Finally, as noted in the introduction, soft keyboards are also the main way to interact and communicate for people with a motor impairment. The interaction device is then adapted to the motor skills of the person. People who still have little motor skills use pointing devices such as a joystick [53], trackball [51], while the most paralyzed use specific devices such as an eye tracker [49], muscle contractions [11], vocal input (non verbal) like humming [35] or hissing [34].

In some scenarios, physical keys are used to move a cursor on the soft keyboard [5,39]. For soft keyboards with single-switch scanning, the cursor moves automatically from zone to zone and, when the cursor is on the right zone, the user validates it through some input mechanism [48].

Finally, we could also take physical keyboards into account in this criterion. Some of them use unconventional layouts or interactions (such as OrbiTouch (by Keybowl, Inc.) or DataHand [17]).

Summary. Table 1 summarizes the possible values for the three criteria of the "Context of use" dimension. It should be noted that the set of possible values is not restricted to those given, but is malleable as per new technologies and applications that arise.

Table 1. Possible values for each criteria of the "Context of use" dimension

Criteria	Possible values
User	Able-bodied, motor impairment, visual impairment, novice, expert
Display	All, screen, projection, touch screen (smartphones, tablets), small touch screen (smartwatches), interactive TV, head-mounted display
Device	Mouse, joystick, touch screen (smartphones, tablets), small touch screen (smartwatches), remote control (Wii), eye tracker, muscle contractions, vocal input (non verbal), hissing, tongue

3.2   Representation

The second dimension of our description space concerns the structure and the graphical representation of a soft keyboard. We use four criteria to describe the representation.

A soft keyboard can sometimes be decomposed into several text input systems. For example, a soft keyboard that includes word prediction or work completion is a combination of two input systems: the keyboard on the one hand and the word list on the other hand. Values are assigned to following criteria separately for each part of the keyboard.

Visibility. Some parts of the keyboard are not permanently visible. For example, the POBox system [29] displays a list of the most probable words but only after the first character of the word is entered. We therefore distinguish between those parts that are permanently visible and those that are visible only occasionally.

Language. The language determines the information that appears in the interactive zones. This can be characters usable on the system, undefined words (for predicted words lists), or codes to represent or extend the character set. For example, EdgeWrite [54] uses codes representing the four corners of a square. All characters have a representation using a sequence of these codes.

Cardinality. Cardinality corresponds to the number of interactive zones on the input system. We write "N" when there are as many interactive areas as there are characters. If there are less zones than elements, the number of zones is given. This can be the case of a soft keyboard using a code (such as EdgeWrite [54] or H4-Writer [22]), or when several characters are associated with the same zone. Examples of the latter are ambiguous keyboards, such as a phone keypad, where multiple letters are associated with each key.

Layout. Here we describe how the different interactive zones are arranged in relation to each other. This can be any grid such as the Qwerty layout, a horizontal or vertical list, a circular layout [28], or a square layout [33].

Summary. Table 2 summarizes the possible values for the four criteria of the "Representation" dimension. As with the Context-of-use dimension, the set of possible values may vary as per new technologies and applications that arise.

3.3   Interaction

Whatever the type of elements produced (codes, characters, or words), the production of these elements occurs in two stages: first, navigating to the desired interactive zone and then validating or confirming the zone.

Table 2. Possible values for each criteria of the "Representation" dimension

Criteria	Possible values
Visibility	None, occasionally, permanent
Language	Characters, words, codes
Cardinality	Full, number
Layout	None, grid, list, square, circle

Navigation. The navigation phase is only present for systems using a pointer or cursor to select the interactive zones. For soft keyboards on smartphones, connected watches, or other devices using a touch screen, there is no pointer: The user directly accesses the zone, for example, using a finger or stylus. In this case, there is no navigation phase. If a pointer or cursor is present, its movement depends on the user's ability to manipulate a pointing device or its equivalence. For users with a motor impairment, navigation uses a cursor that is moved, typically without using a pointing device. One possibility is the use of non-verbal voice input: the user vocalizes sounds which map to virtual arrow and select keys [45].

More commonly, the cursor or hot spot is moved automatically from zone to zone on a soft "scanning keyboard" (aka "single-switch scanning"). When the cursor is on the right zone, the user validates it through some input mechanism. There are two types of movement: *continuous movement* of a pointer using a pointing device, and *discrete movement* of a cursor from zone to zone using directional keys or other discrete actions to realize and control the direction of movement. We therefore distinguish three types of navigation: automatic, direct, or indirect. Each type can be continuous or discrete.

Validation. Finally, the validation of an interactive zone produces the element linked to this zone. For soft keyboards on smartphones or other touch screens, the most common validation consists in directly tapping the desired zone. Pressing a finger on the screen, the user validates the zone under the finger. During an interaction by a gesture stroke, the interactive zones are generally validated by crossing: Each zone crossed by the trace is considered validated. In this case, a language model makes it possible to determine the desired word from the sequence of zone crossings [56]. It is also possible to perform a gesture on the desired zone to validate it. This technique of validation by gesture is sometimes used for zones where there are several characters. The use of gestures to validate the zone allows, in the same action, removing the ambiguity on the desired character [31].

For soft keyboards used with a pointing device, validation is usually done with a button on the pointing device. Similarly, for keyboards where the selection of the zone is done by single-switch scanning, the user validates the selection using a switch or any other input mechanism that produces a discrete action to indicate validation of the selection [48].

Summary. Table 3 summarizes the possible values for the three criteria of the "Interaction" dimension. As before, the set of possible values is not restricted to those given, but can expand as new interaction techniques emerge.

Table 3. Possible values for each criteria of the "Interaction" dimension

Criteria	Possible values
Navigation	Couple (automatic, direct, indirect) × (discrete, continuous)
Validation	Discrete, continuous

3.4 Linguistic System

Finally, the last dimension of our description space determines whether our soft keyboard uses algorithms based on linguistic knowledge. The process combines actions previously performed with linguistic knowledge (rules, statistics, etc.) to complete or modify a string of characters already entered. Alternatively, the process may dynamically modify part of the keyboard to help the user in his text input [30].

These systems are of different types. The most well-known are word prediction algorithms that propose the most probable words according to the given prefix [3]. Prediction systems can also propose characters that are most likely to succeed the prefix already entered.

Soft keyboards can also use a deduction system, whereby information coming from the user's input is used to deduce the intended word. This information can include, for example, the ordered sequence of the zones previously hovered over or validated. From this information and linguistic knowledge, the system will then deduce the word best matching this information.

Summary. Table 4 summarizes the possible values for the three criteria of the "Context of use" dimension. Again, the set of possible values may expand as per new technologies and applications that arise.

Table 4. Possible values for each criteria of the "Context of use" dimension

Criteria	Possible values
Linguistic system	Characters prediction, words prediction, words deduction

4 Putting DESSK into Practice

Our description space is presented in the form of a table with one criterion per line, as shown above in Fig. 1. In populating the description space, the objective is to show the dynamics of the soft keyboard and possible interactions between the different parts of the keyboard. We use green circles to represent the possible productions, with C, W, or S displayed in these circles to infer that the system produces characters, words, or strings. Blue lines represent the interactions between the different criteria of the soft keyboard: The circle at one end indicates which criterion generates the interaction while the diamond at the other end indicates the criterion impacted by this interaction. Green and blue rectangles, respectively, define the information that is sent to the linguistic system, and the modification that is made on the soft keyboard in reaction to the information sent by the linguistic system.

The modifications can be of different types: The most common consist of modifying the set of words displayed in the list [3] or the set of characters displayed on additional keys [37], or altering the character positions on a "scanning keyboard" [48]. It is also possible to modify the key sizes [1] or shapes [2] to facilitate access to the most probable characters. Other modifications have also been tried, for example, changing the font to highlight the most probable characters to assist searching for novice users [26], or modifying the transfer function of the pointing device to improve navigating to keys [38].

Modifications to the keyboard can also occur depending on user interactions. For example, the FishEye keyboard is a full keyboard designed to be displayed on a smartphone or PDA and used with the finger or a stylus [41]. When the user (or stylus) touches the screen, the keys around this point magnify to make them easier to read (see Fig. 2a).

Context	User	able-bodied
	Display	touch screen
	Device	
Representation	Visibility	permanent
	Language	characters
	Cardinality	full
	Layout	grid [key size]
Interaction	Navigation	direct – continuous
	Validation	discrete [C]
Linguistic system		none

(a) Implementation [42]   (b) DESSK description

Fig. 2. FishEye keyboard

The user can then move his finger (or stylus) on the screen until hovering over the desired character. When he lifts his finger, the character is validated. Figure 2b is the description with DESSK of the FishEye Keyboard.

Another example is F.O.C.L., a soft keyboard designed in the late 90s to be implemented on a cell phone, pager, or other mobile device [5]. The user moves a cursor from key to key using four directional keys. After each character is entered, the character layout changes so that the most likely characters are as close as possible to the cursor. Figure 3 shows the description of this keyboard in our space. We can observe that the characters entered are added to the text produced (green circle with a C) and sent, in parallel, to the character prediction system which returns the list of characters ordered according to the probability of each one to be entered. With this information, the system updates the character layout.

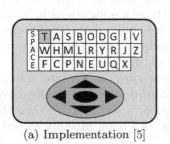

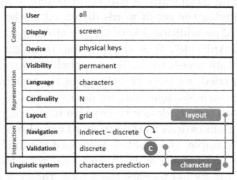

(a) Implementation [5]   (b) DESSK description

Fig. 3. FOCL system.

If the soft keyboard uses regions to enter elements, they will be presented in additional columns. See Fig. 4. For example, a soft keyboard with a word list includes two regions: the soft keyboard and the list of predicted words. The border between the regions describes the relationship between these two parts. On the one hand, the two systems are used in parallel (dotted border) whereby the user switches between the keyboard and the prediction list during the input of a word. Or, the two systems are used separately and sequentially (solid border). For example, in the DUCK keyboard [40], the user enters an approximate set of characters for a word and then selects the correct word from a set of words proposed by the deduction system.

The example in Fig. 4 is SIBYLLE [48] which is an assistive communication system for people with motor disabilities who cannot use a pointing device. Navigation on the soft keyboard is done by automatic switch scanning. The user validates the selection with a contact that is activated when the cursor is on the desired key. SIBYLLE is a complete text entry system which proposes all the characters and functionalities proposed on a standard keyboard, but also complementary keys which propose additional functionalities. It includes regions for character input, a word list, a numeric keypad, and a menu bar. Two linguistic prediction systems are included, a character prediction system which rearranges characters after each character entered, and a word prediction system which proposes a list of the most probable words.

The representation of SIBYLLE in DESSK (Fig. 4) presents only the part of SIBYLLE that evolves dynamically during the input; that is, the character input block whose layout is rearranged after each character input, and the word list (on the left) that is updated after each new character entered.

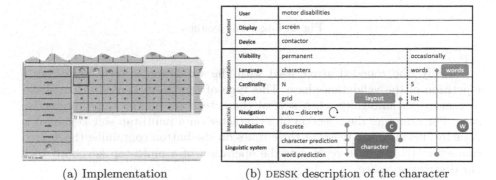

(a) Implementation   (b) DESSK description of the character

Fig. 4. SIBYLLE system.

For many soft keyboards, zone validation produces a character or code. In the case of code-based keyboards, a sequence of codes is produced before being sent to a deduction algorithm that determines the character corresponding to the sequence. This sequence is produced by validating several interactive zones. To show this in our description space, we use a black rounded arrow between the selection and validation criteria. The number of repetitions necessary to achieve the sequence is given as an interval near the arrows. For example, in EdgeWrite [54], each character is coded by a sequence of corners the user has passed through (see Fig. 5a). The right part of Fig. 5 shows the description of EdgeWrite in DESSK .

a b c ç d e f g
h i j k l m n o
p q r s t u v w
x y z capitalization
Context
User
motor disabilities
Display
none
Device
stylus
Representation
Visibility
none
Language
corners
Cardinality
4
Layout
square
Interaction
Navigation
direct - continuous
Validation
crossing
[2,5]
Linguistic system
characters deduction
corners
C

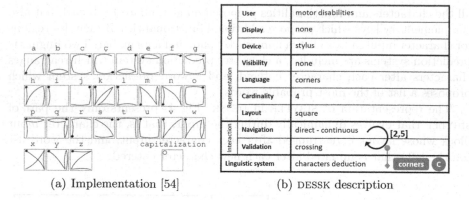

(a) Implementation [54]   (b) DESSK description

Fig. 5. EdgeWrite system.

Finally, the rounded arrow used with the validation criteria represents a repetition of the validation phase. This type of repetition is used in particular to remove an ambiguity when several characters are on the same interactive zone. For example, the selection of a character on a multi-tap soft keyboard is done by clicking once, twice, or three times on the button containing the desired character [47]. Figure 6 represents the operation of a multi-tap keyboard with our description space.

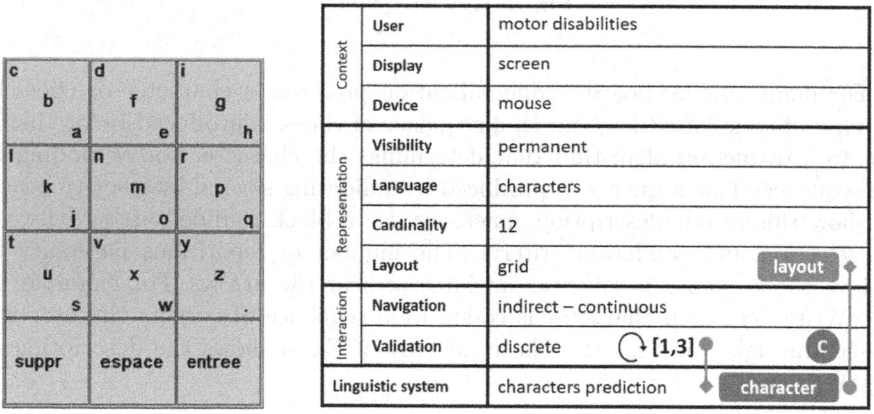

c b a
d f e
i g h
l k j
n m o
r p q
t u s
v x w
y z .
suppr
espace
entree
Context
User
motor disabilities
Display
screen
Device
mouse
Representation
Visibility
permanent
Language
characters
Cardinality
12
Layout
grid
layout
Interaction
Navigation
indirect – continuous
Validation
discrete
[1,3]
C
Linguistic system
characters prediction
character

(a) Implementation [47]   (b) DESSK description

Fig. 6. Multi-tap keyboard.

5 Conclusion

We present DESSK, a description space for text entry with soft keyboards. The space is divided into four regions, Context, Representation, Interaction, and Linguistic system. The regions include sub-regions which are populated with labels and symbols to describe the operation of the keyboard, including dynamic and linguistics features and the context of use.

In order to serve the community working in text entry, we have designed and developed a website dedicated to text entry systems: http://text-entry.com/.

This website is primarily a showcase of the various existing soft keyboard entry systems and aims to bring together as many research prototypes as possible. Beyond a simple catalog of existing solutions, the goal of our website is also to allow the exploration of this set of systems according to the desired characteristics. To do this, our website includes all the criteria from our description area to allow all solutions to be filtered according to these criteria. The description in our description space is available for each system presented on our page. All of these descriptions are available on our site http://text-entry.com/.

Our goal in proposing this descriptive model is to provoke thought about the problem space for the design of text input systems. We built our model from a large set of keyboards found in the literature. However, our descriptive model (certainly) has limits; some systems may be difficult to map into the DESSK model. Our description space will evolve over time depending on the feedback we get and the new systems we learn about.

References

1. Al Faraj, K., Mojahid, M., Vigouroux, N.: BigKey: a virtual keyboard for mobile devices. In: Jacko, J.A. (ed.) HCI 2009. LNCS, vol. 5612, pp. 3–10. Springer, Heidelberg (2009). https://doi.org/10.1007/978-3-642-02580-8_1
2. Aulagner, G., François, R., Martin, B., Michel, D., Raynal, M.: FloodKey: increasing software keyboard keys by reducing needless ones without occultation. In: Proceedings of the 10th WSEAS International Conference on Applied Computer Science, pp. 412–417. World Scientific and Engineering Academy and Society (WSEAS), ACM, New York (2010)
3. Badr, G., Raynal, M.: WordTree: results of a word prediction system presented thanks to a tree. In: Stephanidis, C. (ed.) UAHCI 2009. LNCS, vol. 5616, pp. 463–471. Springer, Heidelberg (2009). https://doi.org/10.1007/978-3-642-02713-0_49
4. Banubakode, S., Dhawale, C.: Survey of eye-free text entry techniques of touch screen mobile devices designed for visually impaired users. Covenant J. Inform. Commun. Technol. 2(1) (2013)
5. Bellman, T., MacKenzie, I.S.: A probabilistic character layout strategy for mobile text entry. In: Proceedings of Graphics Interface 1998 - GI 1998, pp. 168–176. Canadian Information Processing Society (CIPS), Toronto (1998)
6. Buxton, W.A.S.: A three-state model for graphic input. In: Proceedings of the IFIP TC13 International Conference on Human-Computer Interaction - INTERACT 1990, pp. 449–456. Elsevier, Amsterdam (1990)

7. Card, S.K., Moran, T.P., Newell, A.: The Psychology of Human-Computer Interaction. Erlbaum, Hillsdale (1983)
8. Chen, X., Grossman, T., Fitzmaurice, G.: SwipeBoard: a text entry technique for ultra-small interfaces that supports novice to expert transitions. In: Proceedings of the 27th Annual ACM Symposium on User Interface Software and Technology - UIST 2014, pp. 615–620. ACM, New York (2014)
9. Damper, R.: Text composition by the physically disabled: a rate prediction model for scanning input. Appl. Ergon. **15**(4), 289–296 (1984)
10. Dube, T.J., Arif, A.S.: Text entry in virtual reality: a comprehensive review of the literature. In: Kurosu, M. (ed.) HCII 2019. LNCS, vol. 11567, pp. 419–437. Springer, Cham (2019). https://doi.org/10.1007/978-3-030-22643-5_33
11. Felzer, T., MacKenzie, I.S., Beckerle, P., Rinderknecht, S.: Qanti: a software tool for quick ambiguous non-standard text input. In: Miesenberger, K., Klaus, J., Zagler, W., Karshmer, A. (eds.) ICCHP 2010. LNCS, vol. 6180, pp. 128–135. Springer, Heidelberg (2010). https://doi.org/10.1007/978-3-642-14100-3_20
12. Frey, L.A., White, K., Hutchison, T.: Eye-gaze word processing. IEEE Trans. Syst. Man Cybern. **20**(4), 944–950 (1990)
13. Isokoski, P.: Performance of menu-augmented soft keyboards. In: Proceedings of the SIGCHI Conference on Human Factors in Computing Systems - CHI 2004, pp. 423–430. ACM, New York (2004)
14. Isokoski, P., Raisamo, R.: Quikwriting as a multi-device text entry method. In: Proceedings of the Third Nordic Conference on Human-Computer Interaction - NordiCHI 2004, pp. 105–108. ACM, New York (2004)
15. Johansen, R.: Groupware: future directions and wild cards. J. Organ. Comput. Electron. Commer. **1**(2), 219–227 (1991)
16. Jones, E., Alexander, J., Andreou, A., Irani, P., Subramanian, S.: GesText: accelerometer-based gestural text-entry systems. In: Proceedings of the ACM SIGCHI Conference on Human Factors in Computing Systems - CHI 2010, pp. 2173–2182. ACM, New York (2010)
17. Knight, L.W., Retter, D.: DataHand: design, potential performance, and improvements in the computer keyboard and mouse. In: Proceedings of the Human Factors Society Annual Meeting, vol. 33, pp. 450–454. SAGE Publications, Los Angeles (1989)
18. Kristensson, P.O., et al.: Grand challenges in text entry. In: Extended Abstracts of the ACM SIGCHI Conference on Human Factors in Computing Systems - CHI 2013, pp. 3315–3318. ACM, New York (2013)
19. MacKenzie, I.S.: Motor behaviour models for human computer interaction. In: Carroll, J.M. (ed.) HCI Models, Theories, and Frameworks: Toward a Multidisciplinary Science, pp. 27–54. Morgan Kaufmann, San Francisco (2003)
20. MacKenzie, I.S.: Human-Computer Interaction: An Empirical Research Perspective. Elsevier, Amsterdam (2013)
21. MacKenzie, I.S., Castellucci, S.J.: Eye on the message: reducing attention demand for touch-based text entry. Int. J. Virtual Worlds Hum.-Comput. Interact. **1**, 1–9 (2013)
22. MacKenzie, I.S., Soukoreff, R.W., Helga, J.: 1 thumb, 4 buttons, 20 words per minute: design and evaluation of H4-Writer. In: Proceedings of the 24th Annual ACM Symposium on User Interface Software and Technology - UIST 2011, pp. 471–480. ACM, New York (2011)
23. MacKenzie, I.S., Tanaka-Ishii, K.: Text entry using a small number of buttons. In: MacKenzie, I.S., Tanaka-Ishii, K. (eds.) Text Entry Systems: Mobility, Accessibility, Universality, pp. 105–121. Morgan Kaufmann, San Francisco (2007)

24. MacKenzie, I.S., Tanaka-Ishii, K.: Text Entry Systems: Mobility, Accessibility, Universality. Elsevier, Amsterdam (2010)
25. MacKenzie, I.S., Zhang, S.X.: The design and evaluation of a high-performance soft keyboard. In: Proceedings of the SIGCHI Conference on Human Factors in Computing Systems, pp. 25–31. ACM, New York (1999)
26. Magnien, L., Bouraoui, J.L., Vigouroux, N.: Mobile text input with soft keyboards: optimization by means of visual clues. In: Brewster, S., Dunlop, M. (eds.) Mobile HCI 2004. LNCS, vol. 3160, pp. 337–341. Springer, Heidelberg (2004). https://doi.org/10.1007/978-3-540-28637-0_33
27. Majaranta, P., Räihä, K.J.: Twenty years of eye typing: systems and design issues. In: Proceedings of the ACM Symposium on Eye Tracking Research and Applications - ETRA 2002, pp. 15–22. ACM, New York (2002)
28. Mankoff, J., Abowd, G.D.: Cirrin: a word-level unistroke keyboard for pen input. In: Proceedings of the ACM Symposium on User Interface Software and Technology - UIST 1998, pp. 213–214. ACM, New York (1998)
29. Masui, T.: POBox: an efficient text input method for handheld and ubiquitous computers. In: Gellersen, H.-W. (ed.) HUC 1999. LNCS, vol. 1707, pp. 289–300. Springer, Heidelberg (1999). https://doi.org/10.1007/3-540-48157-5_27
30. Merlin, B., Raynal, M.: SpreadKey: increasing software keyboard key by recycling needless ones. In: 10th European Conference for the Advancement of Assistive Technology in Europe (AAATE 2009), pp. 138–143. IOS Press, Amsterdam (2009)
31. Nesbat, S.B.: A system for fast, full-text entry for small electronic devices. In: Proceedings of the 5th International Conference on Multimodal Interfaces - ICMI 2003, pp. 4–11. ACM, New York (2003)
32. Nigay, L., Coutaz, J.: A design space for multimodal systems: concurrent processing and data fusion. In: Proceedings of the INTERACT 1993 and CHI 1993 Conference on Human Factors in Computing Systems, pp. 172–178. ACM, New York (1993)
33. Perlin, K.: QuikWriting: continuous stylus-based text entry. In: Proceedings of the ACM Symposium on User Interface Software and Technology - UIST 1998, pp. 215–216. ACM, New York (1998)
34. Poláček, O., Míkovec, Z., Slavík, P.: Predictive scanning keyboard operated by hissing. In: Proceedings of the 2nd IASTED International Conference Assistive Technologies, pp. 862–869. ACTA Press, Calgary (2012)
35. Polacek, O., Mikovec, Z., Sporka, A.J., Slavik, P.: Humsher: a predictive keyboard operated by humming. In: The Proceedings of the 13th International ACM SIGACCESS Conference on Computers and Accessibility, pp. 75–82. ACM, New York (2011)
36. Polacek, O., Sporka, A.J., Slavik, P.: Text input for motor-impaired people. Univ. Access Inf. Soc. 16(1), 51–72 (2015). https://doi.org/10.1007/s10209-015-0433-0
37. Raynal, M.: Keyglasses: semi-transparent keys on soft keyboard. In: Proceedings of the 16th International ACM SIGACCESS Conference on Computers and Accessibility, pp. 347–349. ACM, New York (2014)
38. Raynal, M., MacKenzie, I.S., Merlin, B.: Semantic keyboard: fast movements between keys of a soft keyboard. In: Miesenberger, K., Fels, D., Archambault, D., Peňáz, P., Zagler, W. (eds.) ICCHP 2014. LNCS, vol. 8548, pp. 195–202. Springer, Cham (2014). https://doi.org/10.1007/978-3-319-08599-9_30
39. Raynal, M., Martin, B.: SlideKey: impact of in-depth previews for a predictive text entry method. In: Miesenberger, K., Manduchi, R., Covarrubias Rodriguez, M., Peňáz, P. (eds.) ICCHP 2020. LNCS, vol. 12377, pp. 363–370. Springer, Cham (2020). https://doi.org/10.1007/978-3-030-58805-2_43

40. Raynal, M., Roussille, P.: DUCK: a DeDUCtive soft Keyboard for visually impaired users. In: Harnessing the Power of Technology to Improve Lives, pp. 902–909. IOS Press, Amsterdam (2017)

41. Raynal, M., Truillet, P.: Fisheye keyboard: whole keyboard displayed on PDA. In: Jacko, J.A. (ed.) HCI 2007. LNCS, vol. 4551, pp. 452–459. Springer, Heidelberg (2007). https://doi.org/10.1007/978-3-540-73107-8_51

42. Raynal, M., Vinot, J.L., Truillet, P.: Fisheye keyboard: whole keyboard displayed on small device. In: UIST 2007, 20th Annual ACM Symposium on User Interface Software and Technology - UIST 2007, p. 65. ACM, New York (2007)

43. Siqueira, J., et al.: Braille text entry on smartphones: a systematic review of the literature. In: 2016 IEEE 40th Annual Computer Software and Applications Conference - COMPSAC 2016, vol. 2, pp. 521–526. IEEE, New York (2016)

44. Soukoreff, R.W., MacKenzie, I.S.: Recent developments in text-entry error rate measurement. In: Extended Abstracts of the ACM SIGCHI Conference on Human Factors in Computing System - CHI 2004, pp. 1425–1428. ACM, New York (2004)

45. Sporka, A.J., et al.: Chanti: predictive text entry using non-verbal vocal input. In: Proceedings of the ACM SIGCHI Conference on Human Factors in Computing Systems - CHI 2011, pp. 2463–2472. ACM, New York (2011)

46. Tinwala, H., MacKenzie, I.S.: Eyes-free text entry with error correction on touchscreen mobile devices. In: Proceedings of the 6th Nordic Conference on Human-Computer Interaction - NordiCHI 2010, pp. 511–520. ACM, New York (2010)

47. Vigouroux, N., Vella, F., Truillet, P., Raynal, M.: Evaluation of AAC for text input by two groups of subjects: able-bodied subjects and disabled motor subjects. In: 8th ERCIM Workshop, User Interface for All, Vienne, Autriche, pp. 28–29. Springer, Berlin (2004)

48. Wandmacher, T., Antoine, J.Y., Poirier, F., Départe, J.P.: Sibylle, an assistive communication system adapting to the context and its user. ACM Trans. Access. Comput. (TACCESS) 1(1), 1–30 (2008)

49. Ward, D.J., Blackwell, A.F., MacKay, D.J.: Dasher: a data entry interface using continuous gestures and language models. In: Proceedings of the 13th Annual ACM Symposium on User Interface Software and Technology - UIST 2000, pp. 129–137. ACM, New York (2000)

50. Wigdor, D., Balakrishnan, R.: A comparison of consecutive and concurrent input text entry techniques for mobile phones. In: Proceedings of the ACM SIGCHI Conference on Human Factors in Computing Systems - CHI 2004, pp. 81–88. ACM, New York (2004)

51. Wobbrock, J., Myers, B.: Trackball text entry for people with motor impairments. In: Proceedings of the ACM SIGCHI Conference on Human Factors in Computing Systems - CHI 2006, pp. 479–488. ACM, New York (2006)

52. Wobbrock, J.O., Myers, B.A., Aung, H.H.: Writing with a joystick: a comparison of date stamp, selection keyboard, and edgewrite. In: Proceedings of Graphics Interface - GI 2004, pp. 1–8. CIPS, Toronto (2004)

53. Wobbrock, J.O., Myers, B.A., Aung, H.H., LoPresti, E.F.: Text entry from power wheelchairs: edgewrite for joysticks and touchpads. In: Proceedings of the 6th International ACM SIGACCESS Conference on Computers and Accessibility - ACCESS 2003, pp. 110–117. ACM, New York (2003)

54. Wobbrock, J.O., Myers, B.A., Kembel, J.A.: EdgeWrite: a stylus-based text entry method designed for high accuracy and stability of motion. In: Proceedings of the 16th Annual ACM Symposium on User Interface Software and Technology - UIST 2003, pp. 61–70. ACM, New York (2003)

55. Ye, L., Sandnes, F.E., MacKenzie, I.S.: QB-gest: qwerty bimanual gestural input for eyes-free smartphone text input. In: Antona, M., Stephanidis, C. (eds.) HCII 2020. LNCS, vol. 12188, pp. 223–242. Springer, Cham (2020). https://doi.org/10.1007/978-3-030-49282-3_16

56. Zhai, S., Kristensson, P.O.: Shorthand writing on stylus keyboard. In: Proceedings of the ACM SIGCHI Conference on Human Factors in Computing Systems - CHI 2003, pp. 97–104. ACM, New York (2003)

LuxBoard: Ambient Light Manipulation for Contactless Text Entry on Mobile Devices

Alen Salkanovic[1,2] and Sandi Ljubic[1,2](✉)

[1] Faculty of Engineering, University of Rijeka,
Vukovarska 58, 51000 Rijeka, Croatia
{alen.salkanovic,sandi.ljubic}@riteh.hr
[2] Center for Artificial Intelligence and Cybersecurity, University of Rijeka,
R. Matejcic 2, 51000 Rijeka, Croatia

Abstract. In this paper, we present a proof-of-concept for text entry technique that requires no direct contact with the mobile device and relies exclusively on built-in light sensor utilization. Simple in-air gestures, performed above the smartphone screen, alter the current level of ambient lighting. This allows adjusting the keyboard cursor position based on the sensor readings. The idea of this work is in accordance with the Around-Device Interaction (ADI) concept, currently attracting a lot of attention in the Human-Computer Interaction field. The proposed solution successfully augments an input area of a mobile device without the use of sophisticated peripherals. Two different methods can be used to select the target character, depending on how the keyboard cursor is operated. While manual control requires continuous hand gestures to directly adjust the cursor position, automatic control is based on stopping the cursor along its predefined route. In the conducted experiment, 32 participants utilized the touchless interaction technique for both text entry methods on their own smartphone devices. The outcomes of this empirical research are reported, with a special emphasis on text entry speed, total error rate, usability attributes, and perceived workload.

Keywords: Text entry · Around Device Interaction · Ambient light sensor · Contactless interaction · Mobile devices

1 Introduction and Related Work

Text entry on contemporary touchscreen mobile devices is accomplished through a virtual keyboard. In addition to the standard keyboards that come as preinstalled, there are many alternative designs, each with its unique character layout. Many of these alternative solutions try to make better use of the relatively small screen of a mobile device by saving space intended for the keyboard and, at the same time, freeing up the area for the content of the underlying application. For example, Li et al. [2] introduced a virtual keyboard for tablet devices with

© The Author(s), under exclusive license to Springer Nature Switzerland AG 2022
M. Kurosu (Ed.): HCII 2022, LNCS 13303, pp. 126–139, 2022.
https://doi.org/10.1007/978-3-031-05409-9_10

QWERTY-based layout in a single line. Similarly, Sharif et al. [7] presented a single-row reduced conventional QWERTY keyboard that takes up only 7% of the available screen space on a typical smartphone. *Tap and Slide* [5] represents another solution that supports text entry using a zone-based keyboard visualized on a smaller part of the screen.

However, the majority of available text entry methods are fundamentally dependent on touching the screen to select the required character. Certain issues associated with this type of interaction occur, including fat-finger syndrome and different occlusion conditions. In general, these well-known drawbacks negatively affect the speed and accuracy of text entry in the mobile domain. To circumvent mentioned difficulties, many authors utilize the Around-Device Interaction (ADI) techniques. ADI usually refers to contactless interaction with the device, mostly relying on additional sensors or handheld accessories. *TypingRing* [4] is an example of a solution in which several external sensors are incorporated into a custom-developed wearable ring that facilitates touchless text entry.

In addition to research that investigates the possibility of applying external sensors for ADI, we are particularly interested in solutions that use exclusively built-in sensors to achieve contactless interaction with a mobile device. For example, *TiltWriter* [1] and *SWiM* [12] represent tilt-based text entry methods that rely on readings from integrated orientation sensors - specifically, accelerometers and gyroscopes. *CamK* [13] is a solution that enables text input using the built-in camera of a mobile device. While text entry is performed on the mock-up paper keyboard, images are captured by the camera and processed to recognize typing behavior. *Sandwich keyboard* [6] is a novel keyboard design that utilizes a touch sensor on the back side of a device to allow ten-finger typing. The solution folds any three-row keyboard layout and does not require a peripheral device. *UbiK* [9], *EchoType* [11], and *SoundWrite* [15] solutions leverage the embedded microphone to collect subtle audio signals which are subsequently used to identify text typing actions.

As opposed to other sensors, an ambient light sensor is generally less used for augmenting the interaction with mobile devices. Zhang et al. [14] proposed a system called *Okuli* that extends the tablet interaction surface and locates the user's finger inside the workspace using two photodetectors and a low-power LED transmitter. This solution does not use a sensor embedded within the mobile device but instead requires sophisticated peripheral hardware. On the other hand, *UbiTouch* [10] utilizes proximity and ambient light built-in sensors to enhance smartphones with virtual touchpads. However, this solution requires a modification of the OS kernel in order to access the raw sensor readings.

In this paper, we present a *LuxBoard*, text entry technique based on the utilization of an integrated ambient light sensor. The proposed technique entails character selection without touching the screen and does not require any external sensing hardware or additional accessories. The LuxBoard is implemented as an Android IME (Input Method Editor) service which enables text entry in any existing mobile application, using only hand gestures above the mobile device. We applied the proposed technique to two different character selection methods: manual and automatic.

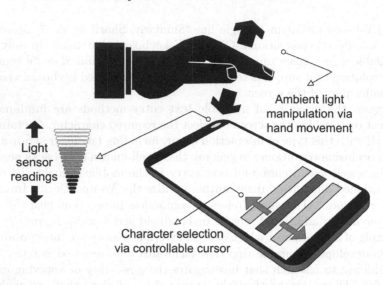

Fig. 1. The concept of contactless text entry is based on the use of a built-in ambient light sensor.

2   LuxBoard: Contactless Text Entry

Both text entry methods presented in this paper are based on the current readings of the ambient light sensor. The related concept is illustrated in Fig. 1. The layout and number of keyboard components (character groups) vary according to whether the user employs manual or automatic cursor control.

Luxboard automatic method, as shown in Fig. 2a, utilizes six keyboard components. The target group/element is triggered in response to an abrupt decrease in ambient light intensity. More specifically, it is activated when the illumination level drops below a predefined threshold. This prevents the unintentional activation of keyboard components. As opposed to manual control, which requires continuous hand movements, this approach activates the target component by simply placing a hand over the light sensor.

Figure 2b shows the layout for *Luxboard manual* method, which utilizes only three components. The reason for this is the increasing gap between the different light intensity thresholds that activate the target element. As a consequence, it is simpler and less error-prone to manually manipulate the keyboard cursor when the number of layout elements is smaller. Manual control involves more physical effort as the cursor's location is being continuously determined by the position of the user's hand relative to the light sensor.

Regardless of the utilized text entry method, the user is initially required to perform an automated and one-time sensor calibration step that involves determining the current maximum value of light intensity in a given environment. The virtual keyboard then appears at its default position at the bottom of the screen.

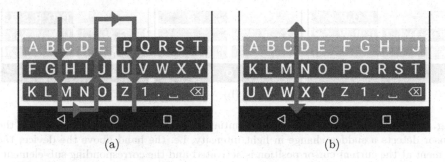

(a)   (b)

Fig. 2. *Luxboard automatic*: keyboard layout with six elements and a predefined path of the self-traveling cursor (a). *Luxboard manual*: keyboard layout consists of three elements only, but the cursor can be intentionally moved downwards or upwards (b).

Luxboard automatic, therefore, allows the keyboard cursor to move along a predefined (cyclic) 6-elements path without explicit user interaction. The position of the cursor directly determines the currently active letters group. The cursor trajectory starts in the top-left keyboard element. The cursor moves down the keyboard layout until it reaches the bottom left component. When this occurs, it is automatically repositioned to the top right element and continues to move downwards. If the bottom right component is reached, the cursor returns to its initial position, from which the cycle repeats. When the sensor detects the abrupt change in light intensity, the keyboard element currently selected by the cursor is activated. This could be the corresponding letters group or the target character. It should be mentioned here that the cursor scan time, or the pace at which it moves automatically between adjacent keyboard elements, is specified at 850 ms. We empirically determined this value within the development phase.

Character entry with *Luxboard automatic* is visualized in Fig. 3. The selection of the target element, either a letter group or a specific character, is accomplished by placing the hand above the light sensor at the appropriate moment, which results in sensing a sudden change in light intensity. Hence, automatic cursor control does not require continuous hand movement above the light sensor, but allows the user to manipulate ambient lighting only when target selection is required.

Unlike automatic control, manual cursor control refers to the procedure of finding a target character by moving the hand closer or further away from the light sensor. The corresponding navigation process starts when a sensor detects changes in light intensity. As the user's hand approaches the mobile device, the sensor data indicates a decrease in light intensity, and the cursor begins to move downwards. Likewise, as the user's hand moves away from the sensor, the light intensity level increases, in which case the keyboard cursor moves upwards. A predefined period (dwell time) is used to activate a specific keyboard element. This actually means that the hand must be kept in a certain position above the device, with the light intensity not changing significantly during the dwell time.

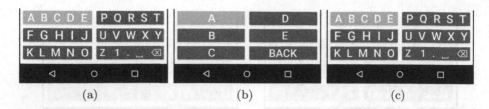

(a)   (b)   (c)

Fig. 3. *Luxboard automatic* displays the initial layout with six elements (a). When the sensor detects a sudden change in light intensity, i.e. the hand above the device, the element at the current cursor position is activated and the corresponding sub-elements are displayed. At this stage, the user can select the BACK button to explicitly return to the previous layout or can select the target character (b). After selecting the target character, the keyboard implicitly returns to its initial layout (c).

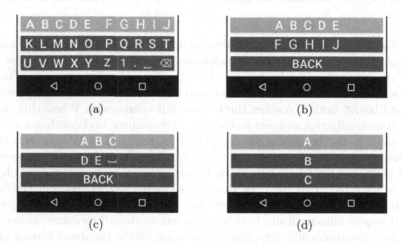

Fig. 4. The initial keyboard layout for *Luxboard manual* consists of only three interactive elements (a). If a certain element is activated via dwell-time, the current layout is replaced with the corresponding sub-elements (b). Navigation towards the target character continues in the same way, with the number of characters in the group being reduced accordingly (c). In case the target element is finally selected (d), character entry is performed and the keyboard returns to its initial layout.

Following the initial testing in the development phase, we set the dwell time value to 1700 ms.

In case the selected keyboard element contains a group of characters, the current keyboard layout is replaced with the corresponding characters of the selected group. On the other hand, if the target character is selected, then it will be applied to the input stream of the underlying application. This equally holds for both the automatic and manual control, with the difference that the *Luxboard manual* uses only three elements in each of its layouts.

The previously described text entry method is visualized in more detail in Fig. 4. As with the automatic modality, the unique keyboard element labeled

BACK allows the user to revert to the previous keyboard layout, in case the incorrect element is inadvertently activated.

3 Empirical Evaluation

By performing an experiment with altogether 32 participants, we comparatively evaluated two text entry methods, i.e. two presented Luxboard designs. The results of the related empirical research are reported in this section. Special attention is paid to the following aspects: text entry speed (measured in Words Per Minute, WPM), total error rate (TER), usability attributes, and perceived workload.

3.1 Participants, Apparatus, and the Procedure

Of the 32 individuals who participated in our experiment, there were nine women and twenty-three men. The majority of the participants were students aged 22 to 27, with an average of 23.3 years (SD = 1.3).

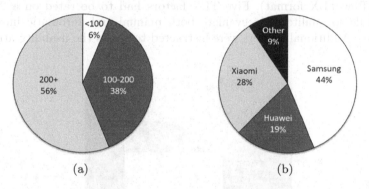

(a)   (b)

Fig. 5. About the participants: the number of typing tasks on a smartphone on a daily basis (a) and the manufacturer of their personal smartphone device (b).

As shown in Fig. 5a, over half of the users reported performing more than 200 typing activities every day, indicating that they have extensive experience and a pronounced habit of entering text on their mobile devices. However, since the proposed text input methods are not based on typical touch interaction, participants were advised to conduct a 30-min training session using both types of Luxboard keyboards. The intention of the short training was to get acquainted with keyboard layouts, contactless interaction based on a light sensor, and the principles of automatic and manual cursor control. Users were provided with detailed instructions on how to install and configure the LuxBoard solution, and the only requirement for participation was owning a smartphone with Android OS. Namely, in addition to insight into the efficiency and usability of the proposed text entry methods, we wanted to check whether the solution can be applied to a wider range of Android mobile devices. Since all modern smartphones come with a built-in light sensor, we assumed that there would be no obstacles in installing and using Luxboard keyboards. The manufacturers of mobile devices utilized in the experiment are shown in Fig. 5b.

After the training, the actual data collection began, with participants having to complete a total of ten text entry tasks. Five activities required the manual cursor control within the 3-elements keyboard layout, while the other five required automatic cursor control within the 6-elements keyboard layout. In order to cancel out the order effect, a trivial counterbalancing method was utilized. Namely, one half of the users started with the *Luxboard automatic*, and the other half with the *Luxboard manual*. During empirical testing, standard text entry metrics [8] such as WPM and TER were gathered using our own logging application – *Text Input Logger*. Each task involved the rewriting of a random text phrase from a 500 samples set prepared by MacKenzie and Soukoreff [3].

After completing all tasks utilizing both text entry methods, subjects were invited to fill out a post-study questionnaire based on the NASA-TLX rating section (Raw-TLX format). Five TLX factors had to be rated on a 21-point Likert scale to qualitatively evaluate both manual and automatic interaction modalities. Additionally, users were instructed to assess the usability attributes

Fig. 6. LuxBoard keyboard, with automatic cursor control, being used for text entry within *Text Input Logger* application

of LuxBoard keyboards using 7-point Likert scales. Specifically, we were interested in perceived ease of use, learnability, and overall satisfaction when working with two different Luxboard designs.

All experiment activities were carried out while respecting epidemiological measures due to the COVID-19 pandemic. The average ambient illuminance, obtained from the initial calibration data of each device in the experiment, was 508 lux for *Luxboard manual* and 577 lux when *Luxboard automatic* was tested. Figure 6 shows a participant's hand while utilizing the LuxBoard keyboard with automatic cursor control within the data-gathering application.

3.2 Results and Discussion

Text entry speed and total error rate obtained across five consecutive transcription tasks are shown in Fig. 7. It can be seen that there are trends of slightly increasing text entry speed and decreasing error rate, with these trends being somewhat more pronounced for manual cursor control. Based on this outcome alone, we can assume that eventual longer training would have a better effect on the *Luxboard manual* efficiency.

Figure 8 shows average values of text entry speed and total error rate, achieved by utilizing the provided Luxboard keyboards. Based on descriptive statistics indicators, it can be noted that a design with automatic cursor control is more efficient than the one with manual control, both in terms of WPM (1.2 ± 0.06 vs. 1.0 ± 0.17) and total error rate (2.2% ± 1.8% vs. 3.4% ± 2.5%). The dependent t-test (paired-samples t-test) was used to formally compare the efficiency of two Luxboard keyboards, according to the obtained data. The t-test revealed a statistically significant difference between the two text entry methods in terms of input speed: $t(31) = 6.403, p < .001$. Furthermore, the difference in total error rate between the two conditions was also found to be statistically significant: $t(31) = -2.748, p < .05$.

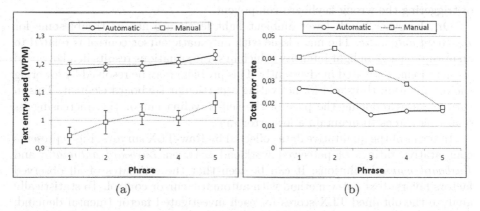

(a)   (b)

Fig. 7. Text entry speed (a) and total error rate (b) achieved across five consecutive transcription tasks employing automatic and manual cursor control

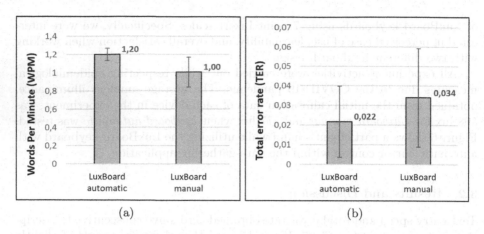

Fig. 8. Average text entry speeds achieved with two Luxboard keyboards (a), and the corresponding average total error rates (b)

The predetermined dwell time, used for target selection via steady hand hovering, could be a factor for lower WPM and higher TER while manually controlling the keyboard cursor. Reduced dwell time value would presumably result in enhanced text entry speed, but could, at the same time, increase the number of incorrectly triggered elements. An additional experiment, in which users could select from a range of custom dwell time values, would be the logical next step in assessing how exactly dwelling gesture affects the *Luxboard manual* efficiency.

Furthermore, we have noticed that current ambient lighting affects the character selection speed when manual cursor control is utilized. Namely, in low light intensity conditions, it is more difficult to manipulate the keyboard cursor manually. Since the illumination thresholds related to the activation of certain keyboard elements are very close in such conditions, there is a higher probability of triggering the wrong keyboard component.

On the other hand, lower ambient light levels are not as troublesome for *Luxboard automatic*. The main issue with automatic cursor control is related to an abrupt change in light intensity, which in some situations results in a keyboard element being activated inadvertently. This problem may be resolved by lowering the illumination threshold for activating a particular keyboard element. This in turn requires reducing the pace of the self-traveling cursor (i.e. increasing its scan time) so as to maintain a low error rate.

In terms of the qualitative data collected by Raw-TLX surveys, Fig. 9 presents comparative ratings of perceived workload between *Luxboard automatic* and *Luxboard manual* solutions. It can be seen that the estimates of all observed factors favor a text entry method with automatic cursor control. To statistically analyze the obtained TLX scores for each investigated factor (mental demand, physical demand, level of frustration, perceived performance, and overall effort invested in experiment tasks), the Wilcoxon signed-rank tests were utilized.

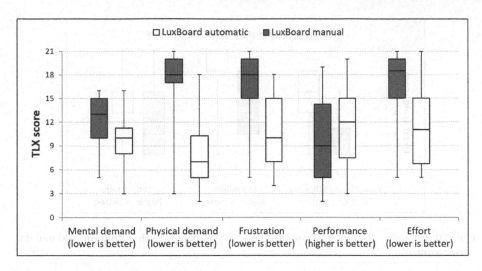

Fig. 9. Users' comparative ratings on perceived workload between different Luxboard designs (automatic and manual cursor control)

The results of the statistical analysis confirm that the participants clearly prefer automatic cursor control. The Wilcoxon signed-rank tests revealed statistically significant differences for all TLX factors except for perceived performance. This can be explained by the fact that both Luxboard keyboards have a fairly low text entry speed and, as expected, cannot come close to touch-based solutions. Also, after a period of prolonged use of automatic control, the cursor movement may become too slow for a trained or advanced user. By analogy, a predefined dwell time value in manual cursor control can also be a limiting factor for text entry performance.

When compared to *Luxboard manual*, it was confirmed that *Luxboard automatic* implies significantly lower mental demand ($Z = -2.788, p < .01$), physical demand ($Z = -4.452, p < .001$), and level of frustration ($Z = -3.379, p < .05$). Knowing this, it is not surprising that the perceived total effort was also significantly lower for automatic cursor control ($Z = -4.013, p < .001$).

As mentioned before, at the end of the experiment the participants rated two text entry methods on a seven-point Likert scale against the ease of use, learnability, and overall satisfaction. Figure 10 depicts the results obtained from the respective questionnaires. Once again the Wilcoxon signed-rank tests revealed statistically significant differences between the two Luxboard keyboards, this time considering all the usability attributes observed. Namely, the participants perceive *Luxboard automatic* both significantly easier to use ($Z = -4.289, p < .001$) and easier to learn ($Z = -4.110, p < .001$). This automatically explains the fact that users are significantly more satisfied when entering text with the support of automatic cursor movement ($Z = -3.334, p < .05$).

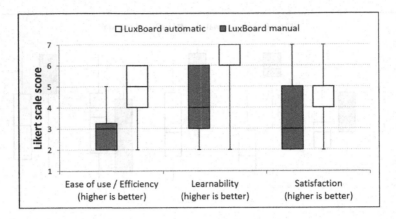

Fig. 10. Usability attributes of the LuxBoard keyboard for both automatic and manual cursor control

In conclusion, we can confirm that the findings based on quantitative metrics (WPM, TER) fully correspond to the outcomes of the questionnaire, i.e. to the qualitative part of the research. Between the two presented methods for contactless text entry, *Luxboard automatic* can be considered the clear winner. Although the difference in text entry speed, when compared to the *Luxboard manual*, is relatively small (at the level of one character per minute), it is nevertheless found as statistically significant. Furthermore, the automatic cursor contributes to better usability and lower workload in text entry tasks. 75% of participants stated that they would use automatic cursor control and the matching 6-element keyboard layout on a daily basis if they had to choose between the two proposed methods.

4   Conclusion

In this paper, we introduced an interaction technique that enables contactless text entry by utilizing only an embedded ambient light sensor of a mobile device. Simple hand gestures above the smartphone screen can alter the light intensity detected by the sensor, and this (intentional) change is then used for touchless control of the target application. By making use of the proposed solution, ADI can be successfully augmented without the need for any external sensing hardware or additional accessories.

Two different text entry methods are proposed that apply the mentioned interaction technique: *Luxboard automatic* and *Luxboard manual*. While both methods are based on keyboard cursor control, they differ both in layout (i.e. the number of keyboard elements) and in the way the cursor is controlled. Namely, a manual cursor control requires continuous hand gestures to be made above the light sensor, in order to position the cursor at a specific location within a 3-element keyboard layout. Hand dwelling is subsequently used for selecting the target element, either a letter group or a specific character. Contrariwise, automatic control assumes programmatically invoked cursor repositioning, allowing users to make hover gesture (causing an abrupt change in sensed illumination) only when the target element needs to be selected. The pace of the automatic cursor is predefined, and its route is based on a 6-element keyboard layout.

The results obtained from a conducted experiment involving 32 participants have shown that the *Luxboard automatic* approach was significantly more efficient than the *Luxboard manual*, both in terms of text entry speed and total error rate. The qualitative data analysis, which was based on both the NASA TLX scores and the usability questionnaire answers, further confirmed that users clearly prefer automatic cursor control. This could be due to the fact that the *Luxboard automatic* delivers a more straightforward and physically less troublesome cursor control than the *Luxboard manual*. In other words, it is unsurprising that the overall effort is substantially higher when text entry requires constant manual control of the keyboard cursor.

The text entry speed achieved by the proposed methods can hardly be brought into a common context with the speeds achieved on standard touch-based keyboards. However, despite the low WPM attained, our proof-of-concept solution demonstrates the feasibility of using only a light sensor for ADI-based contactless text input. Furthermore, LuxBoard has been proven to operate on a wide range of Android smartphones, regardless of manufacturer or device model. None of the participants in the study had any issues with the installation, configuration, or proper use of the Luxboard keyboards.

With more practice and longer use of both proposed methods, a corresponding improvement in text entry efficiency can be expected. In this context, additional studies can be carried out to analyze the effect of cursor movement pace on input speed and error rate when using the *Luxboard automatic*. Similarly, different dwell time values can be evaluated for *Luxboard manual* method, in order to determine their impact on WPM and TER metrics. Since only alphabetical character layouts were used in our study, it would also be interesting to investigate how alternative character layouts and/or different group layouts may affect the text entry efficiency. Finally, future work should engage different demographic groups and user types with varying abilities to interact with the proposed solution.

References

1. Castellucci, S.J., MacKenzie, I.S., Misra, M., Pandey, L., Arif, A.S.: TilTwriter: design and evaluation of a no-touch tilt-based text entry method for handheld devices. In: Proceedings of the 18th International Conference on Mobile and Ubiquitous Multimedia. MUM 2019. Association for Computing Machinery, New York (2019). https://doi.org/10.1145/3365610.3365629
2. Li, F.C.Y., Guy, R.T., Yatani, K., Truong, K.N.: The 1line keyboard: a qwerty layout in a single line. In: Proceedings of the 24th Annual ACM Symposium on User Interface Software and Technology. UIST 2011, pp. 461–470. Association for Computing Machinery, New York (2011). https://doi.org/10.1145/2047196.2047257

3. MacKenzie, I.S., Soukoreff, R.W.: Phrase sets for evaluating text entry techniques. In: CHI 2003 Extended Abstracts on Human Factors in Computing Systems. CHI EA 2003, pp. 754–755. Association for Computing Machinery, New York (2003). https://doi.org/10.1145/765891.765971

4. Nirjon, S., Gummeson, J., Gelb, D., Kim, K.H.: TypingRing: a wearable ring platform for text input. In: Proceedings of the 13th Annual International Conference on Mobile Systems, Applications, and Services. MobiSys 2015, pp. 227–239. Association for Computing Machinery, New York (2015). https://doi.org/10.1145/2742647.2742665

5. Romano, M., Paolino, L., Tortora, G., Vitiello, G.: The tap and slide keyboard: a new interaction method for mobile device text entry. Int. J. Hum.-Comput. Interact. **30**(12), 935–945 (2014). https://doi.org/10.1080/10447318.2014.924349

6. Schoenleben, O., Oulasvirta, A.: Sandwich keyboard: fast ten-finger typing on a mobile device with adaptive touch sensing on the back side. In: Proceedings of the 15th International Conference on Human-Computer Interaction with Mobile Devices and Services. MobileHCI 2013, pp. 175–178. Association for Computing Machinery, New York (2013). https://doi.org/10.1145/2493190.2493233

7. Sharif, M.A., Rakhmetulla, G., Arif, A.S.: TapSTR: a tap and stroke reduced-qwerty for smartphones. In: Companion Proceedings of the 2020 Conference on Interactive Surfaces and Spaces. ISS 2020, pp. 47–50. Association for Computing Machinery, New York (2020). https://doi.org/10.1145/3380867.3426208

8. Soukoreff, R.W., MacKenzie, I.S.: Metrics for text entry research: an evaluation of MSD and KSPC, and a new unified error metric. In: Proceedings of the SIGCHI Conference on Human Factors in Computing Systems. CHI 2003, pp. 113–120. Association for Computing Machinery, New York (2003). https://doi.org/10.1145/642611.642632

9. Wang, J., Zhao, K., Zhang, X., Peng, C.: Ubiquitous keyboard for small mobile devices: harnessing multipath fading for fine-grained keystroke localization. In: Proceedings of the 12th Annual International Conference on Mobile Systems, Applications, and Services. MobiSys 2014, pp. 14–27. Association for Computing Machinery, New York (2014). https://doi.org/10.1145/2594368.2594384

10. Wen, E., Seah, W., Ng, B., Liu, X., Cao, J.: Ubitouch: ubiquitous smartphone touchpads using built-in proximity and ambient light sensors. In: Proceedings of the 2016 ACM International Joint Conference on Pervasive and Ubiquitous Computing. UbiComp 2016, pp. 286–297. Association for Computing Machinery, New York (2016). https://doi.org/10.1145/2971648.2971678

11. Yang, Q., Fu, H., Zou, Y., Wu, K.: A novel finger-assisted touch-free text input system without training. In: Proceedings of the 16th Annual International Conference on Mobile Systems, Applications, and Services. MobiSys 2018, p. 533. Association for Computing Machinery, New York (2018). https://doi.org/10.1145/3210240.3211107

12. Yeo, H.S., Phang, X.S., Castellucci, S.J., Kristensson, P.O., Quigley, A.: Investigating tilt-based gesture keyboard entry for single-handed text entry on large devices. In: Proceedings of the 2017 CHI Conference on Human Factors in Computing Systems. CHI 2017, pp. 4194–4202. Association for Computing Machinery, New York (2017). https://doi.org/10.1145/3025453.3025520

13. Yin, Y., Li, Q., Xie, L., Yi, S., Novak, E., Lu, S.: CAMK: Camera-based keystroke detection and localization for small mobile devices. IEEE Trans. Mob. Comput. **17**(10), 2236–2251 (2018). https://doi.org/10.1109/TMC.2018.2798635

14. Zhang, C., Tabor, J., Zhang, J., Zhang, X.: Extending mobile interaction through near-field visible light sensing. In: Proceedings of the 21st Annual International Conference on Mobile Computing and Networking. MobiCom 2015, pp. 345–357. Association for Computing Machinery, New York (2015). https://doi.org/10.1145/2789168.2790115

15. Zhang, M., Yang, P., Tian, C., Shi, L., Tang, S., Xiao, F.: SoundWrite: text input on surfaces through mobile acoustic sensing. In: Proceedings of the 1st International Workshop on Experiences with the Design and Implementation of Smart Objects. SmartObjects 2015, pp. 13–17. Association for Computing Machinery, New York (2015). https://doi.org/10.1145/2797044.2797045

Evaluation of Draw and Use Buttons Methods for Curve Plot Using a Facial Tracker

Ivana Bandeira[1] and Fernando H. G. Zucatelli[2]

[1] Institute of Mathematics and Statistics (IME),
R. do Matão 1010, 05508-090 São Paulo, SP, Brazil
[2] School of Mechanical Engineering (FEM – Unicamp),
Rua Mendeleyev, 200, Campinas, 13083-860 São Paulo, Brazil
f193303@dac.unicamp.br

Abstract. This paper presents the evaluation of two methods to plot three dimensional polygonal curves with the aid of a face tracker (eViacam). We compared a pointing method to select points forming polygons on a 3D grid, called "Draw" and the other method was denominated "Use Buttons" and used to type three coordinates and plot the curves.

The experiment evaluates the new feature of "Use Buttons" in contrast with the original "Draw" method. A total of forty-six volunteers including six users with disabilities participated in the tests which have taken place in São Paulo University and Federal University of ABC. We evaluated average time, the amount of errors and effort of participants to draw previously defined figures along three sessions such as training and affinity could be carried on through sessions. The obtained results show that the method "Use Buttons" does not imply better usability, despite being an interesting alternative input method. Although time demand is greater with this method than the original one, it is still not a big problem when volunteers focus on the activity.

Keywords: Human-computer interaction · Design and evaluation · User experience · Empirical studies of user behavior · Accessibility

1 Introduction

Face tracking has been implemented in systems as an assistive technology for communication with patients with motor impairments [1], disabled students [2,3] and as low cost assistive technology providing computational accessibility for disabled people in general [4]. In Brazil, in particular, about 92% of students with disabilities are included in regular classes [5]. In this sense, we aim to contribute and provide options that can be used for art processes, study of Mathematics and games including students with disabilities in the upper limbs.

This study was financed in part by the Coordenação de Aperfeiçoamento de Pessoal de Nível Superior - Brasil (CAPES) - Finance Code 001.

© The Author(s), under exclusive license to Springer Nature Switzerland AG 2022
M. Kurosu (Ed.): HCII 2022, LNCS 13303, pp. 140–151, 2022.
https://doi.org/10.1007/978-3-031-05409-9_11

In a previous article titled "A Human-Computer Interface and an Analyze about the Drawing of Curves with a Face Tracker Mouse" [6] we showed our results about the study of plotting curves using specific face tracker called Enable Viacam (eViacam) [7]. We investigated the needs of the users since the beginning of the project, identified the usability goals and user experience. In that experiment, 16 participants collaborated on our understanding about the needs, forms of interaction and user experience. As a suggestion of some participants in the previous experiment, we have improved our interface including buttons to type three coordinates and plot some polygonal curves using a face tracker. This kind of design using eye and head movements for pointing and selection is also analyzed in other studies as in [8,9].

Thenceforth, we created a totally new experiment with an updated interface, 46 volunteers and two input methods for the curves using another face tracker, before it was used HeadMouse [10] and now eViacam [7]. The first method is selecting the vertices directly on the grid and the second is typing the coordinates clicking on big buttons on a numeric virtual keyboard embedded on the interface screen.

The graphical interface is similar to that seen in the previous experiment. The update was the inclusion of the buttons: "Use Buttons", "0", "1" and "2". They allow users to enter coordinates without the need to click directly on the grid, which was considered a difficulty in the previous experiment because of the small size of the target. This study is not just a new version of the previous interface. The first aim was verifying if this new tool would facilitate the task of plotting curves.

In order to evaluate the performance, the usability of the interface and the experience of the user, we have executed this experiment. In it we aimed to compare the "Draw", methods where the selection of the point in the grid is made by time, and "Use Buttons", with which there is a need of typing the three coordinates to select the point in the grid. So, three groups of volunteers were interviewed, they also answered questionnaires and were evaluated with respect to performance and user experience. Another fact we would like to investigate was whether there would be a difference in participants performance and amount of error with a small difference in latency time.

2 Methodology

Users Characteristics
In total, forty-six volunteers are part of the following demographic composition: Gender: 60.86% female and 39.13% male; Age group: 15.21% over 40 years old and 84.78% over 20 years old. Data were collected from users with physical disabilities (6) and healthy participants (40). All with normal or corrected vision with the use of glasses. Among the physically challenged volunteers there were disabled athletes (2), researchers in Applied Mathematics (2), a Marketing student and an employee of IBM. The group of physically capable participants includes students from undergraduate and graduate programs at São Paulo University and Federal University of ABC, as well as professors from IME/USP (6)

and some volunteers who are not from academia. But they can be considered stakeholders for surrounding potential users of the programs.

All forty-six volunteers answered our survey. Eight of them had already participated in the previous experiment. Before starting the sessions, the same interview from the previous experiment was proposed. We intended to evaluate the experience of drawing curves using a computer, the needs during the task, the benefits and the difficulties in performing this action. In addition, we were interested to know about: the practice in programming, the difficulty in controlling the conventional mouse and keyboard, also about other forms of interaction and the experience with software to obtain geometric figures.

In this experiment, about 54.35% declared to know how to program in one or more languages. Among the programming languages mentioned, we have: C (13), Java (11), Matlab (11), Python (7), C++(5), Assembly (4), Fortran (4), R (4), Html (2), Ladder (2), Pascal (1), Prolog (1) SQL (1), Scilab (1), VHDL (1). Only 3 volunteers stated to have difficulty handling the mouse conventional, 2 of them were disabled people.

Twenty-three participants mentioned to have already used other devices to interact with the computer, such as: Enable Viacam (9), Touchscreen (6), Video Game Controls (6), Voice Command (3), Graphics Tablet (3), HeadMouse (2), Kinect (2), Pupil (2), EyeTribe (1), PCB (1). As for software for obtaining geometric figures, we obtain the following results: twenty-one use one or more of these programs: GeoGebra (4), AutoCAD (3), SolidWorks (3), ArcGIS (2), CorelDraw (2), Maple (2), Matlab (2), Surface Evolver (2), Paint (2), Inkscape (2), GIMP (2), InfraWorks (1), Aimsun (1), Photoshop (1), COMOS (1), Craft Edge (1), Wolfram/Alpha (1), Xfig (1), LaTexDraw (1), Winplot (1).

As difficulties faced in using software cited stand out: learning the windows and functions to generate the desired figure, discovering all the features, finding the applications, controlling the tools for editing curves, for example, the need of programming scripts to plot curves and surfaces.

In this experiment, the participants were divided into three groups:

1. **Group 1** – Users without Motor Impairment: Undergraduate students and teachers and postgraduate studies at the University of São Paulo (USP).
2. **Group 2** – Users with Motor Impairment: Two volunteers from IME-USP, an external participant and two swimmers from the Association for Sports Integration of the Physically Disabled (Ciedef).
   These two groups have used the face tracker Enable Viacam, setting 10 ds (ten tenths of a second) for dwell time.
3. **Group 3** – Users without Motor Impairment: Undergraduate and graduate students and professors at the Federal University of ABC. They have controlled the face tracker Enable Viacam, setting 15 ds for dwell time.

The volunteers were asked to reproduce curves with a facial tracker (Enable Viacam) polygonal with 4, 6 and 9 vertices, in different positions in each session but with the same amount of points. During all sessions, the image to be copied was placed beside the interface for both steps named as "Draw" and in "Use Button", according to Fig. 1.

Fig. 1. User during a session

2.1   Use Buttons New Input Method

The previous interface had only one input method, the so called "Draw". This method enables data input from direct mouse clicking on the desired point on the 3D-Cube. Following suggestions from previous volunteers, we added a new input method, the so called "Use Buttons" (Fig. 2). This method presents to users a set of 5 buttons. The "Use Buttons" button starts the process of inserting data into the 3D-Cube as presented in Fig. 3. The interface deactivates the buttons "Draw" and "Save next". These buttons are only re-activated when the "Use Buttons" button is pressed again. Above the now green-colored "Use Buttons" is displayed the coordinates in the form $(x, y, z) = (, ,)$.

Each button is associated with a color, "0" with yellow, "1" with magenta and "2" with cyan. Since it's necessary to select one coordinate in each plan at a time, each button is presented with the respective color of the associated plane, in order to make easier to any user to identify coordinates and buttons. Figure 3(a) presents the interface to insert an x-coordinate, Fig. 3(b) for y-coordinate and Fig. 3(c) for z-coordinate. There is also a button called "Remove Last". This button removes the last inserted coordinate, except for the last coordinate. If the last coordinate has been wrongly inserted, then the user should remove the whole point by using the "Undo" button.

This input method was a suggestion from previous users, therefore, one objective of this article is to test and compare user's experiences in each input method.

3   Discussion

The groups had different characteristics. This fact impacted the results so it is necessary to analyze separately. For example, in the first session, for Group 1 the average time was 51.2 s by selecting five points to plot the curve. Although this is similar to most volunteers, we could detect some outliers performing 22.0 s and another 88.3 s. Thereafter, the average value has just decreased to 44.0 s

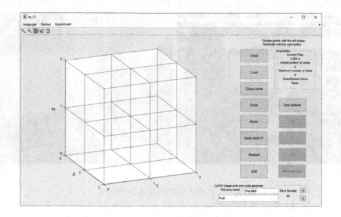

Fig. 2. Interface – overview

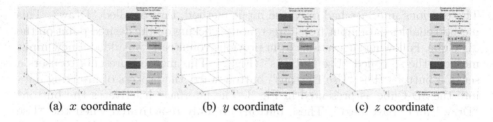

(a) x coordinate   (b) y coordinate   (c) z coordinate

Fig. 3. "Use Buttons" highlighted coordinates (Color figure online)

in the second session and 39.8 in the third session. About the other method, "Use Buttons", typing the coordinates, we also observed the same behavior: 83.7 s in the first session, 74.1 s in the second and 72.9 in the third. It is curious that the minimum and maximum time for this method were 21.0 s and 165.9 s, respectively in the first session. Nevertheless, they were not the same outliers cited before. In this sense, we can see that some volunteers had better time even if they needed clicking two times more. The behavior was similar to the chains with 6 vertices using the method "Draw", the average time declined from 68.8 s to 62.5 s and then 61.3 s. But, the chains with 6 and 9 vertices performed by "Use Buttons" decreased from the first to second sessions and increased again in the third session.

This situation illustrates that although training and learning processes were carried out as we will see in the analysis of subjective measures, the complexity of the figures with nine vertices influences significantly over time. As we can verify in Fig. 4.

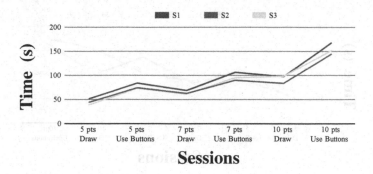

Fig. 4. Average time per figure and input method for Group 1

For Group 2, we have changed the chart style aiming to be able to compare the three sessions with two methods. Contrasting the average time from this group against Group 1, which was in the same conditions for dwell time and identical pictures, we observe a better performance. Probably because two participants were experts using a face tracker. However, when the complexity of edges increased, as in the chains with 9 edges, there were not big differences within the groups, expert or novice participants achieved around 167.5 s. Checking Fig. 5, the bars for the first and third sessions, which the used method was "Draw", are proportional to the chains with 4 and 6 edges, around 42 s and 60 s, respectively.

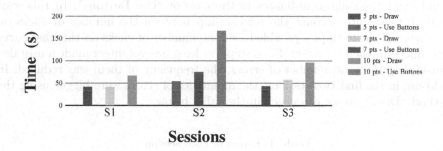

Fig. 5. Average time per season for Group 2

As expected, Group 3 presented the highest time averages due to 5 ds more for the dwell time. Comparing the first and third session, the time average was reduced for all cases, as we can see on Fig. 6.

Though, differently from Group 1, the average time during the performance for the chains with 6 and 9 vertices adopting the method "Use Buttons" increased from the first to second sessions and decreased in the third session.

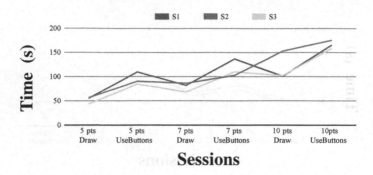

Fig. 6. Average time per figure and input method for Group 3

3.1 Error Analysis

In this section we will discuss the mistakes made by the volunteers during the previous sessions. First, we shall list what was considered an error in this experiment:

1. Coordinates different from those shown in the test examples;
2. Amount of "Undo" and "Redo" uses;
3. Click on the same point.

We were concerned about whether the participant would be able to plot curves with the amount of clicks provided in the method "Draw" and if they would enter the same coordinates in the case of "Use Buttons". In this way, we have taken into account the relationship between the number of clicks on the curves of the examples provided and the number of clicks on the final curve reproduced by each volunteer. In all steps, at least one volunteer made a mistake. Considering the total number of errors, the frequency of them was reduced. In addition, in the first two sessions, the quantities of errors were bigger using the method "Draw", as we can check in the table below.

Table 1. Errors in each session

Interaction method	Session 1		Session 2		Session 3	
	$G_1 \cup G_2$	G_3	$G_1 \cup G_2$	G_3	$G_1 \cup G_2$	G_3
Draw	51	15	57	11	19	6
Use Buttons	44	29	48	32	32	21

Figure 7 presents the number of errors done by each set of groups, the union of **Group 1** and **Group 2** ($G_1 \cup G_2$) and **Group 3** (G_3), in this sense, Fig. 7 shows how the errors from Table 1 spread along each figure used during the sessions. Figures are numbered in the sequence they were presented to volunteers, it means, the sequential figure number 1 has 5 pts and is the same as number 4; number 2 and number 5 are the 7 pts pair; and numbers 3 and 6 are the 10 pts pair for Session 1. For Session 2 the pairs are $(7, 10)$, $(8, 11)$ and $(9, 12)$; for Session 3 the pairs are $(13, 16)$, $(14, 17)$ and $(15, 18)$.

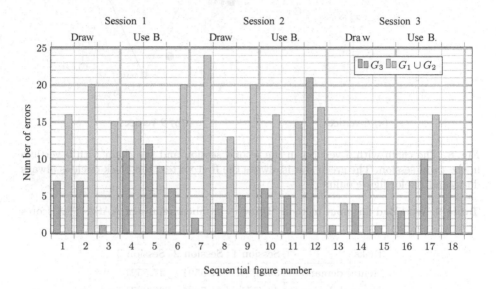

Fig. 7. Number of errors of each tested figure separated by researcher

For Group 1 and Group 2, the most difficult step was a chain with 6 vertices in the second session and for Group 3, it was a chain with 9 vertices in the third session, Fig. 8(a) and (b), respectively.

There were also five volunteers who clicked on buttons that were not part of the curve design, such as: "Read" or "Restart". Some participants have justified their mistakes saying that it was difficult to look at the picture beside and remember the points and others said it would be easier if the researcher could dictate the coordinates.

3.2 Demand Analysis

The following tables show the results of the demands of the participants with the application of the NASA-TLX questionnaire. Results for input method "Draw" are summarized in Table 2 and for input method "Use Buttons" in Table 3. For the subjective analysis we followed the NASA Task Load Index that uses six dimensions to estimate mental workload: mental demand, physical demand, temporal demand, performance, effort, and frustration. For more detailed information, it is possible checking [11].

The evaluation of factors considered most important in the creation of the workload in the task gave greater weight to the performance during two of the

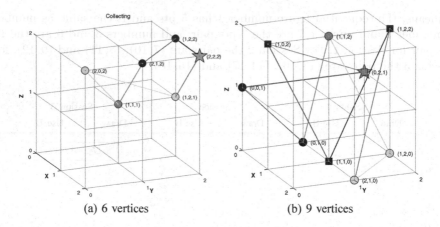

(a) 6 vertices   (b) 9 vertices

Fig. 8. The chain with 6 vertices in the second session and the chain with 9 vertices in the third session. The green star is always the first vertex, the black circle is always de second (Color figure online)

Table 2. Workload for input method "Draw" – numbers represent NASA-TLX scores

Tasks	Session 1	Session 2	Session 3
Mental demand	36.1084	47.5591	47.5591
Physical demand	43.4551	41.7831	36.0071
Temporal demand	44.7893	34.2169	38.6418
Performance	55.9933	57.5556	58.6720
Effort	50.1600	48.1502	45.3467
Frustration	21.3138	14.5920	17.7840

three sessions using the method "Draw": 55.99 in the first session, 57.55 in the second session and 58.67 in the third session. By the parameters, we may infer that the most part has considered the performance good. The effort received the second highest estimations for the tasks in the first and second sessions, 50.16 and 48.15, respectively. But the score in the third session was 47.55 for the mental demand. When we analyze the scores for the method "Use Buttons" the overload is also the performance for the first and second sessions, however, for the third was the temporal demand. This may be a consequence of a comparison done by the participants considering the time they were able to reproduce the pictures during previous sessions.

The rates associated to temporal demand were similar for both methods in the first session for all groups. It is interesting to point out that the mental demand was considered more relevant than the physical demand with "Use Buttons", even though they needed to click twice more. This is endorsed by some commentaries from volunteers, we can cite: 'can you dictate the points?'

Table 3. Workload for input method "Use Buttons" – numbers represent NASA-TLX scores

Tasks	Session 1	Session 2	Session 3
Mental demand	48.1502	29.1342	55.3449
Physical demand	42.6107	44.3004	31.9031
Temporal demand	42.6107	73.5390	37.5609
Performance	50.8133	67.0320	60.5129
Effort	47.9982	48.1502	45.4987
Frustration	21.1111	14.5920	22.5129

or 'it requires a lot of reasoning and concentration'. On the other hand, using the method "Draw", physical demand was more significant. Some of them commented: 'when moving the neck then it is easy losing the mouse position', or 'In some moments I spent a long time trying to hit a point and it started to bother me physically.'. The level of frustration was low, in general, around 25% but it was not a factor that interfered in their performances. Most of them felt themselves secure to do the activities and they were more interested in reproducing the picture correctly.

A curious fact about the second session is a higher level of effort when we asked to choose between 'effort' and 'temporal demand' to know the overload. The level of temporal pressure felt decreased considerably between the first session and the second for the method "Draw" and oscillating for the method "Use Buttons", the score was 73.53 in the second session. A volunteer from Group 1 commented: "the dwell time is too fast and for this reason I made mistakes increasing my time for redoing the curves".

Dimensions as looking, searching the points on the grid and typing the coordinates estimated mental demand as an important source of workload for both methods in the third session, the scores were 47.55 using "Draw" and 55.34 for "Use Buttons". The level of concentration required was said as high by some volunteers, one of them cited: "it is possible applying this software as a group dynamic for candidates in a job application.".

The statistical survey on the expertise of all volunteers in relation to the forms of interaction also shows us that many of those with experience in other methods of interaction had lower mental demand and frustration indices and higher rates of performance.

Another interesting fact is that almost all participants commented they believed this interface is a useful tool for people with physical disabilities, even those considered healthy.

4   Conclusion

In the present article, we discussed about the plotting of curves using a face tracker using two forms of interaction. It is explicit that just adding big a button does not presuppose better usability in our case. Other questions as training and affinity with the tool impact much more. It was emphasized by the rates, mistakes and subjective evaluation in our experiment. Even the target to be clicked with the method "Draw" is tiny, it was considered by the participants as easier and less stressful like the method "Use Buttons". On the other hand, it is clear that typing the coordinates imply in a greater temporal demand but this is not a big problem when the participant focus on the activity. As many volunteers said, the main goal of this interface is the fact it can be used for people with or without disabilities. Also, some possibilities of applications have arose during the session, such as: a memory game, teaching of polygons and job dynamic. In addition to the characteristic of an inclusive design tool for people with limitations in the upper limbs, it may provide applications related to people with cognitive impairment. For example, executive functions where we can work from the game mentioned above to work on sequencing, inhibitory control, logical reasoning and memorization not only of static sequences, but with sequencing in motion, spatial memory, visual perception.

References

1. Kaya, A., Özcan, F.: Communication with the patients of amyotrophic lateral sclerosis and current technology. J. Turk. Family Phys. (2017)
2. Bakken, J.P., Varidireddy, N., Uskov, V.L.: Smart university: software/hardware systems for college students with severe motion/mobility issues. In: Uskov, V.L., Howlett, R.J., Jain, L.C. (eds.) Smart Education and e-Learning 2019. SIST, vol. 144, pp. 471–487. Springer, Singapore (2019). https://doi.org/10.1007/978-981-13-8260-4_42
3. Acessibilidade Digital no Programa Um Computador por Aluno: A Experiência da Paraíba Mariano Castro Neto. 5ºSENID. ISSN 2238-5916
4. da Rocha Perris, P.A., da Fonseca de Souza, F.: Integrated assistive auxiliary system - developing low cost assistive technology to provide computational accessibility for disabled people. In: Antona, M., Stephanidis, C. (eds.) HCII 2020. LNCS, vol. 12188, pp. 33–47. Springer, Cham (2020). https://doi.org/10.1007/978-3-030-49282-3_3
5. INEP Brasil: Censo Escolar: notas estatísticas. Brasília. Instituto Nacional de Estudos e Pesquisas Educacionais Anísio Teixeira, pp. 15–44 (2018)
6. Bandeira, I.S., Zucatelli, F.H.G.: A human-computer interface and an analysis on the drawing of curves with a face tracker mouse. In: Antona, M., Stephanidis, C. (eds.) UAHCI 2016. LNCS, vol. 9738, pp. 3–14. Springer, Cham (2016). https://doi.org/10.1007/978-3-319-40244-4_1
7. eViacam: Enable Viacam. https://eviacam.crea-si.com/
8. Penkar, A.M., Lutteroth, C., Weber, G.: Designing for the eye: design parameters for dwell in gaze interaction. Association for Computing Machinery (2012). https://doi.org/10.1145/2414536.2414609
9. Sidenmark, L., Gellersen, H.: Eye&Head: synergetic eye and head movement for gaze pointing and selection. Association for Computing Machinery (2019). https://doi.org/10.1145/3332165.3347921

10. HeadMouse. http://robotica.udl.cat/catedra/headmouse/version42/headmouse42 pt.pdf
11. Hancock, P.A., Meshkati, N.: Development of NASA-TLX (task load index): results of empirical and theoretical research, **52**, 139–183 (1988). https://doi.org/10.1016/ S0166-4115(08)62386-9

Retinal Viewfinder: Preliminary Study of Retinal Projection-Based Electric Viewfinder for Camera Devices

Ippei Suzuki[✉], Yuta Itoh, and Yoichi Ochiai

Research and Development Center for Digital Nature, University of Tsukuba, Tsukuba, Japan
1heisuzuki@digitalnature.slis.tsukuba.ac.jp

Abstract. This paper presents a prototype of a new type of electronic viewfinder (EVF) that uses a retinal projection system. A viewfinder that enables users to preview an image is one of the characteristics and important interfaces of a camera. However, people who require glasses or contact lenses face a problem when using a viewfinder as they cannot see the image easily. In the retinal projection system, a large depth of field projection will enable users to focus on the displayed image easily. To investigate the above hypothesis, we compared the existing EVF with the proposed method from the perspective of ease of focusing on subjects. The user study employed a person with bad eyesight who uses a visual aid. Experimental results indicate that in certain situations, the proposed method has an advantage in focusing when users look through the viewfinder without glasses or contact lenses.

Keywords: Photography · Camera hardware · Viewfinder · Display · Interface · User experience

1 Introduction

Smartphones and compact digital cameras have made photography accessible to many, allowing people to take photographs regularly. When taking a photo with a camera, the main steps followed are:

1. look around to choose what to photograph
2. adjust photography parameters (e.g., exposure, framing, and lighting)
3. preview the expected result in real-time or through playback of previous photographs
4. take the photograph.

An important step in this process is the preview. Digital cameras generally have the capability to display a preview by utilizing either a viewfinder or a display screen. Viewfinders, especially, are characteristic and important interfaces of cameras (Fig. 1 (a)). In this paper, we define the viewfinder as (1) something

M. Kurosu (Ed.): HCII 2022, LNCS 13303, pp. 152–164, 2022.
https://doi.org/10.1007/978-3-031-05409-9_12

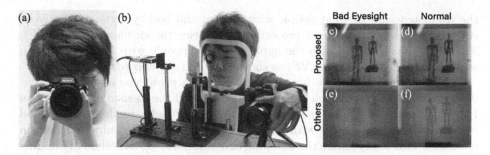

Fig. 1. (a) An individual using an existing camera with an electric viewfinder. (b) An individual using our prototype in the user study. (c), (d), (e) and (f) Simulated views of what a user sees with the viewfinder in the user study. Our method has the advantage of providing a large depth of field projection. (c) and (e) were taken with an incorrect focus target to simulate the vision of a person with bad eyesight.

that provides a viewpoint for an in-focus image to the user, and (2) something that the photographer looks through to compose the framing, adjust exposure, and focus the image.

Viewfinders have three advantages compared to the display screen. First, viewfinders effectively block the user's eye from surrounding light. When a camera is used in bright sunlight, it is difficult to see the image on the display screen due to the reflection of the surrounding light. However, viewfinders are not affected by such light. Second, the user can stabilize the camera by bracing it against their face and keeping their upper arm close to the body. Third, the user can concentrate on taking photos. Taking photographs by using the display screen allows the scenery around the camera to enter the photographer's peripheral visual field. In contrast, the viewfinder restricts the field of view, enabling concentration. Therefore, the viewfinder plays an important role in the process of taking photos.

However, people with bad eyesight find viewfinders difficult to use as they often cannot see the image clearly. First, focusing on the image displayed in a viewfinder can be problematic. Although viewfinders of current commercially available cameras have a diopter adjustment to help those who have myopia or hyperopia, its adjustment range is limited. Second, if the user wears glasses, the glasses collide with the eyepiece or the eyecup of the viewfinder. Thus, viewfinders must be redesigned in order for such people to be able to take advantage of their benefits.

This paper proposes a new mechanism for the viewfinder: a retinal projection-based electric viewfinder (R-EVF). Currently, retinal projection is one of the main research fields for head-mounted displays (HMDs) or augmented reality (AR) smart glasses. The retinal projection system is an image presentation technique that contributes to the solution of vergence-accommodation conflict by providing a large depth of field projection. In essence, a large depth of field projection enables one to focus on the displayed image easily. Figs. 1 (e) and (f) show the simulated view of what people with normal and bad eyesight, respectively, see when using a non-retinal projection-based electric viewfinder (NR-EVF). This study was initiated with the hypothesis that people with bad eyesight can see images easily via the R-EVF, as shown in Fig. 1 (c) and (d).

To investigate the above hypothesis, we built a prototype system and conducted a user study in which participants performed the focusing task using an R-EVF and an NR-EVF. The results of this study indicate that our method has an advantage for people with bad eyesight focusing on the subject in certain instances. This study makes the following contributions: (1) a method of building the R-EVF prototype; (2) an investigation of the effects of using the prototype through a user study; and (3) a discussion of the results and limitations of the current prototype.

2   Related Work

2.1   Current Systems of the Viewfinder

Several types of viewfinders have been developed and implemented in commercially available cameras. There are two main types of viewfinders: an optical viewfinder (OVF) and an electric viewfinder (EVF). This section describes them and cites relevant patents and technical reports.

Optical Viewfinder. An OVF [10,13] displays images optically. Because an OVF requires no electric power to show the images, users can see the image even if the power of the camera is turned off. On the other hand, an OVF cannot use any photography support that uses image processing, such as manual focus magnification assist, focus peaking, and increasing the brightness of the preview. OVFs are mainly divided into three types.

Direct OVFs [6] show images using a lens independent from the main lens of the camera, which is used for photography. It is a type of telescope in which the angle of view is designed to match the main lens. The viewfinder of a single-use camera is a typical example of this category of viewfinders [19].

Rangefinders, typically split-image rangefinders [3], use a range-finding focusing mechanism while showing images using the same method as direct OVFs. Most of them show two images of the same subject: one moves when a focusing ring is turned while the other one remains static. When the two images converge into one, the subjects are in focus. Compared to other OVFs, this method visually indicates whether the subject is in focus or not.

Reflex finders [1] show images using a mirror placed behind the main lens. A pentaprism device receives and transfers reflected images to display them to users. The viewfinder of the single-lens reflex (SLR) camera is a typical example of this category. Compared to other OVFs, reflex finders show the image from the same viewing angle and viewpoint as the main lens.

Electric Viewfinder. An EVF [2,20,26,28] uses electric displays to show the image. The image is captured by an image sensor, processed by an image processing unit, and displayed on the display device. EVFs are mainly divided by the type of display: liquid crystal display (LCD) [26] and organic light-emitting diode (OLED) display [27].

An EVF has three major advantages over an OVF. First, an EVF can provide photography support through image processing such as manual focus magnification assist, focus peaking, and increasing brightness of the preview. Second, because an EVF does not depend on the real-world optics of the main lens, its system can be downsized and placed freely, independent of the main lens. Third, in the case of digital photography, users can preview the image using the "what you see is what you get" (WYSIWYG) method. One of the limitations of the EVF is that it requires electric power and computing resources for image processing. This affects battery life, and users cannot see the image without turning on the camera.

Other Methods. There are some other approaches for building viewfinders. FUJIFILM Corporation proposed a hybrid viewfinder that combines an OVF and an EVF [17]. There exist external viewfinders that use either an OVF or an EVF. An LCD magnification viewfinder [9] enables one to see a larger image on a display screen without hindrance or light from the environment.

2.2 Comparison of Cameras in Specific Applications

Evaluation experiments of cameras in specific applications have been reported. As a first example, research is being carried out on reproducing radiographic images. Sistrom et al. conducted an evaluation experiment using three cameras to reproduce a radiographic image for educational purposes [25]. Brault et al. evaluated the ability to reproduce high-quality radiographic images with seven cameras and its cost performance [5]. As a second example, research is being conducted on dental photography. Bister et al. tested ten digital cameras for use in intra- and extra-oral photography used in orthodontics [4].

In terms of accessibility, a mechanism to improve the camera has also been reported. Mott et al. focused on the accessibility of smartphone photography for people with motor impairments and explored how photography interfaces can be improved for such users [16].

In this research, we conducted a user study on camera viewfinders for a specific purpose. Because viewfinder use is reliant on human vision, problems arise when visual acuity deteriorates. The proposed method provided a large depth of field projection, so we hypothesized that it could display the image more clearly than previous methods for people with bad eyesight.

2.3 Retinal Projection

Retinal projection is one of the methods that allow people to see clear images regardless of their eyesight. The retinal projection has been studied in the area

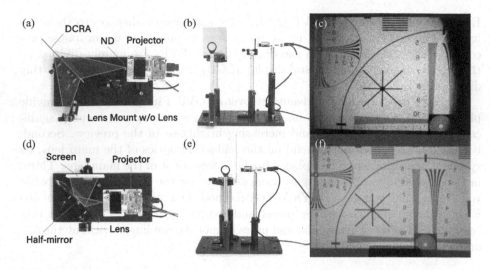

Fig. 2. Setups for the user study. Upper: Retinal projection-based electric viewfinder (proposed). Lower: Non-retinal projection-based electric viewfinder. Photos (c) and (f) are taken from the lens mount position.

of HMDs, and several methods have been proposed. For example, methods with Maxwellian optics [12], methods are based on laser scanning [14], or methods with Fourier hologram using spatial light modulator (SLM) or holographic optical element (HOE) [8]. In this study, we apply the method using a dihedral corner reflector array [18] to an electronic viewfinder. This method can achieve retinal projection without designing a complex optical system, and has a larger eyebox than conventional retinal projection systems.

3   Implementation

In this paper, we propose an R-EVF as a new type of viewfinder. For evaluation purposes, two types of viewfinders were prepared for the user study: one is our R-EVF, and the other is an NR-EVF. This section describes the two setups in detail.

3.1   Retinal Projection Based Electric Viewfinder

We prototyped the new type of electronic viewfinder that uses the retinal projection method. The setup is shown in Fig. 2 (a), (b) and (c). We refer to the implementation proposed in [18]. The image shown in this viewfinder was flipped horizontally owing to the use of a dihedral corner reflector array (DCRA). The DCRA consists of two layers of micromirrors that are orthogonal to each other. By reflection in each micromirror, the DCRA creates the real image of a light source at a plane-symmetric position. In a previous work [11,15], the DCRA was used for aerial imaging and in an aerial interaction system. Recently, it was used for near-eye optical systems [21,22]. The DCRA used in this paper is 140 mm × 115 mm × 2 mm. The distance between each micromirror is 0.3 mm.

As a light source, a laser pico projector with a micro-electro-mechanical systems (MEMS) mirror (HD301; Ultimates, Inc.) was employed. Its resolution is 1280 × 720 pixels, the luminance is 20 lumens ± 10%, and the contrast ratio is 5000:1. The real-time preview image from the camera is an input to the projector. We inserted a neutral-density filter (ND) to reduce the intensity with a value of 1/10000.

For physical support to see the image, a fixed lens mount and chin rest were used. A fixed lens mount without a lens was used to indicate the position of the viewpoint. An ophthalmological chin rest was placed in front of the eyecup because the range from which the image can be seen was limited. The setup with the chin rest is shown in Fig. 1 (b). It was re-positioned for each participant based on their dominant eye. Any calibration other than eye positioning is not required for this system.

3.2 Non-retinal Projection Based Electric Viewfinder

In this study, a non-retinal projection viewfinder was developed using the same laser pico projector as used for R-EVFs in order to match certain conditions (e.g., resolution). If we had used commercially available viewfinders for comparison, a significant difference in resolution would have affected our results.

The setup of the NR-EVF is shown in Fig. 2 (d), (e) and (f). The same projector was used with an R-EVF. A drawing paper was fixed in front of the viewpoint to act as a screen. A half-mirror was used to project images onto the screen from the viewing direction. The image shown in this viewfinder was flipped horizontally because of the reflection of the half-mirror. A plano-convex lens (LA1433-A-ML; Thorlabs, Inc.) with a 150 mm focal length was used as an eyepiece in order to increase the distance between the eyes and the drawing paper as their distance was too close to focus.

4 User Study

4.1 Study Design

We conducted a user study to explore the effectiveness of our method for focusing. The study was conducted using a repeated measures design with two independent variables: (1) the mechanism of the viewfinder system (proposed R-EVF and NR-EVF); (2) whether each participant used a visual aid (with glasses, contact lenses, or without). To contrast with the proposed method, we implemented an NR-EVF as described in the previous section using the same projector with R-EVF. This is owing to the fact that our R-EVF system can currently only display a low-resolution image.

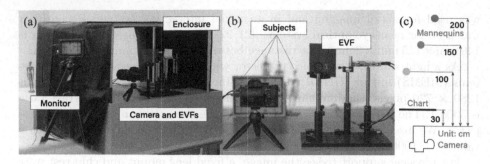

Fig. 3. (a) (b) Setups for user study. (c) Positional relationships between the camera and target subjects.

Two setups for photography were prepared for the user study. One was for taking a photograph of the IEEE Reflection Target[1]. The other is assuming a practical environment which includes three drawing mannequins. The setup of the user study is shown in Fig. 3. The resolution test target was set to be able to move between in-frame and out-of-frame.

4.2   Procedure

The study was conducted in a room with no source of natural light from the outside present. Each participant was briefly informed of the purpose of the study and that they could abort the study and take a break at any time. Further, all participants were provided with a consent form to sign.

As a first step, a quick eye test[2] was conducted. The uncorrected eyesight and corrected eyesight of each participant were measured. We determined the participants' eye dominance by using the Miles test [24] and asked participants to use their dominant eye in this experiment. The participants answered a questionnaire about their daily photography activities, their purpose for taking photographs, how often they use cameras, and the camera they predominantly use.

Next, they were instructed on how to use the two types of viewfinders in this study. The only parameter they could change was the focus ring. Therefore, the position, exposure, and other values were fixed. They could adjust the position of their eyes but could not move the position of the viewfinders.

Then, the following process was repeated for each subject: (1) The experimenter set the camera's focus to the minimum focusing distance. (2) Participants were asked to focus on each subject using a viewfinder. (3) While keeping the focus setting as adjusted by participants, the experimenter pressed the shutter of the camera, which was set to a 2-s delay self-timer to prevent camera shake. Participants repeated the process:

---

[1] https://www.edmundoptics.com/p/ieee-reflection-target/11533/ (last accessed Feb. 11, 2022).

[2] https://eyeportal.jp/60siryokukensa/siryokukennsa.html (last accessed Feb. 11, 2022, in Japanese).

1. With a visual aid/Using R-EVF
2. Without a visual aid/Using R-EVF
3. With a visual aid/Using NR-EVF
4. Without a visual aid/Using NR-EVF

One photo was taken per condition per participant. We conducted an interview with participants after each experiment to collect qualitative data. The order of target subjects, viewfinders, and whether a visual aid was used, were randomly changed.

Finally, participants were interviewed again about how they experienced the experiment, and they openly discussed their feelings. The entire experiment was recorded in both notes and video. The experiment was conducted in less than 30 min.

4.3 Participants and Apparatus

Twelve participants (three females and nine males, including six laboratory members) aged between 19 and 30 years (M = 21.7, SD = 3.78) participated in the experiment. All participants used a visual aid; ten participants wore glasses, and two participants wore contact lenses. Six participants were right-eye dominant, and the others were left-eye dominant. Four participants were first-time users of digital cameras with manual focus.

In this user study, the two viewfinders described in Sect. 3 were connected to one digital camera (ILCE-7SM2; SONY Corp.). Experimental setups are shown in Fig. 3. To protect the optical circuits of the viewfinder from external light, an enclosure was installed. The two viewfinders were allowed to be interchanged by the experimenter. A macro lens, 90 mm F/2.8 (SEL90M28G; SONY Corp.) was mounted on the camera. The setting of the camera was fixed to full-manual mode. The shutter speed was set at 1/200 s, the aperture at F/2.8, and the ISO value at 1000. To record the process of focusing, an external display, which had loop-through output, was inserted between the camera and the viewfinder's projector.

4.4 Result

Focus Accuracy. We post-processed photos captured by participants to calculate the focus measure, which attributes a higher value for a more focused image. There was some out-of-alignment effects on each photo captured in the user study due to the operation of the focus ring. Therefore, we stabilized the photos from each participant using Adobe After Effects. Next, we cropped the photos to trim the blank space caused by the stabilization, as shown in the second line of Fig. 4. Finally, we calculated the focus measure using Python 3.8.2 and OpenCV 4.2.0. We loaded an image by a single channel grayscale. The image was convolved with the 3×3 Laplacian kernel, and then the variance was taken as a focus measure [23]. The focus measure indicates how in-focus the image is (higher is more in-focus).

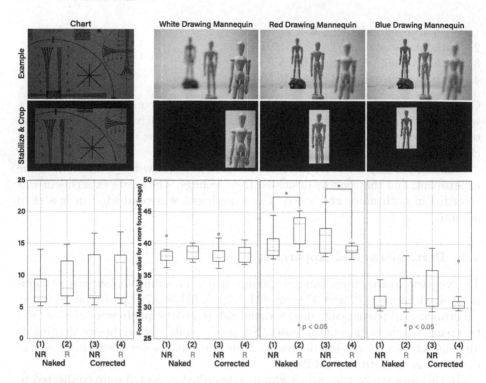

Fig. 4. Upper: Examples of original photos captured in each experimental condition. Middle: Examples of stabilized and cropped photos for quantitative analysis. Bottom: Boxplots of the results of the experiment. The vertical axis represents the focus measure, which indicates how in-focus the image is (higher is more in-focus). The orange line represents the median, the box represents the quartile range, whiskers indicate minimum and maximum, and dots indicate outliers. The red U-shaped line with * indicates that there is a significant difference between the two conditions ($p < 0.05$). NR indicates the non-retinal projection-based electric viewfinder (NR-EVF), and R indicates the retinal projection-based electric viewfinder (R-EVF; proposed). (Color figure online)

The boxplots for each condition are depicted in Fig. 4. The Wilcoxon rank-sum test was used to analyze the experimental results between R-EVF (ours) and NR-EVF in each condition with a significant difference of 5%. There was no significant difference between R-EVF (ours) and NR-EVF when the subject was the chart, the white drawing mannequin, and the blue drawing mannequin. For the red drawing mannequin, some significant differences were noted. When participants performed the task with their uncorrected vision, our R-EVF (2) achieved a better focus measure score than NR-EVF (1). Comparatively, when the tasks were performed with visual aids, the NR-EVF (3) showed a better focus measure score.

Feedback Comments. The participants described the difference in the performance of each viewfinder. P4: *"I didn't feel the difference on each viewfinder when I used it with a contact lens. However, in the NR-EVF tasks without a contact lens, the image that focused on the target seemed to be blurred. In contrast, in the R-EVF tasks, the image that focussed on the target seemed clear."* P10: *"In R-EVF tasks with glasses, lattices (author note: lattice caused by DCRA) could be seen in the image. So I felt that NR-EVF was easier to adjust focus compared to R-EVF. However, without glasses, I felt that the R-EVF was easier than NR-EVF."* P1: *"In the NR-EVF tasks, I felt as though the target was out of focus when I focused on the target without glasses."* P2: *"I felt that R-EVF's field of view is narrow, and its image quality is not very high."*

A few participants described the difference in the process of focusing on targets. P5: *"In NR-EVF tasks without contact lenses, I could not see the image clearly. However, I judged whether in focus or not by repeating the focus adjustment."* P6: *"In NR-EVF tasks without glasses, I focused on the chart following my intuition because it is difficult to judge whether or not in focus."*

5 Discussion and Future Work

5.1 Positioning Problem

From the results of the task to capture the drawing mannequins, we determined that there were significant differences in the focus measures between NR-EVF and R-EVF when the subject was near the center of the frame. Viewing the image through R-EVF requires that the emitted light rays from the light source pass through the center of the pupil. This means that the eyebox is restricted to a specific area. The eyebox is the space within which a viewable image can be seen. Since previous types of viewfinders display the image on a screen, they do not have the limitations of an eyebox and have some viewing angle. When people use the camera, the position relationship between the device and the user changes frequently. Therefore, the available area for seeing the image from the proposed R-EVF system is limited and may be problematic for applications such as cameras.

Some participants mentioned that the R-EVF has a narrow field of view when they see the image with glasses. This is an issue particular to retinal projection systems. When the eye is in a position with the light source, with the DCRA as a plane of symmetry, the obtained image is clearly displayed with a wide field of view. However, when the eye is on the back or forward position of the plane-symmetry, then the field of view becomes narrow. In the user study, we employed the chin rest to fix the viewing position of the image from R-EVF, as shown in Fig. 1 (b). Participants wearing glasses had difficulty adjusting their eye position, due to the fact that the frame of their glasses hit the chin rest.

In the future, we plan to explore how to make the eyebox larger in the retinal projection system. For example, Jang et al. proposed the first practical eyebox expansion method using pupil tracking for holographic near-eye display [7]. The optimal shape for a camera using the R-EVF may be different from the traditional camera shape, for one example, following the AR glass style viewfinder, which shows a preview when people pose for photography.

5.2 Resolution

As some participants mentioned, the resolution of the image from the R-EVF was lower than the ones available on commercial viewfinders. This is a limitation caused by the pitch size of the DCRA and the resolution of the laser pico projector. In the future, the DCRA and projectors with higher resolution may solve this problem. For other solutions, Yahagi et al. proposed a method of suppressing degradations such as lattices using mechanical vibration [29]. In addition, we may consider the transformation of the input image to the projector to complement the resolution.

As a result of the task to capture the chart, there was no significant difference for each pair of conditions. The resolution of the target chart may have been too high for the viewfinder resolution. In practical situations, EVF can compensate for resolution problems by image processing such as magnification or focus peaking.

5.3 Effects of the Focusing Process

Some participants mentioned that when they use the NR-EVF, the judgment of whether the image is in focus or not is relative. This is because their eyes could not accurately focus on the image shown by the NR-EVF. So they adjusted the focusing ring from front to rear repeatedly.

This becomes a problem when using autofocus as the manual focusing process is omitted in autofocus, and the user cannot judge whether the image is in focus during the focusing process. Comparatively, when using the R-EVF, the image that focused on the subject seemed clear in the case of uncorrected vision for shooting the red drawing mannequin. Therefore, R-EVF can sometimes be an appropriate viewfinder for users with bad eyesight.

In this study, we conducted the experiment under specific conditions: the viewfinder was independent from the camera, the camera was fixed, and the target subjects were not moving. In future work, we would like to develop an R-EVF that is attached to the camera, like commercially available viewfinders, and conduct further experiments under conditions closer to the practical applications.

6 Conclusion

This paper presented a prototype of a new type of electronic viewfinder that uses the retinal projection method. We conducted a user study to investigate the hypothesis that a large depth of field retinal projection will enable users to focus on the displayed image easily. We employed a DCRA-based retinal projection method. Experimental results indicated that the proposed method has an advantage in certain situations in focusing when users look through the viewfinder without visual aids. Finally, we discussed the possibility of using it as a viewfinder.

Acknowledgements. This work was supported by JST CREST Grant Number JPMJCR19F2.

References

1. Andre, D.L.J.E.: Verifier finder system for reflex camera. US Patent 2,887,019, 19 May 1959
2. Aoki, T.: Electronic viewfinder. US Patent 5,164,833, 17 November 1992
3. Arpad, B.: Photographic camera. US Patent 1,998,568, 23 April 1935
4. Bister, D., Mordarai, F., Aveling, R.M.: Comparison of 10 digital SLR cameras for orthodontic photography. J. Orthod. **33**(3), 223–230 (2006). https://doi.org/10.1179/146531205225021687, pMID: 16926316
5. Brault, B., Hoskinson, J., Armbrust, L., Milliken, G.: Comparison of seven digital cameras for digitizing radiographs. Vet. Radiol. Ultrasound **45**(4), 298–304 (2004)
6. Brown, S.: Direct-view finder for cameras. US Patent 1,140,108, 18 May 1915
7. Jang, C., Bang, K., Li, G., Lee, B.: Holographic near-eye display with expanded eye-box. ACM Trans. Graph. **37**(6), 195:1–195:14 (2018). https://doi.org/10.1145/3272127.3275069
8. Jang, C., Bang, K., Moon, S., Kim, J., Lee, S., Lee, B.: Retinal 3D: augmented reality near-eye display via pupil-tracked light field projection on retina. ACM Trans. Graph. **36**(6) (2017). https://doi.org/10.1145/3130800.3130889
9. Kamiya, M.: Digital camera diopter adjustment loupe hooded (2010). jP3159548U
10. Kato, S.: Real image mode variable magnification finder optical system. US Patent 5,323,264, 21 June 1994
11. Kim, H., et al.: MARIO: mid-air augmented RealityInteraction with objects. In: Reidsma, D., Katayose, H., Nijholt, A. (eds.) ACE 2013. LNCS, vol. 8253, pp. 560–563. Springer, Cham (2013). https://doi.org/10.1007/978-3-319-03161-3_53
12. Kollin, J.S.: A retinal display for virtual-environment applications (1993)
13. Koyama, T., Yamazaki, S.: Viewfinder device. US Patent 5,640,632, 17 June 1997
14. Liao, C.D., Tsai, J.C.: The evolution of mems displays. IEEE Trans. Industr. Electron. **56**(4), 1057–1065 (2009). https://doi.org/10.1109/TIE.2008.2005684
15. Makino, Y., Furuyama, Y., Inoue, S., Shinoda, H.: Haptoclone (haptic-optical clone) for mutual tele-environment by real-time 3D image transfer with midair force feedback. In: Proceedings of the 2016 CHI Conference on Human Factors in Computing Systems. CHI 2016, pp. 1980–1990. ACM, New York (2016). https://doi.org/10.1145/2858036.2858481
16. Mott, M.E., Jane, E., Bennett, C.L., Cutrell, E., Morris, M.R.: Understanding the accessibility of smartphone photography for people with motor impairments. In: Proceedings of the 2018 CHI Conference on Human Factors in Computing Systems. CHI 2018, pp. 520:1–520:12. ACM, New York (2018). https://doi.org/10.1145/3173574.3174094
17. Nakao, S.: Hybrid finder (1990). jP2691050B2
18. Ochiai, Y., et al.: Make your own retinal projector: retinal near-eye displays via metamaterials. In: ACM SIGGRAPH 2018 Emerging Technologies. SIGGRAPH 2018, pp. 13:1–13:2. ACM, New York (2018). https://doi.org/10.1145/3214907.3214910

19. Ohmura, H., Ushiro, S., Hara, H., Asano, S., Yoshida, T.: Lens-fitted photographic film package. US Patent 4,855,774, 8 August 1989

20. Onoyama, Y., et al.: 70.4l: late-news paper: 0.5-inch XGA micro-oled display on a silicon backplane with high-definition technologies. In: SID Symposium Digest of Technical Papers, vol. 43, no. 1, pp. 950–953 (2012). https://doi.org/10.1002/j.2168-0159.2012.tb05947.x

21. Otao, K., Itoh, Y., Osone, H., Takazawa, K., Kataoka, S., Ochiai, Y.: Light field blender: designing optics and rendering methods for see-through and aerial near-eye display. In: SIGGRAPH Asia 2017 Technical Briefs. SA 2017, pp. 9:1–9:4. ACM, New York (2017). https://doi.org/10.1145/3145749.3149425

22. Otao, K., Itoh, Y., Takazawa, K., Osone, H., Ochiai, Y.: Air mounted eyepiece: optical see-through HMD design with aerial optical functions. In: Proceedings of the 9th Augmented Human International Conference. AH 2018, pp. 1:1–1:7. ACM, New York (2018). https://doi.org/10.1145/3174910.3174911

23. Pech-Pacheco, J.L., Cristobal, G., Chamorro-Martinez, J., Fernandez-Valdivia, J.: Diatom autofocusing in brightfield microscopy: a comparative study. In: Proceedings 15th International Conference on Pattern Recognition. ICPR-2000, vol. 3, pp. 314–317 (2000). https://doi.org/10.1109/ICPR.2000.903548

24. Roth, H.L., Lora, A.N., Heilman, K.M.: Effects of monocular viewing and eye dominance on spatial attention. Brain 125(9), 2023–2035 (2002). https://doi.org/10.1093/brain/awf210

25. Sistrom, C., Gay, S.: Digital cameras for reproducing radiologic images: evaluation of three cameras. AJR Am. J. Roentgenol. 170(2), 279–284 (1998)

26. Stempeck, J.W.: Electronic viewfinder. US Patent 4,571,627, 18 February 1986

27. Ueda, H., Hisamitsu, A., Kitahora, T., Terasaka, Y., Furukawa, K.: Organic electroluminescent display element, finder screen display device, finder and optical device. US Patent 6,468,676, 22 October 2002

28. Weissman, P., Handschy, M.A.: Compact electronic viewfinder. US Patent 7,206,134, 17 April 2007

29. Yahagi, Y., Fukushima, S., Sakaguchi, S., Naemura, T.: Suppression of floating image degradation using a mechanical vibration of a dihedral corner reflector array. Opt. Express 28(22), 33145–33156 (2020). https://doi.org/10.1364/OE.406005

One-Handed Character Input Method for Smart Glasses that Does Not Require Visual Confirmation of Fingertip Position

Toshimitsu Tanaka^(✉), Natsumi Ogawa, Ryota Tsuboi, and Yuji Sagawa

Faculty of Information Engineering, Meijo University, Shiogamaguchi 1-501, Tenpaku-ku, Nagoya 468-8502, Japan
toshitnk@meijo-u.ac.jp

Abstract. We have developed a way for users to enter characters with one hand without looking at their fingers. The user grabs the input device with one hand and taps or strokes with the thumb. The device is covered with a thin plate with holes. The plate limits the area that can be touched, and the boundaries of the holes allow the user to recognize the position of the finger by the tactile sensation of the finger. The text entered by the user is displayed on the smart glasses. Guide images that assist the user's input are also displayed here. This guide shows the status of the input operation and what the user can do next.

Enter one character in two steps. First, the stroke selects a group of characters. Then flick or tap to select one letter from the group. Ten groups are defined that can contain up to 5 characters. Therefore, up 50 characters can be assigned. This number is sufficient to allocate Japanese unvoiced hiragana. However, voiced, semi-voiced, and lowercase hiragana cannot be covered. These characters can be entered after tapping the button to change the selected group to that group.

In the beginners experiment, the average input speed after inputting 50 words was 22.9 [CPM], and the error rate was 8%. In an experiment in which 10 words were entered daily for 30 days, the input speed of two participants was 35 [CPM] and the other participant was 25 [CPM].

Keywords: Character input · One-hand operation · Touch typing · Smart glasses · Mobile

1 Introduction

Recently, smart glasses, which are optical see-through type head mounted displays, are on the market. Smart glasses provide a large virtual screen in a mobile environment. Because the screen size is much larger than a smartphone, users can see more information at once. However, in order to enter text in the posture shown in Fig. 1 (natural posture when walking on a street or riding urban traffic), a method that can be operated without looking at the finger is required. In addition, one-handed operation is required in order to carry luggage or to grab the train strap with the other hand. Two years ago, we developed a character input method that meets this requirement [1]. However, the rate of erroneous

© The Author(s), under exclusive license to Springer Nature Switzerland AG 2022
M. Kurosu (Ed.): HCII 2022, LNCS 13303, pp. 165–179, 2022.
https://doi.org/10.1007/978-3-031-05409-9_13

operation was high. Many of the errors were caused by selecting the wrong character group. The reason for the error was expected to be that each edge of the square input area was divided into two segments, each assigned to a different group. Therefore, we redesigned the input operation to reduce erroneous operation.

Fig. 1. An example of posture when using the proposed method.

2   Related Researches

To date, many techniques have been developed for entering text outdoors or on the move.

Speech recognition technology [2–4], which is widely used in smartphones and PCs, is a common way to enter text without using a keyboard. It is used as the standard input method for car navigation systems. The recognition rate is sufficiently high in private rooms and private cars with little background noise. However, speaking in the crowd increases the number of incorrect inputs. Also, the privacy of the speaker is not protected because the speaker's voice is heard around. It takes a lot of time and effort to correct typos with only voice commands. Silence is required in some places and situations.

Input methods by gestures are available also on mobile environment. However, in the method of drawing characters in the space by moving the arm [5], there is a risk that the arm will hit a nearby person or object. Some methods require devices such as glove type [6] or ring type [5, 7] to detect motion. A camera is required for methods based on image processing. Users need to carry these devices.

Several methods have been developed that allow users to select characters on the on-screen keyboard that appear on a head-mounted display with finger, hand, or arm gestures [8–10]. These methods use a game controller, motion sensor, depth camera, etc. to measure your posture, so you'll need to carry these devices with you when using them outdoors. When using a camera, it is also necessary to take measures against the background and lighting. Another problem is that the on-screen keyboard takes up a lot of screen space. A virtual keyboard is essential to visually confirm the touch position. Touch typing in the air is very difficult.

There have been proposed methods of projecting a keyboard pattern to the back of the user's hand [11] or projecting it on the arm [12]. However, it is necessary to use both hands to enter characters in these ways. Devices to measure the position of fingers are also needed. Touch typing is also difficult.

The methods of detecting the position of the thumb by attaching touch sensors to other fingers [13, 14] can be operated with one hand. The method of attaching the micro touch panel to the fingertip [15] is the same. However, when the user tries to grab something, the touch sensor gets in the way, comes off, or breaks. However, it is not practical to attach the sensor or wear sensor gloves every time you enter text. For this reason, these are difficult techniques to use in a mobile environment.

Tap Strap 2 [16] is a device with five rings connected by a string, and each finger is inserted into the ring for use. Select a character with the combination of tapped fingers. Therefore, it takes a long time to learn the combination. It can be operated with one hand, but since the tapped finger is detected by its vibration, a flat plate for tapping is required.

Some methods have been proposed to specify the character from the orientation and rotation of the wrist [17–19]. These are also one-handed operations, but as the number of input characters increases, the wrist gets tired considerably. It also takes a long time to learn because it is necessary to remember the wrist movements assigned to each letter.

The following conditions are required for the character input system used for smart glasses outdoors. The input device should be small enough to be portable. It must be able to operate with one hand, because the other hand is used to hold a bag, hold a strap, hold an umbrella, open a door, and so on. It also requires that there is no need to visually check the finger position during operation. This is to eliminate the frequent movement of the line of sight between what is displayed on the smart glasses and the input device. Users can focus on what they see on their smart glasses, so eye strain is reduced. We developed such a system two years ago. An overview of the system is given in the next section.

3 Previous Method

A small smartphone that you can grasp in one hand is used as an input device. As shown in Fig. 2, its touch screen is covered with a partially cut plastic sheet, so you can know the position of your finger by tactile perception of fingertips. Touch operation is performed with the thumb. Stroke gestures are performed within the large square opening. The functions assigned to the three small openings are selected with a tap. An input guide showing the functions or character groups assigned to each area is displayed on the smart glasses to assist the user. Figure 3 is a simulation image of the input guide. The guide image changes according to the input state.

Fig. 2. Cover design of the previous method.

Fig. 3. A simulation image that displays an input guide on a smart glasses.

Table 1. Grouping of hiragana and alphanumeric characters. 5 characters are grouped together. First the group is selected, then the members of the group. **CL** in this table means *Caps Lock*.

		Group (selected in the 1st step)																	
		Hiragana mode										*Alphanumeric mode*							
Member (2nd)	あ	か	さ	た	な	は	ま	や	ら	わ	a	f	k	p	u	z	0	5
	い	き	し	ち	に	ひ	み	—	り	。	b	g	l	q	v	CL	1	6
	う	く	す	つ	ぬ	ふ	む	ゆ	る	を	c	h	m	r	w	.	2	7
	え	け	せ	て	ね	へ	め		れ	、	d	i	n	s	x	,	3	8
	お	こ	そ	と	の	ほ	も	よ	ろ	ん	e	j	o	t	y	-	4	9

One character is entered in two steps. First select a group of characters, then select one character in the group. For Japanese hiragana input, first select one Gyou (row of the Japanese syllabary table shown in Table 1) and then one Dan (column of the table). In alphanumeric mode, five characters are stored in one group in alphabetical order. The numbers are divided into 0–4 and 5–9 and stored in each group.

In the group selection, the left, top, and right edges of the large square are each split into two segments, and two character-groups are assigned to each. Figure 4 shows the motion of the finger to input the Japanese "さ" and the accompanying change of the input guide. Slide-in is the action of sliding your finger from the outside to the inside of the opening. As the slide-in passes through one segment, the square is split into two regions, each of which displays one of the two groups assigned to the segment as shown in Fig. 4 (b). In hiragana mode, the name of the group is written here. When the finger moves into one region, its background turns green. By leaving the finger from the screen, the group written in the region is selected.

Then select one character from the group. As shown in Fig. 4 (c), the first character of the selected group is centered and the other characters are assigned in the order left, top, right, bottom. Tap the character in the center to select it. Surrounding characters are selected by flicking in each direction. If you notice that the wrong group is selected before selecting character you can cancel the group selection by tapping the left button.

Up to 50 characters (10 groups × 5 characters) can be assigned by this two-step operation. However, it cannot cover voiced, semi-voiced, or lowercase hiragana shown in Table 2. Each of these characters is converted from the original characters shown in Table 1. After selecting a group, tap the right button to add a voiced or semi-voiced sound mark to the displayed characters, or change the text to lowercase. In Fig. 4(d), "さ" group is converted to the associated "ざ" group by adding the Japanese voiced sound mark. On the standby screen, Backspace, Space, and Enter are assigned to each of the three buttons. However, they are not used in member selection (column selection), so the button functionality is replaced.

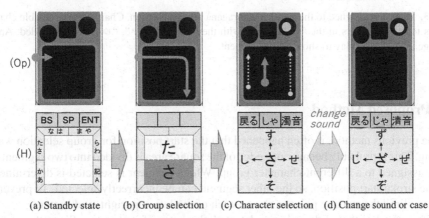

(a) Standby state (b) Group selection (c) Character selection (d) Change sound or case

Fig. 4. A series of operations to select one character of the previous method. The upper row shows the operations, and the lower row shows the guide images in hiragana mode. First select one group of characters, then select one character in the selected group.

Table 2. Voiced, semi-voiced, and lowercase characters in hiragana. These selections are available after tapping the bottom right cell of the member selection to change the display.

			Group					
type	L	V	V	V	L	V	SV	L
Member	あ	が	ざ	だ		ば	ぱ	や
	い	ぎ	じ	ぢ		び	ぴ	
	う	ぐ	ず	づ	っ	ぶ	ぷ	ゆ
	え	げ	ぜ	で		べ	ぺ	
	お	ご	ぞ	ど		ぼ	ぽ	よ

type	meaning
V	Voiced sound
SV	Semi-voiced sound
L	Lowercase

By tapping the middle button, as shown in Fig. 5, the combinations of two characters are displayed on the guide. Each is the "い" column character of the selected group followed by a lowercase "ゃ", "ゅ", or "ょ". Each combination is selected by tapping or flicking like a single letter. This option was installed to enter these character pairs in a single operation. You can enter them separately, but more steps are required. The middle button and left button can be used in combination.

All operations of the proposed method do not need to visually identify the fingertip. Therefore, characters can be entered without visual confirmation.

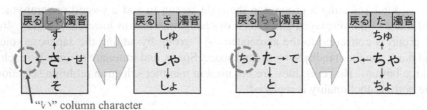

"い" column character

Fig. 5. Function assigned to the buttons in hiragana group selection. Change the selectable characters to the characters in the "い" column with the lowercase "ゃ", "ゅ", or "ょ" added. And change the guide display to show the assignment.

4 Proposed Method

In the previous method, it often happened that the start position for group selection was wrong. This is probably because one edge of the square area is divided into two segments, each assigned to a different character group. Which segment is selected is determined by the stroke start position, so the other segment can be incorrectly selected. To prevent this, we limit the starting point to one on each of the left, top, right, and bottom.

The mistakes that slide-in is not detected also were often happen. Since the touch panel is covered with a plastic sheet, there is a step at the boundary of the input area. The step is small but the first touch position shifts inward when the thumb moves faster. As a result, the slide-in is not detected because the touch position goes inside beyond the slide-in detection area assigned to the boundary. It is possible to increase the detection range, but doing so will increase the number of false positives for slide-in edges.

We solved these problems by changing the stroke gesture and cover design. Figure 6 shows our cover design. The black parts are where the cover is cut out. Strokes are made in the cross-shaped area. The circles arranged in the four corners are function buttons. The size of the operation area is 28 mm × 28 mm, so it fits within the reach of the user's thumb while holding the smartphone.

As shown in Fig. 7 (a), each of the four ends of the cross-shaped area is the stroke start position. And the stroke ends at one of the other three ends. Therefore, the same as the previous method, a total of 12 strokes can be defined. To enter a stroke, touch the start position with your thumb, move your thumb to the end position while still in contact with the screen, and then move it away from the screen.

Since the start position is given by touching instead of sliding in, the deviation of the initial position is considered to be small. Therefore, it is thought that the detection omission of the start position can be reduced. The start positions of our strokes in Fig. 7 (a) are sufficiently separated, although that of the previous method in (b) are close to each other. This reduces the mistake of accidentally tapping another start position.

The curved edges of the cross-shaped opening are designed to assist the finger reach the end position. Moving a finger along the edge reaches to the adjacent end point. Even if the direction of movement is off the opposite end point, you can reach there by moving your finger until it stops.

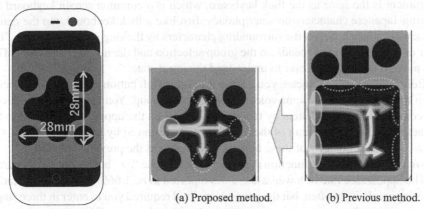

Fig. 6. Cover design of the proposed method.

Fig. 7. Improved stroke. The number of starting positions is reduced to 4, which is half of the previous method, to separate them. Instead, the end position of the stroke is increased to 3 per start position.

(a) Proposed method. (b) Previous method.

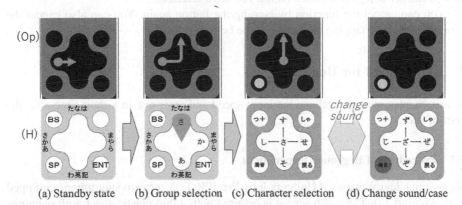

(a) Standby state   (b) Group selection   (c) Character selection   (d) Change sound/case

Fig. 8. A series of operations to select one character by the proposed method. First, select a character group by a stroke from one end of the cross-shaped area to another end. The selected group can be changed to a related voiced, semi-voiced, or lowercase group by tapping the button. The color changes to red while the button is active. Then tap or flick to select a character. (Color figure online)

Figure 8 shows the movement of the finger to input the Japanese "さ" and the accompanying change of the input guide. First, tap the left end where "さ" is written. At this time, the guide display changes to Fig. 8 (b). The group names written on the left end are displayed one by one at the other three end points. Move your fingertip up along the edge of the cover and the area will turn green. If you take your finger off the touch device at this time, the Japanese "さ" group will be selected.

Next, the characters contained in the selected group are displayed in the cross-shaped area. As shown in Fig. 8(c), the first character " さ " of the " さ " group is displayed in the center, and the other characters are displayed in the order of left, top, right, bottom. This assignment is the same as the flick keyboard, which is a common screen keyboard for entering Japanese characters on smartphones. Just like a flick keyboard, tap the center character to select it. Select the surrounding characters by flicking in each direction. The color of the input guide depends on the group selection and the member selection. This is to make it easier for the user to understand the input state.

Before selecting a character, you can tap the bottom left button to change the selected group to a related voiced, semi-voiced, or lowercase group. You can change the group to a combination of two letters by tapping the button on the upper right. These are the characters in the " い " column of the selected group followed by lowercase " や ", " ゆ ", or " よ ". The functionality of these buttons is the same as the previous method.

We also provide a new function that inserts a lowercase " つ " before the input character. The appearance rate of lowercase " つ " is reported to be 1.66% [21]. It's a character that is input relatively often, but the previous method required you to enter in three steps: select a group, change it to lowercase, and select the character. With our system, you can enter it by simply tapping the button on the upper left.

These three buttons can be used in combination. The combination is a bit complicated, but the button color changes to red while the function assigned to the button is active, so you can see at a glance which button you have selected.

You can cancel the function by tapping the button again. You can also cancel the group selection by tapping the button at the bottom right.

5   Experiment for Beginners

In this chapter, we will evaluate the input speed and error rate in a short time after the start of use.

5.1   Procedure of Beginner Experiment

As an input device, we used Unihertz Jelly Pro JPRO-03, a micro smartphone equipped with Android 7.0. The touch screen is covered with a thin plastic sheet with openings shown in Fig. 6. In the experiment, Jelly Pro detects touch gestures, updates input guides, displays task words, and records their time.

Images from Jelly Pro are displayed on the Sony HMZ-T2 via the USB-HDMI adapter 500-KC024HD. Sony HMZ-T2 is a sea-closed type head-mounted display (HMD). It completely covers the user's eyes, obscuring the surroundings. The reason for not using a see-through type HMD is to eliminate the possibility of the subject seeing the finger. The reason for connecting the smartphone and the HMD with a cable is to reduce the display delay. I've tested wireless connections on both Miracast and Chromecast, but the delay was too long for interactive operation.

We evaluated the input speed of 10 beginners. They never used our system and the previous system before this experiment. At the beginning of the experiment, we gave a 10-min presentation on the operation procedure for inputting characters, the meaning of the display of the input guide, the experiment procedure, and precautions. And we asked subjects enter characters as accurately as possible. Each subject sat in a chair in a normal posture and wore an HMD. After confirming that the subject was unable to see the surroundings, the input device was handed over to the dominant hand. The subject checked the locations of the openings with the touch of his/her thumb. Then the experiment was started.

Subjects enter 5 hiragana words in one task. In the experiment, this task is repeated 10 times every between with a 3-min break. Each task starts when a subject touches the cross-shaped opening on the input device. One of the task words written in hiragana is displayed on the HMD screen. The characters entered by the test subject appear immediately below the task word. After entering all the characters of the task word, tap the Enter button located at the bottom right. The Enter button is accepted even if some of the input characters do not match the task word. Then the next word will be displayed. Enter 5 words to complete one task.

The task words were selected from the word list of the Balanced Corpus of Contemporary Written Japanese (BCCWJ) [20] of the National Institute for Japanese Language and Linguistics. From each of the 4, 5, and 6-letter nouns in hiragana notation, 100 words were extracted in order of frequency, excluding numbers and quantifiers. Then words which are same in hiragana notation but different in Kanji notation were merged. Frequency of the merged word is sum of frequency of the original words. Finally, the top 50 words in frequency from each of 4, 5, and 6-letter words were selected.

In the experiment, those 150 words are gathered in one list and randomly sorted for each test subject. The word list is then split every 5 words from the beginning of the list. The different set of the 5 words is used in each task. Therefore, one test subject does not enter the same word twice.

5.2 Results of Beginner Experiment

The thin lines in Fig. 9 are the input speed of each test subject. The thick line is the average input speed of 10 subjects. The input speed of each test subject varies greatly from task to task. The average input speed also fluctuates, but basically increases with the number of tasks. The average input speed of the first task is about 11 [CPM: characters per minute]. In the tenth task, it reached 22.9 [CPM]. The total usage time averaged 15.5 min.

In one task, each subject only enters about 25 characters. This means that entering one wrong character will increase the total error rate (TER) [22] by about 4%. Since the TER of each subject is too volatile to read the trend, Fig. 10 shows only the average TER. The graph fluctuates greatly with the average value of 10 subjects. TER tends to decrease, but it is very slow.

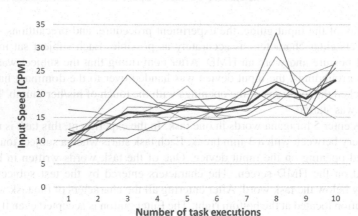

Fig. 9. Input speed for beginners. The thin line is the speed of each subject. The thick line is the average input speed of 10 subjects. The average speed basically increases with the number of tasks.

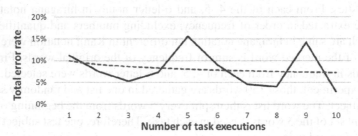

Fig. 10. Average total error rate for 10 subjects. The dotted line is an approximate curve.

6   30-Day Experiment

When this system becomes practical, it is expected to be used every day to answer SMS or e-mail etc. in outdoor, but the number of input characters per day will not be large. Therefore, we investigated how the input speed and error rate change by entering 10 words every day for 30 days.

6.1   Procedure of the 30-Day Experiment

The experimental participants were three university students, who used the system for the first time in this experiment. The tasks in this experiment are the same as the beginner's tasks in Sect. 5. It is the same for a 3-min break between tasks. However, it is repeated only twice.

The task words are also the same as those used in the experiments in Sect. 5. They are randomly sorted by subject on the first day of the experiment. Next, cut out 10 words from the top of the word list every day and use them as task words for the experiment. The number of task words is 150, so the list will be empty in 15 days. When the list is empty or the participant restarts the input system, the task words are randomly re-sorted and reused.

6.2 Result of the 30-Day Experiment

Figure 11 is a graph of input speed smoothed by a simple moving average (SMA). The averaging period is 5 days, that is, from 2 days before to 2 days after. Since the number of characters that can be input per day is only 50, if the subject makes a mistake in one character, the input speed and error rate will fluctuate greatly. Therefore, this section shows the experimental results after 5-day SMA.

The logarithmic approximation curves of the input speeds of subjects T2 and T3 are almost the same. The input speed on the 5th day is almost the same as the speed on the 10th task of the beginner experiment. In both experiments, a total of 50 words were entered at that time, so it can be said that the speed change is the same. The input speed reached 35 [CPM] in 30 days. The total usage time for subjects T2 and T3 is 59 min and 57 min, respectively. Users who can easily learn how to use it are expected to be able to enter 35 characters per minute after using it for an hour. The increase in input speed of subject T1 was slower than that of the other two subjects, but the speed reached 25 [CPM] on day 30.

Even on the 30th day, the input speed of all subjects is still increasing. Experts in this system have recorded 46.8 [CPM], so continued use may increase the speed even further.

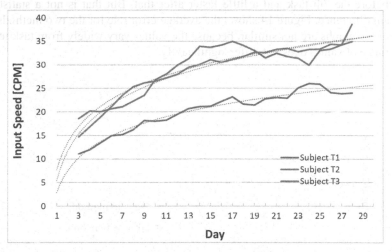

Fig. 11. Input speed of 3 subjects in a 30-day experiment. Each is smoothed by a 5-day simple moving average.

Figure 12 shows the error rates for the three test subjects. This graph is after processing with 5-day simple moving average, but the fluctuation is still large. Subject T2 has a low error rate, almost less than 4%. The error rates for subjects T1 and T3 are high, ranging from approximately 8–10% over the last 10 days of the experiment. The cause of the difference in input speed between T1 and T2 is considered to be the difference in error rate. The error rate of subject T3 is higher than that of T2, but the input speed is the same as T2. This is probably because subject T3 moved his finger faster at the expense of accuracy.

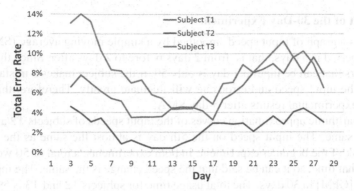

Fig. 12. Total error rate of 3 subjects in a 30-day experiment. These graphs are also smoothed with a 5-day simple moving average, but the variability is still large.

7 Comparison with the Previous Method

Figure 13 shows the average input speed for beginners in our method and the previous method. The shapes of both graphs are very similar. The speed of our method is a little slower before the 7th task and a little faster after that. But that is not a statistically significant difference. Figure 14 shows the average error rate for the two methods. The shapes of the graphs are not similar, because the values vary widely from task to task, but the range of values does not differ significantly.

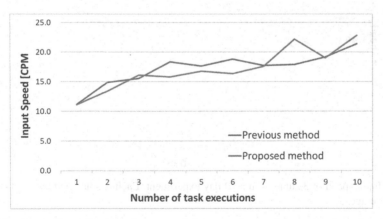

Fig. 13. Comparison of average input speeds between the previous and proposed methods.

Unwanted group selections are group selections that have been canceled by the user. If the user notices that they have selected the wrong group and cancels it, the error rate does not increase because the wrong characters have not been entered. However, the input speed will be slower because the work time will be longer by the unnecessary stroke and tap. Therefore, we investigated the number of times unwanted groups were selected.

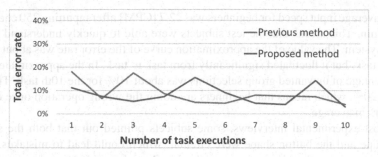

Fig. 14. Comparison of average total error rate between the previous and proposed methods.

Figure 15 shows the ratio of unwanted group selections to the number of task characters. The percentage of unwanted group selections in the previous method is about twice that of our method. This difference is due to the effect of limiting the starting position to one in each of the four directions. The start position ambiguity caused by two keys sharing one edge has been resolved.

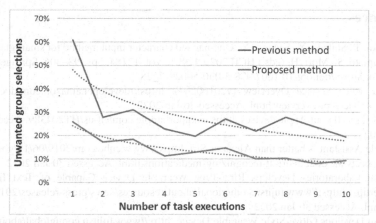

Fig. 15. Comparison of the percentage of unwanted group selection between the previous and proposed methods.

8 Conclusion

We have developed a one-hand character input method that can be operated without looking at the finger. In this method the shape of screen cover and the definition of strokes for selecting character group were renewed from the previous method. This change eliminated the position ambiguity caused by having to select the top or bottom of the edge, or the right or left side of the edge in the previous way. As a result, the selection of unwanted groups has been cut in half. Unfortunately, there were no statistically significant changes in input speed or error rate.

The average input speed for beginners was 22.7 [CPM] after inputting 250 characters in 15.5 min. This means that the test subjects were able to quickly understand how to use our system. The value of the approximation curve of the error rate was about 8% for the 10th task, but it fluctuated significantly from task to task. In the approximate curve, the percentage of unwanted group selections was about 10% for the 10th task. The total is about 20%, which means that beginners are doing the wrong operation once every 5 characters in average.

In post-experimental interviews, some subjects pointed out that both the starting point shape and the button shape were circular, which could lead to mistakes. There was also an opinion that the group name displayed on the guide screen was small and the location was difficult to understand. Therefore, we plan to change the shape of the starting point to a square. Also, the placement of character groups will change. These names will be larger in the input guide. We believe that these improvements can reduce the incidence of erroneous operations.

In a 30-day experiment, the input speed of the two subjects reached 35 [CPM]. It was achieved after 1 h of use. The expert's speed record is 46.8 [CPM], so practice may increase the speed.

References

1. Tanaka, T., Shibata, Y., Sagawa, Y.: One-handed character input method for smart glasses. In: Yamamoto, S., Mori, H. (eds.) HCII 2020. LNCS, vol. 12184, pp. 393–406. Springer, Cham (2020). https://doi.org/10.1007/978-3-030-50020-7_28
2. Alexa Voice Service Overview (v20160207). https://developer.amazon.com/docs/alexa-voice-service/api-overview.html. Accessed 30 Jan 2022
3. Use Siri on all your Apple devices. https://support.apple.com/en-us/HT204389. Accessed 30 Jan 2022
4. Google Assistant is better than Alexa or Siri. https://www.cnbc.com/2019/06/19/google-assistant-beats-alexa-and-siri-at-recognizing-medications.html. Accessed 30 Jan 2022
5. Fujitsu Laboratories Develops Ring-Type Wearable Device Capable of Text Input by Fingertip. https://www.fujitsu.com/global/about/resources/news/press-releases/2015/0113-01.html. Accessed 30 Jan 2022
6. Fujitsu Develops Glove-Style Wearable Device. http://www.fujitsu.com/global/about/resources/news/press-releases/2014/0218-01.html. Accessed 30 Jan 2022
7. Ring Zero. https://logbar.jp/ja/index.html, https://www.techinasia.com/ring-zero-new-start-japanese-wearable, https://www.g-mark.org/award/describe/42290?locale=en. Accessed 30 Jan 2022
8. Grubert, J., Witzani, L., Ofek, E., Pahud, M., Kranz, M., Kristensson, P.O.: Text entry in immersive head-mounted display-based virtual reality using standard keyboards. In: 25th IEEE Conference on Virtual Reality and 3D User Interfaces, VR 2018 - Proceedings, pp. 159–166 (2018)
9. Boletsis, C., Kongsvik, S.: Text input in virtual reality: a preliminary evaluation of the drum-like VR keyboard. Technologies 7(2), 31:1–31:10 (2019)
10. Yu, C., Gu, Y., Yang, Z., Yi, X., Luo, H., Shi, Y.: Tap, dwell or gesture?: Exploring head-based text entry techniques for HMDS. In: Proceedings of the 2017 CHI Conference on Human Factors in Computing Systems, pp. 4479–4488 (2017)
11. Haier Asu Smartwatch. https://www.digitaltrends.com/smartwatch-reviews/haier-asu-review/. Accessed 30 Jan 2022

12. NEC develops ARmKeypad Air, a contact-free virtual keyboard for a user's arm. https://www.nec.com/en/press/201607/global_20160713_01.html. Accessed 30 Jan 2022

13. Wong, P., Zhu, K., Fu, H.: FingerT9: leveraging thumb-to-finger interaction for same-side-hand text entry on smartwatches. In: Proceedings of CHI 2018, Paper No. 178 (2017)

14. Whitmier, E., et al.: DigiTouch: reconfigurable thumb-to-finger input and text entry on head-mounted displays. In: Proceedings of ACM IMWUT 2017, vol. 1, no. 3, Article 133 (2017)

15. Xu, Z., et al.: TipText: eyes-free text entry on a fingertip keyboard. In: Proceedings of the 32nd ACM Symposium on User Interface Software and Technology, pp. 883–899 (2019)

16. TAP STRAP 2.http://www.tapwithus.com. Accessed 30 Jan 2022

17. Sun, K., Wang, Y., Yu, C., Yan, Y., Wen, H., Shi, Y.: Float: one-handed and touch-free target selection on smartwatches. In: Proceedings of CHI 2017, pp. 692–704 (2017)

18. Gong, J., Yang, X., Irani, P.: WristWhirl: one-handed continuous smartwatch input using wrist gesture. In: Proceedings of UIST 2016, pp. 861–872 (2016)

19. Gong, J., et al.: WrisText: one-handed text entry on smartwatch using wrist gestures. In: Proceedings of CHI 2018, Paper No. 181 (2018)

20. The word list of the Balanced Corpus of Contemporary Written Japanese of the National Institute for Japanese Language and Linguistics. https://ccd.ninjal.ac.jp/bccwj/en/freq-list.html. Accessed 30 Jan 2022

21. Let's check the "frequency of hiragana appearance" on your blog using your computer!(in Japanese). https://ena.hatenablog.jp/entry/20070604/1180930739. Accessed 30 Jan 2022

22. Soukoreff, R.W., MacKenzie, I.S.: Metrics for text entry research: an evaluation of MSD and KSPC, and a new unified error metric. In: Proceedings of ACM CHI 2003, pp. 113–120 (2003)

Ambient Light Tolerant Laser-Pen Based Interaction with Curved Multi-projector Displays

Sarvesh Thakur(✉), Meghana Urs, Muhammad Twaha Ibrahim,
Alexander Sidenko, and Aditi Majumder

Summit Technology Laboratory, Irvine, CA, USA
marsar24@terpmail.umd.edu
{sarvesh,meghana,twaha,sasha,aditi}@summittechlab.com

Abstract. Large multi-projector displays allow users to be immersed in the data at a grand scale without wearing AR/VR headsets. There has been tremendous advancement in automated projection mapping that uses multiple feedback cameras to stitch and blend images from multiple projectors on curved surfaces of different shapes and sizes. Yet, there is still no easy way to interact with such displays. In this paper, we present a scalable technique that uses the same feedback cameras used for projection mapping to enable multi-user interaction with these displays using multi-colored laser-pens. We also devise methods to achieve the projection mapping and the laser based interaction in the presence of ambient light. This results in an interactive multi-projector system that can be set up and used in an interactive manner in regular illuminated conditions without any disruptions.

Keywords: Interaction · Laser-pen · Human-computer interaction · Multi-projector system

1 Introduction

Immersive multi-projector displays are used in many applications (e.g. training, simulation, visualization, edutainment). A large amount of work has been done on camera-based registration of multiple projectors, both for geometry and color [1–11, 20–22]. This is commonly referred to as projection mapping and has resulted in easy deployment and maintenance of such displays. However, a suitable interaction paradigm for multi-projector displays that can be scaled across multiple users, devices, and applications is still not available. Most prior works focus on single projector-camera systems [12–15] while others focus on completely centralized methods or flat displays that cannot scale easily to different shapes or displays with a large number of projectors [18, 19, 23–37]. Further, the aforementioned techniques assume no ambient light which makes the setup of these displays disruptive and further interaction with them fraught with inaccuracies. This impacts the user experience negatively thereby inhibiting the adoption of this useful technology.

© The Author(s), under exclusive license to Springer Nature Switzerland AG 2022
M. Kurosu (Ed.): HCII 2022, LNCS 13303, pp. 180–194, 2022.
https://doi.org/10.1007/978-3-031-05409-9_14

In this paper we propose a multi-projector system that uses camera based registration techniques but with an added component of using appropriate camera exposure based on the ambient lighting conditions when acquiring the data required for registration. This allows ambient light tolerant multi-projector display setup without the disruptions of darkening the environment. We also present a laser-pen based interaction paradigm which uses the same cameras used during registration to provide real time interaction with the display by multiple users. Further, the same ambient light tolerance capability allows the interaction to continue at high accuracy in presence of surround illumination. *In summary, we present the first multi-projector system on immersive non-flat shapes that is interactive and is operational at high accuracy in the presence of ambient light.*

Related Work: The use of laser-pens for interaction with projection based displays has been explored in a limited manner for a single projector-camera unit [12,13], often needing IR filters on cameras for tracking the laser spot. [14,15] extends such techniques to flat multi-projector systems. However, single camera based solutions are not scalable to large and complex shapes, especially surround displays. [16] uses a centralized algorithm that takes input from multiple cameras and processes it. Centralized methods impact the real time performance and scalability that can be offset by Kalman filter based prediction of laser location at the cost of compromised performance. [17] presents a distributed system that assumes one camera atop each projector and uses message passing across multiple projector-camera units for handing off interactions between the units or drawing out responses from units which don't see the interaction in their field-of-view (FoV). To the best of our knowledge, there is no ambient light tolerant multi-projector system designed till date.

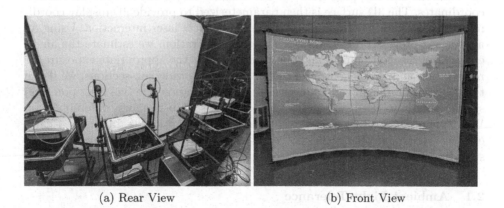

(a) Rear View   (b) Front View

Fig. 1. Our example multi-projector system is a rear projected curved display ($10'W \times 8'H$) surface illuminated by superposition of 2 sets of 2×2 array of projectors (total of 8 projectors), observed by 4 cameras in a linear array. All results in this paper are from this system. In (a), one of the projectors (blue) and all four cameras (red) are marked. (Color figure online)

Our Contributions: We present a method that is a hybrid of completely centralized [16] and completely distributed [17] methods and is therefore the most efficient not only in terms of real-time performance but also in terms of communication and memory usage. This also enables scalability to m projectors and n cameras, unlike [17] where m = n. (a) Using parallelism across devices we achieve real time performance for laser tracking that does not impact camera frame rate. (b) Using a state machine based action detector (example actions are drag; single, double or triple clicks; custom gestures/shapes) we enable lucid real-time reaction to laser based gesture. (c) We can scale to complex curved surfaces by accurate surface reconstruction during calibration and surface parametrization that maps 3D display coordinates to 2D parametrized coordinates through the cameras. (d) Using a structured light based ambient light estimation method we enable our calibration and the laser pen based interaction to work in the presence of significant ambient light. (e) Using different colored lasers we can allow multi-user interaction. Since our method is completely scalable, the number of users does not impact the latency of the laser tracking and consecutive system reaction, unlike [16,17]. (f) Finally, we provide capabilities of mirroring the content of a laptop connected to the multi-projector system on its display and allow the laser interaction on the multi-projector display to control the content mirrored from the tethered laptop.

2   System

Our multi-projector display is observed by multiple cameras and registered automatically using [1–5]. This automated registration provides the 3D location of the cameras and mapping from the 2D camera coordinates to the 3D surface coordinates. The 3D surface is then parameterized to provide 2D display coordinates and is the input to our method that conducts laser interaction. Using an automated process prior to the start of the registration, we estimate the ambient light of the environment and set the cameras at the appropriate exposure for registration and subsequent interaction. In the following sub-sections, we detail the process of achieving an ambient light tolerant interactive (via laser pointers) system. We have used projectors and cameras set up in many different ways. We explain our method with the configuration shown in Fig. 1a where 4 cameras in a horizontal array observe a curved display made of 8 projectors (two superimposing arrays of 2 × 2 projectors).

2.1   Ambient Light Tolerance

Any camera based registration technique uses some structured light patterns to estimate the shape of the display. The accuracy of detecting features in the structured patterns captured by the observing cameras is the key to an accurate registration. However, detecting features in the presence of ambient light demands acquisition at an exposure that is appropriate for the display illuminated by the ambient light. Most cameras have an auto-exposure control that measures the ambient light using some low resolution sensor (e.g. photo diode). This estimation is adequate for taking pictures of humans or objects illuminated by the ambient light. However, the situation is quite different when a digital display device is captured. The display creates its own somewhat directional lighting conditions. Therefore, as the displayed image changes (as is usual in any structured light patterns), the exposure needs to adapt even if the low resolution measurement of the ambient light from the sensor does not change.

Our approach handles all the above scenarios and has three steps. (a) First, we automatically estimate the ambient light; (b) Next, we predict the appropriate camera exposure to be used for a specific pattern using the estimated ambient light and the average brightness of the pattern. (c) Finally, using the data from the aforementioned steps, we can predict the correct exposure for any other image or pattern. This assures that the captured patterns are neither over nor under exposed and features thereof can be detected accurately to enable an accurate registration.

Estimating Ambient Light: The fundamental concept behind this step is to record the gray of the surface captured by the cameras when a black is projected from the projectors in the presence of ambient light. When black is projected by the projector and captured in the dark (with no ambient light) by a camera, it is captured as relatively black. However, in the presence of ambient light, the captured image of a projected black is a gray that increases with the increase in ambient light due to the added light on the surface itself. This captured black is subtracted from any subsequent images captured by the camera to remove the impact of ambient light.

Relating Exposure Time to Image Brightness: Exposure time required to capture an image that is not over or under saturated is not only proportional to the ambient light, but also to the average brightness of the image. Therefore, in order to estimate the dependence of the exposure to the average brightness of an image, we first find the appropriate exposure of a specific image P with a known average brightness. P is any image that has around x% black and (100-x)% any other color pixels, where x is a number between 25–75%. The pattern can be stripes, blobs, patches of different sizes or anything else as shown in Fig. 2.

Let the known average brightness of P be B_r. We then capture this image from a camera at multiple exposures and detect the appropriate exposure E_r to be the one that yields an image with minimum over or under exposed values. Also, the ambient light, A, is estimated from the black portions of P.

Predicting Exposure Time for Other Patterns: Using the above, we can now correctly predict the exposure time of any other pattern of image S. Let the average brightness of S be B_s. Then the appropriate exposure E_s should decrease with increase in B_s and A. Therefore,

$$E_s \propto E_r(A + B_r)/(A + B_s) \tag{1}$$

Every structured light pattern used for registration is captured using the predicted exposure to yield an appropriately exposed image.

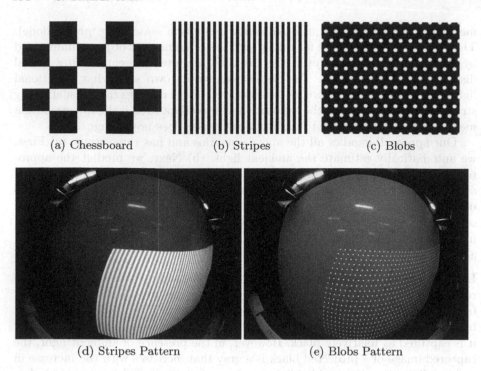

(a) Chessboard   (b) Stripes   (c) Blobs

(d) Stripes Pattern   (e) Blobs Pattern

Fig. 2. (a–c) Shows three different examples of patterns than can be used for the ambient light estimation; (d) shows stripes pattern being projected on to the display system showed in Fig. 1; (e) shows a different structured light pattern made of blobs (c) whose appropriate exposure can be predicted using our method.

2.2   Laser-Pen Interaction

Our laser-pen based interaction on the multi-projector display is enabled by tracking of the laser-pen as it travels across the display. Multiple cameras work together and share the responsibility of tracking using a 2-step method: (a) a one-time partitioning of the display where only one camera is responsible for tracking the laser-pen in each partition; (b) a real-time camera hand off as the laser-pen moves from one partition to another. We also detect camera failures so that an active camera takes over the regions covered by the failed cameras in a seamless manner. Therefore, the interaction continues uninterrupted, even if some cameras fail.

Display Partitioning: The data generated during registration provides us with the camera extrinsic parameters, and a mapping between the 3D surface points and the 2D display coordinates. Using these, we compute the distance of every camera from each 2D display coordinate. The camera which is closest to the 2D display coordinate is assigned the responsibility of tracking the display at that coordinate. Therefore, each camera is now responsible for tracking the laser-pen at the surface points that are closer to it than any other camera. Figure 3 shows

the partitions generated by the four cameras in the 2D display coordinate system
(bottom left in Fig. 3), where each partition is shown in a different color.

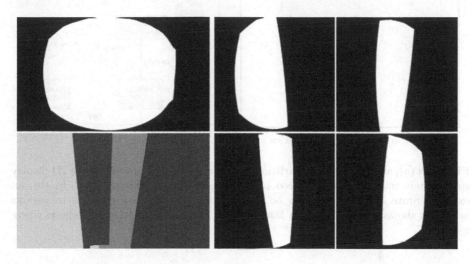

Fig. 3. (Top left) Entire display region marked in white as seen by one of the cameras;
(Bottom left) Partitions of the 4 observing cameras in the 2D display space where the
ROI of each camera is shown with a different color; (Right) The different partitions
from (Bottom left) shown in each camera's 2D space. If every camera was responsible
for the entire display, these images would look like (Top left). (Color figure online)

Laser-Pen Detection: Once the display is registered and being used, users
can point to any region of the display using the laser-pen – just like a mouse
– to drag, click, double click and so on. We use a threshold based technique to
detect the bright laser spot from the background content on the display. Other
methods based on shape of the laser (e.g. Hough circle) can also be used. To
account for ambient light, the black image taken during ambient light estimation
is subtracted from each frame.

Real-Time Camera Hand-Off: As the laser moves around the 3D surface,
different cameras need to be polled to get the detected 2D laser coordinates
using the mapping from 2D camera coordinates to the 2D display coordinates
generated during the registration process. We identify a small boundary region
for each partition where it is adjacent to another partition (Fig. 4a). When the
laser moves in the interior of the partition, only the camera assigned to the
partition is polled. However, in the boundary region, the adjacent camera is also
polled. As the laser moves to the partition of the adjacent camera, the former
camera is no longer polled. This way, a smooth and efficient hand-off occurs from
one camera to another as the laser moves from one camera's region to another's.

Understanding User's Intended Action: The interaction capabilities are
estimated from the user action based on a state machine that monitors the pause
between clicks or lack thereof to assign different meaning to the user actions.

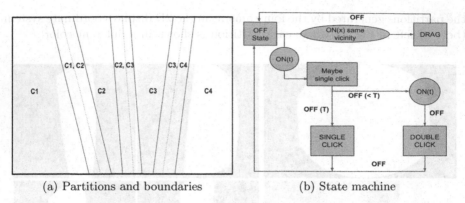

(a) Partitions and boundaries   (b) State machine

Fig. 4. In (a), an illustration of partitions and the boundaries thereof in the 2D display space where multiple cameras need to be polled for a smooth hand-off. In (b), an example State Machine that can be implemented to map user gestures to various actions is shown. Here, the time a laser is ON is denoted inside the parenthesis where $t < x < T$.

Figure 4b shows an example of such a state machine. It has three major states: (a) OFF state, (b) Drag state and (c) Click state. Off state is simply when the laser pen is not used. Click state is entered when the pen is turned on/off just like regular mouse clicks. In this state, Single click is encountered when the laser has been ON for some time ($<t$ seconds), then turned off for a longer time ($\geq T$ seconds). Double click is encountered when second instance of single click pattern starts before the action trigger time ($<T$ seconds). Holding the laser pen around a same location for a slightly longer time ($<x$ seconds, $x > t$) locks the system in Drag mode. While in Click state, the state machine determines the number of clicks the user intends to make based on the previous recorded pattern. This interaction modality can be mapped to any event in the application. For example, a regular laser-pen can be imparted a scrolling ability, which it usually doesn't have, by mapping a triple click to a scroll wheel down modality offered in a mouse with a scroll wheel.

3   Implementation

Our hardware setup consists of a desktop workstation with an Intel Core i7-11700K CPU @ 3.6 GHz with 32 GB of RAM and two NVIDIA Quadro RTX A4000 graphics cards. We experimented with a variety of cameras and projectors. For cameras, we tested with ELPs, Logitech C920, Logitech Brio and FLIR blackfly cameras. For projectors, we experimented with ultra short throw projectors such as Optoma GT5600 DLP and Optoma ZH500. Our laser interaction module is scalable and can be used with any camera (C) and projector (P) configuration and following configurations were successfully tested: 4P-1C, 4P-2C, 4P-3C, 4P-4C and 8P-4C.

In our implementation, we used FLIR Black-Fly Cameras because of their robustness and high FPS (45–55). The cameras could be arranged in any configuration across the display as long as each display surface point is seen by at least 2 cameras. We tested them in two configurations: horizontal arrangement (Fig. 1) and vertical arrangement (Fig. 5).

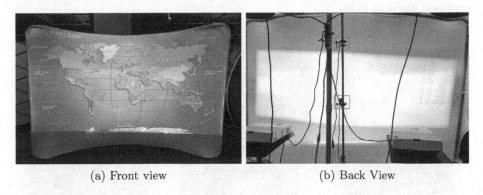

| (a) Front view | (b) Back View |

Fig. 5. Our second multi-projector system of size $10'W \times 8'H$ is a rear projected pringle-shaped display, with three cameras in a vertical configuration (marked in red in b). Results in Sect. 4.1 Ambient Light Tolerance are from this display. (Color figure online)

4 Results

4.1 Ambient Light Tolerance

In our tests, we measured the ambient light using a light meter for the setup shown in Fig. 5. The ambient light was increased by increasing the brightness of adjustable overhead stage lights from 0 to 750 lux. Table 1 shows E_r, the exposure predicted for the reference image and E_i, the exposure predicted for calibration patterns using ambient light estimated (A). Note that as A increases, E_r decreases. Further, E_i maintains a constant ratio with E_r, as expected.

Table 1. Exposures predicted for different ambient light settings

Ambient light (Lux)	E_r (ms)	E_i (ms)
0	320	320
97	80	160
190	80	160
325	40	160
415	40	160
590	40	80
735	40	80

We achieved equally accurate aggregation with high ambient light as with no ambient light, irrespective of the kind of camera configuration used. Figure 6 shows the results in the presence of both low and high ambient light. Note that the accuracy of the results are maintained even in the presence of the high ambient light. As the brightness increases, the display in Fig. 6 looks more and more whitewashed. This loss in contrast in the picture quality is only due to increased ambient light.

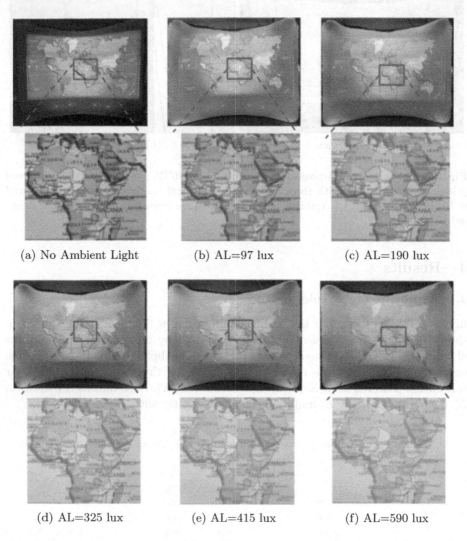

(a) No Ambient Light   (b) AL=97 lux   (c) AL=190 lux

(d) AL=325 lux   (e) AL=415 lux   (f) AL=590 lux

Fig. 6. Results at progressively higher ambient lights (AL). Even at such high ambient light conditions, registration of the images are accurate. NOTE: Loss in contrast in the picture quality is only due to the increased ambient light.

4.2   Laser Interaction

Interaction module with FLIR cameras operates at around 45–55 FPS and has no perceptible latency. Users have the option to choose the number of cameras to use for interaction. If any camera fails, others pick up its responsibility by recomputing their partitions to cover the entire region. Results are better seen in the video here. Please note how user is able to interact with various kinds of applications like web browsing, navigating Google Maps, etc. The module is generalized to adapt to different applications and can be customized based on user requirements.

Actions triggered by each gesture can be modified based on user requirements as well. We mapped (a) single laser click to Mouse's Left Click, (b) double laser click to double Left Click, and (c) laser initial hold and then drag to Mouse's drag (left click hold and movement). While executing a dragging gesture, the laser movement is recorded and can be matched to a similar recorded pattern. Thus, the drag gesture allows custom actions to be taken in an application. Laser-pen based interaction allows distal interaction till up to 10 ft distance from the display. For larger distances, performance is compromised only at the edges where the diminishing brightness of the laser-pen makes the laser spot harder to detect with the camera's grazing view of the 3D surface. For quantifying the performance of laser interaction module, we performed the following tests: (a) Laser detection accuracy test, (b) User gesture accuracy test, and (c) Location of action accuracy test.

Laser Detection Accuracy Test: For this test, we partitioned the display into an 8×8 grid. A user manually pressed the clicks 100 times in each region and the program recorded the number of times it successfully detected the laser-pen. The user maintained a distance between $5' - 10'$ while pointing the laser across the grid region. In Fig. 7a, the results in each grid region are shown as percentages. In Fig. 7b, a higher resolution heat map reflects the performance across the entire 2D display region. Average accuracy for the entire 2D display region is 98.21%, with an average accuracy of 99.94% in the central 6×6 grid and average accuracy of 96% in the edge grid regions. The lower accuracy in the periphery is due to cameras observing these regions at grazing angles. Note the camera placement as shown in red circle in Fig. 1a and note that our display sharply curves away from the outermost cameras making the edge regions to lie at grazing angles with respect to the cameras. To better cover the regions at a grazing angle to the current cameras, either additional cameras can be placed to focus on those areas or the current camera positions can be modified so that the grazing regions are smaller if not eliminated.

User Gesture Accuracy Test: For this test, a user performs each gesture and the program registers the type of action detected based on the state machine. During this test, the user also maintains a distance between $5'-10'$ while pointing the laser-pen. The user performs each gesture 100 times and the program logs the gesture it estimates. Results for Single Clicks and Double Clicks are shown in the form of heat-maps in Fig. 7(c,d). Note that the average estimation for all

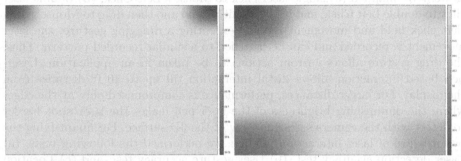

(a) 8 × 8 grid results for detection test(%) (b) Heatmap over display for detection test

(c) Single Clicks test results in heatmap (d) Double Clicks test results in heatmap

Fig. 7. Results from laser detection (a, b) and gesture accuracy (c, d) tests. In (b), the yellow regions show laser detection accuracy of about 100%. Average accuracy for all edge grid regions is 98.21% with highest of 100% and lowest of 65% at the top left corner. (c) shows the Single Click recognition accuracy, with a maximum of 100% and minimum of 99.55%. (d) shows Double Click recognition accuracy, with a maximum of 100% and minimum of 98%. (Color figure online)

the gestures is greater than 98% across the entire 2D display region. For Single Clicks, accuracy is highest, ranging from 99% across the top corners to 100% in all central regions. Double Click's accuracy ranges from 98% across the corners to 100% in the center region. This is directly correlated to the detection accuracy in the corners. The accuracy of the Drag behaves similarly and is therefore not shown explicitly.

Location of Action Accuracy Test: In order to estimate the error between the actual laser location and the detected laser location, we used the mouse cursor to point at the detected laser location. In these tests, the mouse cursor followed the laser very closely. We measured the Manhattan distance in pixels between the cursor and the laser spot using a camera to measure the error. The min, mean and max errors were 0.5, 0.94 and 1.5 pixels respectively. This shows a sub-pixel error in the detected location of the laser-pen which also attests to the sub-pixel accuracy of our automated registration.

4.3   Other Results

Here we show results of multi-user interaction and mirroring capabilities which can be better seen in the video here.

Multi-user Interaction: To test multi-user interaction, we designed a balloon popping game application where two players use two different colored laser-pens to pop balloons flying through the scene. To properly display the scores for each player, different colored lasers to be attributed to different users were necessary as shown in Fig. 8a.

(a) Multi-User Interaction   (b) Mirroring Application

Fig. 8. (a) Two kids interact with the display using different colored lasers (blue and green). (b) Using a laser on the curved display, the user interacts with the laptop via a VNC connection. (Color figure online)

Mirroring Applications: We use a capture card to tether a laptop or a VR headset to the multi-projector display via HDMI. This mirrors the content from the laptop/headset onto the large display and through a VNC connection, the user can use the laser interaction on the display to control the application on the laptop (Fig. 8b).

5   Conclusion and Future Work

In summary, we present a scalable laser-pen based interaction paradigm for auto-registered multi-projector displays that can operate in a large range of ambient light conditions, allowing users to robustly and smoothly interact with huge displays without any disruptions.

For future work, we plan to introduce a real-time custom gesture library for users. Such a gesture library (e.g. circular movement, swiping left, right) can allow for deeper analysis of movement profiles to reduce ambiguity (such as people tracing ovals when a there is a gesture for circles) and therefore increase accuracy of the detected gesture, possibly through AI/ML. A library can also offer us easy ways to marry different gestures with an intended action. For example, the same movement of hand to the right can be paired with a pan action in an image visualization software, but can be paired with drawing a stroke in a painting software. We plan to test scaling of our methods on more stressing configurations of massive (more than 30 projectors) surround displays. We also plan to parallelize our methods across multiple servers. Currently, our display is driven by a single server that can render at most 8–16 projectors in real-time (30–60 FPS). Using a large number of projectors for a massive display would need the use of multiple servers and our methods should scale to such situations.

References

1. Tehrani, M.A., Gopi, M., Majumder, A.: Automated geometric registration for multi-projector displays on arbitrary 3D shapes using uncalibrated devices. In: IEEE Transactions on Visualization and Computer Graphics, vol. 27, no. 4, pp. 2265–2279, 1 April 2021. https://doi.org/10.1109/TVCG.2019.2950942
2. Majumder, A., Sajadi, B.: Large area displays: the changing face of visualization. Computer **46**(5), 26–33 (2013). https://doi.org/10.1109/MC.2012.429
3. Aliaga, D.G., Yeung, Y.H., Law, A., Sajadi, B., Majumder, A.: Fast high-resolution appearance editing using superimposed projections. ACM Trans. Graph. **31**, 2, 1–13 (2012). Article 13. https://doi.org/10.1145/2159516.2159518
4. Sajadi, B., Majumder, A.: Autocalibrating tiled projectors on piecewise smooth vertically extruded surfaces. IEEE Trans. Visual Comput. Graphics **17**(9), 1209–1222 (2011). https://doi.org/10.1109/TVCG.2011.33
5. Sajadi, B., Majumder, A.: Markerless view-independent registration of multiple distorted projectors on extruded surfaces using an uncalibrated camera. IEEE Trans. Vis. Comput, Graph. **15**(6), 1307–1316 (2009). PMID: 19834203. https://doi.org/10.1109/TVCG.2009.166
6. Sajadi, B., Tehrani, M.A., Rahimzadeh, M., Majumder, A.: High-resolution lighting of 3D reliefs using a network of projectors and cameras. In: 2015 3DTV-Conference: The True Vision - Capture, Transmission and Display of 3D Video (3DTV-CON), pp. 1–4 (2015). https://doi.org/10.1109/3DTV.2015.7169372
7. Majumder, A., Brown, R.G., El-Ghoroury, H.S.: Display gamut reshaping for color emulation and balancing. In: IEEE Computer Society Conference on Computer Vision and Pattern Recognition - Workshops 2010, pp. 17–24 (2010). https://doi.org/10.1109/CVPRW.2010.5543467
8. Muhammad Twaha, I., Gopi, M., Aditi, M.: Dynamic projection mapping of deformable stretchable materials. In: 26th ACM Symposium on Virtual Reality Software and Technology (VRST 2020), 01–04 November 2020, Virtual Event, Canada. ACM, New York (2020). https://doi.org/10.1145/3385956.3418970
9. Kurth, P., Lange, V., Siegl, C., Stamminger, M., Bauer, F.: Auto-calibration for dynamic multi-projection mapping on arbitrary surfaces. IEEE Trans. Vis. Comput. Graph. **24**(11), 2886–2894 (2018). https://doi.org/10.1109/TVCG.2018.2868530
10. Siegl, C., Colaianni, M., Stamminger, M., Bauer, F.: Adaptive stray-light compensation in dynamic multi-projection mapping. Comput. Vis. Media **3**(3), 263–271 (2017). https://doi.org/10.1007/s41095-017-0090-8

11. Lange, V., Siegl, C., Colaianni, M., Stamminger, M., Bauer, F.: Robust blending and occlusion compensation in dynamic multi-projection mapping. In: Proceedings of the European Association for Computer Graphics: Short Papers (EG 2017), pp. 1–4. Eurographics Association, Goslar, DEU (2017). https://doi.org/10.2312/egsh. 20171000

12. Sun, Z., Wang, Y., Ye, L.: Research on human-computer interaction with laser-pen in projection display. In: 2008 11th IEEE International Conference on Communication Technology, pp. 620–622 (2008). https://doi.org/10.1109/ICCT.2008.4716152

13. Kirstein, C., Muller, H.: Interaction with a projection screen using a camera-tracked laser pointer. In: Proceedings 1998 Multimedia Modeling. MMM 1998 (Cat. No. 98EX200), p. 191–192 (1998). https://doi.org/10.1109/MULMM.1998.723001

14. Ahlborn, B.A.: A practical system for laser pointer interaction on large displays. In: Proceedings of the ACM Symposium on Virtual Reality Software and Technology - VRST 2005. ACM Press (2005)

15. Stuetzle, C.S., Cutler, B., Sammann, T.: Identifying inexpensive off-the-shelf laser pointers for multi-user interaction on large scale displays (2017)

16. Davis, J., Chen, X.: Lumipoint: multi-user laser-based interaction on large tiled displays. Displays **23**, 205–211 (2001). https://doi.org/10.1016/S0141-9382(02)00039-2

17. Roman, P., Lazarov, M., Majumder, A.: A scalable distributed paradigm for multi-user interaction with tiled rear projection display walls. In: IEEE Transactions on Visualization and Computer Graphics, vol. 16, no. 6, pp. 1623–1632, November–December 2010. https://doi.org/10.1109/TVCG.2010.128

18. Sajadi, B., Aditi, M.: Automatic registration of multiple projectors on swept surfaces. In: VRST 2010 (2010)

19. Sajadi, B., Majumder, A.: Markerless view-independent registration of multiple distorted projectors on extruded surfaces using an uncalibrated camera. IEEE Trans. Vis. Comput. Graph. **15**(6), 1307–1316 (2009). https://doi.org/10.1109/TVCG. 2009.166

20. Sajadi, B., Lazarov, M., Majumder, A., Gopi, M.: Color seamlessness in multi-projector displays using constrained gamut morphing. IEEE Trans. Vis. Comput. Graph. **15**, 1317–25 (2009). https://doi.org/10.1109/TVCG.2009.124

21. Majumder, A., Stevens, R.: Color nonuniformity in projection-based displays: analysis and solutions. In: IEEE Transactions on Visualization and Computer Graphics, vol. 10, no. 2, pp. 177–188, March–April 2004. https://doi.org/10.1109/TVCG. 2004.1260769

22. Aditi, M., Rick, S.: Perceptual photometric seamlessness in projection-based tiled displays. ACM Trans. Graph. **24**(1), 118–139 (2005). https://doi.org/10.1145/ 1037957.1037964

23. Sajadi, B., Majumder, A.: Auto-calibration of cylindrical multi-projector systems. IEEE Virtual Reality Conference (VR) 2010, pp. 155–162 (2010)

24. Sajadi, B., Majumder, A.: Scalable multi-view registration for multi-projector displays on vertically extruded surfaces. Comput. Graph. Forum. **29**, 1063–1072 (2010). https://doi.org/10.1111/j.1467-8659.2009.01676.x

25. Cao, X., Balakrishnan, R.: Interacting with dynamically defined information spaces using a handheld projector and a pen. In: Proceedings of the 19th Annual ACM Symposium on User Interface Software and Technology, pp. 225–234, October 2006

26. Cao, X., Forlines, C., Balakrishnan, R.: Multi-user interaction using handheld projectors. In: Proceedings of the 20th Annual ACM Symposium on User Interface Software and Technology, pp. 43–52, October 2007

27. Davis, J., Chen, X.: Lumipoint: multi-user laser-based interaction on large tiled displays. Displays **23**(5), 205–211 (2002)
28. Izadi, S., Brignull, H., Rodden, T., Rogers, Y., Underwood, M.: Dynamo: a public interactive surface supporting the cooperative sharing and exchange of media. In: Proceedings of the 16th Annual ACM Symposium on User Interface Software and Technology, pp. 159–168, November 2003
29. Jiang, H., Ofek, E., Moraveji, N., Shi, Y.: Direct pointer: direct manipulation for large-display interaction using handheld cameras. In: Proceedings of the SIGCHI Conference on Human Factors in Computing Systems, pp. 1107–1110, April 2006
30. Kim, J., Park, J., Kim, H., Lee, C.: HCI (human computer interaction) using multi-touch tabletop display. In: Pacific RIM Conference on Communications, Computers and Signal Processing, pp. 391–394 (2007)
31. Krumbholz, C., Leigh, J., Johnson, A., Renambot, L., Kooima, R.: Lambda table: high resolution tiled display table for interacting with large visualizations. In: Workshop for Advanced Collaborative Environments (WACE) (2005)
32. Shen, C., Vernier, F.D., Forlines, C., Ringel, M.: Diamondspin: an extensible toolkit for around-the-table interaction. In: SIGCHI Conference on Human Factors in Computing Systems, pp. 167–174 (2004)
33. Stødle, D., Bjørndalen, J.M., Anshus, O.J.: A system for hybrid vision- and sound-based interaction with distal and proximal targets on wall-sized, high-resolution tiled displays. In: IEEE International Workshop on Human Computer Interaction, pp. 59–68 (2007)
34. Stødle, D., Tor-Magne, S., Hagen, J., Bjørndalen, M., Anshus, O.J.: Gesture-based, touch-free multi-user gaming on wall-sized, high resolution tiled displays. In: 4th International Symposium on Pervasive Gaming Applications, PerGames, pp. 75–83 (2007)
35. Stødle, D., Troyanskaya, O., Li, K., Anshus, O.J.: Device-free interaction spaces. In: IEEE Symposium on 3D User Interfaces, pp. 39–42 (2009)
36. Wong, C.-O., Kyoung, D., Jung, K.: Adaptive context aware attentive interaction in large tiled display. In: IEEE International Workshop on Human Computer Interaction, pp. 1016–1025 (2007)
37. Wu, M., Balakrishnan, R.: Multi-finger and whole hand gestural interaction techniques for multi-user tabletop displays. In: ACM Symposium on User Interface Software and Technology, pp. 193–202 (2003)

A Paper-Based Keyboard Using ArUco Codes: ArUco Keyboard

Onur Toker[✉], Bayazit Karaman, and Doga Demirel

Florida Polytechnic University, Lakeland, FL 33805, USA
{otoker,bkaraman,ddemirel}@floridapoly.edu

Abstract. Object tracking in computer vision can be done either by using a marker-less or marker-based approach. Computer vision systems have been using Fiducial markers for pose estimation in different applications such as augmented reality [5] and robot navigation [4]. With the advancements in Augmented Reality (AR), new tools such as AugmentedReality uco (ArUco) [6] markers have been introduced to the literature. ArUco markers, are used to tackle the localization problem in AR, allowing camera pose estimation to be carried out by a binary matrix. Using a binary matrix not just simplifies the process but also increases the efficiency. As a part of our initiative to create a cost-efficient, 24/7 accessible, Virtual Reality (VR) based chemistry lab for underprivileged students, we wanted to create an alternative way of interacting with the virtual scene. In this study, we used ArUco markers to create a low-cost keyboard only using a piece of paper and an off-the-shelf webcam. We believe this method of keyboard will be more beneficial to the user as they can see the keys before they are typing in the corner of the screen instead of an insufficient on the screen VR keyboard or a regular keyboard where the user can't see what they are typing with a VR headset. As potential extensions of the base system, we have also designed and evaluated a stereo camera and an IMU sensor based system with various sensor fusion techniques. In summary, the stereo camera reduces occlusion related problems, and the IMU sensor detects vibrations which in turn simplifies the KeyPress detection problem. It has been observed that use of any of these additional sensors improves the overall system performance.

Keywords: ArUco codes · IMU sensors · Sensor fusion

1 Introduction

Object tracking in computer vision can be done either by using a marker-less or marker-based approach. Computer vision systems have been using Fiducial markers for pose estimation in different applications such as augmented reality [5] and robot navigation [4]. With the advancements in Augmented Reality (AR), new tools such as AugmentedReality uco (ArUco) [6] markers have been introduced to the literature. ArUco markers, are used to tackle the localization

M. Kurosu (Ed.): HCII 2022, LNCS 13303, pp. 195–208, 2022.
https://doi.org/10.1007/978-3-031-05409-9_15

problem in AR, allowing camera pose estimation to be carried out by a binary matrix. Using a binary matrix not just simplifies the process but also increases the efficiency. As a part of our initiative to create a cost-efficient, 24/7 accessible, Virtual Reality (VR) based chemistry lab for underprivileged students, we wanted to create an alternative way of interacting with the virtual scene. In this study, we used ArUco markers to create a low-cost keyboard only using a piece of paper and an off-the-shelf webcam. We believe this method of keyboard will be more beneficial to the user as they can see the keys before they are typing in the corner of the screen instead of an insufficient on the screen VR keyboard or a regular keyboard where the user can't see what they are typing with a VR headset.

Our setup is straightforward and consists of a webcam and a piece of paper with a keyboard-like pattern printed on it, see [4]. Basically, there is a numeric keypad with rectangular regions labeled from 0 to 9, and each region has the ArUco code for the corresponding key value. When the system is running in "live" mode, users can use this printed paper as a keypad. All "touched" key values will be translated to keypress events and the printed paper will act as a regular keyboard. This system needs both computer vision and smoothing/filtering techniques which can be fine-tuned for an average user or a specific user.

In this paper, we propose using a real-time OpenCV-based computer vision approach and a specific state-machine based fast smoothing/filtering algorithm. The filter has a parameter, N, which represents the filter strength. We have first created a dataset using six-digit numbers typed by the same user using this paper-based keyboard. Then we varied the filter strength parameter N from 1 to 10 and measured the accuracy of the proposed paper-based keyboard. For a specific trained user, and for a specific dataset of size ten, the system accuracy is measured as 0.0 for N less than 4, 0.6 for $N = 4$, 1.0 for $N = 5, 6, 7$, 0.3 for $N = 8$, 0.10 for $N = 9$, and finally 0.0 for $N = 10$. Optimal values seem to be $N = 5, 6, 7$, but if we eliminate $N = 5$ and 7 as potential boundary cases, we get $N = 6$ as the optimal choice for this specific trained user.

The ArUco keyboard used in this study is shown in Fig. 1, and the base system demo is presented in Fig. 4. As potential extensions of the base system, we have also designed and evaluated a stereo camera and an IMU sensor based system with various sensor fusion techniques. The specific stereo camera used for this research was a USB3 ZED camera, see Fig. 2, tested with a GeForce GTX 1050 Ti Max-Q 4 GB laptop running Ubuntu 18 LTS. It has been observed that the stereo camera reduces occlusion related issues, and results more robust detection performance. The IMU sensor used in this research is a GY-521 accelerometer and gyro sensor, see Fig. 3, interfaced to an Arduino Uno board over the SPI

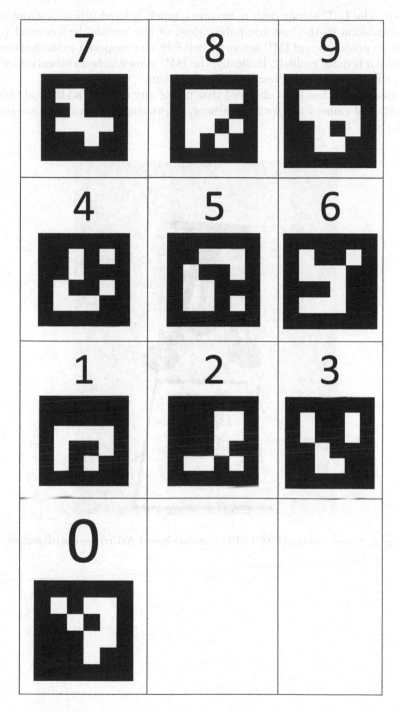

Fig. 1. ArUco keyboard.

interface. The IMU sensor detects keypress/touch related vibrations and sends this information to the host computer. Most of the mobile devices used today do have a camera(s) and IMU sensors, therefore the proposed extensions to our base system is quite realistic. Basically, the IMU sensor detects vibrations which in turn simplifies the KeyPress detection problem.

In summary, it has been observed that use of any of these additional sensors, i.e. additional camera and/or IMU sensor, improves the overall system performance.

Fig. 2. Stereo camera (USB3 ZED camera) based ArUco keyboard system.

Fig. 3. GY521: InvenSense MPU-6050 based IMU sensor board interfaced to an Arduino Uno over SPI.

2   Base System

Our base system [1] shown in, Fig. 4, has a single webcam. The algorithm used in this base implementation is shown in Algorithm 1. In each OpenCV frame, we first detect all visible ArUco markers and then determine all blocked ArUco markers. For each frame, we also determine the highest blocked marker value. If the highest blocked marker is the same during the past N frames, then we generate a KeyPress event. A KeyRelease event is generated in the first frame having all ArUco markers visible.

The detection performance of the system depends on the value of N. For a specific trained user, $N = 6$ value is found to be optimal for a webcam running at 25 frames/s. In general, the optimal N value depends on the frame rate and the user.

Algorithm 1: Algorithm used for the base system

Input: OpenCV frame img as a numpy array
Result: Keyboard event and key code
1 Find all visible ArUco markers in the frame img
2 Determine all blocked ArUco markers
3 Memorize the list of blocked markers for the past N frames
4 Find the highest blocked marker for all of the past N frames
5 If the highest blocked marker does not change, trigger a KeyPress event and use the highest blocked marker as the key value
6 Generate a KeyRelease event in the first frame having all ArUco markers visible
7 Goto Step 1

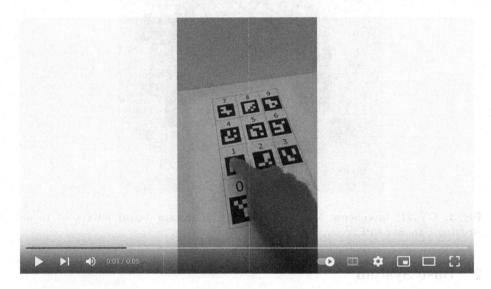

Fig. 4. ArUco keyboard: Base system, https://youtu.be/tnKc6zvXliY

3   IMU Sensor Based System

The base system presented in the previous section works by detecting blocked ArUco markers in each frame. However, this single camera based system cannot differentiate between blocked without touch and blocked because of touch cases. Because of this technical difficulty, a user should be trained not to keep his/her hand stationary for a "long" period of time (5/25 s) while being visible by the camera. Although this is technically possible, and the training process is observed to be not that difficult, we have developed an alternative approach to overcome this problem.

This new approach [2] is based on using an IMU sensor, see Fig. 5, to differentiate between blocked without touch and blocked because of touch. IMU sensors have acceleration sensors in x, y and z directions, and can be used to detect even a slight tap on a surface. We have used an InvenSense MPU6050 chip as our IMU sensor. A first order digital low-pass filter is used for smoothing, and a thresholding with hysteresis is used for tap detection. In this case, the microcontroller sends the tap events to the host device, and only after this stage the host device starts executing Algorithm 1. See the full source code given in the appendix for digital low-pass filter, thresholding and hysteresis parameters.

Fig. 5. ArUco keyboard: IMU sensor based version, https://youtu.be/sIuhZQpu0AE

4   Stereo Camera Based System

As a final improvement of the proposed ArUco keyboard system, we have implemented a stereo camera based solution [3] shown in Fig. 6. A stereo camera based system provides more data which can be used to improve the overall system performance, and this is true with or without using an IMU sensor. Sometimes, we may have certain ArUco markers being blocked because of occlusion, and not because of touch. Basically, after a touch or tap is detected we may still have multiple ArUco markers being blocked. The priority scheme used in Algorithm 1 seems to work for most cases, but the failure rate is non-zero and becomes more noticeable if the ArUco keyboard is rotated significantly. A stereo camera greatly improves detection performance for such cases.

Fig. 6. ArUco keyboard: Stereo camera version (USB3 ZED camera), https://youtu.be/ssbv2NqfAJg

If both cameras report a particular ArUco marker as not detected, then the probability of failure, i.e. being not-detected because of occlusion, will be smaller compared to a single camera system. Therefore, use of a stereo camera reduces false KeyPress events and also key value errors. But it requires more processing power and more complex hardware which may not be practical for all possible use cases.

5   Conclusion

In this paper, we have presented a paper based numeric keypad using ArUco markers. Full details of all source codes are given in the appendix. This system can be quite useful as a low-cost disposable keyboard for VR systems and mobile devices equipped with a camera. It has been observed that, the use of an IMU sensor greatly improves the overall system performance. Since almost all mobile devices, whether it is a phone or a tablet, do have IMU sensors, the improved IMU based keyboard can be used without any additional sensor or equipment. We have also implemented a stereo camera based system, but to the best of our knowledge mobile devices with stereo cameras are not widely available. The stereo camera based implementation is a feasible alternative for VR systems.

Acknowledgments. Funding is provided by NSF-1919855, Advanced Mobility Institute grants GR-2000028, GR-2000029, and Florida Polytechnic University startup grant GR-1900022.

Appendix I: ArUco Code Detection Module `aruco_tools.py`

```
import cv2
from cv2 import aruco
import numpy as np

# Module constants
my_aruco_dictionary = aruco.DICT_4X4_50

def detect_markers(image):
    gray = cv2.cvtColor(image, cv2.COLOR_BGR2GRAY)

    # OTSU threshold

    # aruco_dict = aruco.Dictionary_get(aruco.DICT_ARUCO_ORIGINAL)
    aruco_dict = aruco.Dictionary_get(my_aruco_dictionary)
    parameters = aruco.DetectorParameters_create()
    corners, ids, rejectedImgPoints = aruco.detectMarkers(gray, aruco_dict, parameters=parameters)
    frame_markers = aruco.drawDetectedMarkers(gray.copy(), corners, ids)
    ids = np.array(ids)
    ids = ids.reshape((-1,))
    ls = []
    for k, mid in enumerate(ids):
        if not (mid == None):
            # print(k, mid, corners[k])
            c = corners[k][0]
            x_pixel = int(np.round(c[:, 0].mean()))
            y_pixel = int(np.round(c[:, 1].mean()))
            ls.append((mid, x_pixel, y_pixel))

    return ls
```

Appendix II: Base System `minikdb_mono.py`

```
import cv2
from aruco_tools import detect_markers
import winsound
import pyttsx3

# initialize Text-to-speech engine
engine = pyttsx3.init()

# openCV
cap = cv2.VideoCapture(0)

mid_list = [0,1,2,3,4,5,6,7,8,9]
tts = {0:'zero', 1:'one', 2:'two', 3:'three', 4:'four', 5:'five', 6:'six', 7:'seven', 8:'eight', 9:'nine'}

frame_counter = 0
num_rep=7
key_pressed = False
key_value = -1

hist_list = num_rep*[-1]
while True:
    frame_counter += 1

    success, color_frame = cap.read()
    if not success:
        print("Ignoring empty camera frame.")
        continue

    # To improve performance, optionally mark the image as not writeable to pass by reference.
    color_frame.flags.writeable = False

    L = detect_markers(color_frame)
    try:
        dL = []
        for mid, x_pixel, y_pixel in L:
            dL.append(mid)
            cv2.circle(color_frame, (x_pixel, y_pixel), 5, (0, 0, 255), 3)
    except Exception as e:
        print(e)

    keypress_set = set(mid_list).difference(set(dL))
    if len(keypress_set) > 0:
        # print(frame_counter, max(keypress_set))
```

```
        hist_list.pop(0)
        hist_list.append(max(keypress_set))
        hist_set = set(hist_list)
        print(hist_list, key_pressed)

        if len(hist_set) == 1:
            ckey_value = min(hist_list)
            if key_pressed == False:
                key_value = ckey_value
                key_pressed = True
                # print('KeyPress', key_value)
                # pyautogui.keyDown(str(key_value))    #Key press event
                # print(key_value, end='')              #Write to console
                # winsound.Beep(2500, 200)              #Audio feedback
                engine.say(tts[key_value])
                engine.runAndWait()

    elif (key_pressed == True):
        key_pressed = False
        # Key release event
        print('KeyRelease')

    cv2.imshow('ARUCO', color_frame)
    key = cv2.waitKey(1)
    # Press esc or 'q' to close the image window
    if key & 0xFF == ord('q') or key == 27:
        cv2.destroyAllWindows()
        break

cap.release()
cv2.destroyAllWindows()
```

Appendix III: IMU Based System `minikbd_imu.py`

```
import cv2
from aruco_tools import detect_markers
import winsound
import pyttsx3
import pyautogui
import serial
import winsound
import random

# initialize Text-to-speech engine
engine = pyttsx3.init()

# openCV
cap = cv2.VideoCapture(0)

mid_list = [0,1,2,3,4,5,6,7,8,9]
tts = {0:'zero', 1:'one', 2:'two', 3:'three', 4:'four', 5:'five', 6:'six', 7:'seven', 8:'eight', 9:'nine'}

frame_counter = 0
num_rep=5
key_pressed = False
key_value = -1
armed = False

# configure the serial connections (the parameters differs on the device you are connecting to)
ser = serial.Serial(port='COM3', baudrate=57600)
ser.isOpen()

num_fail = 0
for test_num in range(100):

    rnd_num = int(random.uniform(100,999))
    engine.say(str(rnd_num)), engine.runAndWait()
    print(rnd_num)

    in_str=''
    for digit_no in range(3):

        hist_list = num_rep*[-1]
        while True:
            frame_counter += 1

            success, color_frame = cap.read()
            if not success:
                print("Ignoring empty camera frame.")
                continue

            # To improve performance, optionally mark the image as not writeable to pass by reference.
            # color_frame.flags.writeable = False

            L = detect_markers(color_frame)
            try:
                dL = []
```

```
                for mid, x_pixel, y_pixel in L:
                    dL.append(mid)
                    cv2.circle(color_frame, (x_pixel, y_pixel), 5, (0, 0, 255), 3)
            except Exception as e:
                print(e)

            if armed == False:
                if ser.inWaiting() == 0:
                    pass
                else:
                    # print('beep')
                    ser.read(ser.inWaiting())
                    if armed == False:
                        armed = True
                        hist_list = num_rep * [-1]

            if armed == True:
                keypress_set = set(mid_list).difference(set(dL))
                if len(keypress_set) > 0:
                    # print(frame_counter, max(keypress_set))
                    hist_list.pop(0)
                    hist_list.append(max(keypress_set))
                    hist_set = set(hist_list)
                    # print(hist_set, hist_list, key_pressed)

                    if len(hist_set) == 1:
                        ckey_value = min(hist_list)
                        key_value = ckey_value
                        # print('KeyPress', key_value)
                        # pyautogui.keyDown(str(key_value))
                        print(key_value, end='')
                        in_str = in_str + str(key_value)
                        # winsound.Beep(5000, 200)
                        # engine.say(tts[key_value])
                        # engine.runAndWait()

                        armed = False
                        # ser.read(ser.inWaiting())
                        # Key release event
                        # print('KeyRelease')
                        winsound.Beep(2500, 200)
                        break

            cv2.imshow('ARUCO', color_frame)
            key = cv2.waitKey(1)
            # Press esc or 'q' to close the image window
            if key & 0xFF == ord('q') or key == 27:
                cv2.destroyAllWindows()
                break

        #end of digit_num

    if (str(rnd_num) == in_str):
        print(' ok    ', end='')
    else:
        print(' failed', end='')
        num_fail += 1
    print('       ', num_fail, ' fails in', test_num + 1, ' pf = %', round(100*num_fail / (test_num + 1)))

    # end of test_num
cap.release()
cv2.destroyAllWindows()
```

Appendix IV: Stereo Camera Based System `minikbd_zed.py`

```
import cv2
import pyzed.sl as sl
from aruco_tools import detect_markers
import beepy
import serial
import random

# ZEDCAM
init = sl.InitParameters()
cam = sl.Camera()
if not cam.is_opened():
    print("Opening ZED Camera...")
status = cam.open(init)
if status != sl.ERROR_CODE.SUCCESS:
    print(repr(status))
    exit()

runtime = sl.RuntimeParameters()
mat = sl.Mat()

# ArUco
```

```
mid_list = [0,1,2,3,4,5,6,7,8,9]
tts = {0:'zero', 1:'one', 2:'two', 3:'three', 4:'four', 5:'five', 6:'six', 7:'seven', 8:'eight', 9:'nine'}

frame_counter = 0
num_rep=5
key_pressed = False
key_value = -1
armed = False

# configure the serial connections (the parameters differs on the device you are connecting to)
ser = serial.Serial(port='/dev/ttyACM0', baudrate=57600)
ser.isOpen()

num_fail = 0
for test_num in range(100):

    rnd_num = int(random.uniform(100,999))
    print(rnd_num)

    in_str=''
    for digit_no in range(3):

        hist_list = num_rep*[-1]
        while True:
            frame_counter += 1

            err = cam.grab(runtime)
            if err == sl.ERROR_CODE.SUCCESS:
                cam.retrieve_image(mat, sl.VIEW.LEFT)
                imgL = mat.get_data()
                cam.retrieve_image(mat, sl.VIEW.RIGHT)
                imgR = mat.get_data()

            L = detect_markers(imgL)
            mL = []
            for mid, x_pixel, y_pixel in L:
                mL.append(mid)
                cv2.circle(imgL, (x_pixel, y_pixel), 5, (0, 0, 255), 3)

            L = detect_markers(imgR)
            mR = []
            for mid, x_pixel, y_pixel in L:
                mR.append(mid)
                cv2.circle(imgR, (x_pixel, y_pixel), 5, (0, 0, 255), 3)

            if armed == False:
                if ser.inWaiting() == 0:
                    pass
                else:
                    # print('beep')
                    ser.read(ser.inWaiting())
                    if armed == False:
                        armed = True
                        hist_list = num_rep * [-1]

            if armed == True:

                mC = set(mL).union(set(mR))
                keypress_set = set(mid_list).difference(mC)
                if len(keypress_set) > 0:
                    # print(frame_counter, max(keypress_set))
                    hist_list.pop(0)
                    hist_list.append(max(keypress_set))
                    hist_set = set(hist_list)
                    # print(hist_set, hist_list, key_pressed)

                    if len(hist_set) == 1:
                        ckey_value = min(hist_list)
                        key_value = ckey_value
                        # print('KeyPress', key_value)
                        # pyautogui.keyDown(str(key_value))
                        print(key_value, end='')
                        in_str = in_str + str(key_value)
                        beepy.beep(sound='coin')  # string as argument

                        armed = False
                        break

        cv2.imshow("ZED LEFT", imgL)
        cv2.imshow("ZED RIGHT", imgR)
        key = cv2.waitKey(1)
        # Press esc or 'q' to close the image window
        if key & 0xFF == ord('q') or key == 27:
            cv2.destroyAllWindows()
            break

    #end of digit_num

    if (str(rnd_num) == in_str):
        print(' ok    ', end='')
```

```
else:
    print(' failed', end='')
    num_fail += 1
print('        ', num_fail, ' fails in', test_num + 1, ' pf = %', round(100*num_fail / (test_num + 1)))

# end of test_num

cv2.destroyAllWindows()
cam.close()
```

Appendix V: IMU Sensor Code for Arduino Uno

```
#include<Wire.h>
const int MPU=0x68;
const int LED=13;
const int BUZZER=5;
int16_t AcX,AcY,AcZ,Tmp,GyX,GyY,GyZ;
int16_t AcZp = 0;
float d = 0;
int key_state = 0;
int count = 0;

void setup(){
  pinMode(LED, OUTPUT);
  pinMode(BUZZER, OUTPUT);
  digitalWrite(LED, LOW);
  Wire.begin();
  Wire.beginTransmission(MPU);
  Wire.write(0x6B);
  Wire.write(0);
  Wire.endTransmission(true);
  Serial.begin(57600);
}

void loop(){
  Wire.beginTransmission(MPU);
  Wire.write(0x3B);
  Wire.endTransmission(false);
  Wire.requestFrom(MPU,12,true);
  AcX=Wire.read()<<8|Wire.read();
  AcY=Wire.read()<<8|Wire.read();
  AcZ=Wire.read()<<8|Wire.read();

  // Digital low-pass filtering
  d = 0.8 * d + 0.2 * abs(AcZ - AcZp);
  // Saturation/Limiter/Hysteresis
  if (d > 300) {
    d = 300;
    digitalWrite(LED, HIGH);
    analogWrite(BUZZER, 1);
    if (key_state == 0) {
      //Serial.println(count++);
      Serial.print('x'); // keypress notification
    }
    key_state = 1;
  }
  if (d < 150) {
    d = 0;
    digitalWrite(LED, LOW);
    analogWrite(BUZZER, 0);
    key_state = 0;
  }
  //Serial.println(round(d));
  AcZp = AcZ;

  delay(10);
}
```

References

1. ArUco keyboard demo video: Base system. https://youtu.be/tnKc6zvXliY
2. ArUco keyboard demo video: IMU sensor based version. https://youtu.be/sIuhZQpu0AE
3. ArUco keyboard demo video: Stereo camera version (USB3 ZED camera). https://youtu.be/ssbv2NqfAJg

4. Bacik, J., Durovsky, F., Fedor, P., Perdukova, D.: Autonomous flying with quadrocopter using fuzzy control and ArUco markers. Intell. Serv. Robot. **10**(3), 185–194 (2017). https://doi.org/10.1007/s11370-017-0219-8
5. Billinghurst, M., Clark, A., Lee, G.: A survey of augmented reality. Found. Trends Hum.-Comput. Interact. **8**(2–3), 73–272 (2015). http://dx.doi.org/10.1561/1100000049
6. Garrido-Jurado, S., Muñoz-Salinas, R., Madrid-Cuevas, F., Marín-Jiménez, M.: Automatic generation and detection of highly reliable fiducial markers under occlusion. Pattern Recogn. **47**(6), 2280–2292 (2014). https://doi.org/10.1016/j.patcog.2014.01.005

Text, Speech and Image Processing
in HCI

Visualizing and Processing Information Not Uttered in Spoken Political and Journalistic Data: From Graphical Representations to Knowledge Graphs in an Interactive Application

Christina Alexandris[1,3](✉), Jiali Du[2], and Vasilios Floros[1,3]

[1] National and Kapodistrian University of Athens, Athens, Greece
calexandris@gs.uoa.gr

[2] Lab of Language Engineering and Computing, Faculty of Chinese Language and Culture, Guangdong University of Foreign Studies, Guangzhou, China

[3] European Communication Institute (ECI), Danube University Krems and National Technical University of Athens, Athens, Greece

Abstract. The present interactive application targets to the processing and direct generation and use of information not uttered, converting it into "visible", processable information in the form of knowledge graphs and, subsequently, training data, for neural networks and other uses. In-depth understanding and un-biased evaluation of interviews and discussions in spoken political and journalistic texts is targeted, especially when an international public is concerned. Special emphasis is placed on parameters concerning Chinese speakers within the international media and community.

Keywords: Spoken journalistic texts · Spoken interaction · Knowledge graphs · Graphic representations · Cognitive Bias

1 Spoken Interaction as Graphical Representations

Previous research focused in generating graphic representations for interactions involving persuasion and negotiations. The generated graphic representations are targeted to enabling the visibility of information not uttered, in particular, tension and the overall behavior of speakers-participants in spoken political and journalistic texts, especially where the elements of persuasion and negotiations are involved [1]. The generated graphic representations are intended to assist evaluation, training and decision-making processes and for the construction of respective models. In particular, the graphic representations generated from the processed wav.file or video files may be used to evaluate persuasion tactics employed in spoken interaction involving negotiations (a), their possible employment in the construction of training data and negotiation models (b) and for evaluating a trainee's performance (c).

M. Kurosu (Ed.): HCII 2022, LNCS 13303, pp. 211–226, 2022.
https://doi.org/10.1007/978-3-031-05409-9_16

Data was collected from transcribed spoken political and journalistic texts processed by an interactive, user-friendly annotation tool. The data was enriched with observations provided by professional journalists (European Communication Institute (ECI)-Quality Journalism and Digital Technologies, Danube University at Krems, Austria, the Athena-Research and Innovation Center in Information, Communication and Knowledge Technologies, Athens, the Institution of Promotion of Journalism Ath.Vas. Botsi, Athens and the National and Technical University of Athens, Greece.

The correct perception and evaluation of information not uttered in spoken interaction can pose challenges to applications processing spoken texts that are not domain-specific, as in the case of spoken political and journalistic texts. In addition to their characteristic richness in socio-linguistic and socio-cultural elements, spoken political and journalistic texts pose challenges for their evaluation, processing and translation due to their content concerning discussions and interactions beyond a defined agenda, and also in regard to the possibility of different types of targeted audiences - including non-native speakers and the international community [3]. This is considered a crucial complexity factor since essential information, presented either in a subtle form or in an indirect way, is being often undetected, especially by the international public. However, previous research has demonstrated that information that is not uttered can be derived from the overall behavior of speakers-participants in a discussion or interview. Spontaneous turn-taking [31, 41], another complexity factor in spoken political and journalistic texts, has resulted to implementation of strategies concerning the analysis and processing of discourse structure and rhetorical relations with the aid of graphical generations, complementing previous research and previous approaches [11, 21, 35, 43].

Previous research [4, 5, 7, 24] concerned an implemented processing and evaluation framework allowing the graphic representation to be presented in conjunction with the parallel depiction of speech signals and transcribed texts, designed to operate with most commercial transcription tools. Specifically, the alignment of the generated graphic representation with the respective segments of the spoken text enables a possible integration in existing transcription tools. The processing and evaluation framework and interactive annotation tool is adapted from strategies still employed in most traditional Spoken Dialog Systems, such as keyword processing in the form of topic detection [25] (constituting the basis for the development of approaches using neural networks [40]). The generated visual representations depict topics avoided, introduced or repeatedly referred to by each Speaker-Participant, and in specific types of cases may indicate the existence of additional, "hidden" [24] Illocutionary Acts [10, 14, 15, 32] other than "Obtaining Information Asked" or "Providing Information Asked" in a discussion or interview. The output of the processing and evaluation framework also included functions and respective values reflecting the degree in which the speakers-participants address or avoid the topics in the dialog structure as well as the degree of tension in their interaction. Data was collected from transcribed spoken political and journalistic texts processed by an interactive, user-friendly annotation tool, with the aid of professional journalists [1, 2, 24].

The interactive function of the framework and annotation tool monitors and controls the Confidence Bias [18] of the user-evaluator, especially if multiple users-evaluators may produce different forms of generated visual representations for the same conversation and interaction. In particular, the user chooses relations between topics in each conversation segment defined by speaker-turns [1, 2, 24]: "Repetition", "Association", "Generalization" and "Topic Switch". Chosen relations between words may describe Lexical Bias [37] and may differ according to political, socio-cultural and linguistic characteristics of the user-evaluator, especially if international users are concerned [20, 26, 27, 42] due to lack of world knowledge of a language community [8, 16, 39]. A high frequency of Repetitions (value 1), Generalizations (value 3) and Topic Switches (value -1) in comparison to the duration of the spoken interaction is connected to the "(Topic) Relevance" benchmarks with a value of "Relevance (X)" [4, 5]. In spoken interaction concerning persuasion and types of negotiation based on persuasion [13, 30, 34], perceived affirmative ("Yes") and negative ("No") answers receive the "0" (zero) and "−2" values. Thus, a negotiation with a sequence of negative answers and several attempts to change a topic or to approach a (seemly) different topic will generate a graphic representation below the "0" (zero) value (Fig. 1).

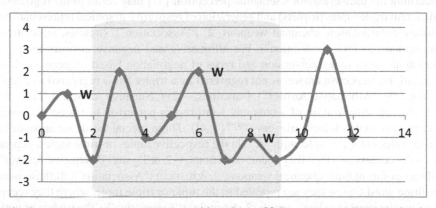

Fig. 1. Generated graphic representation with multiple "No" answers and Word-Topic triggers ("W") and Tension (shaded area between topics) in generated graphic representation and signalized "tension trigger" word ("W") (Alexandris et al. 2021).

2 Perception, Visibility, Processability of Information Not Uttered and Knowledge Graphs

The "Association" relation played a central role in the interactively generated graphic representations of spoken interactions constituting persuasion and types of negotiation based on persuasion [34], especially if emotion is used as a tool for persuasion [30], establishing a link between persuasion, emotion and language (Fig. 2).

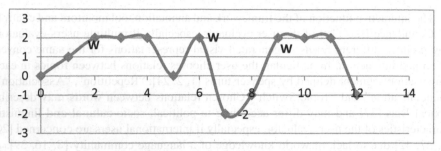

Fig. 2. Generated graphic representation with multiple "Association" relations and signalized Word-Topic triggers ("W") (Alexandris et al. 2021).

Diverse types of negotiation skills, apart from persuasion tactics [13, 30, 34], including "value creating"/"value claiming" tactics and "defensive" tactics [34] use emotion as a tool for persuasion. "Association" (and "Generalization", "Repetition" and "Topic-Switch") relations between word-topics are measured in the form of triple tuples as perceived relations-distances between word-topics [5]. Lexical Bias (Cognitive Bias) concerning the user-evaluator's semantic perception [37] may result to the registration of different triple tuples (triplets) and generation of respective graphical representations: (military confrontation, chemical weapons, 2) ("Association"), (treaties, international commitment, 3) ("Generalization"). For affirmative and negative answers in spoken interactions constituting persuasion and types of negotiation based on persuasion, the topic and the respective answer is not registered as a triplet but is registered as a tuple: (stability, 0) ("Affirmative Answer"), (sanctions, −2) ("Negative Answer"). There was an additional signalization of words and word-topics perceived to trigger tension or other reactions (Word-Topic triggers -"W" [1, 4]). These special words are appended as marked values (for example, with "&") in the respective tuples or triple tuples, depending on the context in which they occur: (sanctions, −2, &dignity) ("Negative Answer"), (military confrontation, chemical weapons, 2, &justice) ("Association"). If these words constitute word-topics, they are repeated in the tuple or triple tuple, where they receive the respective mark: (country, people, 2, &people) ("Association"). The triplets or tuples and the sequences they form may be converted into vectors (or other forms and models) [22, 23, 36, 38], used as training data for creating negotiation models and their variations.

2.1 Association Relations, Argument Structure and Knowledge Graphs

Spoken political and journalistic texts do not always provide clear-cut models of argumentation and argument structure, if the factor of subjectivity, information perceived and socio-cultural elements of the international community are taken into account. For negotiation applications, identifying "Association" relations between words and their related topics contributes to strategies targeting to directing the Speaker-Participant into addressing the topic of interest and/or to produce the desired answers and the avoidance of unwanted "Association" types, as well as unwanted other types of relations -"Repetitions", "Topic Switch" and "Generalizations". "Generalization" may also be used for the same purpose, as a means of introducing a (not directly related) topic of interest. As previously described, the perceived relations-distances between word-topics are linked to socio-cultural factors and Cognitive Bias [1–3]. Additionally, in regard to "Association", words and their related topics may contain two types of information content: (Assoc-1) "Association" (or other) relations that are context-specific, connected to current events and state-of-affairs, (Assoc-2) "Association" (or other) relations that concern words with inherent socio-culturally determined linguistic features and are usually independent from current events and state-of-affairs [1–3].

We note that relations between words perceived as topics of each individual utterance in speaker turns – especially "Association" - and the link of words and word-topics to persuasion and tension may also be regarded as an alternative way of depicting and understanding argument structure, especially if spontaneous turn-taking [31, 41] is concerned.

Generated argument structure and the overall discourse structure may be compared to predicted argument structure and the overall discourse structure. In this case, not a generation of all possible matches is created, but possible matches according to speakers' perceptions. For example, the above-presented application allows the generated graphical representations of perceived word-topic relations to be converted into the following sequences depicted in Fig. 3, which may subsequently be modelled into knowledge graphs for their subsequent conversion into vectors or other forms of data for neural networks and Machine Learning applications [22, 23, 36, 38].

The interface of the interactive application for the generation of knowledge graphs is presented in Sect. 4.

(treaties, international commitment,3) : treaties -> GEN-> international commitment
(treaties, international commitment, 2): treaties -> ASSOC-> international commitment

(military confrontation, chemical weapons, 2):
military confrontation -> ASSOC-> chemical weapons
(military confrontation, chemical weapons, -1):
military confrontation -> SWITCH-> chemical weapons

Fig. 3. Registering alternative perceptions of topic relations and conversion of triple tuples and tuples for creating knowledge graphs.

2.2 Registering Associations: Resolving Implicit Statements, Omission and Ambiguity in Spoken Mandarin Chinese

The registration of perceived Association relations and their role in argumentation bypassed typical problems encountered in high-context language languages such as Mandarin Chinese [12] where there is a tendency for native speakers to express themselves implicitly and economically (1, Implicit statements). This feature can persist in the communication in a foreign language, for example, English. The Principle of Least Effort can be well applied to the Chinese spoken communication where "less words can mean more sense" [12]. Common features observed in spoken Mandarin Chinese are implicit statements (Implicit Statements 1), the omission of syntactic elements as well as Zero anaphora in Chinese discourse cohesion. (2, Omission) [12]. We note that Chinese native speakers are used to omitting the subject, especially the animate subject; Chinese antecedent is usually considered to be the subject of a sentence, and the omitted anaphora phenomenon often appears at the following clause. Mandarin Chinese is considered to be more like a topic-focused language, where speakers have to guess the potential meaning by the limited syntactic information [12].

The registration of perceived Association relations allows the depiction of argument structure based on the topics perceived and the retrieval of possible types of essential information based on the registered reactions and responses of the speakers-participants. This registration may also contribute to the management of lexical ambiguity of perceived word-topics for Mandarin Chinese native speakers communicating in a foreign language (3, Ambiguity), as well as word types containing socio-cultural information, as described in the following section.

2.3 Registering Associations and Implied Socio-cultural Information as Tension Triggers and Emotion in Spoken Interaction

Association relations and argumentation can also be related to inherent yet subtle socio-culturally determined linguistic features in commonly occurring words, referred to "Gravity" and "Evocative" words [3, 6]. The subtlety of their content is often unconsciously used or perceived (mostly) by native speakers.

"Gravity" words are may contribute to the degree of formality or intensity of conveyed information in a spoken utterance whereas "Evocative" words usually contribute to a descriptive or emotional tone in an utterance [3, 6].

"Gravity" and "Evocative" words play a remarkable role in interactions involving persuasion and negotiations, considering that, according to Rockledge et al. 2018, "the more extremely positive the word, the greater the probability individuals were to associate that word with persuasion" [30]. "Gravity" and "Evocative" words [3, 6] (signalized as "W" [1, 4]), may constitute triggers in respect to the areas of perceived tension or other types of reactions in the processed dialog segment with two (or multiple) speakers-participants. This case may be compared to multiple factors contributing to a creation of a particular state or situation.

Generated graphical representations of perceived word-topic relations and registered "Gravity" and "Evocative" words (signalized as "W" in previous research [1, 4]) and can be converted into sequences for their subsequent conversion into knowledge graphs or other forms of data for neural networks and Machine Learning applications [22, 23, 36, 38]. As described above, registered "Gravity" and "Evocative" words are appended as marked values with "&" in the respective tuples or triple tuples. In the sequences, the "&" indication is converted into a "CONTEXT" relation.

For example, a "No" answer (−2) preceded by "sanctions" as a perceived word topic accompanied with a perceived "Gravity" word (W)"dignity" (sanctions, −2, &dignity), is converted into the following sequences depicted in Fig. 4. If the perceived word-topic also constitutes a perceived "Gravity" or "Evocative" word (W), the "&" indication is converted into a "CONTEXT" relation with the same word (Fig. 4, ii).

Therefore, the existence of a "Gravity" or an "Evocative" word is signalized by the "Context" relation itself. There is no signalization of the word's additional content and/or interpretation (for example, "important" – for a "Gravity" word or "heartfelt" for an "Evocative" word), at least not in the current stage of the present research. This is because any additional content is may not be limited to a singular interpretation summarized by a particular expression-keyword.

As in the case of "Gravity" and "Evocative" words, words and word-topics perceived to trigger tension or other reactions ("W") can be depicted as sequences for their subsequent modelling into knowledge graphs or other forms of data with the "&" indication (in the respective tuples or triple tuples) converted into a "CONTEXT" relation. Figure 5 depicts two tension triggers from a speech segment with perceived tension.

We note that the interface of the interactive application for the generation of knowledge graphs is presented in Sect. 4 (Fig. 6).

(i) (sanctions, -2, &dignity):

sanctions ->NO -> SWITCH-> treaties
sanctions -> CONTEXT -> dignity

(ii) (country, people, 2, &people) ("Association")

country -> ASSOC-> people
people ->CONTEXT-> people

Fig. 4. Conversion of triple tuples and tuples with "Gravity" and "Evocative" words for the generation of knowledge graphs. The "Gravity" word "dignity" contributes to the "No" answer and subsequent topic switch (SWITCH).

(sanctions, -2, &dignity) (military confrontation, chemical weapons, 2, &justice):

TENSION {
sanctions ->NO -> SWITCH -> treaties ->GEN -> international commitment
sanctions -> CONTEXT -> dignity

military confrontation -> ASSOC-> chemical weapons
military confrontation -> CONTEXT -> justice
chemical weapons ->CONTEXT -> justice
} TENSION

Fig. 5. Triple tuples and tuples with perceptions of topic relations and "Gravity" and "Evocative" words in speech segments with registered tension. Conversion of the triple tuples and tuples for the generation of knowledge graphs.

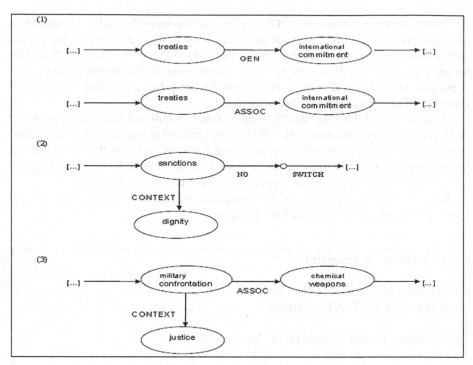

Fig. 6. Fragment of a Knowledge Graph from generated graphic representation with alternative "Association" (2) and "Generalization" (3) relations, "No" Answer (−2) and "Gravity" and "Evocative" words as "tension-triggers" (&), the latter signalized by the "Context" relation.

As presented in previous research [4, 5], multiple points of tension ("hot spots"- consisting of a question-answer pair or a statement-response pair or any other type of relation between speaker turns [4]) indicate a more argumentative than a collaborative interaction, even if speakers-participants display a calm and composed behavior. These points of tension ("hot spots") involving, among others, the registration of words and word-topics and the reactions they provoke, can contribute to the detection and identification of more subtle emotions, in the middle and outer zones of the Plutchik Wheel of Emotions [28]. For example, for subtle negative reactions in the Plutchik Wheel of Emotions, namely "Apprehension", "Annoyance", "Disapproval", "Contempt", "Aggressiveness" [28]. These emotions are usually too subtle to be easily extracted by sensor and/or speech signal data. However, such subtle emotions may play a crucial role in spoken interactions involving persuasion and negotiations, although they are not always easily detectable or "visible".

Points of possible tension and/or conflict between speakers-participants ("hot-spots") are identified by a set of criteria based on the Gricean Cooperative Principle [4, 5] and signalized in generated graphic representations of registered negotiations (or other type of spoken interaction concerning persuasion), with special emphasis on words and topics triggering tension and non-collaborative speaker-participant behavior. The detection of "hot spots" - points of tension implemented in previous research [4, 5], facilitates the detection of words and word-topics associated with Persuasion and/or Tension, according to the factor of perception, subjectivity, socio-cultural factors and the current state-of-affairs (summarized as the above-presented "Assoc-1" and "Assoc-2" types of information content).

3   Visibility and Processability for Paralinguistic Elements: Knowledge Graphs

The registered words include respective information from perceived paralinguistic elements. In previous research [7], the use of linguistic information with or without a link to paralinguistic features is proposed as a more reliable source of a speaker's attitude, behavior and intentions than stand-alone paralinguistic features. For example, for spoken information content with paralinguistic features depicting contradictory information, annotations such as "[! facial-expr: eye-roll]" and "[! gesture: clenched-fist]" were proposed [1, 6]. The Gricean Cooperative Principle is violated if the information conveyed is perceived as not complete (Violation of Quantity or Manner) or even contradicted by paralinguistic features (Violation of Quality) [14, 15].

Paralinguistic features may often contribute to the correct detection and identification of subtle emotions, complementing or intensifying the information content of the word or word-topic, however, they are not always reliable, especially if international speakers and/or an international public are concerned. Paralinguistic features constituting information that is not uttered is also problematic in Data Mining and Sentiment Analysis-Opinion Mining applications. These applications mostly rely on word groups, word sequences and/or sentiment lexica [19], including recent approaches with the use of neural networks [9, 17, 33], especially if Sentiment Analysis from videos (text, audio and video) is concerned. However, even if context dependent multimodal utterance features are extracted, as proposed in recent research [29], the semantic content of a spoken utterance may be either complemented or contradicted by a gesture, facial expression or movement.

As described in previous research [1, 4], the interactive annotation of paralinguistic features is proposed, depicting information complementing the information content of the spoken utterance (for example, "[+ facial-expr: eyebrow-raise]" and "[+ gesture: low-hand-raise]") or constituting "stand-alone" information [3, 6]. In the latter case, information was interactively annotated with the insertion of a separate message or response [Message/Response]. For example, the raising of eyebrows with the interpretation "I am surprised" [and / but this surprises me] [3, 6] may be indicated either as [I am surprised], as a pointer to information content or as [Message /Response: I am surprised] (a), as a substitute of spoken information, a "stand-alone" paralinguistic feature [1]. The alternative interpretations of the paralinguistic feature (namely, "I am listening very carefully" (b), "What I am saying is important"(c) or "I have no intention of doing otherwise" (d)) [3, 6] could be indicated with the annotations "[I am listening], [Please pay attention], [No] and [Message/Response: I am listening], [Message/Response: Please pay attention], [Message /Response: No]" respectively.

The insertion of the respective type of annotation depended on whether paralinguistic feature constitute "Pointer" (A) or "Stand-Alone" (B) paralinguistic features, according to the parameters of the language(s) and the speaker(s) concerned [4].

As in the case of perceived "Gravity" and "Evocative" words and tension-triggers ("W"), paralinguistic elements can be similarly annotated as appended messages and processed with a "CONTEXT" relation for their subsequent modelling into knowledge graphs for neural networks and Machine Learning applications [22, 23, 36, 38].

We note that during the conversion process, appended messages linked to the "W" annotation are signalized with the "&&" indication in the respective tuples or triple tuples and subsequently converted into a "CONTEXT" relation.

The "CONTEXT" relation connects the chosen word-topic from the speech segment with a word-expression emphasizing / complementing the spoken content such as "indeed" or respective word summarizing the message.

For example, for the paralinguistic element [eyebrow-raise], possible options are: word-topic -> CONTEXT -> indeed, word-topic -> CONTEXT - > surprised, word-topic -> CONTEXT -> important, or word-topic -> CONTEXT -> "No".

Figure 7 depicts examples of registered paralinguistic elements and their respective messages from speech segments.

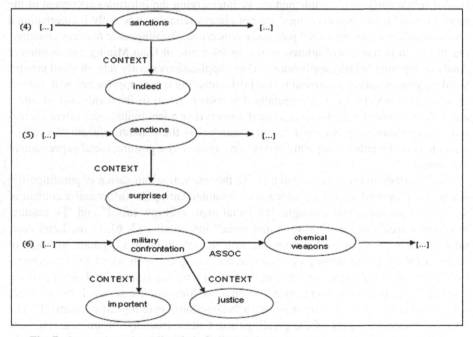

Fig. 7. Integration of paralinguistic features information content in knowledge graphs.

3.1 Contradictory Information in Paralinguistic Features

For paralinguistic features depicting contradictory information to the information content of the spoken utterance, the additional signalization of "!" was proposed in previous research [1, 4] for example, "[! facial-expr: eye-roll]" and "[! gesture: clenched-fist]" [1, 4]. In this case, the "CONTEXT" relation connects the chosen word-topic from the speech segment with a word-expression contradicting the spoken content with the expression "not really" as a special indication (Fig. 8).

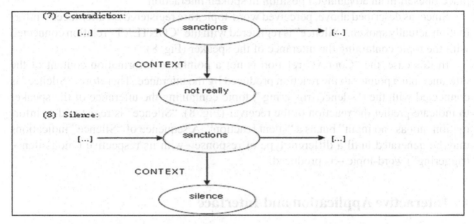

Fig. 8. Integration of paralinguistic features information content in knowledge graphs.

3.2 "Silence" in Spoken Mandarin Chinese: Knowledge Graphs

The above-described registration of paralinguistic features enabling their conversion into knowledge graphs or other models allows the indication and processing of two additional typical features of Spoken Mandarin Chinese, namely Silence as an answer and an overall passive role in spoken interaction (4, Silence, 5. Passive role in Dialog) [12]. For Mandarin Chinese native speakers, Silence is an effective way to show the modest behavior. This principle also applies to the tendency to seldom take the role of the dialog pace-setter and playing a more passive role (5, Passive role in Dialog). Based on Confucianism, the modesty can be shown by keeping silence. Furthermore, it is considered that common assumed knowledge is seldom to blame and speaking aloud can be a signal of weakness and vulnerability [12]. This is one of the reasons why it is common for Chinese native speakers to seldom take the role of dialogue pace-setter in the international communication [12].

In other words, "Silence" sometimes is considered to be a form of nonverbal communication in China. Both intentional and unintentional silence are usually used as an effective strategy to help people out of an uncomfortable situation and interaction causing anxiety or embarrassment. Under the influence of Confucian ideas, native Chinese speakers are encouraged to keep intentional or "active" silence especially when the speaker-participant knows more than the other speakers-participants. This behavior is intended to be considerate and/or respectful of the other party/parties. Specifically, the speaker-participant must conceal one's better knowledge of a matter and avoid embarrassing the other party or parties concerned. However, native Chinese speakers are still encouraged to keep unintentional or passive silence also in the case in which the speaker-participant does not consider him/herself not as smart and wise as the other party/parties. It is believed that listening carefully will help a speaker-participant to have access to more information from the speakers and plan future interactions accordingly. In other words, "Silence", remains a traditional means with which a speaker-participant may place oneself in an advantaged position in spoken interaction.

Since, as described above, perceived word-topics are registered on utterances – information actually spoken, "Silence" is registered with the "CONTEXT" relation connected with the topic containing the utterance of the speaker (Fig. 8).

In this case, the "Context" relation is not a pointer to information content of the utterance but a pointer to the reaction produced by the utterance. Therefore, "Silence" is connected with the ("silence triggering") topic containing the utterance of the speaker to indicate/predict the reaction of the receiver (Fig. 8). "Silence" is registered as information, not as "no input" but as a "silent reaction". A sequence of "Silence" indications may be generated until a different type of response –with its respective ("non-silence triggering") word-topic – is produced.

4   Interactive Application and Interface

The interactive application presented and analyzed above is depicted in Fig. 9 and Fig. 10. The application generates the knowledge graphs (Fig. 9) with the "Create Graph" (black) button of the interface (Fig. 10).

In the interface, the user choses the perceived relation between word-topics with the "Topic Relation" button and signalizes "Gravity", "Evocative" words and paralinguistic elements with the respective buttons "Tension-Emotion Trigger (W) and "Paralinguistic Info". With the "Create Graph" button of the interface, the knowledge graphs are generated (Fig. 10).

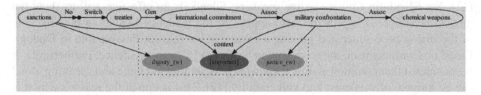

Fig. 9. Generated knowledge graph by the implemented application and interface.

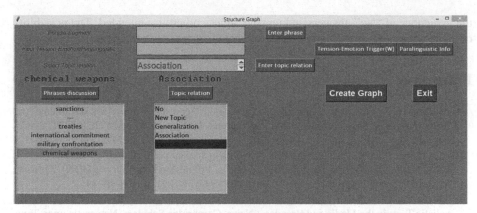

Fig. 10. Overview of interface of the implemented application.

5 Conclusions and Further Research

The present approach and interactive application target to the processing and direct generation and use of information not uttered, converting it into "visible" and processable information. This subtle information not uttered includes overall speaker behavior and paralinguistic elements, allowing the monitoring of fairness in interviews and discussions in spoken political and journalistic texts, contributing both to the detection and the avoidance of Cognitive Bias (detecting Lexical Bias and avoiding Confidence Bias). The present approach also targets to the visibility and processability of perceived information as well as varieties of subjective, perceived information according to socio-cultural factors and the current state-of-affairs.

The annotated relations between words and their topics [1, 2] can be converted into knowledge graphs [22, 23, 36, 38], based on the values of the triple tuples (triplets) and tuples (and respective distances). As described in recent studies [22, 23, 36, 38], knowledge graphs may be converted into vectors or other forms of data for neural networks and Machine Learning applications. The created knowledge graphs may depict multiple/alternative variations of possible associations and other relations between words and their topics.

The generated data allows the integration in Natural Language Processing (NLP) applications, for example, in the enrichment of "Bag-of-Words" approaches in Sentiment Analysis and their subsequent integration in training data for statistical models and neural networks. The perception, registration and visualization of the above presented categories of "invisible" information not uttered and their integration in training data contributes to refining various Natural Language Processing (NLP) tasks such as Sentiment Analysis and Opinion Mining. The processed information may serve as (initial) training and test sets or for Speaker (User) behavior and expectations in Human-Computer Interaction and even in special types of Human-Robot Interaction systems.

The processed information and generated data may also serve for directing the user for creating a simulation of interaction. For example, for training-simulation providing the user with directions for what words and word-topics to avoid ("what not to say") for the avoidance of "No" answers and tension, unless otherwise intended. The possibility of these types of implementations are a subject of further investigation.

References

1. Alexandris, C., Floros, V., Mourouzidis, D.: Graphic representations of spoken interactions from journalistic data: persuasion and negotiations. In: Kurosu, M. (ed.) HCII 2021. LNCS, vol. 12764, pp. 3–17. Springer, Cham (2021). https://doi.org/10.1007/978-3-030-78468-3_1
2. Alexandris, C.: Registering the impact of words in spoken political and journalistic texts. J. Hum. Lang. Rights Secur. 26–48 (2021). Peoples Friendship University (RUDN), Moscow, Russian Federation. https://doi.org/10.22363/2713-0614-2021-1-1-26-48
3. Alexandris, C.: Issues in Multilingual Information Processing of Spoken Political and Journalistic Texts in the Media and Broadcast News, Cambridge Scholars, Newcastle upon Tyne, UK (2020)
4. Alexandris, C., Mourouzidis, D., Floros, V.: Generating graphic representations of spoken interactions revisited: the tension factor and information not uttered in journalistic data. In: Kurosu, M. (ed.) HCII 2020. LNCS, vol. 12181, pp. 523–537. Springer, Cham (2020). https://doi.org/10.1007/978-3-030-49059-1_39
5. Alexandris, C.: Evaluating cognitive bias in two-party and multi-party spoken interactions. In: Proceedings of Interpretable AI for Well-Being: Understanding Cognitive Bias and Social Embeddedness (IAW 2019) in Conjunction with AAAI Spring Symposium (SS-19-03), Stanford University, Palo Alto, CA. http://ceur-ws.org/Vol-2448
6. Alexandris, C.: Visualizing pragmatic features in spoken interaction: intentions, behavior and evaluation. In: Proceedings of the 1st International Conference on Linguistics Research on the Era of Artificial Intelligence – LREAI, Dalian, 25–27 October 2019. Dalian Maritime University (2019)
7. Alexandris, C.: Measuring cognitive bias in Spoken interaction and conversation: generating visual representations. In: Beyond Machine Intelligence: Understanding Cognitive Bias and Humanity for Well-Being AI Papers from the AAAI Spring Symposium, Stanford University, Technical report SS-18-03, pp. 204–206. AAAI Press, Palo Alto (2018)
8. Alexandris, C.: English, German and the international "semi-professional" translator: a morphological approach to implied connotative features. J. Lang. Transl. 11(2), 7–46 (2010). Sejong University, Korea
9. Arockiaraj, C.M.: Applications of neural networks in data mining. Int. J. Eng. Sci. 3(1), 8–11 (2013)
10. Austin, J.L.: How to Do Things with Words, 2nd edn. University Press, Oxford Paperbacks, Oxford (1976). Urmson, J.O., Sbisà, M. (eds.) (1962)
11. Carlson, L., Marcu, D., Okurowski, M.E.: Building a discourse-tagged corpus in the framework of rhetorical structure theory. In: Proceedings of the 2nd SIGDIAL Workshop on Discourse and Dialogue, Eurospeech 2001, Denmark, September 2001
12. Du, J., Alexandris, C., Mourouzidis, D., Floros, V., Iliakis, A.: Controlling interaction in multilingual conversation revisited: a perspective for services and interviews in Mandarin Chinese. In: Kurosu, M. (ed.) HCI 2017. LNCS, vol. 10271, pp. 573–583. Springer, Cham (2017). https://doi.org/10.1007/978-3-319-58071-5_43
13. Evans, N.J., Park, D.: Rethinking the persuasion knowledge model: schematic antecedents and associative outcomes of persuasion knowledge activation for covert advertising. J. Curr. Issues Res. Advert. 36(2), 157–176 (2015). https://doi.org/10.1080/10641734.2015.1023873
14. Grice, H.P.: Studies in the Way of Words. Harvard University Press, Cambridge (1989)

15. Grice, H.P.: Logic and conversation. In: Cole, P., Morgan, J. (eds.) Syntax and Semantics, vol. 3. Academic Press, New York (1975)

16. Hatim, B.: Communication Across Cultures: Translation Theory and Contrastive Text Linguistics. University of Exeter Press, Exeter (1997)

17. Hedderich, M.A., Klakow, D.: Training a neural network in a low-resource setting on automatically annotated noisy data. In: Proceedings of the Workshop on Deep Learning Approaches for Low-Resource NLP, Melbourne, Australia, pp. 12–18. Association for Computational Linguistics-ACL (2018)

18. Hilbert, M.: Toward a synthesis of cognitive biases: how noisy information processing can bias human decision making. Psychol. Bull. **138**(2), 211–237 (2012)

19. Liu, B.: Sentiment Analysis and Opinion Mining. Morgan & Claypool, San Rafael (2012)

20. Ma, J.: A comparative analysis of the ambiguity resolution of two English-Chinese MT approaches: RBMT and SMT. Dalian Univ. Technol. J. **31**(3), 114–119 (2010)

21. Marcu, D.: Discourse trees are good indicators of importance in text. In: Mani, I., Maybury, M. (eds.) Advances in Automatic Text Summarization, pp. 123–136. The MIT Press, Cambridge (1999)

22. Mittal, S., Joshi, A., Finin, T.: Thinking, Fast and Slow: Combining Vector Spaces and Knowledge Graphs. arXiv:1708.03310v2 [cs.AI] (2017)

23. Mountantonakis, M., Tzitzikas, Y.: Knowledge graph embeddings over hundreds of linked datasets. In: Garoufallou, E., Fallucchi, F., William De Luca, E. (eds.) MTSR 2019. CCIS, vol. 1057, pp. 150–162. Springer, Cham (2019). https://doi.org/10.1007/978-3-030-36599-8_13

24. Mourouzidis, D., Floros, V., Alexandris, C.: Generating graphic representations of spoken interactions from journalistic data. In: Kurosu, M. (ed.) HCII 2019. LNCS, vol. 11566, pp. 559–570. Springer, Cham (2019). https://doi.org/10.1007/978-3-030-22646-6_42

25. Nass, C., Brave, S.: Wired for Speech: How Voice Activates and Advances the Human-Computer Relationship. The MIT Press, Cambridge (2005)

26. Paltridge, B.: Discourse Analysis: An Introduction. Bloomsbury Publishing, London (2012)

27. Pan, Y.: Politeness in Chinese face-to-face interaction. In: Advances in Discourse Processes Series, vol. 67. Ablex Publishing Corporation, Stamford (2000)

28. Plutchik, R.: A psychoevolutionary theory of emotions. Soc. Sci. Inf. **21**, 529–553 (1982). https://doi.org/10.1177/053901882021004003

29. Poria, S., Cambria, E., Hazarika, D., Mazumder, N., Zadeh, A., Morency, L.-P.: Context-dependent sentiment analysis in user-generated videos. In: Proceedings of the 55th Annual Meeting of the Association for Computational Linguistics, Vancouver, Canada, 30 July–4 August 2017, pp. 873–888. Association for Computational Linguistics – ACL (2017). https://doi.org/10.18653/v1/P17-1081

30. Rocklage, M.D., Rucker, D.D., Nordgren, L.F.: Psychol. Sci. **29**(5), 749–760 (2018). https://doi.org/10.1177/0956797617744797

31. Sacks, H., Schegloff, E.A., Jefferson, G.: A simplest systematics for the organization of turn-taking for conversation. Language **50**, 696–735 (1974)

32. Searle, J.R.: Speech Acts: An Essay in the Philosophy of Language. Cambridge University Press, Cambridge (1969)

33. Shah, K., Kopru, S., Ruvini, J.-D.: Neural network based extreme classification and similarity models for product matching. In: Proceedings of NAACL-HLT 2018, New Orleans, Louisiana, 1–6 June 2018, pp. 8–15. Association for Computational Linguistics-ACL (2018)

34. Skonk, K.: 5 Types of Negotiation Skills, Program on Negotiation Daily Blog. Harvard Law School, 14th May 2020. https://www.pon.harvard.edu/daily/negotiation-skills-daily/types-of-negotiation-skills/. Accessed 11 Nov 2020

35. Stede, M., Taboada, M., Das, D.: Annotation Guidelines for Rhetorical Structure. Manuscript. University of Potsdam and Simon Fraser University, March 2017

36. Tran, H.N., Takashu, A.: Analyzing knowledge graph embedding methods from a multi-embedding interaction perspective. In: Proceedings of the 1st International Workshop on Data Science for Industry 4.0 (DSI4) at EDBT/ICDT 2019 Joint Conference (2019). https://arxiv.org/abs/1903.11406

37. Trofimova, I.: Observer bias: an interaction of temperament traits with biases in the semantic perception of lexical material. PloS ONE 9(1), e85677 (2014)

38. Wang, M., Qiu, L.: A survey on knowledge graph embeddings for link prediction. Symmetry 13, 485 (2021). https://doi.org/10.3390/sym13030485

39. Wardhaugh, R.: An Introduction to Sociolinguistics, 2nd edn. Blackwell, Oxford (1992)

40. Williams, J.D., Asadi, K., Zweig, G.: Hybrid code networks: practical and efficient end-to-end dialog control with supervised and reinforcement learning. In: Proceedings of the 55th Annual Meeting of the Association for Computational Linguistics, Vancouver, Canada, 30 July–4 August 2017, pp. 665–677. Association for Computational Linguistics (ACL) (2017)

41. Wilson, M., Wilson, T.P.: An oscillator model of the timing of turn taking. Psychonomic Bull. Rev. 12(6), 957–968 (2005)

42. Yu, Z., Yu, Z., Aoyama, H., Ozeki, M., Nakamura, Y.: Capture, recognition, and visualization of human semantic interactions in meetings. In: Proceedings of PerCom, Mannheim, Germany (2010)

43. Zeldes, A.: rstWeb - a browser-based annotation interface for rhetorical structure theory and discourse relations. In: Proceedings of NAACL-HLT 2016 System Demonstrations, San Diego, CA, pp. 1–5 (2016). http://aclweb.org/anthology/N/N16/N16-3001.pdf

Preliminary Evidence of Sexual Bias in Voice over Internet Protocol Audio Compression

Matthew L. Bolton(✉)

University of Virginia, Charlottesville, VA 22903, USA
mlb4b@virginia.edu

Abstract. Voice over internet protocol (VoIP) has become critical to professional communication through its use in office phone systems and video teleconferencing. In this environment, it is critical that VoIP represent everybody's voices with equal fidelity. This will allow all demographics to have the opportunity for equal participation. This research investigated whether there was evidence of sexism in the way VoIP compresses vocal data. This was accomplished by measuring the similarity of a large database of vocal samples between their original and compressed forms and statistically comparing their differences between females and males. Multiple measure showed significant evidence of reduced audio quality for female voices compared to male voices. We discuss these results and propose future research.

Keywords: Access to on-line communities and eServices · Universal access and accessibility requirements · Voice communication · Audio compression

1 Introduction

Even before the COVID-19 pandemic, voice over internet protocol (VoIP) was important for people conducting business. This is because it allows voice communication (with or without video) to occur with nearly anybody in the world over the internet. Since the COVID-19 outbreak and the associated social distancing, VoIP has become critical for enabling remote operations. Even when this situation resolves, VoIP will remain an integral part of modern work. It is thus critical that the understandability and quality of VoIP presented speech be equal for all demographics of people. However, in my own subjective experience using VoIP to communicate with my wife, students, and colleagues, I have had more trouble understanding female voices (for people I had no trouble understanding in person) over VoIP than male voices.

This research sought to be a preliminary investigation into whether there is evidence of sexist performance in VoIP communication. Below, we present background for understanding the presented approach, the study's scientific objectives, methods, and results. Ultimately, findings are discussed and future research directions are identified.

M. Kurosu (Ed.): HCII 2022, LNCS 13303, pp. 227–237, 2022.
https://doi.org/10.1007/978-3-031-05409-9_17

2   Background

To the best of my knowledge, no study has investigated whether there are differences in how VoIP handles female and male voices. Thus, no literature on this subject is reviewed. However, an understanding of VoIP and "lossy" audio codec (compression decompression) technology is topical to the research. These are discussed below.

In VoIP, a voice is processed by a microphone, encoded into a digital format, transmitted over the internet to a recipient device, and decoded and played on a speaker. Audio codecs are critical to the performance of VoIP's encoding process. Audio codecs constitute methods for compressing audio files so that they can be transmitted efficiently. While lossless codec's exist (codecs that loose no audio data), most VoIP system codecs are lossy. That is, they eliminate audio data to reduce the amount of information that needs to be transmitted. The way that codecs do this can range from using filtering techniques to more sophisticated approaches that use psychoacoustics to eliminate frequencies that are simultaneously masked (rendered inaudible) by other concurrent sounds due to limitations of the human sensory system [1]. Most codecs can also support varying bitrates, a measure of how many bits are used to represent a second of audio data. The lower the bitrate, the smaller the file. When used in many modern VoIP systems [5], the bandwidth or ping of the connection will be used to dynamically vary the bitrate to ensure the audio is delivered continuously.

There are a number of different codecs used in VoIP such as G.711, G.719, OPUS, G.722, G.729 and AMR. For the purpose of this work, I focus on OPUS [17]. This is because OPUS is the audio codec used in a number of popular VoIP applications including ZOOM, Skype, Microsoft Teams, and WhatsApp. It is also extremely flexible as it is low latency, offers sophisticated lossy audio compression specifically tuned for speech, and can use bitrates ranging from 6 to 510 kbps that can be varied based on bandwidth availability [5,17].

3   Objective

This work sought to determine if there was evidence of sexism in VoIP. To accomplish this we made use of an online database of English speaking for males and females with varying ages and native languages. These were each processed in accordance with minimal quality settings using the OPUS audio codec. These settings were used because they would constitute the largest possible distortion of the original signal. The *original* and resulting *compressed* files were compared across a number of standard auditory similarity measures. These measures were then statistically compared between male and female voices to understand which was the most distorted or degraded and identify the nature of the change.

4 Methods

4.1 Data and Apparatus

The data used in this experiment constituted the full set of audio samples (files) from the Speech Accent Archive [19,20]. This is a resource available online through a Creative Commons License. The archive contains 2,933 separate audio files (when pruned for blank entries and computer generated voices), where each is a speech sample from a unique person. The samples were taken from people of different sexes, ages, and language backgrounds. The sample ultimately included 1494 females and 1439 males with an age range of [6] with a median of 27. In every audio sample, the speaker recites the same paragraph in English:

> Please call Stella. Ask her to bring these things with her from the store: Six spoons of fresh snow peas, five thick slabs of blue cheese, and maybe a snack for her brother Bob. We also need a small plastic snake and a big toy frog for the kids. She can scoop these things into three red bags, and we will go meet her Wednesday at the train station.

All the samples were encoded in monaural MP3 with a 48,000 Hz sample rate and 256 kbps bitrate. Note that MP3 is itself a lossy audio codec. However, the sample rate and bitrate of these files are well above thresholds that would influence audio quality perception in normal listeners.

To simulate the effect of the audio being broadcast over VoIP using a slow internet connection, each *original* MP3 was *compressed* using the OPUS audio codec using the lowest possible settings: a constant bitrate of 6 kbps. The option for optimizing for speech was also selected.

4.2 Independent Variables

In all the presented analyses, *Sex*, with Female and Male levels, was the independent variable.

4.3 Dependent Measures

In this research, metrics were selected that would measure the similarity between an individual's *original* and *compressed* audio samples. There are many metrics for accomplishing this [12]. In this work, ten metrics were selected that appeared to have the most precedent in the literature. All are described below along with how they were computed.

Cross Correlation. The cross correlation was a measure of the correlation of raw waveform data of *original* and *compressed*. This was computed as the value returned for zero lag by MATLAB's xcorr function. The higher the produced correlation the more similar *original* is to *compressed*.

Signal-to-Noise Ratio (in dB). Signal-to-noise ratio was computed with MATLAB's snr function: the ratio of the power of *compressed* ("signal") to that of *original* ("noise") in dB. The lower the value, the more power lost in *compressed*.

Euclidian Distance. The Euclidian distance between *original* and *compressed* was computed as the norm (or vector magnitude) of the vector formed by *original* − *compressed*. This was calculated using MATLAB's norm function. The smaller the distance, the more similar the audio samples.

Mean Coherence. Mean coherence was computed as the average of the magnitude-squared coherence of *original* and *compressed* with a window size of 25 ms, an overlap of 12.5 ms, and 256 sample points, all parameters for the required Fourier transform. These parameters were selected because they are the standard for analyzing speech audio data [11]. This was computed as the average of the vector returned by MATLAB's mscohere function. The higher the coherence, the more similar the two audio signals.

Compression Error Rate. The compression error rate was introduced by Siegert et al. [13] as a measure for quantifying data loss from lossy audio codecs. This was computed using the formulation from [13] as the absolute error obtained by comparing the spectrograms of *original* and *compressed*, using the standard Fourier transform parameters defined above. The lower the error rate, the more similar the audio samples.

Spectral Entropy Correlation. Spectrally entropy is a measure of a signal's irregularity [8]. Thus, spectral entropy correlation represents a measure of the correspondence between the signal irregularities of *original* and *compressed*. This was computed as the correlation between the vectors returned by MATLAB's pentropy function. The higher the correlation, the more similar the samples.

Structural Similarity. Structural similarity is commonly used to measure the similarity between original on compressed images [18]. However, it can also be used for similar purposes for audio [3,7]. Structural similarly was computed here using MATLAB's ssim function. The higher the structural similarity score, the more similar the two audio signals.

Objective Difference Grade. The objective different grade (ODG) is meant as an objective measure of perceived audio quality. It is computed in accordance with the ITU BS.1387-1. (PEAQ) algorithm [15]. This was designed to simulate the human ear and incorporate psychophysical concepts to produce a single metric of perceived audio quality when comparing an original signal to a degraded or compressed one. This metric ranges from 0 (imperceptible difference) to −4 (annoying). This metric, and the algorithm for computing it, are an international standard and are thus used in a number of scientific studies and the development of many audio technologies. In this work, we used the MATLAB ODG implementation called PQevalAudio provided by Kabal [6].

Centroid Difference (in Hz). The spectral centroid is a measure for characterizing the mean or average of a signal's frequencies [12]. It has been experimentally shown to have a robust relationship with the perceived brightness of sounds [4]. It is ultimately calculated as the weighted average of a signal's frequencies based on a Fourier transform [12]. In this work, the centroid difference is calculated as the spectral centroid of *original* minus the spectral centroid of *compressed*, both computed using MATLAB's spectralCentroid function with the Fourier transform parameters from above. Thus, centroid difference represents a measure of how the frequency or perceived brightness of the sound changed when the sound was compressed. The larger the magnitude of the centroid difference, the more of a shift occurred. A positive results means *compressed* is less bright (favors lower frequencies) than *original*. A negative results means *compressed* is brighter (favors high frequencies) than *original*.

Spread Difference (in Hz). The spectral spread of a sound is a measure of the variance of a signal's frequencies, the "spread" of the sound around its spectral centroid [12]. Noisy sounds usually exhibit a large spectral spread. Tonal sounds usually have lower spectral spreads. In this research, the spread difference is calculated as the spectral spread of *original* minus the spectral spread of *compressed*, where spreads are computed with MATLAB's spectralSpread function with the Fourier transform parameters from above. The larger the spread difference, the more spectral variation is lost. A positive value implies that *compressed* has less variance than *original*. A negative value implies the opposite.

4.4 Data Analysis

A two-sample Mann-Whitney U Test was used to compare differences between each of the computed measures for samples taken from female and male speakers. This nonparametric test was used due to the failure of the dependent measures to show evidence of normal distribution using Anderson Darling tests. A significance level of 0.05 was used. However, to compensate for multiple tests (one for all ten dependent measures), we employed a Bonferoni correction that lowered the significance level to $0.05/10 = 0.005$.

5 Results

Results (Table 1) revealed significant differences between females and males for signal-to-noise ratio, Euclidian distance, compression error rate, spectral entropy correlation, objective difference grade, and spread difference.

Table 1. Results comparing females and males for each dependent measure

Measure	M_{Females}	M_{Males}	$U_{1494,1439}$	z	p	r
Cross correlation	0.791	0.783	1032591.0	−1.850	0.065	0.034
Signal-to-noise ratio (dB)	−1.373	−1.718	653834.0	−18.400	< 0.001 *	0.340
Euclidian distance	48.843	45.958	930913.0	−6.280	< 0.001 *	0.116
Mean coherence	0.195	0.191	1074740.5	−0.008	0.993	< 0.001
Compression error rate	0.195	0.183	989949.0	−3.710	< 0.001 *	0.069
Spectral entropy correlation	0.784	0.827	1270719.0	8.540	< 0.001 *	−0.158
Structural similarity	0.699	0.697	1048410.0	−1.160	0.247	0.021
Objective difference grade	−3.913	−3.913	1198438.5	6.050	< 0.001 *	−0.112
Centroid difference (Hz)	122.770	99.207	1013949.0	−2.660	0.008	0.049
Spread difference (Hz)	579.573	435.738	957807.0	−5.110	< 0.001 *	0.094

Note. M_{Females} and M_{Males} represent the median values for females and males respectively for each measure. U is the Mann-Whitney U test statistics with sample sizes $n_{\text{Female}} = 1494$ and $n_{\text{Male}} = 1439$. z is the associated z-score test statistic. p is the test's p-value. A p-value is labeled with a * if it was significant at a 0.005 level. r, rank-biserial correlation [2], is the effect size.

A closer comparison of the results (Fig. 1) revealed that, for all but signal-to-noise ratio (where the higher value observed for females indicates more correspondence between *original* and *compressed*), the *compressed* sound resulted in more of a change for female voices than for males. For female samples, there was a significantly larger Euclidian distance between *original* and *compressed*, a significantly larger compression error rate, a significantly lower spectral entropy correlation, a significantly lower objective difference grade, and a significantly higher spread difference. It should be noted that objective difference grade (Fig. 1(E)) showed very little variance in the results: [−3.9132, −3.837] for females and [−3.9132, −3.8275] for males. In fact, 1729 of the computations (58.95%) exhibited the minimum value of −3.9132.

6   Discussion

The results show clear evidence of bias in the OPUS VoIP audio codec at the low bitrate used in the analysis. Given that five of the six significant measures showed a bias that favored male over female voices, this suggest that the OPUS codec is likely, unintentionally, sexist towards women. This is a potentially serious issue given that OPUS is used as the primary audio codec of ZOOM, Skype, Microsoft Teams, WhatsApp, Playstation Network, and many VoIP phone service vendors and it may be limiting women's ability to communicate.

A possible explanation for the observed differences is illustrated in Fig. 2. This compares the spectrum of an *original* and *compressed* pair for a female speaker. While there are clear differences, the biggest occurs above 4,500 Hz. Specifically, the *compressed* sample contains no frequencies greater than this value, while the *original* clearly does. This suggests that OPUS (at least with the selected parameters) uses a low pass filter to eliminate audio data. Given that women tend to have higher pitched voices than men [16], this would likely impact females more

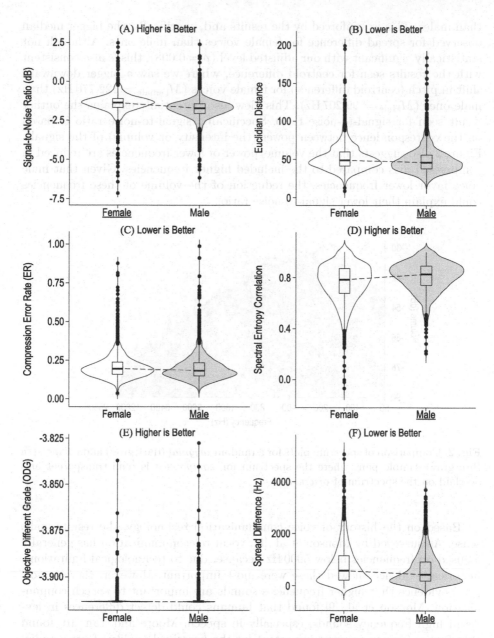

Fig. 1. Violin plots for dependent measures that showed significant differences between Females and Males. Each entry contains a box and whisker plot surround by kernel density plots. The box depicts the interquartile range (IQR) bisected horizontally by a line at the median (M); whiskers represent the extremum within 1.5 of the IQR; outliers (filled dots) are points outside of 1.5 of the IQR. A dotted line between plot medians illustrates changes between the values between levels. Underlined x-axis labels indicate which category (Female or Male) saw better median performance.

than males. This is reinforced by the results and, specifically, the bigger median observed for spread difference for female voices than male ones. Although not statistically significant with our adjusted level ($p = 0.008$), this is also consistent with the results seen for centroid difference, where we saw a bigger downward shift in pitch (centroid difference) for female voices ($M_{\text{Female}} = 122.770\,\text{Hz}$) than male ones ($M_{\text{Male}} = 99.207\,\text{Hz}$). This view also potentially explains the outlier result seen for signal-to-noise ratio. Specifically, signal-to-noise ratio is based on the correspondence between power (the intensity or volume) of the signals. Figure 2 also suggests that the volume/power of lower frequencies are reduced in compressed files compared to the included higher frequencies. Given that male voice favor lower frequencies, the reduction of the volume of these frequencies could explain their lower signal-to-noise ratio.

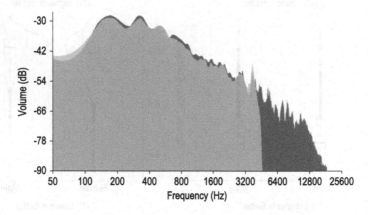

Fig. 2. Comparison of spectrum plots for a random *original* (dark gray) and *compressed* (lite gray) sample pair, where the spectrum for *compressed* is semi-transparent and overlaid on the spectrum of *original*.

Based on the history of voice communication technology, the results make sense. As surveyed by Monson et al. [9], vocal telecommunication has generally focused on frequencies below 5000 Hz because, due to technological limitations, historical evidence showed these were most important. However, there is now good evidence that higher frequencies sounds are important to speech communication. Monson et al. [9] found that humans could detect differences in levels in high frequency sounds, especially in speech. Moore and Tan [10] found that higher frequencies were important for the perceived quality of voice audio. Finally, Snow [14] found significant increases in speech discrimination when low pass filter cutoffs were increased. This was especially true for female voices, which required higher cutoffs (well above 5000 Hz) for comparable discrimination rates with male voices. All of this provides more evidence that the loss of higher frequencies in VoIP is disadvantageous to effective and natural communication for women.

The effect sizes observed in the results are small. However, the above discussion shows that even these small difference may impact an individual's ability to communicate. Beyond this, the scale at which VoIP technology like OPUS is used suggests that, as marginal as individual impacts could be, there is very likely an aggregate detrimental impact on female users.

The results presented here are preliminary. There are many avenues for future investigation. These are discussed below.

6.1 Objective Difference Grade

The extremely small range of values obtained for the objective difference grade measure suggest that the OPUS codec is specifically designed to achieve specific levels of objective difference grade performance. Thus, even though significant difference were observed between male and female voices, there was not a practically significant difference between median scores. This suggests that the objective difference grade may not be the most appropriate metric for determining how to scale speech. Future work should investigate if there are other measure that would better suited for understand the quality of speech signals while accounting for the sex of the speaker.

6.2 Other Settings, Codecs, and VoIP Considerations

The analysis presented here is far from complete. The OPUS codec offers bitrates all the way up to 512 kbps, which will likely reduce differences between signals significantly. Additionally, as discussed earlier, there are other common codecs used in VoIP applications, each with their own variable settings. Beyond this, there may be other factors that could impact speech comprehension and quality in VoIP such as the rate of packets being dropped and the amount of information loss this constitutes in the audio signal. Future work should investigate to what extent the biases reported here manifest with other settings, codecs, and VoIP considerations.

6.3 Additional Voice Considerations

Beyond sex, there are other factors that could influence how humans use different frequencies in voice communications. This could suggest that their may be biases against people with different accents or communicating in different languages. This should be explored in future efforts.

6.4 Experimental Validation

While the results presented here are compelling and there is literature suggesting significant real world impact, the magnitude of this impact is not entirely clear. Thus, future work should conduct an experiment with human subjects to validate our results and assess real word effects.

References

1. Bosi, M., Goldberg, R.E.: Introduction to Digital Audio Coding and Standards. Springer, Heidelberg (2012)
2. Cureton, E.E.: Rank-biserial correlation. Psychometrika **21**(3), 287–290 (1956)
3. Gan, C., Wang, X., Zhu, M., Yu, X.: Audio quality evaluation using frequency structural similarity measure. In: IET International Communication Conference on Wireless Mobile and Computing (CCWMC 2011), pp. 299–303. IET (2011). https://doi.org/10.1049/cp.2011.0896
4. Grey, J.M., Gordon, J.W.: Perceptual effects of spectral modifications on musical timbres. J. Acoust. Soc. Am. **63**(5), 1493–1500 (1978)
5. Han, Y., Magoni, D., McDonagh, P., Murphy, L.: Determination of bit-rate adaptation thresholds for the OPUS codec for VoIP services. In: 2014 IEEE Symposium on Computers and Communications (ISCC), pp. 1–7. IEEE (2014)
6. Kabal, P.: An examination and interpretation of ITU-R BS. 1387: perceptual evaluation of audio quality. Technical report, Telecommunications and Signal Processing Laboratory, McGill University, Montreal (2002)
7. Kandadai, S., Hardin, J., Creusere, C.D.: Audio quality assessment using the mean structural similarity measure. In: 2008 IEEE International Conference on Acoustics, Speech and Signal Processing, pp. 221–224. IEEE (2008)
8. Llanos, F., Alexander, J.M., Stilp, C.E., Kluender, K.R.: Power spectral entropy as an information-theoretic correlate of manner of articulation in American English. J. Acoust. Soc. Am. **141**(2), EL127–EL133 (2017)
9. Monson, B.B., Hunter, E.J., Lotto, A.J., Story, B.H.: The perceptual significance of high-frequency energy in the human voice. Front. Psychol. **5**(587) (2014). 11 pages
10. Moore, B.C., Tan, C.T.: Perceived naturalness of spectrally distorted speech and music. J. Acoust. Soc. Am. **114**(1), 408–419 (2003)
11. Paliwal, K.K., Lyons, J.G., Wójcicki, K.K.: Preference for 20–40 ms window duration in speech analysis. In: 2010 4th International Conference on Signal Processing and Communication Systems, pp. 1–4. IEEE (2010)
12. Peeters, G.: A large set of audio features for sound description (similarity and classification) in the CUIDADO project. Technical report 23/04/04, Ircam, Analysis/Synthesis Team, Paris (2004)
13. Siegert, I., Lotz, A.F., Duong, L.L., Wendemuth, A.: Measuring the impact of audio compression on the spectral quality of speech data. In: Jokisch, O. (ed.) Elektronische Sprachsignalverarbeitung (ESSV 2016). Proceedings of the 27th ESSV Conference (Studientexte zur Sprachkommunikation, vol. 81), pp. 229–236. TUDpress, Dresden (2016)
14. Snow, W.B.: Audible frequency ranges of music, speech and noise. Bell Syst. Tech. J. **10**(4), 616–627 (1931)
15. Thiede, T., et al.: PEAQ-the ITU standard for objective measurement of perceived audio quality. J. Audio Eng. Soc. **48**(1/2), 3–29 (2000)
16. Titze, I.R.: Physiologic and acoustic differences between male and female voices. J. Acoust. Soc. Am. **85**(4), 1699–1707 (1989)
17. Vos, K., Sørensen, K.V., Jensen, S.S., Valin, J.M.: Voice coding with opus. In: Audio Engineering Society Convention 135. Audio Engineering Society (2013)
18. Wang, Z., Bovik, A.C., Sheikh, H.R., Simoncelli, E.P.: Image quality assessment: from error visibility to structural similarity. IEEE Trans. Image Process. **13**(4), 600–612 (2004)

19. Weinberger, S.H.: Speech accent archive (2015). George Mason University. http://accent.gmu.edu
20. Weinberger, S.H., Kunath, S.A.: The speech accent archive: towards a typology of English accents. In: Corpus-Based Studies in Language Use, Language Learning, and Language Documentation, pp. 265–281. Brill Rodopi (2011)

Corpus Construction for Aviation Speech Recognition

Yiyi Cui, Zhen Wang$^{(\boxtimes)}$, Yanyu Lu, and Shan Fu

School of Electronic Information and Electrical Engineering,
Shanghai Jiao Tong University, Shanghai, People's Republic of China
b2wz@sjtu.edu.cn

Abstract. In the aviation field, safety is always the top priority. Human error is one of the important factors affecting flight safety, which may cause serious consequences. Since voice conversation is the primary way of communication in the cockpit, speech recognition technology can be applied to detect possible human error, and this technology requires carefully annotated speech text for model training. This paper proposes a small-scale Chinese civil aviation professional corpus, which is constructed from civil aviation flight manuals and speech data in real flight scenarios with manual audio filtering and text annotation, thorough preprocessing and cleansing procedures. Besides, we identify keywords to extract the corpus, so that we can make the topics of our corpus more focused on the aviation domain, thus allowing the model to better learn the unique features of aviation speech such as aviation terms, quantity words, etc. Moreover, we contrast the WER of the speech recognition results before and after using our corpus. The experimental results have shown that our proposed corpus can improve the effect of aviation speech recognition.

Keywords: Aviation safety · ASR · Aviation corpus

1 Introduction

With the increase of the civil aviation industry, safety issue has become social focus with constant concern. Human factor is an important part of the aviation safety problem and has received much attention from academic and industrial experts in recent years, as human error has been recognized rather than technical failure to underlie most aviation accidents and [1] (Airplanes et al. 2007). For example, from 1996 to 2005, of the 32 civil aviation accidents in China, 56.25% were related to the crew [2] (Ku et al. 2020). In 2006, of the fatal accidents in the United States, 79% were attributed to pilot error [3] (Kharoufah et al. 2018). Common human factors in aviation accidents and incidents include fatigue, situational awareness, communication and so on. Voice conversation is the primary way of communication in the cockpit, therefore, we can detect pilot workload and productivity to determine fatigue and ineffective communication through automatic speech recognition.

M. Kurosu (Ed.): HCII 2022, LNCS 13303, pp. 238–250, 2022.
https://doi.org/10.1007/978-3-031-05409-9_18

Nevertheless, there still remains a great challenge for aviation automatic speech recognition. At present, there is a lack of qualified corpora to train practical ASR systems in aviation. Most of the existing corpora such as Twitter Corpus [4] (Ritter et al. 2011), Ubuntu Dialogue Corpus [5] (Kadlec et al. 2015), etc. cannot be used to train aviation language models due to different domains. Building a well-annotated aviation corpus is a very difficult task: on the one hand, due to the unique characteristics of aviation speech, such as special terms in the vocabulary, position-related vocabulary and unstable speech rate, it relies heavily on professional knowledge, only professional practitioners can be competent for this job [6] (Lin et al. 2020). As a result, annotating aviation speech data is a costly, laborious, and time-consuming work. On the other hand, aviation audio data often contains a lot of noise, which greatly interferes with the training of aviation language models. Therefore, a qualified aviation domain corpus is urgently needed to train practical ASR systems in aviation domain.

To address the above issues, we propose a small-sample Chinese civil aviation professional corpus constructed from civil aviation flight manuals and speech data in real flight scenarios. We screened and annotated a large number of aviation audios with high-quality audio, and proposed a small-scale aviation Chinese corpus, which includes 3318 human-annotated sentences. By decomposing the reading method of quantitative words to extract quantitative keywords, it solves the problem of special reading and changing reading of numbers in aviation data. By determining the keywords of aviation terms through the common word exclusion method, we solve the problem of identifying aviation terms. This article provides a reference for the subsequent design and construction of small-sample Chinese civil aviation professional corpus.

2   Method of Corpus Construction

To the best of our knowledge, there are few high-quality Chinese corpora designed for civil aviation speech recognition before our work. We believe that corpus with higher quality will promote greater breakthroughs in civil aviation speech recognition. In this paper, we use real cockpit speech data as the corpus source. Our intention is to make the corpus build on this basis more realistic while maintaining professionalism. We construct our civil aviation corpus following four steps: 1) cockpit speech data acquisition, 2) data pre-processing, 3) corpus extraction and 4) text cleaning [7] (Xu et al. 2018).

2.1   Data Processing

The speech data processing includes audio filtering, text annotation and text segmentation.

2.2   Data Acquisition

There are 11 crews participated in a simulator flight. Each crew performed one simulated flight mission in level-D flight simulator. Speech of the participants was recorded during the flight and used as speech data in the study. We collected a total of 29 flight scenarios, including normal flight scenarios and flight scenarios in emergency situations.

The voice data is collected by the embedded microphone of the eye tracker Tobii Pro Glasses3, the recording format is MP4, the sampling length is 2 byte, the sampling frequency 16000 Hz.

The collected cockpit voice data inevitably contains some non-flight-related dialogues, and some audio that cannot be identified with semantics. These audios cannot be used as corpus, so we first filter the voice data, judge the quality of the audio according to the designed principles, and remove low-quality audio. The designed principles are as follows: 1) If the audio is incomplete, and it can be clearly judged that the semantics are incomplete, then it is low-quality audio. 2) If the voice volume of the audio is too small or the pronunciation is ambiguous, or the content of the speech cannot be determined, it is low-quality audio. 3) If it can be clearly judged that the speech is not related to the cockpit or flying the aircraft, it is low-quality audio. The filtered audio will be labeled in sentence units and segmented into words using the jieba toolkit.

2.3   Keyword Identification and Text Extraction

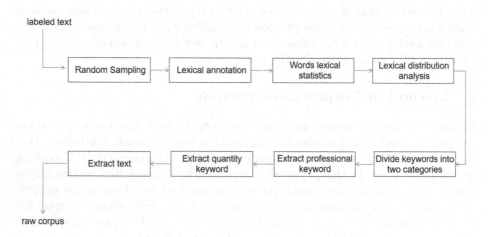

Fig. 1. Raw corpus extraction processing.

Previous researches indicate that more focused topics are helpful to guide NRG models away from the state of producing universal responses (Mou et al. 2016; Xing et al. 2017), so we set keywords to topics of our corpus more focused on the field of civil aviation. In order to allow the neural network model to better learn the specific terms and special pronunciation of civil aviation, we first extract keywords from the civil aviation flight manual and delete or add some words as

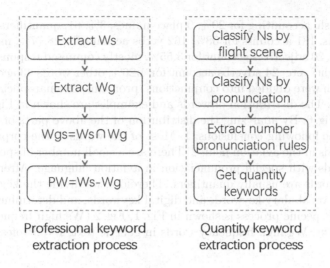

Fig. 2. Professional keyword and quantity keyword extraction processing.

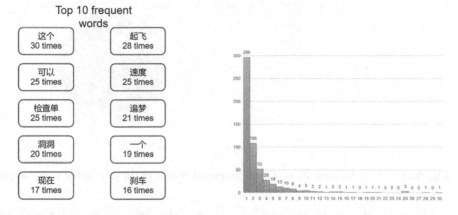

Fig. 3. Top ten frequency words of the annotated text samples.

Fig. 4. The word frequency distribution of annotated text samples.

appropriate, and then use these keywords to extract sentences from the annotated text as the raw corpus. We randomly selected 10% of the labeled texts as samples, annotated the sample with lexicality, and then counted the distribution of words with high frequency in the samples (the occurrences of more than 5 times were considered as high-frequency words), there are 563 high-frequency words in the statistical sample, which are divided into nouns, verbs, adjectives, adverbs, and other words. There are 314 nouns, accounting for 55.77%, which are divided into English, place names, numerals and proper nouns. Among them,

63 are English, accounting for 20%, 9 place names, 3%, 61, quantifiers, 19%, and proper nouns. 181 accounts for 58%; 162 verbs account for 28.77%, mostly flight instructions, 20 adjectives account for 3.55%, mostly command responses, such as "good", "right", etc. 24 adverbs account for 4.26%, other words 43 accounted for 7.64%, which were divided into conjunctions, pronouns, onomatopoeia, and auxiliary words. The distribution of words and examples are shown in Fig. 3, Fig. 4, Fig. 5 and Fig. 6. By analyzing the distribution of the above parts of speech, we can draw the following conclusions: 1. Most of the words in the corpus are specialized words in the aviation field. 2. There are a small number of special words, that is, words with special pronunciation in aviation language. After investigation, such words are usually quantifiers. Therefore, we divide the keywords into professional vocabulary keywords and digital keywords, and determine them separately. The specific process is shown in Fig. 1, Fig. 2 (Ws:high frequency words in sample text, Wg:high frequency words in generic text, PW:Professional keywords).

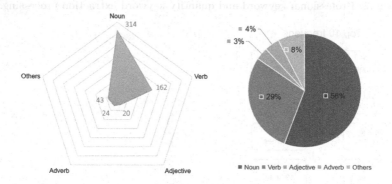

Fig. 5. The lexical distribution of high-frequency words in the annotated text samples.

Professional Keywords: From the perspective of professionalism and field relevance, we choose to extract professional keywords from the flight crew training manual. Since the 29 flight scenarios of the voice data are all carried out with the A321 aircraft as the carrier, therefore we extracted professional keywords from the "A321 Flight Crew Training Manual".

The steps to extract professional keywords are as follows:

1) Tokenize the text.

2) Count the word frequency, sort the words according to the order of word frequency from high to low, and form the raw key word list.

3) Screen out the words with low degree of professionalism in the raw keywords.

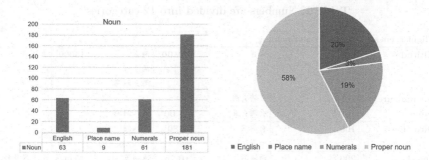

Fig. 6. The distribution of the noun in the annotated text samples.

The degree of vocabulary professionalism is obviously negatively correlated with its generality, that is, the higher the degree of vocabulary generality, the lower the degree of professionalism. Therefore, we adopted the following method to filter out words with low degree of professionalism: extracting high-frequency words in general texts as the degree of professionalism Low-level words, and then delete these words from the raw keywords list to get professional keywords.

Quantity Keywords: Due to the changeable pronunciation of quantifiers, there are situations where the same number corresponds to many different expressions. For example, "5700" has various pronunciations such as Wu guai, Wu guai dong dong, Wu qian guai, and Wu qian qi at the same time. According to the section on the reading of numbers in <Civil Aviation Radio Land-Air Communication for Chinese Textbooks>, the reading of numbers is determined by the flight scene, so we divide the numbers that appear in the sample audio into the following 12 categories according to the flight scene: altitude value, air pressure value, time, heading, speed, wind direction and speed, frequency, runway, distance, bearing, transponder, type. Table 1 gives a summary of all categories.

We found that it was feasible to distinguish pronunciation according to scenes, but it was too tedious and complicated. We categorized the pronunciation cases twice according to their pronunciation, and in order to make the pronunciation rules clearer, only one of each case following the same pronunciation rules was kept. Table 2 shows our twice categorized result. Observing Table 2, we summarize the rules of pronunciation as follows:

1) The numbers 3, 4, 5, 6, 8 and 9 are pronounced in three, four, five, six, eight and nine fixed ways Table 3
2) The numbers 2, 7 and 0 are pronounced in various ways Table 3
3) 10, 100, 1000 pronunciation is also fixed Table 3
4) Decimal point fixed reading 'dian' Table 3

Table 1. Numbers are divided into 12 categories.

Flight scenes	Numbers and reading					
Altitude	600	六百	2100	两幺 两千一 两幺洞洞	18000	幺八洞
Air pressure	1012	幺洞幺两				
Time	10:15	幺洞幺五	8:00	洞八洞洞		
Direction	100	幺洞洞 一百度	180	幺八洞		
Speed	200	两洞洞 两百节	0.75	点拐五	15 m/s	十五米每秒
Wind speed Wind direction	Wind direction20 Wind speed 7 m/s gust 12 m/s	风洞两洞 拐米 阵风十二米				
Frequency	118.1	幺幺八点幺	245	两四五		
Track	2	洞两	17	幺拐	18R	幺八右
Distance	17 nm	幺拐海里	30 km	三洞公里		
Position	1	一点钟方向	12	十二点钟方向		
Responder code	5271	五两拐幺	1200	幺两洞洞		
Aircraft mode	B737-800	波音七三七杠八百	A320	空客三二零	A321	空客三二幺

Table 2. Twice categorized result.

	Numbers and reading					
1	600	六百	12	十二	380	三百八十
			200	两百		
			2100	两千一		
2	737	七三七	320	三二零	321	三二幺
3	1012	幺洞幺两	17	幺拐	5271	五两拐幺
4	0.75	点拐五	118.1	幺幺八点幺		

According to the above pronunciation rules, we determined sixteen quantity keywords, which can cover all the quantity words after the pronunciation of these quantity keyword combinations.

Table 3. The rules of pronunciation

Number/Symbol	Reading	Number/Symbol	Reading	Number/Symbol	Reading
3	三	2	二	10	十
4	四		两	100	百
5	五	7	七	1000	千
6	六		拐		
8	八	0	零		
9	九		洞		
			No pronunciation		
			点		

2.4   Text Cleaning

We conduct the following cleansing operations:

1) Replicated words or characters (e.g., "好的好的好的" and "啊啊啊啊啊啊", etc.) are substituted with its normal form using regular expressions.

2) Replicated sentence are removed to avoid redundancy.

3) Sentences longer than 60 are deleted (Too long sentences will make it difficult for the decoder to converge, so we delete long sentences)

After the above operations, we obtained the final corpus, and the scale comparison between the keyword extracted text and the text before and after text cleaning is shown in the Table 4. There are 9088 sentences in the annotated text, with an average sentence length of 11.075 words per sentence. After the steps of keyword extraction text and text cleaning, our small-scale aerial corpus has 3318 sentences with an average sentence length of 7.2 words per sentence.

Table 4. The scale comparison.

	Scale	Sentence length
Raw text	9088 sentence	11.075 words
Final corpus	3318 sentence	7.2 words

3   Experiment

To verify the quality of the corpus, we analyze the word frequency and lexical distribution and the WER of the speech recognition results before and after using the corpus.

3.1   Word Frequency and Lexical Distribution Comparison

We compared the word frequency distributions and lexical distributions of the annotated text samples, the airline flight manuals and the corpus. Figure 4, Fig. 8 and Fig. 10 show the word frequency distributions of the annotated text sample, the aviation flight manual and the corpus, respectively. From Figs. 1, 2 and 3, we can find that the word frequency distribution trends are more or less the same, with most words appearing less frequently, mostly in the frequency range of 1–50, and the high frequency range often corresponds to only one or two words.

Figure 3, Fig. 7 and Fig. 9 show the top ten words in the frequency of the annotated text samples, the aviation flight manual and the corpus respectively. The most descriptive words appear in Fig. 4, including "this, can, now, a", while there are almost no such words in Figs. 5 and 6, because such descriptive words are indeed more common in the annotated text, and they are often intonation words, pronouns, and status words that are unconsciously added in the course of spoken conversation. These words are sometimes repeated unconsciously by

Fig. 7. The word frequency distribution of aviation flight manual.

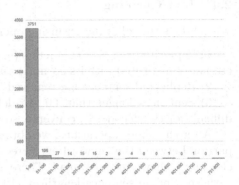

Fig. 8. Top ten frequency words of the aviation flight manual.

Fig. 9. The word frequency distribution of our corpus.

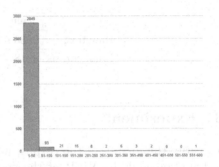

Fig. 10. Top ten frequency words of the corpus.

the speaker, so they appear more frequently. In contrast, airline flight manuals are written normative texts with written and precise characteristics, so such descriptive and imprecise words appear less frequently in airline flight manuals. The corpus was built to strengthen the recognition performance of the professional aspects of the model aviation, and in the process of building the thesaurus, the daily common words were deleted when the key words were determined, so the frequency of such colloquial, non-professional related words was reduced to a greater extent.

Figure 5, Fig. 11, Fig. 12 show the lexical distribution of high-frequency words in the annotated text samples, the aviation flight manual and the corpus respectively. The distribution of all three is generally consistent, with nouns being the most frequent, followed by verbs, and adjectives and adverbs and other words together accounting for 10%–15%. This phenomenon is in line with the actual situation that aviation conversations are more concise consisting of directives of proper nouns and corresponding operations. However, the distribution of the three words is not identical. The percentage of other words in the aviation flight manual is less than that of the annotated text sample and the corpus, which indicates that there are fewer words of colloquial auxiliaries, conjunctions, onomatopoeia, etc. in the manual compared to the actual conversation in the cockpit, which is in line with the actual situation that the manual is highly written and professional. The proportion of other words in the corpus is lower than that of the labeled text sample, indicating that it is effective to enhance the professionalism and aviation relevance of the corpus by identifying key words to extract the corpus.

Figure 6, Fig. 13, Fig. 14 show the distributions of English, place names, quantifiers, and proper nouns in the annotated text samples, airline flight manuals, and corpus, respectively. In these three distributions, what remains consistent is that proper nouns account for more than 50%, while the difference is in the distribution of quantifiers and place names. The percentage of quantifiers in both the airline flight manual and the labeled text samples is less than 20%, and the percentage of quantifiers in the airline flight manual is smaller than that in

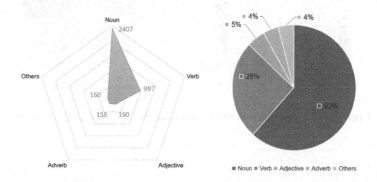

Fig. 11. The lexical distribution of high-frequency words in the aviation flight manual.

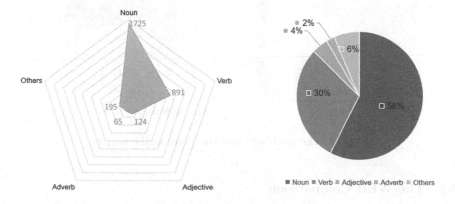

Fig. 12. The lexical distribution of high-frequency words in the corpus.

the labeled text samples, and the percentage of quantifiers in the corpus is the largest among the three texts with more than 20%. Given that the aviation flight manual is an instructional text, which is mainly rule-based and professional, and the quantity words are mostly practical and specific, so there will not be many quantity words in the manual, so it is reasonable that the percentage of quantity words in the aviation flight manual is the least among the three cases. In order to solve the problem of variable reading of quantity words, we deliberately added quantity keywords in the step of keyword determination, so the percentage of quantity words in the corpus is significantly higher than the other two cases reflecting that the determination of quantity keywords is effective, and the final extracted corpus contains more quantity words, which can cover more quantity word readings, thus strengthening the training of the model quantity word readings.

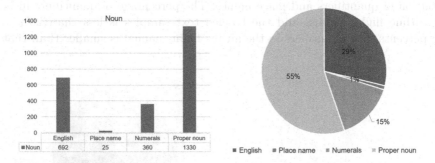

Fig. 13. The distribution of the noun in the aviation flight manual.

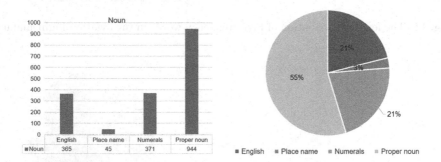

Fig. 14. The distribution of the noun in the corpus.

3.2 The WER Comparision

WER (Word Error Rate) is the most commonly used error measurement in ASR [8] (Park et al. 2008). In order to make the recognized word sequence consistent with the standard word sequence, some words need to be replaced, deleted or inserted. The total number of words inserted, replaced or deleted is divided by the number of words in the standard word sequence. The percentage of the total number is WER. It calculated as $WER = (S + I + D)/N \times 100$, where S is the number of substitutions, I is the number of insertions, D is the number of deletions, and N is the total number of words in the actual transcript. The interpretation of WER is that the lower the WER, the better the speech recognition is.

We use the model from AISPEECH to train and obtain the speech recognition results. After testing, the WER of speech recognition results before adding the corpus is 23.8%, and after adding the corpus the speech recognition results are 19.4%, and the recognition results are improved by 5.4% after adding the corpus, which indicates that our corpus does play an optimization role for the neural network model.

4   Conclusion

In this paper, we propose a small-scale Chinese civil aviation professional corpus for training aviation speech models. We collected flight speech data and screened the aviation audio to remove excessively noisy audio and audio that is not relevant to flight mission dialogue. In addition, we also perform text annotation on high-quality audio data and perform necessary text data cleaning and pruning work to remove text noise. Moreover, we also identified keywords of aviation terms and keywords of quantifiers to improve the recognition of aviation terms and solve the problem of variable pronunciation of quantifiers.

Furthermore, we conduct the frequency and lexical distribution statistics of the words with high frequency in the annotated text, and test and contrast the WER of the speech recognition results before and after using the corpus.

References

1. Boeing Commercial Airplanes. Statistical summary of commercial jet airplane accidents-worldwide operations 1959–2006 (2007)
2. Kuć, J., Żendzian-Piotrowska, M.: A pilot study evaluating the prevalence of cervical spine dysfunction among students of dentistry at the medical university. Front. Neurol. **11**, 200 (2020)
3. Kharoufah, H., Murray, J., Baxter, G., Wild, G.: A review of human factors causations in commercial air transport accidents and incidents: from to 2000–2016. Prog. Aerosp. Sci. **99**, 1–13 (2018)
4. Ritter, A., Cherry, C., Dolan, B.: Data-driven response generation in social media. In: Empirical Methods in Natural Language Processing (EMNLP) (2011)
5. Kadlec, R., Schmid, M., Kleindienst, J.: Improved deep learning baselines for ubuntu corpus dialogs. arXiv preprint arXiv:1510.03753 (2015)
6. Lin, Y., Guo, D., Zhang, J., Chen, Z., Yang, B.: A unified framework for multilingual speech recognition in air traffic control systems. IEEE Trans. Neural Netw. Learn. Syst. **32**, 3608–3620 (2020)

7. Xu, Z., et al.: LSDSCC: a large scale domain-specific conversational corpus for response generation with diversity oriented evaluation metrics (2018)
8. Park, Y., Patwardhan, S., Visweswariah, K., Gates, S.C.: An empirical analysis of word error rate and keyword error rate (2008)

DICOM-Based Voxel-Supported Blood-Vessel-Avoiding Scalpel Navigation

Takahiro Kunii[1](✉), Miho Asano[2], and Hiroshi Noborio[3]

[1] Kashina System Co., Hikone, Japan
kunii@tetera.jp
[2] Preemptive Medicine and Lifestyle-Related Disease Research Center, Kyoto University Hospital, Kyoto-shi, Japan
[3] Department of Computer Science, Osaka Electro-Communication University, Shijyo-Nawate, Japan

Abstract. In this study, we propose a navigation algorithm that directly depicts a safe path for malignant tumors and cerebral thrombi while avoiding obstacles such as blood vessels, directly from DICOM data without using STL. For this purpose, we use a voxel-based algorithm, which we have recently proposed. In the voxel-based algorithm, the organ STL polyhedron is converted into a voxel lattice structure model, which is used to search for a safe path to the malignant tumor while avoiding blood vessels. Each voxel has a density that is the percentage of obstacles in its own space, and this density is used for retrieval, but such a density can also be created from a series of DICOM tomographic images placed in 3D space. Once the voxel lattice structure model is generated, the search can be performed using the voxel-based algorithm. It is possible to adjust which range of values in the DICOM data is considered as an obstacle, and it can be checked on the personal computer (PC) monitor.

Keywords: Navigation · Surgical path · Three-dimensional voxel space

1 Introduction

In surgical operations, tumors and other malignancies must be quickly removed from organs that are lined with complex networks of blood vessels. Thus, in past works, we created a navigation algorithm to guide the scalpel to the periphery of the tumor to limit bleeding, further aiding the clinician. This process mimics a car navigation system, in which the driver's burden of monitoring the surrounding environment is alleviated.

In past works, these navigation algorithms require the standard triangulated language (STL) [2] to be created using the patient's DICOM (Digital Imaging and Communications in Medicine) data [1] acquired by computed tomography (CT) [9] or magnetic resonance imaging (MRI) [8] in the pre-processing step. Then, the Euclidean distances from the polyhedral scalpel to the polyhedral organs and blood vessels, which were separately acquired by a 3D scanner, were rapidly calculated by parallel processing based

© The Author(s), under exclusive license to Springer Nature Switzerland AG 2022
M. Kurosu (Ed.): HCII 2022, LNCS 13303, pp. 251–263, 2022.
https://doi.org/10.1007/978-3-031-05409-9_19

on the depth values of the Z-buffer generated by orthogonal projection onto the poly-hedron using a GPU (Graphical Processing Unit) [3]. Subsequently, using potential [4] and sensor-based methods [5], we created a navigation algorithm to guide the scalpel to the periphery of the tumor to limit bleeding, further aiding the clinician.

Even with these notable advancements, the operation still requires careful attention, expertise, time, and effort. Hence, to eliminate the preprocessing steps and further relieve clinician pressure, we replaced the original navigation algorithm with one that eliminates the STL polyhedra from our real-time surgical navigation system and began directly with DICOM. Most recently, we proposed a navigation voxel-based algorithm [6] that converts an organ STL polyhedron into a voxel lattice structure model, manages it in memory as an organ voxel map, and finds a safe path to the malignant tumor while avoiding blood vessels. The voxel-based algorithm converts the STL polyhedron of an organ into a voxel lattice structure model and manages it in memory as an organ voxel map to find a safe path to the malignant tumor while avoiding obstacles (blood vessels). The organ voxel map has a density for each voxel that indicates the percentage of obstacles in voxel space, and the path to be followed is determined by evaluating this density in pathfinding.

We propose an improved voxel-based algorithm, in which this organ voxel map is created from consecutive DICOM tomographic images instead of STL polyhedra, as a navigation algorithm using DICOM data. In addition, in order for clinicians to confirm what values in the DICOM data are obstacles to be avoided, the area corresponding to the specified range of values in the DICOM data is displayed on the PC monitor using the ray-marching method. The organ voxel map is then created based on the range of values used for the DICOM data display. Once the organ voxel map is generated, it can be searched using the voxel-based algorithm. The process after the organ voxel map is generated is the same as in the case of STL, so we do not evaluate the routes found. We visually check whether the obstacle areas taken from the DICOM data displayed on the screen and the created organ voxel maps are linked. Therefore, the organ voxel map can also be displayed on the screen.

The DICOM data used were 128 consecutive tomographic images taken by MRI, with measurements separated into a grid of 256 horizontal and 256 vertical lines. All files are loaded in a few seconds and can be rotated, enlarged, and moved on the PC monitor in the same way as STL polyhedral models. There was no lagging behind the hand operation. It also responded in real-time when changing the range of the measured values. In this way, it became possible to identify obstacles to be avoided from the DICOM data and to search for a safe route. In this study, the obstacles were determined only by specifying the range of DICOM data values, so it was not possible to strictly distinguish between blood vessels and lymphatic vessels. We are thinking of combining MRI, CT, and multiple DICOM data. The visibility of whether or not the pathway avoids obstacles was lower than STL in that the pathway display was not synthesized on the screen. We are considering whether we can incorporate the path into the DICOM raymarching.

The created voxel group was also displayed on the PC monitor, and we were able to confirm that the voxel group changed in conjunction with the region of the DICOM data determined from the specified range of values. After the voxel lattice structure model is generated, the process is the same as in the STL case, so we do not evaluate the path we found. The ability for clinicians to determine obstacles directly from DICOM data and make adjustments on the fly would be scalable and immediate in a way that STL, with its fixed geometry, cannot be.

We first describe why we use our voxel-based navigation algorithm for navigation with DICOM data in Sect. 2. In Sect. 3, we describe our voxel-based navigation algorithm. In Sect. 4, we conclude our present research and discuss the scope for future work.

2 Why Do We Use Voxel-Based Navigation Algorithms for Navigation with DICOM Data?

In the potential method mentioned earlier, the repulsive force received from the planes that make up the polyhedron is defined and used for obstacle avoidance. The sensor method uses the collision with the plane and its surface normal to determine the direction of the obstacle avoidance path. Therefore, it was necessary to convert the DICOM data to STL.

In contrast, the voxel-based algorithm divides the 3D space along an arbitrary axis and determines the obstacle avoidance path by evaluating the density as the percentage of obstacles in each divided voxel space. The density of such obstacles can also be calculated by how many particles are in each voxel space. By placing successive DICOM tomographic images in 3D space and considering each value of DICOM data as a particle, a group of voxels can be created instead of STL. Once the voxel group is created, the voxel-based method can be used.

3 Voxel-Based Method

In our voxel-based method, the 3D space is divided into voxel cubes of approximately $10 \, mm^2$, where the z-axis is a straight line connecting the center of the tumor to a position specified by the doctor (Fig. 1(a)). The STL models of the blood vessels and bile ducts are divided as such (Fig. 1(a)).

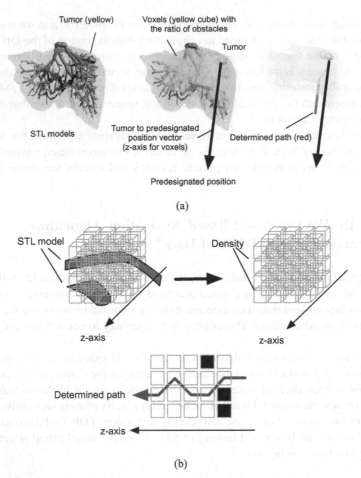

(a)

(b)

Fig. 1. Routing using the voxel-based method: (a) The space is divided into a group of voxels along the specified z-axis and the path is explored; (b) The voxel series is selected and moved to where the standard triangulated language (STL) model (blood vessel) occupies a low percentage of voxels.

The voxel grid structure, transformed from a set of consecutive DICOM tomographic images (Fig. 2), is used as a map for navigation.

Fig. 2. Sequential digital-imaging-and-communications-in-medicine tomographic images.

3.1 Handling 3D DICOM Tomographic Images

With a polyhedral STL model, the normal vectors and internal and external boundaries are clear. Thus, the model can be used as-is to display a 3D polygon mesh [7] on a PC monitor. When using 3D-stacked DICOM images, it is also necessary to consider the construction of the 3D voxel map for route-searching.

First, DICOM tomographic images are obtained by virtually cutting the human body, a 3D object, into a circle and dividing it into 100 sections horizontally and 100 sections vertically (Fig. 3). Then, the measurement values for each section of the grid are recorded. The DICOM tomographic images that are generally viewed on a PC monitor comprise measurement values recorded on each grid, which are converted to gray or colored images and arranged according to the grid arrangement. For example, when MRI or CT is used, each grid contains measured values are recorded in the range of 0–255 (1 byte) or 0–65535 (2 bytes), expressed in shades of a gray two-dimensional (2D) image.

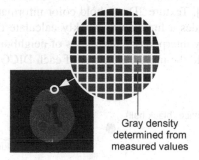

Gray density
determined from
measured values

Fig. 3. Digital-imaging-and-communications-in-medicine tomographic measurements.

Because each image contains the positional information of the human body cut into circles, if each image plane is rearranged in a 3D space based on this information, the measurement values recorded for each grid can be distributed as an information grid. The 3D space into which this grid is distributed (Fig. 4) is referred to as the "DICOM volume."

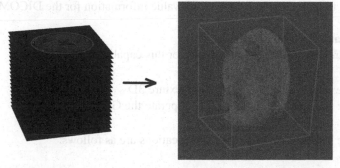

Fig. 4. Digital-imaging-and-communications-in-medicine volume constructed in a three-dimensional space based on recorded location information.

Surgically assisted navigation based on the voxel method on a DICOM volume is the subject of this study. Hence, the following issues must be resolved:

1. Management of the DICOM Volume in PC Memory
2. Display of the DICOM Volume on the PC Monitor
3. Voxel Creation from the DICOM Volume

3.2 Management of DICOM Volumes in PC Memory

Considering the PC display and manipulation of the DICOM volume space, we opted to manage the DICOM volume as a 3D texture in the PC memory.

Texture 3D
Current graphics processing units (GPUs) employ a standard 2D-handling process for images called "Texture 2D" [10]. Additionally, there is a standard for adding depth to obtain "Texture 3D" [11]. Texture 2D can hold color information for displaying a 2D grid, and the GPU provides a function to quickly calculate the value of an arbitrary position between grids by interpolating the values of neighboring grids (Fig. 5). Thus, we use Texture 2D to hold the measured values of each DICOM tomogram grid in the PC memory.

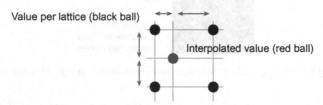

Fig. 5. Value of an arbitrary position between lattices is found by interpolating the values of neighboring lattices.

Similarly, Texture 3D can hold color and other information for display as 3D particles. It also provides the ability to interpolate values between particles. Thus, we opted to use this method to hold the grid measurement value information for the DICOM volume.

Hardware and Software Requirements
The hardware and software requirements for this capability are as follows:

- Hardware: GPU capable of providing Texture 3D
- Software: A programming interface to operate the GPU

The specific hardware and software specifications are as follows:

- MacBook Pro (16 in, 2019)
- CPU: Intel Core i9 2.3-GHz 8 Cores

- Memory: 64 GB
- GPU: AMD Radeon Pro 5500M 8 GB
- OS: macOS Version 12.1
- Software development platform: Unity[12] 2020.3
- Translated with www.DeepL.com/Translator (free version)

3.3 Displaying the DICOM Volume on a PC Monitor

The DICOM volume is a collection of measured value information particles. When this is displayed on a PC monitor, it is best to use an algorithm to determine the color from the measured values, as with DICOM tomographic images. They can then be displayed as small particles in 3D (Fig. 6(a)).

The ray-marching method [13] accounts for the relationship between particles. Hence, a line of sight is generated for each pixel on the PC monitor (Fig. 7), the space in the DICOM volume is searched by the line of sight, and the color of the pixel is determined from the particle information around the line of sight (Fig. 6(b)). The pixel colors on the PC monitor are determined from the particles in the vicinity of the eye (Fig. 6(b)). Thus, the pseudo-normals set for each particle (described later) are used to emphasize the 3D effect (Fig. 6(c)). This ray-marching method using pseudo-normals is used to display the DICOM volume in this study.

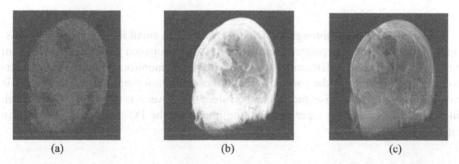

(a)　　　　　　　　(b)　　　　　　　　(c)

Fig. 6. Example of three-dimensional display of a digital-imaging-and-communications-in-medicine volume on a computer monitor: (a) Particle intake; (b) Ray-marching method; (c) Ray-marching method with pseudo-normal.

Ray-Marching Method

In the ray-marching method, the line of sight is created from the pixels on the PC monitor, and the color is determined by searching the DICOM volume along the line of sight (Fig. 7).

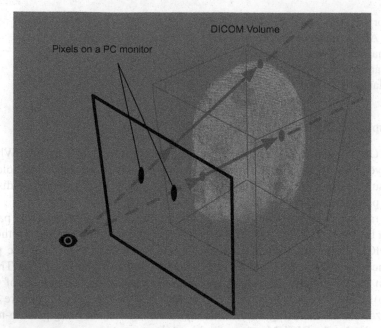

Fig. 7. Searching the digital-imaging-and-communications-in-medicine (DICOM) volume along the line of sight. PC: personal computer.

The search proceeds through the DICOM volume in small increments at fixed distances to extract the interpolated measurement values between particles at the current point (Fig. 8). It further determines the color of the PC monitor. When the value interpolated by the values of the particles around the extraction point is zero, the image is made transparent; otherwise, the higher the value, the closer it is to opaque white. When all determined colors are superimposed, the image on the PC monitor is as shown in Fig. 6(b).

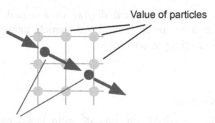

Fig. 8. Searching the digital-imaging-and-communications-in-medicine volume in small increments at fixed distances and extracting measurements interpolated between particles per location.

Pseudo-Normals

The pseudo-normals are the gradients of the values between particles in the x-, y-, and z-axes (Fig. 9(a)), which are used as the coefficients of the 3D basis vectors of the normals for each particle (Fig. 9(b)). The pseudo-normal is created from the value gradients. The angle to the light source can then be determined, and shading can be applied.

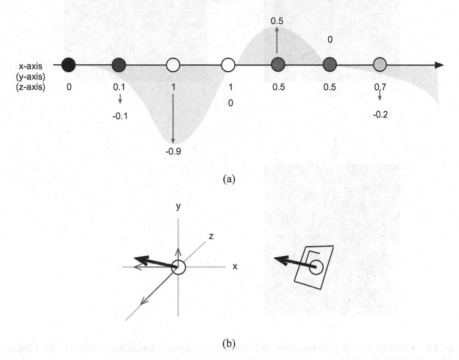

(a)

(b)

Fig. 9. Taking the gradient of the values between particles for each of the x, y, and z axes (a) and creating the coefficients of the three-dimensional basis vectors of particle normals (b).

Operating DICOM Volume Images

The DICOM volume is displayed on the screen, and the color and illumination are adjusted to improve the visibility of the DICOM volume, as shown in Fig. 10(a). This is done by reading the DICOM tomogram taken by MRI and using the ray-marching method to display only the DICOM volume particles in the range 0.2–0.5 (normalized to 0–1; Figs. 10(a) and (b)) when the measured values of DICOM volume particles change from 0.35 to 0.65.

In this study, only a simple volume is realized. However, because it can specify the distribution area of particles in a 3D space, it is possible to scrape off a part of the DICOM volume in an arbitrary 3D space region represented as a sphere, hexahedron, or STL model (Fig. 10(c)).

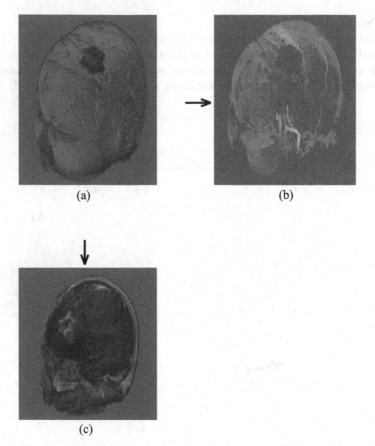

(a)

(b)

(c)

Fig. 10. Viewing the digital-imaging-and-communications-in-medicine volume: (a) Display range (0.2–0.5); (b) Display range (0.35–0.65); (c) Cut-out front.

The clinician performs these operations via the DICOM volume display on the PC monitor and finally determines the area of the obstacle (e.g., blood vessels, bile ducts, lymph nodes, and nerves). In the future, we plan to use Leap Motion, a small motion-controlled 3D motion-capture system, to allow clinicians to perform non-contact operations during surgery. Additionally, in the polyhedral STL model, the tumor will be separated as one model in advance, allowing the position and posture of the malignancy to be determined. However, in the current DICOM volume, position and posture must be determined by the clinician in advance or online. In the present study, the position and posture are confirmed by the practitioner on the PC monitor and specified using mouse clicks or directly with coordinate values. Thus, it is possible to make decisions online while viewing real tissues during surgery. Mutual information exchange between real and virtual organs (i.e., online modification of the obstacle object area) is also possible.

Here, the obstacles around the specified coordinates are colored yellow to show the position and posture of the specified tumor (Fig. 11). Finally, the desired cutting position is specified, and the voxel-based method is executed.

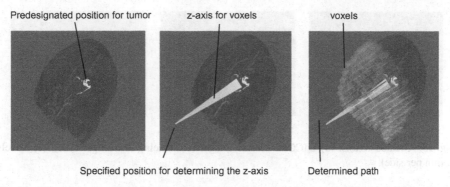

Predesignated position for tumor   z-axis for voxels   voxels

Specified position for determining the z-axis   Determined path

Fig. 11. Voxel-based method for specifying the tumor and desired cutting location (Color figure online)

3.4 Voxel Creation from the DICOM Volume

The ray-marching method is also used to create voxels from a DICOM volume. In this case, the line of sight used for ray-marching is the z-axis connecting the tumor position specified by the clinician and the desired cutting position. Along this axis, the ray-marching method is performed by limiting the search start position and depth for each layer of voxels (Fig. 12). From this, we determine the density of obstacles for each voxel. This can be regarded as a "virtual tomography" performed on a DICOM volume instead of a human body.

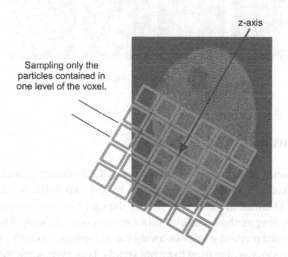

z-axis

Sampling only the particles contained in one level of the voxel.

Fig. 12. Voxel creation from digital-imaging-and-communications-in-medicine volume

Regarding the generated voxels, one piece is 10 mm in size (Fig. 13b), and the other is 2 mm (Fig. 13c). High-density voxels are reddish-black, and the lower voxels are nearly transparent. Although the 2-mm path is inappropriate for human cutting, it is convenient to use to check whether the area of obstacles is voxelized properly.

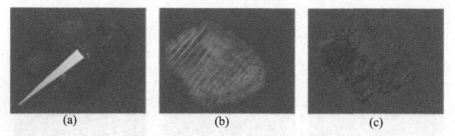

Fig. 13. Created voxels: (a) DICOM volume image; (b) Voxels (10 mm per side); (c) Voxels (2 mm per side).

The path found by this method is combined and displayed in the DICOM volume. The practitioner can then move the viewpoint in any direction and distance to further study the path (Fig. 14).

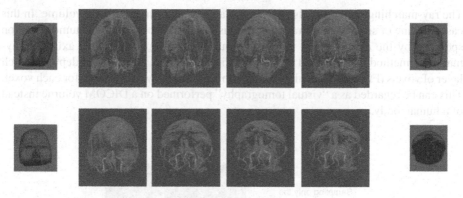

Fig. 14. Pathway validation

4   Conclusions and Future Works

In this study, a group of particles (lattice) of a DICOM volume was created from consecutive 3D stacked DICOM images obtained by CT and MRI. Next, obstacles were identified in the 3D lattice model by specifying the range of measurement values. Then, using the ray-marching method, we selected a route to guide the scalpel to the malignancy using the voxel-based method while observing the movement through a PC monitor. The ray-marching method was also used to create voxels. However, accurate identification is an issue that we leave for future study; here, we demonstrated that it is possible to search for obstacle avoidance routes using the voxel-based method from 3D stacked DICOM images, texture 3D, and ray-marching without requiring STL models.

By further improving the accuracy of obstacle identification, it may become possible to identify bones, blood vessels, and lymph nodes more precisely by combining multiple DICOM tomographic images of the same patient. This may further rely on calibrating imaging parameters and determining the types of contrast media and their presence or absence in CT and MRI images.

For this purpose, it is necessary to adjust the position, orientation, and scale of various DICOM tomographic images by, for example, matching the shape of the skeleton. We plan to test how well the system can discriminate obstacles from measurements obtained by multiple imaging methods, including accounting for their necessary visual adjustments. This mechanism may also be used for the automatic extraction of tumor areas.

The quality of the 3D display and the front-back relationship between the path and the obstacles may be further improved by incorporating the path as a particle of the DICOM volume, rather than combining the path and the DICOM volume display on the screen. We also plan to introduce an immersive display using a virtual-reality head-mounted display with binocular parallax capability.

Acknowledgment. This study was supported partly by the 2017 Grants-in-Aid for Scientific Research (No. 20K04407 and 20K12053) from the Ministry of Education, Culture, Sports, Science and Technology, Japan.

References

1. DICOM. https://en.wikipedia.org/wiki/DICOM
2. STL (file format). https://en.wikipedia.org/wiki/STL_(file_format)
3. Noborio, H., Kunii, T., Mizushino, K.: GPU-based shortest distance algorithm for liver surgery navigation. In: Proceedings of the 10th Anniversary Asian Conference on Computer Aided Surgery, Kyusyu University, Fukuoka Japan, pp. 42–43, 24–25 June 2014
4. Noborio, H., Aoki, K., Kunii, T., Mizushino, K.: A potential function-based scalpel navigation method that avoids blood vessel groups during excision of cancerous tissue. In: Proceedings of the 38th Annual International Conference of the IEEE Engineering in Medicine and Biology Society (EMBC 2016), Orlando Florida USA, pp. 6106–6112, 16–20 August 2016
5. Kunii, T., Asano, M., Fujita, K., Tachibana, K., Noborio, H.: Comparative study of potential-based and sensor-based surgical navigation in several liver environments. In: Kurosu, M. (ed.) HCII 2021. LNCS, vol. 12763, pp. 551–565. Springer, Cham (2021). https://doi.org/10.1007/978-3-030-78465-2_40
6. Kunii, T., Asano, M., Noborio, H.: Voxel-based route-search algorithm for tumor navigation and blood vessel avoidance. In: Kurosu, M. (ed.) HCII 2021. LNCS, vol. 12763, pp. 566–581. Springer, Cham (2021). https://doi.org/10.1007/978-3-030-78465-2_41
7. Polygon mesh. https://en.wikipedia.org/wiki/Polygon_mesh
8. Magnetic resonance imaging. https://en.wikipedia.org/wiki/Magnetic_resonance_imaging
9. CT scan. https://en.wikipedia.org/wiki/CT_scan
10. Three-dimensional texture image. https://www.khronos.org/registry/OpenGL-Refpages/gl4/html/glTexImage3D.xhtml
11. Two-dimensional texture image. https://www.khronos.org/registry/OpenGL-Refpages/gl4/html/glTexImage2D.xhtml
12. Unity. https://unity.com
13. Unity Documentation. https://docs.unity3d.com/2020.3/Documentation/Manual/class-Texture3D.html. Graphics Runner. http://graphicsrunner.blogspot.com/2009/01/volume-rendering-102-transfer-functions.html

Fine-Grained Sentiment Analysis
of Multi-domain Online Reviews

Panagiotis Theodoropoulos[✉] and Christina Alexandris

National and Kapodistrian University of Athens, Athens, Greece
panagtheodor@gmail.com, calexandris@gs.uoa.gr

Abstract. We propose a fine-grained Sentiment Analysis application focusing in multiple domains and text types. The present approach concerns sentiment analysis implemented at a fine-grained level, beyond the typical polarity of "positive", "negative" and "neutral" as evaluations of user input, introducing intermediate sentiments community. Fine-grained sentiment analysis is applied on movie reviews, Tripadvisor reviews and Coursera reviews. The implemented application is accessed by a web graphical user interface.

Keywords: Sentiment analysis · Classification models · Machine learning · Graphical user interface

1 Introduction

Sentiment Analysis is a rapidly growing field in the research areas of Artificial Intelligence (AI)-Machine Learning (ML) and Computational Linguistics-Natural Language Processing (NLP). Developments in Sentiment Analysis and Opinion Mining systems are directly connected to developments in Social Media applications, with a constantly expanding variety of user-groups. Targeting to the correct and efficient detection and processing of user responses and human emotions - often in non-specialized texts, Sentiment Analysis and Opinion Mining may be considered a particularly challenging field in Natural Language Processing.

Here, we propose a fine-grained Sentiment Analysis application focusing in multiple domains and text types. Typical Sentiment Analysis applications focus on one domain such as commercial products, films or organizations and concern the detection of positive or negative attitudes based on authors' articles or blogs. In the proposed fine-grained sentiment analysis classification, there are more sentiment classes, for example: "negative", "slightly negative", "neutral", "slightly positive", "positive". This type of classification, concerning the detection and processing of additional sentiment types, is considered to be more challenging to implement, than the typically encountered sentiment analysis that detects, classifies and processes three sentiments, namely "positive", "negative" and "neutral".

In particular, the present approach concerns sentiment analysis implemented at a fine-grained level, beyond the typical polarity of "positive", "negative" and "neutral" as evaluations of user input. We introduce intermediate sentiments such as "slightly

M. Kurosu (Ed.): HCII 2022, LNCS 13303, pp. 264–278, 2022.
https://doi.org/10.1007/978-3-031-05409-9_20

positive" and "slightly negative". Here, a more rigorous, in-depth processing of user input is targeted. The sentiment "slightly positive", expressing a positive but not overly enthusiastic review, is placed between sentiments "positive" and "neutral". The sentiment "slightly negative" expresses a negative review which does not escalate to anger, disgust or deep disappointment and is placed between sentiments "neutral" and "negative".

2 Data

The text types concerned involve movie reviews (Stanford Sentiment Treebank - SST5 [10] dataset), Tripadvisor reviews (Tripadvisor dataset) [8] and Coursera reviews (Coursera dataset) [9] from an English-speaking public and/or English-speaking international public. The corresponding datasets are publicly available on the Kaggle platform. Figures 1, 2, 3, 4, 5 and 6 illustrate the balance of training and testing labels of each dataset.

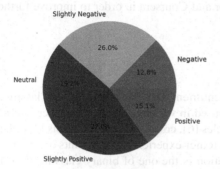

Fig. 1. Training labels' balance, 9645 examples (SST5)

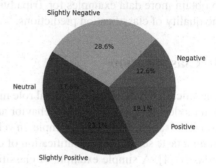

Fig. 2. Testing labels' balance, 2210 examples (SST5)

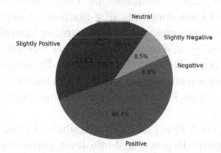

Fig. 3. Training labels' balance, 15367 examples (Tripadvisor)

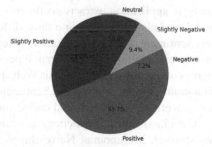

Fig. 4. Testing labels' balance, 5124 examples (Tripadvisor)

Based on the pie charts depicting the labels' balance within the training and testing sets, it is apparent that not all datasets are well balanced. For instance, the Movies (SST5) dataset is very well balanced, due to the fact that, each label category represents approximately one fifth of the entire dataset. This situation changes for the Tripadvisor dataset, with the positive labels exceeding 40% of the entire dataset. The Coursera

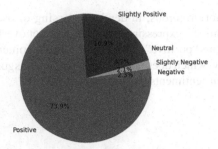

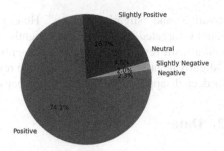

Fig. 5. Training labels' balance, 80263 examples (Coursera)

Fig. 6. Testing labels' balance, 26755 examples (Coursera)

dataset is badly balanced with the positive labels representing more than 70% of the entire dataset. Based on these observations, we understand that there is significant need to obtain more data examples for Tripadvisor and Coursera in order to improve further the quality of classification predictions.

3   Classification

Classification models play a crucial role in Sentiment Analysis applications. Classification models concerning human behavior are used in various Human-Computer Interaction (HCI) applications, for example, in vehicles [6], coffee satisfaction levels [3] (when using a taste sensor) and identification of customer experience touchpoints on the hotel industry [4]. A simple example of classification is the one of binary classification. In that example of a learning task, the classifier has to choose between two categories. For example, if a client is convinced or not [1]. In [2] Sentiment Analysis is performed for multiple social media types and language-specific customizations. Their Sentiment Analysis application extracts sentiments from texts consisting of a machine learning model, and classifies input into three different categories: positive, negative or neutral. This sentiment analysis application is realized by a Web application. That web platform receives input to two different types of text: tweets and movie reviews. The online sources of this Sentiment Analysis Web application are: Twitter, Reddit and Youtube. In [5] a multi-domain fine-grained Sentiment Analysis is implemented for online reviews that concern movies, hotels and online courses.

The classification predictions are based on 5 (five) different classifiers: Pytorch Transformer, Multinomial Naïve Bayes, Logistic Regression, Multi-layer Perceptron and Adaboost. The first classifier is based on Pytorch and the next four classifiers are based on the scikit-learn machine learning Python library. The evaluation is performed based on well-known classification evaluation metrics, such as Precision, Recall, F1-Score and Accuracy. In particular, Precision is a classification metric, which measures the proportion of positive identifications that were actually correct. Recall is a classification metric, which measures the proportion of actual positives identified correctly. F1-score or F-score, is defined as the harmonic mean of a model's precision and recall. F1-score is widely used in the evaluation of information retrieval systems like search engines and other kinds of machine learning models, for instance, models used in natural language processing. Accuracy defines the fraction of a model's correct predictions.

3.1 Evaluating Classifiers

Finally, an evaluation and comparison of the classifiers used is presented. We present and discuss the performance evaluation based on classification accuracies collected from the classification reports. The classification reports are linked to the implementation of the proposed fine-grained Sentiment Analysis application processing online reviews from the Movies, Tripadvisor and Coursera datasets (Tables 1, 2 and 3).

Table 1. Example of classification report for Pytorch Transformer for the Coursera dataset.

Coursera (Pytorch Transfomer training details)			
Epochs	Accuracies	Losses	Hours:Minutes:Seconds
Epoch 1	79.166%	0.282	16:46:02
Epoch 2	79.386%	0.251	17:03:49
Epoch 3	79.483%	0.218	17:35:46
Test results	80.288%		

Table 2. Example of classification report for multi-layer perceptron for the Coursera dataset.

Classes	Precision	Recall	F1-score	Support
Negative	0.39	0.37	0.38	615 (2.3%)
Slightly Negative	0.21	0.21	0.21	546 (2.0%)
Neutral	0.27	0.23	0.25	1288 (4.8%)
Slightly Positive	0.36	0.28	0.32	4476 (16.7%)
Positive	0.85	0.89	0.87	19830 (74.1%)

Testing accuracy: 73%. Testing time approximately 27 minutes

Table 3. Summary of testing accuracies

Classifier	Movies/SST5	Tripadvisor	Coursera
Pytorch Transformer	49.457% (49.9%)	65.418%	80.288%
Multinomial Naïve Bayes	39%	44%	74%
Logistic Regression	40%	62%	78%
Multi-layer Perceptron	35%	56%	73%
Adaboost	30%	55%	75%

The testing accuracy score of 49.9% refers to the published accuracy about the SST5 dataset [12], whereas the 49.457% accuracy is the one retrieved by us, after training and testing the Pytorch transformer on the same dataset in our machine.

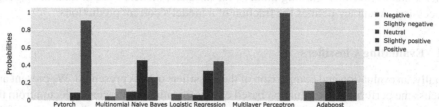

Fig. 7. Example of positive review sentiment prediction probabilities: "wonderful and amusing movie"

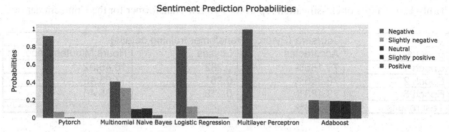

Fig. 8. Example of negative review sentiment prediction probabilities: "horrible and bad movie"

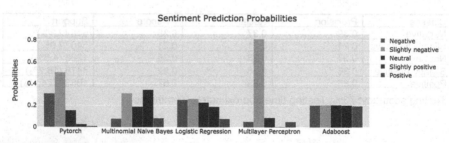

Fig. 9. Example of slightly negative review sentiment prediction probabilities: "not so amusing movie"

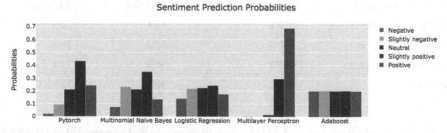

Fig. 10. Example of slightly positive review sentiment prediction probabilities: "quite creative movie"

Sentiment Prediction Probabilities

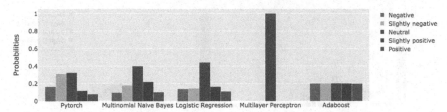

Fig. 11. Example of neutral review sentiment prediction probabilities: "OK movie"

Figures 7, 8, 9, 10 and 11 demonstrate Plotly [11] bar charts for a single review input. These plots concern the movies dataset.

These bar charts demonstrate the probabilities for each classifier. As mentioned above we use 5 classifiers, therefore we have 5 bar charts. Due to the fact that, we perform fine-grained sentiment analysis of 5 emotions, we have 5 bars within each bar chart. The y-axis depicts the prediction probabilities, which add up to 1, in each bar chart.

To commence with the figures' description, we see that Fig. 7 concerns an example review "wonderful and amusing movie". This review was typed in the HTML form created for the movies dataset. After typing the review entry, the "Submit" button is pressed and then the linguistic computation commences. After just a few seconds the interactive – Plotly - bar chart appears in the User Interface (UI). The true label of the typed movie review "wonderful and amusing movie" is Positive. We see that Pytorch, Logistic Regression, Multilayer Perceptron and Adaboost correctly identify this review as Positive. However, Multinomial Naïve Bayes identifies it as Slightly Positive.

In Fig. 8 the probabilities for the negative movie review change dramatically. We see that all classifiers have predicted for the label Negative, which is the correct prediction outcome.

Similarly, in Fig. 9, 10 and 11 the probabilities change when evaluating other types of reviews, such as Slightly Negative, Slightly Positive and Neutral.

Figures 12, 13, 14, 15 and 16 demonstrate Plotly bar charts for a single review input. These plots concern the Tripadvisor dataset.

Sentiment Prediction Probabilities

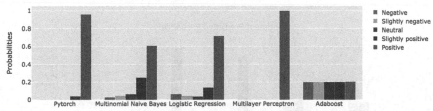

Fig. 12. Example of positive review sentiment prediction probabilities: "amazing and admirable hotel"

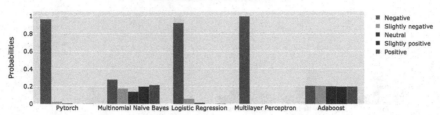

Fig. 13. Example of negative review sentiment prediction probabilities: "awful and terrible hotel"

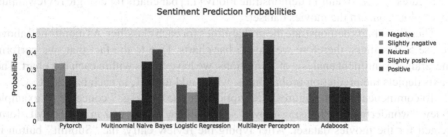

Fig. 14. Example of slightly negative review sentiment prediction probabilities: "not so good hotel"

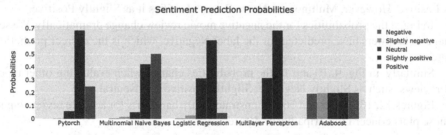

Fig. 15. Example of slightly positive review sentiment prediction probabilities: "quite good hotel"

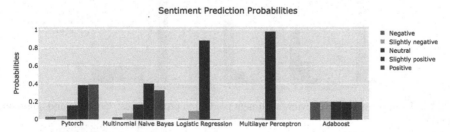

Fig. 16. Example of neutral review sentiment prediction probabilities: "OK hotel"

Figures 17, 18, 19, 20 and 21 demonstrate Plotly bar charts for a single review input. These plots concern the Coursera dataset.

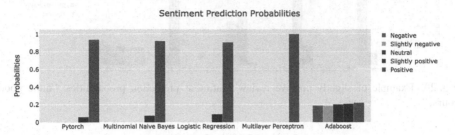

Fig. 17. Example of positive review sentiment prediction probabilities: "wonderful and worthy course"

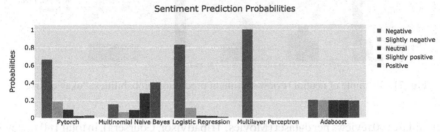

Fig. 18. Example of negative review sentiment prediction probabilities: "poor course"

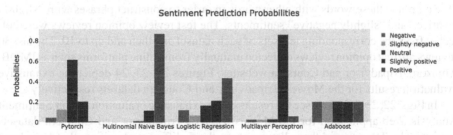

Fig. 19. Example of slightly negative review sentiment prediction probabilities: "not so detailed course"

In Fig. 19 we observe that no classifier managed to classify successfully this new review, as Slightly Negative. This happens due to the fact that Coursera is imbalanced dataset, with Slightly Negative labels representing only 2.0–2.1% of the training – testing sets. There is need to collect more data for this particular label.

4 Exhaustive Evaluation

An exhaustive evaluation per dataset, is performed, based on manually constructed opinion reviews, test review opinion reviews, and real review opinion reviews. The evaluation

Sentiment Prediction Probabilities

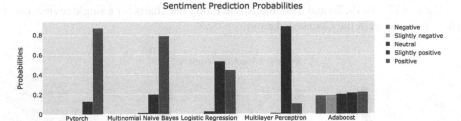

Fig. 20. Example of slightly positive review sentiment prediction probabilities: "quite good course"

Sentiment Prediction Probabilities

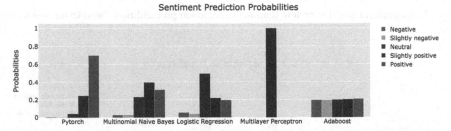

Fig. 21. Example of neutral review sentiment prediction probabilities: "okay course"

accumulates 60 reviews per dataset (Movies, Tripadvisor, Coursera), in total 180 reviews. The manually constructed reviews add up to 20 and they follow specific linguistic rules. These rules introduce specific words with positive, negative or neutral meaning and they combine these words with other words in order to construct phrases with "slightly positive" and "slightly negative" sentiments. The test review opinion reviews were collected from the corresponding test sets of each dataset and then add up to 10. The last 30 reviews are real opinion reviews collected manually from online platforms such as IMDB, Amazon, Tripadvisor and Coursera websites. Figures 22, 23, 24 depict the exhaustive evaluation results for the Movies, Tripadvisor and Coursera datasets respectively.

In Figs. 22, 23 and 24 we see the results of the exhaustive evaluation for our Sentiment Analysis Web application for the Movies (SST5), Tripadvisor and Coursera datasets respectively. The rows in these lists concern the 5 different classifiers that have been used and the columns concern the types of the reviews that were evaluated. The first column is related to the reviews that were constructed by us. These reviews follow specific linguistic rules that we consider, in order to gain a better understanding on the quality of the classification predictions.

Positive words such as, *amazing, wonderful, amusing, astonishing, breathtaking, incredible* were used in order to generate sentences with positive sentiments. On the other hand, negative words such as, *horrible, bad, awful, poor, terrible, terrifying, sad* were used for achieving the opposite, namely sentences with negative sentiment. For the intermediate sentiments (slightly positive and slightly negative), the aforementioned words were combined with *not/so, quite, above, beyond* in order to generate the corresponding sentences accordingly. Last but not least, the simplest form of sentences were

Classifier	Constructed Reviews Score	Test Reviews (Selected) Score	Real Reviews Score	Overall Score
Pytorch	19/20	10/10	30/30	59/60
Multinomial Naive Bayes	8/20	2/10	11/30	21/60
Logistic Regression	12/20	5/10	14/30	31/60
Multilayer Perceptron	8/20	6/10	11/30	25/60
Adaboost	7/20	4/10	9/30	20/60

Fig. 22. Exhaustive evaluation for movies dataset

Classifier	Constructed Reviews Score	Test Reviews (Selected) Score	Real Reviews Score	Overall Score
Pytorch	13/20	10/10	19/30	42/60
Multinomial Naive Bayes	7/20	5/10	4/30	16/60
Logistic Regression	13/20	9/10	12/30	34/60
Multilayer Perceptron	12/20	8/10	11/30	31/60
Adaboost	11/20	9/10	8/30	28/60

Fig. 23. Exhaustive evaluation for Tripadvisor dataset

the neutral ones. These sentences simply used the words: *adequate, average, decent, OK, satisfactory*.

For instance, for the Movie reviews (Fig. 22), the classifier Pytorch Transformer scored 19 out of 20 (19/20). This means that from the 20 constructed reviews, 19 were predicted correctly by this particular classifier. This was the best score for constructed reviews for the Movies dataset. The second-best score was achieved by Logistic Regression (12/20). The next columns concern reviews collected from the test sets and the third column concerns reviews collected from online platforms, such as IMDB and Amazon.

Classifier	Constructed Reviews Score	Test Reviews (Selected) Score	Real Reviews Score	Overall Score
Pytorch	9/20	10/10	17/30	36/60
Multinomial Naive Bayes	4/20	6/10	2/30	12/60
Logistic Regression	11/20	8/10	7/30	26/60
Multilayer Perceptron	14/20	10/10	19/30	43/60
Adaboost	5/20	8/10	5/30	18/60

Fig. 24. Exhaustive evaluation for Coursera dataset

For the test set reviews the best score was recorded again by Pytorch Transformer (10/10). This was also the case for the third column, namely the real reviews (Pytorch scored 30/30). In the last column the overall score is provided, demonstrating that Pytorch transformer was the best performing classifier for Movies and the second best was the Logistic Regression.

In Fig. 23 we see the same type of results for the Tripadvisor reviews. Pytorch scores overall 42/60 and Logistic Regression 34/60. This tell us that Pytorch is still the best but Logistic Regression gains performance on the Tripadvisor dataset, when compared to the Movies dataset.

In Fig. 24 the situation changes. Logistic Regression scores the best (43/60) and Pytorch Transformer is the second best with score 36/60.

5   Interface

Our implemented application is accessed by a web graphical user interface. This application is coded in Python and uses HTML templates with Data Visualizations using the aforementioned Plotly library. The Web server application is based on Flask and Jinja web template engine. Figure 25 demonstrates the interaction with the Web application.

Figure 25 is a System Sequence Diagram (SSD) used in general in software engineering to describe interaction between different role entities. There are three roles: The user of the Application Programming Interface (API), the role of the User Interface (UI) and the role of the Backend. The user is an entity that describes an individual interested in evaluating in real time reviews in terms of sentiment. Such users can be described using Personas, as Fig. 26 demonstrates.

The UI is a software visualization interface enabling user interaction. The user uses the UI in order to enter a new review or trigger an automated evaluation of many reviews.

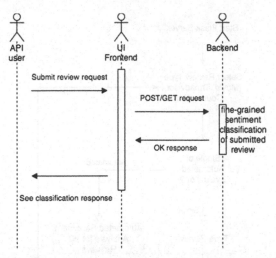

Fig. 25. The Application Programming Interface (API)

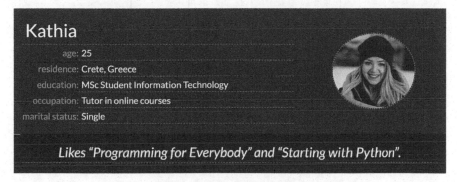

Fig. 26. Kathia's Persona

Then, the backend will read the user request, through the UI, and it will execute the corresponding linguistic computations.

Figure 27 is a flowchart describing the execution flow of the Web application and the available options for the targeted user. There are basically two flows per dataset type. One flow for a single (individual) review evaluation, submitted manually from the user, and one flow for an automated evaluation procedure. This automated evaluation procedure contains 60 reviews, hardcoded in the backend of the Flask server. The dataset type can be: Movies, Tripadvisor or Coursera.

Figure 28 depicts one instance of the UI, in this case for a single movie review submission. The submission is done by pressing the button "Submit" once the user manually types a single movie review, for example "wonderful and amusing movie". The user is given also the option to reset the manually typed review or to trigger an automated evaluation (so-called exhaustive evaluation) of many (60) movie reviews. This UI is replicated accordingly for the Tripadvisor and Coursera review types.

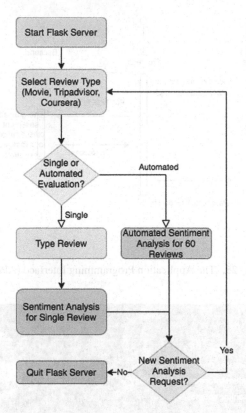

Fig. 27. The flowchart

Enter Your Movie Review for Sentiment Analysis

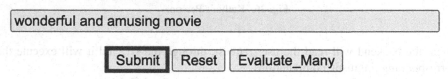

Fig. 28. Enter a single movie review

6 Conclusions and Further Research

The present research paper and implemented application targets sentiment analysis at a more fine-grained level, beyond the typical polarity of "positive", "negative" and "neutral" as evaluations of user input - and with three different datasets, with varying levels of domain-specific content. The fine-grained sentiment analysis was investigated having as a basis three different datasets: SST5 (Movies), Tripadvisor and Coursera. A Pytorch Transformer classifier was used, due to the fact that it performed very well on manually constructed sentiment queries. In addition to the Pytorch Transformer, 4 scikit-learn classifiers were used. The entire classification processing work was embedded in the backend of a Flask server. Through specific buttons in the UI/Frontend, the Flask server can execute specific classification requests and then push the classification outcomes to the frontend.

Therefore, the present research paper attempts to investigate user data and to produce results beyond polarity in Sentiment Analysis – targeting the processing of more subtle emotions and text types with richer content. The implemented application processes multiple categories of emotions and user responses, beyond "positive", "negative" and "neutral", including more subtle elements corresponding to "slightly positive" and "slightly negative". This type of classification is directly linked to inclusion of text types with richer content. In particular, the training data set used ranges from typical domain-specific text types to less domain-specific text types, with a larger variety of expressions. Specifically, the training data involves three datasets, namely Movie reviews, Tripadvisor reviews, and, finally, Coursera reviews.

During the development of this research paper several obstacles were met, with the most severe being the high need in computational resources. The training of the classifiers required several hours, in order to be completed. This means that all classifiers combined for all datasets needed several days in order to be trained, tested and export their corresponding pipeline models in files. These files are quickly loaded by the Flask server in order to predict the new reviews for our sentiment analysis purposes. The Pytorch Transformer was very difficult to run on a machine with 8 gigabytes of Random Access Memory (RAM) and, therefore, another machine was used with 16 gigabytes of RAM, which completed the training process of Pytorch Transformer successfully.

Finally, it should be noted that it is necessary to collect more data for the labels that represent a very small portion of the datasets investigated in this research paper. The portion of examples per dataset is shown in Figs. 1, 2, 3, 4, 5 and 6. Based on these pie charts it can be concluded that Movies (SST5) is well balanced. Tripadvisor is less balanced than Movies (SST5), however more balanced than the Coursera dataset. The Coursera dataset is heavily imbalanced with a very small portion of examples for the Neutral, Slightly Negative and Negative labels.

As future work, several areas for further investigation, application improvement and development are identified in the Thesis. One point for further improvement is the further fine-tuning of Multi-layer Perceptron in the training phase (to avoid overfitting), so that it performs better in the testing phase. Changing the Pytorch Transformer parameters could also be investigated. Additionally, another tokenizer may be used to speed up the preprocessing process, because the current tokenizer is very time consuming. Furthermore, a machine translation feature could be used in order to support reviews in languages other than English. For instance, there are specific Python libraries that support machine translation and can be used for translation purposes. One example of such a library is "Deep-Translator" [7], which is available online. Further research may contribute to overcoming the challenges in Sentiment Analysis and Opinion Mining involving data from varied user groups and human emotions.

References

1. Amari, Y., Okada, S., Matsumoto, M., Sadamitsu, K., Nakamoto, A.: Multimodal analysis of client persuasion in consulting interactions: toward understanding successful consulting. In: Meiselwitz, G. (eds.) HCII 2021. LNCS, vol. 12775, pp. 29–40. Springer, Cham (2021). https://doi.org/10.1007/978-3-030-77685-5_3
2. Giannakis, S.: Sentiment analysis application with social media network integration. Master's thesis, Department of Informatics and Telecommunications, National University of Athens, Greece (2020)
3. Nakahara, T.: Why do we love coffee even though it is bitter? In: Meiselwitz, G. (ed.) HCII 2021. LNCS, vol. 12774, pp. 450–460. Springer, Cham (2021). https://doi.org/10.1007/978-3-030-77626-8_30
4. Rojas, L., Quiñones, D., Rusu, C.: Identifying customer eXperience touchpoints in tourism on the hotel industry. In: Meiselwitz, G. (eds.) HCII 2021. LNCS, vol. 12774, pp. 484–499. Springer, Cham (2021). https://doi.org/10.1007/978-3-030-77626-8_33
5. Theodoropoulos, P.: Fine-grained sentiment analysis of multidomain online reviews. Master's thesis, Department of Informatics and Telecommunications, National University of Athens, Greece (2021)
6. Xing, Y., Lv, C., Wang, H., Cao, D., Velenis, E., Wang, F.-Y.: Driver activity recognition for intelligent vehicles: a deep learning approach. IEEE Trans. Veh. Technol. **68**, 5379–5390 (2019)
7. Deep Translator. https://pypi.org/project/deep-translator/. Accessed 7 Nov 2021
8. Kaggle. https://www.kaggle.com/andrewmvd/trip-advisor-hotel-reviews. Accessed 7 Nov 2021
9. Kaggle. https://www.kaggle.com/septa97/100k-courseras-course-reviews-dataset. Accessed 7 Nov 2021
10. Papers With Code. https://paperswithcode.com/dataset/sst. Accessed 7 Nov 2021
11. Plotly. https://plotly.com/python/bar-charts/. Accessed 7 Nov 2021
12. Towards Data Science. https://towardsdatascience.com/fine-grained-sentiment-analysis-part-3-fine-tuning-transformers-1ae6574f25a6. Accessed 7 Nov 2021

Prediction of Personality Traits Through Instagram Photo HSV

Chu-Chien Wu[1], Ping-Yu Hsu[1], Ni Xu[1], Ming-Shien Cheng[2(✉)], and Yen-Yu Chen[1]

[1] Department of Business Administration, National Central University, No. 300, Jhongda Road, Jhongli, Taoyuan 32001, Taiwan (R.O.C.)
nicoxu@g.ncu.edu.tw

[2] Department of Industrial Engineering and Management, Ming Chi University of Technology, No. 84, Gongzhuan Road, Taishan District, New Taipei City 24301, Taiwan (R.O.C.)
mscheng@mail.mcut.edu.tw

Abstract. Instagram is a popular social networking application for young people nowadays. Users can publish and share photos and apply different photo filters to adjust the appearance of pictures. The adjusted photos turn into works with personal characteristics, and users can share their feelings with viewers. This study aimed to infer the user's personality traits through the analysis of the user's photo hue. To explore the relationship between photo hue and personality traits, a questionnaire survey was conducted. The subjects were asked to fill in the personality traits questionnaire, and the Instagram photos of the subjects were obtained with their consent. The photo hue was input in the SVM classifier and CNN model, and finally, the personality traits classification results were obtained.

Keywords: Instagram · Photo hue · Personality traits · Support Vector Machine (SVM) · Convolutional Neural Network (CNN)

1 Introduction

Modern people's life is almost inseparable from community websites. As far as Instagram is concerned, the number of users worldwide has exceeded 1 billion by January 2020. From sharing community photos to following the updates of relatives and friends, Instagram has been widely used and integrated into people's lives, which can be said to be an indispensable and influential social way.

People intend to present their best on social media, so as many as 90% of users need to do some work (Meitu 2019) before publishing a picture. According to a survey report by Georgia Tech, the number of posts using filters is 21% higher than that without using filters. Undoubtedly, the adjustment of color hue is the most necessary thing. The adjusted photos turn into works with personal characteristics, demonstrating the unique style of each user.

Past studies have found that hues can reflect personality traits (Cerbus and Nichols 1963). Some studies have found that hues have psychological significance for human beings. For example, people with melancholy psychological characteristics prefer black

M. Kurosu (Ed.): HCII 2022, LNCS 13303, pp. 279–287, 2022.
https://doi.org/10.1007/978-3-031-05409-9_21

and often use black to represent themselves (Nolan et al. 1995). Yellow gives a warm but non-stimulating feeling (Clifton 2006). People who are more stubborn and strong prefer warm colors (Fernando et al. 1992). People who like blue are quiet, focused and thoughtful (Hartman 2000).

Meanwhile, many psychological studies explored the relationship between personality and realistic behavior. Personality is a stable structure that can capture individual characteristics and explain behavioral differences (Matthews et al. 2003). Costa & McCrae believed that individual behavior reflects an individual's unique personality characteristics. If these characteristics continue to appear in certain situations, we can call them "personality traits". Therefore, personality traits are stable and important main factors in life.

How to acquire personality traits according to behavior is a topic attracting great concern. One of the acquisition methods is to obtain personality information from the social network (Vinciarelli and Mohammadi 2014). For example, texts can be used to detect Facebook behavior (Chang 2013), Twitter behavior (Golbeck et al. 2011) and analyze Facebook and Twitter personal data image content (Celli et al. 2014). Since Instagram is a social network dominated by photo sharing, texts are not necessary. Thus, it is difficult to make judgments and predictions. Recent studies have used hues to judge personality traits, but the accuracy rate is only about 20%. Moreover, there is little research to explore the relationship between the style of photos posted on Instagram and personality traits.

To solve the above-mentioned research issues, this study conducted personality analysis for Instagram users and accepted the Big Five Inventory widely used by John and Srivastava. The five personality traits are divided into five categories: Extraversion, Agreeableness, Conscientiousness, Neuroticism and Openness. Personality traits on social networks were analyzed from styles of photos posted to Instagram. In this study, the support vector machine (SVM) and the convolutional neural network (CNN) were used to analyze the photos shared on social networks to predict personality traits, which can be used as a reference for subsequent research and enterprise recruitment of employees.

2   Related Work

2.1   HSV

H is hue, S is saturation, and V is value. Hue (H) is the basic attribute of color, such as the commonly used color blue, yellow, etc. Saturation (S) is the purity of the color, and the higher the value is, the brighter the color will be. Value (V) will change with saturation (S), ranging from 0 to 100%. When the value is 0, the color space will turn black completely. As the value increases, the value of the color space increases and various colors are displayed.

RGB and CMYK are additive primary colors and subtractive primary colors respectively, and define colors in the way of primary color combination. Unlike them, HSV is like the way human beings feel colors and has a strong perception. It presents information about colors in a way more familiar to human beings: "What color is this? How is the depth? How is the value?" (Fig. 1).

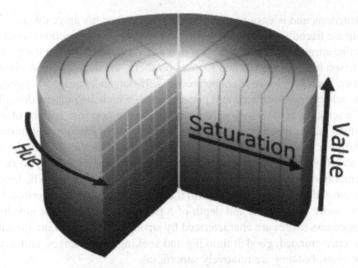

Fig. 1. HSV color model

Different from the above two comparisons, HSV decomposes value from color. Each component of RGB has a high correlation, while HSV color space is less susceptible to light and HSV color space is independent of each other, so HSV can better perceive the color of the photo when adjusting the value, contrast, saturation, hue, etc. (image enhancement algorithm) of the photo. This study predicted personality traits through the hue of photos, and HSV color space was used to interpret photos.

2.2 Five Personality Traits

Personality traits are an abstract concept and have a variety of types. To show the differences between personalities, researchers classified many personality traits and formed the theory of personality traits.

Although different personality traits have appeared in the literature, with the use of factor analysis technology, especially in the 1970s and 1980s, personality psychologists gradually came up with the five main traits or factors, called Big Five, and then gradually formed the so-called five factor model (FFM) hierarchy (taxonomy). These five traits are respectively extraversion, agreeableness, conscientiousness, neuroticism, openness to experience or openness in short. If the order is not considered, the initial letter can be used to form OCEAN (ocean) to facilitate memory. The following are the conceptual definitions of these five traits.

Extraversion is mainly used to measure a person's love for communicating with others and participating in social activities. If a person likes to contact people and participate in social activities, the extraversion will be high. People will be confident, active, outgoing, talkative and achieve outstanding performance. Besides, they also like to make friends and participate in lively occasions and like excitement and stimulation. Agreeableness is mainly used to measure whether a person's interpersonal interaction pattern tends to be friendly or aggressive. If a person is willing to cooperate with others and follow instructions and is easy to communicate with, then his agreeableness is strong. Such people are friendly, polite, easy-going and tolerant. Conscientiousness means the degree of concentration and concentration that a person is focused on the goals he pursues. If a person has fewer goals and focuses on them, the degree of conscientiousness will be higher. Such people are characterized by self-demand, hard work, concentration, orderliness, achievement-oriented and perseverance, which also means discipline, prudence and a sense of responsibility. Neuroticism is the opposite feature of emotional stability, which means that a person can withstand negative emotional stimulation. The less stimulation a person can withstand, the higher his neuroticism and the lower his emotional stability. A high degree of neuroticism indicates a tendency to be nervous, depressed, emotional and insecure. Those with low neuroticism tend to be less nervous, relaxed, secure and able to properly control their temper, and are less excited. Openness is used to measure the amount and depth of a person's acceptance of novelty. People with high openness scores are characterized by strong curiosity and imagination. Most of them are open-minded, good at thinking and seeking new changes, and have a wide range of interests, but they are relatively superficial.

Past studies over years have proved that the five personality traits do exist and are effective. These traits can help to understand oneself and others. Many studies have developed tools to measure personality traits according to the theory of the five personality traits. Such tools may be used to judge the relationship between personality traits and behavior. For example, they can be used to discuss the influence of employees' personality traits on work, the relationship between personality traits and career success in the industry, the positive correlation between extroverted personality traits and salary, promotion and job satisfaction, the negative correlation between neuroticism and job satisfaction, indicating that personal career success is related to his personality traits, or the relationship between personality traits and personal career satisfaction and life satisfaction. Therefore, the correlation between personality traits and the hue of published photos is the emphasis of this study.

2.3 Support Vector Machine (SVM)

SVM is an optimal separating hyperplane (OSH) between two different classes of data or regression between estimated data. The reason why SVM is valued is that it is equivalent to solving a quadratic programming problem (QP problem). For QP problem, there is already a quite solid mathematical theoretical basis. If it satisfies some characteristics, the solution found is a global solution rather than a local solution.

SVM has good performance in classification and prediction, and has been widely used in different fields, such as 3D image recognition, text classification, handwritten character discrimination and classification problems related to biotechnology. In addition to the above reasons, since the feature inputs are all composed of numbers, this study used SVM to predict users' personality traits (Fig. 2).

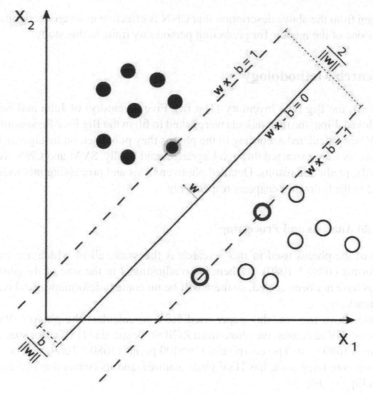

Fig. 2. SVM model

2.4 Convolutional Neural Network (CNN) Method Architecture

CNN is an important and popular technology in the field of deep learning, which has been widely used to solve various problems related to identification and classification. As three-dimensional data can be input, some important spatial information in the image can be preserved, and different spatial arrangements also represent different image features, which is helpful to find out the correlation among them.

The general CNN is a three-tier architecture, which consists of convolution, pooling and full connection. The purpose of convolution operation is to extract different features of input data. In the process, corner angles and lines will be extracted through Filter, and these features will be stored in feature maps. The function of the pooling layer is to reduce sampling, which compresses the picture and retains important information. Pooling can effectively reduce the number of parameters and reduce the amount of computation by reducing the dimension of feature maps. Finally, it is classified by the full connection layer.

CNN is of the function of extracting two-dimensional feature information. It is widely applied in image recognition, such as handwritten character recognition, with an error rate of 0.7% from the LeNet architecture proposed by LeCun. Later, other architectures were also developed. CNN has also been successfully applied to speech recognition. It can be seen from the above description that CNN is effective in image recognition, so it is used as one of the models for predicting personality traits in this study.

3 Research Methodology

In this study, the Big Five Inventory (The Big Five Inventory) of John and Srivastava was employed. First, the respondents were asked to fill in the Big Five Personality Scale, then HSV was calculated according to the photos they published on Instagram, then the photo features were extracted through Lagrange, and finally, SVM and CNN were used to obtain the prediction results. Detailed photo analysis and processing methods will be described in the following chapters respectively.

3.1 Photo Analysis and Processing

The size of the photos used in this research is the same, all of which are Instagram unified format (1080 * 1080), so there is no adjustment in the size of the photos, and the photos have not been scaled, so there will be no content deformation and resolution inconsistency.

For the above reasons, this paper used HSV to calculate the photo features and adopted OpenCV to convert the photo from RGB color space to HSV color space. As the photo size is 1080 * 1080 pixels (pixel), 1166400 points (1080 * 1080) will be obtained after conversion. Each point has HSV three features, and its conversion definition is as shown in Eq. (1) (Fig. 3):

h (Hue): in the range [0, 360], the angle in degrees,
s (Saturation): in the range [0, 1],
v (Value) is in the range [0, 1],
as follows:

$max = \max \{r, g, b\}$
$min = \min \{r, g, b\}$

$$h = \begin{cases} 0° & \text{if } max = min \\ 60° \times \frac{g-b}{max-min} + 0°, & \text{if } max = r \text{ and } g \geq b \\ 60° \times \frac{g-b}{max-min} + 360°, & \text{if } max = r \text{ and } g < b \\ 60° \times \frac{b-r}{max-min} + 120°, & \text{if } max = g \\ 60° \times \frac{r-g}{max-min} + 240°, & \text{if } max = b \end{cases}$$

$$s = \begin{cases} 0, & \text{if } max = 0 \\ \frac{max-min}{max} = 1 - \frac{min}{max}, & \text{otherwise} \end{cases}$$

$$v = max \tag{1}$$

Three continuous functions can be obtained by arranging HSV values in sequence in a photo, representing H, S and V respectively. As there are too many features (1080 * 1080 * 3), this paper used principal components analysis (PCA) to extract the

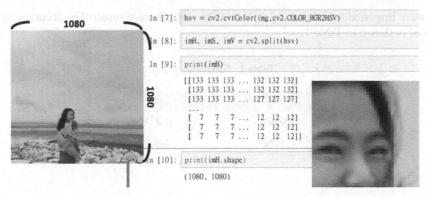

Fig. 3. Photo to HSV

features of a photo, reducing the features of a photo to 3 * 3, i.e. Finding its minimum or maximum eigenvalue (extreme value) in 1080 * 1080 points, as shown in Eq. (2):

$$L(x_1, x_2, \lambda) = f(x_1, x_2) + \lambda g(x_1, x_2)$$
$$\frac{\partial L}{\partial x_1} = 0, \frac{\partial L}{\partial x_2} = 0, \frac{\partial L}{\partial \lambda} = 0, \tag{2}$$

3.2 Classification Model

This study used two models, SVM and CNN, of which SVM is the main classification model, hoping that a simple and time-consuming regression model can predict personality traits.

CNN is often used in various problems related to image recognition and classification, and it can be seen from the above that it is effective.

3.3 Data Collection

In this study, the BFI Personality Scale was used as a psychological test with credibility recognized by the international psychological circle. The accuracy of the test is calculated based on the test results.

Google Forms were used for questionnaire design and recycling. A total of 291 questionnaires were collected, of which 28 were invalid (Instagram photos of respondents could not be obtained), and 263 were valid, of which 42 were men. The main age group was 20–25 years old, accounting for 71.8%, with a total of 43,132 photos (excluding films). According to the 80/20 rule, the photo database was divided into training sets and test sets, i.e. 34,505 as training data sets and 8,627 as TEST data sets.

4 Research Results

80% of the original data set was taken as the training set and the remaining 20% as the test set. After the training of the classification model was completed, the data of the test set were imported into the model to obtain the classification result. The accuracy of the model is shown in Table 1:

Table 1. Model accuracy

Accuracy	
SVM	42.8%
CNN	48.3%

Based on the results of the above experiments, we can find that the method of convolution neural network can use the color hue of photos for effective classification, and the accuracy performance of convolution neural network is better than that of SVM classifier commonly used.

5 Conclusion and Future Research

Research on personality traits has always been popular. For example, there are many related researches on purchasing behavior analysis in marketing field or reference basis for enterprise candidates. However, the acquisition method of personality traits is difficult, and it is often obtained by filling in personality traits.

This study excluded the previous manual standardized tests, and used photo hue to make five personality classification predictions based on psychology, social network, data mining and statistics. The image hue was used as the input of SVM classifier and CNN model, and finally the personality traits classification results were obtained. According to the experimental results, the accuracy of the model used can reach 40%, which indicates that the photo hue may serve as a tool to distinguish personality traits.

Based on the results of this experiment, the color hue of photos can be used as the basis for judging personality traits, which not only solve the problem that manual standardized tests can hardly obtain personality traits and are complicated, but also obtain the personality traits of interviewers in real time for enterprise recruitment. Due to the rise of awareness of personal data privacy and security in recent years, many people's social network platforms are set as closed accounts, that is, photos and videos released by them cannot be seen without permission, so it is also difficult to obtain such photos and videos to a certain extent. For example, the invalid questionnaires were caused due to the provision of invalid Instagram accounts (which does not exist) or Instagram accounts that cannot be accessed. Even the purpose of this study has been indicated on the questionnaire and it is also promised that no personal data will be leaked, some subjects may still worry about security. This also shows that network users are sensitive to information security, and future research can be used as a reference for this topic.

Moreover, the traditional method of filling in the personality characteristics inventory does not guarantee correct answers due to insufficient self-understanding or ideal self-understanding. Thus, the calculated personality traits may not be correct. Future research can also consider this problem.

In addition, the interpretation and meaning of color may be influenced by cultural factors, so culture may lead to different behaviors of photographing angle and hue application.

References

Meitu Inc. 2019 US Photo Taiwan Selfie Pink Book (2019)

Matthews, G., Deary, I.J., Whiteman, M.C.: Personality Traits. Cambridge University Press, Cambridge (2003)

Cerbus, G., Nichols, R.C.: Personality variables and response to color. Psychol. Bull. **60**(6), 566–575 (1963)

Nolan, R.F., Dai, Y., Stanley, P.D.: An investigation of the relationship between color choice and depression measured by the beck depression inventory. Percept. Mot. Skills **81**(3_suppl), 1195–1200 (1995)

Clifton, D.: Basic need in a new light – a colorful diagnosis. Int. J. Real. Ther. **26**(1), 18–19 (2006)

Fernando, M.L.D., Cernovsky, Z.Z., Harricharan, R.: Color preference of DSM-III-R bipolars and normal controls. Soc. Behav. Pers. **20**(4), 247–250 (1992)

Hartman, T.: Color your future: using the character code to enhance your life. Simon and Schuster (2000)

Vinciarelli, A., Mohammadi, G.: More personality in personality computing. IEEE Trans. Affect. Comput. **5**(3), 297–300 (2014). ISSN 1949-3045

Chang, X.Z.: Using text mining to predict personality based on social behavior (2013)

Golbeck, J., Robles, C., Turner, K.: Predicting personality with social media. In: Proceedings of the 29th ACM Conference on Human Factors in Computing Systems (CHI), May 2011 (2011)

Celli, F., Pianesi, F., Stillwell, D., Kosinski, M.: Workshop on computational personality recognition. In: Proceedings of the 22nd ACM International Conference on Multimedia, pp. 1245–1246 (2014)

Emotion and Physiological Reactions Recognition

Analyzing Facial Expressions and Body Gestures Through Multimodal Metaphors: An Intelligent E-feedback Interface

Abdulrhman Alharbi(✉) [iD]

Taibah University, Madina, Kingdom of Saudi Arabia
aamharbi@taibahu.edu.sa

Abstract. Humans develop facial expressions to transmit a variety of meanings in a variety of settings. The facial expression is in charge of transmitting not just concepts or information, but also sentiments. What makes emotional communication fascinating is that it seems as if certain of emotional states are biologically programmed and are exhibited in much the same way among all individuals of all societies. Humans employ facial expressions in a variety of circumstances, ranging from reactions to environmental events to specific linguistic formulations under sign languages. This research presented the experimental effort carried out in order to examine creatively the viewpoints of individuals on distinct facial expressions and body language (neutral, happy, thinking, hand clenching, arms folded, chin-stroking, and arms pointing) when used to deliver different feedback types in an e-feedback interface. Also, it investigated usability aspects and the engagement of users with feedback in platforms that presented feedback types through three different e-feedback interfaces. The first interface incorporated face-to-face (video) vibrant facial structure while generated voice with text was used for the second interface. In the third interface, the interface made use of half body animated avatar with facial expression. The assessed usability measures included efficiency where the task is measured in completing time, effectiveness where the task is measured correctly completed, and user satisfaction.

Keywords: Usability · E-feedback interface · User engagement · Synthesized speech · Facial expressions · Body gestures

1 Introduction

Internet technology has changed the everyday routines and lifestyles of college students across the globe. The interaction of physical and technical settings has necessitated the development of new methodologies for the creation and evaluation of student-targeted solutions. Modern educational systems and assistive technology have been developed to support both healthy and impaired people enhance their learning processes and cognitive capacities. Video streaming, online learning, and remotely operated research are all making inroads into the Web-based education field. Together with the advancement of second-generation virtual learning facilities, it would be important to consider modifying

© The Author(s), under exclusive license to Springer Nature Switzerland AG 2022
M. Kurosu (Ed.): HCII 2022, LNCS 13303, pp. 291–302, 2022.
https://doi.org/10.1007/978-3-031-05409-9_22

the user experience of learning teaching strategies for the innovative interface, such as multimedia and interactive media advancements, as well as creating the academic standards required for widespread implementation.

The development of interfaces for educational technology and technology-enhanced learning is increasing rapidly. This is because of the importance of delivering information to students effectively and the significance of feedback to students. Therefore, feedback is considered to be one of the most important issues in the learning process. Students wish to receive feedback from tutors in a clear and easily understandable manner. There is a general lack of e-feedback interfaces that deliver effective feedback. This indicates that written feedback is not always helpful and that the use of multimodal metaphors (audio and visual) can potentially have a better performance in terms of efficiency at least in some cases. The feedback interface in an educational setting is depicted in Fig. 1. The top section (a) depicts positive feedback, while the bottom section (b) depicts negative feedback.

The use of multimodal metaphors also allows users to read selectively by browsing through the audio and visual materials by skipping parts of little interest [1 and 2]. In addition, the learning styles of students often differ. Therefore, the use of multimodal metaphors enhances the learning capabilities of students by providing different means of learning such as audio, video, mp3, and screenshots [3–5]. The e-feedback should be in such a manner that it should enhance the learning capabilities of the students as well as ease the process of human-computer interaction. Recently, e-feedback systems using multimodal metaphors have gained significant importance.

The remaining part of the work is organized as: Sect. 2 designates the background and related works. Section 3 describes the experimental setup for conducting the research. Section 4 describes the methodology and hypothesis of the proposed research work. Section 5 depicts the experimental results and discussion. The research work is concluded in Sect. 6.

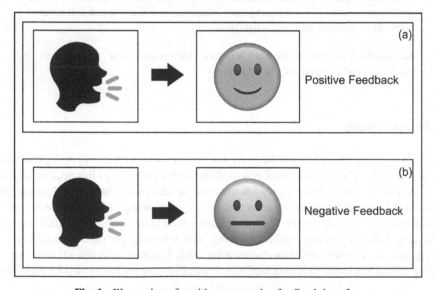

Fig. 1. Illustration of positive or negative feedback interface

2 Background and Related Work

In the context of e-feedback, the student's responses to the audio and visual feedback often lead to encouraging results in terms of understanding the subject and enhancing the learning and its efficiency [1]. It was demonstrated that student arts-based students are good in terms of selecting the subjects that help them later in boosting their interests. However, activities and actions related to writing content are not as actively participating by the art and design student compared to the activities involving the use of the audio and visual senses [6]. Also, students were more comfortable with accomplishing activities using the audio and visuals marks in order to remember lessons and understand the concepts rather than relying largely on the text that is often cumbersome to read [6]. Furthermore, the word blindness condition also called dyslexia is a condition in which a student is unable to differentiate among different kinds of words and this difficulty can be removed by using audio feedback [4, 5, 7, 8]. The concept of multimodal feedback has been utilized to help to get the small targets in the realm of graphical user interfaces during the human-computer interaction [9]. The feedback was provided in three types called the non-speech, tactile, and pseudo-haptic. In the tactile type of the feedback, the simulation was performed by making use of the vibration and the sticky conditions were performed by dynamically reconfiguring the display controlled by the mouse when the cursor was used to enter the target. The conclusion drawn indicated that for all the three types of feedback systems, the target time was reduced as long as the targets were located close to one another rather than being at a reasonable distance.

There is a great need to have a presentation system that structures the data in such a manner that it is presented well to the students [10, 11]. The presentation data is often in the form of multimodal metaphors and enhancing the ways of presentation would certainly help the students in understanding the presentation better. The work of a master thesis also argues in the same direction [12]. The thesis proposes the design of a presentation recording system that is based on multimodal metaphors. The obvious advantage of the proposed system is that it can be used to save the presentation and students can access it anytime. For example, a student can play the audio or video files of the presentation at different times. The lecture can be listened by the student repeatedly until the underlying concepts are fully clarified. A specific presentation is recorded and managed. All the contained information can be saved and retrieved in a number of multimedia formats. Special software is used to perform all these actions for the proposed system [13–15].

3 Experiment

This experiment examined and compared the use of characters in e-feedback platforms as virtual academics, presenting six sorts of feedback. In addition to graphical and textual communications metaphors, synthesized speeches, as well as animated speech-speaking avatars, were used in three modes of presentations that talk face-to-face video, synthesize speech, and speak avatars with facial movements and body language interface. This study aims to investigate the effect of multimodal metaphors (synthesized speech, natural facial expressive, natural recorded speech, and facial expressive avatar with body gestures) and feedback type in an e-feedback interface on usability. Moreover, it is aimed to obtain the user's perspective about the interface which is delivering different feedback types more effective in terms of using face to face, synthesized speech, and avatar with body gestures. It is also evaluating usability in aspects of efficiency, effectiveness, and satisfaction by utilizing the platforms listed below:

3.1 Feedback Types

Six different types of feedback were communicated to users by the experimental interfaces. The first type of feedback was about the location of error that the tutor identified within the assessed work. The second type was about the tutor's expressed comments that may demonstrate techniques or procedures that the student has not followed or used appropriately. The third type was about student's engaged thinking that enables the user to reason and reflect upon the merits or shortfalls of their written or presented work. The fourth feedback type was about explaining ideas or concepts that are primarily used to clarify issues to students. The fifth type was about further suggestions that refer users to further study or reading. The final type was the mark with the justification for the assigned marks or grades.

3.2 Using of Non-speech Metaphors

Samples of facial expressions and physical actions employed in the experiment are shown in Fig. 2 [16]. Four types of facial expressions were commonly used in both face-to-face platform and avatar body gestures, [17] whereas four body movements were utilized in the avatar body gestures platform. Such typical expressions, as well as gestures, are often utilized by teachers or instructors when feedback is communicated to students [17]. Facial expressions and body gestures are classified into three groups; positive, neutral, and negative [18, 19]. The software eSpeack was used to present the synthesized speech [20, 21].

3.3 Usability Criteria

Usability relates to the characteristics and quality of a user engagement using items or systems like sites, applications, equipment, or activities. Usability concerns with user view, efficiency, effectiveness, and user satisfaction. The evaluation of usability deals with how individuals can understand and use a system to achieve their objectives. It also relates to the satisfaction of users [27, 28]. Specialists are using many approaches to obtain feedback from users on an existing interface or plans connected to a new system to support the findings.

a. *User view*
   It is assessed by the percentage of positive and negative users' views regarding each of the modalities that used in each interface.
b. *Efficiency*
   This is the time taken by users to complete a task.

c. **Effectiveness**
It is the number of successfully performed tasks.
d. **User Satisfaction**

It is obtained by the user's responses to the post-experimental questionnaire.

a) Face-to-face platform feedback.
b) Synthesized speech platform feedback.
c) Avatar with body gestures platform feedback.

The proposed experiment comprised of significant levels such as identifications of different feedback types, and further use of non-speech metaphors, and lastly the identification of usability criteria. These levels are discussed in the following sub-sections.

Fig. 2. Facial expressions and body gestures used in the experiment

4   Methodology

In conducting this empirical work, the internal design technique was employed. This design enables the users to participate in the evaluation of all systems and consequently influences any other external factors which may affect the user effectiveness from one treatment to another [22]. Consequently, an evaluation of the new e-feedback systems included one of our users: face-to-face, synthesized speech, and platforms for body gestures. A final tally of 36 users participated individually in the experiment. This research consisted of four basic components. The first section concerns the pre-experimental user characterization questions and obtaining their views on past feedback understanding as well as its categories. The second portion presented test platforms to describe how the research should be done by exhibiting a 2-min recorded video. In the third phase of this research, users were instructed on the innovative platforms, and users were dynamically provided with empirical feedback. The last phase received total feedback from users regarding the usefulness, preferred experimental platform, and commentary on the multimodal metaphors employed.

4.1 Hypothesis

The introduction of this new approach to communicating different types of e-feedback in the context of e-learning interfaces will affect the usability of these interfaces. Therefore, the hypotheses proposed are:

H1
Positive facial expressions as part of a facially expressive avatar that communicates e-feedback will be rated positively by users in terms of being meaningful and understood for all feedback types.

H2
Positive body gestures as part of a facially expressive avatar with body gestures that communicate e-feedback will be rated positively by users in terms of being meaningful and understood for all feedback types.

H3
Voice expression using synthesized speech as a means to communicate e-feedback will be rated negatively by users in terms of being meaningful and understood for feedback types.

H4
When e-feedback is communicated using different multimodal metaphors (e.g. face to face, avatar body gestures or synthesized speech) for the different types of feedback, variable efficiency (i.e. time taken by users to complete tasks), effectiveness (i.e. successfully completed tasks), and user satisfaction rates will be observed.

H5
There will be a good fit between multimodal metaphors used and feedback types in terms of usability parameters of efficiency, effectiveness, and satisfaction.

5 Results and Discussion

In order to investigate the relevance of category data variations as user opinions, the nonparametric Chi-square test was applied in the statistical analysis [22, 23]. The Kolmogorov-Smirnov test revealed that the residual data were not normally dispersed and ANOVA was consequently utilized by Friedman. In the event of a violation of normal data distribution [24, 25], this test may be used to examine changes among experimental circumstances within subjects. Furthermore, the Wilcoxon signed-rank test was utilized to conduct follow-up pairs between the experimental circumstances of this research when a p-value of the Friedman test is higher than 0.05 as the non-parametric counterpart of the dependent t-test [22, 26].

The findings indicate that the users also perceived facial expressions as well as body gestures generally as favorable. The findings suggest that special facial expressions and movements may be more enticing to students, but certain other emotions may not be ideal for students. The virtual body movements' platform was a highly efficient, effective, and successful presentation method. Furthermore, when the entire body of avatar speakers was animated by the conversation, the users were more engaged, happier, and worried. Findings also indicated that the degrees of usability of face-to-face, as well as virtual body movements, are similar. However, it was not so important to users as the Avatar Body Gestures system that the incorporations of face-to-face conversation into an interface component other than that used to provide textual feedback (as implemented in the Avatar Body Gestures system). In general, the virtual body management platform was far more pleasant to users than the users and the synthesized voice platforms and encouraged them for evaluation. They consequently assessed the function that e-feedback systems could perform.

The results showed that facial expressions have been highly regarded by users (happiness was rated significantly high). The percentage of positive rating for this expression is about 69%. On the other side, the most favorable views were neutral terms by the users, where they were 86% thinking as well as 75% neutral. The test findings from Chi-square supported what was hypothesized with H1 when neutral and positive phrases were significantly acceptable for users. These findings provide additional support to H1.

It was assumed that voice expression will be rated negatively in H3. The synthesized speech is usually used to give instructions to users and it should be used for short statements. The results were not significant for the most voice expression used to communicate e-feedback. A sequence of tones was rated negatively by most users (64%). While the rate of the remaining voice expressions was close to each other. On the other hand, volume expression was the only significant positive rate. On the whole, it is clear these results support the H3. The number of questions that were answered correctly and the satisfaction of users varied across these interfaces. The illustration of this can be seen in Fig. 4. The ANOVA computations of Friedman revealed this variation to be significant. The avatar body motions platform was judged to be the highly efficient, effective, and most acceptable presenting option through many evaluations. The way in which avatar corporeal actions are carried out in order to provide feedback for the students encouraged the usage of feedback, similar to the actual human contact between lecturers and students.

Furthermore, when the entire group of speakers was animated, people immersed themselves more and became more involved in the engagement. In addition, it assisted users to view both feedback forms simultaneously in the Avatar lecturer's background inside one interface element of the avatar body movements' platform. The comparing of face-to-face with avatar body motions shows that the usability levels are the same. However, it was significant even though, using avatar body gestures performed better than using face to face and their usefulness was rated higher.

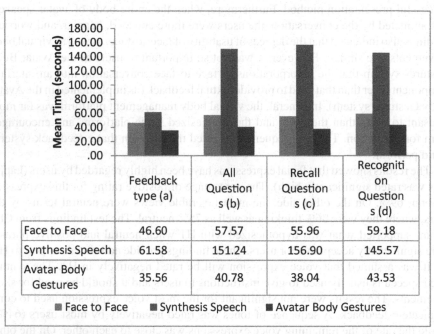

	Feedback type (a)	All Questions (b)	Recall Questions (c)	Recognition Questions (d)
Face to Face	46.60	57.57	55.96	59.18
Synthesis Speech	61.58	151.24	156.90	145.57
Avatar Body Gestures	35.56	40.78	38.04	43.53

■ Face to Face   ■ Synthesis Speech   ■ Avatar Body Gestures

Fig. 3. Mean values of time of all feedback types (a), all questions (b), feedback recall questions (c), feedback recognition (d).

Overall the users have taken less time responding to the identification question than their time answering the reminder questions. The illustration of this can be seen in Fig. 3. The mean time that users spent answering feedback recognition questions was 82.78 and for recall, questions were 83.63. However, lower time was spent by users to answer questions in feedback recall questions in synthesized speech and avatar body gestures platforms. Users were impressed and satisfied with the diverse aspects of the avatar body gestures platform as well as the learning skill they extended using this platform. The illustration of this can be seen in Fig. 5.

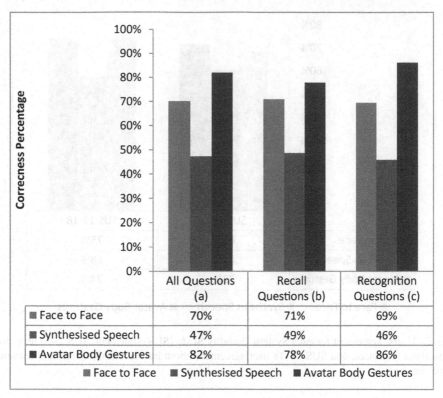

	All Questions (a)	Recall Questions (b)	Recognition Questions (c)
■ Face to Face	70%	71%	69%
■ Synthesised Speech	47%	49%	46%
■ Avatar Body Gestures	82%	78%	86%

■ Face to Face   ■ Synthesised Speech   ■ Avatar Body Gestures

Fig. 4. Correctness percentage of all questions (a), feedback recall questions (b), feedback recognition questions (c).

The findings presented that the users also perceived facial expressions as well as body gestures generally as favourable. These results advocate using these terms and movements in the designing of avatars to display an appealing and pleasant persona as an instructor. The findings of this experiment also gave genuine suggestions for better efficacy, efficiency, and more satisfaction than the other two e-feedback platforms, while using half-body animation of the speaker, together with feedback in the same text at the same platform.

Regarding different types of feedback (i.e. Error and Further Suggestions), the multimodal audio-visual demonstration of the feedback types as implemented in the avatar body gestures platform, also, feedback questions types (feedback recall question and feedback recognition questions). However, the results appeal to extra questions such as: would adding auditory non-speech metaphors to avatar body gestures platform enhance the student's engagement with different feedback types. This will be investigated more in the next experimental stage. These results are in agreement with other reported results in the literature that recorded natural speech is better than synthesized speech.

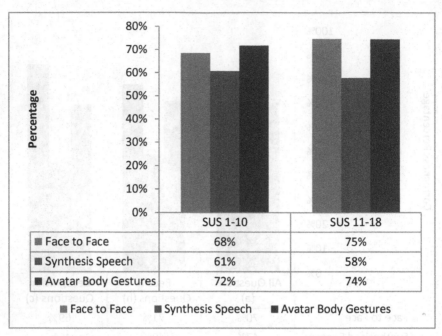

Fig. 5. Users' agreement for each System Usability Scale (SUS) statement, SUS 1–10 user attitude about interfaces, and SUS 11–18 user agreement about interface components and learning experience.

6 Conclusion

The research in this paper suggests that combining tones and pitches to stress particular words and phrases within the delivered speech is aiding user comprehension. The research in this paper suggests that synthesized speech should only be used for short messages to communicate e-feedback. For example, to give instructions to users and even, in this case, it should be in very short sentences. The usage of a recorded speaking face with facial gestures in a different interaction component than that used to offer textual feedback (as utilized in the avatar body gestures system) did not attract users more than the facially expressive avatar with body gestures. It is therefore suggested to use face-to-face (video) to deliver Mark and Comment feedback type. on the basis of the empirical data, it is suggested to use facial expression to animate avatars particularly when further suggestions and engage thinking feedback types are communicated. Positive body gestures should be included in the design of an expressive avatar that communicates feedback and it was found to be particularly useful when error, further suggestions, and marks need to be communicated.

The obtained results showed that the gestures (e.g. pointing, walking and arms folded) used contributed to the learning process and engaged the users with the different types of the communicated feedback. However, there were some body gestures (e.g. chin-stroking and hands clenching) that according to data and observations are less likely to have contributed to the comprehension and engagement of users with the feedback communicated by the virtual tutors. Users also did not find these gestures particularly helpful.

References

1. Chipps, R., Lowe, J.: Students responses to audio and visual feedback. De Montfort University (2012)
2. Vitense, H.S., Jacko, J.A., Emery, V.K.: Multimodal feedback: establishing a performance baseline for improved access by individuals with visual impairments. In: Proceedings of the Fifth International ACM Conference on Assistive Technologies, pp. 49–56 (2002)
3. Nortcliffe, A., Middleton, A.: Smartphone feedback: using an iPhone to improve the distribution of audio feedback. Int. J. Electr. Eng. Educ. **48**, 280–293 (2011)
4. Rotheram, B.: Using an MP3 recorder to give feedback on student assignments. Educ. Dev. **8**, 7 (2007)
5. van der Kleij, F.M., Eggen, T.J.H.M., Timmers, C.F., Veldkamp, B.P.: Effects of feedback in a computer-based assessment for learning. Comput. Educ. **58**, 263–272 (2012)
6. Glover, C., Brown, E.: Written feedback for students: too much, too detailed or too incomprehensible to be effective. Biosci. Educ. e-J. **7**, 1–6 (2006)
7. Chang, N.: Can students improve learning with their use of an instructor's extensive feedback assessment process? Instruct. Technol. **6**, 49 (2009)
8. Schum, T.R., Krippendorf, R.L., Biernat, K.A.: Simple feedback notes enhance specificity of feedback to learners. Ambul. Pediatr. **3**, 9–11 (2003)
9. Cockburn, A., Brewster, S.: Multimodal feedback for the acquisition of small targets. Human-Computer Interaction Lab, Dept of Computer Science, University of Canterbury, New Zealand (2012)
10. Heinrich, E., Milne, J.: Applying a framework to evaluate assignment marking software: a case study on Lightwork. Res. Learn. Technol. **20**, n2 (2012)
11. Burrows, S., Shortis, M.: An evaluation of semi-automated, collaborative marking and feedback systems: academic staff perspectives. Australas. J. Educ. Technol. **27**, 1135–1154 (2011)
12. Funchal: Improved Management. Retrieval and Access of Presentation Recordings for Enhanced Learning Processes, Master thesis, University of Maderia (2008)
13. Heinrich, E., Milne, J., Moore, M.: An Investigation into E-Tool Use for Formative Assignment Assessment–Status and Recommendations. Образовательные технологии и общество, **12** (2009)
14. Hepplestone, S., Holden, G., Irwin, B., Parkin, H.J., Thorpe, L.: Using technology to encourage student engagement with feedback: a literature review. Res. Learn. Technol. **19**, 117–127 (2011)
15. Gibson, D., B. Dodge, D.: Social Learning through the Avatar in the Virtual World: The Effect of Experience Type and Personality Type on Achievement Motivation
16. Beale, R., Creed, C.: Affective interaction: How emotional agents affect users. Int. J. Hum Comput Stud. **67**, 755–776 (2009)
17. Wang, Y., Geigel, J.: Using facial emotional signals for communication between emotionally expressive avatars in virtual worlds. Affect. Comput. Intell. Interact. 297–304 (2011)
18. Power, M.R.: Non-verbal communication (1998)
19. Korte, B.: Body Language in Literature. Univ of Toronto Pr (1997)

20. Palmer, M.: Face recognition software gaining a broader canvas. Financ. Times **22**, 74 (2010)
21. Janse, E.: Time-compressing natural and synthetic speech. In: Seventh International Conference on Spoken Language Processing (2002)
22. Lazar, J., Feng, J.H., Hochheiser, H.: Research Methods in Human-Computer Interaction. Wiley, London (2009)
23. Clark-Carter, D.: 7 quantitative research methods: gathering and making sense of numbers. In: Healthcare Research: A Textbook for Students and Practitioners, p. 130 (2010)
24. Argyrous, G.: Statistics for Research: With a Guide to SPSS. Sage Publications Ltd, London (2011)
25. A. P. Field, Discovering Statistics using SPSS. SAGE publications Ltd, 2009
26. Pathak, D.C.: Comparing Two Means using SPSS (T-Test) (2009)
27. Ansari, M.T.J., Baz, A., Alhakami, H., Alhakami, W., Kumar, R., Khan, R.: P-STORE: extension of STORE methodology to elicit privacy requirements. Arab. J. Sci. Eng. **46**(9), 8287–8310 (2021). https://doi.org/10.1007/s13369-021-05476-z
28. Ansari, M.T.J., Al-Zahrani, F.A., Pandey, D., Agrawal, A.: A fuzzy TOPSIS based analysis toward selection of effective security requirements engineering approach for trustworthy healthcare software development. BMC Med. Inform. Decis. Mak. **20**(1), 1–13 (2020)

A Swarm Intelligence Approach: Combination of Different EEG-Channel Optimization Techniques to Enhance Emotion Recognition

Sabahudin Balic[✉], Lukas Kleybolte[✉], and Christian Märtin

Faculty of Computer Science, Augsburg University of Applied Sciences, An der Hochschule 1, 86161 Augsburg, Germany
{sabahudin.balic,lukas.kleybolte,
christian.maertin}@hs-augsburg.de

Abstract. This paper describes well-known classification techniques which are evaluated for emotion classification. The aim of this work is the comparison of different channel selection techniques to achieve fast computation for electroencephalogram (EEG) data. Swarm intelligence algorithms belong to the class of nature-inspired algorithms which are very useful in achieving high accuracies while reducing the computing cost. In this paper different channel optimization techniques are compared to each other. They are applied to the DEAP dataset to find the most suitable channels in the context of emotion recognition. For channel selection, principal component analysis (PCA), maximum relevance-minimum redundancy (mRMR), particle swarm optimization (PSO), cuckoo search (CS) and grey wolf optimization (GWO) were investigated. By applying these optimization algorithms, the number of EEG channels could be reduced from 32 to 20 while the accuracy remained nearly the same. The proposed optimizations techniques saved between two- and seven-hours of computing time in training the Bidirectional Long Short-Term Memory model to classify emotions, while the computing time without channel selection took 18 h. Among these algorithms, mRMR and CS obtained the most promising results. By using mRMR a total computing time of 11 h with an accuracy of 92.74% for arousal and 92.36% for valence was achieved. For CS a total computing time of 15 h was achieved, with an accuracy of 93.33% for arousal and 93.67% for valence.

Keywords: Emotion recognition · Channel selection · Swarm intelligence · EEG · mRMR · Cuckoo search · Computing time reduction

1 Introduction

Human-computer interaction holds an outstanding position in society and research. Whether in the field of psychology, medicine or market research, significant progress has been made by applying HCI technologies and methods to these disciplines. These days emotion recognition has gained much interest in the context of human-machine interaction. Being able to identify the true current emotional state of patients – especially those with expressive difficulties – would not only contribute to better communication and understanding, but also to better diagnosis and adequate medical care. Knowing exactly the varying emotions of individual users and customers could both improve user experience and commercial goals of the providers of interactive games, entertainment services, and e-commerce sites.

One way to detect emotions is by using brain waves, where physiological signals from the brain can be analyzed and evaluated using the electroencephalogram (EEG). The signals are measured by electrodes, which are usually applied in 10–20 [1], 10–10 [2] or 10–5 [3] schemes, whereby these schemes distribute the electrodes evenly over the top of the skull. However, a reduction of electrodes or a specific selection of the electrodes in relation to the goals of the application could increase the accuracy and decrease the computational effort.

This paper describes well-known techniques that are normally applied in other classification areas, e.g., in motor imagery, but are used here in emotion classification. The aim of this work is to compare different channel selection techniques to obtain the most suitable selection method to achieve a fast-computing process with high accuracy. In Sect. 2 we update the state-of-the-art channel selection methods by focusing on filter methods and wrapper methods. In Sect. 3, we describe our emotion model, the used DEAP dataset, and the swarm intelligence process with its preprocessing approach, and the Bidirectional Long Short-Term Memory classification model. In Sect. 4 we present and discuss our applied approach with its achievements. In the final section we express our thoughts on further research potentials.

2 Related Work

There are several approaches to increase the effectiveness of EEG-based emotion recognition processes. One important method is the *EEG Channel Selection Method* [4, 5]. The Channel Selection Method describes a complex automated process to select suitable EEG channels that provide the most reliable EEG values in correlation. Different algorithms are used for interacting with different parameters.

Three different approaches can be applied to select channels in EEG data leading to better performance and accuracy. One is the *filtering method*, where statistical evaluation criteria are used to find the best possible channels. Advantageous is the high performance of this method and the independence of the classifier. However, the disadvantage of this method is the low accuracy, since possible channel combinations are ignored.

Another approach is the *wrapper method*, where the selection of the best channels takes place during the machine learning process. This is also the most computation-intensive method and can be prone to overfitting. A classic example for wrapper methods is the *Genetic Algorithm* based on the natural theory of evolution.

In contrast to the wrapper method, the third method is embedded into the model building process, i.e., it is located between the filter and the wrapper method. The method is based mainly on recursive channel elimination and has a lower risk of over-fitting compared to the wrapper method.

In 2015, Alotaiby et al. published a review of established evaluation methods for channel selection methods in the areas of seizure detection, motor imagery classification, emotion classification, mental task classification, sleep state classification, and drug effect classification [6]. However, the above research paper lists only two evaluation methods for the emotion classification domain and needs a small extension. One of the two methods is a filtering method by Rizon et al. [7], which uses a fuzzy c-model to obtain the following values, assuming five different basic emotions: Fuzziness performance index $= 0.150051$, modified partition entropy $= 0.154724$, separable distance $= 0.328312$. The other method listed is a wrapper approach by Jatupaiboon et al. [8] which achieves an accuracy of 84.18% with five channel pairs and 85.41% with seven channel pairs by using a Gaussian *Support Vector Machine (SVM)* classifier. The project distinguishes between a positive and a negative emotion.

Ansari-Asl et al. [9] try to select the best channels using a synchronization likelihood method and three different classifiers *(linear discriminant analysis (LDA)*, SVM, *(SVM+Radial Basis Functions)*. In this project three basic emotions are distinguished (exciting-positive, exciting-negative and neutral). It turns out that with the help of the LDA classifier no higher accuracy value than 68.7% was achieved. Yildirim et al. [10] achieved an accuracy of 87.17% using a new approach called *swarm intelligence* with the help of *random forest classifiers*. The swarm intelligence approach includes the feature selection methods *particle swarm optimization (PSO), cuckoo search, grey wolf optimizer* and *dragonfly algorithm*.

Wang et al. [11] achieved 74.53% using a convolutional neural network. Here, a squeeze-excitation is used to additionally evaluate the EEG channels. It consists of an average pooling part across 32 channels, then an excitation part, which evaluates the interdependencies between the channels. For emotion classification, an SVM is applied. Wang et al. [12] using a *normalized mutual information* approach achieve 74.41% with an SVM emotion classifier.

Pane et al. [13] achieve an accuracy value of 99.85% using a *stepwise discriminant analysis (SDA)* approach for a pairing of 15 channels. The SDA is derived from the statistical method of discriminant analysis. In this project three basic emotions are distinguished (positive, negative, and neutral). The channel selection strategy is equipped with the Wilks lambda score.

Al-Qazzaz et al. [14] achieve an accuracy of 86.85% using the *differential evolution algorithm* approach with the help of an LDA as discriminant. *The Savitzky-Golay (SG)* filter and the power of the individual frequency bands (alpha, beta, gamma, delta, theta) were used as features. Tong et al. [15] obtain a value of 72.03% using a ReliefF algorithm while Zhao et al. [16] obtain a value of 89.37% using an approach consisting of SVM, KNN, and the F-score. Finally, the researchers Xu et al. [17] achieve a value of 80.83% using the *max-relevance and min-redundancy (mRMR)* method.

3 Methods

The overall concept of the pipeline to classify emotions is shown schematically in Fig. 1. The approach is comparable in most papers: First, a new EEG dataset is created if no existing one is used. This is followed by a feature extraction phase. Normally, the most relevant features from the extracted ones are selected for classification. However, we are concerned with the question of whether some EEG channels can be rejected to achieve better results, which is why we want to establish channel selection instead of feature selection. For this purpose, we use different approaches based on classical feature selection and swarm optimization.

The resulting adjusted dataset is then used for emotion determination using a classification algorithm, which classifies according to a chosen emotion model.

In the following section we will explain the proposed steps for emotion recognition and describe the used operations in detail.

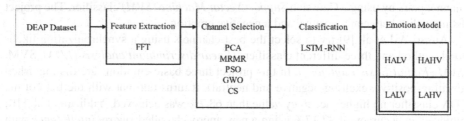

Fig. 1. Proposed model architecture for emotion recognition.

3.1 Emotion Model

In this paper, we use Russel's two dimensional circumplex model, which represents a coordinate system in which the individual emotions are represented. Russell's model is one of the best known bipolar dimensional models, in which he defines two axes, each with a scale from −24 to +24. The valence axis defines the range of negative and positive emotions, while the arousal axis defines the range of calm and excitement. In total, there are 28 emotions in Russel's model. However, we have not used the model in such detail, instead we classify according to the quadrants of the model. In other words, the axes Valence (x) and Arousal (y) represent the individual quadrants of the Russel model, and so also the individual emotion tendencies as shown in Table 1.

Table 1. Emotion's quadrants in Russel's circumplex model.

Quadrants	Emotions
High arousal low valence (HALV)	Angry, Nervous
High arousal high valence (HAHV)	Happy, Excited
Low arousal high valence (LAHV)	Relaced, Calm
Low arousal low valence (LALV)	Sad, Bored

3.2 DEAP Dataset

The DEAP dataset is one of the most widely used datasets in the field of emotion recognition research. This dataset resulted of a study conducted by Koelstra et al. in 2012

[18]. In this study, 40 subjects watched 32 music videos, with a duration of one minute, while their brain waves (EEG) were recorded. Besides their brain waves, eye movements (EOG), muscle movements (EMG), skin temperature, heartbeat, and galvanic skin response (GSR) were also recorded. However, only the EEG data is used in our paper.

To record the EEG data, a 32-channel headset was used with 32 active AgCl electrodes placed in the standardized 10–20 structure on the head of the subjects. The sample rate was 512 Hz and resulted in a dataset with the shape $(32 \times 40 \times 40 \times 32256)$, which is defined by (subject $\times$ video/trail $\times$ channel $\times$ data). This collected data was then pre-processed by down sampling the data to 128 Hz and filtering out the eye movements and applying a bandpass filter from 4.0 Hz to 45.0 Hz.

Since we "only" used 32 EEG channels, the remaining eight channels, which had measured other physical signals, were removed. This resulted in the dataset used here with the dimension of $(32 \times 40 \times 32 \times 8064)$.

3.3 Feature Extraction

The feature extraction is an important part in data analysis to find correlations or to extract important data, therefore we also conducted feature extraction in this paper. Individual frequencies were extracted out of the recorded EEG data using the Fast Fourier Transformation (FFT). The used frequency bands were δ (1–4 Hz), θ (4–8 Hz), α (8–14 Hz), β (14–31 Hz), and γ (31–45 Hz). Via FFT, the data is converted from time domain into frequency domain. In our case FFT was applied to small data "windows" with a fixed size of 2 s, also defined as 256 data points. The spectral power in each frequency domain was then calculated from this window. Subsequently, the window was shifted by 0.125 s, i.e., 16 data points.

Thus, the complexity of the data was reduced from $(32 \times 40 \times 32 \times 8064)$ to a $(32 \times 624640 \times 160)$ shaped dataset. The value 160 in the new dataset dimension represents the 32 channels times the respective 5 frequency bands.

3.4 Classical Channel Selection Based on Classical Feature Selection

As mentioned before, the aim of this work is to develop a classical channel selection, where in our case the whole of the five frequency bands is selected, instead of a usually performed feature selection, where the individual frequency bands are selected. We used the following techniques that are normally used to select features such as statistical features or entropy features. Generally, the EEG channels can also be defined as features, therefore a "feature" selection can be applied to them. By selecting and subsequent reduction of channels, the accuracy, and the speed of learning processes can be increased. In this work we applied the channel selection algorithms after extracting the features. For this purpose, we transformed the dataset from $(32 \times 624640 \times 160)$ to a $(32 \times 3123200 \times 32)$ shape, to obtain 32 separated EEG channels that appear separated in the dataset again. This enabled us to evaluate the channels and to avoid the selection of the individual frequency bands of the channels.

In feature selection, there are two methods that are used frequently, since the idea behind the algorithms is relatively simple, and they operate efficiently. We used the common methods principal component analysis and minimum redundancy and maximum relevance for our channel selection approach.

Principal Component Analysis. The principal component analysis (PCA) is a statistical method for representing the information content of large datasets using a smaller set of summary indices. It is an orthogonal basis transformation which calculates the covariance matrix of the given dataset and finds the *eigenvalues* and *eigenvectors* of this matrix. However, this algorithm preserves the first principal components most of the dataset's variance which is an unarguably advantage. Then, the PCA selects the best *eigenvalues* and *eigenvectors* to form the transformation matrix for dimension reduction. Suppose the origin of the coordinate system is placed in the center of mass of the point cloud. Then, the coordinate system is rotated so that the first coordinate points to the direction of the largest variance of the point cloud, thus the first coordinate represents the first principal axis. In the next step, the coordinate system is rotated again so that the second coordinate and so the second major axis points in the direction of the remaining largest variance. This step is repeated until all coordinates have been processed [19, 20].

Maximum Relevance – Minimum Redundancy. The Maximum Relevance – Minimum Redundancy algorithm (mRMR) invented by Peng et al. [21, 22] calculates the importance of classification variables and low correlations by excluding useless and redundant features in a large date set. To be more precise the main objective of mRMR is to select features with a high correlation with the classification variables and low correlation between themselves, then determine the importance of each feature and to return the n most important features by calculating *Mutual Information I*. When the condition of given marginal probabilities $p(a)$ and $p(b)$ is fulfilled and the joint probability $p(a, b)$ is known the Mutual Information I can be calculated as follows:

$$I(A; B) = \sum_{b \in B} \sum_{a \in A} p(a, b) \log\left(\frac{p(a,b)}{p(a)p(b)}\right).$$ (1)

3.5 Swarm-Intelligence Based Channel Selection

Swarm Intelligence algorithms are based on research on biological behavioral intelligence and different organisms acting in swarms to gain best profit in nature life. Thus, swarm intelligence algorithms arise from nature-inspired algorithms which are hierarchically structured in biology-based algorithms, physic-based algorithms, evolution-based algorithms and human behavior-based algorithms. In this paper we focus on the behavior of particle swarms, cuckoos and grey-wolves [23].

Particle Swarm Optimization. Particle Swarm Optimization PSO is based on a stochastic computational method which optimizes a target problem by iteratively trying to improve a solution candidate. The PSO algorithm is inspired by simulated social behavior of birds or fishes. Each individual represents a PSO particle. Originally the PSO optimizes nonlinear continuous functions and has no evolution operators for crossover and mutation.

The PSO algorithm initially sets the baseline position of each individual representing random solutions (particles) as a swarm ready for propagating global optimal solution over a number of iterations. All particles fit and share information for their further search places.

With the following equations each particle k has a position x_k^n and a velocity v_k^n in iteration $n(n = 1, 2, \ldots, W)$ and flies through on the solution space for finding their best positions:

$$v_k^n = \omega v_k^{n-1} + c_1 \theta_1 \left(x_k^* - x_k^{n-1} \right) + c_2 \theta_2 \left\{ \left(\min_{k \in S} x_k^* \right) - x_k^{n-1} \right\}, \tag{2}$$

$$x_k^n = x_k^{n-1} + v_k^n. \tag{3}$$

The iteration is controlled by the inertia weight factor ω. Additionally, c_1 and c_2 represent the cognitive factors for trust between each particle and the swarm. θ_1 and θ_2 are randomly created numbers in the range $[0, 1]$. x_k^* stands for the best particle while $\min_{k \in S} x_k^*$ is the best swarm at the last iteration [24].

Cuckoo Search. Cuckoo search (CS) [25] belongs to the latest nature-inspired meta-heuristic algorithms, developed in 2009 by Xin-She Yang and Suash Deb. CS is inspired by the brood parasitism of some cuckoo species. CS might potentially be more efficient than PSO and Genetic Algorithms. The Ani and Guira cuckoos lay their eggs in communal nests, though they may remove others' eggs to increase the hatching probability of their own eggs. The Cuckoo Search could be normalized in three rules, where each cuckoo firstly lays one egg at a time and dumps it in a randomly chosen nest. Then, the best nests with high-quality eggs will be carried over to the next generations. The number of available host nests is fixed, and the egg laid by a cuckoo is discovered by the host bird with a probability $p_a \geq (0, 1)$. In this case, the host bird can either get rid of the egg, or simply abandon the nest and build a completely new nest.

The Cuckoo Search Algorithm contains a balanced combination of a local random walk and the global explorative random walk, controlled by a switching parameter p_a while $\alpha > 0$ (step size scaling factor):

$$x_i^{t+1} = x_i^t + \alpha s \otimes H(p_a - \epsilon) \otimes \left(x_j^t - x_k^t \right), \tag{4}$$

defined by x_j^t and x_k^t. These are two different solutions randomly selected by random permutation, while $H(u)$ is a *Heaviside function*, ϵ is a random number drawn from a uniform distribution, and s is the step size. The global random walk uses Lévy flights:

$$x_i^{t+1} = x_i^t + \alpha L(s, \lambda), \tag{5}$$

where

$$L(s, \lambda) = \frac{\lambda \Gamma(\lambda) \sin\left(\frac{\pi \lambda}{2} \right)}{\pi} \frac{1}{s^{1+\lambda}}, (s \gg s_0 > 0). \tag{6}$$

L represents the characteristic scale of the problem of interest, while $\Gamma(\lambda)$ is defined by an integral function, and λ is defined as $0 \leq \lambda \leq 2$ [26].

Grey Wolf Optimizer. The Grey Wolf Optimizer algorithm (GWO) [27] simulates an attacking scenario where a group of wolves tries to catch a prey. This group is separated into a leader (alpha), sub-leader (beta), wolves which follow leader and sub-leader (delta), and omega wolves as lowest rank (omega). This nature inspired algorithm has mainly three steps: tracking and chasing the prey (exploration phase in the GWO algorithm), harassing and encircling the prey (evaluating phase for finding the best candidate during each iteration – Eq. (7)), and attacking towards the prey (exploitation phase – Eq. (9), (10), (11)). Alpha represents the best candidate solution, while Beta and Delta are the second and third solutions. Omega stands for any other solutions:

$$\vec{D} = \left| \vec{C_1} \vec{X_p}(t) - \vec{X}(t) \right|, \vec{X}(t+1) = \vec{X}_p(t) - \vec{A}\,\vec{D}, \tag{7}$$

where t represents the number of the current iteration, $\vec{A}$ and $\vec{C}$ represent the coefficient vectors, $\vec{X}_p$ stands for the position vector of the prey and $\vec{X}$ is a position vector of a grey wolf.

$$\vec{A} = 2\vec{d}\,\vec{r_1} - a, \vec{C} = 2\vec{r_2}, \tag{8}$$

where $\vec{d}$ is a linearly decreasing vector from 2 to 0 over iteration course and $\vec{r_1}, \vec{r_2}$ are random vectors in the range of [0,1]. For the mentioned exploitation phase:

$$\vec{D}_\alpha = \left| \vec{C_1}\vec{X_\alpha} - \vec{X} \right|, \vec{D}_\beta = \left| \vec{C_2}\vec{X_\beta} - \vec{X} \right|, \vec{D}_\delta = \left| \vec{C_3}\vec{X_\delta} - \vec{X} \right|, \tag{9}$$

$$\vec{X}_1 = \vec{X}_\alpha - \vec{A}_1\left(\vec{D}_\alpha\right), \vec{X}_2 = \vec{X}_\beta - \vec{A}_2\left(\vec{D}_\beta\right), \vec{X}_3 = \vec{X}_\delta - \vec{A}_3\left(\vec{D}_\delta\right), \tag{10}$$

$$\vec{X}(t+1) = \frac{\vec{X}_1 + \vec{X}_2 + \vec{X}_3}{3}. \tag{11}$$

3.6 Classification

To extract emotions from EEG data, the features must be classified, i.e., assigned in a dimensional emotion model. Usually, the data is clustered into arousal and valence to determine emotions by using Russel's circumplex model [28]. In general, many algorithms to classify emotions are available.

We decided to use a Bidirectional Long Short-Term Memory (LSTM) model, which is an extension of the basic LSTM, which was introduced 1997 by Hochreiter and Schmidhuber [29]. The LSTMs belong to the family of recurrent neural networks (RNN). In contrast to the RNNs, the LSTMs have a memory pool with two key factors: the short-term and the long-term state. So, the short-term state keeps the output of the current step of the LSTM and the long-term state manages the final elements of the LSTM, whereby the storing, reading, and writing depends on the activation function of the LSTM cell. The architecture of a single LSTM cell is visualized in Fig. 2.

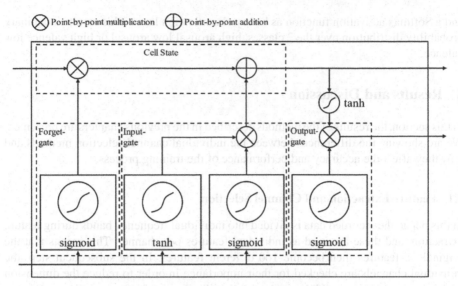

Fig. 2. Architecture of a single LSTM cell.

The first gate in an LSTM cell is the forget gate, it decides which information to remove from the cell state, these decisions are made with a sigmoid layer. The second gate is an input gate, which uses a sigmoid layer to decide which values to update and additionally a tangent hyperbolic layer to create a new vector from the updated values. In the end, the output of the current state is calculated based on the updated cell state and a sigmoid layer that decides which parts of the cell state become the final output.

The difference between a normal LSTM and a bidirectional LSTM is that in a bidirectional LSTM a layer is duplicated, where one layer takes input in the forward direction and the other in the reverse direction. This effectively increases the amount of information available to the network.

We use the architecture of the LSTM defined by Acharya et al. [30] in their publication, where they designed a bidirectional LSTM to classify multiple classes of emotion. They achieved an accuracy of 81.91% for Arousal and 84.39% for Valence. However, in contrast to us, they classified labels from 1 to 10 for arousal and valence respectively, while we classified the emotions by high arousal, low arousal and high valence and low valence, so we have a binary classification problem.

The LSTM model consists of four LSTM layers and two dense layers, with dropout layers between each LSTM layer. The first LSTM layer is the bidirectional layer, which has 128 neurons, but since the layer is duplicated, it has a total of 256 neurons. This is followed by a dropout layer with a probability of 60%. This layer helps to avoid the overfitting, thereby random variables are set to zero. Next comes another LSTM layer with 256 neurons and a dropout layer with a probability of 60%. Afterwards there are two LSTM layers with 64 neurons each, whereby the first one is followed by a dropout layer with a probability of 60%, while the second one is followed by a dropout layer with a probability of 40%. Last comes a Dense layer with 16 classes, and with a Rectified Linear Activation function (Relu). The next layer is a Dens layer with 2 classes and a Softmax activation function as binary classification layer. This results in a binary probability distribution over the 2 classes, high arousal low arousal or high valence low valence.

4   Results and Discussion

In this section, the results of the methods described in the previous chapters are presented. We are showing the differences between the individual channel selection methods and how they affect the accuracy and performance of the training process.

4.1   Feature Extraction and Channel Selection

In this paper, the recorded data is divided into individual frequency bands during feature extraction, and these are used as individual features per channel. This means that the original 32 features then become 160 different features. In the subsequent step, the individual channels are checked for their importance in order to reduce the dimension of the dataset and to possibly increase the classification performance and speed up the classification.

First, a distinction must be made between unsupervised and supervised channel selection algorithms. The PCA algorithm is the only one that is an unsupervised algorithm, and as such it does not require any labeled data. This makes the algorithm generally universally suitable, but in our case, it achieved the worst result, as shown in Table 1. In addition, it is not even possible to describe this as a channel selection algorithm, since the original data of the selected channels are not used for the classification, instead a new dataset with entirely new values is created.

All other algorithms are supervised algorithms and accordingly require a labeled dataset to be applied. The particle-based algorithms and the mRMR algorithm, which belongs to the classical selection algorithms, are to be distinguished here again. Because when applying the algorithms, the particle-based algorithms were many times more computationally intensive than the classical algorithms.

Each of the algorithms was implemented in Python, using the *Scikit-learn* library [31] and the open source code of Jingwei Too [32]. For each subject, each channel optimization algorithm was executed, where each algorithm selected a fixed number of 20 channels, so in the end all subject-datasets could be combined into one large dataset.

A comparison of the results of the different channel selection algorithms used to classify the subjects according to arousal and for the 14th subject is shown in Fig. 3.

4.2   Classification

For the classification, a bidirectional LSTM model was used as already mentioned in Sect. 3.5. This was also implemented in Python using the Python library *TensorFlow*. To train the model, the dataset was split into two parts. 25% of the data was used for validation, and the rest for training. Thereby, the classification algorithm has no knowledge about the validation dataset and so it cannot train the model especially for this dataset. Only at the end the trained model is evaluated by the validation dataset, so

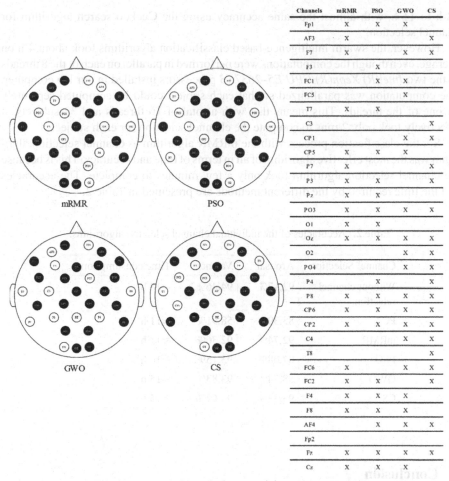

Channels	mRMR	PSO	GWO	CS
Fp1	X	X	X	
AF3	X			X
F7	X		X	X
F3		X		
FC1		X	X	
FC5			X	
T7	X	X		
C3				X
CP1			X	X
CP5	X	X	X	
P7	X			X
P3	X	X		X
Pz	X	X		
PO3	X	X	X	X
O1	X	X		
Oz	X	X	X	X
O2			X	X
PO4			X	X
P4		X		X
P8	X	X	X	X
CP6	X	X	X	X
CP2	X	X	X	X
C4			X	X
T8				X
FC6	X		X	X
FC2	X	X		X
F4	X	X	X	
F8	X	X	X	
AF4		X	X	X
Fp2				
Fz	X	X	X	X
Cz	X	X	X	

Fig. 3. Selected channels from participant 14 (Arousal)

that it can be verified that the model is able to correctly classify data it has never seen before.

The LSTM model was trained equally for each run with the different datasets that resulted after the channel selection process. The training was performed on 200 epochs with an initial learning rate of 0.001 using *Adam* as the optimizer function. *Adam* is an optimization algorithm that can be used instead of the classical stochastic gradient descent to iteratively update the network weights based on the training data [33].

When training with the 75% training data without performing a channel selection before, an epoch took 324 s on a system with two *GeForce GTX TITAN X* as graphics cards on which training was performed. This results in a complete training time of about 18 h.

By reducing the size of the dataset using the channel selection process before training, an epoch required only 197 s, so that the complete training time could be reduced from

18 h to 11 h, with almost the same accuracy using the Cuckoo search algorithm for channel selection.

However, the swarm intelligence-based classification algorithms took about 4 h on average, even though the computations were performed in parallel on each of the 8 threads of the two *Intel(R) Xeon(R) CPU E5–2637 v3* processors installed in our lab computer. The computation was parallelized so that each subject could be computed separately on one of the threads. This means that with a total of 16 threads and 32 subjects, it effectively took only 2 runs to compute the channel selection for each subject.

So, the classification process with the mRMR algorithm as channel selection algorithm was the most effective algorithm of all in terms of time and accuracy. This is because the channel selection algorithm took only a few minutes to complete. The accuracies and the time required by the different methods are presented in Table 2.

Table 2. Accuracies of the individual channel selection algorithms.

Channel Selection	Arousal	Valence	Time consumption
Without channel selection	92,17%	94,46%	≈18 h
PCA	83,39%	58,91%	≈11 h
mRMR	92,74%	92,36%	≈11 h
PSO	87,08%	93,15%	≈16 h
GWO	88,74%	93,83%	≈15 h
CS	93,33%	93,67%	≈15 h

5   Conclusion

In this work, we were able to successfully investigate which specific channel selection techniques applied on EEG recordings have a positive impact on emotion categorization. This allowed us to obtain accurate results without high computing power and time requirements.

We therefore used different channel selection techniques such as mRMR, PCA, PSO, GWO and CS from different subdomains of EEG classification to eject unnecessary channels and consequently reduce the size of a dataset. It was found that the mRMR channel selection algorithm saved the most computing power while decreasing negligibly with respect to classification accuracy: The average accuracy was 92.55% instead of 93.32%, achieved by the method without channel selection. Using the equally promising cuckoo search algorithm for channel selection did not save as much computing power as the mRMR algorithm but achieves a slightly higher average accuracy of 93.5%. To be more precisely, when reducing the dataset from 32 channels to 20 channels, an average of 132 s per training epoch could be saved when training the classification algorithm. However, the CS algorithm itself takes about 4 h to calculate the optimal channel set. So, this method reduces the total computing time, but not as much as the mRMR method, where channel selection takes only a few minutes.

Since both methods significantly reduced computing power and influenced the accuracy negligible, we further modified the CS and mRMR channel selection algorithm to select the most important 10 channels from the 32 EEG channels.

Using the new CS algorithm, we were able to reduce the required time for training the classification algorithm from 18 h to approximately 4 h, while the accuracy for arousal slightly decreased from 92.17% to 91.32% and for valence from 94.46% to 91.84%. The also modified mRMR algorithm on the other hand, achieved almost the same accuracy as the CS algorithm, with 91.29% accuracy for valence and 90.04% accuracy for arousal, whereby the training of the classifier also took only 4 h. These findings show how promising and versatile channel optimization methods are. Further research on optimization and modifying channel selection methods regarding computation time and accuracy is therefore of great interest.

For future research it is conceivable to define individually varying quantities for the selection of the channels. In this work we fixed the selected channels to a certain length to get a homogeneous dataset. This simplifies the handling of the classification mechanism, but also uniformizes the datasets without considering data loss or unnecessary computational work.

Swarm intelligence-based channel selection algorithms are inherently designed to select only the needed channels, which can vary from subject to subject, therefore they seem to be very promising regarding further modifications.

Furthermore, there are other classification models that can be used in this context to improve emotion recognition.

Combining nature-inspired algorithms with other filtering methods is adaptive and therefore also very promising. However, channel selection methods can also be combined with feature selection methods, e.g., such that channels are selected first and then the optimal features from this reduced dataset are used.

All in all, there are many possibilities to optimize emotion recognition using EEG data with channel selection methods and to create a precise, efficient dataset.

References

1. Jasper, H.: Report of the committee on methods of clinical examination in electroencephalography. The ten-twenty electrode system of the International Federation. Electroencephalography Clin. Neurophysiol. **10**, 370–375 (1958). https://doi.org/10.1016/0013-4694(58)900 53-1
2. Nuwer, M.R.: 10–10 electrode system for EEG recording. Clin. Neurophysiol. Offic. J. Int. Fed. Clin. Neurophysiol. **129**, 1103 (2018). https://doi.org/10.1016/j.clinph.2018.01.065
3. Silva, J., Burgos, F., Shin-Ting, W.: Interactive visualization of the cranio-cerebral correspondences for 10/20, 10/10 and 10/5 systems. In: 2016 29th SIBGRAPI Conference on Graphics, Patterns and Images - SIBGRAPI 2016, pp. 424–431 (2017)
4. Torres-García, A.A., Reyes-García, C.A., Villaseñor-Pineda, L., García-Aguilar, G.: Implementing a fuzzy inference system in a multi-objective EEG channel selection model for imagined speech classification. Expert Syst. Appl. **59**, 1–12 (2016). https://doi.org/10.1016/j.eswa.2016.04.011

5. He, L., Hu, Y., Li, Y., Li, D.: Channel selection by Rayleigh coefficient maximization based genetic algorithm for classifying single-trial motor imagery EEG. Neurocomputing **121**, 423–433 (2013). https://doi.org/10.1016/j.neucom.2013.05.005

6. Alotaiby, T., El-Samie, F.E.A., Alshebeili, S.A., Ahmad, I.: A review of channel selection algorithms for EEG signal processing. EURASIP J. Adv. Sig. Process. **2015**(1), 1–21 (2015). https://doi.org/10.1186/s13634-015-0251-9

7. Rizon, M., Murugappan, R., Nagarajan, R., Yacoob, S.: Asymmetric ratio and FCM based salient channel selection for human emotion detection using EEG. WSEAS Trans. Signal Process. **4**, 596–603 (2008)

8. Jatupaiboon, N., Pan-ngum, S., Israsena, P.: Emotion classification using minimal EEG channels and frequency bands. In: Proceedings of 10th International Joint Conference on Computer Science and Software Engineering (JCSSE 2013) (Khon Kaen, Thailand, 2013), vol. (2013)

9. Ansari-Asl, K., Chanel, G., Pun, T.: A channel selection method for EEG classification in emotion assessment based on synchronization likelihood. In: 15th European Signal Processing Conference (EUSIPCO 2007), Poznan, Poland, 3–7 September 2007 (2007)

10. Yildirim, E., Kaya, Y., Kilic, F.: A channel selection method for emotion recognition from EEG based on swarm-intelligence algorithms. IEEE Access **9**, 109889–109902 (2021). https://doi.org/10.1109/ACCESS.2021.3100638

11. Wang, Z., Hu, S., Liu, G., Song, H.: Channel selection method based on CNNSE for EEG emotion recognition. In: Proceedings of IEEE 14th International Conference on Intelligent Systems and Knowledge Engineering (ISKE 2019). (2019)

12. Wang, Z., Hu, S., Song, H.: Channel selection method for EEG emotion recognition using normalized mutual information. IEEE Access **7**, 143303–143311 (2019). https://doi.org/10.1109/ACCESS.2019.2944273

13. Pane, E., Wibawa, A., Purnomo, M.: Channel selection of EEG emotion recognition using stepwise discriminant analysis. In: International Conference on Computer Engineering, Network and Intelligent Multimedia (CENIM) (2018)

14. Al-Qazzaz, N., Sabir, M., Ali, S., Ahmad, S., Grammer, K.: Effective EEG channels for emotion identification over the brain regions using differential evolution algorithm. In: 2019 41st Annual International Conference of the IEEE Engineering in Medicine and Biology Society (EMBC), pp. 4703–4706 (2019)

15. Tong, L., Zhao, J., Fu, W.: Emotion recognition and channel selection based on EEG signal. In: 2018 11th International Conference on Intelligent Computation Technology and Automation (ICICTA), 101–105 (2018). https://doi.org/10.1109/ICICTA.2018.00031

16. Zhao, C., et al.: F-score based EEG channel selection methods for emotion recognition. In: 2020 IEEE International Conference on E-health Networking, Application & Services (HEALTHCOM) (2021)

17. Xu, H., Wang, X., Li, W., Wang, H., Bi, Q.: Research on EEG channel selection method for emotion recognition. In: Proceeding of the IEEE International Conference on Robotics and Biomimetics. Dali, China, December 2019 (2019)

18. Koelstra, S., et al.: DEAP: a database for emotion analysis; using physiological signals. IEEE Trans. Affect. Comput. **3**, 18–31 (2012). https://doi.org/10.1109/T-AFFC.2011.15

19. Jolliffe, I.T.: Principal Component Analysis. Springer Series in Statistics. Springer, New York (2002). https://doi.org/10.1007/b98835

20. Naik, G.R.: Advances in Principal Component Analysis. Springer, Singapore (2018). https://doi.org/10.1007/978-981-10-6704-4

21. Peng, H., Long, F., Ding, C.: Feature selection based on mutual information: criteria of max-dependency, max-relevance, and min-redundancy. IEEE Trans. Pattern Anal. Machine Intell. **27**, 1226–1238 (2005). https://doi.org/10.1109/tpami.2005.159

22. Ramírez-Gallego, S., et al.: Fast-mRMR: fast minimum redundancy maximum relevance algorithm for high-dimensional big data. Int. J. Intell. Syst. **32**, 134–152 (2017). https://doi.org/10.1002/int.21833

23. Tang, J., Liu, G., Pan, Q.: A review on representative swarm intelligence algorithms for solving optimization problems: applications and trends. IEEE/CAA J. Autom. Sinica **8**, 1627–1643 (2021). https://doi.org/10.1109/JAS.2021.1004129

24. Carbas, S., Toktas, A., Ustun, D.: Nature-Inspired Metaheuristic Algorithms for Engineering Optimization Applications. Springer, Singapore (2021). https://doi.org/10.1007/978-981-33-6773-9

25. Yang, X.-S. (ed.): Cuckoo Search and Firefly Algorithm. SCI, vol. 516. Springer, Cham (2014). https://doi.org/10.1007/978-3-319-02141-6

26. Nature-Inspired Computation and Swarm Intelligence, vol.. Elsevier (2020)

27. Ali, M., El-Hameed, M.A., Farahat, M.A.: Effective parameters' identification for polymer electrolyte membrane fuel cell models using grey wolf optimizer. Renew. Energy **111**, 455–462 (2017). https://doi.org/10.1016/j.renene.2017.04.036

28. Russell, J.A.: A circumplex model of affect. J. Pers. Soc. Psychol. **39**, 1161–1178 (1980). https://doi.org/10.1037/h0077714

29. Hochreiter, S., Schmidhuber, J.: Long short-term memory. Neural Comput. **9**, 1735–1780 (1997). https://doi.org/10.1162/neco.1997.9.8.1735

30. Acharya, D., et al.: Multi-class emotion classification using EEG signals. In: Garg, D., Wong, K., Sarangapani, J., Gupta, S.K. (eds.) IACC 2020. CCIS, vol. 1367, pp. 474–491. Springer, Singapore (2021). https://doi.org/10.1007/978-981-16-0401-0_38

31. Pedregosa, F., et al.: Scikit-learn: machine learning in Python. J. Mach. Learn. Res. **12**, 2825–2830 (2011)

32. Jingwei, T.: Wrapper-Feature-Selection-Toolbox-Python. GitHub. GitHub repository, (2021)

33. Kingma, D.P., Ba, J.: Adam: a method for stochastic optimization (2014)

A System for Graphical Visualization of Brainwaves to Analyse Media Content Consumption

Valdecir Becker(✉) , Matheus Cavalcanti , Thiago Silva ,
Edvaldo Vasconcelos , Alessandro Pinon , and Felipe Melo

Laboratory of Interaction and Media, Informatics Center, Federal University of Paraíba,
João Pessoa, PB, Brazil
contato@lim.ci.ufpb.br

Abstract. This article reports the development of a software for capturing, analyzing and graphically visualizing brainwaves from electroencephalographic reading, during the consumption of media content. Within the scope of the Design Science Research method, brainwaves naturally produced will be mapped, categorized, stored and graphically printed. The interface is used as input for fruition analysis in various systems, such as evaluation of movies and series, art pieces evaluation and neural marketing. As the perception and experience of media fruition is variable and subjective among individuals, this research contributes to obtaining relevant data in the context of multimedia interactions study and development.

Keywords: Audiovisual fruition · Brain computer interfaces · DSR

1 Introduction

Brain Machine Interfaces (BCI) consist of a direct connection between the brain and a computer or an external device, without muscular stimuli [9]. According to the European Commission for the Coordination of Research in BCI, six main thematic axes for applications are feasible and promising [2]. Among them, the use of BCI as a research and development tool stands out, by obtaining implicit feedback in real time.

In the field of Human Computer Interaction, the Electroencephalogram (EEG) was incorporated as a BCI to provide input data for computer systems. Non-invasively, without the need to insert electrodes inside the skull, EEG measures the voltage fluctuations resulting from ionic currents within the brain neurons. It obtains information from spontaneously generated brainwaves and enables its transformation into manipulable data.

This article describes the development of a graphical visualization tool to interpret brainwaves in real time, with emphasis on observation of media content consumption, based on the Design Science Research (DSR) methodology. DSR legitimizes the development of problem-solving artifacts as an important way to produce scientific and technological knowledge [4–6]. The research steps consist of identifying and defining classes

M. Kurosu (Ed.): HCII 2022, LNCS 13303, pp. 318–328, 2022.
https://doi.org/10.1007/978-3-031-05409-9_24

of problems, developing artifacts to transform situations, and changing their initial status to satisfactory or desirable conditions. It also considers the evaluation of artifacts and the dissemination of the learned lessons.

Due to the complex nature of interdependence between waves and their simultaneous emission at different points in brain, the Emotiv Insight electroencephalographic reader was used to obtain and process data. In addition, the device can read signals from all cortical lobes of the human brain.

The use of EEG in Computer Brain Interactions shows promising in the field of audiovisual production and consumption, since the feedback about a workpiece can be collected in a pervasive and immediate way, that is, without considering user's subjectivity in the evaluation process. As practical examples about using the obtained data, improvement in accuracy of content recommender systems or a creation of a system capable of validating evaluations of works of art can be cited.

2 Electroencephalography as a BCI

Electroencephalography (EEG) can be defined as the measurement of electrical activity in an active (living) brain. The first EEG recordings date back to 1924, when scientist Hans Berger, using a galvanometer, discovered Berger waves (now named Alpha waves) by attaching an electrode to a person's head [8]. Although there are specific cases, it is usually a non-invasive method, without the need to attach sensors directly to the brain surface via surgery.

An EEG measures how voltage fluctuations result from ionic current within neurons in the brain. For medical purposes, in modern electroencephalography, more than 21 sensors are used with a fundamental purpose of gauging five waves. However, with the development of studies on BCIs and neural feedback outside clinical settings, cheaper devices with simplified readings became available.

2.1 Meanings of Brainwaves

Humans simultaneously emit five different types of electrical patterns in the cerebral cortex. Each of the waves has a specific purpose and their harmony contributes to healthy mental functioning. Through EEG measurement, the impact of an interaction can be highlighted by detecting changes in an individual's brain patterns. The waves can be classified according to frequency of neural spectrum [1, 3, 7].

In the lowest region of the spectrum, between 0 and 4 Hz, there are the Delta waves, associated with the deepest levels of relaxation (Fig. 1). They are involved in regulatory functions such as heartbeat and digestion. Its proper functioning helps, for example, in the restorative effect of a good night's sleep.

Between 4 and 8 Hz the Theta waves are located. They are particularly linked to our connection to the perception of emotions, representing an almost hypnotic human state when detected in excess. In a regular state, they bring benefits to creativity and what is usually called intuition.

Historically first detected, the Alpha waves can be observed in the spectrum between 8 to 12 Hz. They are the link between conscious and subconscious thinking. In states of stress or absolute excitement, a phenomenon named "Alpha Blocking" can occur. This effect causes an almost totally disconnection between conscious and subconscious stimuli due to the suppression of Alpha waves by the overproduction of Beta waves.

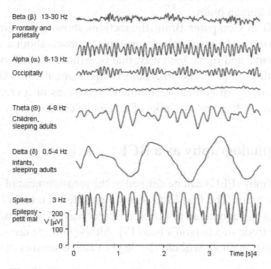

Fig. 1. Visual example of brainwaves patterns in Hz.

Known as high-frequency/low-amplitude waves, between 12 and 40 Hz, Beta waves are commonly observed while we are awake. They are involved in critical, conscious, and logical thinking processes. These waves are amplified by substances such as caffeine and other stimulants. Excessive production of Beta waves is linked to ongoing stress and anxiety.

Related to cognitive functioning, Gamma waves are vitally important for learning, memory, and information processing. They are located at the top of the spectrum, between 40 and 100 Hz, directly linked to the connection between the senses and perception. Individuals with cognitive difficulties normally have low production of Gamma waves.

2.2 Hardware Specifications

The Emotiv Insight headset (Fig. 2) is projected to be used in scientific research and personal applications. It is not suitable for diagnosis and treatment of medical conditions [12]. The headset offers electronic components optimized for clean and robust reading and data transmission, while, due to its compact presentation, it can be used anywhere. It uses five channels of electroencephalography, being the only headset in its market niche to read signals from all cortical lobes of the human brain and, therefore, suitable for scientific research. It also has a nine-axis sensor, capable of mapping user movements during interactions. Altogether, it can provide unprocessed EEG data, mental commands, performance metrics and facial expression detection.

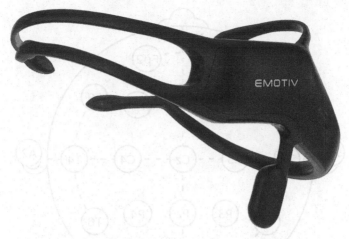

Fig. 2. Emitiv insight headser.

In addition to the rechargeable battery, capable of providing up to nine hours of device operation, the headset has wireless connectivity via native Bluetooth and its own USB adapter. It can be used in both desktop and mobile applications. The easiness in the process of assembling and connecting the device allows interactions to be started in less than five minutes.

2.3 Brainwave Reading

Emitted spontaneously and interdependently, brainwaves are commonly read from specific points on the human skull, in a non-invasive way using electrodes. Respecting the international 10–20 encephalographic reading system, which refers to the arrangement of electrodes on the contact surface, the Emotiv Insight headset has total neural feedback at positions F3, F4, PZ, T7 and T8, located respectively in the left frontal lobe, right parietal lobe, and left and right temporal lobes. It also has two reference sensors, located in the left mastoid region (Fig. 3).

Readings are taken at a rate of 128 samples per second per channel, with a resolution of 14 bits and spectrum responses between 0.5 and 43 Hz. They occur through electrodes manufactured with a proprietary polymer, which offers good conductivity with minimal assembly required. The hydrophilic nature of the material eliminates the need for extensive priming or contact-enhancing gels typically found in other similar-level reading devices.

In this way, the electroencephalographic reader is capable to export four types of data streams. In mental commands mode, it is capable of recording four commands per user profile, in addition to a neutral position. In the case of facial expressions, it can capture eye blinks, surprise, displeasure, smiles and chin clenching. In its performance metrics, it can identify agitation, engagement, relaxation, interest, stress, and focus. For the capture and return of raw EEG data, i.e., without processing, a license payment is required, which also enables the use of the "EmotivPro" application.

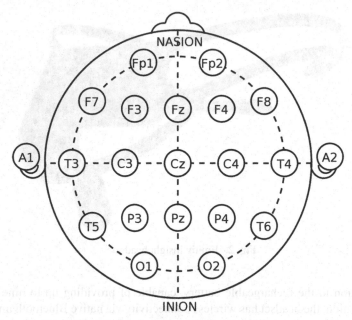

Fig. 3. 10–20 electroencephalographic reading system.

2.4 Brain Regions and Lobe Functions

The human brain is traditionally divided into two hemispheres, left and right, connected by the corpus callosum (Fig. 4). Usually, the left hemisphere is considered dominant as it is responsible for activities related to the right side of the body. In this hemisphere are concentrated two main regions related to verbal comprehension and production, Wernicke and Broca's areas, respectively. The right hemisphere is related to creativity, perception, and visual-spatial processing, and directly involved with facial recognition.

The outermost layer of the brain, the cortex, can be divided into lobes, distributed over the surfaces of the hemispheres. From the placement of electrodes using the 10–20 system, it is possible to extract information about mental states of observed users. With the Emotiv Insight device, reading and analysis can be done in the frontal, temporal, and parietal lobes.

Frontal lobes are responsible for immediate and sustained attention, memory, and initiative. They are strongly linked to the region of the brain that controls emotions, thus being responsible for empathic perception and social skills. In the left hemisphere, covered by electrodes Fp1, F3 and F7, it delivers information about concentration, working memory and positive emotions. In the right hemisphere, in electrodes Fp2, F4 and F8, it is linked to episodic memory and social awareness.

Parietal lobes are responsible for solving problems introduced by the frontal lobes. In the left hemisphere, in P3, it deals with aspects related to logical problem solving, complex grammar and attention, while in the right hemisphere it deals with spatial orientation in P4.

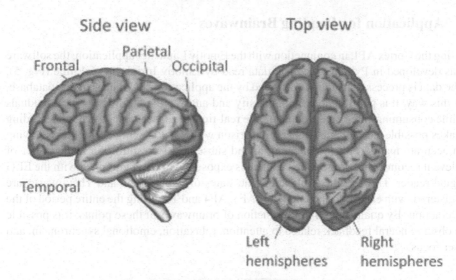

Fig. 4. Brain regions and lobes.

Finally, temporal lobes are situated in the region close to the human auditory system. In T3 and T5, in the left hemisphere, the assimilation of words, reading and memory can be seen. The right hemisphere, in T4 and T6, is related to the recognition of objects, music, faces and customs.

2.5 Cortex API

"Cortex" is the application programming interface (API) responsible for the software routines and standards that make it possible to interpret the electroencephalographic signals obtained through Emotiv brand products. According to the manufacturer, "Cortex" is the centerpiece of the company's technology, capable of bringing brain-computer interfaces closer to the consumer. It is aimed at anyone who has programming skills and wants to develop custom applications that interact with Emotiv products. Compliant with a focus on scientific research, the company provides extensive documentation about the software, openly available on the product's website.

The API was built on the standard of returning data in JSON format through Web-Sockets, facilitating coupling to a wide range of programming languages and platforms. The main requirement is access to create an account, personal or corporate, to validate a paid or free license. Communication between API and application takes place through an intermediary program, Emotiv Launcher, which manages connected devices, credentials, and settings. All accreditation and data processing are done in the cloud, requiring a constant internet connection to use the platform.

3 Application for Reading Brainwaves

Using the Cortex API, in conjunction with the Emotiv Launcher application, the software was developed in Python, to collect data read by Emotiv Insight in real time (Fig. 5). The data is processed by the API, filtered by the application, and then sent to a database. In this way, it is possible to obtain, classify and analyze the brainwaves of individuals while consuming some media content. The real-time electroencephalographic recording makes possible a direct and deeper comparison with what is being consumed, allowing an accurate mapping of the interaction, and subsequently resulting in instant offer of relevant recommendations. A first content is exposed to the user equipped with the EEG signal reader. Through the application, the states of Alpha, Beta and Theta waves are registered, with electrodes positioned at AF3, AF4 and T7 during the entire period of the interaction. By quantifying forces of action of brainwaves at these points, it is possible to observe neural feedback related to attention, relaxation, emotional synchronism, and user focus.

Fig. 5. Application running during lab tests.

3.1 Definition of Artifact Objectives and Development

Considering that the central problem of this research lies in the visualization and interpretation of the brain's natural reaction to media stimuli, it is possible to outline a series of objectives to guide the development of the artifact, based on EEG usage. The first one is to be able to capture the brainwaves of an individual, filtering the relevant data for a future analysis, and arranging them in a database that will be used to feed the application. One of the most important objectives can be associated with the need for graphic visualization of brainwaves, so that it is possible to analyze the data obtained from users based on time, to understand the effects of each stage of fruition in a clear and precise way.

For this, the Python programming language was used to build a graph with data obtained by the Emotiv Insight headset, which is updated in real time, during the user's enjoyment. After a complete session it is possible to have access to the final graph for analysis of the results and comparison with the results of other individuals.

4 Artifact Demonstration and Validation

Fifteen males participated in the experiments, aged between 18 and 55 years. Eliminating the time of placing the electrodes of the Emotiv Insight reader on the scalp of the participants and optimizing the signal acquisition, through positioning assistant provided by the manufacturer, each interaction lasted about four minutes. During this time, images were automatically made available for viewing and judgment by the participants for a period of approximately four seconds each.

The first day of laboratory testing sought a broader understanding of the mental states of interest, attention, disgust, and repulsion. A set of images was presented, composed of both photos of appetizing foods and representations characterized by beings or objects culturally considered repulsive in situations related to food. Users were instructed, before enjoying the images, to assess their state of hunger and think of their favorite dish, to incite interest in what would be presented next.

For the second day of tests, perpetuating the focus on observation in states of interest, a new presentation was prepared consisting of products that, based on the sociocultural profile of the group, could be desired by the participants. Next to the images, creating an ad format, prices were attached that did not always represent the real value of the product.

During the experiments, users' Alpha, Beta, Theta, Delta, and Gamma waves were observed in real time and stored in the database, allowing for investigation and comparison at later times. In real-time graphics format, the Alpha, Beta and Theta waves were displayed on the F3, F4 and T7 position sensors, located to perform readings in the frontal lobe. Such an arrangement allows the observation of neural feedback related to the user's attention, relaxation, emotional synchronism, and focus.

In parallel, tests were carried out during the enjoyment of videos with football matches. Videos of crucial moments in the defeat of the team for which the user cheers were analyzed, as well as throws of the defeat that demoted a rival team. Peaks of attention could be observed during the anticipation of the moments of climax of the bids, the biggest being in the celebration of the goal against the rival team.

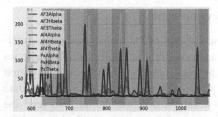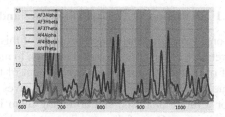

Fig. 6. Comparison between electroencephalographic readings.

Although the images presented to all participants were the same, there was a discrepancy between the neural response graphs registered (Fig. 6). During the next step, application of questionnaires about the interaction, it was also possible to notice differences in the perception of the spectators about the same topic. These results can be justified by differences in viewer's focus, resulting from their individuality during the enjoyment of media contents. According to the participants' reports, while some users looked for links among specific elements in each image, others tried to correlate the content on the screen with past personal experiences.

At this moment, it was difficult to identify patterns, including comparing waves for the same test applied consecutively with the same viewer, since the way in which it interacts with an image will always be unique. Even though the user has seen it before, he unconsciously seeks new forms of interpretation.

5   Discussion About the Learned Lessons

Based on the results obtained during the test phase with users, it is possible to affirm that there is feasibility in the combination between the functioning of an EEG device and the ability to concatenate and make data available from a computer application such as BCI, aimed at understanding the enjoyment in the consumption of audiovisual content.

The temporal overlap of brainwave monitoring results with the consumed content makes it possible to perceive changes in user behavior motivated by what was seen on screen. Such aspects of media enjoyment could be ignored, omitted or even unknown by the user himself as an evaluator of an audiovisual workpiece. Considering such aspects, subjective and related to the individuality of each human being, contributes to the personalization experience of content consumption, attributed to the depth of analysis of user behavior during the interaction.

From the proposed system, there is the possibility of coupling other services that use the information collected and interpreted in real time, such as personalized content recommendations, neural marketing, and art evaluation. Nuances such as the attention and desynchronization of a spectator's focus in relation to the exhibition of a picture or film can be monitored and transformed into heuristics, enabling the formation of a catalog of other contents that reach a minimum level of correlation.

6 Conclusion

This article described the use of an EEG-based BCI for reading, processing, storing, and retrieving data about the behavior of user's brainwaves during audiovisual enjoyment, to obtain accurate information about the interaction. To carry out the research, an EEG device was used to obtain data regarding brainwaves. Tests were carried out with users, using the device, to assess the possibility of extracting relevant information for the development of a recommender system based on a BCI. The results were displayed graphically, through an application developed in Python, and proved to be satisfactory for the purposes of this article.

It is necessary to emphasize limitations in the tests with users, which were restricted to fifteen individuals. This is an insufficient number to generate more precise conclusions about the efficiency and effectiveness of the system, indicating only a potential use of the software.

The next steps for the evolution of the research will be to define a pattern of heuristics contemplating emotional involvement, or how much the individual liked or disliked the workpieces (and parts of them) through the analysis of brainwaves. In addition, it is necessary to consolidate the system used for the graphic analysis of read waves, since the tests were carried out with a small number of participants. The coupling of accessory technologies, such as the user's eye monitoring in relation to the screen or the capture of facial expressions during media enjoyment, could be promising in increasing the accuracy in the representation of the user's emotional state during the moment of interaction.

Finally, it is necessary to highlight some ethical elements about the present research. In the context of BCIs, as described by [11], the responsible use of technologies that aim to obtain access to data regarding the functioning and brain dynamics of an individual is necessary, given its sensitive nature to user's privacy. Technological systems need to behave in ways that are beneficial to people, beyond simply achieving functional goals or solving technical problems [10]. For this, it is important to emphasize care related to protection of this data was and should be taken in research using this technology. Likewise, ethical and legal elements, such as the General Data Protection Law, are prerequisites, both for research and for the dissemination of results. As a result, the challenges regarding ethics, privacy and security, described by [10], are present in the research, especially to inhibit inappropriate or irresponsible uses.

References

1. Becker, V., et al.: Potencial das interfaces cérebro máquina no aprimoramento da recomendação de conteúdos em sistemas de áudio e vídeo sob demanda. In: Ferraz de Abreu, J., Abásolo Guerrero, M.J., Almeida, P., Silva, T. (eds.) Proceedings of the 9th Iberoamerican Conference on Applications and Usability of Interactive TV-jAUTI 2020, Aveiro (2020)
2. Brunner, C., et al.: BNCI Horizon 2020: towards a roadmap for the BCI community. Brain-Comput. Interfaces 2(1), 1–10 (2015)
3. Demos, J.: Getting Started with Neurofeedback. W. W. Norton & Company, New York (2005)
4. Dresch, A., Lacerda, D.P., Antunes, J.A.V.: Design Science Research: A Method for Science and Technology Advancement. Springer, Cham (2015). https://doi.org/10.1007/978-3-319-07374-3

5. Hevner, A.R., March, S.T., Park, K.: Design research in information systems research. MIS Q. **28**(1), 76–105 (2004)
6. Järvinen, P.: Action research is similar to design science. Qual. Quant. **41**(1), 37–54 (2007)
7. Monori, F., Oniga, S.: Processing EEG signals acquired from a consumer grade BCI device. Carpathian J. Electron. Comput. Eng. **11**(2), 29–34 (2018)
8. Sałabun, W.: Processing and spectral analysis of the raw EEG signal from the MindWave. Przeglad Elektrotechniczny **90**(2), 169–174 (2014)
9. Silversmith, D., et al.: Plug-and-play control of a brain–computer interface through neural map stabilization. Nat. Biotechnol. **39**(3), 326–335 (2021)
10. Stephanidis, C., et al.: Seven HCI grand challenges. Int. J. Hum.-Comput. Interact. **35**(14), 1229–1269 (2019)
11. Zeng, Y., Sun, K., Lu, E.: Declaration on the ethics of brain–computer interfaces and augment intelligence. AI Ethics **1**(3), 209–211 (2021). https://doi.org/10.1007/s43681-020-00036-x
12. Emotiv Insight headset. https://www.emotiv.com/insight/. Accessed 10 Feb 2022

Support of Virtual Human Interactions Based on Facial Emotion Recognition Software

Bärbel Bissinger[1,2]([✉]), Christian Märtin[1,2], and Michael Fellmann[1,2]

[1] Computer Science, Augsburg University of Applied Sciences, Augsburg, Germany
{baerbel.bissinger,christian.maertin}@hs-augsburg.de
[2] Business Information Systems, University of Rostock, Rostock, Germany
michael.fellmann@uni-rostock.de

Abstract. Emotion recognition based on facial expressions is an increasingly important area in Human-Computer Interaction Research. Despite the many challenges of computer-based facial emotion recognition like, e.g., the huge variability of human facial features, cultural differences, and the differentiation between primary and secondary emotions, there are more and more systems and approaches focusing on facial emotion recognition. These technologies already offer many possibilities to automatically recognize human emotions. As part of a research project described in this paper, these technologies are used to investigate whether and how they can support virtual human interactions. More and more meetings are taking place virtually due to the Covid-19 pandemic and the advancing digitalization. Therefore, the face of the attendees is often the only visible part that indicates emotional states. This paper focuses on outlining why emotions and their recognition are important and in which areas the use of automated emotion detection tools seems to be promising. We do so by showing potential use cases for visual emotion recognition in the professional environment. In a nutshell, the research project aims to investigate whether facial emotion recognition software can help to improve self-reflection on emotions and the quality and experience of virtual human interactions.

Keywords: Facial emotion recognition · Facial expressions · Human emotions · Professional environment · Virtual human interaction

1 Introduction

This chapter briefly describes the motivation and background of the importance of emotion recognition and facial expressions.

1.1 Importance of Emotions

In our society and specifically in the business context, emotional reactions are often perceived negatively even though emotions play an important role in all human actions. Emotions directly influence interactions between humans as well as Human-Computer

M. Kurosu (Ed.): HCII 2022, LNCS 13303, pp. 329–339, 2022.
https://doi.org/10.1007/978-3-031-05409-9_25

Interaction. This means that emotions are not only linked to social environments or the entertainment industry, but that they are essential for human communication, human perception and decision-making. In the past, scientists were assuming that human beings primarily behave rationally. Today's expertise and research prove the opposite. Nowadays it is known that emotions trigger actions and are involved in human processes like the following [1]:

- *Evaluation of situations*
- *Motivation*
- *Preparation*
- *Actions*
- *Regulations*
- *Social Tasks*

These processes cover a broad field of behavior and activities. It can be seen that the power of emotions influences the decision-making processes in many situations and areas of life [2].

1.2 Signs of Emotional States via Facial Expressions

People communicate most emotionally and most directly in face-to-face conversations. This happens unconsciously and automatically via facial expressions. Within a group, facial expressions are used to trigger specific behavior or to organize the group. People have always lived in social networks, and therefore it always was important to inform others quickly about one's emotional state. Emotions visible through the face can therefore be powerful, and they can encourage other people to take action [3].

Especially in the face, the shown expressions can differ, depending on the context. For example, people show other facial expressions in the professional environment than in their free time. Ekman explained this with the so-called *social display rules*, which must be considered when measuring emotions. In 1990, Duchenne identified different facial muscles, which represent different expressions, such as attention, pleasure, doubt, joy, or contempt [4]. Based on these muscles and Ekman's universally valid basic emotions, he and colleagues developed the *Facial Action Coding System (FACS)*, a description of facial expressions. In addition, they developed the *Emotion FACS (EmFACS)* that can be used to determine correlations between muscle movements in the face and emotions. With the help of the FACS and the EmFACS, facial expressions can be assessed in a standardized manner [3]. Many of today's facial emotion recognition approaches, which are used to automatically recognize facial expressions, are based on this system [4].

1.3 Emotional Intelligence and Importance for the Business Sector

Emotional intelligence (EI) is an important success factor in many areas of life and work. The psychologist Salovey identified five main domains of EI [5]:

1. *Knowing one's emotions*
2. *Managing emotions*

3. *Motivating oneself*
4. *Recognizing emotions in others*
5. *Handling relationships*

According to a recent study by the Capgemini Research Institute [6], EI skills will be indispensable in the workforce in the future. The demand for these skills in the professional environment is expected to continue to increase and will be up to six times higher in 2024 than in 2019. Therefore, it is important to create a culture that promotes EI.

2 Problem Statement and Research Questions

Due to the Covid-19 pandemic, more and more meetings and workshops are taking place virtually, and the trend of working remotely is likely to continue in the future [7]. Tools for online communication and collaboration support these virtual set-ups. However, studies show that video conferences are more exhausting than meetings with other communication media [8]. This phenomenon is also called *Zoom Fatigue*, which generally stands for video conference fatigue [9].

In virtual environments, the communication of non-verbal messages can be difficult or impossible for both the sender and the receiver [10]. When it comes to human interactions, there is a huge difference between virtual and on-site events, especially in showing and recognizing emotions. In digitally mediated interactions, only a small part of a person's expressions, like the face and the voice, can be involved in the interactions, and therefore a lot of social cues can get lost. For virtual teams, these missing social cues may lead, for example, to difficulties with coordination, planning, and clarity of roles and tasks, reduced quality of decision-making, and challenges to build trust within a team [11]. Moreover, technical issues during video conferences can lead to boredom or disengagement of participants [10].

Even though many attributes for emotions are shown via facial expressions (see Sect. 1.2), we are not used or trained to recognize emotions by only seeing the signs of the faces. Participants of video conferences report that it is difficult for them to read social signals on the video screens and feel pressured to provide those to others [8]. Therefore, tools analyzing facial expressions can help us recognize emotional states.

The question of how these technologies can help to support virtual human interactions by training human beings in identifying emotions via the face and by visualizing emotional states of online meeting participants' will be evaluated with the help of concrete use cases. Examples of our use cases are described in the paper at hand and are the basis for the iterative development of a prototype and guidelines for assisting in emotion recognition in virtual environments. The question how such a system should be designed, also regarding its user experience, will be evaluated by experiments and user feedback. In the following, we describe how we envision to answer those research questions.

3   Project Intention and Target Perspective

The following gives an overview of our research project.

3.1   Project Objective

The main goal of our project is to first explore technical possibilities and limits and, based on that, to create a prototype. The system will help people recognize emotional states in themselves and others and assess their effects more easily. This in turn could be the basis to optimize communication processes and human energy, which is a recently proposed single-item metric to measure the energetic activation or vitality of humans [12]. Second, we intend to develop design guidelines that should inform the future development of emotion-sensitive communication systems. In sum, we aim to contribute to the following objectives:

- Increase awareness of the importance of recognizing one's emotional state
- Assist in recognizing one's own and other people's emotional states
- Determine how emotional states can influence communication and energy levels
- Use gained insights to be able to react in a way so that communication and energy levels can be improved

In this paper, we focus on how software can help humans read emotions and how we can contribute to that by presenting concrete use cases and a conceptual framework which we will evaluate and further develop.

3.2   Strategy, Approach, and Methods

We will give a brief overview on our strategy, approach, and methods in the following. Our project aims to help humans read facial expressions and capture interaction data with the support of software to make virtual activities and interactions more collaborative and enjoyable. Since it is not that easy for us humans to read emotions by facial signs only, software that automatically analyzes facial expressions has a huge potential. For that purpose, we integrate the software *FaceReader* from Noldus Information Technology. Furthermore, we measure other interaction data like the share of speech of participants in online meetings, which can provide insights into interaction quality. The measured data is visualized so that people can see this information immediately. This visualization is intended to help reflect on virtual interaction quality. To visualize the right information in the best possible way, we will continuously incorporate user feedback into the framework and the type of visualization and follow an iterative development approach. Furthermore, we have identified use cases on individual and group level for qualitative and empirical data collection. Interaction data will be measured for these use cases, and people will be asked to participate in a survey. The results of the analysis of the measurements and the surveys are the basis for the framework's design and visualizations. The outlined strategy is summarized in Fig. 1 as a golden circle model based on the concept of Simon Sinek [13].

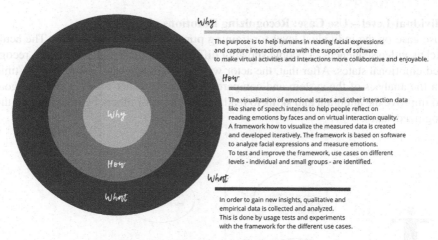

Fig. 1. Golden circle strategy of our project

The first phase of this project is the definition of use cases and the conceptual framework. Experiments follow this to collect empirical data to gain insights to develop the prototype design, as shown in Fig. 2.

Fig. 2. Project steps

This research project is in its initial phase. One use case on the individual level and one on the group level as examples and the conceptual frameworks are described in the next section. The envisioned collection of qualitative empirical data with user tests and experiments is not covered in this paper.

3.3 Use Cases

One of the first steps was to identify use cases for our experiments to collect qualitative empirical data and feedback to develop the prototype and the guidelines iteratively. We analyze two different areas. One is the individual level, where we evaluate whether the use of such technologies is helpful in self-reflection and communication training. The second area is the group level, where we focus on the measurement and analysis of participants' emotional states in small group meetings and other interaction data to analyze and optimize the quality of these meetings. One use case of each level is presented briefly in the following.

Individual-Level – Use Case: Recognizing Emotions of Others
A use case on the individual level for training purposes is shown in Fig. 3. The actor watches video sequences of people showing different emotions and notes down recognized emotional states. After that, the actor watches the sequences again, but this time with the analysis of the system and compares it with his or her own results. The goal is to improve the attention and skills to read the emotions of others by reflecting on the recognized states.

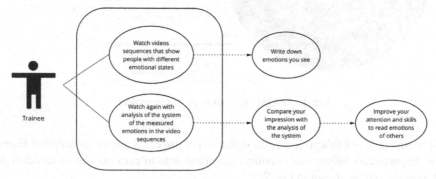

Fig. 3. Use case on the individual level

Group Level – Use Case: Remote Meeting Moderation
A use case on the group level is illustrated in Fig. 4. The set-up is a remote meeting where only the moderator uses the system to get support for moderation and get help to reflect on the quality of the meeting while considering emotional states and speaking time of participants, which are visualized by the system.

Group Level – Use Case: Remote Meeting
Figure 5 shows another use case on group level. The situation is the same as in the previous use case, except that besides the moderator, *all* participants use the system to reflect on the quality of the meeting while considering emotional states and speaking time of participants.

The experiments on these use cases are evaluated to determine if the visualization of interaction data is helpful to improve the quality of virtual interactions and how this information should be presented.

3.4 Conceptual Framework

For use cases on the individual level, the conceptual framework is shown in Fig. 6. The purpose of the framework is to support the identification of emotional states by analyzing the system and the personal impressions when seeing only faces on videos.

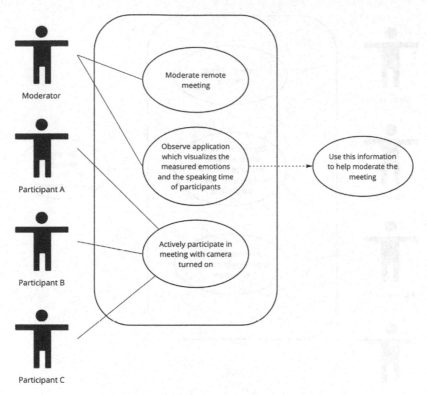

Fig. 4. Use case on group level

On the group level, the framework intends to improve the quality of virtual interactions by the visualization of the system analysis and the self-assessments of participants. The conceptual framework is illustrated in Fig. 7. In addition to emotional states, related data like valence, arousal, and speaking time which can be indicators for the activeness of the participants, will be included.

3.5 First Prototype

We test our approach with the use cases and a first prototype that indicates for example emotional states and speaking time of meeting participants. Figure 8 shows a screenshot of the prototype with the analysis of the different emotional states of all participants. On the right side it sums up, for example, the number of participants, the dominant emotion, the second most recognized emotion in brackets as well as the mean valence and arousal. It is possible to select emotions of interest, participants, and the preferred type of visualization.

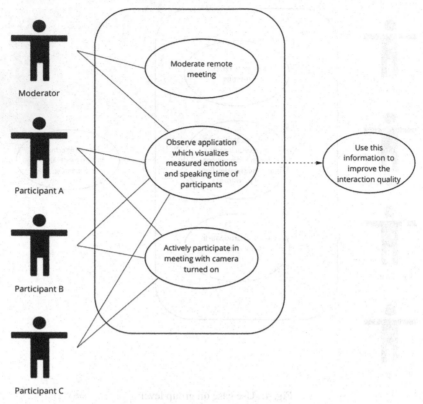

Fig. 5. Use case on group level variance

Fig. 6. Conceptual framework individual level

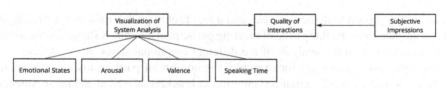

Fig. 7. Conceptual framework group level

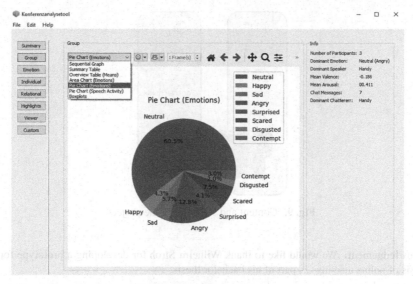

Fig. 8. Screenshot of prototype

4 Conclusion and Future Work

This paper describes an approach to answering the research questions of how emotion recognition software can help support virtual human interactions and how a system should be designed for that purpose. To answer these questions, the results of the experiments are needed, which are part of future work.

The focus of the future work of this research project is the socio-technical system design for supporting emotion-sensitive interaction. Another paper will summarize different attempts and products for facial emotion recognition in science and industry and provide an overview of the state of the art. The challenges and opportunities of our framework will be presented and evaluated based on the results of planned experiments on the different use cases. This will be the basis for devising the conceptual and socio-technical design. The research project will also cover the acceptance and ethics of such an approach. The main areas of future work are visualized in Fig. 9.

Future analysis will also answer questions like when the visualization of interaction data is helpful or when it could distract, which information is necessary or which information could lead to cognitive overload or even technostress, and how the information should be visualized best. This will be done by research, by the specification of requirements, and by human-centered evaluation of created wireframes, prototypes, or existing solutions. For example, A/B tests will be executed to test if simple charts should be used for the visualization or rather metaphors which represent, for example, emotional states, arousal, and speaking time.

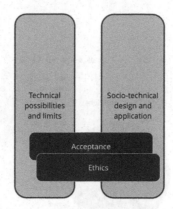

Fig. 9. Content and structure of the project

Acknowledgement. We would like to thank Wilhelm Stroh for developing a prototype for the analysis of online meetings as part of his bachelor thesis.

References

1. Broschart, S., Monschein, R.: Der Content Faktor. Franzis Verlag, München (2017)
2. Märtin, C., Bissinger, B.C., Asta, P.: Optimizing the digital customer journey—improving user experience by exploiting emotions, personas and situations for individualized user interface adaptations. J. Consum. Behav. (2021). https://doi.org/10.1002/cb.1964
3. Stürmer, R., Schmidt, J.: Erfolgreiches Marketing durch Emotionsforschung. Haufe, Freiburg (2014)
4. Picard, R.W.: Affective Computing, July 2000. https://doi.org/10.7551/mitpress/1140.001.0001
5. Goleman, D.: Emotional intelligence: why it can matter more than IQ, 1. Bloomsbury, London (1996)
6. Capgemini Research Institute. Emotional intelligence– the essential skillset for the age of AI (2019)
7. McKinsey Global Institute. The future of work after COVID-19 | McKinsey (2021)
8. Nesher Shoshan, H., Wehrt, W.: Understanding 'Zoom fatigue': a mixed-method approach. Appl. Psychol. apps.12360 (2021). https://doi.org/10.1111/apps.12360
9. Riedl, R.: On the stress potential of videoconferencing: definition and root causes of Zoom fatigue. Electron. Markets (2021). https://doi.org/10.1007/s12525-021-00501-3
10. Oeppen, R.S., Shaw, G., Brennan, P.A.: Human factors recognition at virtual meetings and video conferencing: how to get the best performance from yourself and others. Br. J. Oral Maxillofac. Surg. **58**(6), 643–646 (2020). https://doi.org/10.1016/j.bjoms.2020.04.046
11. Acai, A., Sonnadara, R.R., O'Neill, T.A.: Getting with the times: a narrative review of the literature on group decision making in virtual environments and implications for promotions committees. Perspect. Med. Educ. **7**(3), 147–155 (2018). https://doi.org/10.1007/s40037-018-0434-9

12. Lambusch, F., Weigelt, O., Fellmann, M., Siestrup, K.: Application of a pictorial scale of human energy in ecological momentary assessment research. In: Harris, D., Li, W.-C. (eds.) HCII 2020. LNCS (LNAI), vol. 12186, pp. 171–189. Springer, Cham (2020). https://doi.org/10.1007/978-3-030-49044-7_16
13. Sinek, S.: Start with Why: How Great Leaders Inspire Everyone to Take Action. Penguin, London (2009)

Partner's Gaze with Duchenne Smile in Social Interaction Promotes Successive Cooperative Decision

Xiaoqi Deng, Hosseini Sarinasadat [ID], Miyake Yoshihiro, and Nozawa Takayuki[✉] [ID]

Tokyo Institute of Technology, Tokyo, Japan
nozawa.t.ac@m.titech.ac.jp

Abstract. Smile has been conceptualized as a signal of cooperative intent. However, given that smile is easy to fake, how smiling conveys the cooperative intention has long been a question of great interest. Although previous work suggests that people tend to mimic other's smile and interpersonal synchrony is linked to prosocial behaviors, how synchronized smiling will influence cooperation is yet to be studied. What's more, the impact of gaze direction during smiling on prosocial outcomes is still unclear. The authors investigated gaze direction and synchronized smiling across the course of 5-min conversation among pairs of same-sex strangers, and cooperation in a one-shot, two-person Prisoner's Dilemma game occurring directly following the conversation. Consistent with previous works, Duchenne smiling predict their cooperation of the receiver in the Prisoner's Dilemma game. It was found that greater direct gaze during synchronized Duchenne smiling predicts greater likelihood of cooperation by both the signaler and the receiver in the prisoner's dilemma game. The results indicate that the Duchenne smiling with direct gaze may be an honest signal of cooperative intent.

Keywords: Smile · Gaze · Cooperation · Communication · Synchronization

1 Introduction

1.1 Smiling and Cooperation

The human smile is a common social display in daily life. Understanding what a smile communicate is important because smiles are involved in cooperative interactions, and related to decision making about who to cooperate with [1, 2].

Smiling influence receiver's level of trust in the sender of the smiles. Individuals displaying enjoyment smiles tend to be rated as more trustworthy and to be cooperated with [3]. People are more cooperative with strangers represented by a smiling photograph in a trust game [4].

Smiling is also related to the sender's cooperative intent. Some studies have found that cooperative and altruistic individuals display higher levels of smiles than non-cooperators [2, 5]. In addition, a study that investigated the role of facial expressions in Prisoner's Dilemma games showed that smiles were predictive of cooperative decisions in dyads [6].

M. Kurosu (Ed.): HCII 2022, LNCS 13303, pp. 340–351, 2022.
https://doi.org/10.1007/978-3-031-05409-9_26

However, given that smiles are easy to fake [7], how smiling convey the cooperative intention has long been a question of great interest in the field of nonverbal-communication. Previous research suggests that Duchenne smiles (characterized by use of the orbicularis oculi and the zygomatic major which presents the raise up of the corners of the mouth as well as the winkles around eyes) could play a crucial role, as it is considered a rather reliable indicator of cooperative intent. Because the activation of muscles around the eyes (orbicularis oculi) is believed to be under emotional control but not under straightforward voluntary control [8, 9], Duchenne smiles are therefore difficult to fake. Additionally, people tend to judge faces with the presence of Duchenne smiles as more generous [10]. Senders expressing smiles would be more likely to cooperate, and this effect was particularly stronger for Duchenne smiles compared to non-Duchenne smiles [6]. As previous studies suggested, Duchenne smiles are considered to be a rather reliable indicators of cooperative intent [2, 5].

1.2 Honest Signal of Cooperative Intent

According to Scott-Phillips [14], signals should be beneficial to both the signaler and the receiver. Because smiles (especially non-Duchenne ones) are easy to fake, smiling is not widely acknowledged as a costly signal that impose significant cost on the smiler. However, previous research suggested that Duchenne smiling is a reliable indicator of cooperative intent as well as a reliable basis of judgement of others' cooperative intent. For these reasons, Duchenne smiling could be conceptualized as a signal of cooperative intent [6, 11].

Many research about models of signaling demonstrated that a signal's honesty can be maintained by imposing a cost on the sender of the signal [12, 13]. Pentland and Heibeck [15] proposed that honest signals should be signals that are processed unconsciously or uncontrollably that can change other people's impression of the signaler's attention, trust, interest and focus. Meanwhile, the signals should be easy to read in noisy environment. Considering these factors, Duchenne smiling itself might not be enough to serve as an honest signal of cooperative intent.

Prior studies shed light on honest signals in human communication indicating that conversations between people are a likely place to find honest signals in the form of mimicry, synchrony, or related to attention level [6, 15]. In this study, we investigated the following displays that might be engaged in processing honest signals in conversation.

Gaze Direction. Gaze direction is an important cue in human's social interaction, providing information about attention, interests, and intentions [16, 17]. Gaze direction indicates where someone's attention is focused [18], and gaze direction is able to evoke an observer's attention shifts [19]. Additionally, gaze direction influences the perception of facial expressions of emotion that when gaze direction matches the underlying behavioral intent, the perception of that expression would be enhanced [20]. Gaze direction plays an important role in guiding people's attention and focus, as well as facilitating the reading of expression. In the case of smiling, sending direct gaze while smiling would enhance the other people's perception of the smile [20].

Given that a potential honest signal should be unconscious to change other people's attention, as well as easy to read, when taking into account the gaze direction, smiling may become an honest signal. Although some work suggests that Duchenne smiling may be predictive of cooperative intent, to our knowledge, prior research has not yet investigated on how gaze direction during Duchenne smiling will influence cooperation.

Synchronized Smiles. Interpersonal synchrony and mimicry have also been suggested to be linked to prosocial outcomes such as cooperation and coordination [16], acting in synchrony with others can increase cooperation by strengthening social attachment [17]. Studies also suggest that people tend to mimic smiles, and mimicry is linked to more prosocial behavior. For example, in interactive social settings, Duchenne smiling by speakers were mimicked by listeners [18]. Recent study showed that dynamically engaged smiling predicted cooperation on the part of the receiver of the smiles [19]. Additionally, Duchenne smile were often displayed mutually between participants while they were making commitments to cooperate [6]. Although these works suggest that people tend to mimic other's smile and interpersonal synchrony is linked to prosocial behaviors, how synchronized smiling will influence cooperation is yet to be studied. Previous research has established that individuals tend to mimic partner's smile and smile together in social interaction, that interpersonal synchrony generally can lead to prosocial outcomes, and that synchrony may be an honest signal. In the current study, we try to apply these insights in answering the question of how gaze direction during synchronized smiling influences smile's function of signaling cooperative intent.

1.3 The Current Study

In this study, we examined gaze direction and synchronized smiling across the course of a five-minute conversation among pairs of same-sex strangers. Participants' cooperative intents are measured by the results of a one-shot prisoner's dilemma game within pair after the conversation. We were interested in the relationship between synchronized smiling across the conversation with direct or avoided gaze direction and the cooperation on the prisoner's dilemma game. Based on previous research, we expected that the measure of amount of Duchenne smiling across the conversation displayed by the signaler would (1) be related to the likelihood of the signaler's cooperation [6]; (2) predict higher likelihood of the receiver's (the person being smiled at) cooperation [4]. It was hypothesized that synchronized Duchenne smile would be predictive of individual's cooperative intent, moreover, direct gaze during synchronized Duchenne smile would be an honesty signal of cooperative intent. If a display is an honest signal, then that display will predict both the behavior of the signaler and the behavior of the receiver, and both are beneficial from the signal. In the current study, if greater direct gaze during synchronized Duchenne smiling predicts greater likelihood of cooperation by both the signaler and the receiver in the prisoner's dilemma game, then this means that the direct gaze in Duchenne smiling is an honest signal of cooperative intent. Therefore, the authors expected that direct gaze during synchronized Duchenne smile predict likelihood of cooperation for both the signaler and the receiver.

2   Methods

2.1   Participants

68 university and college students (34 female participants and 34 male participants) in Tokyo, Japan were recruited for this study. Participants received JPY 2,000 (approximate $17.5) as payment for participation. They were able to win up to JPY 450 (approximate $3.9) more based on the outcome of the prisoner's dilemma (see below). Participants were randomly assigned to form 34 same sex dyads, without any knowledge of their assigned partners prior to the experiment.

Participants ranged in age from 20 to 30 years, with an average age of 22 years old. 68.9% of participants were Japanese, 31.1% of participants were Chinese.

2.2   Procedure

Upon arrival to the experiment room, participants were individually greeted by an experimenter, and were taken to their seats that were separated by a divider to insure they would not make any communication before experiment started. Participants were then given a description of the study, and the procedures to be undertaken in the study. Participants were aware that they were being videotaped but were not informed that their expression would be coded for further analysis. Participants were informed of the plan for facial coding after completion of the experiment. After the introduction session, participants were given a consent form to review and sign.

After signed the consent form, participants were asked to complete questionnaires assessing their current emotion. Then participants were asked to participate in a one-shot prisoner's dilemma game with an experimenter who they did not see or talk to, nor did they know other individuals' decisions. The participants were not informed about the partner's decisions or their own profits.

Participants then took part in a ten-minute, unstructured conversation, during which they were told they could talk about any topic. During the conversation session, participants were seated on opposite ends of a meeting table with 1-m distance in between. Two Sony FDR-AX45 digital camcorders were placed approximately 0.5 m behind of each participant and were used to record the facial behavior of the participant on the opposite end of the table. Participant's facial behavior during the conversation session were video-recorded for the full 10 min at 30 frames per second with participants' knowledge and consent. Directly after the conversation, a visual divider was placed between participants, and they were asked to participate in a one-shot prisoner's dilemma game with their conversation partners and completed the questionnaire assessing emotion.

In order to avoid the influence of participants' awareness of smiles, before the experiment, the participants were informed that they would participate in a research about the relationship between personalities and cooperation. Participants were informed of the true objective of the study and the results of the prisoner's dilemma game after finishing the experiment, and were asked to sign the consent of agreement.

However, the results of the questionnaires and prisoner's dilemma game before conversation were saved for future analysis. The results were not relevant to and were not shown in the current study.

2.3 Prisoner's Dilemma Game

The prisoner's dilemma game was conducted using an exchange protocol following Mizuho, S., & Toshio, Y. [21], in which instead of choosing cooperation or defection, participants could choose different levels of cooperation. The incentive structure corresponding with the PDG was presented to the participants in an exchange form.

Each participant was provided an endowment of JPY 150 (approximately US$1.31) and was asked to decided how much of the endowment to give to an experimenter who they would not interact with or know each other's information. The provided money was then doubled and given to the partner. The participant retained the money that he/she did not give away.

If both participants provided JPY 150 (fully cooperated), each received JPY 300. If one participant fully cooperated and provided JPY 150, and the other participant offered no money, the one who fully cooperated earned nothing, and the one who completely defected earned JPY 450. If both participants chose to give nothing, each earned JPY150 (mutual defection). The participant earned more by giving less regardless of the partner's offer level. Therefore, these outcomes corresponded to the four cells in the standard PD matrix. Outcome possibilities (Table 1) were clearly outlined for participants in a chart. We used the proportion of money that each participant offered his or her partner as a measure of individual's cooperation.

Table 1. The incentive structure of the Prisoner's dilemma game used in the current study expressed as a payoff matrix.

Participant A's cooperation level (i.e., how much A gives)					
Participant B's cooperation level		150	100	...	0
	150	300R300	200R350		0R450
	100	350R200	250R250		50R350
	...				
	0	450R0	350R50		150R150

2.4 Behavior Analysis

Analyses of facial behavior were only conducted for 5 min directly before the prisoner's dilemma game. By focusing analysis on the 5 min of the clip that directly before the prisoner's dilemma game, we aimed to capture facial actions during the conversation, which were highly relevant to cooperative intent. Ekman and Friesen's Facial Action Coding System (FACS) was used to measure facial behavior [22].

FACS Coding. Individual participants' smiling during the 5-min clip of conversations was coded in 1-s intervals following the FACS. In each second, smiles were coded as Duchenne smile (AUs 6 + 12, lip corner raising up as well as presence of cheek movement and "crow's feet" wrinkles indicating contraction of the orbicularis oculi muscles), non-Duchenne smile (AU 12, raise up of lip corner). Smiles were coded as either present or absent for each second of the 5-min clip. If a Duchenne or non-Duchenne smile was present during a second, that smile was coded as 1 for the present for that second. This resulted in two series of binary coding for both Duchenne and non-Duchenne smile per participant.

All videos of the 5-min clip were coded by a certified coder. Approximately 20 percent of the overlapping videos were coded by another certified coder, in order to assess reliability. Average pairwise reliability across coders, based on the intraclass correlation coefficient (ICC) was 0.913 using random effects.

Gaze Direction Coding. Individual participants' gaze direction was coded as direct gaze (if looking at the partner) or averted gaze (if not looking at the partner) in 1-s intervals for the 5-min clip by a coder. In each second, gaze direction was given a score of 1 (direct gaze) or 0 (averted gaze). Thus, generate a series of binary data.

Approximately 10% of the videos were coded by another coder overlapped, in order to assess reliability. Average pairwise reliability across coders, based on the intraclass correlation coefficient (ICC) was 0.759 using random effects.

3   Results

3.1   Smiles, Gaze Direction and Cooperation

The level of smiles and gaze was calculated as the sum of time with code 1 in total 300 s for individuals. Individual's cooperation level was measured by the proportion of money that each participant offered his or her partner. Display time level of different types of smiles was significant different ($t(67) = 2.96$, $p = 0.004$), generally individuals display significantly more non-Duchenne smile ($M = 78.794$, $SD = 5.063$) than Duchenne smile ($M = 56.602$, $SD = 6.035$). The mean direct gaze level was 176.588 ($SD = 5.954$), mean mutual gaze level was 97.147 ($SD = 3.864$). On average, the participants provided their partners with 74.1% of the endowment of the JPY 150 ($M = 111.102$, $SD = 5.731$). Descriptive statistics for variables are shown in Table 2.

Table 2. Descriptive statistics for variables.

	N	M	SD
Duchenne smile	68	56.602	6.035
Non-Duchenne smile	68	78.794	5.063
Direct gaze	68	176.588	5.945
Mutual gaze	34	97.147	3.864
Cooperation	68	111.102	5.731

Linear regression analysis was performed with smiling level as predictor variables and the cooperation level as response variable. Analysis showed that there was a trend, although non-significant, suggesting that the smiler's cooperation level after conversation was positively associated with his or her own Duchenne smiles displayed during that interaction (t(66) = 1.72 p = 0.08). Consistent with prior studies, cooperation level of the receiver of the Duchenne smile was positively affected by the Duchenne smile level of the smiler in the conversation session (t(66) = 2.03, p = 0.04). This indicates that the participants tended to be more likely to cooperate if they had shown more Duchenne smiles while conversation, and that people would be more likely to cooperate if their partner displayed more Duchenne smiles during conversation. Correlation was not observed either between sender's cooperation level and non-Duchenne smiling (t(66) = 0.9, p = 0.36), or receiver's cooperation level and non-Duchenne smiling (t(66) = −0.78, p = 0.43).

In order to check if direct gaze affect the successive cooperation, we performed linear regression analysis between direct gaze level and cooperation level of either sender and receiver of the direct gaze. Results showed that cooperation level of both sender (t(66) = −0.6, p = 0.54) and receiver (t(66) = −0.43, p = 0.66) of the direct gaze were not influenced by direct gaze level, indicating that direct gaze might not be a potential signal of cooperative intent.

These results suggest that Duchenne smiling might be an important factor in finding potential honest signal of cooperative intent.

3.2 Synchronized Smiling and Cooperation

Synchronized smiles are defined as a series of smiling displayed by the two individuals in a group simultaneously. At each second, if the two individuals' smiles were both presented, then we counted 1. The counts were summed up as the measure of synchronized smiles. The mean synchronized smile level was 91.029 (SD = 7.482), the mean synchronized Duchenne smile level was 30.647 (SD = 4.221).

The results of linear regression analysis showed a marginally significant positive correlation between synchronized Duchenne smile and cooperation level (t(66) = 1.94, p = 0.05). However, correlation between synchronized smile and cooperation level was not observed (t(66) = 1.26, p = 0.21). When the index of synchronized Duchenne smiling was calculated as the proportion of time within synchronized smiling of dyads, the result of a linear regression showed that cooperation of dyads were significantly affected by their synchronized Duchenne smiling (t(66) = 2.32, p = 0.02). These results indicate that, synchronized Duchenne smile might be a signal of cooperative intent.

3.3 Gaze Direction During Synchronized Duchenne Smiling and Cooperation

Direct gaze during synchronized Duchenne smiling was measured as the proportion of time that individuals send direct gaze during synchronized Duchenne smiling in the pair's synchronized smiling (M = 0.109, SD = 0.012).

In order to test the hypothesis that direct gaze during synchronized Duchenne smile predict likelihood of cooperation for both the signaler and the receiver, we performed linear regression analysis with direct gaze during synchronized Duchenne smiling level as predictors and the cooperation level as criteria. The results showed significant positive association between direct gaze during synchronized Duchenne smiling level and the cooperation level of the sender of the gaze (t(66) = 2.12, p = 0.03, Fig. 1), and receiver of the gaze (t(66) = 2.47, p = 0.01, Fig. 2). This indicates that, the individuals were more likely to cooperate if the proportion of direct gaze during synchronized Duchenne smiling in total synchronized smiling while conversation is higher, and that individuals would be more likely to cooperate if the proportion of their partner's direct gaze during synchronized Duchenne smiling was higher in total synchronized smiling.

These results supported our hypothesis that direct gaze during synchronized Duchenne smile is an honest signal of cooperative intent.

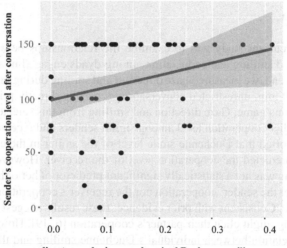

Fig. 1. Relationship between direct gaze during synchronized Duchenne smiling and the cooperation level of the sender of the gaze.

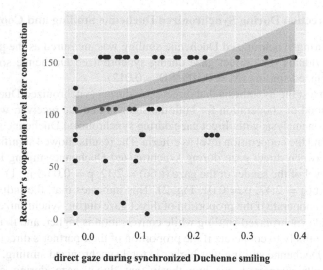

Fig. 2. Relationship between direct gaze during synchronized Duchenne smiling and the cooperation level of the receiver of the gaze.

4 Discussion

The aim of the current study was to examine the relationships between gaze direction, synchronized smiling and cooperation among dyads engaged in a one-shot social dilemma. To this end, we measured gaze direction and smiling during the last 5-min segment within a 10-min, unrestricted conversation occurring directly prior to a one-shot Prisoner's Dilemma game. Gaze direction and smiling from this selected segment were then used to predict cooperation level among signal senders and receivers.

Results supported that Duchenne smile level of the smiler in the conversation session positively predicted the cooperation level of the receiver. However, sender's own Duchenne smiling was not a statistically significant predictor of her or his own cooperation level. Neither the sender' cooperation nor the receiver's cooperation were predicted by the direct gaze. Consistent with prior evidence, these results suggest that individual's Duchenne smiling might elicit their partner's cooperation [6, 19]. However, we did not observe the correlation between individual's Duchenne smiling and their own cooperation as reported in prior studies. Under the evolutionary signaling framework, signals should be beneficial to both senders and receivers when they cooperate. If signals are beneficial to the senders but not the receivers, these signals are considered "manipulative display". Because Duchenne smiling predicted the receiver's cooperation but not the sender's cooperation, Duchenne smiling in conversations might be a manipulative display. This does not mean that the smilers are doing so under conscious calculation. It is the result of the process of evolution that selected the display because it benefits the sender from other organisms [27]. However, it is only a tentative explanation that Duchenne smiling might be a manipulative display. Because although the effect was not statistically significant, the direction of parameter estimate indicated that senders were more likely to cooperate if they display more Duchenne smiling. That is, the direction was in line with the hypothesis that Duchenne smiling are honest signals. Considering our limited and less diverse sample, this result should be replicated with a larger sample before we can reach a conclusion about whether Duchenne smiling is an honest signal.

In our results, mutual gaze didn't have an effect on cooperation. However, as we expected and in line with prior research, synchronized Duchenne smiling predicted the cooperation in dyads. Consistent with our hypothesis, results supported the hypothesis that signaler sending direct gaze during synchronized Duchenne smiling would be more likely to cooperate. Results also supported the hypothesis that signaler sending direct gaze during synchronized Duchenne smiling would be more likely to elicit cooperation from their partners. Much previous research suggests that interpersonal synchrony and mimicry is linked to prosocial behavior [16, 17, 29]. In the current study, the result that synchronized Duchenne smiling predicted cooperation are in line with a growing body of work suggesting the correlation between interpersonal synchrony and prosocial outcomes. Positive emotions need to be generated for synchrony to foster cooperation [17]. Prior works provides evidence that cooperation is linked to facial expression related to positive emotion [6, 31]. Duchenne smile is an indicator of positive emotion [8], therefore, synchronized Duchenne smiling indicating shared positive emotion during interaction for eliciting cooperation. On the other hand, our results show that although gaze is not associated with cooperation, direct gaze during synchronized Duchenne smiling is positively correlated with cooperation of both the sender and the receivers. Gaze has rarely been reported as a signal of cooperation. However, gaze indicates attention direction [23], and enhances the perception of facial expression [24]. These reasons can serve as a possible explanation why direct gaze during synchronized Duchenne smiling predicted cooperation in dyads, because gaze indicates attention direction of individuals during synchronized Duchenne smiling, and helpes perceiving the facial action. Additionally, we cannot reject the possibility that people would send direct gaze to their partner during synchronized Duchenne smiling. Further analysis such as surrogate data testing need to be conducted to investigate the relationship between gaze and synchronized Duchenne smiling, examining if direct gaze tends to co-occur with synchronized Duchenne smiling.

It is also important to note that our results do not suggest a casual correlation between smiling and cooperation. Much prior research provides evidence that cooperative individuals are seen as more likely to express positive emotion than non-cooperative individuals [2, 10, 32]. It is possible that individuals who are more cooperative display more Duchenne smiles. Further research need to be conducted to clarify the casual relationship.

Limitation of the Current Study and Future Research. Like much work on smiling and cooperation, our participants are limited to university and college students. What's more, although our participants are Chinese and Japanese, they are limited in one ethnic group, East Asian, and share much in culture. This specific nature of the sample in addition to the limited sample size, makes it difficult to infer the generality of the observed results. Further research should be conducted on a more diverse and representative population.

We did not include the analysis of emotion in this study. Given that emotion plays an important role in promoting cooperation, and smile as an indicator of positive emotion, further research considering emotion as a factor might give better insight into the mechanism of smiles as a signal of cooperation.

Altruism is another factor need to be considered in future research. In the current study, we did not take in to account the effect of altruism on prosocial outcomes. Future research should control the effect of altruism in analysis of smiling and cooperation.

5   Conclusion

In conclusion, the current study investigated the relationships between gaze direction, smiling and cooperation. It is found that direct gaze during synchronized Duchenne smiling in conversation predicted the cooperation of both sender and receiver, indicating that direct gaze during synchronized Duchenne smiling may be an honest signal of cooperative intent. Our work confirms previous findings on smiling and cooperation, and adds to a growing body of research on smiles from an evolutionary signaling perspective.

Acknowledgements. This study was partially supported by KAKENHI (Grant Numbers 20H03553) from JSPS/MEXT, Japan, and by the Center of Innovation Program from Japan Science and Technology Agency (JST), Japan.

References

1. Brown, W.M., Moore, C.: Smile asymmetries and reputation as reliable indicators of likelihood to cooperate: an evolutionary analysis. In: Shohov, S.P. (ed.) Advances in Psychology Research, vol. 11, pp.59–78. Nova Science Publishers, Huntington, New York (2002)
2. Mehu, M., Grammer, K., Dunbar, R.: Smiles when sharing. Evol. Hum. Behav. **28**, 415–422 (2007)
3. Johnston, L., Miles, L., Macrae, C.N.: Why are you smiling at me? Social functions of enjoyment and non-enjoyment smiles. Br. J. Soc. Psychol. **49**, 107–127 (2010)
4. Scharlemann, J.P.W., Eckel, C.C., Kacelnik, A., Wilson, R.K.: The value of a smile: game theory with a human face. J. Econ. Psychol. **22**, 617–640 (2001)
5. Brown, W.M., Palameta, B., Moore, C.: Are there non-verbal cues to commitment? An exploratory study using the zero-acquaintance video presentation paradigm. Evol. Psychol. **1**, 42–69 (2003)
6. Reed, L.I., Zeglen, K.N., Schmidt, K.L.: Facial expressions as honest signals of cooperative intent in a one-shot anonymous Prisoner's Dilemma game. Evol. Hum. Behav. **33**, 200–209 (2012)
7. Gunnery, S.D., Hall, J.A., Ruben, M.A.: The deliberate Duchenne smile: individual differences in expressive control. J Nonverbal Behav **37**, 29–41 (2013)
8. Ekman, P., Friesen, W.V.: Felt, false, and miserable smiles. J. Nonverbal Behav. **6**, 238–258 (1982)
9. Schmidt, K.L., Cohn, J.F.: Human facial expressions as adaptations: evolutionary questions in facial expression research. Yearb. Phys. Anthropol. **44**, 3–24 (2001)
10. Mehu, M., Little, A.C., Dunbar, R.I.M.: Duchenne smiles and the perception of generosity and sociability in faces. J. Evol. Psychol. **5**, 133–146 (2007)

11. Centorrino, S., Djemai, E., Hopfensitz, A., Milinski, M., Seabright, P.: Honest signalling in trust interactions: smiles rated as genuine induce trust and signal higher earning opportunities. Evol. Hum. Behav. **36**, 8–16 (2015)

12. McCullough, M.E., Reed, L.I.: What the face communicates: clearing the conceptual ground. Curr. Opin. Psychol. **7**, 110–114 (2016)

13. Centorrino, S., Djemai, E., Hopfensitz, A., Milinski, M., Seabright, P.: A model of smiling as a costly signal of cooperation opportunities. Adapt. Hum. Behav. Physiol. **1**(3), 325–340 (2015). https://doi.org/10.1007/s40750-015-0026-4

14. Scott-Phillips, T.C.: Defining biological communication. J. Evol. Biol. **21**, 387–395 (2008)

15. Pentland, A., Heibeck, T.: Honest signals: How they shape our world. MIT press, Cambridge (2010)

16. Cirelli, L.K.: How interpersonal synchrony facilitates early prosocial behavior Curr. Opin. Psychol. **20**, 35–39 (2018)

17. Wiltermuth, S.S., Heath, C.: Synchrony and cooperation. Psychol. Sci. **20**, 1–5 (2009)

18. Hess, U., Bourgeois, P.: You smile–I smile: emotion expression in social interaction. Biol. Psychol. **84**(3), 514–520 (2010)

19. Danvers, A.F., Shiota, M.N.: Dynamically engaged smiling predicts cooperation above and beyond average smiling levels. Evol. Hum. Behav. **39**, 112–119 (2018)

20. Emery, N.J.: The eyes have it: the neuroethology, function and evolution of social gaze. Neurosci. Biobehav. Rev. **24**, 581–604 (2000)

21. Langton, S.R.H.: The mutual influence of gaze and head orientation in the analysis of social attention direction Q. J. Exp. Psychol. A **53**, 825–845 (2000)

22. Frischen, A., Bayliss, A.P., Tipper, S.P.: Gaze cueing of attention: visual attention, social cognition, and individual differences. Psychol. Bull. **133**, 694–724 (2007)

23. Langton, S.R.H., et al.: Do the eyes have it? Cues to the direction of social attention. Trends Cognit. Sci. **4**, 50–59 (2000)

24. Adams, R.B., Jr., Kleck, R.E.: Effects of direct and averted gaze on the perception of facially communicated emotion. Emotion **5**(1), 3–11 (2005)

25. Mizuho, S., Toshio, Y.: Physical attractiveness and cooperation in a prisoner's dilemma game. Evol. Hum. Behav. **35**, 451–455 (2014)

26. Ekman, P., Friesen,W.V., Hager, J.C.: Facial action coding system (FACS). A technique for the measurement of facial action, pp. 22. Consulting, Palo Alto (1978)

27. Maynard Smith, J., Harper, D.: Animal Signals. Oxford University Press, Oxford (2003)

28. Jarick, M., Bencic, R.: Eye contact is a two-way street: arousal is elicited by the sending and receiving of eye gaze information. Front. Psychol. **10**, 1262 (2019)

29. Lumsden, J., Miles, L.K., Richardson, M.J., Smith, C.A., Macrae, C.N.: Who syncs? Social motives and interpersonal coordination. J. Exp. Soc. Psychol. **48**, 746–751 (2012)

30. Lang, M., et al.: Sync to link: endorphin-mediated synchrony effects on cooperation. Biol. Psychol. **127**, 191–197 (2017)

31. Schug, J., Matsumoto, D., Horita, Y., Yamagishi, T., Bonnet, K.: Emotional expressivity as a signal of cooperation. Evol. Hum. Behav. **31**, 87–94 (2010)

32. Gueguen, N., De Gail, M.: The effect of smiling on helping behavior: smiling and good Samaritan behavior. Commun. Rep. **16**(2), 133–140 (2003)

Enabling Situation-Aware User Interface Behavior by Exploiting Emotions and Advanced Adaptation Techniques

Christian Herdin[1]([⊠]) and Christian Märtin[2]

[1] Department of Computer Science, University of Rostock, Albert-Einstein-Str. 22, 18059 Rostock, Germany
Christian.Herdin@uni-rostock.de

[2] Faculty of Computer Science, Augsburg University of Applied Sciences, An der Hochschule 1, 86161 Augsburg, Germany
Christian.Maertin@hs-augsburg.de

Abstract. SitAdapt is an architecture and runtime system for building adaptive interactive applications. The system is integrated into the PaMGIS framework for pattern- and model-based user interface construction and generation. This paper focuses on the situation-rule-based adaptation process and discusses the different categories of adaptations. As the system observes the user during sessions and collects visual, bio-physical, and emotional data about the user that may vary over time, SitAdapt, in contrast to other adaptive system environments, is able to create situation-aware adaptations in real-time that reflect the user's changing physical, cognitive, and emotional state. With this advanced adaptation process, both, task accomplishment and user experience can be significantly improved. The operation of the system is demonstrated with an example from an adaptive travel-booking application.

Keywords: Adaptive user interface · Situation analytics · Situation awareness · Model-based user interface development · Situation-aware adaptations

1 Introduction and Related Work

Sensing and recognizing user emotions and generating emotionally intelligent responses to user actions during a session are capabilities that are on their way to become necessary and significant for the success of all sorts of advanced context- and situation-aware interactive systems.

Current research in this area is diverse and most approaches that exploit emotions build upon the groundwork established by [11] that initiated the field of affective computing. Emotions can be evaluated for many different purposes. The goal of the work presented in this paper is to exploit user emotions in real-time for improving user experience (UX) and task accomplishment mainly for responsive interactive web-based business applications. Our approach can be applied to online-shops, travel-booking sites, help

M. Kurosu (Ed.): HCII 2022, LNCS 13303, pp. 352–361, 2022.
https://doi.org/10.1007/978-3-031-05409-9_27

desks, and other types of information systems, but is not generally limited to such applications. It could also be used in technical environments, e.g., automotive safety and infotainment systems. Our approach provides domain-independent and domain-dependent situation-awareness functionality [3] and observation data for interactive applications. It can be helpful, both for users and service providers. It even works in environments, where the standard tracking mechanisms of web browsers are disabled, and no data analytics tools are applied due to privacy reasons. However, it very well can also be combined with all sorts of business intelligence and tracking methods.

For creating a flexible environment for experimental studies and for prototyping, we did not integrate the affective components and situation-awareness functionality into the target application software, but used instead PaMGIS, a model-based framework for providing components and repositories for models and patterns that support context- and situation-awareness and enable advanced real-time adaptation. SitAdapt can be seen as an integrated component within the PaMGIS framework. The system provides a multi-faceted monitoring platform for observing users in their interactive working environment and allows for emotion-recognition, situation awareness and rule-based decision-making for adapting the target application. The adaptation process is based on the observed user-characteristics, user-behavior, user actions and real-time meta-information from the target application. In [8] we extensively discussed related work on situation-awareness and affective computing. In [9] we presented the results of using SitAdapt for optimizing the digital customer journey in two related studies carried out in a real-world e-commerce portal for beauty products. These studies provided us with valuable data about potential application areas. We could demonstrate that situation-aware adaptive applications – enabled through close monitoring of the emotional state, eye-movements, gaze-tracking, bio-physical data of the user and of application meta-data – can lead to better user-experience. We could experimentally show that this type of situation-aware interactive work can also lead to better identify mission-critical application parts, improve task-accomplishment and achieve the business-goals of the service-providers.

In this paper we examine the current version of the system, into which SitAdapt has evolved over the last years. The paper focuses on the system features and discusses the underlying technologies and the adaptation process.

1.1 Context- and Situation-Awareness

The concept of context-aware computing was first proposed for distributed mobile computing in [12]. In addition to software and communication aspects to be solved when dynamically migrating an application to various devices and locations, the notion of context then also included aspects related to the interacting people and the environment.

Early definitions of the term situation-awareness appearing in psychology and the cognitive sciences were aimed at supporting human operators in complex situations. By defining situation-dependent requirements correct and smooth interactive task accomplishment could be facilitated [6, 7].

Context is a complex and not easily tangible concept. In [13] it is shown that context can either be focused on the semantics of every relevant object surrounding the entities engaged in interactions or can play a deeper role in interactions, where it must be considered, when users are forming meanings over time by also interpreting pragmatic contextual information contained in utterances of all types.

To capture the individual requirements of a situation, Chang in [3] has suggested that a situation specification must cover the user's operational environment E, the user's social behavior B, by interpreting his or her actions, and a hidden context M that includes the user's mental states and emotions. A situation Sit at a given time t can thus be defined as $Sit = <M, B, E>_t$. A user's intention for using a specific software service for reaching a goal can then be formulated as a temporal sequence $<Sit_1, Sit_2, ..., Sit_n>$, where Sit_1 is the situation that triggers the usage of a service or the execution of an activity and Sit_n is the goal-satisfying situation. For recognizing and evaluating situations adaptive runtime environments must provide the cognitive and analytic capabilities to interpret the multitude of available signals and meta-data and to infer a goal-oriented set of adaptations.

Our system can be seen as a high-quality and practicable software engineering environment for building situation-aware target systems. Therefore, we followed a combined approach by linking the *PaMGIS (Pattern-Based Modeling and Generation of Interactive Systems)* MBUID-framework and its domain and user interface models with a high-resolution observation component and a user-centric, situation-aware adaptation component. For integrating the necessary reasoning capabilities, we have introduced *situation rules* that have access to both, the observed raw-situations, and the modeling resources of the MBUID.

1.2 Different Types of Adaptations

The current version of the PaMGIS framework architecture is based on [5] and combines pattern- and model-based user interface construction tools with our situation analytics platform *SitAdapt* to build runtime-adaptive interactive applications that react to context changes in the user's environment as well as situational changes that include the user's behavior and emotional state. In this section we discuss user interface adaptation mechanisms in general and with respect to their implementation within the Sit-Adapt platform. In general, three different categories of user interface adaptations are distinguished [1, 14]:

- *Adaptable user interfaces.* The user customizes the user interface to his or her personal preferences.
- *Semi-automated adaptive user interfaces.* The user interface provides recommendations for adaptations. The user must decide whether he or she wants to accept the recommendation or not.
- *Automated adaptive user interfaces.* The user interface automatically reacts to changes in the context-of-use

With the integrated SitAdapt component (Fig. 1) such different types of adaptations can be modeled by the developer and generated at runtime. The SitAdapt system allows different types of automated user interface adaptations.

- *Changes of media and interaction object types.* Such changes modify the way of the information presentation. Different types of charts (mosaic or a bar charts), personalized areas or functions (areas with functions frequently used by the individual) can be chosen by situation-aware adaptations. Other possibilities for adaptations can, e.g., be the replacement of a form with a wizard or the change of the input media from text to speech.
- *Changes in content.* The system can adapt the content presented to the user. Thus, it is possible to change button labels or offer help texts. In the e-commerce domain, specific advertising and offers, as well as additional elements or pop-ups such as vouchers can be presented to the user. Different users can also be offered different content, e.g., variably detailed text information or product images, or variably detailed content presentations, by adding or removing content attributes.
- *Changes in design and layout.* SitAdapt can adapt the design of the program or website, e.g., colors, background colors, images and the contrast or change text layout and font size and type. The system can also change the layout of the user interface objects.
- *Changes in structure.* SitAdapt can change the number of objects displayed on the interface, for example the number of input fields of a form.
- *Personalized information.* The system can change the content of the text. For example, more formal or easier language.
- There is also the possibility of combining the various types of adaptations.

1.3 Different Times of Adaptations

Depending on the adaptation types and the available data about the user in a situation, the SitAdapt system can modify the user interface at different times:

- Before the first display of the user interface
- While the user interacts with the interface
- When the user at a later time revisits the interface

2 Integrated Development Environment

In this section the relationships of the PaMGIS framework to the integrated SitAdapt platform are discussed.

2.1 The PaMGIS Framework

The PaMGIS framework uses the domain- and context models as proposed by the CAMELEON reference framework (CRF). The CRF [2] is the most common standard architecture for the model-driven construction of interactive systems. This reference framework also includes structural guidelines for adapting software to the requirements of different platforms and for migrating an application from a device to another device.

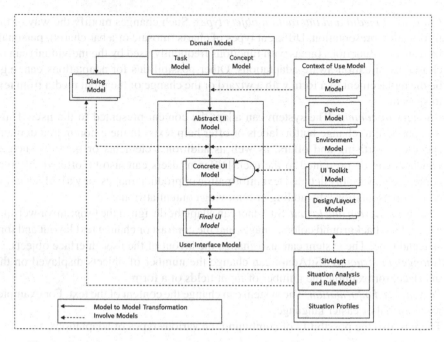

Fig. 1. Interplay between PaMGIS modeling components and SitAdapt modeling

2.2 The PaMGIS Models

The *abstract user interface model (AUI)* is generated by using information from the task model based on *Concur Task Trees (CTT)* [10] and the concept model contained in the domain model. The AUI includes the specifications of the abstract user interface objects. In the domain model and the originally rendered AUI the user interface is still independent of the usage context. After the completion of AUI modeling, the AUI model can be transformed into a *concrete user interface model (CUI)* in the next step. The information of the context model and the structure of the dialog model are exploited by this process. For defining the dynamic aspects of the user interface, PaMGIS uses a dialog model. The dialog model is based on *dialog graphs* that were originally introduced by the TADEUS system [4]. In the next step the *final user interface model (FUI)* is generated from the CUI model. In this step information from the design model and the context model is integrated into the generation process. Depending on the target implementation language, the FUI must either be compiled, or can be executed directly by an interpreter (Execute UI). The specification of the models is done in conformity with the Extensible Markup Language (XML) [5].

2.3 The SitAdapt Component

The SitAdapt system in the PaMGIS framework offers a situation analysis and rule model for development and runtime support for multiple-adaptive user interfaces and can react to context changes in the user's environment, the user's behavior, and emotional state in real-time. To allow the different types of adaptations, the system collects data from different types of inputs (eye-tracker, wristband, facial expression recognition software interface, metadata from the application regarding the user and the environment). SitAdapt uses two different data types. Atomic data types as constant attribute values (e.g., *age range* = 30–32, or *glasses* = *true*) and temporal data types (*blood pressure* or *eye* positions). With the aid of the SitAdapt rule editor, these atomic and temporal data can be used to create rules, that influence the adaptation of the user interface.

For an adaption of the user interface, SitAdapt requires the following components:

- The *situation analytics component* analyzes and assesses situations by exploiting the observed data that have been stored as situation profiles in the SitAdapt database.
- The *rule editor* allows the definition and modification of rules, e.g., for specifying the different user states and the resulting actions. The rules are triggered by the situation analytics component when the rule conditions are satisfied. Situation rules interact with the situation profiles stored in the SitAdapt database.
- The *evaluation and decision component* uses the data that are provided by the situation analytics component to decide, whether an adaptation of the user interface is currently meaningful and necessary. For this purpose, the component evaluates one or more rules and solves conflicts that may occur between the rules. Whether an adaptation is meaningful depends on the predefined purpose of the situation-aware target application. Such goals can be detected, if one or more situations in the situation profile trigger an application dependent or domain independent situation rule. If the decision component decides that a complex adaptation is necessary, it must provide the artifacts from the PaMGIS pattern and model repositories to allow for the modification of the target application by the adaptation component.

3   The SitAdapt Adaptation Process

The different types of adaptations, have different effects on the models in the PaMGIS framework. The models must be updated or must be re-generated.

To demonstrate the possibilities of the adaptive PaMGIS framework, an experimental travel portal based on different existing travel booking portals was developed. For example, during the Covid-19 pandemic, it can be useful for risk groups, such as elderly people, to get additional information for the planned travel. The SitAdapt travel platform offers various options to support these special users. To make these adaptations, SitAdapt must collect information about the users. With the help of the API of the FaceReader software the *situation analytics component*, e.g., receives data about the age range (atomic data) of the user from the database. In the rule editor (Fig. 2) an adaptation rule is stored if an age over 50 years is observed for the current user.

In this example, the user is in the first part of the booking process and fills the first form with the basic travel information, such as place of departure and arrival, and the travel date. In this step, the FaceReader software observes the user at the same time and determines the possible age range of the user in the background and stores this information in the database. If the user wants to display the search results on the next screen, the adaptation takes place before the first display of the new site. The

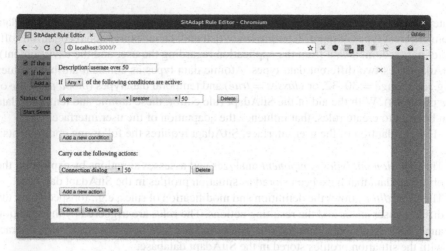

Fig. 2. SitAdapt example rule for people over 50 years

evaluation and decision component uses the data that are provided by the situation analytics component and the defined rules for the modification of the search results page.

For the generation of the search results, the *evaluation and decision component* chooses the special dialog models (Fig. 3) for users over 50 years. In this dialog it is possible to display additional information for travel connections. From this dialog model and the AUI the CUI can be created in the next step. In the following step the FUI is generated from the CUI model (Fig. 4) and the UI-Toolkit and Design/Layout-model. All UI models – from AUI to CUI to FUI – have access to modeling resources on different abstraction levels, i.e., they can use generic and application-specific HCI patterns for constructing the required user interface structure and functionality as requested by the task and dialog models during the original user interface generation process and later adaptations [5]. For the FUI templates can be available that comply with the used UI toolkits and web development tools and are still open for design and layout modifications.

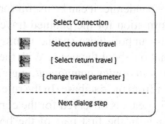

Fig. 3. Dialog model for search results

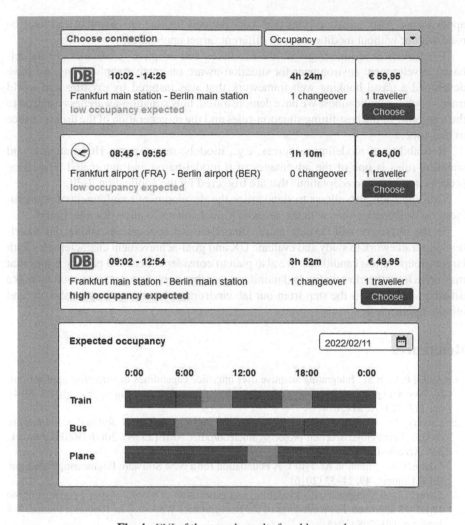

Fig. 4. FUI of the search results for older people

The newly generated user interface contains additional information on the utilization of each individual connection (Fig. 4). In addition, a graphical diagram is given to the user with the respective occupancy rates of the individual means of transport on this day to provide a possible decision-making aid for a means of transport.

4   Conclusion

This paper has discussed the interplay between the SitAdapt component, and the modeling resources provided by the PaMGIS framework. Our integrated approach allows the reuse of resources like user interface patterns and model fragments over different target applications. Also, situation-rules that were defined for one environment can later be used with or without modifications in different target applications.

For further experimenting with the resources and adaptive features of our model-based development environment for situation-aware interactive applications, we have developed a travel-booking web framework that was inspired by existing real-world travel-booking applications. We have demonstrated, how situation-awareness can lead to the triggering of the best-fitting situation-rules and the re-generation of the user interface in real-time.

Reusability of modeling resources, e.g., models, model-parts, HCI patterns, and situation-rules is one of the advantages of a model-based and automated adaptation process in contrast to adaptations that are triggered by the application itself.

Our approach also allows to standardize the development requirements for instrumenting web applications with the necessary mechanisms to allow for adaptivity.

In the future we will develop more comprehensive applications within our travel-booking framework to study and evaluate UX and goal-achievement characteristics with larger groups of test candidates. We also plan to consider ethical and privacy issues that may arise from the close individual monitoring of the users. Our goal is to soon let make SitAdapt-applications the step from our lab environment to the end-users of web- and mobile applications.

References

1. Akiki, P.A., et al.: Integrating adaptive user interface capabilities in enterprise applications. In: Proceedings of the 36th International Conference on Software Engineering (ICSE 2014), pp. 712–723. ACM (2014)
2. Calvary, G., Coutaz, J., Bouillon, L., et al.: The CAMELEON Reference Framework (2002). http://giove.isti.cnr.it/projects/cameleon/pdf/CAMELEON%20D1.1RefFramework.pdf. Accessed 08 Dec 2021
3. Chang, C.K.: Situation Analytics: A Foundation for a New Software Engineering Paradigm. IEEE Comput. **49**, 24–33 (2016)
4. Elwert, T., Schlungbaum, E.: Modelling and generation of graphical user interfaces in the TADEUS approach. In Proceedings of the Eurographics Workshop in Toulouse, France, 7–9 June, pp. 193–208 (2015)
5. Engel, J., Märtin, C., Forbrig, P.: A concerted model-driven and pattern-based framework for developing user interfaces of interactive ubiquitous applications. In: Proceedings of the First International Workshop on Large-scale and Model-Based Interactive Systems, Duisburg, pp. 35–41 (2015)
6. Flach, J.M.: Situation awareness: the emperor's new clothes. In: Mouloua, M., Parasuaman, R. (eds.) Human performance in Automated Systems: Current Research and Trends, pp. 241–248, Erlbaum (1994)
7. Flach, J.M., Mulder, M., Van Paassen, M.M.: The concept of the situation in psychology. In: Branbury, S., Tremblay, S. (eds.) A Cognitive Appraoch to Situation Awareness: Theory and Applications, pp. 42–60. Ashgate Publishing, Oxon (UK) (2004)
8. Herdin, C., Märtin, C.: Modeling and runtime generation of situation-aware adaptations. In: Proceedings of the HCI 2020, Part I, LNCS 12181, pp. 71–81, Springer (2020)
9. Märtin, C., Bissinger, B.C., Asta, P.: Optimizing the digital customer journey—improving user experience by exploiting emotions, personas and situations for individualized user interface adaptations. J. Consum. Behav. (Jun. 2021). https://doi.org/10.1002/cb.1964

10. Paternò, F.: The ConcurTaskTrees notation. In: Model-Based Design and Evaluation of Interactive Applications, pp. 39–66, Springer, Heidelberg (2000). https://doi.org/10.1007/978-1-4471-0445-2_4
11. Picard, R.: Recognizing Stress, Engagement, and Positive Emotion. In: Proceedings of the IUI 2015, Atlanta, USA, pp. 3–4 (2015)
12. Schilit, B.N., Theimer, M.M.: disseminating active map information to mobile hosts. IEEE Network 8(5), 22–32 (1994)
13. Vieweg, S., Hodges, A.: Rethinking context: leveraging human and machine computation in disaster response. Computer 47(4), 22–27 (2014)
14. Yigitbas, E., Sauer, S., Engels, G.: A model-based framework for multi-adaptive migratory user interfaces. In: Kurosu, M. (ed.) HCI 2015. LNCS, vol. 9170, pp. 563–572. Springer, Cham (2015). https://doi.org/10.1007/978-3-319-20916-6_52

Practical Suitability of Emotion Recognition from Physiological Signals by Mainstream Smartwatches

Rainer Lutze[1]([✉]) and Klemens Waldhör[2]

[1] Dr.-Ing. Rainer Lutze Consulting, Wachtlerhof, Langenzenn, Germany
`rainer.lutze@lustcon.eu`
[2] FOM University of Applied Sciences, Nuremberg, Germany
`klemens.waldhoer@fom.de`

Abstract. In the paper, we analyze the current opportunities and limitations of emotion recognition in real-life situations via mainstream smartwatches (e.g. Apple Watch™). We have identified and taken into account specific real-life situations capable to be recognized by a smartwatch app, where emotion articulation will be superimposed by physiological reactions of the human body. If not handled, such situation would result in misinterpreted emotions. Unfortunately, only one dimension of emotion, *tension* resp. stress, today can be securely recognized by mainstream smartwatches and only for more strong emotion articulations. To pave the way for the recognition of the other motion dimensions, *arousal* and *valence*, we propose a new test scenario, watching *soccer games*, as an internationally useable, highly scalable and extensively automatable test field. Only with broader experiments in this proposed field the targeted progress in emotion recognition by mainstream smartwatches will be achievable.

Keywords: Emotion recognition via mainstream smartwatches · Possibilities and limitations of cost-efficient emotion recognition · Stress recognition in real-life situations · Watching soccer games as a test scenario for emotion recognition

1 Background and Motivation

Emotion recognition by wearables is commonly seen as one of the most practical as well as cost-efficient ways of considering the user's current emotion for the purpose of a more user centered and empathic design of human computer interfaces [1–5, 7, 8]. Wearables, especially smartwatches, are widely spread, unobtrusive, affordable, mobile and allow for emotion recognition not only in the lab, but also in non-controlled everyday situations.

One – unfortunately not sufficient – constituent of emotion recognition is the observation of changes in the blood volume pulse (BVP), often denominated as heart rate (HR), and measured by wearables via photoplethysmography (PPT) [6]. The details of emotion recognition will be described in Sect. 2 of this paper.

M. Kurosu (Ed.): HCII 2022, LNCS 13303, pp. 362–375, 2022.
https://doi.org/10.1007/978-3-031-05409-9_28

It is known that emotion recognition via BVP must also consider the HR increase caused by physical activity, which superimposes the emotion response of the autonomous nervous system (ANS) and disables emotion recognition for that period. Fortunately, such physical activity can be precisely detected and considered via standard smartwatch accelerometers, barometers and GPS sensors.

A second dimension of situations, which superimpose the normal ANS emotion response, are current health hazards of the user. An onset dehydration caused by low intake of fluids - a common situation for the elderly -, a prior fall, straying around by lost spatial orientation, a bradycardia/tachycardia attack for physiological reasons beyond the smartwatch sensorics horizon, ... are stress situations where the negative emotion elicitation is of secondary importance, and the management of the concluded health hazard is of premium importance. Together with the emotion recognition considering also physical activity we present an integrated concept for the systematic determination of such health hazards, which likely cause the negative emotion elicitation occurring and require priority management.

Therefore, practical emotion recognition from physiological signals by mainstream smartwatches is more demanding and complex than passively observing and analyzing the emotion elicitation.

- First, it includes machine learning for acquiring nominal resp. baseline values. Those values need be learned during the course of the day and for a specific day of the week, thus considering the individual life style (e.g. coffee intake, ...) of the smartwatch wearer. Unusual geographic whereabouts – typically also causing excitement or stress - need also the be considered via analysis of the GPS sensor.
- Second, it needs tracking of physical activity above the acquired baseline level for the specific time and day of the week, in order to consider the effects on emotion elicitation.
- Third, it needs continuous monitoring of known health hazards affecting emotion elicitation in order to react on those health hazard and not only to register the emotional stress caused by the hazards. Upfront smartwatches include suitable actuator instruments: vibration alerts, acoustic alerts, and external communication via an integrated cellular radio.

When emotion recognition delimited by the facts described below in Sect. 3 takes place on a smartwatch, we use this information to control an empathic dialog with the user based on the principles presented in [9, 10]. Our domain of application is the support of a safe and self-determined living of elderly people – or people in need of care - in their familiar home until very old age. The support will be delivered by an embedded, autonomous app running on this smartwatch [11]. Empathic dialogues target at more successful joint actions improving the performance and actions of the smartwatch wearer. The *critical dialogue sections* (CDS) - introduced in [9] as basic structures of the dialogue with the smartwatch user - are categorized in [10] and controlled in their execution by i) the *severity* of the health hazard associated with the CDS and ii) the learned social acceptance of smartwatch initiated dialogues with the user in classified real-life situations. Now, the recognized emotional situation of the user will be used as an additional control dimension ([10], Table 4) *when* and *in which way* to initiate dialogues with the user. In general, recognized stress emotion will cancel resp. postpone planned dialogue executions other in cases of immediate urgency of a concluded health hazard presently jeopardizing the user.

2 Prior Work

Emotions have been originally described by the German psychologist Wilhelm M. Wundt 1896 in the three dimensions of arousal (*inhibition, tranquility* <--> *excitement*), valence (*unpleasure* <--> *pleasure*), and tension (*relaxation* <--> *tension* [12, 13]. The principle claim of Wundt is that all possible emotions can be expressed by specific locations in this three dimensional space. Russell inaugurated 1980 a planar, circular representation of emotions in his *circumflex* model [14]. In 1992, P. Ekman published his concept of six basic emotions: *anger, disgust, fear, joy, sadness* and *surprise,* based on an analysis of facial expressions [15]. A discussion of the different emotion theories will be found in [16]. For computational effectivity, the three dimensional Wundt model is typically contracted to the arousal and valence dimension - a two dimensional plane compliant to the Russel circumplex - and emotions will be mapped into the four quadrants of this plane. They will be associated with positive/negative arousal and positive/negative valence values. In this approach, Wundt's tension dimension will be expressed as a scalar attribute, *intensity,* of the emotions in the two dimensional space. Intensity will be physiologically articulated by *stress,* which can be comfortably measured by increased HR, decreased heart rate variability (HRV) values. In [16], a corresponding approach is described to locate emotionally denoted words in such vectors space and to visualize them accordingly.

[17–19] present an encompassing, up-to-date review of all current technic possibilities for sensory emotion recognition and recognition, classification algorithms. [19] illustrates the specific potential of the different sensors in detail. With respect to practicality and widespread use for real life situation, one may only conclude disillusioned, that still there is no silver bullet for emotion recognition with present-day technology. The sensor aggregation and fusion recommended in general for achieving more precise results is not the answer a practitioner can and will accept.

For wearables and their physiological sensors, numerous studies have elaborated that an emotion recognition is possible, if at least the following physiological data will be available [4]:

i)   BPV resp. HR,
ii) the skin conductivity (electrodermal activity, EDA), and
iii) the skin temperature (ST).

Together with the BVP, mostly the heart rate variability will be acquired, which measures the interbeat intervals (IBIs) between two succeeding R rises of the QRS-complex in the scope of the ventricular depolarization of the heart. The standard deviation SDNN of the IBIs is also a relevant aspect of emotion elicitation. HRV can be calculated in the scope of BPV with a correlation of about 90% to the electrocardiogram (ECG) [2]. ECG is the "gold standard" for the lab / controlled environments, but impractical for field use. A medical grade wristband delivering these data i) – iii) is the Empatica M4™ [2, 3]. But, current mainstream smartwatches (e.g. Apple Watch™ and Polar Vantage V2™) measure only the BVP and SDNN. With these data, only the arousal and intense of emotion can be measured. The valence of the emotion, describing a negative or positive emotion type, cannot be concluded. Moreover, the Apple Watch™ delivers HRV values only from time to time and is not suited for continuous HRV monitoring in the scope of the envisioned emotion monitoring. The Polar smartwatches are no programmable smartwatches.

In [20], a completely different approach to emotion recognition is presented, which uses a RF radio signal to extract the HR, the individual heartbeat IBIs and the derived SDNN as well as the breathing cycle from the reflected signals. The system can determine HR and SDNN with a quality comparable to a ECG. By additionally considering the breathing cycle, a classifier could be built for the four basic emotions: *joy, pleasure, sadness* and *anger* in the quadrants of the arousal, valence plane. The machine learning based classifier was trained by experienced actors expressing the specific emotions. After being trained, the classifier achieves a person independent recognition rate of the *four* emotions with a classification accuracy of 70 to 75%. We do mention this approach, in order to clarify what will be needed in addition to HR, in order to achieve a realistic emotion recognition.

There is a broad range of potential application areas of smartwatch-based emotion recognition. [7] describes a utilization in the recommendation of best suited tourist locations. In [8], smartwatch based emotion recognition will be applied for emotional self-regulation of people with autism spectrum disorder ("affective computing").

3 System Requirements Specifications and Design

Our requirement specifications regarding emotion recognition is limited to potential implementations on *widespread programmable smartwatches* like AppleWatch™, Samsung Galaxy™, Huawei smartwatches, ... Only for this product group we see realistic changes for a wide dissemination of a corresponding product in the foreseeable future. Such up-to-date smartwatches are typically equipped with 3D *accelerometers, 3D gyrometers,* a *magnetometer*, a *barometric* sensor, an *ambient light* sensor, a *GPS* resp. GLONASS, GALILEO, BEIDOU sensor for global positioning, *a* photoplethysmographic sensor for determining the current *heart rate* and atrial *oxygene saturation* (S_pO_2), and a sensor for deriving a *1-channel ECG* via a bipolar lead according to W. Einthoven in position I (both upper extremities) [21]. Sensors for *ambient* or *skin temperature* as well as *skin conductivity* are currently not common for these smartwatches and thus cannot be presupposed in the following. Additionally, nearly all smartwatches provide a synthetic *"pedometer"* sensor, by which passed daily steps will be counted. For communication purposes, the smartwatches are equipped with low energy *Bluetooth, WiFi, NFC,* and optionally an *integrated cellular radio*.

Following the rationales from Sect. 1, a *continuous monitoring* of the user activities between attaching the smartwatch after rising in the morning until dropping the smartwatch when retiring to bed at nighttime shall take place. At nighttime, the smartwatch typically needs to be charged. Thus, the corresponding smartwatch monitoring app realizing these requirements must ensure a *minimal daily runtime of* 16 h. This poses very substantial demands on the *energy efficiency* of the monitoring algorithms used.

The ongoing monitoring task on the smartwatch shall not affect the smartwatch user, wearer, in utilizing his/her devices. All programmable smartwatches feature a *"background operation"* mode for such tasks, which concurrently can run which other tasks running in the foreground of the smartwatch and currently utilizing the display of the watch, for example – and most prominently - the display of current time.

3.1 Smartwatch Operating System Support for Emotion Recognition

Unfortunately, long hours continuous monitoring of user activities is not compliant with the smartwatch manufacturer's vision of an app for such wearables. For example, in Apple's finite state machine life cycle model for WatchOS™ apps [22], after a complete startup from the initial state »not running«, apps do have a short, visible activation period of usually two minutes in the *foreground*, after which they can continue (invisible) cleanup work in the *background* and finally will be transferred to the»suspended« state. Suspended apps do not perform any further work, but will be kept in smartwatch memory – as long as resources will be available -, in order to be reactivated in short term upon user request or arriving notifications. If the smartwatch OS will run short on resources (memory), an app finally would be purged from memory, state:»not running«. For specific uses case, an app can be granted an extended one-time activation time in foreground or background of up to one hour (*self-care, mindfulness, physical therapy* apps). Additionally, *"smart alarm"* type apps may require a scheduled 30 min extended runtime in the background and can schedule themselves consecutively for (nearly) continuous operation of a monitoring algorithm. Therefore, *smart alarm* is the application type of choice for our monitoring purpose. The deliberate price for this on the WatchOS™ platform is a haptic alarm within each 30 min activation session, in order to keep the user aware that the monitoring process is still operating in the background. The monitoring app also needs to be actively started by the user once a day.

The Google Wear™ OS background operation concept is less restrictive [23].

3.2 Communicating with the Smartwatch User

Even though the user activity monitoring and emotion recognition app runs in the *background* of the smartwatch, the app can inform other apps running on the smartwatch – or a companion app running on the user's smartphone – about recognized emotional situations of significance. For Apple's SwiftUI framework, the *UserDefaults* class and the definition of a common app *suite* [24] allows communication of predefined emotional situation across all apps belonging to the specific *suite* and running on the wearable. With *remote notifications,* addressing as well the user's smartphone or smartwatch, whatever device is currently unlocked and in the view of the user, the user can be given applicable hints for the specific emotional situation. Remote notification utilize the *Apple Push Notification Service (APN),* an asynchronous message queueing service. A comparable notification service is available for the Wear™ OS platform.

3.3 The Monitoring Process

The recognition of extraordinary emotional situations of a user (negative or positive stress) will be done by identifying a significant increase in the HR, which cannot be explained by other factors within the event horizon of the smartwatch (see Sect. 3.4). In doing this, the smartwatch app needs a user reference profile of nominal values for the "typical" HR development during the specific day of the week. A separate HR reference profile for each day of the week will be sampled each 2 min and tabulated by the smartwatch app. There are different situations, which can be recognized by a smartwatch app and for which HR values are not tabulated, because they do not constitute the "typical" situation of everyday life and cause a stress situation by their own:

- ongoing *substantial physical activity* which an HR over 100 bpm and a *recovery period* of 5 min after the termination of these physical activities
- ongoing activities with a *fast change in altitude* (e.g. riding in an elevator, climbing long stairs, air plane takeoff or landing, ...)
- ongoing activities on the road with a *high moving velocity* greater 130 km/h [the smartwatch GPS sensor will not only deliver the current *global position*, but also *speed* and *heading*]

If gaps in the tabulated HR data remain, they will be closed by suitable *interpolation*. The weekly *extrapolation* of the nominal HR values of the past for the current time, for which still no tabulated data exist, will be done via *time series analysis* [25].

3.4 Limited Possibilities of Emotion Recognitions via Smartwatches

In addition to the extraordinary HR situations evoked by physical activity or external factors described in the prior Sect. 3.3, there are other intrinsic factors, which will inhibit the recognition of emotion via HR increase, because they superimpose the HR variation. These factors, which again can be securely detected by the smartwatch [25], include:

- an *awakening user* after a sleeping period resp. taking a nap (the reduced HR for the sleep period will be substantially increased within the awakening process),
- a tumble of the user, after which the physiologic response to this event for some minutes will overlay emotion elicitation,
- a progressing dehydration of the user due to low intake of fluids (only 3% loss of body fluids can cause mental disorder and a substantially increased HR).

One should be aware, that beyond the smartwatch's event horizon additionally there are a plenitude of pathophysiologic processes, which will also cause (substantially) increased HR rates. Extreme HR increases (tachycardia) will be excluded from being interpreted as a pure emotional reactions, although they could be caused also by anxiety disorders or a panic attacks and thus have an emotional constituent. But, unfortunately many purely physiologically caused HR increases (e.g. caused by antihistamine drugs or hyperthyroidism) would in deed be misinterpreted as emotional manifestations of the user. This is an principal and inherent limitation of the approach, which would probably not be alleviated if additional skin temperature and conductivity sensor would be available for a smartwatch.

4 Experiment

In order to get a first impression if emotion detection is achievable based on smartwatches in real life situations an experiment was conducted and a qualitative analysis made. When evaluating the influence of emotions on heartrate anchors are required which associate heartrates, emotions and time. Several methods could be used: a) self-description and monitoring by the person wearing the smartwatch, b) supervision by a second person and c) making usage of external data. Method a) and b) are relatively time-consuming and the esp. with a) an interaction between the self-writing process and emotion/heartrate may occur. For this study method c) was chosen.

The next question was how to find a setup which provides the necessary external – objective – data and where the heartrate could be recorded with the necessary precision and timing. It should also adhere ethical standards. E.g. it was considered unethical providing participants with negative connotated events like illness or death messages. The usual laboratory method to present to the participants standardized, emotionally connotated image catalogues / video clips (e.g. from *international affective picture system* (IAPS), *emotional movie data base* (EMDB)) was also rejected, because it does not reflect at all a realistic everyday scenario. Finally it was decided using sport events, in this case it was decided to use soccer. Although other sports like ice hockey or handball could be used also but these sports have a relative short action cycle, meaning different actions follow within a short period of time – within 5–10 s. In contrast actions in *soccer* require more time, in most cases at least 30 s. This gives a good chance that an emotion can be attributed towards an event as the average heartrate time measurement takes place every five seconds. A decisive advantage of using soccer sport matches is that at least for more important events *live tickers* with date and time information and containing the relevant episodes of the match are available. These tickers are produced by professional, rather objective sports journalists and provide the necessary *ground truth* for emotion recognition. Only articulated emotions in timely proximity of the commented episodes of the match will be accounted for a later in-depth emotion analysis of the match. In the following two typical examples are described.

The participant – a fan of FC Bayern - was watching the soccer game FC Bayern München vs. RB Leipzig taking place on February, 5th, 2022 starting at 18:30 in Munich. The participant was sitting in a chair and watching the game on TV. This was important as interactions of the heartrate with physical movements could be avoided. The participant was wearing an Apple Watch and as control a Fitbit Surge. Both wearables were running a sports app which collected the heartrate about every 5 s. To summarize the goal the participant noted that the game as such was not really exciting although five goals were shot. So the emotional involvement was little bit limited.

For providing ground truth, the ARD sport live ticker for the game (https://livece nter.sportschau.de/fussball/deutschland-bundesliga/ma9242650/ bayern-muenchen_rb-leipzig/liveticker) was used. The advantage of the ticker is that it can be downloaded and it contains a minute based description of the game, esp. also the goals (Fig. 1).

44.

Robert Lewandowski
Bayern

Tooor für Bayern München, 2:1 durch Robert Lewandowski
Aus dem Mittelkreis spielt Corentin Tolisso den Pass auf die
linke Seite, schickt damit Kingsley Coman in den freien Raum.
Der Franzose hat jede Menge Platz und Zeit für eine präzise
Flanke. Die kommt auf den Punkt. Robert Lewandowski kann
mit Anlauf in die Hereingabe springen und aus etwa zehn
Metern einköpfen. Péter Gulácsi hat da noch die rechte Hand
dran, vermag den Einschlag aber nicht zu verhindern. Saisontor
Nummer 24 für den FIFA-Weltfußballer!

41.   Nach einer Flanke von Kingsley Coman geht Robert
Lewandowski mit dem Schädel zu Werke, bekommt seinen
Kopfball aber nicht auf die Kiste platziert. Da muss Péter
Gulácsi keinen Finger krümmen.

Fig. 1. Example Sportschau Live Ticker excerpt (Source: https://livecenter.sportschau.de/fus sball/deutschland-bundesliga/ma9242650/bayern-muenchen_rb-leipzig/liveticker/)

Data preparation was done partially automatically, partially manually. The data of the wearables were exported, the time stamps and heartrates extracted from the export file as csv. The live ticker was manually adapted so that it contained only the date time, game minute and ticker message. In a next step both files were imported into a SQL database and both files outer joined based on the time stamp and reexported into an csv/xlsx file. For each heart rate measurement goal a binary marker was added for each ticker event if a ticker message was available or a goal was fallen. Overall 1465 annotated measures were generated based on one minute precision. For each minute several heartrate measured are available. The measurement started at 18:30 and was finished at 2026 resulting in 12 measures per minute. An example of the data set used in given in Table 1. Table 2 displays the main statistical properties of the heartrate for this game and Figs. 2 and 3 give graphical representation of the time series.

Table 1. Excerpt of data used for analyzing the heartrate data: "Live Ticker" indicates if a message was available for heartrate measure, "Goal" if a goal has fallen at this heartrate measure.

Time	Heartrate	Minute	LiveTickerMessage	LiveTicker	Goal
17:31	82	1	Spielbeginn	1	0
17:31	81	1	Spielbeginn	1	0
17:31	82	1	Spielbeginn	1	0

(continued)

Table 1. (*continued*)

Time	Heartrate	Minute	LiveTickerMessage	LiveTicker	Goal
...					
17:32	73			0	0
17:32	74			0	0
...					
17:34	77	4	Sportlich geht das Duell zwischen dem 16. und 18. eher ruhig los. ...	1	0
17:34	76	4	Sportlich geht das Duell zwischen dem 16. und 18. eher ruhig los	1	0
17:34	75	4	Sportlich geht das Duell zwischen dem 16. und 18. eher ruhig los	1	0
...					
17:38	76	7	Tooor für VfL Wolfsburg, 1:0 durch Aster Vranckx	1	1
17:38	75	7	Tooor für VfL Wolfsburg, 1:0 durch Aster Vranckx	1	1
...					

Table 2. Main statistical properties of the heartrate measures for the FC Bayern – RB Leipzig and VfL Wolfsburg vs. Greuther Fürth game

FC Bayern – RB Leipzig	Heartrate
Mean	60,68
Min	53,00
Max	76,00
Stddev	3,62
VfL Wolfsburg vs. Greuther Fürth	
Mean	68,15
Min	56,00
Max	95,00
Stddev	6,34

The blue line shows the heartrate, the red line the time stamps of the goals labelled with the team and the orange line shows the live ticker messages. The green part represents the game break, it is marked separately as during this period a physical movement occurred.

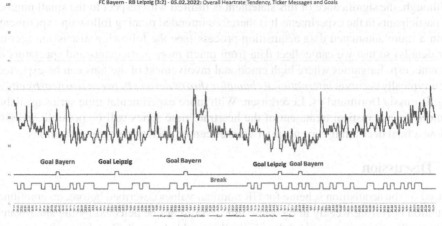

Fig. 2. Graphical display of the heartrate data and events for the FC Bayern – RB Leipzig game (Color figure online)

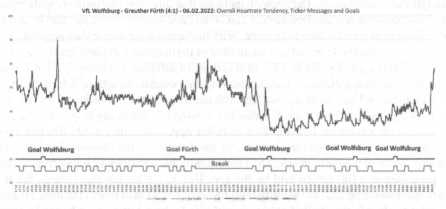

Fig. 3. Graphical display of the heartrate data and events for the VfL Wolfsburg – Greuther Fürth game (Color figure online)

A similar experiment was done with another game, VfL Wolfsburg vs. Greuther Fürth (see Fig. 3) taking place on Sunday, February, 6th at 17:30 in Wolfsburg. The participant is a Greuther Fürth fan. In contrast to the FC Bayern game the participants favorited team lost.

As just two time series were available only a qualitative analysis could be done. Visual inspection shows that positive correlations between the goals and heartrate exist, e.g.. for the first four goals of the Bayern game and the first three goals of the Wolfsburg game. As time tickers are only present if some notable event occurred there is also some parallelism between ticker events and the heartrate. Both games had no real highlights which could result in high emotions.

Overall, the real-life experiment shows that a measurable heartrate increase coincides in the dimension of 66 to 80% with the emotionally thrilling episode of the matches.

Although, the significance of this statement is limited with respect to the small number of participants in the experiment. It is therefore intended running follow up experiments with a more automated data acquisition process (see the following discussion section for details) so that we can collect data from much more participants and spectators of a game, esp. for games where high emotional involvement of the fans can be expected. This typically occurs at *international championship* or *derbies between two nearby cities,* e.g. Borussia Dortmund vs. Leverkusen. With more experimental time series available a more rigor statistical treatment of the heartrate time series will be possible and will allow a final decision if current smartwatches can be used to recognize emotions.

5 Discussion

Based on the acquisition scheme for HR nominal values described before, an emotional situation occurring weekly at the same time, would not be detected by the smartwatch because this situation would be classified a "normal behavior". This definitely is a week point of our present approach without apparent cure.

The proposed utilization of watching *soccer games* as a test ground for emotions has strengths and weaknesses. The strength includes that this sport discipline is widespread liked and thus this test implementation can be utilized in many countries and by a very large number of sports interested people. With the planned automatic data acquisition, a test is very well scalable in that a great number of participants can participate. Watching a soccer game typically elicits a broad spectrum of different emotions, so that further analysis of motion patterns of participants will be possible, which goes beyond stress measurement and targets at arousal and valence recognition. In order to provide the necessary *ground truth* for such experiments, it would be necessary to provide the participants with a connected smartphone or tablet app, where they could disclose their felt emotions by simply tapping on the app touchscreen in the moment this emotions became aware to the participants. The field all *possible emotions* to select from would be presented as a full screen grid by the app. Before the soccer game starts, the test participant would be asked to identify himself/herself as a fan of one of the match teams, in order to classify the elicited emotions in the right way. Although, it has to be taken into account that the elicitation of emotion and affection by the participant will be individually different and that also unintended blunders in operating the app will occur in the heat of the moment. Therefore a substantial number of test participants will be necessary, in order to conclude significant results from such a test. The advantage of the approach is that the test processing can be highly automated and the necessary hardware: *mainstream smartwatches* and *smartphones/tablets* are widely available and must not separately procured for the experiments.

The weaknesses of the approach include that a repetition of a test in short-term by watching the same game more than once is impossible. If the result and course of the soccer game is already known to the test participants, a repetition of the test will not elicit comparable emotions than watching the unknown game before, for the first time and with unknown result. Each game will be different and make direct comparisons difficult.

We have scored our experiment with the GARAFED (Graphical Assessment for RealLife Application-Focused Emotional Datasets) [26]. This assessment methodology targets for an standardized evaluation of *emotion, mood and stress recognition* (EMSR) experiment. Best scorings will be easily revealed by an even proportioned octagon. The corresponding scoring result for our presented experiment is depicted in Fig. 4. The experiment achieves maximum scoring in the O dimension *(real-life emotions, ambulatory (i.e. out of lab) monitoring)*, the I dimension *(Portable and non-invasive: The system is light and does not have an impact on everyday activities ... It is similar to a commonly worn object such as a watch, a belt etc.)*, and the P dimension *(Non-intrusive data: non personal and does not allow for identification)*. Otherwise our experiment show clear deficiencies and achieves only minimal scoring with respect to *duration* and number of participants.

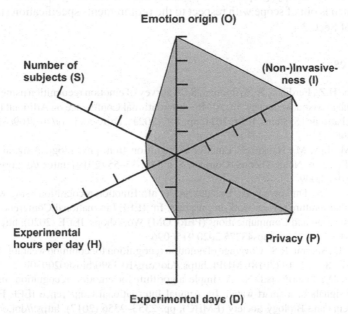

Fig. 4. GARAFED diagram with respect to [26] for the experiment

6 Conclusions

Our work has shown that at present only *one* dimension of emotion, the *tension resp. stress* can be monitored via mainstream smartwatches. Capturing of the other two emotion dimensions: *arousal* and *valence* from smartwatch motion pattern *in real-life situations* seems not to be impossible, but will require broader and more basic research work. For entering into this field, we propose a new common test ground for emotion measurements: watching *soccer games*.

The experiments have shown, that *in real-life situations* only more strong tension situations will evoke unambiguous stress recognition patterns for the smartwatch. This is not really surprising taking into account that even with the sensorially more rich instrumented Empatica M4 smartwatch the reported stress recognition [27] accuracy rate of 84,13% could only be achieved in complete static lab conditions.

It has also to be kept in mind, that even the *tension* dimension measurements of emotion by smartwatches have to account for the fact, that tension might be also caused by a plenitude of pathophysiologic processes within the user or extraordinary behavior (e.g. substantial *physical activity*) of the user. By utilizing the smartwatch capabilities, we have excluded an increased number of such situation from our emotion monitoring process, which otherwise would have led to misinterpretation of stress as primarily emotional articulation of the user. The only known working alternative for recognition of emotion in the condition of substantial physical activity is a far reaching-instrumentation of the user including electromyographic (EMG) and electroencephalographic (EEG) sensors … [28], which is out of scope with respect to the requirements specification stated at the beginning of Sect. 3.

References

1. Wijasena, H.Z., Ferdiana, R., Wibirama, S.: A survey of emotion recognition using physiological signal in wearable devices. In: AIMS - International Conference on Artificial Intelligence and Mechatronics Systems, IEEE 2021, pp. 1–6 (2021). https://doi.org/10.1109/AIMS52415.2021.9466092
2. Egger, M., Ley, M., Hanke, S.: Emotion recognition from physiological signal analysis: a review. Electron. Notes Theoret. Comput. Sci. **343**, 35–55 (2019). https://doi.org/10.1016/j.entcs.2019.04.009
3. Saganowski, S., Dutkowiak, A., Dziadek, A., et al.: Emotion recognition using wearables: a systematic literature review-work-in-progress. In: IEEE International Conference on Pervasive Computing and Communications (PERCOM) Workshops. IEEE (2020). https://doi.org/10.1109/PerComWorkshops48775.2020.9156096
4. Hui, T.K.L., Sherrat, R.S.: Coverage of emotion recognition for common wearable biosensors. Biosensors **8**(2), 1–19 (2018). MDPI, https://doi.org/10.3390/bios8020030
5. Pollreisz, D., TaheriNejad, N.: A simple algorithm for emotion recognition, using physiological signals of a smart watch. In: Annual International Conference IEEE Engineering in Medicine and Biology Society (EMBC), pp. 2353–2356 (2017). https://doi.org/10.1109/EMBC.2017.8037328
6. Beckmann, N.: Photoplethysmographie-basierte Messung der Pulswellenlaufzeit für die Emotionserkennung, dissertation (in German), University Essen-Duisburg 2019, pp. 1–160
7. Satamaria-Granados, L., Mendoza-Moreno, J.F., Ramirez-Gonzalez, G.: Tourist recommender systems based on emotion recognition – a scientometric rewiew. Future Internet **13**(2), 1–37 (2021). https://doi.org/10.3390/fi13010002
8. Torrado, J.C., Montoro, G., Gomez, J.: The potential of smartwatches for emotional self-regulation for people with autism spectrum disorder. In: Proceedings of the 9th International Joint Conference on Biomedical Engineering Systems and Technologies, vol. 5, SCITEPRESS, pp. 444–449 (2016). https://doi.org/10.5220/0005818104440449
9. Lutze, R., Waldhör, K.: Model based dialogue control for smartwatches. In: Kurosu, M. (ed.) HCI 2017. LNCS, vol. 10272, pp. 225–239. Springer, Cham (2017). https://doi.org/10.1007/978-3-319-58077-7_18
10. Lutze, R., Waldhör, K.: Improving dialogue design and control for smartwatches by reinforcement learning based behavioral acceptance patterns. In: Kurosu, M. (ed.) HCII 2020. LNCS, vol. 12183, pp. 75–85. Springer, Cham (2020). https://doi.org/10.1007/978-3-030-49065-2_6

11. Lutze, R., Waldhör, K.: Personal health assistance for elderly people via smartwatch based motion analysis. In: IEEE International Conference on Healthcare Informatics (ICHI), pp. 124–133. IEEE (2017). https://doi.org/10.1109/ICHI.2017.79
12. Wundt, W.M.: Outlines of Psychology (in German). Engelmann Publishers, Leipzig (1896)
13. Reisenstein, R.: A structuralist reconstruction of wundt's three-dimensional theory of emotion. In: Westmeyer, H. (ed.) The Structuralist Program in Psychology: Foundations and Applications, pp. 141–189. Hogrefe & Huber Publishers, Toronto, CN (1992)
14. Russell, J.A.: A circumplex modell of affect. J. Person. Soc. Psychol. **39**(6), 1161–1178 (1980). https://doi.org/10.1037/h0077714
15. Ekman, P.: An argument for basic emotions. Cogn. Emot. **6**(3/4), 169–200 (1992). https://doi.org/10.1080/02699939208411068
16. Liu, Z., Xu, A., Guo, Y., et al.: SEEMO: a computational approach to see emotions. In: Conference on Human Factors in Computing Systems (CHI), Montreal, CN, Paper 464, pp. 1–12, ACM (2018). https://doi.org/10.1145/3173574.3173938
17. Pal, S., Mukhopadhyay, S., Suryadevara, N.: Development and progress in sensors and technologies for human emotion recognition. MDPI Sens. **21**(16), 1–21 (2021). https://doi.org/10.3390/s21165554
18. Shu, L., Xie, J., Yang, M., et al.: A review of emotion recognition using physiological signals. MDPI Sens. **18**(7), 1–41 (12018). https://doi.org/10.3390/s18072074
19. Dzedzickis, A., Kaklauskas, A., Bucinskas, V.: Human emotion recognition: review of sensors and methods. MDPI Sens. **20**(3), 1–40 (2020). https://doi.org/10.3390/s20030592
20. Zhao, M., Fadel, A., Katabi, D.: Emotion recognition using wireless signals. ACM Commun. **61**(9), 91–100 (2018). https://doi.org/10.1145/3236621
21. Barold, S.S.: Willem Einthoven and the birth of clinical electrocardiography a hundred years ago. Cardiac Electrophysiol. Rev. **7**, 99–104 (2003). https://doi.org/10.1023/A:1023667812925
22. NN: Working with the watchOS App Life Cycle, Developer Information, Apple Inc. https://developer.apple.com/documentation/watchkit/wkextensiondelegate/working_with_the_watchos_app_life_cycle. Accessed 5 Feb 2022
23. NN: Guide to Background Work, Android Developers, Google Inc. https://developer.android.com/guide/background. Accessed 5 Feb 2022
24. NN: User Defaults, Developer Information, Apple Inc. https://developer.apple.com/documentation/foundation/userdefaults. Accessed 5 Feb 2022
25. Lutze, R., Waldhör, K.: Integration of stationary and wearable support services for an actively assisted living of elderly people: capabilities, achievements, limitations, prospects—a case study. In: Wichert, R., Mand, B. (eds.) Ambient Assisted Living. ATSC, pp. 3–26. Springer, Cham (2017). https://doi.org/10.1007/978-3-319-52322-4_1
26. Larradet, F., Niewiadomski, R., Barresi, G., et al.: Towards emotion recognition from physiological signals in the wild: approaching the methodological issues in real-life data collection. Front. Psychol. **11**(7), 1–23 (2020). Article 1111 https://doi.org/10.3389/fpsyg.2020.01111
27. Montesinos, V., Dell'Agnola, F., Arza, A. et al.: Multi-modal acute stress recognition using off-the-shelf wearable devices. In: Annual International Conference IEEE Engineering in Medicine and Biology Society (EMBC), pp. 2196–2201 (2019). https://doi.org/10.1109/EMBC.2019.8857130
28. Heinisch, J.S., Anderson, C., David, K.: Angry of climbing stars? Towards physiological emotion recognition in the wild. In: IEEE International Workshop on Emotion Awareness for Pervasive Computing with Mobile and wearable Devices, p. 486–491 (2019), DOI: https://doi.org/10.1109/PERCOMW.2019.8730725

Algorithm for Automatic Brain-Shift Detection Using the Distance Between Feature Descriptors

Takumi Mori[1], Masahiro Nonaka[2], Takahiro Kunii[3], Masanao Koeda[4], Kaoru Watanabe[1], and Hiroshi Noborio[1(✉)]

[1] Osaka Electro-Communication University, Osaka 575-0063, Japan
nobori@osakac.ac.jp
[2] Kansai Medical University, Osaka 573-1191, Japan
[3] KASINA System Co., Shiga 522-0041, Japan
[4] Okayama Prefectural University, Okayama 719-1197, Japan

Abstract. In this study, we conducted basic research to accurately detect intraoperative brain shifts using preoperative and postoperative normalized (position, posture, and scale aligned) patient Digital Imaging and Communications in Medicine and aimed to develop a brain model that could be used online along with intraoperative sensor basting. For accurate brain-shift detections, we evaluated the agreement between the local brain shifts detected by several feature-point matching algorithms and their parameters and the artificially produced local brain shifts. The results indicated that the scale-invariant feature transform algorithm proved unsuitable for detecting brain shifts, while the accelerated-KAZE algorithm produced good results. Thus, this study identified a suitable feature-point detection algorithm and its parameters for the detection of brain shifts.

Keywords: DICOM · Open CV · Brain-shift

1 Introduction

The brain is the most important organ in the human body, and unnecessary damage during surgery must be avoided to prevent complications and sequelae following surgery. Hence, the brain must be skillfully handled. Generally, it is difficult to determine the boundary between normal and abnormal areas during surgery. For example, surgeons might go too far while removing a malignant tumor and thus reduce the survival rate of patients. Alternatively, if too much of the malignant tumor is left behind, recurrence arises.

In general, before neurosurgery, a patient's brain image is captured using computed tomography (CT) or magnetic resonance imaging (MRI) as Digital Imaging and Communications in Medicine (DICOM) (represented by 124 2D shading-value images stacked on top and bottom). These images are represented in a three-dimensional hierarchical structure of the shading value voxels. Employing the CT and MRI techniques, malignant tumors and aneurysms along with vessels and nerves can be detected. During operations, the neurosurgical navigation system reveals to the physician the relationship between

M. Kurosu (Ed.): HCII 2022, LNCS 13303, pp. 376–387, 2022.
https://doi.org/10.1007/978-3-031-05409-9_29

areas of malignant tumors and blood vessels and the position and posture of the scalpel in real-time.

However, because the brain is a soft organ, the brain itself deforms during surgery, resulting in a brain shift wherein the brain images captured before surgery do not match the actual brain during surgery. Brain shift is a phenomenon in which the brain deforms in a manner such that it sinks. When spinal fluid is lost, the brain sinks toward the base of the skull. In addition, when a malignant tumor or brain clot is removed, the surrounding tissues move into the void. Consequently, the location, position, and morphology of malignant tumors change during neurosurgery, degrading the accuracy of navigation guidance. Because current neurosurgical navigation systems cannot accurately predict and represent this brain shift, it is often impossible to perform surgeries per the preoperative surgical plan. Rather, surgeries are performed solely based on the surgeon's experience while looking at actual surgical fields.

To solve this problem, we aimed to develop a neurosurgical navigation system and create a brain model that deforms appropriately from that in video images captured during the operation. Previous organ models have not been backed up by actual intraoperative data; hence, their deformations have not been evaluated for veracity [1–8]. We aimed to create a brain model that deforms similarly to the intraoperative data by quantitatively detecting the brain misalignment based on the preoperative and postoperative brain DICOM images recorded in several hospitals. Therefore, for the past few years, we have been using feature-point detection algorithms [9–17] (e.g., accelerated-KAZE (AKAZE), oriented features from the accelerated segment test (FAST) and rotated binary robust independent elementary features (BRIEF) (ORB), binary robust invariant scalable keypoints (BRISK), scale-invariant feature transform (SIFT)) in preoperative and postoperative DICOMs to extract a mapping set of similar feature points, which we subsequently employed as the brain shift. However, we could not confirm the correctness of this extracted brain shift [18, 19].

Therefore, we first developed an algorithm that could artificially and locally deform a DICOM image [20]. Subsequently, as part of this study, we identified the local brain shifts detected by feature-point matching algorithms that agreed well with the artificially generated local brain shifts. Based on this, we determined the most suitable feature-point detection algorithm for detecting brain shifts.

The remainder of the paper is organized as follows. We first describe conventional feature-point extraction algorithms in Sect. 2. In Sect. 3, we explain the brain-shift detection method based on the feature-point extraction algorithms and their methods for visualizing the local brain-shift region in color. In Sect. 4, we compare the artificially generated local brain shifts with the detected local brain shifts and identify the feature-point detection algorithm that is most suitable for detecting brain shifts. Finally, we summarize our research in Sect. 5.

2   Feature-Point Extraction Algorithms

A feature-point detection algorithm is employed to detect feature points in an image [9]. Features are generally detected in the form of corners, blobs, edges, junctions, lines, etc. SIFT, speeded-up robust features (SURF), KAZE, AKAZE, ORB, BRISK, etc., are basic feature detection algorithms that are scale, rotation, and affine invariant, each of which has a specified feature descriptor and has its own advantages and disadvantages.

Feature matching is performed using the L1- or L2-norms for feature-point detection algorithms (SIFT, SURF, KAZE, etc.) and Hamming distance for binary descriptors (AKAZE, ORB, BRISK, etc.). Various matching strategies are employed for feature matching, each with its advantages and disadvantages, such as threshold-based matching, nearest neighbor, and nearest neighbor distance ratio [10].

2.1 KAZE

The KAZE algorithm was proposed by Alcantarilla et al. in 2012 [11]. KAZE employs a nonlinear scale space of features based on nonlinear diffusion filtering. Image blurring is locally adapted to the feature points to reduce noise while preserving the boundaries of the regions in the subject image. The feature points are computed based on the scale-normalized determinant of the Hessian matrix computed at multiple scale levels.

The maximum value of the detector response is selected as a feature point using a moving window. The feature description introduces the property of rotational invariance by identifying the dominant direction in a circular neighborhood around each detected feature. KAZE features are invariant to rotation, scale, and limited affine transformations, and they appear more distinctly at various scales at the cost of a modest increase in computational time.

2.2 AKAZE

The AKAZE algorithm was presented by Alcantarilla et al. in 2013 [12]. Like KAZE, AKAZE is based on nonlinear diffusion filtering, but its nonlinear scale space is built in a computationally efficient framework called fast explicit diffusion. AKAZE is based on the determinant of the Hessian matrix detector. AKAZE possesses a response threshold for the detector, which was tuned as a parameter in this study. The features of AKAZE are invariant to scale, rotation, and limited affine transformations, and owing to its nonlinear scale space, it has more distinct features at various scales.

2.3 ORB

The ORB algorithm was presented by Rublee et al. in 2011 [13]. The ORB algorithm combines the modified FAST [14] detection method and the oriented normalized BRIEF [15] description method. FAST corners are detected at each layer of the scale pyramid, the angles of the detected points are evaluated using the Harris corner score, and the highest-quality points are filtered. A modified version of the BRIEF descriptor is employed because the BRIEF descriptor is highly unstable concerning rotations. The ORB features are invariant to scale, rotation, and limited affine transformations.

It should be noted that in this study, the number appearing in front of the experimental results represents the edge threshold (the size of the border where no feature is detected), and the number appearing behind represents the FAST threshold (the threshold of the difference in intensity between the center pixel and the pixels in a circle around this pixel).

2.4 BRISK

BRISK was presented by Leutenegger et al. in 2011. BRISK uses the AGAST algorithm to detect corners and locate the maximum of the scale-space pyramid while filtering the detected corners using the FAST corner score [16]. Thus, BRISK allows a selection of the AGAST detection threshold, which is the threshold of the difference in intensity between the center pixel and the pixels in a circle around this pixel.

The description of BRISK is based on identifying the characteristic direction of each feature to achieve rotational invariance. The results of a simple brightness test are concatenated to form the descriptor as a binary string such that it is indepen-dent of illumination. BRISK features are invariant to scale, rotation, and limited affine transformations.

2.5 SIFT

SIFT was proposed by D. G. Lowe in 2004 [17]. It is a well-known feature detection and description algorithm. Herein, feature points are detected using the difference-of-Gaussian operator, which approximates the Laplacian-of-Gaussian operator, by search-ing for local maxima at various scales of the subject image. A 16×16 neighborhood is extracted around each detected feature point, and the region is further divided into sub-blocks to obtain a total of 128 values. SIFT is robust to image rotation, scale, and limited affine transformations, but it has the drawback of being computationally expensive.

3 Feature-Point Extraction Algorithms

Currently, even if a brain shift is detected, it is impossible to confirm whether the detected brain shift is correct. In this study, we examine the ability of our method to detect the position and posture of the brain shift using a brain shift created by artificially processing a real DICOM [20] as an answer of this algorithm.

The virtual DICOM holds the feature-point coordinates of the original DICOM and the coordinates of the shifted feature points as internal data. We used these internal data as the correct answer data to evaluate the accuracy of the brain-shift detection algorithms.

1. For the pre-deformed DICOM, we extracted the feature point group (A) using a feature-point extraction algorithm (AKAZE, ORB, BRISK, SIFT, etc.)
2. According to the feature-point group (denoted as A), a local brain shift of DICOM was created using the artificial brain-shift algorithm [20] to obtain the post-deformed DICOM and its feature-point group (denoted as A′).
3. Because there exists a one-to-one correspondence between feature-point groups A and A′, we can extract the pair group AA′ and visualized the answer brain-shift C′ by displaying the white vector aiai′ and the colored Euclidean distance |aiai′| [mm] in the experimental Figs. 2, 3, 4, 5, 6,7, 8 and 9 for the elements of A∋ai and A′ ∋ ai′ (i = 1,…, m) (Fig. 1).
4. For the post-deformed DICOM, we newly extracted a new set A″ of feature points (ai″) using the same feature-point extraction algorithm.

5. We can extract the pair group AA'' and visualized the answer brain-shift C'' by displaying the white vector aiai'' and the colored Euclidean distance |aiai''| [mm] in the experimental Figs. 2, 3, 4, 5, 6,7, 8 and 9 for a pair of elements of A∋ai and A'' ∋ai'' (i = 1,..., n) whose neighbor pixel pattern is similar (Fig. 1).
6. Subsequently, the pairs were sorted by the distance |aiai''| and were displayed by a given threshold number in the experimental Figs. 2, 3, 4, 5, 6,7, 8 and 9.

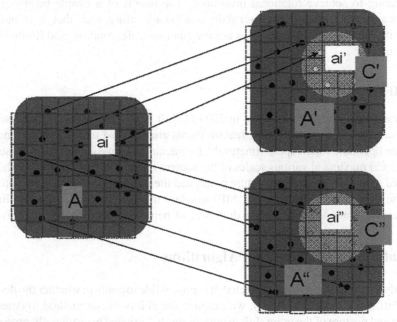

Fig. 1. The pre-deformation DICOM before deformation, feature point group A, and individual feature point ai, and the post-deformation DICOM, feature point group A', and individual feature point ai'. The newly detected feature point group A'' and individual feature points ai'' in the post-deformation DICOM.

4   Feature-Point Extraction Algorithms

In a Delaunay diagram consisting of grid points divided into 10×10 feature points, we first generated an artificial brain displacement by moving any vertex. AKAZE, ORB, BRISK, and SIFT were used as feature-point extraction algorithms, and large, medium, and small parameters were selected and implemented for each algorithm (however, multiple patterns were used for SIFT because the parameters used for feature-point extraction could not be set) (Table 1).

Table 1. Parameters used for each algorithm.

ORB		AKAZE	BRISK	SIFT
10	21	0.001	30	None
10	31			
10	41			
20	21	0.0005	20	None
20	31			
20	41			
30	21	0.0001	10	None
30	31			
30	41			

4.1 Feature-Point Detection Algorithm SIFT

Because this feature-point detection algorithm has no parameters, only one type of brain shift can be detected. Compared to the correct brain shift, illustrated in Fig. 2(a), the detected brain shift, illustrated in Fig. 2(b), exhibits excessive detection in the middle and bottom regions and accurate detection in the upper right region. It should be noted that the color indicator on the right represents the Euclidean distance [mm] of the difference between the correct and detected feature points, which shifts to warmer colors as the distance increases.

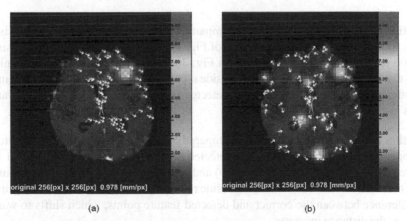

(a)   (b)

Fig. 2. Comparison results when using the feature point detection algorithm SIFT, (a) Brain shift C' detected from feature point group A and feature point group A', (b) Brain shift C" detected from feature point group A and feature point group A" (500 points in decreasing order of similarity). (b) Brain shift C" detected from feature point group A and feature point group A" (1000 points in decreasing order of similarity). (Color figure online)

4.2   Feature-Point Detection Algorithm AKAZE

Because this feature-point detection algorithm has no parameters, only one type of brain shift can be detected. Compared to the correct brain shift, illustrated in Fig. 2(a), the detected brain shift, illustrated in Fig. 2(b), exhibits excessive detection in the middle and bottom regions and accurate detection in the upper right region. It should be noted that the color indicator on the right represents the Euclidean distance [mm] of the difference between the correct and detected feature points, which shifts to warmer colors as the distance increases.

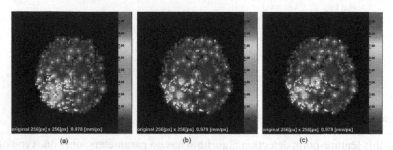

(a)   (b)   (c)

Fig. 3. Comparison results when using the feature point detection algorithm AKAZE (parameter 0.0001), (a) Brain shift C' detected from feature point group A and feature point group A', (b) Brain shift detected from feature point group A and feature point group A'' (500 points in decreasing order of similarity). (b) Brain shift C'' detected from feature point group A and feature point group A', (c) Brain shift C'' detected from feature point group A and feature point group A'' (1000 points in decreasing order of similarity). (Color figure online)

Selection of the Parameter 0.0001. Compared to the correct brain shift, which is primarily identified in the lower-left corner of Fig. 3(a), the detected brain shift consisting of 1000 feature point pairs, illustrated in Fig. 3(c), is relatively accurate. It should be noted that the color indicator on the right side represents the Euclidean distance [mm] of the difference between the correct and detected feature points, which shifts to warmer colors as the distance increases.

Selection of the Parameter 0.0005. Compared to the correct brain shift, depicted in the upper right corner of Fig. 4(a), the detected brain shifts consisting of 500 and 1000 feature point pairs, illustrated in Figs. 4(b) and 4(c) are extremely accurate. It should be noted that the color indicator on the right side represents the Euclidean distance [mm] of the difference between the correct and detected feature points, which shifts to warmer colors as the distance increases.

Selection of the Parameter 0.001. Compared to the correct brain shift, depicted at the bottom of Fig. 5(a), the detected brain shifts consisting of 500 and 1000 feature point pairs, illustrated in Figs. 5(a) and 5(b), are both extremely accurate.

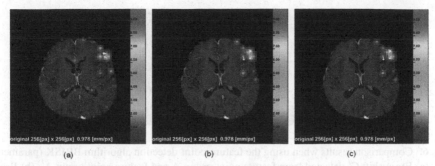

(a)   (b)   (c)

Fig. 4. Comparison results when using the feature point detection algorithm AKAZE (parameter 0.0005), (a) Brain shift C' detected from feature point group A and feature point group A', (b) Brain shift detected from feature point group A and feature point group A'' (500 points in decreasing order of similarity). (b) Brain shift C'' detected from feature point group A and feature point group A', (c) Brain shift C'' detected from feature point group A and feature point group A'' (1000 points in decreasing order of similarity). (Color figure online)

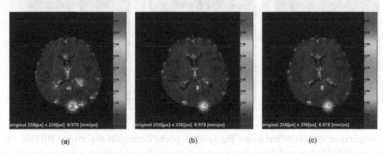

(a)   (b)   (c)

Fig. 5. Comparison results when using the feature point detection algorithm AKAZE (parameter 0.001), (a) Brain shift C' detected from feature point group A and feature point group A', (b) Brain shift detected from feature point group A and feature point group A'' (500 points in decreasing order of similarity). (b) Brain shift C" detected from feature point group A and feature point group A', (c) Brain shift C'' detected from feature point group A and feature point group A'' (1000 points in decreasing order of similarity). (Color figure online)

4.3 Feature-Point Detection Algorithm BRISK

Because this feature-point detection algorithm has parameters, an infinite number of brain shifts can be detected. However, owing to time constraints, we considered only two different parameters.

Selection of the Parameter 20. Compared to the correct brain shift, depicted in Fig. 6(a), the detected brain shifts, illustrated in Figs. 6(b) and 6(c), exhibit an overestimated detection of the correct shift in the upper left corner and an excessive detection in the upper right corner.

Selection of the Parameter 30. The detected brain-shift C'' illustrated in Fig. 7(b) and Fig. 7(c) captures the correct brain shift C' illustrated in Fig. 7(a), relatively accurately.

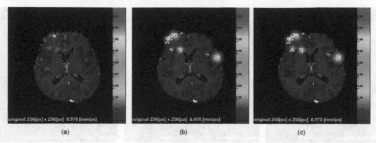

(a)   (b)   (c)

Fig. 6. Comparison results when using the feature point detection algorithm BRISK (parameter 20), (a) Brain shift C′ detected from feature point group A and feature point group A′, (b) Brain shift detected from feature point group A and feature point group A″ (500 points in decreasing order of similarity). (b) Brain shift C″ detected from feature point group A and feature point group A′, (c) Brain shift C″ detected from feature point group A and feature point group A″ (1000 points in decreasing order of similarity). (Color figure online)

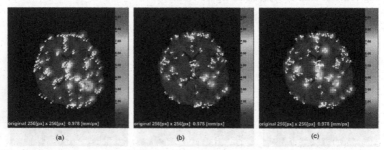

(a)   (b)   (c)

Fig. 7. Comparison results when using the feature point detection algorithm BRISK (parameter 30), (a) Brain shift C' detected from feature point group A and feature point group A′, (b) Brain shift detected from feature point group A and feature point group A″ (500 points in decreasing order of similarity). (b) Brain shift C″ detected from feature point group A and feature point group A″ (1000 points in decreasing order of similarity). (Color figure online)

4.4 Feature-Point Detection Algorithm ORB

Because this feature-point detection algorithm has parameters, an infinite number of brain shifts can be detected. However, owing to time constraints, we considered only two different parameters.

Selection of the Parameter (20, 21).
The detected brain shift, illustrated in Fig. 8(b),(c), captures the correct brain shift, illustrated in Fig. 8(a), relatively accurately.

Selection of the Parameter (20, 41). For the correct brain shift, illustrated in Fig. 9(a), neither the brain shifts depicted in Fig. 9(b) nor (c) accurately capture the brain shift.

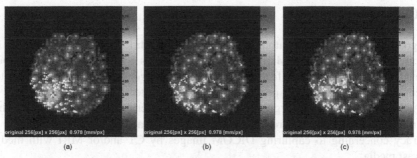

Fig. 8. Comparison results when using the feature point detection algorithm ORB (parameters 20,21), (a) Brain shift C' detected from feature point group A and feature point group A′, (b) Brain shift detected from feature point group A and feature point group A″ (500 points in decreasing order of similarity). (b) Brain shift C″ detected from feature point group A and feature point group A′, (c) Brain shift C″ detected from feature point group A and feature point group A″ (1000 points in decreasing order of similarity). (Color figure online)

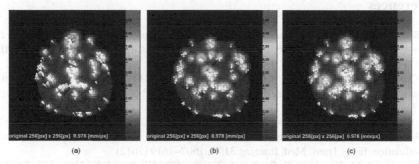

Fig. 9. Comparison results when using the feature point detection algorithm ORB (parameters 20, 41), (a) Brain shift C′ detected from feature point group A and feature point group A′, (b) Brain shift detected from feature point group A and feature point group A″ (300 points in decreasing order of similarity). (b) Brain shift C″ detected from feature point group A and feature point group A′, (c) Brain shift C″ detected from feature point group A and feature point group A″ (1000 points in decreasing order of similarity). (Color figure online)

In most cases, the location of the brain shift was generally identified with an error of less than 5 mm, but no effective results were obtained for detecting the direction in which the brain shift occurred or the direction of the brain shift. However, in terms of identifying the position of the brain shift, SIFT was not accurate, but the other three algorithms captured the range of the brain shift relatively accurately, although it depended on the parameter identification (some parameters captured it excessively). On the other hand, ORB was superior among the four algorithms in accurately depicting how the brain shift occurred.

In future studies, we plan to devise better methods to accurately estimate the direction of brain shifts and generalizations to several DICOM sites in many patients.

5 Conclusions

The goal of our study was to automatically extract brain shifts from the preoperative and postoperative recorded DICOM images of several patients in a hospital. For this purpose, we evaluated several suitable feature-point detection algorithms and their parameters. Based on our findings, SIFT proved unsuitable for detecting brain shifts, while the AKAZE algorithm produced good results; however, verifying the accuracy of these findings for multiple patients remains a crucial task. In addition, we should verify the accuracy concerning to capturing DICOM images by CT and/or MRI with medical contrast media.

Acknowledgment. This study was supported partly by the 2020 Grants-in-Aid for Scientific Research (No. 20K04407 and 20K12053) from the Ministry of Education, Culture, Sports, Science and Technology, Japan.

References

1. Sun, K., Pheiffer, T.S., Simpson, A.L., Weis, J.A., Thompson, R.C., Miga, M.I.: Near real-time computer assisted surgery for brain shift correction using biomechanical models. IEEE J. Transl. Eng. Health Med. **2**, 1–13 (2014)
2. Chen, I., Ong, R.E., Simpson, A.L., Sun, K., Thompson, R.C., Miga, M.I.: Integrating retraction modeling into an atlas-based framework for brain shift prediction. IEEE Trans. Biomed. Eng. **60**(12), 3494–3504 (2013)
3. DeLorenzo, C., Papademetris, X., Staib, L.H., Vives, K.P., Spencer, D.D., Duncan, J.S.: Volumetric intraoperative brain deformation compensation: model development and phantom validation. IEEE Trans. Med. Imaging **31**(8), 1607–1619 (2012)
4. Vigneron, L.M., Boman, R.C., Ponthot, J.-P., Robe, P.A., Warfield, S.K., Verly, J.G.: Enhanced FEM-based modeling of brain shift deformation in image-guided neurosurgery. J. Comput. Appl. Math. **234**(7), 2046–2053 (2010)
5. Zacharaki, E.I., Hogea, C.S., Biros, G., Davatzikos, C.: A comparative study of biomechanical simulators in deformable registration of brain tumor images. IEEE Trans. Biomed. Eng. **55**(3), 1233–1236 (2008). International Journal of Pharma Medicine and Biological Sciences Vol. 8, No. 3, July 201977
6. Payan, Y.: Soft Tissue Biomechanical Modeling for Computer Assisted Surgery, Part of the Studies in Mechanobiology, Tissue Engineering and Biomaterials book series (SMTEB, volume 11)
7. Valencia, A., Blas, B., Ortega, J.H.: Modeling of brain shift phenomenon for different craniotomies and solid models. J. Appl. Math. **2012**(12), 20 (2012). Article ID 409127
8. Lowe, D.: Distinctive image features from scale-invariant keypoints. Int. J. Comput. Vis. **60**(2), 91–110 (2004)
9. Hassaballah, M., et al.: Image features detection description and matching. In: Image Feature Detectors and Descriptors, Springer International Publishing, pp. 11–45 (2016)
10. Mikolajczyk, K., Schmid, C.: A performance evaluation of local descriptors. IEEE Trans. Pattern Anal. Mach. Intell. **27**(10), 1615–1630 (2005)
11. Alcantarilla, P.F., et al.: KAZE features. In: European Conference on Computer Vision, pp. 214–227 (2012)
12. Alcantarilla, P.F., Nuevo, J., Bartoli, A.: Fast explicit diffusion for accelerated features in nonlinear scale spaces. Trans. Pattern Anal. Mach. Intell. **34**(7), 1281–1298 (2011)

13. Rublee, E., et al.: ORB: an efficient alternative to SIFT or SURF. In: IEEE International Conference on Computer Vision, pp. 2564–2571 (2011)
14. Rosten, E., Drummond, T.: Machine learning for high-speed corner detection. In: European Conference on Computer Vision, pp. 430–443 (2006)
15. Calonder, M., et al.: Brief: binary robust independent elementary features. In: European Conference on Computer Vision, pp. 778–792 (2010)
16. Leutenegger, S., et al.: BRISK: Binary robust invariant scalable keypoints. In: IEEE International Conference on Computer Vision, pp. 2548–2555 (2011)
17. Lowe, D.G.: Distinctive image features from scale-invariant keypoints. Int. J. Comput. Vision 60(2), 91–110 (2004)
18. Noborio, H., Uchibori, S., Koeda, M., Watanabe, K.: Two-dimensional DICOM feature points and their mapping extraction for identifying brain shifts. Int. J. Pharma Med. Biol. Sci. 8(3), 71–78 (2019). http://www.ijpmbs.com/uploadfile/2019/0723/20190723045554314.pdf,pp.71-78,July
19. Noborio, H., Uchibori, S., Koeda, M., Watanabe, K.: Visualizing the correspondence of feature point mapping between DICOM images before and after surgery. In: Proceedings of the 2019 11th International Conference on Bioinformatics and Biomedical Technology, pp.1–7. ACM, New York (2019). https://doi.org/10.1145/3340074.3340075, ISBN: 978-1-4503-6231-3. Stockholm Sweden, 29–31 May, 2019
20. Mori, T., Nonaka, M., Kunii, T., Koeda, M., Noborio, H.: Development of an algorithm to artificially create virtual brain deformations for brain DICOM. In: Kurosu, M. (ed.) HCII 2022. LNCS, vol. 13303, pp. 388–402. Springer, Cham (2022, to appear)

Development of an Algorithm to Artificially Create Virtual Brain Deformations for Brain DICOM

Takumi Mori[1], Masahiro Nonaka[2], Takahiro Kunii[3], Masanao Koeda[4], and Hiroshi Noborio[1(✉)]

[1] Osaka Electro-Communication University, Osaka 575-0063, Japan
nobori@osakac.ac.jp
[2] Kansai Medical University, Osaka 573-1191, Japan
[3] KASINA System Co., Shiga 522-0041, Japan
[4] Okayama Prefectural University, Okayama 719-1197, Japan

Abstract. This study proposes an algorithm to artificially create brain shifts in patients' brain DICOM images. Then, we evaluate the SIFT, AKAZE, ORB, and BRISK feature point extraction algorithms for the automatic detection of local brain shifts from a patient's pre-and postoperative DICOM images. Accurate and automatic detection of brain shifts could contribute toward the generation of accurate brain deformation models. The evaluation results suggested that the BRISK and AKAZE algorithms are most suitable for the above purpose.

Keywords: DICOM · Open CV · Brain-shift

1 Introduction

Brain shift always occurs during neurosurgery, and it degrades the accuracy of current neurosurgical navigators. This is because the position, posture, and shape of blood vessels and malignant tumors taken preoperatively using digital imaging and communications in medicine (DICOM) system change intraoperatively. To solve this problem, we incorporate a brain model that is appropriately triggered by intraoperative video images into our original neurosurgical navigator.

For this purpose, a model that can reflect the true brain deformation in real-time is needed. Numerous organ models have been proposed [1–8]; however, hardly any can simulate true deformations. In this study, we model the brain deformation using a pair of pre-and postoperative brain DICOM images. Unfortunately, the number of segments and resolution of DICOM images taken by computed tomography (CT) and magnetic resonance imaging (MRI) is not standardized, and the pre-and postoperative conditions for taking DICOM images are very different. Further, it is very difficult to determine where the brain deformation occurs. To address these issues, we first compare a large number of pre-and postoperative DICOM images captured by CT and MRI and stored in hospitals to locally detect the brain shift to build a brain deformation model.

M. Kurosu (Ed.): HCII 2022, LNCS 13303, pp. 388–402, 2022.
https://doi.org/10.1007/978-3-031-05409-9_30

We have pre-and postoperatively applied various feature point detection algorithms like scale-invariant feature transform (SIFT), accelerated KAZE (AKAZE), oriented FAST and rotated BRIEF (ORB), and binary robust invariant scalable key-points (BRISK) [9–17] to DICOM images, extracted a set of feature points with close shading arrangement and Euclidean distance, and examined their correspondence in 124 DICOM images [18, 19]. Although this allowed us to somewhat detect local deformations, we could not confirm whether these were brain shifts. This is because even if brain shifts are confirmed by an experienced neurosurgeon by visually comparing pre-and postoperative brain DICOM images, the shading values in these images are so small that only obviously large brain shifts can be detected. Further, this manual process requires considerable time and effort, making it impractical considering that neurosurgeons have to examine and treat a large number of patients. Therefore, numerous pre-and postoperative brain DICOM image pairs of patients remain unexamined in the workstations of medical schools.

We propose an algorithm to artificially create brain shifts in a patient's brain DICOM image and then evaluate the detection ability of four feature point extraction algorithms -SIFT, AKAZE, ORB, and BRISK- for these shifts. The rest of this paper is organized as follows. Section 2 discusses these four feature point extraction algorithms [9–17]. Section 3 describes how DICOM brain models are obtained using Delaunay diagrams. In Sect. 4, after creating artificial brain shifts using the above four feature point extraction algorithms, we examine whether enough feature points can be extracted from the pre-and postoperative DICOM image pairs to extract brain shifts and evaluate the best and optimal feature point extraction algorithm [21]. Finally, Sect. 5 summarizes this study.

2 Feature Point Extraction Algorithm

An algorithm for detecting feature points in a grayscale image is called a feature point extraction algorithm [9]. These features are detected as corners, blobs, edges, junctions, lines, etc. in the image. Feature point extraction algorithms SIFT, SURF, KAZE, AKAZE, ORB, BRISK, etc. have scale, rotation, and affine invariant feature detectors, and each feature descriptor has its advantages and disadvantages.

SIFT, SURF, KAZE, etc. use L1-norm and L2-norm, while AKAZE, ORB, BRISK, etc. are algorithms that use Hamming distance. Various matching strategies such as threshold matching, nearest-neighbor matching, and nearest neighbor distance ratio are employed for feature matching, and each has its advantages and disadvantages [10].

2.1 KAZE

Algorithm KAZE [11], proposed by P. F. Alcantarilla et al. in 2012, uses a nonlinear scale space of features based on nonlinear diffusion filtering. By adopting local image blurring to feature points, it can reduce noise and at the same time preserve the boundaries of regions in the subject image. The feature points are based on the scale-normalized determinant of the Hessian matrix computed at multiple scale levels. the KAZE features are invariant to rotation, scale, and limiting affine, and have more distinct features at various scales, although the computation time increases slightly. the KAZE features are invariant to rotation, scale, and The KAZE feature is invariant to rotation, scale, and limiting affine.

2.2 AKAZE

The algorithm Accelerated-KAZE (AKAZE) [12], presented by P. F. Alcantarilla et al. in 2013, is based on nonlinear diffusion filtering, similar to KAZE. This nonlinear scale space is built in a computationally efficient framework called Fast Explicit Diffusion (FED) AKAZE is based on a deterministic detector of the Hessian matrix. The quality of this rotational invariance is improved by using the SCHAAL filter. The AKAZE has a detector response threshold, which is tuned as a parameter in this work. A unique feature of AKAZE is that it is invariant to scale, rotation, and limiting affine.

2.3 ORB

The algorithm Oriented FAST and Rotated BRIEF (ORB) [13], presented by E. Rublee et al. in 2011, is a combination of the modified FAST (Features from Accelerated Segment Test) [14] detection method and the Oriented Normalized BRIEF (Binary Robust Independent Elementary Features) [15] description method.

The ORB algorithm is a combination of the Modified FAST (Features from Accelerated Segment Test) [14] detection method and the ORIEF (Binary Robust Independent Elementary Features) description method, and the ORB algorithm is a combination of the modified FAST (Features from Accelerated Segment Test) [14] detection method and the ORIEF description method, and the ORB features are invariant to scale rotation and limited affine transformations.

In this study, the numbers in front of the experimental results are the edge threshold (the size of the boundary where no feature is detected), and the numbers behind are the fast threshold (the threshold of the intensity difference between the center pixel and the pixels in the circle around it).

2.4 BRISK

The feature point extraction algorithm BRISK (Binary Robust Invariant Scalable Keypoints) was presented by Leutenegger et al. in 2011. BRISK finds corners with a detector called AGAST, filters them with a FAST corner score, and searches for the maximum of a scale-space pyramid [16]. BRISK finds the corners with a detector called AGAST and filters them with the FAST corner score to find the maximum of the scale-space pyramid [16]. BRISK allows the user to choose the threshold of the AGAST detection. This is the threshold of the intensity difference between the center pixel and its surrounding pixels.

To achieve rotation invariance, the BRISK descriptor is based on identifying the direction of each feature. BRISK descriptors are illumination independent because the results of a simple brightness test are concatenated to form a descriptor as a binary string; BRISK features are invariant to scale, rotation, and limited affine variation.

2.5 SIFT

The feature point extraction algorithm SIFT (Scale Invariant Feature Transform) was proposed by D. G. Lowe in 2004 [17]. Here, feature points are detected using the Difference-of-Gaussians (DoG) operator, which approximates the Laplacian-of-Gaussian (LoG) operator. At various scales of the subject image, feature points are detected by searching for local maxima using DoG. A 16×16 neighborhood is extracted around each detected feature point, and the region is divided into sub-blocks to obtain a total of 128 values. This SIFT is robust to image rotation, scaling, and limited affine transformations, but has the drawback of being computationally expensive.

In this study, the numbers in front of the experimental results are the edge threshold (the size of the boundary where no feature is detected), and the numbers behind are the fast threshold (the threshold of the intensity difference between the center pixel and the pixels in the circle around it).

3 Delaunay Brain Deformation Model with Feature Points and Lattice Points

In this chapter, we describe how the feature and grid points that uniformly divide the space (i.e., vertices when the brain region is divided into squares with uniform length and width) are divided into Delaunay triangulations [20]. The vertex of the Delaunay diagram is manually moved such that the force is inversely proportional to the distance, and the surrounding vertices are linked to it. Finally, all surrounding DICOM pixels are moved in inverse proportion to the Euclidean distance from all moving vertices, thus moving all the pixels that make up the DICOM.

First, feature points are extracted from the real DICOM image (Figs. 1(a) and 4(a)), and the point cloud with grid points added to the feature points is divided into Delaunay triangles (Figs. 1(b)(c) and 4(b)(c)). This is because the area per mesh becomes too large with only the feature points, and unnatural deformations may occur. Therefore, we divide the mesh into a grid, as described above, and then consider feature points to reduce the size per mesh and unnatural deformations. Then, by selecting a vertex from the vertex group and manually moving its position, the surrounding vertex set and the DICOM pixels around the vertex set are deformed (Figs. 2 and 4(d)).

The pre-deformed DICOM feature points ai $(i = 1,...,n)\epsilon$ a point cloud A is deformed to obtain the post-deformed DICOM feature points ai' $(i = 1,...,n)\epsilon$ another point cloud A' that are similar but have different positions, resulting in local brain shifts (Fig. 3). Next, the same feature point extraction algorithm is applied to the post-deformed DICOM to obtain new feature points as the other point cloud A''. Then, feature points ai'' $(i = 1,...,m)\epsilon A''$ that is similar to the feature points ai' $(i = 1,...,m) \epsilon A'$ are found depending on the degree of similarity. Thus, the feature point pair (ai', ai'') is obtained, and from the difference between them, the detection ability of the feature point extraction algorithm for local brain shifts is evaluated (Fig. 3).

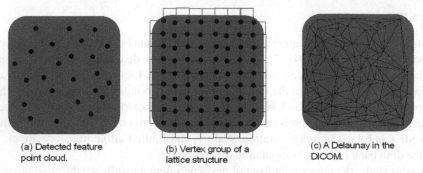

(a) Detected feature point cloud.

(b) Vertex group of a lattice structure

(c) A Delaunay in the DICOM.

Fig. 1. Real DICOM brain model by the Delaunay diagram.

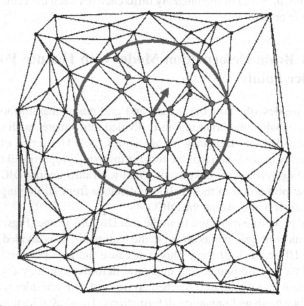

Fig. 2. Brain shift generation by arbitrary point shift in Delaunay diagram.

The deformation is different when the grid (mesh) is large (Fig. 4(e)) and small (Fig. 4(f)). To reduce the loss of feature points (shading pixel array) due to artificial brain shifts, the region around the moving point (consecutive neighbor points and surrounding pixel groups) is deformed in inverse proportion to the Euclidean distance.

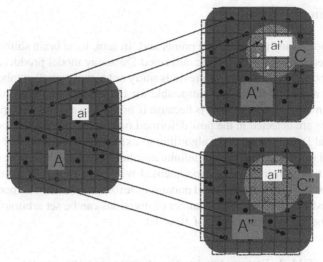

Fig. 3. The pre-deformed DICOM before deformation, feature point group A, and individual feature point ai, and their corresponding post-deformation DICOM after deformation, feature point group A′, and individual feature point ai′. By the same feature detection algorithm, we newly capture feature point group A″ including individual feature points ai″ in the post-deformation DICOM.

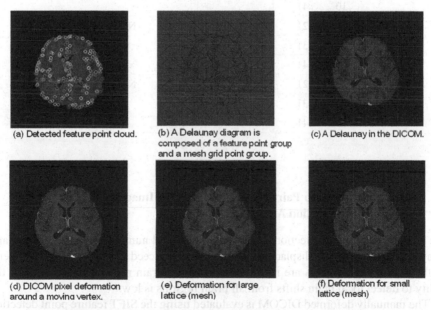

(a) Detected feature point cloud.

(b) A Delaunay diagram is composed of a feature point group and a mesh grid point group.

(c) A Delaunay in the DICOM.

(d) DICOM pixel deformation around a moving vertex.

(e) Deformation for large lattice (mesh)

(f) Deformation for small lattice (mesh)

Fig. 4. Real DICOM deformation by the Delaunay diagram.

4 Experimental Results

We evaluate how many useful feature points and, in turn, local brain shifts are retained in the deformed DICOM image in the deformed Delaunay model produced using each feature point extraction algorithm. A previous study noted that a small number of retained feature points and brain shifts were unsuitable for the evaluation of an automatic brain shift extraction algorithm [21]. This is because if no feature points of the pre-deformed DICOM image are detected in the post-deformed one, no brain shift will be detected.

For the real DICOM image, the algorithm to extract feature points and their parameters are listed in Table 1. Because an infinite number of parameters can be chosen from and owing to time constraints, we experimented with three types of parameters: large, medium, and small (Table 1). To avoid unnatural deformations, the number of divisions in the grid mesh was adjusted. The number of divisions can be set arbitrarily; however, in our experiments, we used a mesh of 10×10.

Table 1. Feature point detection algorithm and its parameters.

ORB		AKAZE	BRISK	SIFT
10	21	0.001	30	None
10	31			
10	41			
20	21	0.0005	20	None
20	31			
20	41			
30	21	0.0001	10	None
30	31			
30	41			

4.1 Feature Point Group Pair (ai′, ai″) in DICOM Image Deformed by SIFT Feature Point Detection Algorithm

The SIFT feature point detection algorithm has a small number of feature points, and many feature points have displacements that greatly exceed the amount of movement. Further, feature point pairs are not distributed in all brain regions, and therefore, the ability to detect local brain shifts from all brain regions is low.

The manually deformed DICOM is evaluated using the SIFT feature point detection algorithm. Feature point ai′ exists in the pre-deformed DICOM and moves, and feature point ai″ is extracted from the post-deformed DICOM. The feature points with similar feature values are paired to form a feature point group pair (ai′, ai″). The deformed DICOM has many such feature point group pairs.

The horizontal lines in Figs. 5(b) and 5(c) indicate the number of feature point pairs. The vertical axes in Figs. 5(b) and 5(c) indicate the X- and Y-axis errors of the feature point pair (mm), respectively. The SIFT feature point detection algorithm has a small number of feature point pairs and no selection parameters; therefore, the number of feature point pairs cannot be increased further.

Figures 5(b) and (c) show that many pairs (ai', ai'') have distances that are much larger than the travel distance of the selected point in the pre-deformed DICOM. Figure 5(a) shows the newly detected feature points ai'' (i = 1,..., m) (dark blue cross) and the original feature points ai' (i = 1,..., m) (green cross) in the artificially deformed DICOM. The results indicate that the SIFT feature point detection algorithm is unsuitable for detecting local brain shifts in the whole brain space because the feature point pairs are spatially nonuniformly distributed.

4.2 Feature Point Group Pair (ai', ai'') in DICOM Image Deformed by AKAZE Feature Point Detection Algorithm

The AKAZE feature point detection algorithm has a large number of feature points, and many feature points have displacements that greatly exceed the amount of movement. Further, feature point pairs are distributed in all brain regions, and therefore, the ability to detect local brain shifts from all brain regions is high.

The manually deformed DICOM is evaluated using the AKAZE feature point detection algorithm Feature point ai' exists in the pre-deformed DICOM and moves, and feature point ai'' is extracted from the post-deformed DICOM. The feature points with similar feature values are paired to form a feature point group pair (ai', ai''). The deformed DICOM has many such feature point group pairs. Feature point ai'' can be derived from pre-deformed DICOM without knowing the feature point ai' of the post-deformed DICOM and can then be used to detect brain shifts in the pre-and postoperative DICOM pairs.

The horizontal lines in Figs. 6(b) and 6(c) indicate the number of feature point pairs. The vertical axes in Figs. 6(b) and 6(c) indicate the X- and Y-axis errors of the feature point pairs (mm), respectively. The AKAZE feature point detection algorithm has a large number of feature point pairs and selection parameters; therefore, the number of feature point pairs can be increased further.

Figures 6(b) and 6(c) show that few pairs (ai', ai'') have distances that are much larger than the travel distance of the selected point in the pre-deformed DICOM. Figure 6(a) show the newly detected feature points ai'' (i = 1,..., m) (dark blue cross) and the original feature points ai' (i = 1,..., m) (green cross) in the artificially deformed DICOM. These results indicate that the AKAZE feature point detection algorithm is suitable for detecting local brain shifts in the whole brain space because the feature point pairs are spatially uniformly distributed.

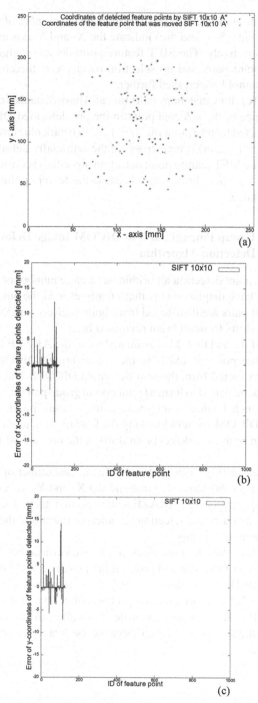

Fig. 5. Comparison results when using the feature point detection algorithm SHFT, (a) feature point group A (dark blue tens) and feature point group A′ (green x), (b) X-axis direction error for feature point correspondence number (mm), (c) Y-axis direction error for feature point correspondence number (mm). (Color figure online)

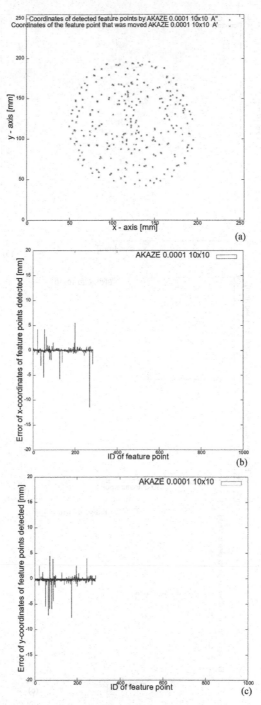

Fig. 6. Comparison results when using the feature point detection algorithm AKAZE_0.0001_10x10, (a) feature point group A (dark blue tens) and feature point group A′ (green x), (b) X-axis direction error for feature point correspondence number (mm), (c) Y-axis direction error for feature point correspondence number (mm). (Color figure online)

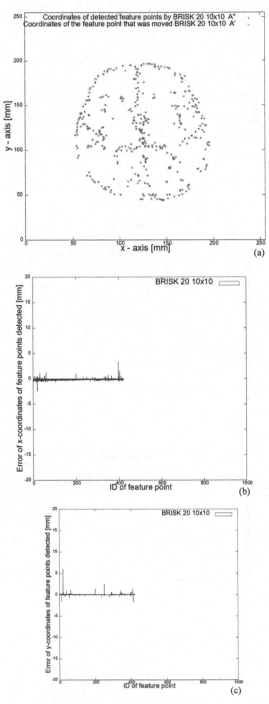

Fig. 7. Comparison results when using the feature point detection algorithm BRISK_20_10x10, (a) feature point group A (dark blue tens) and feature point group A′ (green x), (b) X-axis direction error for feature point correspondence number (mm), (c) Y-axis direction error for feature point correspondence number (mm). (Color figure online)

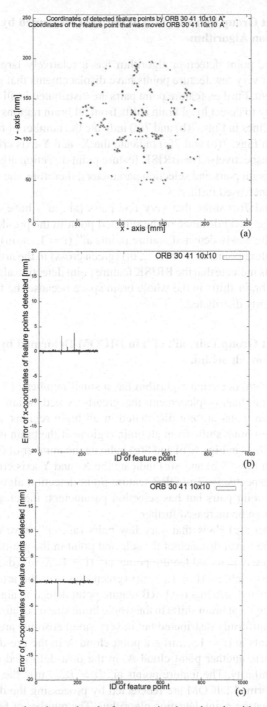

Fig. 8. Comparison results when using the feature point detection algorithm ORB_30_41_10x10, (a) feature point group A (dark blue tens) and feature point group A′ (green x), (b) X-axis direction error for feature point correspondence number (mm), (c) Y-axis direction error for feature point correspondence number (mm). (Color figure online)

4.3   Feature Point Group Pair (ai', ai'') in DICOM Deformed by BRISK Feature Point Detection Algorithm

The BRISK feature point detection algorithm has a relatively large number of feature point pairs, but very few feature points have displacements that greatly exceed the amount of movement. Further, feature point pairs are distributed in all brain regions, and therefore, the ability to detect local brain shifts from all brain regions is relatively high.

The horizontal lines in Figs. 7(b) and 7(c) indicate the number of feature point pairs. The vertical axes in Figs. 7(b) and 7(c) indicate the X- and Y-axis errors of the feature point pairs (mm), respectively. The BRISK feature point detection algorithm has a large number of feature point pairs and selection parameters; therefore, the number of feature point pairs can be increased further.

Figures 7(b) and 7(c) show that very few pairs (ai', ai'') have distances that are much larger than the travel distance of the selected point in the pre-deformed DICOM. Figure 7(a) show the newly detected feature points ai'' (i = 1,..., m) (dark blue cross) and the original feature points ai' (i = 1,..., m) (green cross) in the artificially deformed DICOM. The results indicate that the BRISK feature point detection algorithm is suitable for detecting local brain shifts in the whole brain space because the feature point pairs are spatially uniformly distributed.

4.4   Feature Point Group Pair (ai', ai'') in DICOM Deformed by ORB Feature Point Detection Algorithm

The ORB feature point detection algorithm has a small number of feature points, and very few feature points have displacements that greatly exceed the amount of movement. Further, feature point pairs are not distributed in all brain regions, and therefore, the ability to detect local brain shifts from all brain regions of the brain is low.

The horizontal lines in Figs. 8(b) and 8(c) indicate the number of feature point pairs. The vertical axes in Figs. 8(b) and 8(c) indicate the X- and Y-axis errors of the feature point pair (mm), respectively. The ORB feature point detection algorithm has a small number of feature point pairs but has selection parameters; therefore, the number of feature point pairs can be increased further.

Figures 8(b) and 8(c) show that very few pairs (ai', ai'') have distances that are much larger than the travel distance of the selected point in the pre-deformed DICOM. Figure 8(a) show newly detected feature points ai'' (i = 1,..., m) (dark blue cross) and the original feature points ai' (i = 1,..., m) (green cross) in the artificially deformed DICOM. The results indicate that the ORB feature point detection algorithm is not very suitable for detecting local brain shifts in the whole brain space because the feature point pairs are spatially uniformly distributed but in very small absolute amounts.

The feature points ai (i = 1,..., n) ϵ a point cloud A in the pre-deformed DICOM and ai' (i = 1,..., n)ϵ another point cloud A' in the post-deformed DICOM have the same degree of similarity. The feature points ai'' (i = 1,..., m)ϵ the other point cloud A'' in the post-deformed DICOM are redetected by processing the deformed DICOM using the BRISK feature point detection algorithm. The number of feature point group pairs (ai', ai'') and the errors of their X and Y coordinates vary greatly depending on the parameters of the BRISK feature point detection algorithm.

To summarize these results, SIFT is unsuitable because it does not have many feature point pairs and no selection parameters. Further, ORB has an insufficient number of feature point pairs with a nonuniform distribution in the brain. By contrast, BRISK and AKAZE have a sufficient number of feature point pairs with a uniform distribution in the brain. Between these two, BRISK is better owing to the smaller distance difference between feature point pairs, although the diversity of the brain distribution was slightly lacking. Overall, BRISK and AKAZE are considered suitable for the application considered in this study.

5 Conclusions

We proposed an artificial deformation algorithm that can preserve enough feature points in DICOM images. Further, we evaluated algorithms for the automatic detection of local brain shift from a patient's pre-and postoperative DICOM images. An automatic detection algorithm that can accurately and automatically detect the brain shift from a patient's pre-and postoperative DICOM image pairs can be used to generate accurate brain deformation models.

In this study, we roughly divided the parameters of the feature point detection algorithm into large, medium, and small. However, our results show that each algorithm has an appropriate intensity. Therefore, in the future, we aim to investigate the optimal parameter strength so that the difference in coordinates between the moved and the detected feature points can be reduced.

Acknowledgment. This study was supported partly by the 2020 Grants-in-Aid for Scientific Research (No. 20K04407 and 20K12053) from the Ministry of Education, Culture, Sports, Science and Technology, Japan.

References

1. Sun, K., Pheiffer, T.S., Simpson, A.L., Weis, J.A., Thompson, R.C., Miga, M.I.: Near real-time computer assisted surgery for brain shift correction using biomechanical models. IEEE J. Transl. Eng. Health Med. **2**, 1–13 (2014)
2. Chen, I., Ong, R.E., Simpson, A.L., Sun, K., Thompson, R.C., Miga, M.I.: Integrating retraction modeling into an atlas-based framework for brain shift prediction. IEEE Trans. Biomed. Eng. **60**(12), 3494–3504 (2013)
3. DeLorenzo, C., Papademetris, X., Staib, L.H., Vives, K.P., Spencer, D.D., Duncan, J.S.: Volumetric intraoperative brain deformation compensation: model development and phantom validation. IEEE Trans. Med. Imaging **31**(8), 1607–1619 (2012)
4. Vigneron, L.M., Boman, R.C., Ponthot, J.-P., Robe, P.A., Warfield, S.K., Verly, J.G.: Enhanced FEM-based modeling of brain shift deformation in image-guided neurosurgery. J. Comput. Appl. Math. **234**(7), 2046–2053 (2010)
5. Zacharaki, E.I., Hogea, C.S., Biros, G., Davatzikos, C.: A comparative study of biomechanical simulators in deformable registration of brain tumor images. IEEE Trans. Biomed. Eng. **55**(3), 1233–1236 (2008). International Journal of Pharma Medicine and Biological Sciences, vol. 8, No. 3, July 201977

6. Payan, Y.: Soft Tissue Biomechanical Modeling for Computer Assisted Surgery, Part of the Studies in Mechanobiology, Tissue Engineering and Biomaterials book series (SMTEB, volume 11)
7. Valencia, A., Blas, B., Ortega, J.H.: Modeling of brain shift phenomenon for different craniotomies and solid models. J. Appl. Math. **2012**(12), Article ID 409127, 20 pages, February 2012
8. Lowe, D.: Distinctive image features from scale-invariant keypoints. Int. J. Comput. Vis. **60**(2), 91–110 (2004)
9. Hassaballah, M., et al.: Image features detection description and matching. In: Awad, A., Hassaballah, M. (eds.) Image Feature Detectors and Descriptors. SCI, vol. 630, pp. 11–45. Springer, Cham (2016). https://doi.org/10.1007/978-3-319-28854-3_2
10. Mikolajczyk, K., Schmid, C.: A performance evaluation of local descriptors. IEEE Trans. Pattern Anal. Mach. Intell. **27**(10), 1615–1630 (2005)
11. Alcantarilla, P.F., et al.: KAZE features. In: European Conference on Computer Vision, pp. 214–227 (2012)
12. Alcantarilla, P.F., Nuevo, J., Bartoli, A.: Fast explicit diffusion for accelerated features in nonlinear scale spaces. Trans. Pattern Anal. Mach. Intell. **34**(7), 1281–1298 (2011)
13. Rublee, E., et al.: ORB: An efficient alternative to SIFT or SURF. In: IEEE International Conference on Computer Vision, pp. 2564–2571 (2011)
14. Rosten, E., Drummond, T.: Machine learning for high-speed corner detection. In: Leonardis, A., Bischof, H., Pinz, A. (eds.) ECCV 2006. LNCS, vol. 3951, pp. 430–443. Springer, Heidelberg (2006). https://doi.org/10.1007/11744023_34
15. Calonder, M., et al.: Brief: binary robust independent elementary features. In: European Conference on Computer Vision, pp. 778–792 (2010)
16. Leutenegger, S., et al.: BRISK: Binary robust invariant scalable keypoints. In: IEEE International Conference on Computer Vision, pp. 2548–2555 (2011)
17. Lowe, D.G.: Distinctive image features from scale-invariant keypoints. Int. J. Comput. Vision **60**(2), 91–110 (2004)
18. Noborio, H., Uchibori, S., Koeda, M., Watanabe, K.: Two-dimensional DICOM feature points and their mapping extraction for identifying brain shifts. Int. J. Pharma Med. Biol. Sci. **8**(3), 71–78 (2019). http://www.ijpmbs.com/uploadfile/2019/0723/20190723045554314.pdf
19. Noborio, H., Uchibori, S., Koeda, M., Watanabe, K.: Visualizing the correspondence of feature point mapping between DICOM images before and after surgery. In: Proceedings of the 2019 11th International Conference on Bioinformatics and Biomedical Technology, pp.1–7. ACM New York, Stockholm Sweden, 29–31 May, 2019. https://doi.org/10.1145/3340074.3340075ISBN: 978-1-4503-6231-3
20. Shewchuk, J.R.: Delaunay refinement algorithms for triangular mesh generation. vol. 22, pp. 21–74 (2002). ISSN 0925-7721
21. Mori, T., Nonaka, M., Kunii, T., Koeda, M., Watanabe, K., Noborio, H.: Algorithm for automatic brain-shift detection using the distance between feature descriptors. In: Kurosu, M. (eds.) HCII 2022. LNCS, vol. 13303, pp. 376–387. Springer, Cham (2022, to appear)

Emotion Recognition for Individuals with Autism

Sumedha Seniaray, Trasha Gupta, Payal, and Ravindra Singh$^{(\boxtimes)}$

Delhi Technological University, New Delhi, India
{sumedhaseniaray,trashagupta,payaldabas,ravindra}@dtu.ac.in

Abstract. Individuals suffering from Autism Spectrum Disorder find it challenging to perceive basic human emotions, which deters their communication capabilities. Given this difficulty, we proposed a Kawaii-engineered framework for Individuals with Autism by developing a Machine Learning pipeline using multilabel classification algorithms to identify the emotions from a video. We experimented on two datasets OMGE and DIAEMO. Both datasets have videos of the duration of approximately one minute. After pre-processing, facial expressions and audio content-based features were extracted. Multilabel Classification algorithm like Instance Based Learning by Logistic Regression for Multi-Label Learning, Multi Label k- Nearest Neighbour, Binary Relevance k-Nearest Neighbour, Random k- Label Sets, and Calibrated Label Ranking were used and for sampling, 5-fold Cross-Validation and Leave One Out Cross Validation were employed for both the datasets. We observed that LOOCV based sampling strategy gave the best results for both the datasets with CLR classifier using Gaussian kernel.

Keywords: Multi-label classification · Emotion recognition · Autism · Machine learning

1 Introduction

Many emotions influence our day-to-day interactions with other individuals. We are a slave to the emotions experienced by us at any instant of time. These emotions determine how we respond to others, the choices we make and the decisions we take. Various kinds of emotions experienced by humans have been identified and studied by psychologists. The emotions felt by humans have been categorized by psychologists to give different theories. Psychologist Paul Eckman in 1970s s recognized 6 basic emotions that a human experience globally - happiness, sadness, anger, surprise, fear, and disgust [9]. The basic emotions act as components to form mixed (complex) emotions. Naturally, fully-abled humans develop complex expressions as a combination of two or more emotions, like contempt, anticipation, guilt, envy, pride, and shame. These compound emotions are more existent in the real world and challenging to identify than the basic ones. Another emotion classification system known as the "wheel of emotions"

© The Author(s), under exclusive license to Springer Nature Switzerland AG 2022
M. Kurosu (Ed.): HCII 2022, LNCS 13303, pp. 403–414, 2022.
https://doi.org/10.1007/978-3-031-05409-9_31

was introduced in 1980s s by Robert Plutchik. This model was based on combining different emotions together to form eight primary emotional dimension: happiness vs. sadness, anger vs. fear, trust vs. disgust, and surprise vs. anticipation. These emotions can then be combined to create others (such as happiness + anticipation = excitement). Later in 1999, Eckman expanded his list of emotions to include embarrassment, excitement, contempt, shame, pride, satisfaction, and amusement. In fact, various other basic emotions exist than previously accepted which is seen in a up to date study published in the Proceedings of National Academy of Sciences. In the study, twenty seven different categories of emotion have been identified by the researchers all of which are highly interconnected, i.e., emotions do not occur in isolation rather these different feelings are deeply correlated. Understanding these emotions can help us sail through life with much more ease. Emotions are an essential part of who we are, but they complicated, and perplexing sometimes, hence identifying the emotions is a cumbersome process for any individual. In fact, the most primary signal to understand the feelings of others is through recognition of facial expressions [13,14]. This problem (recognition) even becomes more challenging for people with Autism Spectrum Disorder (ASD) [6]. Autism spectrum disorder (ASD) is a neuro-developmental disability which can cause significant challenges to social, emotional, and communication skills of the individual. People with ASD may converse, act, and comprehend in ways that are different from most other people. They have repetitive behaviors and refuse to change their daily routine. Also, they tend to be less able to accurately identify the complex emotions from facial expressions experienced at a normal real-world pace. Recognizing a facial expression or an emotion in a face depends on what we see and gather from a person's eyes and mouth. It has been observed that people with ASD often avoid looking into other individuals' eyes, thus contributing to difficulty in detecting even the basic emotions.

Across the CDC surveillance sites, an average of 1 in every 44 (2.3%) 8-year-old children were estimated to have ASD in 2018. The Table 1 below shows data from the most recent ADDM Network prevalence estimates (published December 2021).

Table 1. Prevalence of Autism Spectrum Disorder in 8-year-olds (2018) Data Courtesy of CDC*

		Prevalence**	Percent**
Overall		23.0 per 1,000	2.3 %
Sex	Boys	36.5 per 1,000	3.7%
	Girls	8.8 per 1,000	0.9%
Race/Ethnicity	White	21.2 per 1,000	2.1%
	Black	22.3 per 1,000	2.2%
	Asian/Pacific Islander	22.2 per 1,000	2.2%
Hispanic***	22.5 per 1,000	2.3%	

*The percent (i.e., rate per 100) was calculated by NIMH.
** Please see the measurement caveats regarding age below.
***All other groups are non-Hispanic.

Autistic children recognize feelings similar to typically developing children. By the age of 5–7 years, children with autism struggle to recognize simple emotions like happiness and sadness, but challenge multiplies in recognizing elusive expressions like fear and anger [7]. Also, as adults, they may continue to have trouble interpreting certain emotions. Autism also affects communication as some children may face difficulty communicating using speech or language and may have limited speaking skills. Apart from the verbal address, many children or adults with ASD may also have poor nonverbal communication skills [8]. Considering the gravity of the problem, we propose to develop a Kawaii engineered framework (Emoji-based User interface) for Individuals with Autism. At the backend of the framework, we have developed a Machine Learning (ML) pipeline (using multilabel classification algorithms) that identifies the emotion(s) from a video. We performed the experiments on two datasets - a publicly available dataset - (OMGE Dataset) [10] and our own collected dataset (DIAEMO dataset). Both the datasets are taken from YouTube medium. OMGE Dataset is monologue-based, and the DIAEMO dataset is dialogue-based. Both the datasets have videos of the duration of approximately one minute. We pre-processed the video to extract the audio and visual-related information separately. Then we extracted video (facial expressions), audio, and audio content-based features and normalized the features. Then we applied various Multilabel Classification algorithms [1,11] like Instance Based Learning by Logistic Regression for Multi Label Learning (IBLR-ML), Multi Label k- Nearest Neighbour (MLk-NN), Binary Relevance k- Nearest Neighbour (BRk-NN), Random k- Label Sets (RAkEL), and Calibrated Label Ranking (CLR). For Sampling, we used two cross-validation approaches (5-fold Cross-Validation and Leave One Out Cross Validation (LOOCV)) for both datasets.

The rest of the paper is structured as follows. The related work has been discussed in Sect. 2. The Sects. 3.1, 3.2 and 3.3 explain the methodology (feature extraction, Multi-label classifiers and Sampling Strategies and Performance Metrics) followed in the experiments. The experimental framework is described in Sect. 4. The results are stated and analysed in Sect. 5 and concluded in Sect. 6.

2   Review of Literature

Emotion recognition can be thought as an interface between the computer and humans, for which many researchers have applied various techniques. Mainly, these techniques are categorized as appearance-based features and geometry-based features, that are used to extract facial features which can be used for emotion detection. A fully-abled person has no problem in detecting emotions with the help of facial expressions but a differently-abled or an autistic person might not be able to comprehend the emotion of the person that he is witnessing. Appearance-based approach is widely popular, Principal Component Analysis (PCA), Linear Discriminant Analysis (LDA), and Gabor-wavelet are some of the techniques that are used to extract facial expression features and they are applied either to a specific portion of the face or the complete face. In [15], PCA technique was used in order to detect facial features and in order to do that Eigen range was used instead of Eigen values or Eigen vectors. Local Binary Patterns (LBP) is implemented as a local feature extraction method in facial expression recognition They proposed a portable low-complexity emotion detector for autistic children which optimized the computations based on the PCA Eigen value range and achieved a detection accuracy of 82.3%. In [16], authors conducted two experiments for emotion recognition, in one experiment they had used PCA alone and concluded the average recognition rate to be 67.14% and an average accuracy of 91.63% whereas in the second experiment they employed PCA with Singular Value Decomposition and Euclidean Distance Classifier and achieved the system performance with average recognition rate at 78.57% and average accuracy of 94.28%. In [17], authors implemented emotion detection with PCA and LDA with Euclidean distance on JAFFE database with a total of 14 images for 7 facial expressions and both PCA and LDA recognized 9 images with a recognition rate of 70% and 30% respectively. In [18], a framework was proposed where the face area was divided into smaller regions, and LBP, histograms are extracted and concatenated into a single feature vector. Out of 2000 images, 1980 were recognized thus, had a recognition rate of 99%. In geometry-based feature extraction, the location and shape of facial areas are considered which necessitates precise facial features extraction. In [19], Bavkar et al. employed geometry-based approach and evaluated the feature vector by finding the distance between the dynamic and static points. The authors have used Support Vector Machine (SVM) and Radial Basis Function Neural Network (RBFNN) classifiers and attained an average recognition rate of 91%. Murugappan et al. have successfully recognized six emotional expressions in [20]. They have used a mathematical model on various locations on the face in an automated manner. ICC, AoT and ICAT are evaluated to classify the facial emotions. Out of these, ICAT provides a maximum mean classification rate of 98.17% with the help of Random Forest (RF) classifier. After having reviewed the above related work, it was found that there is a scope to explore literature, framework, or methodologies related to Kawaii-engineered framework for emotion recognition for individuals with autism using audio and videos.

3   Methodology

Considering the gravity of the problem, we propose to develop a Kawaii engineered framework (Emoji-based User interface) for Individuals with Autism. At the backend of the framework, we have developed a Machine Learning (ML) pipeline (using multi-label classification algorithms) that identifies and return the emotion(s) of an individual. This would help the disabled person in understanding the human behavior in a rational way. The problem under consideration can be briefly expressed as

find a function f(x) that, given a short video of a
monologue/dialogue, it identifies the emotion(s) from the video.

Figure 1 illustrates the Kawaii engineered framework developed in this paper.

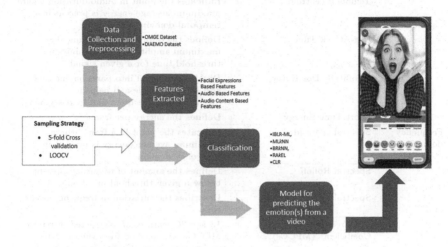

Fig. 1. The experimental ML framework for detecting emotions from a video.

3.1 Features

In this paper, we extracted three sets of features namely, facial expressions-based features, audio based features and, audio content-based features. The features extracted are described below -

– **Facial Expressions Based Features** - We extracted facial Expressions Based Features from the face of the participant(s) at a gap of every 15 15 s in the video. In each facial image, 10 facial landmarks were identified (like chin, cheeks, eyebrows, lips eyes forehead, etc.), around which forms the expression of emotions. The face was then divided into disjoint segments about these landmarks. Uniform Local Binary Pattern (LBP) based features were extracted from these segments separately and then they were concatenated. Also 2 moments - spatial moment and central moment was computed for each segment.

– **Audio Based Features** - We used audio based features defined in Temporal, Frequency, and Modulation Frequency domain. Audio based Features extracted in various domains are briefly described in Table 2.

– **Audio Content Based Features** - Six Audio Content Based Features were extracted from the content spoken in the video. The words uttered were recorded textually and stop-words were removed. Remaining words were lemmatized. English Wordnet[1] was used to create dictionary of words related to 6

---

[1] https://wordnet.princeton.edu/.

Table 2. Description of audio based features in various domains.

Domain	Features	Description of these features
Temporal domain	Zero-crossing rate	Defines the number of zero crossings done in a single frame
	Temporal centroid	Indicates the point in audio duration where maximum average energy is present in temporal domain
	Log-Attack Time	Defines the duration of attaining the maximum amplitude from a minimum threshold time for a given signal
	Amplitude Descriptor	Divides the signal into parts having high and low amplitude and helps in distinguishing the quiet and loud segments
	Short Time Energy	Defines the energy per frame
Frequency domain	Spectral centroid	Indicates the point in a frame where maximum average energy is present in frequency domain
	Spectral Rolloff	Defines the amount of frequency present below a given threshold in a frame
	Spectral Flux	Describes the variation in frequency over time
	Mel-Frequency Cepstral Coefficients (MFCCs)	13 MFCC features are extracted. First 13 MFCC's are selected from the discrete cosine transform of MEL scale
Modulation frequency domain	Pulse Metric	Defines the rhythmicness of sound by identifying the peaks
	Beat Histogram	Value of peak in Beat Histogram and sum of histogram bins between 40 and 90, 90 and 140, and 140 and 250 Beats Per Minutes are used as additional features

basic emotions. Word count in the intersection of emotion specific dictionary and the lemmatized audio content was recorded for each basic emotion.

The extracted features were normalized and passed to classifiers for classification.

3.2 Multi-label Classifiers

The problem under study is a Multi-label Classification problem [11]. The task of multi-label training is to learn function $H : X \rightarrow Y$, where Y is a set of emotions relevant to the normalized feature-set X, extracted from a given video. We used 5 well-known algorithms for Multi-label classification, briefly discussed below:

– **Multi-Label k-Nearest Neighbour (MLk-NN)** [2] - MLk-NN uses Maximum a Posterior principle to identify the set of emotions applicable to the given feature-set in the neighbourhood. Prior probability and conditional probability is estimated among frequency of each label's k-nearest neighbours. To predict the emotions of an unseen instance i, the class is predicted separately for each label. It considers the number of neighbours containing the label to be assigned.

- **Binary Relevance k-Nearest Neighbour (BRk-NN)** [2] - BRk-NN for multi-label classification learns binary classifiers for each label in the label set L, where L = happy, sad, angry, surprise, fear, disgust. It creates $|L|$ data subsets D_j, where each D_j, for $j = 1, 2, ..., 6$, contains all the instances as in the original dataset. The instance in the D_j is labelled positive if the label-set of the instance in original dataset contains that label j else is labelled as negative in D_j. Then it learns k Nearest Neighbour classifier for each D_j. BRk-NN outputs the labels that are positively predicted by the 6 k Nearest Neighbour Classifiers.

- **Instance Based Learning by Logistic Regression for Multilabel Learning (IBLR-ML)** [5] - IBLR-ML works on the combination of Instance-Based Learning (IBL) and Logistic Regression. It considers the labels of neighbouring instances as features of a new sample. It reduces the problem from IBL to logistic regression. This method understands the correlation amongst the labels with the help of sign and magnitude of Regression coefficients. Hence it is an improvisation over MLk-NN.

- **Random k-Label Sets (RAkEL)** [3] - RAkEL is an ensemble based method. It breaks a large set of labels, L, into subsets of small size (k), called k-labelsets. It iteratively constructs an ensemble of k Label Power-set (LP) classifiers. Each LP classifier is trained on a small random subset of k-label-sets. It considers the correlation among the labels. During prediction of a new sample the votes given by the individual classifiers are averaged. k should be small enough in order to handle the deficiency of LP classifier.

- **Calibrated Label Ranking (CLR)** [4] - Label Ranking learns $R : x \rightarrow \preceq_x$, where $\preceq_x$ is the ranking defined over labels L = $\lambda_1, ..., \lambda_c$. $\lambda_i \preceq_x \lambda_j$ implies that for an instance x, label λ_i is preferred to λ_j. In CLR, a neutral label is added as a natural zero-point to distinguish between relevant and irrelevant labels. A calibrated ranking $\lambda_{i1} \preceq \lambda_{i2} \preceq ... \lambda_{ij} \preceq \lambda_0 \preceq \lambda_{ij+1} \preceq ... \lambda_{ik}$ is ranking of the labels and produce a partition of relevant $(\lambda_{i1}, ..., \lambda_{ij})$ and irrelevant $(\lambda_{ij+1}, ..., \lambda_{ik})$ labels. Each instance that is annotated with a particular label, is a positive instance for that label and is treated as a negative instance for the calibration label and vice versa.

3.3 Sampling Strategies and Performance Metrics

We considered Accuracy, F-Measure, Hamming Loss, and Subset Accuracy [12] as criteria for evaluating the performance of the model. Accuracy defines the probability of correctly predicting the emotions of a given dialogue/monologue in test sample. F-Measure is calculated as the harmonic mean of sensitivity and specificity. Hamming loss penalizes the difference between predicted and actual class label for the test set using XOR operation. Subset Accuracy is a strict evaluation metric that awards when prediction is absolutely correct. That is neither incorrect class is predicted nor legitimate class is missed by the classifier. The chosen metrics for model performance evaluation are not correlated with each other. The corresponding classifier parameters were considered optimal if they yielded the most considerable Accuracy, F-Measure, Hamming Loss, and Subset Accuracy.

We performed 5-fold cross-validation and Leave-One-Out Cross-Validation (LOOCV) to obtain a more reliable estimate of the performance of the model. The number of samples in training data increases as the value of k increases. With this, the model's performance improves. In LOOCV, in each fold (N-1) samples is used for training the model and remaining one sample is used as test sample.

All the metrics considered during testing of each fold of k-fold cross-validation are averaged to get the final performance of the model. We selected optimal classifier parameters based on their performance using 5-fold and LOOCV strategies.

4   Experimental Design

The experiments were conducted on a computer using Windows 10 operating system with 16GB RAM and i7 (9th generation) Processor. We used Python 3.3 (64 bit) to implement the entire framework and conducting the experiments. Figure 1 illustrates the ML framework followed for conducting the experiments.

We performed our experiments on two video based datasets - a publicly available dataset - OMGE Dataset[2] [10] and our own collected dataset - DIAEMO dataset. Both the datasets are taken from YouTube medium. Both the datasets have videos of the duration of approximately one minute. The collection and pre-processing steps of OMGE and DIAEMO datasets are described below:

- **OMGE Dataset** [10] - OMGE Dataset is a monologue based dataset and publicly available[3]. The dataset available has video instances divided into several utterances such that each utterance is annotated to a basic emotion only. We combined 2–3 utterances of a video to generate instances having compound emotions.
- **DIAEMO Dataset** - DIAEMO Dataset is our own collected dataset from www.youtube.com. It is a dialogue-based video dataset. We used python library - 'pytube', to download the videos using various basic and compound emotions-based hashtags like #happy, #surprise, #happysurprise, #awful, #surpriseangry, #surpriseangrysad etc. Then approximately one minute video was cropped from the middle of the downloaded videos. The cropped videos were also manually annotated by three independent individuals and were assigned emotion(s) based on voting scheme.

The datasets used have a balanced number of samples from each basic emotion for bot the datasets. The statistics of the datasets are stated in Table 3. Also, according to the problem of multi-label classification under consideration, a sample belonging to a basic emotion may also belong to other basic emotions

---

[2] https://www2.informatik.uni-hamburg.de/wtm/OMG-EmotionChallenge/.
[3] https://github.com/knowledgetechnologyuhh/OMGEmotionChallenge.

as well. That is an instance may have one or more basic emotions. After pre-processing the video, we extracted 3081 features described in Sect. 3.1. Then, we normalized the extracted features in the range [0–1].

We finally obtained the 3081-dimensional Multi-label dataset having instances of the pattern (X,y) where X is an input vector extracted from a video and y is a 6-dimensional binary vector where emotions relevant to X are represented by 1 and emotions irrelevant to X are represented by 0.

Table 3. Size of datasets used in the study

DataSets	Type	Happy	Sad	Surprise	Angry	Disgust	Fear	Total samples
OMGE Dataset	Monologue-based	98	91	100	94	93	93	374
DIAEMO Dataset	Dialogue-based	61	65	63	65	62	65	260

Table 4. Description of Multi-label classifier's parameters and their settings in the experiment.

Algorithm	Parameters	Parameters values	Description of these parameters
MLk-NN	k	[1 − 30]	Number of nearest neighbours
	Distance Measure	Euclidean Distance	Similarity measure between instances
BRk-NN	k	[1 − 30]	Number of nearest neighbours
	Distance Measure	Euclidean Distance	Similarity measure between instances
CLR	Kernel	Linear, Gaussian	To transform the input space into higher dimension
RAkEL	k	[1, 2, 3, 4]	The size of label sets

All the features extracted were passed to the commonly used classifiers for multi-label classification - IBLR-ML, MLk-NN, BRk-NN, RAkEL, CLR. We also performed a grid-search with the respective parameters of the classifiers to achieve the best results. The multi-label classifier parameters for grid search are summarized in Table 4.

Data folds for k-fold Cross-Validation were generated only once for all the pipelines that is we divided the data into 5 random stratified partitions, respectively, only once. The partitions were kept same for all pipelines (features extraction, feature selection, classifier, and Cross-Validation combinations). Along with 5-fold Cross-Validation and LOOCV was also done to contrast the behaviour of data. All the results are recorded along with the parameters for which the best accuracy, Hamming Loss, F-Measure and Subset Accuracy are achieved.

5 Result and Discussion

The results of the experiments conducted are stated in Table 5 and illustrated in Fig. 2. Following observations are made from the Table 5 and Fig. 2 obtained:

Table 5. The best results obtained for the given framework on OMGE and DIAEMO Datasets.

OMGE dataset (monologue based)								
Multi-label classifier	5 Fold Cross Validation				LOOCV			
	Accuracy	F-Measure	Hamming Loss	Subset Accuracy	Accuracy	F-Measure	Hamming Loss	Subset Accuracy
IBLR-ML	90.5	90.13	17.21	23.76	93.5	92.13	11.21	26.76
MLk-NN	90.94	83.99	23.83	23.1	93.94	90.99	20.83	25.1
BRk-NN	85.57	89.45	23.93	28.16	91.57	91.45	19.93	30.16
RAkEL	89.33	76.55	23.06	23.3	92.33	83.55	19.06	27.3
CLR	90.33	81.05	18.26	24.4	95.33	85.05	16.26	28.4
DIAEMO Dataset (Dialogue Based)								
Multi-label classifier	5 Fold Cross Validation				LOOCV			
	Accuracy	F-Measure	Hamming Loss	Subset Accuracy	Accuracy	F-Measure	Hamming Loss	Subset Accuracy
IBLR-ML	91.57	86.57	23.64	81.49	93.57	89.57	20.64	83.49
MLk-NN	88.68	84.68	24.93	86.16	92.68	88.68	19.93	89.16
BRkNN	85.55	86.55	27.58	83.85	89.55	89.55	20.58	86.85
RAkEL	83.58	83.58	27.37	65.35	88.58	86.58	20.37	70.35
CLR	92.58	82.78	22.67	69.25	95.58	88.78	17.67	73.25

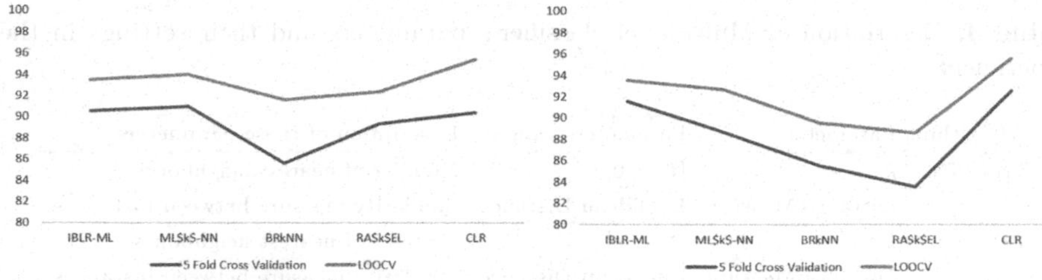

(a) OMGE Datasets   (b) DIAEMO Datasets

Fig. 2. Comparison of classification accuracy values between various cross-validation strategies used in the framework.

- Experiments performed with LOOCV strategy gave the best results for both the datasets as the number of samples available for training is maximum in LOOCV.
- CLR multi-label classifier with Gaussian kernel gave the best result for both the datasets with LOOCV.
- RAkEL and BRk-NN have not performed well for both the datasets. This is due to non consideration of correlation amongst the multiple labels applicable to a sample.
- Amongst the k-NN based algorithms for multilabel classifiers, IBLR-ML have performed best for both the datasets.

The importance of extracted features is also evaluated using the T-statistic. Table 6 states 15 best features with level of significance less than 0.01. Audio and Facial Expression-based features form the relevant feature-set in identifying the emotion(s) applicable to an instance well.

With the help of the proposed ML pipeline, we can recognize the emotion(s) from a given video sample effectively.

Table 6. Set of best features (based on T-Statistic) with level of significance less than 0.01.

cheeks_centralmoment	eyebrows$_s$$patialmoment$	lips$_s$$patialmoment$
eyebrows$_c$$entralmoment$	lips$_c$$entralmoment$	eyes$_L$$BP5$
eyes$_L$$BP8$	forehead$_L$$BP10eyes_L BP12$	eyes$_L$$BP33$
forehead$_L$$BP19$	Temporal centroid	Spectral centroid
MFCC10	MFCC7	Beat$_H$$istogram_peak$

6   Conclusion and Future Work

As we know that recognizing emotions or even facial expressions is unfortunately a difficult task for not only autistic children but also adults with ASD. Considering this, we had proposed a Kawaii-engineered framework for individuals with ASD. We had performed experiments on two separate datasets, OMGE and DIAEMO. Video or facial expressions and audio-based features were extracted and normalized. Multilabel classification algorithms like IBLR-ML, MLkNN, BRkNN, RAkEL, and CLR were implemented for this framework. 5-fold Cross-Validation and LOOCV were employed on both the datasets for data sampling. We evaluated the above experiments using metrics, namely, Accuracy, F-Measure, Hamming Loss, and Subset Accuracy. We observed that LOOCV based sampling strategy gave the best results for both the datasets with CLR classifier using Gaussian kernel. We found that audio and visual-based features form the relevant feature-set in identifying the corresponding emotion(s). It was observed that in the first experiment performed on OMGE dataset, the recognition accuracy was best with 90.94% when MLkNN and 5-fold Cross-Validation was employed, and 95.33% recognition accuracy on exercising CLR technique and LOOCV sampling method. Whereas, in the second experiment executed on DIAEMO dataset, it was perceived that CLR technique enhanced the performance of the system with both 5-fold Cross-Validation and LOOCV sampling with highest accuracy of 92.58% and 95.58%, respectively. This model would help individuals suffering from ASD understand both basic and complex emotions, that any fully-abled person can, effortlessly. In the future, we propose to build a system that recognizes the emotion(s) from a real-time video stream.

References

1. Zhang, M.L., Zhou, Z.H.: ML-KNN: a lazy learning approach to multi-label learning. Pattern Recogn. **40**(7), 2038–2048 (2007)
2. Tsoumakas, G., Katakis, I., Vlahavas, I.: Data mining and knowledge discovery handbook. Mining multi-label data, pp. 667–85 (2010)
3. Kanj, S., Abdallah, F., Denœx, T.: Evidential multi-label classification using the random k-label sets approach. In: Denoeux, T., Masson, MH. (eds) Belief Functions: Theory and Applications. AISC, vol. 164, pp. 21–28. Springer, Heidelberg (2012). https://doi.org/10.1007/978-3-642-29461-7_2

4. Fürnkranz, J., Hüllermeier, E., Loza Mencía, E., Brinker, K.: Multilabel classification via calibrated label ranking. Mach. Learn. **73**(2), 133–153 (2008)
5. Cheng, W., Hüllermeier, E.: Combining instance-based learning and logistic regression for multilabel classification. Mach. Learn. **76**(2), 211–225 (2009)
6. Keating, C.T., Fraser, D.S., Sowden, S., et al.: Differences between autistic and non-autistic adults in the recognition of anger from facial motion remain after controlling for alexithymia. J. Autism Dev. Disord. **52**, 1855–1871 (2021)
7. Rump, K.M., Giovannelli, J.L., Minshew, N.J., Strauss, M.S.: The development of emotion recognition in individuals with autism. Child Development **80**(5), 1434–1447 (2009)
8. Communication Problems in Children with Autism Spectrum Disorder by U.S. DEPARTMENT OF HEALTH AND HUMAN SERVICES. National Institutes of Health
9. Ekman, P., Friesen, W.V.: Constants across cultures in the face and emotion. J. Personality Soc. Psychol. **17**(2), 124 (1971)
10. Barros, P., Churamani, N., Lakomkin, E., Siqueira, H., Sutherland, A., Wermter, S.: The omg-emotion behavior dataset. arXiv preprint arXiv:1803.05434(2018)
11. Herrera, F., Charte, F., Rivera, A.J., del Jesus, M.J.: Multilabel classification. In: Multilabel Classification, pp. 17–31. Springer, Cham (2016). https://doi.org/10.1007/978-3-319-41111-8_2
12. Pereira, R.B., et al.: Correlation analysis of performance measures for multi-label classification. Inf. Process. Manage. **54**(3), 359–369 (2018)
13. Darwin, C.: The Expression of the Emotions in Man and Animals. Oxford University Press, Oxford (1872)
14. Ekman, P.: Emotions Revealed. Owl Books, New York (2003)
15. Smitha, K.G., Vinod, A.P.: Low complexity FPGA implementation of emotion detection for autistic children. 7th International Symposium on Medical Information and Communication Technology (ISMICT), pp. 103–107. IEEE (2013)
16. Gosavi, A.P., Khot, S.R.: Emotion recognition using principal component analysis with singular value decomposition. In: 2014 International Conference on Electronics and Communication Systems (ICECS), pp. 1–5. IEEE (2014)
17. Taqdir, J.K.: Facial expression recognition with PCA and LDA. IJCSIT Int. J. Comput. Sci. Inf. Technol. **5**(6), pp. 6996–6998 (2014)
18. Rahim, M.A., Azam, M.S., Hossain, N., Islam, M.R.: Face recognition using local binary patterns (LBP). Global Journal of Computer Science and Technology (2013)
19. Bavkar, S.S., Rangole, J.S., Deshmukh, V.U.: Geometric approach for human emotion recognition using facial expression. Int. J. Comput. Appl. **118**(14) (2015)
20. Murugappan, M., Mutawa, A.: Facial geometric feature extraction based emotional expression classification using machine learning algorithms. Plos one **16**(2), e0247131 (2021)

Pupil and Electromyography (EMG) Responses to Collision Warning in a Real Driving Environment

Xiaonan Yang[1,2]([mail]) and Jung Hyup Kim[1,2]

[1] Industrial and Systems Engineering Laboratory, School of Mechanical Engineering,
Beijing Institute of Technology, Beijing, China
yangxn@bit.edu.cn
[2] Industrial and Manufacturing Systems Engineering Department, University of Missouri,
Columbia, MO 65211, USA
kijung@missouri.edu

Abstract. The purpose of this study is to assess drivers' upcoming decisions to collision warnings by analyzing their pupil and electromyography (EMG) responses in a real driving environment. Twenty male college students participated in this study. Tobii Glasses2 and electromyography MYO armbands were used to collect the physiological data. Forward collision warning (FCW) and lane departure warning (LDW) were generated from aftermarket CAT devices. According to the results, we found that different fluctuating patterns of pupil and electromyography responses exist when drivers responded to a collision warning. The potential causality between pupil diameter changes and normalized EMG could be applied as a valid indicator of drivers' different cognitive status to the responded warning and ignored warning, which contains valuable or useless information. Findings from this study will contribute to future algorithm development in a next-generation smart vehicle that can not only identify and predict drivers' upcoming responses but also customize warning functions based on drivers' status.

Keywords: Collision warning · Pupillary response · Electromyography (EMG) · Human cognitive behavior

1 Introduction

As collision avoidance technology (CAT) becomes popular to reduce the number of vehicular injuries and deaths, distraction-related crashes caused by frequent false warnings are increased, and drivers' trust in collision warning is likely to deteriorate [1]. Eventually, frequent false alarms lead to driver aversion to the collision warnings. A study showed that a high false alarm rate is often associated with distrust of the system with abrupt unwarranted responses, more errors in driving performance, and a failure to benefit from the warnings, even increasing of risk [2]. Therefore, it is necessary to understand how drivers respond to collision warning in order to develop CAT devices with less false alarm rate.

© The Author(s), under exclusive license to Springer Nature Switzerland AG 2022
M. Kurosu (Ed.): HCII 2022, LNCS 13303, pp. 415–423, 2022.
https://doi.org/10.1007/978-3-031-05409-9_32

Recently studies have investigated various physiological measures to understand human's upcoming actions. Among them, pupillary responses and electromyography (EMG) signals are popular for decoding human cognitive behavior and upcoming reactions [3–5]. The objective of this study is to analyze the different patterns of pupillary and forearm EMG responses when drivers respond to the collision warning. Our hypothesis is that different changing patterns exist in pupillary and EMG data between the warnings in which drivers responded and the ignored warnings. Drivers' pupil and EMG signals to both types of warnings were collected in an open road driving environment.

What we expected from the experiment is that the patterns of pupil dilation and EMG signals could be considered as indicators of drivers' upcoming decision corresponding to collision warnings. The outcomes of this study are beneficial to developing an algorithm for an intelligent CAT device that can assess how drivers treat and respond to the collision warnings. For instance, a smart CAT device could automatically adjust the sensitivity level of collision warnings based on drivers' physiological responses to avoid unnecessary warnings if the CAT device detects that drivers are already aware of the potential hazards based on their pupillary and EMG responses. Additionally, the findings of this study can lead to the improvement of collision warning system development to enhance safety and improved device-user interaction.

2 Method

2.1 Apparatus

A 2008 Chevrolet Malibu was used as the testing vehicle in this experiment. Several aftermarket CAT devices were used to collect drivers' natural responses to the collision warnings under an open road real driving environment. The tested CAT devices generated the forward collision warning (FCW) and lane departure warning (LDW). Also, the warning was provided through auditory and visual warnings to the drivers. Tobii Glasses2 (100 Hz sampling rate) was used as an eye-tracking device to capture pupil diameter of both eyes during the entire driving (see Fig. 1). The high-definition scene camera also recorded a series of pupillary data and driver's scene view. The electromyography MYO armbands were placed on the participant's forearm. It consisted of eight sensors per band. The EMGs represent the amount of arm muscle activity during the experiment. The muscle tension and an inertial measurement unit were collected from EMG sensors with a 3D gyroscope, 3D accelerometer and a magnetometer. This MYO armband provides an integrated and easy-to-use solution to study EMG. Drivers' EMG signals were collected with eight data points per second. Also, an HD camera was attached to the right window of the vehicle to record drivers' physical movements. A 360-degree camera was attached at the top of the vehicle for the driving condition recording. It helped us to understand driving behaviors and traffic conditions at the moment of the collision warnings.

2.2 Experiment Procedure

Twenty male students from the University of Missouri participated in this experiment. The average age was 20.52 (StDev:1.47), and they were all required to provide a valid

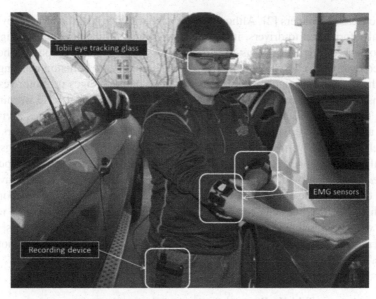

Fig. 1. Experiment devices and setup [6]

driver's license and had at least two years of driving experience. All participants could not wear glasses, except contact lenses.

All participants wore the eye-tracking glasses and drove the vehicle on an open track. The path of this study covers about 9.3 miles of open roads that featured parts of highways, an interstate, rural streets, and roads on campus in Columbia, Missouri. Participants had signed the consent form before the experiment start. The driver was given a full set of instructions at the beginning of the experiment. After that, all recording cameras and eye-tracking devices were set and calibrated. Each participant performed four runs. All drives were conducted in mid-morning (10:00 am–12:30 pm) or mid-afternoon (2:00 pm–4:30 pm) when there was light traffic on the route. The total duration of one run was 15 to 20 min, depending on traffic conditions.

2.3 Warning Categorization

According to the concept of signal detection theory, the warning has been categorized into two outcomes: *responded warning* and *ignored warning*. The collision warnings which drew drivers' visual attention (rapid eye-gaze movement) and lead to physical action changes (braking, accelerating, or steering wheel) were named as a *responded warning*. In this case, the driver seemed to trust the warning and take the appropriate action to avoid any potential hazards. According to the previous study done by Kim [1], *responded warning* could be considered as the most positive and effective warning compared to other types of outcomes since the *responded warning* helps drivers to be aware of the threats and warn them to avoid potential danger. They also defined aware warning which means drivers already detected the potential hazards before the warning occurred. Also, it can be called "*unnecessary warning*" or "*double warning*" from other research papers [2]. Although the aware warning signal did not provide any additional information to drivers, it still indicates potential dangerous and might help drivers to recheck their decisions regarding what kind of motor response should be performed to minimize a vehicle collision. On the contrary, the collision warning which drivers chose to directly ignore it without eye-gaze point changes or motor responses were considered as *ignored warning*s. It is considered as a typical false warning with the most negative impacts compared to other warnings, because it creates a visible or auditory annoyance to drivers as no dangerous at all in the surrounding. Drivers tend to completely ignore the warning after they experienced a high rate of false warnings. In this study, only clear *responded* and *ignored warnings* were considered as valid inputs. The *responded warning* provides productive and useful information to drivers to avoid the potential danger. As the user-device interaction, drivers choose trust *responded warning* and modify their driving behavior. However, drivers considered the *ignored warning* as noise without valuable information for driving. From the recording videos, drivers regarded noise as the distraction and did not give any responses, neither pupil nor motor response.

Table 1. Responded warning and ignored warning

		Physiological Response[a]	
		Yes	No
Physical Response[b]	Yes	*Responded Warning*	
	No		*Ignored Warning*

[a]Rapid eye-gaze movement to check a warning
[b]Any physical motions and motor responses related to breaking, accelerating, or steering wheel caused by a warning.

3   Results

3.1   Warning Segment

The pupillary and EMG responses were analyzed based on the warning categorization at different times. For each warning, there are three different time stages. First, seven seconds before the warning happened. Second, the time for warning, the warning sound was considered lasting for one second. The last one is seven seconds after warning. Normally, the physical responses were following after the 1-s warning segment. From the warning segment timeline in Fig. 2, pupillary and EMG responses under these 1-s warnings were analyzed and compared between *responded warning* and *ignored warning*. T_o here is the time when a warning starts, T_1 represents the start time of drivers' physical response, which occurred within 7 s after warning.

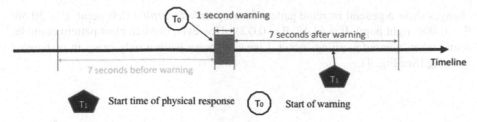

Fig. 2. Warning segment

3.2 Pupil Diameter Changes and Normalized EMG

As each individual has different pupil diameter, in this study, the pupil diameter change (P_d) is considered as a pupillary response. It is calculated by

$$P_d = P_t - P_o \tag{1}$$

P_t is actual pupil diameter data at time t (from 0 to 1)in the one-second warning period. P_o is the average size of the pupil diameter seven seconds before T_0. P_d is the pupil diameter changes based on P_o. If $P_d > 0$, then the current pupil diameter becomes larger than P_o. If $P_d < 0$, then, the actual pupil diameter is smaller than P_o.

For the EMG data analysis, based on the vender's definition, the raw EMG data is unitless, which represents the activation of muscles. So first, all the EMG data were transferred into an absolute value. Moreover, the raw EMG needs to normalized first as participants have different muscle activity ranges. First taking the maximum EMG data among all eight sensors in the absolute value, and then using the following formulation to get normalized EMG:

$$E_n = \frac{E_t - E_{min}}{E_{max} - E_{min}} \tag{2}$$

where E_t is the largest absolute value among all eight EMG sensors at time t (from 0 to 1) in the one-second warning period. E_{min} and E_{max} are respectively the minimum and maximum absolute value of all eight EMG sensors in one experiment trial. The difference between E_{min} and E_{max} represents each individual's muscle activation range. After normalizing, as E_n in the formula, it is the normalized EMG at time t, which is in (0,1) range.

3.3 Time Series Analysis Results

As pupil and EMG data are not two independent data set, they could be represented as two time series. Therefore, the pupil diameter changes and normalized EMG under one-second of the warning duration were analyzed, and the pattern differences were compared between the *responded* and *ignored warning*s. From the video recordings, there were ten clear *responded warning*s and nine *ignored warning*s in this driving experiment. This experiment was conducted in a real driving environment, it is hard to control the number of warnings. From the regression analysis, both eyes' pupil diameter changes show a general increase pattern for *responded warning* (left pupil: F = 30.56, P = 0.000, right pupil: F = 51.12, P = 0.000). However, no such clear pattern could be found when *ignored warnings* occur. Linear increase pattern only exists in *responded warning* (See Fig. 3).

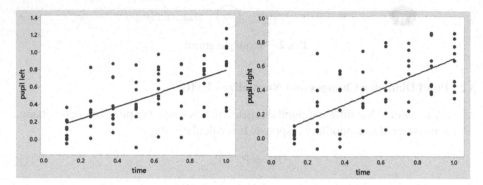

Fig. 3. Pupil diameter changes for responded warning

For the EMG changes under one-second warning duration, only the normalized EMG of the left forearm shows decrement first and then increment pattern for *responded warnings*. Therefore a quadratic regression model was fit with significant results (F = 44.20, P = 0.000). However, for the right forearm, only a positive linear relationship was detected (F = 7.62, P = 0.010) under *responded warnings* instead of a curved pattern. As a comparison, there was no apparent pattern of normalized EMG change for both forearms for *ignored warnings*.

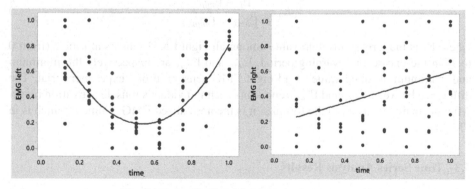

Fig. 4. Normalized EMG for responded warning

As working on time series, one crucial thing that needs to be determined is whether a change in one time series could potentially "cause" a change in another at a given time lag. In other words, is there a strong correlation between pupil diameter changes itself and normalized EMG with given lags? As both pupil diameter changes and normalized

EMG signal show the patterns with time among these participants' *responded warning*. There might be a relationship between these two time series data under *responded warning* as the cross-correlation between two different time series data. Therefore, the cross-correlation function plots were generated in pairs. Running cross-correlation function allows us to determine the lag at which the correlation between two time series is strongest. Figure 5 shows the pupil diameter changes for the left and right eye were explored (Fig. 6).

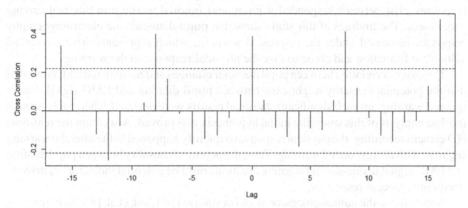

Fig. 5. Cross-correlation function for the left and right pupil diameter changes under responded warning

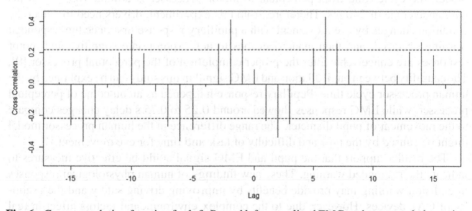

Fig. 6. Cross-correlation function for left P_d and left normalized EMG under responded warning

Examining the cross-correlation plots yields some impressive results. We can see that there is a strong positive correlation at lag $-16, -8, 0, 8, 16$. It indicated that pupil diameter changes from both eyes were highly correlated with no lag difference almost for all *responded warning* data points. While for the left pupil diameter changes and left normalized EMG pair, the strongest positive correlation occurs at the lag 6 and relative significant negative correlation at the lag 2, indicating that causality may exist between left pupil diameter changes and left normalized EMG. For example, a change in the pupil diameter at time t − 6 (or t − 2) may have a positive (or negative) effect on the EMG at time t. As there were eight data samples in one second, one lag time equals 0.125 s. It means there might be around 0.25 to 0.75 s delayed changes in EMG signal compare to the movement of pupil diameter.

4 Discussion and Conclusion

According to results, the different patterns of pupil diameter and electromyography responses exist between responded warning and ignored warning in this real driving experiment. The findings of this study show that pupil diameter and electromyography responses increased under the responded warning, which represents drivers received valuable information and chose to give the physical response to the warning.

The cross-correlation between pupil diameter changes and normalized EMG revealed that the potential causality might exist between pupil dilation and EMG signal. Under ignored warning, no such significant statistical results were detected. Therefore, through the data analysis of this study, the initial hypothesis was proved. Also, from the real-time HD camera recording, the physical response frequently happened in the after the warning segment with the responded warning. Thus, the potential causality between pupil dilation and EMG signal in one-second warning duration could be potential indicators of drivers' upcoming physical responses.

According to the human processor model developed by Card, et al. [8], the human has to use the perceptual, cognitive, and motor processors to perform a task. Each processor has a specific cycle time, and each memory has a decay time. From the human processor model, the cycle time from perceptual to motor processer is around 105 to 470 ms with an average of 240 ms. Therefore, from this experiment, drivers need to detect the condition changes by eye movement with a pupillary response first once the responded warning occurred, and then made decisions to act. Appropriate cognitive and motor responses are conceivable after the proper completion of the perceptual processor [9]. The causality between pupil dilation and EMG signal in this study can be explained by the human processor cycle time. Pupillary response happened as an outcome of perceptual processer, while EMG responses showed around 0.25 to 0.75 s delay changes compare to the movement of pupil diameter. The range difference in the human processor model might be caused by the type and difficulty of task and time for eye movement.

The results support that the pupil and EMG signal could be effective measures to indicate the responded warning. These new findings of human physiological responses in collision warning may provide benefits by improving driving safety and the usability of CAT devices. However, due to the complex environmental factors affect in real driving, only small useful data samples were collected. For the limitations, the number of hazard events we used in this study was small due to the complexity of real driving conditions, and it is impossible to put participants in a dangerous condition. Although it was hard to collect data samples of actual collision conditions in the current study, most of the time drivers only responded to a warning when it helps them identify potential hazards in situations characterized by uncertainty and vulnerability. For future studies, a laboratory-based experiment that simulates several potential hazard events from real car accidents should be considered. Augment reality technology will be used as a completely immersive experience that draws drivers into a focused and rarefied environment all about real driving. Moreover, drivers who participated in the experiment, are college students. People from different age groups and genders should be covered in future studies.

5 Conclusion

This study extended and enhanced past studies to multiple physiological responses to explore drivers' upcoming decisions in collision warning. The findings of this study proved that the pupillary and electromyography responses could be used together as effective indicators when drivers received valuable information and chose to give the physical response to a warning.

References

1. Lee, J.D., Hoffman, J.D., Hayes, E.: Collision warning design to mitigate driver distraction. In: Proceedings of the SIGCHI Conference on Human factors in Computing Systems, pp. 65–72. ACM (2004)
2. Shah, S.J., Bliss, J.P., Chancey, E.T., Brill, J.C.: Effects of alarm modality and alarm reliability on workload, trust, and driving performance. In: Proceedings of the Human Factors and Ergonomics Society Annual Meeting, 2015, vol. 59, no. 1, pp. 1535–1539: SAGE Publications Sage CA: Los Angeles, CA
3. Jang, Y.-M., Mallipeddi, R., Lee, M.: Driver's lane-change intent identification based on pupillary variation. In: 2014 IEEE International Conference on Consumer Electronics (ICCE), 2014, pp. 197–198. IEEE (2014)
4. Liu, Y., Zhang, F., Sun, Y., Huang, H.: Trust sensor interface for improving reliability of EMG-based user intent recognition. In: Engineering in Medicine and Biology Society, EMBC, 2011 Annual International Conference of the IEEE, pp. 7516–7520. IEEE (2011)
5. Tang, R., Kim, J.H.: Evaluating rear-end vehicle accident using pupillary analysis in a driving simulator environment. In: International Conference on Applied Human Factors and Ergonomics, 2019, pp. 176–186. Springer (2019)
6. Kim, J.-H.: Effectiveness of Collision Avoidance Technology, Retrieved from worksafecenter.com, 2016
7. Lees, M.N., Lee, J.D.: The influence of distraction and driving context on driver response to imperfect collision warning systems. Ergonomics 50(8), 1264–1286 (2007)
8. Card, S., Moran, T., Newell, A.: The model human processor- An engineering model of human performance. In: Handbook of Perception and Human Performance, vol. 2, no. 45–1 (1986)
9. Bi, L., Liu, Y.: Modeling driver speed control with the queuing network-model human processor (QN-MHP). In: 17th world Congress on Ergonomics (2009)

Human-Robot Interaction

A Framework for the Classification of Human-Robot Interactions Within the Internet of Production

Ralph Baier[1]([✉]), Hannah Dammers[2]([✉]), Alexander Mertens[1], Mohamed Behery[3], Daniel Gossen[4], Srikanth Nouduri[1], Lukas Pelzer[5], Amir Shahidi[4], Minh Trinh[6], Christian Brecher[6], Burkhard Corves[4], Thomas Gries[2], Christian Hopmann[5], Mathias Hüsing[4], Gerhard Lakemeyer[3], and Verena Nitsch[1,7]

[1] Institute of Industrial Engineering and Ergonomics, RWTH Aachen University, Eilfschornsteinstraße 18, 52062 Aachen, Germany
r.baier@iaw.rwth-aachen.de

[2] Institut für Textiltechnik, RWTH Aachen University, Otto-Blumenthal-Straße 1, 52074 Aachen, Germany
hannah.dammers@ita.rwth-aachen.de

[3] Knowledge-Based Systems Group, RWTH Aachen University, Ahornstraße 55, 52074 Aachen, Germany

[4] Institute of Mechanism Theory, Machine Dynamics and Robotics, RWTH Aachen University, Eilfschornsteinstraße 18, 52062 Aachen, Germany

[5] Institute for Plastics Processing, RWTH Aachen University, Seffenter Weg 201, 52074 Aachen, Germany

[6] Laboratory for Machine Tools and Production Engineering, RWTH Aachen University, Campus-Boulevard 30, 52074 Aachen, Germany

[7] Information Processing and Ergonomics, Department Product and Process Ergonomics, Fraunhofer Institute for Communication, Campus-Boulevard 55-57, 52074 Aachen, Germany

Abstract. An important goal of the Industry 4.0 agenda is increased flexibility in production, which could be achieved, for example, through the use of robot systems that interact with humans. New methods of data acquisition, processing and modeling, such as those developed for the Internet of Production (IoP), open up new possibilities for human-robot interaction (HRI) and in particular human-robot collaboration (HRC). Aiming to support future research in this area and human-oriented work system design in next generation production plants, this paper presents a framework for the classification, analysis and planning of HRI use cases such as those envisioned for the IoP. It uses the dimensions (1) overlap of human and robot workspaces divided into five levels, (2) preconditions and implications in the technical, legal and social domains, and (3) data sources. Using a graphical representation, different variants can be compared and problem areas as well as potentials can be identified easily through color-coded notation.

Keywords: Human-robot interaction · Framework · Internet of Production · Use case-based requirements analysis

© The Author(s), under exclusive license to Springer Nature Switzerland AG 2022
M. Kurosu (Ed.): HCII 2022, LNCS 13303, pp. 427–454, 2022.
https://doi.org/10.1007/978-3-031-05409-9_33

1 Introduction

Industrial robots have become an indispensable part of most production processes. Their demand is growing steadily and with it the range of different applications, as well as their development pace. Originally designed for full automation, the rather inflexible fixed-base industrial robots of the past have evolved into perceptive, sensing robots through the use of sensor technology. The next evolutionary step was triggered with the introduction of autonomous mobile robots, striving towards the development of flexible and adaptive robotics.

Whilst typically robots are employed with the aim to fully automate processes, there are also numerous applications for robots that share a workspace with humans. In this case, humans and robots form a so-called socio-technical work system in which both are integral parts, working together and depending on each other. Conventionally, human-robot interactions are divided into four classes according to the classification model of [1]: full automation, coexistence, cooperation, and collaboration.

However, new fields of robotic applications and innovative forms of human-robot interaction are emerging in research on production of the future, e.g. within the "Internet of Production" (IoP). The IoP aims at reshaping production by using either raw or processed data from different sources in the network through technologies such as machine learning or cloud computing. In this way, fully networked process chains, as well as digital shadows of real production chains, products and human workers are expected to achieve major advantages for production companies [2].

Use cases for robots within the IoP range from their application as kinematic platform for additive manufacturing to create complex three-dimensional parts in a tool-less process in which humans perform auxiliary tasks, to the teleoperation of robots by humans in open die forging processes. In addition, the joint assembly of work pieces by humans and robots using behavior trees to automate planning of robot movements is investigated. Mobile manipulators are considered for assembly tasks too, including autonomous navigation, human tracking, and grasping operations. A further use case examines the processing of limp textile materials, focusing on the complexity- and experience-based division of tasks between humans and robots, as well as the teaching of robots through demonstrations. Furthermore, a soft gripper for HRI applications is being developed. Another use case explores the takeover and manual control of different machines in process steps that are too complex for robots to handle on their own.

Besides the wide variety of use cases, the special characteristics of the IoP (i.e. increased data availability, fully networked process chains and human digital shadows) result in new and more far-reaching aspects of human-robot interaction for the production of the future. Therefore, in this paper we present a new classification framework of the different forms of human-robot interaction, which expands the classification presented in [1] and is derived from the described IoP use cases.

The use cases illustrate the necessity for a new classification to be able to map applications where humans and robots do not only work hand in hand, but also learn from each other or share a common platform (e.g. exoskeleton). Therefore, the original classification is extended by the dimensions of data flow and implications regarding the technical, social and, legal dimension. The obvious advantage of the extended classification is the possibility to classify body-worn or body-connected devices (such as wearables).

Furthermore, the additionally introduced dimensions also allow for the identification of challenges and opportunities in certain areas. Thus, it can be easily shown whether problems are, for example, of a technical nature or rather a question of acceptance, i.e. of a social nature.

Section 2 of this article briefly outlines the process of the framework development. The individual steps are described in more detail in Sects. 3 to 5. The newly created framework is then presented in Sect. 6 and applied to two IoP use cases to illustrate the application of the framework. This section also offers recommendations for applying the framework to a given problem. Subsequently the framework is discussed in Sect. 7. It concludes with an outlook in Sect. 8.

2 Method

This section briefly outlines the process of the framework development (see Fig. 1).

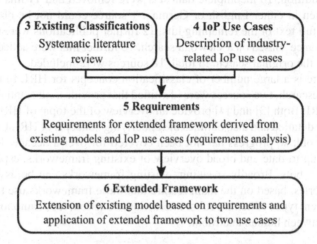

Fig. 1. The process of framework development.

As a first step, a systematic literature review was conducted to ascertain the degree to which existing frameworks would apply to modern HRI use cases, e.g. as they are developed in the IoP. Secondly, a questionnaire was created to survey all HRI applications in the cluster IoP. The subject matter included questions about the degree of cooperation, the reasons for and against HRC for the particular application and the distribution of tasks between human and machine. Thirdly, a requirements analysis was carried out based on the collected use cases. Using these identified requirements, the HRI frameworks found in the literature were evaluated for their suitability. In accordance with the analogy method, usable approaches were identified. One was chosen as the basis for the development of the new framework. As elicitation technique, a workshop was conducted at RWTH Aachen University, with seven subject matter experts from different disciplines – from mechanical and electrical engineering to industrial engineering and ergonomics to computer science. In a first step, they presented their different scenarios (use cases) in detail and, in the second step, applied the extended HRI framework to those use cases for validation. Finally, the advantages and disadvantages as well as the applicability of the framework were discussed. In the course of this debate, some of the dimensions were defined more sharply and borderline cases were identified. These suggestions were incorporated into the framework outlined in this article.

3 Existing Classifications

In order to survey existing HRI classification frameworks, a systematic literature review was conducted. The search term *human-robot AND (interaction OR collaboration OR cooperation) AND (taxonomy OR framework OR spectrum OR system* OR method*)*, resulted in 1914 hits (Web of Science 490, IEEE Xplore 1373 and Google Scholar 51). No time restriction was used for the search results. 5 duplicates were removed. Based on the title, 1800 hits were removed and based on the abstract, another 67 hits were removed. In addition, 10 incomplete data sets were removed and 11 hits because they were not written in either English or German. 1 source could not be obtained. After reviewing the full text of the remaining hits, 12 further publications were removed due to lack of relevance. Based on a snowball search, 10 further hits were added that had not been found by the original search. In total, 18 sources were included.

Today, there is a large number of classification concepts for HRI. In the course of the literature research, two sources were identified that provide a substantial overview of the topic of HRI: Both [3] and [4] provide an overview of the topic of HRI. The second source is more detailed and also outlines the underlying concepts of HRI. Unfortunately, both are quite old, so progress has not been covered for over a decade. Reference [3, 5] provide an up-to-date and broad overview of existing frameworks, especially in the area of social robots. Broadly speaking, existing frameworks can be assigned to one of three categories, based on the main feature that these frameworks use to distinguish between different types of human-robot interaction: Function, robot autonomy and work distribution between human and robot.

(1) Classification according to function: The aspect function is used by [6] to distinguish automation in the four fields of information acquisition, information analysis, decision and action selection, and action implementation. In these areas, automation is scaled over ten levels from low to high.

(2) Classification according to degree of robot autonomy: Reference [7] classifies human-robot systems according to the five stages of bounded autonomy, teleoperation, supervised autonomy, adaptive autonomy, and virtual symbiosis, whereby the complexity of the task increases and thus the autonomy of the robot must also increase in order to fulfil the task sufficiently. For the human operators, the seven generalized functions of labor intensive work, task planning, mission planning, monitoring and intervention, information management, and interactivity are identified. Depending on the stages the proportion of these tasks is distributed differently. The taxonomy described in [8] is an update of [9] and consists of the following eleven dimensions: 1. The type of task being performed, 2. task criticallity describing the priority, 3. robot morphology classifying the appearance of the robot, 4. the

ratio of humans to robots, 5. whether the robotic teams are composed of different or the same robots, 6. level of shared interaction among teams, 7. interaction roles the human can be in, e.g. operator or supervisor, 8. type of human-robot physical proximity, 9. type of decision support for operators, 10. time-space taxonomy of [10], which distinguishes between the same and different time or space, and 11. autonomy level. Reference [11] developed of a framework for social robots. It includes, among other things, autonomy and interactivity to provide guidance for designing social robots. It is also limited to this. Reference [12] developed a framework for identifying the levels of robot autonomy (LORA). It uses guideline questions for this and aspects of HRI are also used to determine the level. They adapted the different autonomy levels – remote control to full, intelligent autonomy – from [13]. This framework was designed for service robots specifically. Reference [14] also use the level of automation as a dimension, which is divided into three levels: fully human controlled, human and robot share task and fully robot controlled. On this basis, a model is developed that primarily addresses the problem of fuzzy task separation between humans and machines.

(3) Classification according to work- and spatial distribution: The framework proposed by [1] divides HRI into four levels according to the overlap of the workspaces: complete separation, coexistence, cooperation and collaboration with full overlap (see Fig. 2 below). Human-robot collaboration (HRC) takes place between the two extremes of manual and fully automated manufacturing, according to [1]. The dimension of physical contact incorporates a safety perspective.

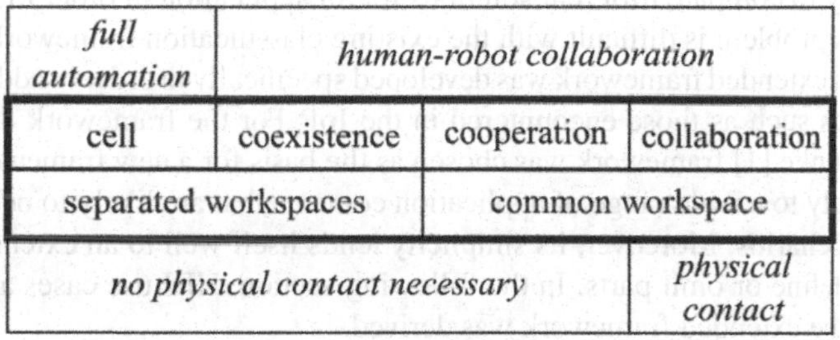

full automation	*human-robot collaboration*		
cell	coexistence	cooperation	collaboration
separated workspaces	common workspace		
no physical contact necessary			*physical contact*

Fig. 2. HRI levels according to Otto & Zunke [1] (own illustration).

Reference [15] distinguishes HRI into the levels coexistence, cooperation and collaboration depending on whether the dimensions working time, workspace, aims and contact are the same for humans and robots The reduction of physical and mental stress is seen as a primary goal for HRI in general. Their HRI model named Human Centered Assistance Applications (HCAA) is designed to cover the application fields exoskeletons, collaborative robots, and orthosis.

Besides these three main categories, [16] added the idea of roles for the human operator to the seven-stage HCI model of [17]. It has the five levels goals, intentions, actions, perception, and evaluation. For the interaction, the human is assigned different roles. These depend on the capabilities of the robot and the area of application. In addition, it is pointed out that for HRI, a certain degree of autonomy must always be existent in the robot. In addition, [5] developed a human-robot interaction taxonomy consisting of three layers that build on each other in a hierarchical way: In the top layer the field of application is specified and the exposure of the robot, i.e. the situation and environment. The robot classification layer covers the tasks the morphology and the autonomy of the robot. The bottom layer classifies the team in terms of the role of the human and the ratio between human and robot, the communication channel and the distance. In addition, a drawing is provided next to the layers to describe the robot in words and with a sketch.

For yet another form of categorization, one can use the perspective of the application domain, the underlying idea or the implementation: For example, the HRI frameworks described in [11] and [5] focus on social robotics, while [18] is limited to the field of home service robots. References [5] and [16] use role concepts for humans in HRI in their frameworks.

In addition to frameworks for classification, [19] presents a framework for evaluation HRI. It is based on the dimensions autonomy, information exchange, team organization, adaptivity and training, task, human factors, ethics as well as cybersecurity. Comparison of existing HRI systems is possible using this framework.

HRI use cases stem from various disciplines and involve the fields of computer science, mechanical engineering and electrical engineering as well as human factors and ergonomics. Therefore, a framework has to be able to cover a broad range of applications. The existing frameworks are typically specialized in certain areas, for which they are also very well suited. A difficulty arises when one is trying to present interdisciplinary use cases clearly in one framework or compare them against each other. In addition, the possibility to compare different solutions for an application in order to find the best solution for a problem is difficult with the existing classification frameworks.

Hence, an extended framework was developed specifically in order to address modern HRI use cases such as those encountered in the IoP. For the framework development, the Otto & Zunke [1] framework was chosen as the basis for a new framework as it was judged to apply to a wide range of application contexts that are likely to occur in future production scenarios. Moreover, its simplicity lends itself well to an extension without having to redefine or omit parts. In the following section, HRI use cases are described from which the extended framework was derived.

4 Use Cases of Human-Robot Interaction Within the Internet of Production

The use cases presented below are all investigated as industry-related use cases within the research Cluster of Excellence "Internet of Production" (IoP). To realize the vision of the IoP, research is currently conducted on how data in the domain of production can be interconnected, processed and finally used for controlling or optimizing production processes – even at different locations if needed [2]. The following section describes seven HRI use cases that are envisioned for the IoP.

4.1 Use Case 1: Robot Teleoperation in Open Die Forging

Some tasks require not only robotic precision but also human flexibility and experience. These tasks can be performed by a human who teleoperates a robot. Sheridan [20] defines teleoperation as the direct continuous control of a robot. This covers a wide spectrum of autonomy to support the operator while performing tasks. Goodrich et al. [21] review different approaches for managing autonomy in robot teleoperation.

Fig. 3. Open die forging process. The robot arm is teleoperated to place the metal ingot between the dies, after which the forging process starts where the dies strike the ingot according to the given process parameters.

Teleoperation tasks within the IoP include, for example, the open die forging see in Fig. 3, which is a fundamental metal forming process that can change the geometric as well as micro structural properties. In this process, an operator controls a robot arm to pick a heated metal ingot from a furnace and position it in front of the dies. Then, an autonomous agent takes over the control of the arm while the human is taking a supervisory role.

According to the classification of [21] the first phase of this task falls under the direct control category in which the operator's commands are directly applied to the robot arm without modification. The direct control paradigm is usually not very intuitive due to the difficulty in mapping the human's commands from a low Degree of Freedom (DoF) input device (such as a joystick) to the relatively high DoF of the robot. The second phase of this task falls under the Supervisory Control category, where the operator defines the task or the motion parameters and initiates the -autonomous- execution by the robot. In the latter phase, the ingot is struck according to a pass schedule, which describes the process parameters such as the number and frequency of strokes as well as the distance between them. Since this process is incremental, meaning these steps are repeated several times before reaching the desired geometry, errors in the placement of the ingot can accumulate over time leading to reduced quality of the product [22, 23]. Throughout the process, the operator makes decisions about the placement of the ingot and correcting the pass schedule to rectify errors. Additionally, due to the lack of nondestructive quality measures, the operator needs to judge whether the ingot should be returned to the furnace for reheating. Some work already exists attempting to either optimize the path schedules [24] or generate them faster [22, 23, 25]. On the other hand, Behery et al. [26] present an approach for discretizing the operator's commands as a step towards building an agent that monitors the process and aids the operator to reduce errors and thus achieve higher quality products.

4.2 Use Case 2: Using a Six-Axis Robot Arm as a Kinematic Platform for Additive Manufacturing

Additive manufacturing (AM) is a production technology, which creates three-dimensional parts by adding material layer by layer. Extrusion based AM with polymers uses an extrusion unit to melt and deposit thermoplastic material through a heated nozzle. The extruded material is applied to a build platform. This enables the production of complex geometries and complete assemblies in a tool-less process [27]. To realize those geometries, the plasticizing unit has to be moved relatively to the build platform. This is done by a kinematics platform which typically allows movement along three linear axes (x, y and z).

Compared to other AM-technologies, extrusion-based systems allow for scaling of the process, both in terms of build volume and material throughput – and therefore processing speed. This has been shown by the Institute for Plastics Processing (IKV) with the development of a hybrid manufacturing cell, as shown in Fig. 4. The manufacturing cell combines a screw-based extruder with a six-axis robot arm to enable the production of large, functional components in a short time. The screw-based extruder allows the machine to process industry-standard pellet material, which reduces cost and widens the usable material spectrum compared to the filaments usually used [28]. Using the six-axis robot arm) as a kinematic platform enables additional degrees of freedom in production and product design. Advanced extrusion units can be mounted and moved with high speed and acceleration. Its six degrees of freedom enable high quality nonplanar AM, because the nozzle can always be oriented perpendicular to curved or inclined surfaces of the part. This way, the staircase effect typically associated with layer-based manufacturing can be avoided and surface quality is improved [29].

The robot-extruder-combination, including the build platform, is situated in an enclosed cell. In a typical use case, the operator prepares the working environment inside the manufacturing cell by cleaning the build platform and, depending on the material to be used, applying a bonding agent to the platform. The next step is the preparation of the machine code, which is done outside of the cell. In this step, process parameters like temperatures, robot movement speeds, screw rotational speed, layer height etc. are being set. In combination with the digital file representing the part's geometry, the layers and tool paths are generated. During production, it is not allowed for anyone to enter the manufacturing cell for safety reasons. There are no sensors on the robot or in the cell which detect humans and the robot is moving a large, heated extruder (up to 380 °C) made from metal at high speeds (up to 5 m/s for travel moves). Therefore, it is necessary to separate the working environments.

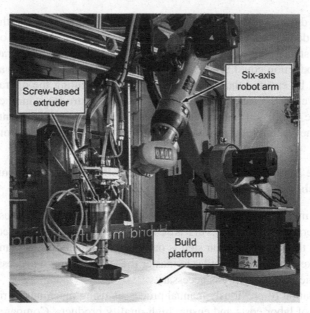

Fig. 4. Hybrid manufacturing cell for large area additive manufacturing.

If the cell door is opened during operation, a switch automatically triggers the stop of the robot. In this case however, only the robot is stopped, while the extrusion process is not affected. This is mainly because material extrusion and temperature processes in general have a high inertia, resulting in an influence on the part regardless of whether they are turned off or not. Therefore, abruptly stopping the robot means ruining the part, since excess material is extruded in that position and too much heat is applied. To remedy a potential problem during production without having to restart the part, it is advised to stop the automatic process and move the robot to a safe position manually (i.e., via user input through the robot's terminal). Afterwards, it is safe for the operator to enter the cell and resolve the problem.

An example of a typical situation that requires the operator to enter the cell is the processing of fiber-filled materials. Parts produced from those materials demonstrate a high stiffness. If there is any excess material, the heated nozzle cannot move past that point. Instead, it will catch on it, preventing movement but not extrusion, therefore creating an even larger spot of excess material. At some point, this spot of excess material is so large that the extruder catching on it means removing the part from the build platform. Those cases have to be detected by the operator to be prevented. Additionally, the process can't be stopped for long since layer bonding highly depends on the temperature between the layers [30]. Stopping the process for too long means that the last layer cooling down, which in turn degrades mechanical properties of the finished part. Once the interruption is over and the operator has left the cell, the process is continued. After production, the robot is automatically moved to a save position and its motors are disabled. Finally, the operator enters the cell safely to retrieve the manufactured part.

Especially during setup of a new material or a new part geometry, this is a tedious process since determining the correct process parameters takes a lot of time. In the process, many small test parts are produced. Here, a safe way for the operator to enter the cell during production could improve the process noticeably. By using a collaborative robot, it could be ensured that the robot itself is not harming the operator in case of collision. However, the robot is still moving a heated extruder, which could burn the operator before a collision is detected. Therefore, even the use of current collaborative robot approaches would require a strict separation of the working environments.

4.3 Use Case 3: Simplified Programming of Robots Using Behavior Trees for Collaborative Assembly

Recent trends in globalization have led to an increased competitive pressure. Furthermore, consumers demand products that are customized to their specific needs. The assembly process as the last production step is particularly affected by demand fluctuations due to its market proximity. In order to master these challenges a process optimization regarding efficiency and agility is necessary.

The automation of previously manual processes using machines or robots can lead to a reduction of labor costs and ensure high-quality products. Compared to assembly machines, robots are characterized by an increased flexibility and lower investments costs. Robots can take over simple assembly tasks, which are repetitive or physically strenuous to the human worker. However, according to [31] some tasks still require high-level reasoning and dexterity which can only be provided by the human. HRC combines the advantages of automated and manual assembly. Figure 5 shows a demonstrator in which the robotic arm preassembles a lamp and a human subsequently carries out the cabling.

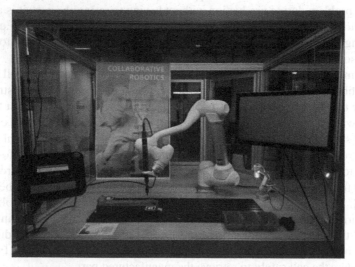

Fig. 5. Extended behavior tree for automatic node ordering and task allocation.

In order to plan collaborative assembly processes, expert knowledge in the field of automation is necessary. An expert must program the robots and ensure safe collaboration with the human. Most small and medium-sized businesses (SMB) lack this expertise. By simplifying the planning process, the advantages of automation are made accessible to SMB which strengthens their resilience towards global competition. Some robot manufacturers such as Franka Emika GmbH or Rethink Robotics Inc. have developed solutions that replace code-based programming with graphical user interfaces. Reference [32] have developed a hardware-based solution using a teach-in tool for intuitive teach-in of robot TCP-positions. Still, these are mostly isolated solutions and not applicable to any robot type.

A promising approach is the use of behavior trees (BT) for automated planning of collaborative assembly tasks. BT organize the behavior of a system in a hierarchical tree structure consisting of action and condition nodes. BT are similar to state machines except that they consist of tasks rather than states. An assembly task can be split into several subtasks (in form of action nodes) and ordered in a sequential or parallel manner. BT are modular since nodes can be easily added or removed. Condition nodes check if a certain condition is met before an action node is executed, which leads to the reactivity of the trees. Finally, BT are intuitive and human-understandable and can therefore be used by non-experts. There are many open source libraries to implement BT using different programming languages. The most common one is py_trees, which is based on Python. Py_trees_ros[1] is an extension for communication with the open source Robot Operating System (ROS) [33], which is becoming a generic framework to program different kinds of robots. [34] Example applications are robotic arm manipulation tasks [35] or mobile robot control [36].

For the IoP, the py_trees_ros library is extended in order to automate the assembly process. A proposed extension are Dynamic Sequence Nodes (DSN), which are used for automatic BT node ordering. In this way, the user does not need to predefine a rigid order of subtasks, because the DNS calculates an optimal order at runtime using a cost function that minimizes the execution time, for instance. A second extension is a Human Action Node (HAN), which automatically distributes subtasks between human and robot depending on the corresponding skills and task requirements. As humans can for example handle limp materials better, they will be assigned handling tasks involving cables or textiles. Furthermore, HAN should enable a fluent task transition between the human worker and the robot. Using e.g. Computer Vision, the robot can detect whether the worker finished her task and continue with the next task. The BT will be displayed on a graphical user interface to visualize as well as simplify the modification of the assembly task. Last but not least, a great focus lies on safety for the human worker. Signals of the camera system as well as sensors of the robot will be evaluated at all times using condition nodes. In case of a condition violation, e.g. an unexpected object enters the robot workspace, the robot will immediately halt or drive into a safe home position.

---

[1] https://github.com/splintered-reality/py_trees_ros.

4.4 Use Case 4: Human-Centered Collaborative Assembly with Mobile Manipulators

Mobile manipulators are redundant robotic systems that are capable of maneuvering in the presence of human coworkers while having the end effector of the robot arm fixed at a specified point or tracing a desired path. Robot task planners exploit these resulting extra degrees of freedom for proactive assistance by making them autonomously navigate and fetch distant objects in its dexterity that are required for sequential operations.

The growing automation needs in the manufacturing industries will demand robotic agents to assist human workers in a proactive manner and work in close proximity. This seeds a necessity for assisting robots to understand human behavior and have improved collaborations in tandem applications that involve autonomous navigation, human tracking and grasping operations. In such interaction scenarios, typical working tasks of robotic agents are perceiving actions of the human worker, predicting when a particular tool is required and bringing necessary toolboxes as the task progresses. A flowchart of how a robot can react to human behavior is shown in Fig. 6.

The conventional production facilities have evolved to be more flexible and self-adaptive with the introduction of smart automation solutions during the fourth industrial revolution. Currently, these industrial configurations are changing from fixed production lines to more agile manufacturing processes having multiple mobile manipulators in autonomous operations. For instance, such an automotive assembly facility will have multiple stations consisting of mobile manipulators with integrated collaborative robot arms to assist the human worker in the machining operations while additional mobile robots bring in the required tools. Here, the chassis frame autonomously navigates through these stations as human workers and collaborative robotic arms share duties to finish the ongoing operations.

Having profound knowledge of the ongoing and consequent tasks, the human worker will drive the assisting robotic agents in most of the tandem operations. While this can be implemented with batch wise scheduling in large production units, further modifications in robot task descriptions will be necessary for customized production units. Although human workers often drive assisting robotic agents in most of the collaborative applications, the leader and follower roles can be exchanged by having profound knowledge of the ongoing and consequent tasks.

Humans at the manufacturing facilities tend to work rather in a comfortable manner with possible task variations and still manage to finish the ongoing operations. As human behavior analysis is a complex entity itself, decoding human intentions is still in pursuit with the current state of the art artificial intelligence algorithms. When an assisting robotic agent perceives these human actions for predicting future outcomes, uncertainties may arise in such interaction scenarios due to task ambiguity, sensor reliability and safety concerns [37]. Humans in general control their movements to the best of their abilities and avoid collisions with moving objects. Despite being cautious around autonomous robots, they tend to make mistakes that may lead to accidents in collaborative workspaces. Uncertainty arises in such situations, as the robotic agents in being the decision maker do not have information on such unpredictable outcomes.

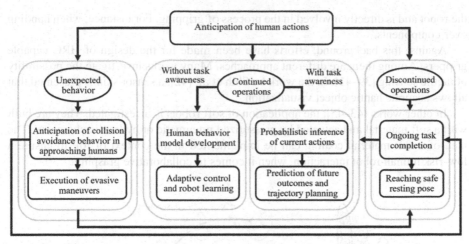

Fig. 6. Action plan for mobile manipulators in tandem applications with possible variations in human behavior.

Bayesian networks are fully comprehensible and efficient in handling these uncertainties and they prevail in most of the probabilistic prediction and planning tasks. With prior knowledge about the ongoing task and duration information, the robotic agent models ongoing operations as sequence of human actions and predict the timing of a future outcome with the help of external sensors [37]. The human actor would be monitored throughout the task execution and as a safety protocol, the assisting robot would first anticipate collision avoidance behavior in the approaching human actor. With a viability assessment of the planned trajectories by verifying if the approaching human falls in this safe boundary, the robot would either re-plan or execute evasive maneuvers, if necessary [38]. This approach can prevent mobile manipulators from stopping for every unexpected encounter of approaching humans, moving obstacles in their way.

4.5   Use Case 5: Development of HRC-Friendly Gripper

Most tasks in production involve gripping of any sort. The gripper is applied to a serial or parallel kinematic robot. Depending on the designated task, different grippers are available and most often customized to the respective needs. The robot thus performs a desired task either on behalf of a human or in cooperation.

In the context of HRC, the level of interaction is important to be distinguished. The robot can either be separated from the human in safety zones and operate in its own workspace, they can share a common workspace but work independently of each other (i.e., cooperate), or last, they work on a common task in close contact (i.e., collaborate).

Considering the latter, the type of interaction further depends on the applied gripping tool. A sucker is comparably harmless for human workers. A component is picked up, moved to the goal pose and placed. Grippers, though, that use a force-, or form-fitted gripping mechanism, can present a greater danger. Without appropriate precautional measures, the human can suffer bruises or worse through direct interaction. This is especially the case in assembly scenarios, in which the human works hand in hand with the robot and is directly involved in the process of gripping. For instance, when handing over components.

Against this background, efforts have been made for the design of HRC capable grippers. Among them are different approaches. Many works investigate the possibility of tactile sensing [39–41]. In the work by Shih et al. [42], a sensor skin is presented that allows accurate haptic object visualization.

In other works [43–45], the application of soft robots is investigated. They are built with a soft material and actuated by pressurized pneumatic or hydraulic chambers. The idea of a soft material coating can be implemented in the context of IoP to ensure a low-risk human-robot interaction, when it comes to collaborative grasping.

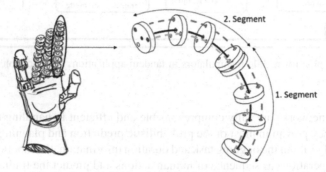

Fig. 7. Continuum robotics-based robot hand with tendon-driven continuum robots for the fingers.

Within the IoP, a continuum robotics-based robotic hand is investigated as a variable industrial gripper. A schematic is presented in Fig. 7. The integration of tendon-driven continuum robotic fingers is evaluated regarding compliant grasping. The flexible and elastic fingers adapt to the grasped object when actuated and thus reduces the required amount of grasping force. Similar work has been performed for discrete tendon-driven finger designs [46]. Further, the implementation of a single tendon in a finger promises the potential to simply "push" a finger away from its position while grasping. For close HRC, this can further reduce the risk of bruises or worse. Last, application of closed-loop force control is investigated to regulate grasping forces and thus ensure safe interactions. A sensor skin, as presented by [42], presents a suitable option for HRC robotic hand regarding both functionality and aesthetics.

4.6 Use Case 6: Human-Robot Collaboration in Textile-Based Composite Preforming

Fiber reinforced plastics are increasingly used in high-performance applications due to their excellent strength-to-weight ratio. However, the existing high demands on component quality, ergonomics and costs can often only be met inadequately by existing production scenarios. To meet all requirements and to avoid expensive, inflexible automation solutions, many companies therefore rely on the manual production of composites [47, 48].

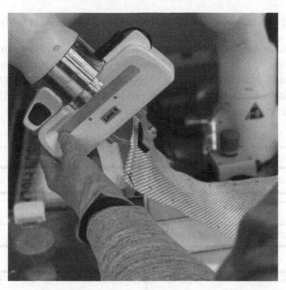

Fig. 8. Human-robot collaboration within textile-based composite production.

In doing so, they rely completely on their experts, who can produce components with a high quality if they are properly trained and have a good sense for the expensive, limp textile materials. However, this type of manual production is characterized by low production speed. In addition, employees often suffer from wrist or back problems due to poor ergonomic conditions. This situation is worsened by a growing shortage of workers as dedicated training for composite production does not exist [48, 49].

Therefore, within this IoP use case we investigate how human workers can be supported by the use of effective human-robot collaboration [50]. The focus is on the preforming process steps handling, draping and joining of the textile layers, as these are particularly experience-intensive and thus prone to errors. A robot is used to take over the pick-and-place of the textiles, i.e. the handling task. In this way, the positioning accuracy can be significantly increased. Furthermore, the robot thus serves as a third hand for the human by fixing the textile at the desired position.

With a special tool, the robot can also be used to take over draping operations (see Fig. 8). For this purpose, a geometry- and complexity-dependent task division is carried out: the robot takes over component areas with low complexity (e.g., slight curvature), while the human takes over the areas with high complexity (e.g., convex-concave curvature). To do so, the robot imitates human hand movements by learning from demonstration. In this way, expert knowledge can be formalized, saved and transferred to other composite production scenarios. An adaption of the robot speed to the working speed of the human harmonizes the collaboration so that waiting time for the robot doesn't cause mental stress in the human.

4.7   Use Case 7: Human-Robot Collaboration in Vehicle Assembly

In 2018, the International Federation of Robotics (IFR) identified the automotive industry as the biggest driver of robot density in Germany [51] and forecasted an annual growth of 5% for the period from 2018 to 2020 [52]. Combined with the fact that HRI will be an increasingly important part of industrial production in the future [53], this will have a particular impact on jobs in the automotive industry.

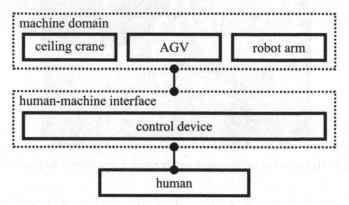

Fig. 9. Schematic diagram of how a human can control different machines via a single control device as a human-machine interface (HMI).

This use case is investigating a single production station in an assembly line from truck production. Here, the drive train gets mounted onto the vehicle frame. For this step, an autonomous ground vehicle (AGV) delivers the prepared vehicle frame and a ceiling crane delivers the preassembled drive train. Each of the two operators control one of the machines and another work person supervises the process and instructs the operators. Since exact positioning is important, the coordination of the three work persons is very important so that no mistakes happen. The consequence would be a complaint or damage to the vehicle in the best and a traffic accident in the worst case. Nevertheless, work must be done fast at this station so that the overall assembly line throughput can be maintained.

For this reason, the aim of this use case is to design an HRI for the described scenario and to scientifically investigate it. As shown in Fig. 9, the approach is to enable a worker to control both machines, the AGV and the overhead crane, with a single control device. As a further option, a robot arm can be integrated into the process as an additional aid. Control is to be taken over for only one machine at a time. The questions that arise in this HRI scenario are, among other things, whether the control of different machines in rapid change overloads the work person cognitively and whether such a system can be operated safely. From an industrial perspective, the question of the productivity of such a work system is also to be answered.

Based on the analysis of the requirements arising from the assembly task and the operation of the individual machines, a corresponding device was designed as a human-machine interface (HMI): The result is a wearable device that can capture all relative movements and register all inputs [54]. In the next step, a simulation of the entire assembly station is created in which various work processes can be modelled. In a study, the new input device will be compared with established input devices. In addition to other objective and subjective parameters, the cognitive load will also be recorded. The knowledge gained from this will be transferred back to the use case. A further research question is how and which data can be used to support the human in the HRI in the best possible way.

5 Requirements

In accordance to [55] a requirements elicitation, analysis, and specification was conducted to determine the requirements for extending the HRI framework. The defined key requirements were divided into five categories: setup, programming, safety, task sharing and interdisciplinarity.

Setup: The described IoP use cases vary not only in the form of human-robot interaction, but also in the addressed target production industry and thus in the robotic setup. Depending on the material to be processed, not only the assembly of solids is considered, but also the processing of plastics or the handling of flexible materials (e.g., textiles or wires). Furthermore, the different applications also result in additional conditions for the robotic setup: the type of robot tool (e.g., hand-like grippers, vacuum grippers, clamp grippers), environment (e.g., high temperatures) and layout (robot cell, production lines). In addition, not only the case of a single robot interacting with a single human is considered, but also multiple robots moving autonomously on the shop floor and interacting with multiple humans.

Programming: Further requirements result from robot programming. Conventionally, robots are programmed once to produce large quantities without necessities for changing their movements. However, in the use cases described, other forms of programming are considered such as direct control of the robot via teleoperation. Other artificial intelligence algorithms are also used, e.g. automatic planning with behavior trees and learning from demonstration.

Safety: According to the level of human-robot interaction, different scenarios of compliance with occupational safety arise. Conventional safety fences or light barriers can be used to prevent human workers from entering the robots' work area. However, it is also possible to improve the perception of the robot by equipping it with sensors and cameras Furthermore, the data recorded by the sensors can be collected, processed and used for analysis and optimization, e.g. via artificial intelligence. Thus, more direct forms of collaboration between humans and robots can be realized while ensuring human safety.

Task Sharing: Efforts are made to achieve a division of tasks between humans and robots in which the respective strengths of human workers and robots are exploited. When analyzing the use cases, it is evident that the type of task sharing and the hierarchy between humans and robots varies from application to application. In some use cases, the human worker takes on a supervisory role and only intervenes in the work process when necessary. In other use cases, the robot is used as a third hand or robot colleague supporting the human, all gradations of task sharing and hierarchy should be considered in the further development of the HRI model.

Interdisciplinarity: Both in conducting the expert workshop, analyzing the use cases and examining the existing HRI models (Sect. 3), it may be noted that specific requirements arise through the various disciplines. The evolved HRI model should thus not only be usable for a specific discipline, but should include aspects that are applicable across disciplines and industries. In addition to purely technical aspects, this also encompasses legal and social factors.

The aforementioned aspects of the five key requirements setup, programming, safety, task sharing and interdisciplinarity shall be considered in the further development and extension of the HRI model by [1] to ensure application to the widest possible number and variation of use cases.

6 Extended Framework

The HRI use cases from the IoP that were described in Sect. 3 involve the fields of computer science, mechanical engineering and electrical engineering as well as human factors and ergonomics. Therefore, a framework has to be able to cover a wide range of applications within the production domain. The existing frameworks are typically specialized in certain areas or disciplines, for which they are also very well suited. A difficulty arises when one is trying to present interdisciplinary use cases clearly in one framework or compare them against each other. However, these are precisely the characteristics of modern HRI applications that they arise from developments in the IoP. Furthermore, the frameworks presented do not support the possibility to compare different approaches for an application in order to find the best solution to a problem.

For the development of the HRI framework, the goal was to be able to cover a wide range of modern HRI applications in the field of production. In order to be accessible and to ensure an overview even for complex systems, it should also have a graphical representation.

For the framework development, the Otto & Zunke [1] framework was chosen as the basis. It was considered applicable to a wide range of application contexts that are likely to occur in future production scenarios based on the mentioned requirements criteria (Sect. 5).

6.1 Description of the HRI-Spectrum

As a derivative of the model by [1], the extended framework has the HRI level as its main axis, to which two additional axes have been added: The axis preconditions and implications cover the whole environment of the HRI system and the axis data sources describes the origin of the required data. Figure 10 shows the structure of the extended framework.

Colored dots mark the different properties in the respective fields of the framework. In addition, these points can also be labeled with text. The level of detail of the textual description depends largely on the individual case and which goals are being pursued: For a comparison on a rather abstract level, the colored marking alone can be sufficient, whereas during the planning of a specific work system or HRI use case, for example, the text should be more detailed. Details can also be directly included in the diagram.

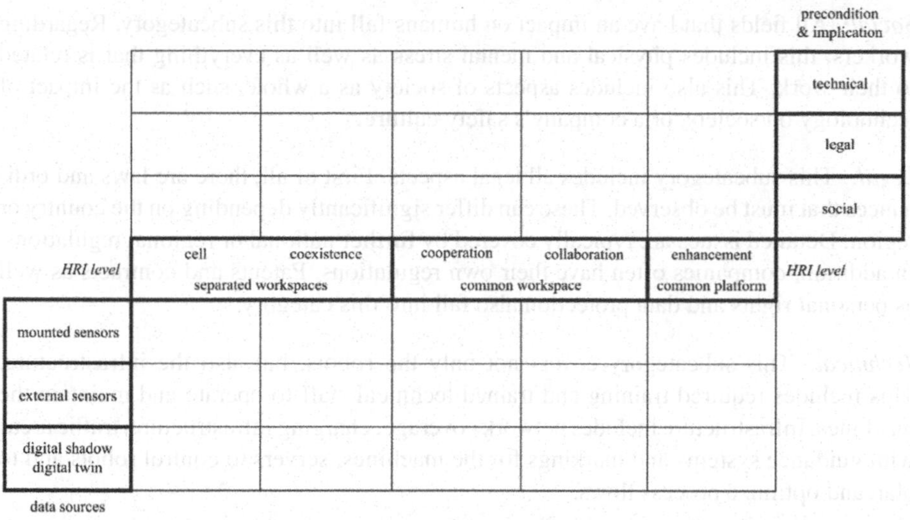

					precondition & implication
					technical
					legal
					social
HRI level	cell coexistence		cooperation collaboration		enhancement	HRI level
	separated workspaces		common workspace		common platform	
mounted sensors						
external sensors						
digital shadow digital twin						
data sources						

Fig. 10. Extended HRI framework.

Dimension Workspace. As mentioned in Sect. 2, [1] divide their classification framework into the areas of separated and common workspaces. Separate workspaces include the cell, where a robot works (physically) isolated from the rest of the production facility. Access to the cell is not possible during the work process, and this is ensured by safety mechanisms of the cell. The second subtype is coexistence, where the robot has presence detection capabilities, so that the work process can be slowed down, limited to a certain area or is stopped if a human enters the workspace of the robot.

The common working area is divided into cooperation and collaboration. Cooperation is characterized by a partial overlap of the workspaces. The work of humans and robots is coupled, but there is no need for physical contact. In collaboration, the workspaces are merged and human-robot contact is necessary for the execution of the task.

Under the term common platform, this classification is expanded to include the category enhancement. It includes all machines or technologies that are worn or are firmly connected to the body, e.g. exoskeletons, prostheses or implants. As these technologies can be used to improve manual work performance [56] or monitor the worker's physiological parameters [57], they are likely to be used in the industry of the future.

Unlike in other classification frameworks, autonomy is not the main axis. Instead, the focus lies on the spatial relationship between humans and robots. Nevertheless, autonomy to some degree is implied as without autonomous capabilities, HRI would not be possible. Therefore, it can be said that with increasing overlap of the workspaces, the autonomy of the robot must also increase.

Dimension Precondition and Implication. This dimension is further divided into the three subcategories social, legal, and technical.

Social: All fields that have an impact on humans fall into this subcategory. Regarding workers, this includes physical and mental stress as well as everything that is related to their work. This also includes aspects of society as a whole, such as the impact of technology on society, or a company's safety culture.

Legal: This subcategory includes all legal aspects. First of all, there are laws and ordinances that must be observed. These can differ significantly depending on the country or region. Detailed issues are typically covered by further national or regional regulations. In addition, companies often have their own regulations. Patents and contracts as well as personal rights and data protection also fall into this category.

Technical: This subcategory covers not only the robots, but also the infrastructure. This includes required training and trained technical staff to operate and maintain the machines. Infrastructure includes network coverage, charging infrastructure, traffic areas with guidance systems and markings for the machines, servers to control robots and to plan and optimize process flows.

For the corresponding HRI level, all potentials are marked in green and obstacles in red in the corresponding categories. This representation allows for problem areas to be easily identified by a cluster of red dots and potentials by a set of green dots. This representation also helps to assess alternative options or supports planning for the future by showing fields with a need for action.

Dimension Data Source. This dimension describes where the robot (primarily) gets its information: mounted or external sensors, and digital twin or digital shadow. In practice, there is usually a combination.

Mounted Sensors: are those that are installed on or permanently connected to the robot, for example force sensors in the joints. Access to the data is always given and the data processing takes place on the robot itself. It is completely independent. The data required for process control is usually supplied by mounted sensors. However, this data can also be made available to the overall system and be used for fleet management, for example.

External Sensors: With external sensors, there is a certain dependence on external infrastructure. These can be stationary or mobile sensors – for example, mounted aboard an AGV. In this context, data processing can also take place outside the robot. An example is motion detection by fixed cameras installed in a building, whereby the object tracking is carried out by a central computer.

Digital Twin/Digital Shadow: Here, the robot accesses (processed) data from the so-called data lake. Data from the data lake usually have a supplementary effect. So, for example, data from quality control or from complaints can be collected and fed back into the manufacturing process in order to increase quality. In addition, there is also the possibility of creating and using a digital shadow for the worker to improve working conditions and enable fluent human-robot collaboration [2].

6.2 Examples of Framework Applications

In the following, two of the use cases described above are presented as examples in the HRI spectrum. Note that the selection does not make any statement about the quality or relevance of the use cases, but only serves to illustrate the applicability of the framework. Also, the level of detail depends on the user's objectives and can be adapted as needed.

Use Case 1 (Robot Teleoperation in Open Die Forging). First, the framework is applied to the HRI Use Case Robot teleoperation in open die forging (see Fig. 11). As this is an example, some key aspects have been extracted.

It is a teleoperation and is assigned to coexistence in its present form. At a glance, it is noticeable that there is only a deficiency on the technical level, specifically, that the entire process cannot be fully automated. This is the reason why an HRI is being planned for this process. Based on this result, problems with the HRI are not to be expected. Other forms of HRI than teleoperation are not listed, but must be discarded because of the lack of separation of workspaces. This is necessary because of the dangers to humans caused by the heat and gases.

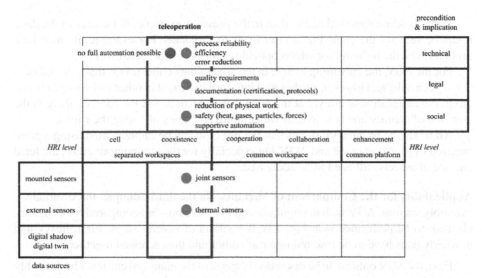

Fig. 11. Use case 1 (with a selection of properties) as an example. (Color figure online)

Use Case 7 (Human-Robot Collaboration in Vehicle Assembly). The application of the extended framework to the use case human-robot collaboration in vehicle assembly is depicted in Fig. 12.

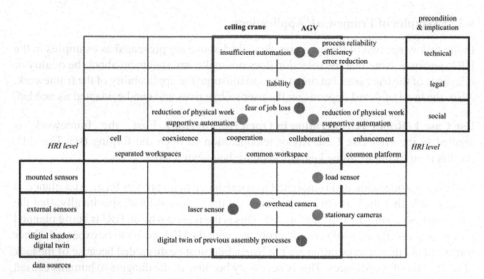

Fig. 12. Use case 7 (with a selection of properties) as an example. (Color figure online)

Here, there are more red marks than in the previous example: In the area of the data, it can be seen for the crane that a laser leads to problems. For example, it could be a problem with the lighting, for which optical sensors can react sensitively.

For the AGV, the only thing to note in the area of data collection is that a digital twin is not yet available. However, further problems are indicated in other categories: for one thing, the automation is not yet at the level that is needed, and for another, there is the question of liability and how to deal with employees' fears of losing their jobs.

All in all, the framework shows that the use case can be implemented using a combination of overhead crane and AGV, but especially for the autonomous AGV, the legal and social aspects still need to be addressed.

Applicability for the Comparison of Variants. In the third example, three variants – assembly stations, AGV with manipulator and exoskeleton – are compared for an assembly task to be performed (see Fig. 13). It consists of several steps: First, heavy and unwieldy parts have to be inserted into each other and then screwed together.

First, the AGV option can be discarded because of the many red entries. The assembly workstation option seems to perform best based on the number of green marks. If one can do without the use of a digital shadow, this solution can be used directly. An exoskeleton is an alternative that does not perform much worse.

Furthermore, it can be seen from the color-coding that the technical and social fields become problematic, especially at high levels of autonomy.

6.3 Guiding Questions for Use

There is no set procedure to use the framework, but the following guiding questions may be useful for its application.

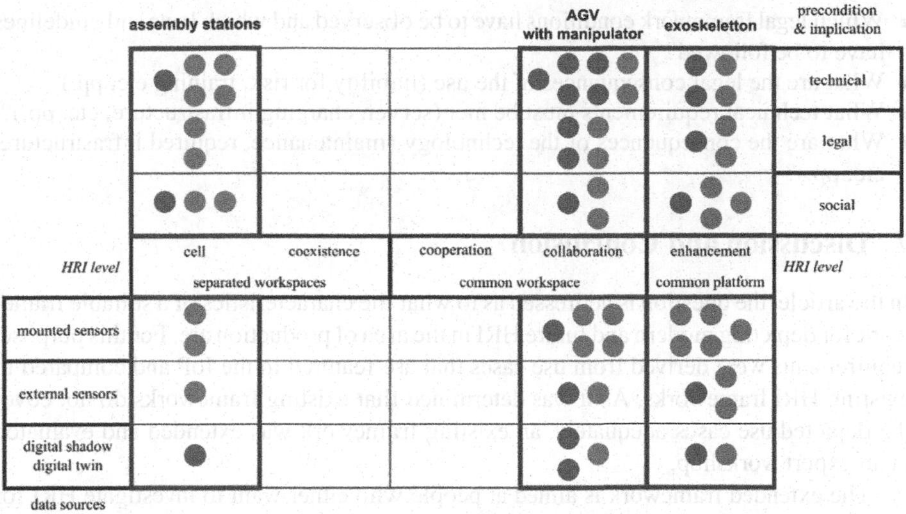

	assembly stations		AGV with manipulator	exoskeletton	precondition & implication
	●●● ●●●		●●●● ●●●●	●● ●●	technical
	● ● ●		●● ●●	● ●	legal
	●●●		● ●	● ●●	social
HRI level	cell	coexistence	cooperation	collaboration	enhancement
	separated workspaces		common workspace		common platform

	cell (separated workspaces)	coexistence	cooperation (common workspace)	collaboration	enhancement (common platform)	HRI level
mounted sensors	● ●			●●● ●●	●●● ●●	
external sensors	●			●●	●● ●	
digital shadow digital twin	●			●● ●	●●	

data sources

Fig. 13. HRI spectrum as a tool for comparing different options. (Color figure online)

Dimension HRI Level

- How large is the spatial overlap of human and robot workspaces?
- To what extent is the robot able to perform tasks independently?
- Can the robot detect the presence of a human?
- Does the robot have interactive capabilities (force sensors in the joints, sensitive skin, etc. pp.)?

Data Source

- Which sensors are mounted on the robot?
- Which external sensors are used by the robot, or to which sensors does it have access?
- Which other sensors are required?
- What other measures or data need to be collected?
- Is there an infrastructure such as a data lake that can be accessed?
- How must the data from a data lake be prepared in order to be used?
- Which data can or should be fed into a data lake for later processing or use?

Preconditions and Implications

- What preconditions must be created among the workers so that they can use the system?
- What are the preconditions for the acceptance of the system by the workers?
- Are there any needs of the workers that are being met or denied by this?
- What are the consequences for the workers (change of work schedule, training, job guarantee etc. pp.)?

- Which legal framework conditions have to be observed and which laws and guidelines have to be followed?
- What are the legal consequences of the use (liability for risk, training etc. pp.)?
- What technical requirements must be met (server, charging infrastructure, etc. pp.)?
- What are the consequences of the technology (maintenance, required infrastructure, etc. pp.)?

7 Discussion and Conclusion

In the article, the question is addressed as to what the characteristics of a suitable framework for depicting modern and future HRI in the area of production are. For this purpose, requirements were derived from use cases that are featured in the IoP and compared to existing HRI frameworks. As it was determined that existing frameworks do not cover the depicted use cases adequately, an existing framework was extended and evaluated in an expert workshop.

The extended framework is aimed at people who either want to investigate HRI for the purpose of description and optimization or who are planning new HRI use cases. Its application is not limited to a specific domain. However, since its development was based on specific use cases, requirements from the domain of production in particular have been incorporated into the design. As such, it may be argued that it is particularly suitable for the classification of HRI within the context of next generation production applications.

The extended HRI framework provides a basis for a structured, yet open approach to the topic of HRI in the field of production. The graphical representation provides easy-to-understand feedback. It also makes it easy to compare several options. Furthermore, it facilitates the identification and consideration of potentials and barriers in the planning phase of collaborative robot development or of socio-technical work systems that include HRI.

However, there are also limitations. First, the framework is intentionally designed to cover a wide range of different applications. As a result of this decision, it does not go into depth, which would be necessary for addressing certain questions, e.g. in particular with regard to collaborative robot development. Yet, this framework can be used to identify critical areas and if combined with a specialized tool, it could be used for targeted in-depth analysis. Second, the openness allows for a high flexibility in use, but also leads to another limitation: The framework itself offers not much guidance on its use. To help users, some questions have been provided in Sect. 6.3 as assistance. Finally, the framework was developed on the basis of the use cases described in Sect. 4 within the scope of the IoP. The workshop with experts from the IoP represented the technical perspective well. Social and legal aspects, on the other hand, have not been taken into account to the same extent. As with any other framework, these limitations should always be taken into account when using it.

8 Outlook

Particularly in production and logistics, workplaces at which people work closely with robots are increasingly in demand. They offer the possibility of combining human skills and abilities with the precise execution of robots in order to make work processes more efficient and flexible. At the same time, they can support healthy working conditions, for example, by relieving workers from forced postures and heavy load handling. The requirements for the design of robots that assist people directly at the workplace differ considerably from those for traditional industrial robots. It is necessary to consider utilization concepts for these workplaces that do not have a negative impact on worker safety, productivity or user acceptance.

Although there are a number of technical standards that apply to HRI workplaces, a lack of empirical knowledge has so far limited the ability to provide concrete design or utilization guidelines, in particular for work with collaborative robots. While research has been concerned with the humane and economically compatible design of human-machine systems for decades, there is still a great need for research into the design of workplaces with highly automated, cooperative robot systems such as those envisioned for next generation production concepts like the IoP.

Acknowledgment. Funded by the Deutsche Forschungsgemeinschaft (DFG, German Research Foundation) under Germany's Excellence Strategy – EXC-2023 Internet of Production – 390621612.

References

1. Otto, M., Zunke, R.: Einsatzmöglichkeiten von Mensch-Roboter-Kooperationen und sensitiven Automatisierungslösungen: Zukunft der Arbeit - die neuen Roboter kommen (2015)
2. Mertens, A., et al.: Human digital shadow: data-based modeling of users and usage in the internet of production. In: 2021 14th International Conference on Human System Interaction (HSI), pp. 1–8. IEEE (2021). https://doi.org/10.1109/HSI52170.2021.9538729
3. Thrun, S.: Toward a framework for human-robot interaction. Human-Computer Interaction **19**, 9–24 (2004)
4. Goodrich, M.A., Schultz, A.C.: Human–Robot Interaction: A Survey (2007)
5. Onnasch, L., Roesler, E.: A taxonomy to structure and analyze human–robot interaction. Int. J. Soc. Robot. **13**(4), 833–849 (2020). https://doi.org/10.1007/s12369-020-00666-5
6. Parasuraman, R., Sheridan, T.B., Wickens, C.D.: A model for types and levels of human interaction with automation. IEEE Transactions on Systems, man, and Cybernetics. Part A, Systems and Humans: a Publication of the IEEE Systems, Man, and Cybernetics Society, vol. 30, 286–297 (2000). https://doi.org/10.1109/3468.844354
7. Granda, T.M., Kirkpatrick, M., Julien, T.D., Peterson, L.A.: The evolutionary role of humans in the human-robot system. Proc. Hum. Factors Soc. Ann. Meeting **34**, 664–668 (1990). https://doi.org/10.1177/154193129003400919
8. Yanco, H.A., Drury, J.L.: Classifying human-robot interaction: an updated taxonomy (2004)
9. Yanco, H.A., Drury, J.L.: A Taxonomy for Human-Robot Interaction (2002)
10. Ellis, C.A., Gibbs, S.J., Rein, G.: Groupware: some issues and experiences. Commun. ACM **34**, 39–58 (1991). https://doi.org/10.1145/99977.99987
11. Bartneck, C., Forlizzi, J.: A design-centred framework for social human-robot interaction. In: RO-MAN 2004. 13th IEEE International Workshop on Robot and Human Interactive Communication (IEEE Catalog No.04TH8759), pp. 591–594 (2004). doi: https://doi.org/10.1109/ROMAN.2004.1374827

12. Beer, J.M., Fisk, A.D., Rogers, W.A.: Toward a framework for levels of robot autonomy in human-robot interaction. J. Hum.-Robot Inter. **3**, 74–99 (2014). https://doi.org/10.5898/JHRI. 3.2.Beer

13. Huang, H.-M., Pavek, K., Albus, J., Messina, E.: Autonomy levels for unmanned systems (ALFUS) framework: an update. In: Gerhart, G.R., Shoemaker, C.M., Gage, D.W. (eds.) Unmanned Ground Vehicle Technology VII. SPIE Proceedings, p. 439. SPIE (2005). https:// doi.org/10.1117/12.603725

14. Kolbeinsson, A., Lagerstedt, E., Lindblom, J.: Classification of Collaboration Levels for Human-Robot Cooperation in Manufacturing, pp. 151–156 (2018). https://doi.org/10.3233/ 978-1-61499-902-7-151

15. Schmidtler, J., Knott, V., Hölzel, C., Bengler, K.: Human Centered Assistance Applications for the working environment of the future. OER **12**, 83–95 (2015). https://doi.org/10.3233/ OER-150226

16. Scholtz, J.: Theory and evaluation of human robot interactions. In: 36th Annual Hawaii International Conference on System Sciences, 2003 (2003)

17. Norman, D., Draper, S.: User Centered System Design: New Perspectives on Human-Computer Interaction (1986)

18. Lee, K.-W., Kim, H.-R., Yoon, W., Yoon, Y., Kwon, D.: Designing a human-robot interaction framework for home service robot (2005)

19. Gervasi, R., Mastrogiacomo, L., Franceschini, F.: A conceptual framework to evaluate human-robot collaboration. Int. J. . Adv. Manuf. Technol. **108**(3), 841–865 (2020). https://doi.org/ 10.1007/s00170-020-05363-1

20. Sheridan, T.: Telerobotics, Automation, and Supervisory Control. MIT Press, Cambridge (1992)

21. Goodrich, M.A., Crandall, J.W., Barakova, E.: Teleoperation and beyond for assistive humanoid robots. Rev. Hum. Factors Ergon. **9**, 175–226 (2013). https://doi.org/10.1177/155 7234X13502463

22. Recker, D.: Entwicklung von schnellen Prozessmodellen und Optimierungsmoeglichkeiten fuer das Freiformschmieden. Aachen, Germany (2014)

23. Rosenstock, D.: Schnelle Prozessmodellierung, Online-Visualisierung und Optimierung beim Freiformschmieden. Verlagshaus Mainz GmbH (2018)

24. Xiu-quan, C., Yu-lin, H., Qin-xiang, X., Bei-gu, K., Wen-xuan, C.: Closing of central cavity in shaft heavy forging. Steel Res. Int. **81**, 330–333 (2010)

25. Wolfgarten, M., Rosenstock, D., Rudolph, F., Hirt, G.: New approach for the optimization of pass-schedules in open-die forging. Int. J. Mater. Form. **12**(6), 973–983 (2019). https://doi. org/10.1007/s12289-019-01471-w

26. Behery, M., Tschesche, M., Rudolph, F., Hirt, G., Lakemeyer, G.: Action discretization for robot arm teleoperation in open-die forging. In: 2020 IEEE International Conference on Systems, Man, and Cybernetics (SMC), pp. 2100–2105 (2020). https://doi.org/10.1109/SMC 42975.2020.9283043

27. Gibson, I., Rosen, D.W., Stucker, B.: Additive Manufacturing Technologies. Springer US, Boston (2010)

28. Hopmann, C., Pelzer, L.: Additive manufacturing of large parts by an extrusion based hybrid approach. In: Polymer Processing Society (ed.) PPS Conference Proceedings (2019)

29. Pelzer, L., Hopmann, C.: Additive manufacturing of non-planar layers with variable layer height. Addit. Manuf. **37**, 101697 (2021). https://doi.org/10.1016/j.addma.2020.101697

30. Seppala, J.E., Hoon Han, S., Hillgartner, K.E., Davis, C.S., Migler, K.B.: Weld formation during material extrusion additive manufacturing. Soft Matter **13**, 6761–6769 (2017). doi: https://doi.org/10.1039/c7sm00950j

31. Pollmann, K., Janssen, D., Vukelic, M., Fronemann, N.: Homo Digitalis: Eine Studie über die Auswirkungen neuer Technologien auf verschiedenen Lebensbereichen für eine menschengerechte Digitalisierung der Arbeitswelt. Fraunhofer Institute for Industrial Engineering (IAO), Stuttgart, Germany (2018)
32. Min, D.H., Hwi-Su, K., Dong Il, P., Yong, C.T., Chanhun, P.: User-friendly teaching tool for a robot manipulator in human robot collaboration. In: 2017 14th International Conference on Ubiquitous Robots and Ambient Intelligence (URAI), pp. 751–752 (2017). https://doi.org/ 10.1109/URAI.2017.7992817
33. Stanford Artificial Intelligence Laboratory et al.: Robotic Operating System. https://www. ros.org
34. Iovino, M., Scukins, E., Styrud, J., Ögren, P., Smith, C.: A Survey of Behavior Trees in Robotics and AI (2020)
35. Colledanchise, M., Ögren, P.: Behavior Trees in Robotics and AI. CRC Press (2018)
36. José Ángel, S.-M., Juan, F.-O.: Integration of an automated hierarchical task planner in ROS using behaviour trees. In: 2017 6th International Conference on Space Mission Challenges for Information Technology (SMC-IT), pp. 20–25 (2017). https://doi.org/10.1109/SMC-IT. 2017.11
37. Hawkins, K.P., Bansal, S., Vo, N.N., Bobick, A.F.: Anticipating human actions for collaboration in the presence of task and sensor uncertainty. In: 2014 IEEE International Conference on Robotics and Automation (ICRA 2014), Hong Kong, China, 31 May–7 June 2014, pp. 2215–2222. IEEE, Piscataway (2014). https://doi.org/10.1109/ICRA.2014.6907165
38. Hawkins, K.P., Tsiotras, P.: Anticipating human collision avoidance behavior for safe robot reaction. In: 2018 IEEE Conference on Decision and Control (CDC), pp. 6301–6306 (2018). https://doi.org/10.1109/CDC.2018.8619849
39. Dario, P., de Rossi, D., Giannotti, C., Vivaldi, F., Pinotti, P.C.: Ferroelectric polymer tactile sensors for prostheses. Ferroelectrics **60**, 199–214 (1984). https://doi.org/10.1080/001501984 08017522
40. Harmon, L.D.: Touch-sensing technology - A review. Technical Report MSR80–03, Dearborn, Michigan: Society of Manufacturing Engineers (1980)
41. Hillis, W.D.: A high-resolution imaging touch sensor. Int. J. Robot. Res. **1**, 33–44 (1982). https://doi.org/10.1177/027836498200100202
42. Shih, B., Drotman, D., Christianson, C., Huo, Z., White, R., Christensen, H.I., Tolley, M.T.: Custom soft robotic gripper sensor skins for haptic object visualization. In: IROS Vancouver 2017. IEEE/RSJ International Conference on Intelligent Robots and Systems, Vancouver, BC, Canada September 24–28, 2017: conference digest, pp. 494–501. IEEE, Piscataway, NJ (2017). https://doi.org/10.1109/IROS.2017.8202199
43. Rus, D., Tolley, M.T.: Design, fabrication and control of soft robots. 0028-0836 (2015)
44. Galloway, K.C., et al.: Soft robotic grippers for biological sampling on deep reefs. Soft Rob. **3**, 23–33 (2016). https://doi.org/10.1089/soro.2015.0019
45. Sinatra, N.R., Teeple, C.B., Vogt, D.M., Parker, K.K., Gruber, D.F., Wood, R.J.: Ultragentle manipulation of delicate structures using a soft robotic gripper. Sci. Robot. **4**, eaax5425 (2019). https://doi.org/10.1126/scirobotics.aax5425
46. Sabetian, P., Feizollahi, A., Cheraghpour, F., Moosavian, S.A.A.: A compound robotic hand with two under-actuated fingers and a continuous finger. In: 2011 IEEE International Symposium on Safety, Security, and Rescue Robotics, pp. 238–244. IEEE (2011). https://doi.org/ 10.1109/SSRR.2011.6106774
47. Fleischer, J., Teti, R., Lanza, G., Mativenga, P., Möhring, H.-C., Caggiano, A.: Composite materials parts manufacturing. CIRP Ann. **67**, 603–626 (2018). https://doi.org/10.1016/j.cirp. 2018.05.005

48. Elkington, M., Bloom, D., Ward, C., Chatzimichali, A., Potter, K.: Hand layup: understanding the manual process. Adv. Manuf. Polymer Composites Sci. **1**, 138–151 (2015). https://doi.org/10.1080/20550340.2015.1114801

49. Chan, W.P., Hanks, G., Sakr, M., Zuo, T., Machiel Van der Loos, H.F., Croft, E.: An augmented reality human-robot physical collaboration interface design for shared, large-scale, labour-intensive manufacturing tasks. In: 2020 IEEE/RSJ International Conference on Intelligent Robots and Systems (IROS), pp. 11308–11313 (2020). https://doi.org/10.1109/IROS45743.2020.9341119

50. Dammers, H., Lennartz, M., Gries, T., Greb, C.: Human-robot collaboration in composite preforming: chances and challenges. Dallas, TX (2021)

51. International Federation of Robotics (IFR): Deutschland zählt zu den Top-10 automatisierten Ländern weltweit (2021). https://ifr.org/downloads/press2018/2021-01-27_IFR_Pressemeldung_Roboterdichte.pdf

52. International Federation of Robotics (IFR): Robot density rises globally (2018). https://ifr.org/img/uploads/2018-FEB-07-IFR-Press_Release_Robot_density_EN.pdf

53. Matheson, E., Minto, R., Zampieri, E.G.G., Faccio, M., Rosati, G.: Human-robot collaboration in manufacturing applications: a review. Robotics **8**, 100 (2019). https://doi.org/10.3390/robotics8040100

54. Baier, R., Mertens, A., Nitsch, V.: Lessons Learned aus dem Prototypendesign einer Mensch-Maschine-Schnittstelle zur Steuerung verschiedenartiger Maschinen für die Produktionslogistik Technologie und Bildung in hybriden Arbeitswelten. 68. GfA-Frühjahrskongress, Dortmund (2022)

55. IEEE Computer Society: Guide to the Software Engineering Body of Knowledge Version 3.0 (SWEBOK Guide V3.0)

56. Fox, S., Aranko, O., Heilala, J., Vahala, P.: Exoskeletons. JMTM **31**, 1261–1280 (2020). https://doi.org/10.1108/JMTM-01-2019-0023

57. Wilson, S., Laing, R.: Wearable Technology: Present and Future (2018)

Social Robots and Digital Humans as Job Interviewers: A Study of Human Reactions Towards a More Naturalistic Interaction

Evangelia Baka[1]([✉]), Nidhi Mishra[2], Emmanouil Sylligardos[3],
and Nadia Magnenat-Thalmann[1]

[1] MIRALab, University of Geneva, Rte de Drize 7, 1227 Geneva, Switzerland
ebaka@miralab.ch
[2] Institute of Media Innovation, Nanyang Technological University, 50 Nanyang Drive,
Singapore, Singapore
[3] Computer Science Department, University of Crete, Voutes University Campus, Heraklion,
Greece

Abstract. More and more companies have started to use nonhuman agents for employment interviews, making the selection process easier, faster, and unbiased. To assess the effectiveness of the above, in this paper, we systematically analyzed, reviewed, and compared human interaction with a social robot, a digital human, and another human under the same scenario simulating the first phase of a job interview. Our purpose is to allow the understanding of human reactions, concluding to a disclosure of the human needs towards human – nonhuman interaction. We also explored how the appearance and the physical presence of an agent can affect human perception, expectations, and emotions. To support our research, we used time-related and acoustic features of audio data, as well as psychometric data. Statistically significant differences were found for almost all extracted features and especially for intensity, speech rate, frequency, and response time. We also developed a Machine Learning model that can recognize the nature of the interlocutor a human interacts with. Although human was generally preferred, the interest level was higher and the shyness level was lower during human-robot interaction. Thus, we believe that, following some improvements, social robots, compared to digital humans, have the potential to act effectively as job interviewers.

Keywords: Social robots · Digital humans · Human reactions · Vocal behavior · Job interview

1 Introduction

We all have experienced, at least once in our life, the procedure of a job interview. Interviewers, up to now, used to be humans specialized for this job. But how we would have reacted if this job interview had been conducted by a robot or a digital human? Employment interviews have come to meet an accelerating digitalization during the last years, making the selection process easier and faster: digital interviews, psychometric online testing, even gamified assessments [1].

M. Kurosu (Ed.): HCII 2022, LNCS 13303, pp. 455–474, 2022.
https://doi.org/10.1007/978-3-031-05409-9_34

In a communication process, such as a job interview, the human factor can trigger unintentionally perceptual biases, influencing the fairness of the decisions. Consequently, this can affect the personnel diversity or the reputation of a company by reducing the practical and financial performance [2]. Here is where social robots and digital humans should help by doing what "people should do but cannot" as Seibt and Vestergaard supported in their study [3]. In this effort of removing implicit biases that can be provoked by visual cues such as gender, nationality, physical appearance, they provided an example proposing a teleoperated robot that can interact with people removing visual cues [3].

The advantage of a social robot over a digital human is the physical presence that can enhance positively the outcome. Studies up to now have demonstrated that a physical present robot can have a bigger influence on psychological responses than telepresent ones or virtual avatars [4]. The difference is in the existence of physical gestures, eye gaze, facial expressions, body direction. Eye gaze is one of the most important features of human behavior as it can serve several purposes and functions like enhancing attention, revealing emotional information, and preserving engagement. Therefore, it has been proved that the physical presence plays a great role in the gaze's perception and thus a robot's eye gaze can be more accurate than the one of a digital avatar [5].

In this effort to eliminate the biases and make the interview process faster and easier, at least in the first phase, robots and digital humans tend to replace the human physical presence. Are nonhuman agents in the position of offering more meritocratic interviews? And if yes, is it really what the candidates prefer? As a response to this, we conducted a study to examine human's reactions towards robot- and digital human-mediated job interviews. Participants interacted with the social humanoid robot Nadine, the digital human Nicole, and a human under the same scenario of the first phase of a job interview. To evaluate our research, we recorded audio data to examine time-related and acoustic features and we used a questionnaire to assess the psychological factors. The nonhuman agents' voice was also recorded to be compared with the humans' ones. Our purpose is to give an insight into how human vocal behavior change when interacting with a social robot or a digital human under a job interview scenario. Moreover, we want to explore the possibility of suggesting some guidelines that will help the design of nonhuman agents to better match the human voice and thus, facilitate the communication process.

1.1 Literature Review

Job interviews are inevitably exposed to implicit subjective biases as they concern usually a face-to-face communication between strangers [6]. Candidates' external appearance, nationality, gender, etc. can dominate their real qualifications and skills. Given that interviewers many times rely on their instinct, they can be affected by cultural similarities or emotional expressions and behavior. Several studies at an experimental level but also several companies have started trying nonhuman agent-mediated interviews to eliminate cues and biases, succeeding a more fair and consistent procedure. The world's first interview social robot and recruitment assistant is Tengai, the robotic head, designed and tested by Furhat Robotics and TNG [7]. Tengai has a database of several validated questions regarding personality and behavioral traits. Social robots have now started to be on the market as job interviewers, covering the lack of the physical presence a video conference or a virtual avatar have.

The potential of NAO robot to act as a job interviewer has also been examined, comparing human-robot interaction (HRI) with the human-human one, but measuring only the duration of human response [8]. The authors didn't manage to find significant differences. The same robot has also been tested in a different context, acting as a physician for a medical interview [9]. The evaluation was only through a questionnaire and participants stated that the social physical presence of the human doctor added more credibility to its role, and they felt comfortable to discuss with him. Credibility is a feature we need to add to nonhuman agents if we really want to enhance trust. Towards this direction, Elkins et al. have presented their plan of an upcoming experiment comparing the efficacy of digital humans as embodied conversational agents versus social humanoid robots [10]. According to these researchers, efficacy will be evaluated mainly through the capability of the agents to induce behavioral cues from human participants, considering that robots' physical presence may affect the outcome.

HireVue is another example of Artificial Intelligence used in the hiring process by the American market [11]. However, candidates have no physical contact with an agent, but they undergo a video interview where the software analyzes their answers, combined with their voice, body language, and facial expressions to decide if the person is suitable for the corresponding position.

To examine the efficacy of nonhuman agents as interviewers, it is important to see how they are perceived from a human point of view. Chapman and Rowe, some years ago, compared a video-based interview with a normal face-to-face one and found that the first one can reduce the anxiety of the participants, forcing them to have better performance [12]. Moreover, shy participants seem to prefer and have better results with computer-mediated communication rather than a direct human one [13]. It has been shown that this personal obscurity promotes a higher motivation to uncover personal information [14]. In this direction, a robot proxy was used in [6], first tested in [3] to examine a robot-mediated job interview. The interviewer and the candidate were never in contact but their voices, their head, and lip movements were transmitted via the robot and the reactions were assessed via a questionnaire. Surprisingly, they found that the robot-mediated is perceived as less fair, but participants felt the lack of the physical presence. In a study of a similar mentality, the authors asked participants to watch and assess a video of a job interview. An autonomous human-like avatar was used as an interviewer and the researchers examined if the level of computer science experience can play a role in the perception and persuasion of a computer-mediated interview [15].

We have found no company, up to now, using digital humans as interviewers [15]. It is of interest to examine if such a possibility could be effective. Virtual characters have mainly been used for training environments. Gebhard et al. examined the perception of people towards two human-like digital avatars of different personalities (polite and demanding respectively), with both verbal and nonverbal cues, acting as job recruiters [16]. The perception of the participants was measured with body, facial, and audio features. As expected, the highest level of stress was stated during the interaction with the demanding avatar, showing that the behavior of an agent can also play a role in the performance of humans during a job interview. The avatar used for this study was a part of the project TARDIS, based on a game-based experience, which aimed at the creation of digital avatars that can respond to humans with relevant verbal and nonverbal behaviors in the context of communication processes [17]. This platform can also be used for interview training. More gaming experience systems have been used to train people for job interviews [18, 19]. Another example of a virtual agent, able to be socially adapted and to emotionally react according to participants' reactions, was used as a recruiter by Youssef et al. [20]. They found that such kind of an agent can provide more naturalness and be more efficient. Participants showed progressively trust in the agent during the interview process, meaning that the adaptation takes time. In a similar work, an adaptive digital human was used as a recruiter which was responding to social cues by mainly imitating the participant [21].

Social robots have also been used for training purposes. Inoue et al. recently tested the humanoid robot ERICA as a job interviewer, targeting to train people for real interviews [22]. They tried to simulate as much as possible a normal human-human interview by generating follow-up questions based on the answers of the participants. They compared the effectiveness of the robot with the one of a digital human and evaluated the results with a questionnaire. Researchers still try to make progress with ERICA, as they try to find the optimal way to generate and follow a job interview [23]. Another example of android, although teleoperated, used for a job interview training is the one of Kumazaki et al. which was addressed to individuals with an autism spectrum disorder [24]. In general, it has been shown that robot-mediated interviews in adults, or even children, with special needs, have an advantage over human interviewers, finding participants more comfortable, familiar, and motivated [24, 25].

1.2 Research Questions

Robots and digital humans can undoubtedly support many roles, being consistent and precise, providing a constant work of high quality, on time, and without discrimination. However, in human-human interactions (HHI), additional features count. The current study aims to examine the acceptance, the provoked reactions, and the perception of these alternative ways of job interviews. Table 1 summarizes studies conducted under the context of a job interview and already applied systems in the same domain. Based on that, to the best of our knowledge, there is no research comparing Human-Computer Interaction (HCI), Human-Robot Interaction (HRI), and Human-Human Interaction (HHI) under the scenario of a job interview and thus, our first research question is:

RQ1: How do humans react in front of a robot- or a digital human-mediated job interview?

After having examined completely humans' reactions towards the three different conditions of the first phase of a job interview, we went a step further comparing the human vocal behavior with the corresponding features of the digital human and the robot. Our goal is to define some guidelines on how such an agent can speak more naturally and humanly, facilitating the procedure for a potential candidate. Thus, our third research question is:

RQ2: What voice/sound features can make an agent speak in a more human-like way, being more approachable and acceptable?

Table 1. Summary of human-robot and human-computer studies as well as already applied systems in the context of a job interview (HRI: Human-Robot Interaction, Hum: Humanoid robot, HVI: Human-Voice Interaction, HHI: Human-Human Interaction)

WORK	OBJECTIVE	FEATURES					CONCLUSIONS
		HRI	Hum	HAI	HVI	HHI	
Inoue et al. (2020) [23]	Comparison between an android (ERICA) and a virtual agent for job interview training	✓	✓	✓	✗	✗	Similar results for both agents, with the virtual one lacking the physical presence - Evaluation only through a questionnaire
Kumazaki et al. (2019) [24]	Use of an android to train non-verbal skills for a job interview	✓	✓	✗	✗	✓	Test to individuals with autism spectrum disorder. High motivation during HRI
Ahmad et al. (2018) [8]	Examining the potential of a NAO robot as job interviewer	✓	✗	✗	✗	✓	No significant results -Measurement only of the duration of human response
Furhat Robotics and TNG (2018) [7]	Tengai - Robot intentionally designed to perform job interviews	✓	✗	✗	✗	✗	First robot specifically designed for job interviews
Youssef et al. (2015) [20]	A socially adaptive virtual agent used as a job recruiter	✗	✗	✓	✗	✗	An adaptive agent ensures more naturalness and better results, but the adaptation takes time
Gebhard et al. (2014) [16]	Study of human perception towards digital humans acting as job recruiters	✗	✗	✓	✗	✗	The behavior of the character has an impact on participants' feelings and reactions
Money et al. (2007) [11]	HireVue – already used AI video interview software	✗	✗	✗	✓	✗	Already used system by the American market
Our work	Comparison of a human, a robot, and a digital human as interviewers	✓	✓	✓	✓	✓	

2   Materials and Methods

2.1   Experimental Design

40 participants (10 female, 30 male), aging from 21 to 65 years old and of several nationalities engaged in our experiment. We selected participants who have no previous experience with robots or similar advanced technology, and of different ages to exclude any kind of bias.

During the experiment, participants experienced three types of interaction, under the same scenario: 1. Interaction with another human (H-H), 2. Interaction with the social robot Nadine (H-N), 3. Interaction with the digital human Nicole (VH).

Fig. 1. LEFT: Example of a participant interacting with the social robot. RIGHT: the two nonhuman agents used in our experiment, Nadine the digital human and Nicole the social robot.

An example of the setup and the nonhuman agents used is presented in Fig. 1. The scenario simulated the first phase of a job interview, where participants had to answer several predefined questions and present themselves. The flow of the interview was based on several predefined thematic areas (TAs) but the sequence of questions and TAs was unique for each agent. The sequence of the interactions was different for each participant to exclude any possible bias and surprise caused by the robot. The whole procedure took place in an isolated room, where external noises were excluded. Our research was held at the Nanyang Technological University (NTU), in the Institute of Media and Innovation (IMI) in Singapore. All the conversations were in English. Our participants though were from different cultural backgrounds, so each style of communication was slightly different.

To examine the acceptance, the provoked reactions, and the perception of these alternative ways of job interviews, we recorded the human vocal behavior and emotional states. The voice of all participants as well as of the three agents was recorded, and we extracted time-related and acoustic features. Firstly, we compared the data among the three interactions to find the differences in human perception and the possible mood shifts. Then, we compared the data extracted from HHI with the ones from the non-human agents, concluding to some guidelines on if and what we could change on an avatar or a robot to speak in a more natural, human-like way. Moreover, an additional feature extraction based on the "pyAudioAnalysis" library in Python was performed on the audio samples to train a K-Nearest Neighbor (KNN) classifier. The latter was trained to categorize the human voice based on the nature of the interlocutor (human, robot, digital human).

Social Robot Nadine and Digital Human Nicole Platform. Nadine the social robot and Nicole the virtual human share the same architecture. They comprise three layers, namely, perception, processing, and interaction layer. Both of them receive audio and visual stimuli from the microphone and 3D camera to perceive user characteristics and her environment, which are then sent to the processing layer. The processing layer is the core module that receives all results from the perception layer about the environment and user to act upon them. Finally, the action/interaction layer consists of a dedicated Agent controller which includes emotion expression, lips synchronization, and gaze generation. The main difference is that Nadine's controller generates physical gestures and Nicole's controller generates gestures as animation. Nadine Controller and Nicole Controller have a similar component – Text to Speech which makes their voice similar.

This architecture allows for modularity in each layer (submodules can be added or removed), task, or environment-based customizations (for example, change in knowledge database). The architecture can be easily deployed to work with other robots and virtual characters by changing the interaction hardware layer. Different gestures and animations can be included in the architecture to help the social robot/virtual human to complete any tasks. This architecture allows Nadine and Nicole to express human-like emotions, personality, behaviors, dialog, etc. and they are capable of perceiving both user/ environmental cues and responding to them in a natural realistic manner.

2.2   Audio Recordings and Analysis

For the recording of the sessions, we used an easy-to-use portable recorder called Zoom H1 Handy recorder. The audio was saved in a.wav format, 24-bit, with a sampling rate of 44.1 kHz. The participants were recorded in a sitting position. The duration of each recording varied for each interaction and each participant from 2 to 6 min.

For the analysis, we used Praat software [26] and Matlab. The pre-processing analysis was conducted in Matlab to clean the possible noise and then, the filtered signal was imported to Praat for further analysis. We annotated the data based on the questions and the TAs and we examined each question/answer separately. For each question, we worked with segments of 40.000 samples each. We examined time-related conversational features and prosodic/acoustic ones as shown in Table 2. The rationale behind the selection of these voice features was based on already established associations with human emotions, like frequency, timing, and volume [27] and already efficiently used vocal features [28–30].

Table 2. Acoustic/Prosodic and Conversational Features used. Yellow: time-related features, Grey: Frequency-related features and Volume, Blue: Acoustic Features

Acoustic / Prosodic Features			Conversational Features		
Human		Agent	Human		Agent
Duration of each answer	T		Voice breaks	VB	
Total duration of each interaction	TD		Response time		Rt
Pause duration	PD		Speechrate (nsyll/sec)		Sr
Fundamental Frequency		F0			
Minimum Fundamental Frequency		F0min			
Maximum Fundamental Frequency		F0max			
Formants		F1, F2			
Intensity		I			
Pulses		Pl			
Jitter		J			
Shimmer		S			
Harmonicity (Harmonics-to-noise ratio)		HNR			

Machine Learning Classification Analysis. To complement the above and to highlight the differences in the vocal behavior, we developed a machine learning (ML) model that can recognize the nature of the interlocutor a human speaks with, taking as input the human vocal behavior. We kept the separation of our data in three classes, according to the nature of the interlocutor.

Participants' reactions to the job interview questions were recorded and labeled according to the nature of the interlocutor. The audio recordings were divided into short-term windows of 100 ms and, for each, a total of 34 distinct features were extracted. Eventually, for each recording, features of each window were combined to compute feature statistics like standard deviation and average values and in total, we have 136 distinct features per sample. To facilitate our work, we used the "pyAudioAnalysis" library in python to extract the audio features [31]. Audio acoustic features both from the time and frequency domain were used. Having verified that all features follow a Gaussian distribution, data were standardized. Subsequently, multiple dimensionality reduction methods were compared to find which one best suited our needs, namely Principal Component Analysis (PCA), Singular Value Decomposition (SVD), Linear Discriminant Analysis (LDA), Isomap Embedding (ISO), and Locally Linear Embedding (LLE). After each reduction, a Support Vector Machine Classifier (SVM) with Radial Basis Function

(RBF) kernel was fitted to the data. Results were acquired via the Stratified 10-Fold Cross Validation (CV) to compare the dimensionality reduction methods. Finally, LDA was selected since it significantly outperformed all other methods.

Regarding the classification task, numerous classification algorithms were compared such as Support Vector Machines, Decision Tree Classifiers and K-nearest Neighbors (KNN) classifiers. To compare them, a 10-Fold Stratified Cross Validation (CV) was employed. Eventually, the KNN classifier with $K = 15$ (number of neighbors) outperformed the others.

Finally, a comparison of the dimensionality reduction methods was repeated using the selected classifier, which verified that LDA outran the other methods in our task. To describe the performance of the classifier and the dimensionality reduction method the precision, recall, and F1-score were extracted.

2.3 Psychometric Data

To complement the audio data, we used a validated questionnaire to assess human emotions and the overall experience of the interactions. The emotion scale was based on the Positive and Negative Affect Schedule with two scales: one measuring positive affect and the other measuring negative. The emotions were based on the emotions scale PANAS X [32].

2.4 Statistics

Statistical analysis was carried out for the audio variables and the questionnaire through SPSS. First, we conducted a Pearson correlation for the questions/thematic areas of each feature for each case, so that we can find the interrelationship among them. Then, we conducted repeated measures ANOVAs for each question of each feature among the three cases as well as a general repeated measures ANOVA for the whole duration of the interview for each feature for each case. A further analysis was carried out concerning possible influences due to gender and nationality but due to the imbalance in the gender of our sample, we decided to not include it. The ANOVA's statistically significant results were followed up by the Bonferroni post-hoc tests. In the rare case where the data did not meet the sphericity requirement, Greenhouse-Geisser and Huynh-Feldt corrections were applied. In the end, we followed the same procedure to assess the differences between the human-human case and the non-human agents.

3 Results

3.1 Audio Data

Time-Related Features. Time – related prosodic and conversational features include the duration of each answer, the total duration of each interaction, the pause duration, voice breaks, response time and speechrate. Table 3 depicts the results for each interaction with their descriptive statistics.

Specifically, firstly we examined the duration of each response. This includes strictly the time starting when participants began to reply to the question until their last word. Expressions of hesitation or uncertainty at the beginning of a response were considered. The longest average time for an answer was noted during H-H interaction with a significant difference among the three interactions (F (2,54) = 44.100, p = < .001, η^2 = .620). Post hoc comparisons indicated that there is a significant difference both between H-H and H-N and, H-H and H-VH. The total duration of each interaction includes the welcome and the goodbye of the agent. H-VH interaction presented the longest total duration of all interactions and was found significantly different from H-H and H-N with p = 0.018 and p < .001 respectively. In general, a significant difference among the three interactions was found (F (2, 54) = 7.805, p = .001, η^2 = .224).

Pause duration refers to the average value of all the pauses done during a participant's speech. We noticed the lower average value during H-H interaction. A significant difference for the three interactions was found (F (2,54) = 4.699, p = 0.013, η^2 = .148) but the post hoc comparisons showed small differences between the pair of groups for the three cases.

In Praat software, voice breaks are described as "the number of distances between consecutive pulses" [26]. H-H presents the highest value and there is a significant difference among the three interactions, (F (1.3, 35.9) = 31.863, p < .001, η^2 = .541). Post hoc comparisons verified the high significance.

Response time refers to the time participants needed to answer a question, starting directly after the end of the agent's sentence until the first sign of response. The lower value was found for H-H whereas in nonhuman interaction the value was significantly higher (F (2,54) = 49.411, p < .001, η^2 = .662). Pairwise analysis showed a difference between H-H and H-N and H-H and H-VH (p < .001 for both). This feature was also examined in the speech of nonhuman agents. The comparison between humans' responses in H-H and the responses of the agents (Nadine, Nicole) showed a significant difference with F (2,54) = 53.828 and p < .001.

Lastly, we examined the speech rate, as the number of syllables per second. The feature presented a significant difference among the interactions (F (2,54) = 11.230, p < .001, η^2 = .294) and the post-hoc comparisons specified them between H-H and H-N as well as between H-N and H-VH. As before, we conducted the comparison between humans' and agents' responses and we found a significant difference among the interactions, F (2,54) = 10.422, p < .001 and η^2 = .278. Post hoc comparisons showed that VH showed significant differences with both other interactions which means that Nicole had a faster speech rate compared to human participants, as well as to Nadine.

Frequency-Related Features and Intensity. As frequency-related features, we extracted the fundamental frequency (F0), the minimum and the maximal value of it (Fmin, Fmax), the first two formants (F1, F2), and the intensity (I). Table 4 presents the results of all the interactions and their descriptive statistics. All features were also extracted from the voice of nonhuman agents.

F0 represents the main frequency used for the transmission of speech and can be related to pitch. Although the frequency is directly related to gender, we took the average value to compare the three interactions. There is a significant difference among the three interaction (F (2, 52) = 33.953, p < .001, η^2 = .566), specifically between H-H and

Table 3. Summary of the descriptive statistics for the acoustic/prosodic and conversational time-relates features

Features	Interac-tions	Mean	SD	p		Agents	Mean	SD	p
Time (sec)	H-H	15.754	4.159						
	H-N	10.464	4.501	<.001					
	H-VH	10.396	4.046						
Total Duration (min)	H-H	3.563	0.920						
	H-N	3.347	1.121	=.001					
	H-VH	4.006	1.081						
Pause Duration (sec)	H-H	0.229	0.059						
	H-N	0.272	0.116	=.013					
	H-VH	0.279	0.124						
Voice Breaks	H-H	30	8						
	H-N	20	9	<.001					
	H-VH	19	8						
Response Time (sec)	H-H	1.147	0.353						
	H-N	2.018	0.545	<.001		NA	1.960	0.599	<.001
	H-VH	2.082	0.765			VH	2.174	0.388	
Speechrate (nsyll/sec)	H-H	3.570	0.352						
	H-N	3.260	0.412	<.001		NA	3.737	0.651	<.001
	H-VH	3.467	0.507			VH	4.474	0.840	

H-VH (p = 0.035) and marginally between H-H and H-N (p = 0.045). Furthermore, we conducted the comparison between humans' and agents' reactions, and we saw that the average value of Nadine's voice was equal to the women's voice but the one of Nicole was significantly higher. The difference between them and the average human value was significant (F (2,54) = 115.623, p < .001, η^2 = .811) with a significance between every pair of interactions.

Given that the differences in frequencies are expected, as the anatomy between women and men is different, we were interested mainly in the changes during the procedure and among the interactions. That is, to assess how and if we adapt to each thematic area and to see if we are affected by our interlocutor. To complete this, we examined the *minimum* and the *maximum* of the F0 range to see the extent of our pitch. It is of interest that the minimum frequency is almost the same for the three interactions. There is no significant difference among the interactions but there is one between humans and agents (F (2,54) = 67.593, p < .001, η^2 = .715). Contrariwise, the maximum value of F0 (Fmax) found to be significant among the interactions (F (2,54) = 12.845, p < .001, η^2 = .322) and post-hoc comparisons showed differences between all pairs with p < .001. Finally, we found a significant difference between the agents and the human (F (2,54) = 27.747, p < .001, η^2 = .593).

Likewise, we examined the first two formants F1 and F2. Formants are frequency peak in the spectrum of the acoustic resonance of the human vocal tract [33]. Regarding the F1, there is a significant difference among the three interactions (F (2,54) = 4.283, p = 0.019, η^2 = .137), and as the post hoc tests indicated, this difference is between H-H and H-VH (p = .021). No significant difference was reported between humans and agents. Regarding F2, which depends on the shape of the mouth and the oral cavity, there

Table 4. Summary of the descriptive statistics for the frequency-related features

Features	Interactions	Mean	SD	p		Agents	Mean	SD	p
F0 (Hz)	H-H	137.710	18.176						
	H-N	144.316	29.600	<.001		NA	180.151	10.553	<.001
	H-VH	144.456	28.817			VH	193.689	10.915	
Fmin (Hz)	H-H	103.719	11.339						
	H-N	106.306	21.134	=.331		NA	132.119	16.132	<.001
	H-VH	102.131	14.737			VH	147.156	13.397	
Fmax (Hz)	H-H	187.537	30.494						
	H-N	212.710	44.942	<.001		NA	224.033	15.979	<.001
	H-VH	220.310	49.212			VH	239.566	32.425	
F1 (Hz)	H-H	586.832	37.287						
	H-N	602.247	27.488	=.019		NA	594.287	45.120	=.521
	H-VH	606.503	24.368			VH	587.325	46.833	
F2 (Hz)	H-H	1785.901	78.427						
	H-N	1742.359	81.141	=.015		NA	1883.986	81.597	<.001
	H-VH	1726.560	65.451			VH	1889.870	83.645	
I (dB)	H-H	39.623	1.834						
	H-N	43.695	3.368	<.001		NA	45.861	3.023	<.001
	H-VH	47.550	4.079			VH	45.238	3.407	

is a significant difference among all interactions (F (1.26, 34.18) = 5.854, p = 0.015, η^2 = .178), specifically between H-H and H-VH (p = .003). Both agents presented similar values and the comparison with the humans' values showed a significance (F (2,54) = 12.583, p < .001, η^2 = .318) between H and N (p < .001) and, H and VH (p = .002).

The last frequency-related feature is the one of the intensity, or volume. There was a great statistical significance among the three cases (F (2,54) = 113.454, p < .001, η^2 = .808), which was confirmed by the post-hoc tests: H-H and H-N (p < .001), H-H and H-VH (p < .001) and, H-N and H-VH (p < .001). For the human-agent comparison, we also got a significance difference (F (2,54) = 39.607, p < .001, η^2 = .595), specifically for H and N (p < .001) and for H and VH (p < .001) which means that both agents tended to speak a bit louder than the humans.

Acoustic Features. Lastly, as acoustic features, we extracted the jitter, shimmer, Harmonics-to-Noise Ratio (HNR), and pulses. Jitter and shimmer have successfully been used in describing the vocal characteristics. Table 5 summarizes the results for the three interactions and their descriptive statistics.

Jitter (J) refers to frequency perturbation which can imply irregularities in the duration of the signal [34]. We found no significant difference among interactions. However, we found a significant difference between Nadine, Nicole, and the humans (F (2.54) = 39.069, p < .001, η^2 = .591) and pairwise comparisons specified it between every pair of interactions. The lower the value of the J, the better. We see that the J of agents is lower compared to humans' response. This is normal, as the human factor and human emotions can affect the human voice compared to the programmed voice of the robot and the avatar. Shimmer, on the other hand, refers to amplitude perturbations. The difference among the three interactions was significant (F (2,54) = 30.310, p < .001, η^2 =

.529) and post-hoc analysis indicated the difference between H-H and H-N (p < .001) as well as H-H and H-VH (p < .001). Although the acoustic features we have chosen are dependent on the human anatomy, we also measured the shimmer for the two agents so that we can conduct the comparisons. The difference between them was found to be significant (p < .001) as well as their difference with the humans (F (2,54) = 69.719, p < .001, η^2 = .721). Although jitter and shimmer are normally measured in a steady voice for each vowel separately, we used the average for the whole voice duration to serve better our purposes.

Table 5. Summary of the descriptive statistics for the acoustic features

Features	Interactions	Mean	SD	p		Agents	Mean	SD	p
Jitter (%)	H-H	1.001%	0.081%						
	H-N	1.002%	0.093%	=.541		NA	0.676%	0.023%	<.001
	H-VH	0.903%	0.101%			VH	0.488%	0.021%	
Shimmer (%)	H-H	13.78%	1.04%						
	H-N	11.84%	2.00%	<.001		NA	17.772%	1.016%	<.001
	H-VH	12.28%	1.58%			VH	15.775%	1.390%	
HNR	H-H	8.314	0.812						
	H-N	9.583	1.692	<.001		NA	6.423	0.770	<.001
	H-VH	9.475	1.503			VH	8.150	1.097	
Pulses	H-H	110	13						
	H-N	114	23	=.438		NA	157	17	<.001
	H-VH	113	22			VH	167	19	

HNR describes the degree of acoustic periodicity, which means that portrays the relationship of two components: the periodic component and the noise [35]. It is usually used to diagnose voice pathological disorders but, in our case, it can be used to demonstrate any kind of perturbation. We found a significant difference among all interactions (F (2,54) = 29.466, p < .001, η^2 = .522) and post-hoc comparisons specified the difference between H-H and H-N and, H-H and H-VH (p < .001). The comparison between humans and agents gave us also significant results (F (2,54) = 35.772, p < .001 and η^2 = .570) with post hoc analysis to indicate that the differences are between H and both N and VH. We can see that Nicole's value is similar to the human's one.

Lastly, the pulse implies the rhythm of the speech. We found no noteworthy differences among the interactions, not even for the questions. The difference between humans and agents was clearly significant (F (2,54) = 100.597, p < .001, η^2 = .788), and our post-hoc analysis showed us the exact differences between H and NA (p < .001) and between H and VH (p < .001).

Machine Learning Model. We developed an ML pipeline that successfully separates our data into 3 clusters, proving that from voice data we can actually distinguish whether somebody is talking to a Human, a Robot, or a Digital Human. The pipeline consists of the LDA dimensionality reduction method and the KNN classifier, as described in the methodology. The former transforms the data to a latent space where they are more easily separable, and the latter finds the best function to fit over the data. Figure 2 shows an approximation of the decision regions of the KNN classifier over the whole dataset. The decision region helps the understanding of how the classifier has decided to divide the input feature space by class label.

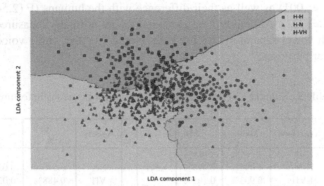

Fig. 2. Results from the KNN classification (decision boundaries) of the two LDA voice features in the three classes with K = 15.

To find the optimal K for the KNN classifier, a 10-Fold CV was employed. The value of K = 15 delivered the most satisfying results. The results of the final model are Precision: 0.818 ± 0.044, Recall: 0.822 ± 0.043, and F1-score: 0.816 ± 0.044.

3.2 Psychometric Data

Seven positive and negative discrete emotions were measured: interested, confident, calm and afraid, nervous, ashamed, surprised respectively. In the meantime, we evaluated participants' perception towards the interviewers.

As it can be seen from Fig. 3a, positive emotions have higher values compared to negative ones. However, we see that H-VH maintained the lowest level of all positive emotions but only the interest showed a significant difference with the other interactions. Although participants felt more confident discussing with the human, the level of calmness presented no significant difference among the three conditions.

On the other hand, the participants felt clearly most surprised during their interaction with the social robot, whereas H-H and H-VH presented the same level of surprise (1.925 and 2.175 respectively). For the fear and the nervousness, there are no significant differences among the interactions, although H-VH had surprisingly the lowest score. Lastly, we noticed that participants felt shyer in front of the other human than the nonhuman agents, with a significant difference.

Figure 3b depicts participants' perception towards their interlocutor/interviewer. The human agent was voted as the most sociable and friendly and consequently less hostile. On the other hand, Nicole was perceived as less friendly and less sociable, whereas Nadine was the one presenting the highest level of hostility, with no significant difference from Nicole.

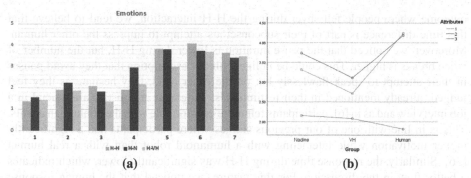

Fig. 3. Left (a): Differences in positive and negative emotions among the three groups. 1 = Afraid, 2 = nervous, 3 = shy, 4 = surprised, 5 = interested, 6 = confident, 7 = calm. Right (b): Mean scores on attributes of the different agents. Attributes' legend: 1 = sociable, 2 = friendly, 3 = hostile

At the end of the questionnaire, participants were asked to evaluate, in words, the performance of each interviewer and to select the most suitable for a job interview. Moreover, their need to change the way and the content of their replies among the three cases was also noted. 76% of the participants felt this need among the interactions. The testimonials were in line with each other, highlighting the lack of naturalness of the two agents. Although they stated that sometimes they felt more comfortable and less nervous discussing with the social robot or the digital human, they found that they need improvements in their reactions. 84.21% of the participants chose the human as the most suitable job interviewer, 10.53% the avatar, and 5.26% the social robot.

4   Discussion and Future Work

In this study, we investigated the potential of nonhuman agents to be used as job interviewers in the first phase of an interview and the human reactions towards such a case. Participants faced three different interactions under the same scenario, allowing us to compare the human natural interaction with a human-robot and a human-avatar one. To evaluate our study, we used audio recordings to assess how different conditions affect human vocal behavior and based on our results, we extracted some guidelines on how an agent's voice can match more naturally the human voice, facilitating the communication process. To validate the above, we also used a questionnaire to assess seven discreet positive and negative emotions. To the best of our knowledge, no previous research has compared these three interactions in the context of a job interview, providing a physical interaction and using a realistic humanoid. We want to believe that our work can support new insights in the human-robot and human-computer interactions as well as their applications.

Our results answer firstly our first research question: *How do humans react in front of a robot- or a digital human-mediated job interview?* We recorded several time-related, frequency-related, and acoustic features and we found a lot of significant differences among the three interactions. First, we noticed that participants spent more time to their answers when interacting with another human. Based also on the questionnaire's outcome where people felt shyer during the H-H interaction, we tend to believe that this time difference is part of their subconscious attempt to impress the other human. Moreover, we noticed that the pause duration is lower during H-H, but the number of voice breaks is higher. This could be in line with our assumption that they avoid pauses in their attempt to speak flawlessly but on the other hand, they hesitate as they feel judged; already mentioned in their testimonials. Judgment and justice are crucial in a job interview and as in [6], participants felt more comfortable with the nonhuman agents. This is in line with one of our previous studies where participants had a significantly higher motivation while interacting with a humanoid robot than with a real human [36]. Similarly, the response time during H-H was significantly lower, which indicates a better flow in the discussion. For this feature, we noticed that the human response was correlated to the agent's response, and we started wondering if our responses are influenced by our interlocutors. To confirm this assumption, we conducted a Pearson correlation for this feature, as shown in Fig. 4, and we found that the higher the response time of the interviewer the higher the value of the participant as well. The same result we noticed for the speech rate but not with such a strong correlation. The highest value of Sr was detected during H-H which means that we tend to speak faster with other people (Fig. 4).

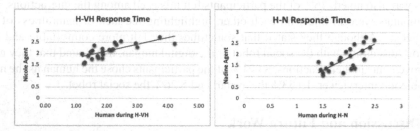

Fig. 4. Response time between the participant and the agent. Pearson r correlation coefficient is equal to 0.744 and 0.740 from left to right.

Of interest is the change in the frequency while interacting with the agents. To make the comparison easier, we used the average value of frequency, men and women included. We took into account that both agents are females, so the comparison is not equal. However, the significant result is that frequency is lower when we speak with humans and higher when we speak with nonhuman agents. We also noticed that the lower values of F presented no significant difference, but the maximum values do. Intensity gave us also interesting results as we found that participants tend to speak louder when interacting with Nadine or Nicole. That could be a sign of stress, but it can also be linked with the fact that participants felt a higher level of shyness interacting with the human. Shyness can decrease the volume. Apparently, the nature of the agent played a role in the human responses as e.g., participants spoke slower and softer to Nadine compared to Nicole.

Lastly, we examined acoustic features to find any perturbations in the voice. Although jitter gave us no significant differences, shimmer was found higher during H-H interaction. HNR is considered a sensitive index of vocal function. In our study, the highest value of HNR was found for the H-N interaction whereas the lowest one for H-H. HNR is also related to hoarseness; the lower the value of HNR, the higher the level of hoarseness [37]. So, we can conclude that participants tend to present some hoarseness while interacting with the human.

In summary, when interacting with nonhuman agents compared to another human in a context of a job interview, we tend to give shorter answers with longer pauses and to speak slower. The frequency and the intensity of the voice are higher, especially the high frequencies. Perturbations in amplitude are less and the value of HNR is bigger. In general, differences in vocal behavior were obvious among the three interactions and that was verified by our classification model.

Our second question is *What voice/sound features can make an agent speak in a more human-like way, being more approachable and acceptable?* We think that it would be very useful to give some guidelines, based on our results, on how an agent can ensure a more natural conversation. Given that we also verified the correlation of some features between humans and agents, we believe that these suggestions would be of a need for a successful interaction. However, these propositions are made based on the features of our nonhuman agents. In general, there is a need of decreasing the values of features like the speech rate, the intensity, the pulses, and the response time to match human voice. The latter needs to be fast enough to keep the discussion in a flowing manner as apparently, our vocal behavior is affected by the response time and the speechrate of our interlocutor. Frequency should follow the need of the relevant task as it depends also on the gender. However, we noticed that the agents are not in the "natural" range of pitch as the low values of frequency are not low enough based on the humans. Thus, a more natural frequency range is of need.

To conclude, interacting with a non-human agent, compared to a real human, triggers different vocal responses in features like intensity, speech rate, response time, and frequency. Moreover, human voice during H-H interaction presents a broader range of values that ensure the normality and the flow, and it is the main point missing from the non-human interaction. Our ML model verified the above as vocal behavior was classified in each interaction with an F1 score of 82%, meaning that our voice is clearly affected by our interlocutor. However, participants felt significantly shyer being interviewed by another real human. The high level of surprise during H-N interaction can be considered in line with our previous work where participants presented the highest motivation while interacting with the humanoid Nadine than with real humans [36]. Surprisingly, questions affected differently our participants during each interaction.

Summing up, this study aims to provide insights regarding human vocal behavior change when interacting with a social robot or an avatar, in a job interview context. Given the proliferation of the use of nonhuman agents in a professional context, such as that of a job interview, we believe that our outcome can help the development and adaptation of job interview systems, as well as future applications of human-robot and human-computer interaction in general. Although technological advances up-to-date do not allow social robots and digital humans to act as job interviewers in full capacity, we argue that studying human reactions in such a context can provide an understanding and meaningful implications for future research in this direction. This is supported by the fact that 72% of the participants admitted to being more comfortable and less nervous discussing with the social robot or the digital human, thus demonstrating the advantages of adapting non-human agents to better match the human voice, facilitating a more natural interaction. We hope that our work will motivate researchers to continue towards this direction of direct comparison between human and nonhuman interactions, covering possible limitations like the use of an adaptive nonhuman agent or the study of digital humans in Virtual Reality.

Acknowledgment. This research is partly supported by the National Research Foundation, Singapore under its International Research Centers in Singapore Funding Initiative, and Institute for Media Innovation, Nanyang Technological University (IMI-NTU). Any opinions, findings and conclusions or recommendations expressed in this material are those of the author(s) and do not reflect the views of National Research Foundation, Singapore.

References

1. Woods, S.A., Ahmed, S., Nikolaou, I., Costa, A.C., Anderson, N.R.: Personnel selection in the digital age: a review of validity and applicant reactions, and future research challenges. Europ. J. Work Organ. Psychol. **29**, 64–77 (2020)
2. Homan, A.C., Van Knippenberg, D., Van Kleef, G.A., De Dreu, C.K.W.: Bridging faultlines by valuing diversity: diversity beliefs, information elaboration, and performance in diverse work groups. J. Appl. Psychol. **92**, 1189 (2007)
3. Seibt, J., Vestergaard, C.: Fair proxy communication: using social robots to modify the mechanisms of implicit social cognition. Research Ideas and Outcomes **4**, e31827 (2018)
4. Li, J.: The benefit of being physically present: a survey of experimental works comparing copresent robots, telepresent robots and virtual agents. Int. J. Hum.-Comput. Stud. **77**, 23–37 (2015)
5. Mollahosseini, A., Abdollahi, H., Sweeny, T.D., Cole, R., Mahoor, M.H.: Role of embodiment and presence in human perception of robots' facial cues. Int. J. Hum.-Comput. Stud. **116**, 25–39 (2018)
6. Nørskov, S., Damholdt, M.F., Ulhøi, J.P., Jensen, M.B., Ess, C., Seibt, J.: Applicant fairness perceptions of a robot-mediated job interview: a video vignette-based experimental survey. Frontiers in Robotics and AI. Frontiers, **163** (2020)
7. Savage, M.: Meet Tengai, the job interview robot who won't judge you. BBC Oline 12 (2019)
8. Ahmad, M.I., Mubin, O., Patel, H.: Exploring the potential of NAO robot as an interviewer. In: Proceedings of the 6th International Conference on Human-Agent Interaction, pp. 324–326 (2018)
9. Edwards, A., Omilion-Hodges, L., Edwards, C.: How do patients in a medical interview perceive a robot versus human physician? In: Proceedings of the companion of the 2017 ACM/IEEE International Conference on Human-Robot Interaction, pp. 109–110 (2017)
10. Elkins, A.C., Gupte, A., Cameron, L.: Humanoid robots as interviewers for automated credibility assessment. In: Nah, F.F.-H., Siau, K. (eds.) HCII 2019, vol. 11589, pp. 316–325. Springer, Cham (2019). https://doi.org/10.1007/978-3-030-22338-0_26
11. HireVue Full Platform. hirevue.com (2022). https://www.hirevue.com/demo/full-platfo rm-em. Accessed 8 Feb
12. Chapman, D.S., Rowe, P.M.: The impact of videoconference technology, interview structure, and interviewer gender on interviewer evaluations in the employment interview: a field experiment. J. Occup. Organ. Psychol. **74**, 279–298 (2001)
13. Stritzke, W.G.K., Nguyen, A., Durkin, K.: Shyness and computer-mediated communication: a self-presentational theory perspective. Media Psychol. **6**, 1–22 (2004)

14. Joinson, A.N.: Self-disclosure in computer-mediated communication: the role of self-awareness and visual anonymity. European journal of social psychology **31**, 177–192 (2001)
15. Langer, M., König, C.J., Fitili, A.: Information as a double-edged sword: the role of computer experience and information on applicant reactions towards novel technologies for personnel selection. Comput. Hum. Behav. **81**, 19–30 (2018)
16. Gebhard, P., Baur, T., Damian, I., Mehlmann, G., Wagner, J., André, E.: Exploring interaction strategies for virtual characters to induce stress in simulated job interviews. In: Proceedings of the 2014 International Conference on Autonomous Agents and Multi-agent Systems, pp. 661–668 (2014)
17. Anderson, K.: The TARDIS framework: intelligent virtual agents for social coaching in job interviews. In: Reidsma, D., Katayose, H., Nijholt, A. (eds.) ACE 2013. LNCS, vol. 8253, pp. 476–491. Springer, Cham (2013). https://doi.org/10.1007/978-3-319-03161-3_35
18. Gebhard, P., et al.: Serious games for training social skills in job interviews. IEEE Trans. Games **11**, 340–351 (2018)
19. Georgiou, K., Gouras, A., Nikolaou, I.: Gamification in employee selection: the development of a gamified assessment. Int. J. Selection Assessment **27**, 91–103 (2019)
20. Youssef, B., Atef, M.C., Jones, H., Sabouret, N., Pelachaud, C., Ochs, M.: Towards a socially adaptive virtual agent. In: International Conference on Intelligent Virtual Agents, pp. 3–16. Springer, Cham (2015). https://doi.org/10.1007/978-3-319-21996-7_1
21. Baur, T., Damian, I., Gebhard, P., Porayska-Pomsta, K., André, E.: A job interview simulation: Social cue-based interaction with a virtual character. In: 2013 International Conference on Social Computing, pp. 220–227. IEEE (2013)
22. Kawahara, T.: Spoken dialogue system for a human-like conversational robot ERICA. In: D'Haro, L.F., Banchs, R.E., Li, H. (eds.) 9th International Workshop on Spoken Dialogue System Technology. LNEE, vol. 579, pp. 65–75. Springer, Cham (2019). https://doi.org/10.1007/978-981-13-9443-0_6
23. Inoue, K., Hara, K., Lala, D., Nakamura, S., Takanashi, K., Kawahara, T.: A job interview dialogue system with autonomous android ERICA. In: Increasing Naturalness and Flexibility in Spoken Dialogue Interaction: 10th International Workshop on Spoken Dialogue Systems, pp. 291–297. Springer Singapore. https://doi.org/10.1007/978-981-15-9323-9_25
24. Kumazaki, H., et al.: Job interview training targeting nonverbal communication using an android robot for individuals with autism spectrum disorder. Autism **23**, 1586–1595 (2019)
25. Wood, L.J., Dautenhahn, K., Lehmann, H., Robins, B., Rainer, A., Syrdal, D.S.: Robot-mediated interviews: Do robots possess advantages over human interviewers when talking to children with special needs? In: Herrmann, G., Pearson, M.J., Lenz, A., Bremner, P., Spiers, A., Leonards, U. (eds.) ICSR 2013, vol. 8239, pp. 54–63. Springer, Cham (2013). https://doi.org/10.1007/978-3-319-02675-6_6
26. Wilson, I.: Using Praat and Moodle for teaching segmental and suprasegmental pronunciation. In: Proceedings of the 3rd international WorldCALL Conference: Using Technologies for Language Learning (WorldCALL 2008) (2008)
27. Crumpton, J., Bethel, C.L.: A survey of using vocal prosody to convey emotion in robot speech. Int. J. Soc. Robot. **8**, 271–285 (2016)
28. Poria, S., Cambria, E., Bajpai, R., Hussain, A.: A review of affective computing: From unimodal analysis to multimodal fusion. Inf. Fusion **37**, 98–125 (2017)
29. Dasgupta, P.B.: Detection and analysis of human emotions through voice and speech pattern processing. arXiv preprint arXiv:1710.10198 (2017)
30. Johnstone, T.: The effect of emotion on voice production and speech acoustics. Thesis Commons (2017)
31. Giannakopoulos, T.: Pyaudioanalysis: An open-source python library for audio signal analysis. PloS One **10**, e0144610 (2015)

32. Watson, D., Clark, L.A.: The PANAS-X: Manual for the positive and negative affect schedule-expanded form (1999)
33. Abhang, P.A., Gawali, B.W., Mehrotra, S.C.: Technological basics of EEG recording and operation of apparatus. Introduction to EEG-and Speech-Based Emotion Recognition, pp. 19–50 . Academic Press (2016)
34. Teixeira, J.P., Oliveira, C., Lopes, C.: Vocal acoustic analysis–jitter, shimmer and hnr parameters. Procedia Technol. **9**, 1112–1122 (2013)
35. de Felippe, A.C.N., Helena, M., Grillo, M.M., Grechi, T.H.: Standardization of acoustic measures for normal voice patterns. Brazilian J. Otorhinolaryngology **72**, 659–664 (2006)
36. Baka, E., Vishwanath, A., Mishra, N., Vleioras, G., Thalmann, N.M.: "Am I talking to a human or a robot?": a preliminary study of human's perception in human-humanoid interaction and its effects in cognitive and emotional states. In: Computer Graphics International Conference, pp. 240–252. Springer (2019)
37. Yumoto, E., Gould, W.J., Baer, T.: Harmonics-to-noise ratio as an index of the degree of hoarseness. The journal of the Acoustical Society of America 71. Acoustical Society of America: 1544–1550 (1982)

Decision-Making Model for Robots that Consider Group Norms and Interests

Yotaro Fuse[1]([✉]) [iD], Biina Ashida[2], Emmanuel Ayedoun[2],
and Masataka Tokumaru[2]

[1] Graduate School of Science and Engineering, Kansai University,
3-3-35 Yamate-cho, Suita-city, Osaka, Japan
k359679@kansai-u.ac.jp
[2] Kansai University, 3-3-35 Yamate-cho, Suita-city, Osaka, Japan
{emay,toku}@kansai-u.ac.jp

Abstract. In this study, we propose a decision-making model that enables a robot to behave socially in groups of people with common interests. Several attempts have been made to develop robots suitable for humans. Robots should act socially in a human-like social manner to help humans live comfortably. However, if robots are completely subservient to humans, it may not have only a positive impact on the humans' social life among their human communities. It is crucial to create robots that are not extremely comfortable for humans as partners. Thus, we propose and evaluate a decision-making model for a robot that can act selfishly and altruistically in a human–robot scenario, while considering mutual interests. This is expected to contribute to the robot's decision-making design in a society where humans and robots coexist in the future. Further, we investigated how a virtual robot equipped with the proposed interest-aware model behaves in interactions with humans in the proposed group-type ultimatum game. The results of the investigation indicate that the robot equipped with our proposed model can combine group and self-oriented behavior in an experimental scenario.

Keywords: Human–robot groups · Sociable robots · Fairness

1 Introduction

A society where humans and robots coexist is expected to emerge in the future. To help humans live comfortably, robots must naturally participate in human communities and behave socially. Sociability is a characteristic of humans who strive to live in a group without conflicts. To create a society where humans and robots can coexist, humans must regard robots as members of their society, community, and group.

However, for robots to be socially accepted, they must exhibit human-like behavior when they interact with people. In social groups, people tend to conform to expectations and common group behavioral patterns. Hence, to exhibit

M. Kurosu (Ed.): HCII 2022, LNCS 13303, pp. 475–485, 2022.
https://doi.org/10.1007/978-3-031-05409-9_35

sociality in human society, robots need to adapt to group norms shared by other group members. Group norms are the informal rules adopted by a group to regulate member behavior [3]. Based on such views, our previous study in human–robot group scenario enables robots to behave socially in human–robot groups during interactions by making decisions based on unspoken and unwritten (i.e., implicit) social rules [1].

Additionally, there are several situations where there is a conflict of interest in human society. In such situations, people need to act equitably. Fairness is the perspective that wealth should be shared by many people and not just a few. It plays a significant role in human behavior within a group, and it is one of the implicit group norms that allow people to live peacefully within a group. If people belonging to a group violate fairness, they will be punished accordingly. Previous research shows that more fortunate people tend to seek fairness [4]. This is because when people are penalized for their mistakes, the more fortunate are punished severely than the less fortunate in unfair situations [4]. However, people who have experienced low social status tend to endorse the values and motivations of fairness than those with high status [5].

Fairness is an essential element of human society. Humans need to be considerate when they interact with each other. However, in the future, humans may become extremely comfortable interacting with socially communication robots, which do not require such consideration.

Here, we consider a situation where humans and robots make decisions collectively in a situation of conflicts of interests. A robot that is completely subordinated to a group might not be regarded as member of another human group. However, if a robot acts in a self-centered manner, it will not be considered a group member. Thus, we hypothesized that a robot capable of combining selfish behavior based on its emotions and personality with altruistic behavior to act like others is likely to be regarded as a group member. This is expected to contribute to the robot's decision-making design in a society where humans and robots coexist in the future.

In our previous study, a robot that acts according to implicit rules in groups is a group-oriented model [1]. This model cannot behave altruistically and selfishly because it does not consider the interests of a group. The robots using the proposed model simply adjusted their behavior to the implicit rules in human–robot groups. Thus, we develop a robot model that can behave in a group and self-oriented way.

We investigated whether our proposed model behaved fairly toward others while ensuring its benefits within the simple group scenario, in which there were interests among group members. It is crucial to propose a robot that can make decisions while considering the interaction between humans and robots under interest. This can lead to exploring new possibilities such as human trust in robots, human treatment of robots, and human feelings and thoughts toward robots.

In this study, we presented a scenario involving humans and robots, and a robot model for altruistic and selfish decision-making. To evaluate the model,

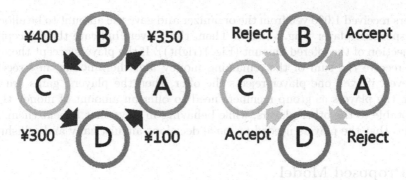

Fig. 1. An example of players offering different amounts in the group-type ultimatum game (Fig. 1 (left)). An example of players' decisions on the offered amounts in the group-type ultimatum game (Fig. 1 (right)).

we proposed a group-type ultimatum game based on the ultimatum game [2] as a scenario where players needed to behave according to their interests. In the scenario, we investigated how a robot equipped with the proposed interest-aware model interacts with humans in the group-type ultimatum game.

2   Methods

We proposed a group-type ultimatum game as an experimental scenario, where participants need to behave based on their interests. The group-type ultimatum game is based on a social psychology game called the ultimatum game [2].

2.1   Ultimatum Game

The ultimatum game is a game for evaluating the fairness of distribution. In the game, the participants are divided into a proposer and a responder, and both make decisions regarding distributing and receiving money. Initially, the organizer of the experiment gives the proposer some money, decides how to divide it between the proposer and the responder, and proposes the divided amount to the responder. If the responder accepts the proposal, the total amount initially given by the organizer is divided as proposed by the proposer. However, if the responder rejects the proposal, both participants will not receive any money. If the proposer offers even a small amount to the responder, the responder should accept the offered amount. However, when the proposer's offer is little, the responder feels unfair and rejects the proposer's offer.

2.2   Group-Type Ultimatum Game

Figure 1 shows the flow of money transactions in one round of the game; A, B, C, and D in the figure represent the players. At the beginning of each round, the players received 1,000 yen from the organizer and gave the amount to be allocated to a specified player (Fig. 1 (left)). Then, the players indicate their acceptance or rejection of the offered amount (Fig. 1(right)). If the players accept the offers, they receive the sum of the remaining money and the amount they received. However, if even one player rejects the offer, then the players' gains are zero. Thus, the players as group members need to offer an amount of money that is acceptable to the other players, while behaving in ways that benefit them. This implies that the players needed to make decisions altruistically and selfishly.

3   Proposed Model

3.1   Overview

In this study, we propose a decision-making model for a robot that acquires interest-based group norms through a group ultimatum game. The proposed model takes as input the amount of money (M_p) offered by others in the group and the decision (j_p) on acceptance or rejection. It outputs the amount of money (M_R) that the robot offers to the counterparty and decision (j_R) on the amount of money offered to the robot. The proposed model's output is the robot's actions to behave fairly while keeping the group norm under interest.

In this experiment, the human players obtain only information about the players related to their transactions based on the rules of the group-type ultimatum game. However, the virtual robot equipped with the proposed model obtains the information of all players' transactions, although their information was not originally available. The robot did not participate in the game under the same conditions as humans. We conducted this experiment to observe how humans and robots in the group behaved in the game.

Figure 2 shows a conceptual diagram of our decision-making model of a robot that behaves in an interest-aware manner through our group-type ultimatum game. The proposed model received the amount of money (M_p) offered by another player and decision (j_p) regarding acceptance or rejection, and outputs the amount of money (M_R) offered to the counterparty and the decision (j_R) regarding the amount of money it received. To estimate the amount of money to be offered in a group under interests, our proposed model accessed the decision-making model of each player who was a group member.

3.2   Estimating Group Norms and Others' Decision-Making

The proposed model enables a robot to make two decisions appropriately; one as a proposer and the other as a responder. The robot with the proposed model learns the criteria of the amount of money that each group member accepts as a responder, and it estimates the degree of the selfishness of the transaction counterpart based on the money. At each round of the game, the robot updates the value function $V(n)$ with the reward function $R(n)$, and it outputs the offered amount (M_R) based on the Q-value that was calculated using $V(n)$. Additionally,

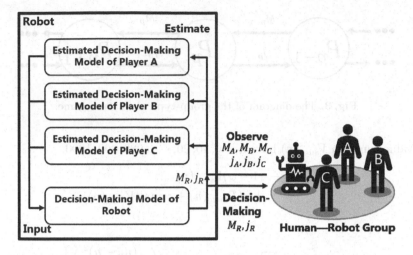

Fig. 2. The diagram of the proposed model.

the robot estimates the tendency of each player's offered amount and rejection amount by constructing an estimation model of the other players in the group. The robot estimates the actions that it should take to behave like a human member by following their tendencies.

The model for estimating the other group members is composed of value function and reward functions. Assuming that other players make decisions based on the value function that is used for the robot's decision-making as described above, then the model for estimating other group members is created for each game using the value function. Therefore, from the value function of the amount of money offered by each player, the proposed model calculates an estimate of the amount of money that a player may propose in the next round, and an estimate of the criteria for the decision of acceptance or rejection. Since the proposed model estimates the amount of money offered by the player and the difference criterion, two models in the proposed model estimate the amount of money offered and the difference criterion. Thus, there are value and reward functions for the offered amount and the difference criterion.

Figure 3 shows the conceptual diagram of the group-type ultimatum game. The counterparty of a group member P_p is $P_{p\pm1}$, and each member inputs and outputs the offered amount M_{p-1}, M_p, and the decision to accept or reject j_p and j_{p+1}. Equation 1 shows that the value of the acceptance or rejection decision j_p is 0 if the group member P_p accepts the offered amount, and 1 if it rejects it.

$$j_p = \begin{cases} 0 \text{ if ACCEPT} \\ 1 \text{ if REJECT} \end{cases} \tag{1}$$

The value function $V_{sugg}(n)$ of the offered amount is defined in Eq. 2, and the reward function $R_{sugg}(n)$ is defined in Eq. 3. The reward function $R_{sugg}(n)$ and

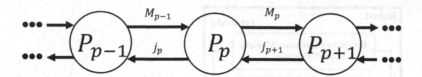

Fig. 3. The diagram of the group-type ultimatum game.

the value function $V_{sugg}(n)$ have $n = 0, 10, 20, \cdots, 980, 990, 1000$.

$$V_{sugg}(n) \leftarrow (1 - \alpha)V_{sugg}(n)$$
$$+\alpha \left(R_{sugg}(n) + \gamma \max V_{sugg}(n)\right) \tag{2}$$

$$R_{sugg}(n) = \sum_{p=1, p' \in P'}^{P} \left\{ (1 - j_{p'}) \exp\left(-\frac{(n_p - n)^2}{kurtosis}\right) \right\}$$
$$+ \sum_{p=1, p' \in P'}^{P} \left\{ j_{p'} \exp\left(-\frac{(n_p + \Delta - n)^2}{kurtosis}\right) \right\} \tag{3}$$

The value and reward functions of the difference criterion are shown in Eqs. 4 and 5. The most valuable tendency of the player's refusal is derived from the value function of the difference criterion. The range of the n is $n = -1000, -990, -980, \cdots, 980, 990, 1000$. Also, the set P' is represented as $P' = \{j_2, j_3, ..., j_P, j_1\}$, so the reward is calculated based on M_p and j_{p+1}.

$$V_{diff}(n) \leftarrow (1 - \alpha)V_{diff}(n)$$
$$+\alpha \left(R_{diff}(n) + \gamma \max V_{diff}(n)\right) \tag{4}$$

$$R_{diff}(n) = \sum_{p=1}^{P} \left\{ (1 - j_p) \exp\left(-\frac{(N(n_p) - n)^2}{kurtosis}\right) \right\}$$
$$+0.5 \sum_{p=1}^{P} \left\{ j_p \exp\left(-\frac{(N(n_p) - n)^2}{kurtosis}\right) \right\} \tag{5}$$

$$N(n) = \frac{n - |n|}{2} = \begin{cases} 0 & (n \geq 0) \\ -n & (n < 0) \end{cases} \tag{6}$$

γ and α represent the discount rate and the learning rate, respectively; n represents the offered amount or the difference. The *kurtosis* represents the degree of flexibility of the Gaussian function. A change in the value of the constant *kurtosis* implies a variation in the assumed degree of adaptation of the group's players. The constant P is the number of group members, excluding the robot, which is the decision-maker in the game. For example, in the group in Fig. 1, $P = 3$.

3.3   Decision-Making Based on Estimating Others

Based on the value function $V_{sugg}(n)$ of the model for estimating the others in the tth round, the robot outputs the amount of money that it proposes by considering the amount of money offered by other players. The robot needs to estimate the amount of money it should offer while adapting to changes in the amount of money offered by the other players in the game. Thus, the robot updates $V_{sugg}(n)$ by calculating $R_{sugg}(n)$ for each round, and makes a decision based on the Q-value obtained using $V_{sugg}(n)$.

The robot makes a decision based on the Q-value obtained using $V_{sugg}(n)$, which is updated every round. Therefore, the amount of money (M_R) offered for the robot's next round is calculated using Eq. 7.

$$M_R = \arg \max Q(n) \tag{7}$$

Equation 7 is determined using the Q-value. Further, the Q-value $(Q(n))$ is expressed using Eq. 8; N_{sugg} is the maximum amount of money that the players proposed.

$$Q(n) = \prod_{n'=0}^{N_{sugg}} \exp\left(-\frac{\left(n' - \arg \max V_{sugg}^R(n)\right)^2}{kurtosis}\right) \tag{8}$$

By adding further conditions as shown in Eqs. 9 and 10, the strategic behavior of the robot in a collective ultimatum game is achieved.

$$Diff'_{p+1} + M'_{p+1} \leq M_p \leq M'_{p-1} - Diff'_p \tag{9}$$

$$V_{sugg}^R(n) \leftarrow 0.5V_{sugg}^R(n) \\ (\text{not if } Diff'_{p+1} + M'_{p+1} \leq n \leq M'_{p-1} - Diff'_p) \tag{10}$$

Using Eqs. 7 and 8, the amount of money M_R offered by the robot in the $t + 1$th round is calculated using the $Q(n)$. However, the value function V_{sugg}^R is updated in the way shown in Eq. 10 before calculating the $Q(n)$. The condition for this case separation is based on Eq. 9, which is derived from the results of the other estimation. This implies that the amounts in the range of Eq. 9 are considered as valuable in the group, and are output on the $t + 1$ turn.

Equation 9 denotes the range of amounts that the robot can accept based on the estimation of the acceptable range difference of the counterparty. The $Diff'_p$ is the optimal amount of the acceptable range of difference for the group member

P_p. M_p is the offered amount for P_p. The acceptable range of the difference denotes the minimum difference that is acceptable for the proposed amount, and corresponds to $Diff'_p$ in Eq. 9. When an amount is proposed, each player has an acceptable range of amounts to accept. The responders decide whether to accept or reject the offered amount based on their acceptable ranges.

We assume that when the group member P_p is a robot, the members P_{p-1} and P_{p+1} make decisions based on Eqs. 2 and 4. In that case, M'_{p-1}, M'_{p+1}, and $Diff_{p+1}$ in Eq. 9 are derived from Eqs. 11, 12, and 13. The $Diff_p$ and M'_p are the acceptable range of difference and the offered amount of the population member P_p is estimated by the robot.

$$Diff_R = \arg \max V^R_{diff} \tag{11}$$

$$M'_{p\pm 1} = \arg \max V^{R \to p \pm 1}_{sugg} \tag{12}$$

$$Diff_{p+1} = \arg \max V^{R \to p+1}_{diff} \tag{13}$$

4 Experiment

4.1 Overview

In this study, a group of three participants and a virtual robot participated in the proposed group ultimatum game in a virtual space. The group consists of participants A, B, and C and a robot R. The participants are unsure whether they are playing alongside a human or a robot. Tables 1 and 2 show that the proposed model worked according to the parameters in the game, and the virtual robot attempted to behave in a human-like and fair manner.

We described that three rules of the group-type ultimatum game applied in this experiment. In the first rule, the player with the most amount of money at the end of the game wins. This goal triggers a sense of competition among the group members and builds interest among them. In the second rule, the trading partners of the participants are fixed at the end of the game. This makes it easier for the participants to estimate the tendency of their counterparties. In the third rule, if at least one player refuses to accept the offer during the approval period of any round, all players' winnings for that round are zero. However, if the players approve the counterparty's offer, they will receive their respective proposed amounts.

4.2 Results and Discussion

Figures 4 and 5 show the transition of the amount of money offered by each player in each round. Tables summarizing the acceptance or rejection status of each player in each round is also included in Figs. 4 and 5. In the tables of Figs. 4 and 5, R denotes the robot. Acceptance and rejection are indicated by ○ and ×, respectively. Table 3 shows the total amount of money obtained by each player in the experiment.

Table 1. Parameters of the proposed model.

Learning rate α	0.1
Discount factor γ	0.9
Δ	20
Number of the players except for robot P	3
Initial $\arg\max Q(n)$	600

Table 2. Experimental conditions.

Number of group members $P+1$	4
The maximum amount of money that a player can propose N_{sugg}	1,000
The minimum amount of money that a player can propose	0
Units of money that a player can propose	10
Amount proposed by non-interaction players	Invisible

Figure 4 shows that in group 1, the players converged on the amount of money they offered as the number of rounds increased. In the first half of the game, there were huge differences in the amounts offered by each player, and there were rounds where players refused the proposals. However, after the fifth round, the number of refusals by the players decreased, and the amounts offered converged. Additionally, B and C, who initially offered small amounts, gradually increased their amounts as the number of transactions increased. In the second round, the robot that lowered its offer significantly increased it. This suggests that the robot was influenced by B and C.

In group 1, we observed that each player converged on the amount of money and did not show an amount that would cause rejection. Thus, the virtual robot equipped with the proposed model in group 1 could play the game based on the group norm formed to avoid causing rejection in each round. Additionally, even in the fifth and sixth rounds, when the deal was concluded, B and C did not lower their offer in the next round, but gradually increased it. This implies that an altruistic group norm that was not focused on pursuing self-interest, was formed. It can be inferred that the group norm will be formed as a relatively altruistic group even if the game continues for more than ten rounds. Additionally, the amount of money offered by the players in Fig. 4 is approximately 400 yen in the 10th round, which implies that the amount of money offered by the players converges to approximately 400 yen.

Figure 5 shows that the amount of money offered varied in the early stages of the game. However, as the game progressed, the players formed a group norm and the amount of money offered gradually converged.

Until the fifth round, the players offered various amounts of money to each other, as if they were trying to discover how much money they should propose. However, after the players accepted the offered amount in the fifth round,

Table 3. The total amount of money obtained by players in each groups. Player R denotes the virtual robot using the proposed model.

Group	Player A	Player B	Player C	Player R
1	¥4,100	¥3,950	¥4,260	¥3,690
2	¥1,080	¥966	¥934	¥1,020

the amounts converged and declined continuously. The gradual decrease in the offered amounts indicates that the players attempted to increase their profits by offering less than their counterparts.

The gradual convergence of group 2 in Fig. 5 indicates that the robot acted according to the implicit group norm of how much to offer in the game. Although the offered amounts converged, the robot offered a relatively high amount compared with the amounts offered by the players. Thus, it is obvious that the robot did not seek profit, but behaved based on the group norm.

Additionally, the amount offered by C in group 2 was lower than that of R. However, R could not tolerate the profit and loss caused by trading with C, and opted to refuse in most cases. Comparing group 1 and 2, we can observe that there is a difference in the amount of money that the entire players can ultimately obtain. Although the amount of money offered tends to converge to a certain amount, inequities occurred in partial transactions within the group, and the entire group lost the opportunity to earn more money.

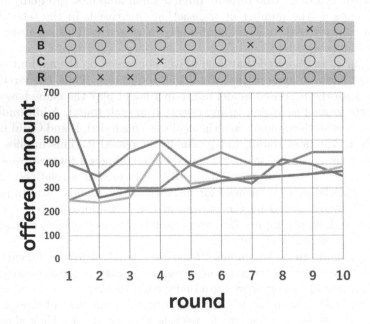

Fig. 4. Amount of money proposed by each player in group 1.

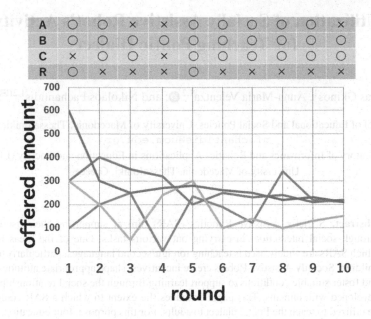

Fig. 5. Amount of money proposed by each player in group 2.

5   Conclusion

In this study, we investigated how a robot that is equipped with the proposed model, which considers interests behave in its interactions with humans. In a group ultimatum game that consists of both robots and human participants, it was confirmed that the amount of money offered converged as the game progressed. Further, we observed that the robot displayed refusal behavior to avoid incurring a huge loss. This indicates that the robot could detect unfair transactions in the group. In the future, we will conduct this game under different conditions and work on improving the proposed model.

Acknowledgments. This work was supported by JSPS KAKENHI Grant Number JP21K12099 and 21J10630.

References

1. Fuse, Y., Tokumaru, M.: Social influence of group norms developed by human-robot groups. IEEE Access **8**, 56081–56091 (2020)
2. Thaler, R.H.: Anomalies: the ultimatum game. J. Econ. Perspectives **2**(4), 195–206 (1988)
3. Feldman, D.C.: The development and enforcement of group norms. Acad. Manag. Rev. **9**(1), 47–53 (1984)
4. Dawes, C.T., et al.: Egalitarian motives in humans. Nature **446**, 794–796 (2007)
5. Guinote, A., et al.: Social status modulates prosocial behavior and egalitarianism in preschool children and adults. Proc. Natl. Acad. Sci. **112**(3), 731–736 (2015)

Utilization of Socially Assistive Robot's Activity for Teaching Pontic Dialect

Minas Gkinos[1], Anna-Maria Velentza[1,2] (iD), and Nikolaos Fachantidis[1,2(✉)] (iD)

[1] School of Educational and Social Policies, University of Macedonia, Thessaloniki, Greece
nfachantidis@uom.edu.gr
[2] Laboratory of Informatics and Robotics Applications in Education and Society (LIRES), University of Macedonia, Thessaloniki, Greece

Abstract. Socially Assistive Robotics (SAR) aim at supporting their users, through social interaction, in carrying out various tasks. One of the areas in which SARs are widely used is teaching foreign/second languages, particularly to children. Socially Assistive Robots create incentives, shape appropriate attitudes, and foster suitable conditions to support learning through the social relationships developed with humans. This paper examines the extent to which a SAR could be utilized to teach the Pontic dialect to adults. For this purpose, four educational activities were designed with specific learning goals incorporated into the curriculum. A total of thirty adult students participated individually in this teaching intervention and then expressed their impressions and attitudes during personal semi-structured interviews. At the same time, the activities were recorded on video. The research data were analyzed based on qualitative research methods. The data analysis found that most participants viewed the endeavor favorably. Interaction with the SAR strengthened a positive learning atmosphere and stirred their interest. All participants made positive remarks on the fact that they had the ability to engage in language activities in an alternative, pleasant manner. However, some of them highlighted the absence of deeper and more substantial communication that is achieved between humans, a shortcoming that is the result of the currently unsolved design weaknesses of robots. Nevertheless, indications are positive and there is interest in further research on the use of SAR in teaching languages to adults.

Keywords: Socially assistive robots (SAR) · Teaching second language · Human robot interaction (HRI) · Pontic dialect · Adults' education

1 Introduction

Socially Assistive Robotics (SAR) have been developed enhanced with social behavior that aim to support their users, through social interaction, in carrying out various tasks. One of the areas in which SAR is utilized is teaching foreign/second languages, particularly to children (Vogt et al. 2019), (Rintjema et al. 2018). Through the social relationships developed with people, Socially Assistive Robots create incentives, shape appropriate attitudes, and foster suitable conditions to support learning (Belpaeme et al.

© The Author(s), under exclusive license to Springer Nature Switzerland AG 2022
M. Kurosu (Ed.): HCII 2022, LNCS 13303, pp. 486–505, 2022.
https://doi.org/10.1007/978-3-031-05409-9_36

2018). Regarding the use of anthropomorphic robots in adults' language learning, it seems that their interaction with the Robot depends on their existing knowledge level and previous knowledge of their peers. Moreover, they are more active through the learning process when the Robot encourages them to do so (Engwall and Lopes 2020).

Gamification techniques has been proposed to enhance the learning of dialects and culture (Burlian et al. 2019). SAR can be perceived as a more pleasant educational activity compared to the traditional one, even perceived as an educational game itself that enhances learning motivation (Boyle et al. 2016). Moreover, SAR may be effective in learning procedures due to its effect in students' attention and triggered reactions such as the cause of surprise (Velentza et al. 2021). Generally, review study on the use of SAR for language learning summarizes that both children and adults have positive attitudes regarding the use of robots, and they seem to be motivated from their role, while enjoying the interaction. On the other hand, the rrobot's social behavior stands in a thin line between being social enough to keep the learners' interest, but not overdoing it, to distract their attention (van den Berghe et al. 2019).

The current study was designed to examine the extent to which a SAR could be utilized to teach the Pontic dialect to adults. For this purpose, four educational activities were designed with specific learning goals incorporated into the educational curriculum. A total of thirty students participated individually in this teaching intervention and then expressed their impressions and views during personal interviews and structured observation strategies. At the same time, the activities were videotaped. The research data were analyzed based on qualitative research methods, leading to the result that most participants viewed the teaching activity and the collaboration with the SAR favorably. Interaction with the SAR strengthened a positive learning atmosphere and sustained their interest. Participants made positive remarks on the fact that they had the ability to engage in language activities in an alternative, pleasant manner. However, they stressed the absence of deeper and more substantial communication that is achieved between humans, a shortcoming that is the result of the currently unsolved design weaknesses of robots. Nevertheless, indications are positive and there is interest in further research of the use of SAR in teaching languages to adults.

1.1 Dialects

It is very common to occur differences and deviations within a language. These differences in intensity and origin are called linguistic diversity and are often associated with specific geographical areas where it is found and are called dialect and idioms. These forms of linguistic diversity are called dialect and idiom. However, there are courses teaching dialects in similar ways to foreign languages. The speakers of a dialect face significant difficulties due to the deviations from the dominant language in the vocabulary and the general structure (Inoue and Hanzawa 2021). Dialects are sometimes underestimated in relation to languages, and that is why it is important for teachers to adopt alternative teaching practices (Wheeler 2019).

The Pontic dialect is one of the main dialects of the Greek language. The characteristics of the dialect are found in phonetic-phonological, morphological, syntactic, and lexical (Tzakosta 2015). A brief record of the characteristics of the dialect could be made based on whether they refer to older linguistic structures (archaisms) or to elements that are newer and constitute deviations from both the origin and the modern Greek.

In June 2016, a memorandum of cooperation was signed between the Pan-pontic Federation of Greece (PSPE) and the University of Macedonia, followed by the establishment and operation of two adult classes on a weekly basis.

2 Related Work

SARs are usually assigned the roles of teacher, peer, care eliciting companion and telepresence robot teacher (Sharkey 2016). The use of SAR in language learning (Robot-Assisted Language Learning - RALL) has some advantages. According to Hirata, Ishiguro's colleague - a pioneer in RALL-related research, SAR can reduce stress levels in students and offer them opportunities for "authentic" learning through close-up interaction (Nazikian 2015). In addition, Kim et al. (2013, mentioned in Nazikian 2015) argue that SAR in the classroom can increase student engagement.

Some of the characteristics of SAR (reproducibility, movement, anthropomorphism, interaction) are directly related to educational goals such as attracting attention, recalling pre-existing knowledge, providing visualized examples, providing feedback, etc. (Aidinlou et al. 2014). Therefore, SAR can be used to provide individualized practice, support the communicative use of language through role-playing games or even the diagnosis and evaluation of students (Nazikian 2015). This can be done through activities such as storytelling, dialogues for practicing pronunciation, question-and-answer or command-execution games, according to the method of Total Physical Reaction (Aidinlou et al. 2014). However, there is a gap in research on how to use SAR in dialect learning.

Despite the similarity of teaching approaches between a second language and a dialect, there are also fundamental differences, as stated in Sect. 1.1. The task of teaching Pontic is relatively recent, as mentioned in the previous section. On the other hand, the domestic literature on the teaching of dialects refers to their use in the direction of critical literacy in school levels of education (Tzakosta 2015). In Greek literature, it was not possible to find any work relevant to the issue of the didactic approach of the Pontic dialect or any other Greek language dialect. In the international literature we found the term 'second dialect', and the way of its conquest is examined. The relevant works refer to a large percentage of the linguistic variants of English, but also to other languages. However, the emphasis is mainly on the phonological part and the vocabulary (Siegel 2010). The second dialect is usually acquired in a natural way, when the speakers meet the dialect in their everyday life, and less in organized didactic circumstances. The literature includes cases of adults learning a second dialect (pronunciation modification) for work reasons (actors) or for better integration into a new environment (Siegel 2010). In most cases of systematic dialect teaching, however, the teachers/designers of the programs act on a case-by-case basis, depending on the nature and the characteristics of the dialect, the target population, and the conditions.

3 Present Study

The present research focuses on the Pontic dialect teaching with the assistance of the SAR Nao. For some of the speakers/participants, this is delayed, systematic teaching of their mother tongue (which is the Pontic dialect, according to their statement). On the contrary, for some others, it is similar to learning a second language (or second dialect) since it can be used, at least to a limited extent, in their environment.

3.1 Hypothesis

H1: SARs carry out educational activities with didactic objectives that are part of dialect learning.

H2: Conducting learning activities with SAR meets the requirements of adult education.

The first two hypotheses stem from the use of SAR in language teaching so far, as evidenced by the bibliographic review, and by the content's peculiarity of the offered language course, and the characteristics of the trainees. In contrast to the presented surveys with adult participants, the courses at UoM are aimed at people who are activated by strong internal motivations (incentives). In addition, the subject of the courses is a dialect that carries the corresponding cultural burden. Learning the dialect is considered in some way a debt to the ancestors for its rescue, and, in addition to the cognitive part, it also has emotional implications. Both motivation and aspiration, as well as emotional reasons are factors that significantly affect adults in the educational process.

H3: SARs can support adult learning environments with interaction and physical participation.

The third hypothesis stems from the literature and specifically from human-robot interaction (HRI) studies. Many people are cautious in their attitudes towards robots. These attitudes have been widely investigated (Xia and LeTendre 2020). Physical contact is an important factor in non-verbal human communication. Tactile is probably the most basic and primitive form of communication, which can nevertheless express positive or negative messages between people (Knapp et al. 2013). Respectively, in the HRI field, physical contact has also been studied (Wullenkord et al. 2016). Tactile contact between humans and robots can increase humans' attachment, emotional expressions and lead to more positive attitudes toward robots (Argall and Billard 2010, Andreasson et al. 2017). Therefore, we are going to examine the aspect of physical contact with the Robot during the process of the educational activity.

H4: SARs can support an adult learning environment capable of extending course participation both time and duration.

Finally, the fourth hypothesis arises from the fact that the lessons took place in the afternoon, at the end of a probably tiring day. Adult learners often face difficulties from their professional and social obligations. Although overall ability to concentrate is not adversely affected over time (Glisky 2007), adults' attention is often distracted either by fatigue or by responsibilities in their extracurricular activities (Wlodkowski and Ginsberg 2017).

4 Methodological Approach

For educational activities, the use of SAR requires building trust and creating a pleasant user experience. In other words, their success is based on their acceptance by people

(Alvin Li et al. 2015). Consequently, the research focuses on the students' perceived emotions from their interaction with the SAR, within the context of Pontic lessons and not in their learning outcomes. It is important for us to gain the students' acceptance towards the Robot and afterward to test their knowledge acquisition. To assess the impact of the interaction on students, we recorded their impressions and opinions, analyzed their thoughts, and drew conclusions to meet the hypotheses. This approach, also known as self-report measures (as opposed to task-performance measure), has been followed in other studies with SAR (Leyzberg et al. 2012, Kidd and Breazeal 2004, Wainer et al. 2007). Additional factors that led us to follow the qualitative approach are the relatively small sample size, and the context in which RALL for dialect teaching took place (Henninget al. 2008). Moreover, the participants' perceptions, interpretations, experiences "constitute important properties" of the research objectives (Bovens et al. 2014).

The current study also shows several similarities with those of the action research. Action research is a "small-scale intervention in the functioning of the real world and a close examination of the effects of this intervention" (Cohen et al. 2008). It attempts to introduce innovative elements into an existing educational situation (which operates in a traditional way) and to consider ways of utilizing these new elements (Cohen et al. 2008). Action research has a dual character that derives from its very name: on the one hand, it improves practices (action) and, on the other produces new knowledge (research) (McNiff 2017).

4.1 Participants

The participants were all adult students in the Pontic dialect courses conducted in the University of Macedonia or other organizations such as schools in Thessaloniki. Apart from their attendance to Pontic dialect courses, there was no other limitation for participation in the study (i.e., gender, age, academic level etc.). The total number of participants was 30, twelve men and eighteen women aged between 20 and 60 years old, from all academic levels, currently studying, working, or being retired, living in big cities, suburbs, or even small villages. More specifically, 13 participants were between 18–29 years old, six between 30–39, four between 40–49, three between 50–59 and four were 60+. Seven participants were Secondary school graduates, and the rest were graduates or students of higher education while (at least) 2 of them had additional studies.

The samples' diversity raised several issues that significantly determined the methodological choices of the research. The issues are summarized in the following points:

The degree of mastery of the Pontic dialect: Some of the participants speak the Pontic dialect with great ease. These are mainly older people (born in the 50s and 60s), who were raised in an environment where Pontic as a code of communication played an important (if not major) role. On the other hand, many participants understand the dialect, but are unable to use it to communicate effectively. Finally, there are participants who have very little knowledge of the dialect (few words or standard phrases).

The individual goals of each trainee: When formulating the goals of an adult training program, the aspirations, and interests of the people to whom the program is addressed should be considered. For some participants, the emphasis is on its deeper knowledge, on exploring its structure and levels, while for others, to achieve functional communication.

Their previous educational experiences: Each of the participants has taken part as a student (or as a teacher) in activities with educational content, having a formed idea about how an educational procedure should be and what helps them in their quest to gain knowledge. Some of the participants draw their experiences from their student years in the 60s (and the educational reality that prevailed then), while the younger ones probably had the opportunity to take a course using ICT. This differentiation, in terms of educational experiences, can be exacerbated by the fact that even among the Pontic teaching departments there are differences in the methods, strategies and techniques used by each instructor, given that the textbook is just a common starting point.

4.2 Measurement Tools

Interview. The main tool of this research is the semi-structured individual interview. The interview, the "discussion for a purpose" (Bovens et al. 2014), gives the researcher the opportunity to draw rich data on the attitudes, experiences, views, and representations of the participants in the research (Iosifidis 2008). Interview in comparison to questionnaires has significant advantages, regarding the depth in the data collection (Cohen et al. 2008; Iosifidis 2008).

A guide with directions was used to conduct the interview, based on the following questions: (a) The trainees' first concerns and impression when they meet the SAR, and how they shape their attitudes towards it. (b) The second relates to the type of interaction that develops between the SAR and the trainees during the activity. In other words, it is examined whether the SAR meets the required criteria, to become accepted by trainees to support the learning process. (c) The third direction revolves around whether the activities with the SAR cover the learning needs of the participants and help them in learning the dialect. (d) Finally, the fourth dimension concerns the ability of the SAR to enhance the involvement of trainees both qualitatively (increased attention) and quantitatively (increased time).

Research questions are related to at least one of the above directions. The wording of the questions follows the logic of the "funnel", i.e., the questions were more general in nature and then, depending on the initial response of the respondent, additional auxiliary questions were asked to obtain additional information. These auxiliary questions belong to the categories of investigation - probes (continuity, processing, clarification, etc.) and continuity - follow-up (Iosifidis 2008).

The content of the guide stems from similar purpose research tools and guides (Lee et al. 2011; Mubin et al. 2013; Serholt and Barendregt 2014). The NAARS, RAS (Nomura et al. 2006) and GODSPEED (Bartneck et al. 2009) questionnaires were also examined.

Observation. Observation is a non-invasive method, where the observer does not attempt to manipulate the observed. However, the subjectivity of the observer, can give inaccurate interpretations of the participants' behaviors and thus, it is suggested that observation be used as a complementary method, in combination with others (Cohen et al. 2008). The data retrieved from the observation may supplement, verify, or even overturn the data collected in parallel with other methods. This makes it a very common tool for enhancing reliability by using multiple data collection methods (Robson 2010).

The observation was made by video recordings, giving the opportunity to examine the execution of the activities and the subsequent of the participants' behavior.

Observation Protocol. The composition of the protocol was mainly based on the list of behaviors that are included in the broader non-verbal behavior listed by Guba and Lincoln (1981) and Includes the Following:

- Eye contact: Eye contact in the context of the present activity was a strong indication of interest, involvement, and interaction.
- Distance from SAR: The inclination of the human body towards SSA is perceived as a sign of intimacy, friendliness and vice versa.
- The orientation of the human body towards the SAR: The face-to-face positioning of the body shows acceptance, intention to stay in the same position, to continue communication, willingness to cooperate.
- Smile-laughter: Feeling of pleasure, cheerful mood.
- Expressions of discomfort: Grimaces that indicate discomfort or embarrassment.
- Reactions to contact with the Robot: The presence or absence of some hesitation is examined when the participant is asked to touch the SAR.
- Reactions to the SAR's movements: The existence of involuntary movements is examined when the SAR performs a movement. The reflex reaction could indicate a lack of trust towards the SAR.
- General signs of nervousness-anxiety: Signs of nervous movements of the foot, hand, occupation of hands with an object, etc.

The hierarchy scale method was used to label and analyse the data. According to this method, the observer draws inference ranging from the simple recording of events to the formulation of judgments (Cohen et al. 2008). The grading of the scales was simple, since the purpose was not the exhaustive and quantitative recording of the behavior, but a rough sketch that will accompany the interview data. There was a prior clarification among the observers on how the events would be prioritized. For example, the label SMILE has the rating range: NOT AT ALL - LITTLE - VERY MUCH. Little was used for behaviors that appeared at least once throughout the activity, i.e., sporadic smiles.

Validity and Reliability. In qualitative methodological research, validity and reliability are evaluated by the credibility, transferability, dependability, and confirmability of the research(Patton 2014). Triangulation, i.e., the use of two or more methods in data collection to study certain dimensions of human behavior, plays a key role in validity and reliability (Cohen et al. 2008). In the present study, triangulation was used to ensure credibility, by collecting data through two methods, qualitative interview, and observation. Also, during the observation, through the recording of the video, another observer was used, who filled in the observation sheets separately. Finally, the research data was given to a fellow language teacher with experience in educational research, who examined their analysis and coding and made her observations and suggestions. After discussion between the researchers involved, some modifications were made to the original approach. Furthermore, the issue of credibility is also supported in terms of Prolonged Engagement, as reported by Guba and Lincoln (1981), since one of the authors is also a teacher with long-term involvement with language teaching. In addition, due to their background, two of the authors know the Pontic dialect quite well and shared experiences with the participants.

The transferability of research can be ensured by what Lincoln and Guba (1985) refer to as a thick description. The presentation of the research findings first focuses on general descriptions and then on detailed reports of the participants' attitudes based on the recordings. The selection of the documents presented reflects the overall assessment of the specific issue each time with a representative report of different points of view and perspectives. Priority was given to views containing richer and more representative data from the situation under consideration.

Finally, for ensuring dependability & confirmability, it is proposed the complete recording (audit trail), the transparent description of all the steps followed during the research process and the preservation of all the data that emerged in the course (primary data, notes, observations, thoughts during the research, etc.) (Lincoln and Guba 1985; Robson 2010).

4.3 Design and Procedure

Robot. The Nao Aldebaran robot served as the educator, as shown in Fig. 1. The Robot was connected to the wi-fi and the coordination of its movements was controlled from the NAOqi OS. The control and planning of the activities were done via the Choreographer and we considered the Pontic culture in the behaviors' design (Shidujaman and Mi 2018; Velentza et al. 2021; Shidujaman et al. 2020). The Robot was named after a traditional Pontic name as 'Giorikas'. An essential factor in shaping the "character" of Giorikas, played the element of humor. The Pontics are very often extroverted, expressive, they like teasing, they often use the language in an "indecent" way (swearing) and they embellish what they say with funny expressions. Since all those who participated in the research (and most students in the classes in general) are of Pontic origin, the effort to match the students' temperament is expected to have positive results. According to Tapus and Matarić (2008), we tried to increase participants' involvement in activities when their character "matches" that of the Robot.

Scripts. The scripts were recorded and uploaded on Nao, combined with movements, to be expressively enriched. The first author, who is also of Pontiac origin, recorded the audio of the activities by his voice. Particular attention was paid to the recording quality. Although it is generally considered more tempting to provide instructions for performing activities in the target language itself (Pontic dialect), it was chosen for all activities that the instructions be in the modern Greek language, to make sure that all participants fully understood what they had to do.

Activities. Four activities were designed, related to different skills in learning a second language and the following factors were considered:

- The possibilities offered by the Robot, but also the limitations set by the functional approach adopted.
- The inhomogeneity of the sample in terms of their characteristics.

– The special features of the dialect, with emphasis on the differences from the colloquial one and the difficulties the students are usually facing.

The content of the activities was based on the Pontic Teaching Manual concerned the following areas (a) vocabulary (b) grammar (c) verbal communication - reading (d) auditory comprehension.

(a) Vocabulary

Thirty (30) words used in the activity retrieved from the vocabulary listed in each chapter of the above-mentioned manual. Fifteen (15) verbs and fifteen (15) nouns (adjectives - nouns) were chosen. The participants were asked to select one of two categories of words. This choice was made to enhance the sense of autonomy and choice that can inspire learning activities for adults. The chosen words cover a wide range of the vocabulary of the Pontic dialect. The implementation of the activity took the form of playful activity. It could be compared to practice exercises from the early stages of the implementation of educational activities in PC (Levy 1997), by adding SAR, which plays the role of peer and indicates the correct meaning of a word, between two versions, through social interaction. SAR takes the role of the knowledgeable social partner, in a variation of a series of tasks that examine the effects of social-type interaction on adult vocabulary learning (Verga and Kotz 2017).

More specifically, after the explanatory pronunciation (in modern Greek), the participant heard a word (depending on the initial category he/she had chosen) and two interpretations, one of which was correct and the other incorrect. At the same time, Nao extended both its hands, one at a time, as it uttered the two possible interpretations. The participant chose the correct interpretation, based on his/her discretion, touching the sensor of the respective hand. The explanation of the whole process was done orally before the start of the activity. In addition to the explanations before the start of the proceedings, Nao was giving recorded instructions. During the execution of the activity in each answer, Nao provided positive or negative (mild) feedback according to the given answer. Adults find it effective and prefer positive feedback because when they try to improve, focusing on their mistakes can discourage them (Wlodkowski and Ginsberg 2017). In the positive answers, a random message was reproduced (out of a total of 4 messages), with a cheerful style and mood-coloring. At the same time, Nao was applauding. Respectively, in the wrong choices, the mistake was pointed out with appropriate (not at all critical) expressions and a parallel negative gesture.

(b) Grammar

The grammatical phenomenon to which it referred was the imperative of the verb. In general, the subject presents peculiarities, due to the completely different way of formation of the precept in the Pontic language in relation to modern Greek. For every one of the six chosen verbs, the following procedure was repeated:

• Nao initially uttered the verb/expression in the definite and waited
• the participant was saying the verb/phrase in the imperative

- Nao (regardless of the answer) said the phrase in the imperative and performed the corresponding action.

The activity was "open", as the answers to be given were not strictly defined. This was clarified before the start of the activity. Nao performing the action says an acceptable (correct) answer that could be given, not the only one, however. It is essentially an alternative treatment of the user's response, in relation to the vocabulary activity, with the recast on the part of the Robot. This type of corrective feedback is an indirect and polite way for students to hear the correct answer, without being embarrassed by pointing out the error (Lightbown and Spada 2021).

(iii) Verbal Communication

The verbal communication activity was a dialogue between the participant and Nao. The original text came from a chapter of the manual and was modified by adding additional phrases to extend its duration. The content was hilarious and fun: the telephone conversation between an elderly woman and her son, Giorika. Users "played" the role of mother, reading the relevant text from a piece of paper.

The purpose of the activity was the practice of reading, but also the utterance of speech with correct pronunciation and coloring of the voice. Dialogues and role-plays are an essential part of the activities, according to modern teaching approaches. In this case Nao serves as a natural speaker of the language, while at the same time his pleasant presence allows students to express themselves in the Pontic language free from possible stress.

(iv) Auditory Comprehension

Auditory comprehension is one of the basic skills required to learn a language. Consequently, language learners must be exposed to a language introduction that is understandable to them (close to the level of knowledge they already have), but somewhat more demanding, to be useful in learning (Doughty and Long 2008). The auditory comprehension activity was done to expose the average trainee to such an introduction. In this activity there were two recorded texts from the Pontic textbook. The texts were not from the preliminary and the first chapters, so they present some difficulty (in terms of vocabulary and meaning). An effort was made to make the pronunciation as expressive as possible, with an appropriate voice tone.

The participant was able to select one of the two texts, according to the instructions at the beginning of the activity. The text was selected again by touching the corresponding Robot's hand. The text was followed by six (6) multiple-choice questions or "True-False". The participant answered orally (i.e., right/wrong or the choice he/she made, depending on the question).

Prior to the activities, the researcher gave detailed information about the procedure, how to interact with the Robot and informed them about GDPR and the use and storage of their data and the right to cancel their participation at any time. No details were revealed about the capabilities, logic, and operation of the SAR. The research was carried out in different rooms in UoM. In each case, the participant was sitting in front of a table with the

SAR being at a short distance in front of him. The procedure was semi-autonomous (in the cases where the participant gave a correct or wrong answer by touching a specific part of the Robot and the Robot replied with corresponding negative or positive feedback). The rest of the activities were instructed by a Wizard of Oz (Engwall et al. 2022), waiting for the participant to finish their answers, and then giving the appropriate feedback from pre-recorded behaviors. The wizard also gave instructions to the Robot to start the activities (via tablet and PC) was sitting in the same place, outside the direct visual radius of the participant.

Immediately after the completion of the process, the interview followed, in a different place. At the same time, the next participant started the activity.

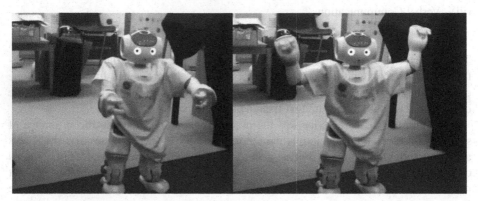

Fig. 1. The Robot performing different movements accompanying its storytelling.

4.4 Data Analysis

The data from the observation were recorded in an excel file per participant. The total observations were written by category. The emerged comments and descriptive remarks were evaluated and presented below, as appropriate. The observation for each participant was contrasted, for cross-reference, with what he/she mentioned in the interview.

The audio transcripts of the interviews were converted into text using a computer program. Prior to their word-for-word transfer, a first hearing of the interviews (mainly the first ones) was held, and notes were made on the main points, to obtain a first supervisory look at the data. During the full recording, the text analysis focused on the content, and additional points were highlighted based on the participants' verbal references, i.e., some statements with emphasis, hesitation, enthusiasm, etc., that were considered important.

The approach followed the typological procedure analysis, in which the construction of quality material is done in categories or thematic fields (Iosifidis 2008). The method of contour approximation was used for the coding. According to this approach, data are categorized based on key-codes, derived from theory, research questions or a first contact with the data. This defines contours based on which the data set is analyzed (Robson 2010).

This method is considered as a set of techniques integrated into the broader approach of thematic text analysis(Cassell and Symon 2004). However, the research cases in the current study overlapped between the categories. For example, the usefulness of SAR in learning is examined in the context of adult learning. So, the existence of evidence that supports case 1 reinforces case 2 at the same time. The element of satisfaction, the reduction of stress, the motivation for participation have a positive effect on the teaching of the language lesson. The division of the categories, in relation to the research cases, was made based on the assumption that each category presents, refers specifically to the language course or general issues of adult education.

The categories and subcategories that emerged during the data analysis were the following (Table 1):

Table 1. The categories and subcategories that emerged during the data analysis.

A. Learning the dialect
The views of the participants
The suitability for language courses
Personalized help
Additional information in relation to the class
Transfer of characteristic elements of the dialect
B. Meeting the requirements of adult education
The views of the participants
Creating a pleasant atmosphere
Ease of use
The removal of stress
The fulfillment of the trainee's expectations
C. Interaction with physical participation
The views of the participants
Preferences for activities
D. Substantial and prolonged involvement in the course
The views of the participants
E. The type of interaction that developed
Visual
Physical
Verbal

5 Results

The results are presenting based on the participants' responses per analyzed category and subcategory as stated above. The number of participants that belong to each category is stated in parenthesis. Participants stated that they have a good (16) or very good (8) relationship with technology, while 6 stated that they have a bad relationship (which is mainly due to their inability to respond to it). In their general assessment of the role and position of robots in society and in education, of the 25 respondents, 19 expressed a positive opinion/attitude, 2 expressed concerns and reservations and maintained a neutral attitude, while 4 had a negative view. The main concern raised by the participants (even among those who had positive general attitudes) was the fear of being replaced by robots at some point in the future.

In relation to the hours of the lessons and whether the participants were overwhelmed by the obligations of the day, overall, they answered that the hours were convenient. Fatigue during the course was reported by 7, however, 3 of them reported strong motivation to attend the course as a compensatory factor. Only 2 reported difficulties in the course due to fatigue and inconvenient schedule. These answers, to some extent opposed the 4th research hypothesis regarding the role of fatigue as an obstacle in attending the course.

Regarding the assessment of the participants' Pontic dialect knowledge level, 12 described themselves as beginners, 9 as intermediate, 7 as good and 2 as very good. The main difficulty mentioned was their speech ability. Many described themselves as "passive speakers", with disproportionate ease of understanding compared to speech production. The more advanced ones focused on writing and elements of the structure of the dialect, grammar, and syntax, which they stated to be the main reason why they attended the courses. Participants also stated that they were interested, in addition to the dialect, in the elements of history and culture.

To the question that asked the general impression of the participants, immediately after the completion of the activity, almost all of them answered with positive comments. There were two answers with doubt (technical difficulties and suitability for children). Most of the answers were more complex than a one-word answer or a simple characterization and included individual evaluative judgments. This content was recorded and integrated with the answers to other questions (provided that the same information was not provided by the same person).

A. Usefulness in Learning Dialect
Generally, participants believe that SAR can contribute to the learning of the Pontic dialect. Almost all of them answered positively to the relevant question, either directly or indirectly. These responses hid a variety of perceptions both about the reasons for which they were given and how strong this belief was.

Usefulness in Language Courses in Language Learning: 23 of the participants answered that they consider the SAR to be suitable for language courses. The other four (4) answered again positively, noting that this technique seems to be suitable for young children. Twenty-nine (29) of the participants answered that the activities could help in learning Pontic. Some (5) assumed with doubts that it could be useful, because as they claimed, the indicative activities did not show them the Robot's full potential. In some cases, the affirmative answer was accompanied by suggestions for future activities. Some answers were also interesting, because although participants expressed some doubts, at the same time they were convinced about the importance of the use of SAR for educational purposes.

Personalized Help: Twenty-four (24) participants answered that the SAR could help them in specific areas of learning. Specifically, most (10) answered that it could help them learn vocabulary, five (5) that it would help them with dialogue activities, two (2) that they could improve their reading ability. As mentioned above, not all participants gave explanations to justify their view of the usefulness of SAR in learning the dialect. Four (4) answered negatively. In one of the negative answers the participant did not seem to consider the indicative nature of the activities, something that was generally perceived by most. In another case, the negative answer was accompanied by the statement that for some people it may be helpful while for others it may not.

Additional Information in Relation to the Class: There is significant diversity between the positive judgments in this subcategory. Most participants (14) highlight elements necessary for a functional classroom that can be found in humans (teacher or class-mates) that the SAR lacks. Several participants "saw" in Giorikas roles that differentiate him from the conventional teaching practice, which are the following: Eleven (11) mentioned the role of the collaborator-examiner in practice. Four (4) emphasized the role of correction-feedback and two (2) the ability of repetition. In addition, some saw in Yorikas a "warehouse" of available, correct knowledge.

Transfer of Language Features: Fifteen (15) of the participants gave positive feedback on the verbal interaction with SAR. The formation of Giorikas' character as a natural speaker of the dialect and, therefore as an acceptable collaborator in the teaching activities was largely based on this element. More specifically, they positively evaluated the comments and answers SAR gave them as feedback or the pronunciation, the comprehensible speech. From the other answers it appeared that either the participants did not like the speech style (3) or that the interaction at the level of verbal communication was not convincing enough, due to the mechanical nature of the activities (6).

B. Meeting the Requirements of Adult Education
Of the twenty-five (25) interviewed, 22 answered that SAR has a place in the adult classroom. The 3 who answered negatively were the same people who also had negative opinion about the language lesson.

Creating a Pleasant Atmosphere: All respondents (30) answered that the activity was enjoyable, even those who expressed doubts and concerns on various issues.

Most of the answers to the participants mentioned described the features of SAR such as funny-playful (12), original-innovative (13) and interactive (9). Some answers were one-word, while others were accompanied by a few comments.

When asked if there is a sense of interaction with a machine and whether it caused discomfort, there were two (2) participants who stated that some characteristics caused them discomfort, although in another question, they stated that the activity was enjoyable and fun. Two more said they felt strongly that they were interacting with an inanimate object, but the sensation gradually subsided, without any discomfort. Seventeen (17) stated that there was a sense of discomfort, but it was not intense and subsided, without feeling it again. Furthermore, eight stated that they felt like talking to a person.

Easy to Use: Most participants did not encounter any difficulties in performing the activities. Only two reported comprehension difficulties.

Stress Relief: Twelve (12) of the participants stated directly or indirectly that SAR helps to relieve stress and that encouraged their participation in the course. In one case, the participant was concerned about how the other participants may felt, although he had a pleasant and stress-relieving experience.

Fulfilling Expectations: All participants who were asked if their expectations were met answered positively. In addition, participants who were asked if they would recommend someone to do similar activities with SAR, 28 answered positively, with five of them clarifying that there must be a teacher accompanying the activity in the class. Many of the participants came to this conclusion rather arbitrarily and thought that they must choose between the SAR and the teacher.

C) Physical Participation

All participants (30) stated that they had no hesitation in encountering the Robot, nor did they have any negative thoughts. The most preferable activity was vocabulary one with 12 (7 unique answers) participants choosing it, which also reinforces the previous answers. The activity of grammar (imperative) followed with 10 (7 unique) preferences, followed by a dialogue with 6 (1) participants choosing it and auditory comprehension with 4 (1) choices. There were two participants who did not point out any activity. Some (3) commented positively on the fact that they touched the SAR.

D) Increase the Engagement Time

Increase Attention and Engagement Time: Most participants (22) answered that the SAR would help them pay more attention and increase their participation in the course. Some pointed out the fact that they wanted to do the activity irrelevantly to the Robot, however the SAR would still help. Of the negative answers (4), only one was fully justified. One of the respondents did not answer and the rest stated that they would be happy to stay in the class shortly after the end to do additional activities with the SAR.

E) Type of Interaction

Participants commented positively or negatively on various aspects of the interaction. The Robot's movements received only positive feedback except for one case. On the contrary, in verbal communication, there were some concerns, as mentioned above. In addition, the Robot's appearance seems to provoke some comments. Participants commended that although they enjoyed the course and found it helpful for dialect learning, they noticed a "lack of human communication". Moreover, they were convinced that a human- tutor has advanced non-verbal communication skills in comparison with the SAR and that they needed a deeper perspective in the learning course such as explanations about the words' etymology, extension of linguistic elements in matters of tradition and culture and solving questions. However, they perceived it as appropriate in activities that aim at low-level skills such as repeating exercises and help them memorize vocabulary. Additionally, they found the SAR ideal for self-assessment, and self-correction.

The data from the observation were examined in parallel with those of the interview.

1. Eye contact: A little: 2 Enough: 21 Continuation: 7
2. Smile-laugh: Not at all: 3 Sometimes: 13 Often: 14
3. Expressions of discomfort: Not at all: 23 Sometimes: 7
4. Position towards SAR: Side: 1 Side, then opposite: 2
5. Distance from SAR: Normal: 11 Nearby: 19
6. Contact (physical) with robots: Without hesitation: 28 Initial hesitation: 2
7. Reaction to the movements of the SAR: No: 29 Yes: 1
8. Signs of nervousness-anxiety No: 27 Yes: 3

The general impression of the interviews agreed with the interview and observation data. The participants' answers during the interview were also reflected in their attitude during the activity. Some were very expressive, gesturing, commenting, and talking to Giorikas. Of additional interest is the fact that when students were at a dead end, they used the same coping strategies with real-world situations. For example, one participant gave the command to the SAR in modern Greek. Other students obviously guessed the right word (swayed between the two hands) and repeated the correct interpretation, after the feedback. This type of self-correction, although not done in the target language, is considered to add more value to the feedback received by the student (Lightbown and Spada 2021).

Contacting the SAR, which was the main target of the observation, did not seem to concern the participants. Only in one case there was a slight hesitation, but only at the beginning, perhaps due to speculation that touch can affect the Robot's stability.

In general, the observed behaviors (signs of discomfort at certain points, e.g., delay in loading the activity) corresponded to relevant reports in the interview. Overall, the cross-use of the observation validated the content of the interviews.

6 Discussion and Conclusions

This research attempted to examine how the use of a SAR can contribute to the teaching of the Pontic dialect to adults. For this purpose, educational activities were designed with specific teaching objectives and the trainees/participants were invited to carry them out, interacting at the same time with the SAR Nao. The activities were suitable for adults' educational needs, emphasizing the communication skills needed when teaching a second language, following the latest didactic language approaches and the role of SAR in the educational process. Their impressions and attitudes were recorded during semi-structured interview and observation.

By analysing the participants' replies, we found that they consider that the activities implemented with a SAR have a place in an adult program, despite some minor objections that it may be more suitable for younger ages.

The combination of technology, with the use of SAR with the dialect teaching according to participants was successful. Giorikas is convincing as a natural speaker of Pontic and is generally accepted as an interlocutor in activities. Key role in Giorikas' acceptance from participants were both the implementation part (voice, pronunciation, clarity of content, rhythm of speech) and the general humanoid dialect-speaking.

Although many participants commented positively in favor of the use of SAR in classroom activities, there were also comments that highlighted the "lack of human communication", the absence of non-verbal communication and the lack of deepening in the learning object (etymology, extension of linguistic elements in matters of tradition and culture, solving questions). This contradiction between the positive attitudes and the concerns at the same time, can be explained as a separation of roles between the traditional course and those performed by SAR. After all, SAR is perceived as more appropriate in activities that aim at low-level skills (practice, memorization assistance) as well as in self-assessment, self-correction, while expressing a clear preference in the traditional classroom and interpretation.

The participants choose as the most popular and most useful, the vocabulary activity that provides them with immediate and tangible results, which is in line with the physiognomy of the adult student. Vocabulary activity activates strategies, provides instant feedback in a third-party environment, provides the opportunity for self-evaluation and self-correction by giving instant feedback, all with a pleasant, interactive approach.

Overall, we can say that the use of SAR, verifying the 2nd research hypothesis, can support dialect learning activities. Regarding the 3rd hypothesis, the collected data showed that it is being verified. Participants responded that they had no problem/hesitation in interacting with physical involvement with SAR. The same facts are also confirmed by the videos' analysis. Regarding the 4th hypothesis, while the participants at the begging answered that the day fatigue did not distract them from the activities, later, most of them admitted that there was fatigue that made it difficult to attend the course. Although the degree of this feeling varied, regardless of the intensity, the participants believe that the presence of SAR helped to alleviate their fatigue.

One of the research limitations is the lack of autonomous interaction between the Robot and the participants that needed to be controlled by a wizard in order to focus on testing the research hypothesis. Moreover, another limitation is the short-term interaction. According to research data in children (Vogt et al., 2019), the result of an interaction examination should be extended over time to manifest, if any, the so-called novelty effect, in which the sense of the unprecedented is initially attracted, but gradually the interest fades. Despite the assurances of the participants to the contrary, this limitation must be considered in order to draw general conclusions.

Acknowledgments. This work is part of a project that has received funding from the Research Committee of the University of Macedonia under the Basic Research 2020–21 funding programme.

References

Aidinlou, N., Alemi, M., Farjami, F., Makhdoumi, M.: Applications of Robot Assisted Language Learning (RALL) in language learning and teaching. Int. J. Lang. Linguist. **2**(3), 12 (2014)

Alvin Li, X., Florendo, M., Luke Miller, E., Ishiguro, H., Ayse Saygin, P.: Robot form and motion influences social attention. In: 2015 10th ACM/IEEE International Conference on Human-Robot Interaction (HRI), pp. 43–50 (2015)

Andreasson, R., Alenljung, B., Billing, E., Lowe, R.: Affective touch in human–robot interaction: conveying emotion to the Nao robot. Int. J. Soc. Robot. **10**(4), 473–491 (2017). https://doi.org/ 10.1007/s12369-017-0446-3

Argall, B.D., Billard, A.G.: A survey of tactile human-robot interactions. Robot. Auton. Syst. **58**(10), 1159–1176 (2010). https://doi.org/10.1016/j.robot.2010.07.002

Bartneck, C., Kulić, D., Croft, E., Zoghbi, S.: Measurement instruments for the anthropomorphism, animacy, likeability, perceived intelligence, and perceived safety of robots. Int. J. Soc. Robot. **1**(1), 71–81 (2009). https://doi.org/10.1007/s12369-008-0001-3

Belpaeme, T., et al.: Guidelines for designing social robots as second language tutors. Int. J. Soc. Robot. **10**(3), 325–341 (2018). https://doi.org/10.1007/s12369-018-0467-6

Bovens, M., Goodin, R.E., Schillemans, T.: The Oxford Handbook of Public Accountability. OUP, Oxford (2014)

Boyle, E.A., et al.: An update to the systematic literature review of empirical evidence of the impacts and outcomes of computer games and serious games. Comput. Educ. **94**, 178–192 (2016). https://doi.org/10.1016/j.compedu.2015.11.003

Burlian, T.D., Sharmila, P., Alavesa, P., Arhippainen, L.: Revitalizing Viena Karelian dialect and culture with gamification, vol. 12 (2019)

Cassell, C., Symon, G.: Essential Guide to Qualitative Methods in Organizational Research. SAGE, London (2004)

Cohen, L., Manion, L., Morrison, K.: Research methods in education. Μεταίχμιο (2008). http:// dspace.lib.uom.gr/handle/2159/13669

Doughty, C.J., Long, M.H.: The Handbook of Second Language Acquisition. Wiley, New York (2008)

Engwall, O., Lopes, J.: Interaction and collaboration in robot-assisted language learning for adults. Comput. Assist. Lang. Learn. **0**, 1–37 (2020). https://doi.org/10.1080/09588221.2020.1799821

Engwall, O., Lopes, J., Cumbal, R.: Is a Wizard-of-Oz required for robot-led conversation practice in a second language? Int. J. Soc. Robot. (2022). https://doi.org/10.1007/s12369-021-00849-8

Glisky, E.L.: Changes in cognitive function in human aging. In: Brain Aging. CRC Press (2007)

Guba, E.G., Lincoln, Y.S.: Effective evaluation: Improving the usefulness of evaluation results through responsive and naturalistic approaches, pp. xxv, 423. Jossey-Bass (1981)

Henning, J.E., Stone, J.M., Kelly, J.L.: Using Action Research to Improve Instruction: An Interactive Guide for Teachers. Routledge (2008). https://doi.org/10.4324/9780203887295

Inoue, F., Hanzawa, Y.: Multivariate analysis of geography and age in dialect vocabulary—Comprehensive analysis of 250 years of language change -. Dialectologia: revista electrònica, 97–160 (2021)

Iosifidis, T.: Qualitative research methods in the social sciences. 'Ποιοτικές μέθοδοι έρευνας στις κοινωνικές επιστήμες'. Κριτική (2008). http://dspace.lib.uom.gr/handle/2159/15539

Kidd, C.D., Breazeal, C.: Effect of a robot on user perceptions. In: 2004 IEEE/RSJ International Conference on Intelligent Robots and Systems (IROS) (IEEE Cat. No.04CH37566), vol. 4, pp. 3559–3564 (2004). https://doi.org/10.1109/IROS.2004.1389967

Knapp, M.L., Hall, J.A., Horgan, T.G.: Nonverbal communication in human interaction. Cengage Learning (2013)

Lee, S., Noh, H., Lee, J., Lee, K.: On the effectiveness of Robot-assisted language learning | ReCALL | Cambridge core. ReCALL **23**(1), 25–58 (2011). https://doi.org/10.1017/S09583440 10000273

Levy, M.: Computer-Assisted Language Learning: Context and Conceptualization. Clarendon Press, Oxford (1997)

Leyzberg, D., Spaulding, S., Toneva, M., Scassellati, B.: The physical presence of a robot tutor increases cognitive learning gains. In: Proceedings of the Annual Meeting of the Cognitive Science Society, vol. 34, no. 34, p. 7 (2012)

Lightbown, P.M., Spada, N.: How Languages Are Learned, 5th edn. Oxford University Press, Oxford (2021)

McNiff, J.: Action Research: All You Need to Know. SAGE, London (2017)

Mubin, O., Stevens, C.J., Shahid, S., Mahmud, A.A., Dong, J.-J.: A review of the applicability of robots in education. Technol. Educ. Learn. 1(1) (2013). https://doi.org/10.2316/Journal.209. 2013.1.209-0015

Nomura, T., Kanda, T., Suzuki, T.: Experimental investigation into influence of negative attitudes toward robots on human–robot interaction. AI Soc. 2(20), 138–150 (2006). https://doi.org/10. 1007/s00146-005-0012-7

Patton, M.Q.: Qualitative Research & Evaluation Methods: Integrating Theory and Practice. SAGE Publications, London (2014)

Rintjema, E., van den Berghe, R., Kessels, A., de Wit, J., Vogt, P.: A robot teaching young children a second language: the effect of multiple interactions on engagement and performance. In: Companion of the 2018 ACM/IEEE International Conference on Human-Robot Interaction, pp. 219–220 (2018). https://doi.org/10.1145/3173386.3177059

Robson, C.: Real-World Research: A Tool for Social Scientists and Professional Researchers. Gutenberg, Athens (2010)

Serholt, S., Barendregt, W.: Students' attitudes towards the possible future of social robots in education. IEEE RO-MAN, 6 (2014)

Sharkey, A.J.C.: Should we welcome robot teachers? Ethics Inf. Technol. 18(4), 283–297 (2016). https://doi.org/10.1007/s10676-016-9387-z

Shidujaman, M., Mi, H.: "Which Country Are You from?" A cross-cultural study on greeting interaction design for social robots. In: Rau, P.-L. (ed.) CCD 2018. LNCS, vol. 10911, pp. 362–374. Springer, Cham (2018). https://doi.org/10.1007/978-3-319-92141-9_28

Shidujaman, M., Mi, H., Jamal, L.: 'I trust you more': a behavioral greeting gesture study on social robots for recommendation tasks. In: 2020 International Conference on Image Processing and Robotics (ICIP), pp. 1–5 (2020). https://doi.org/10.1109/ICIP48927.2020.9367364

Siegel, J.: Second Dialect Acquisition. Cambridge University Press, Cambridge (2010)

Tapus, A., Matarić, M.J.: User personality matching with a hands-off robot for post-stroke rehabilitation therapy. In: Khatib, O., Kumar, V., Rus, D. (eds.), Experimental Robotics: The 10th International Symposium on Experimental Robotics, pp. 165–175. Springer, Cham (2008). https://doi.org/10.1007/978-3-540-77457-0_16

Tzakosta, M. (ed.): The Teaching of Modern Greek Language Varieties and Dialects in Primary and Secondary Education' Η Διδασκαλία των Νεοελληνικών Γλωσσικών Ποικιλιών και Διαλέκτων στην Πρωτοβάθμια και Δευτεροβάθμια Εκπαίδευση'. Gutenberg (2015). https://www.dardanosnet.gr/product/didaskalia-ton-neoellinikon-glossikon-pik ilion-ke-dialekton-stin-protovathmia-ke-defterovathmia-ekpedefsi-i/

van den Berghe, R., Verhagen, J., Oudgenoeg-Paz, O., van der Ven, S., Leseman, P.: Social robots for language learning: a review. Rev. Educ. Res. 89(2), 259–295 (2019). https://doi.org/10. 3102/0034654318821286

Velentza, A.-M., Fachantidis, N., Lefkos, I.: Learn with surprize from a robot professor. Comput. Educ. 173, 104272 (2021). https://doi.org/10.1016/j.compedu.2021.104272

Velentza, A.-M., Ioannidis, S., Georgakopoulou, N., Shidujaman, M., Fachantidis, N.: Educational robot european cross-cultural design. In: Kurosu, M. (ed.) HCII 2021. LNCS, vol. 12763, pp. 341–353. Springer, Cham (2021). https://doi.org/10.1007/978-3-030-78465-2_26

Verga, L., Kotz, S.A.: Help me if I can't: social interaction effects in adult contextual word learning. Cognition 168, 76–90 (2017). https://doi.org/10.1016/j.cognition.2017.06.018

Vogt, P., et al.: Second language tutoring using social robots: a large-scale study. In: 2019 14th ACM/IEEE International Conference on Human-Robot Interaction (HRI), pp. 497–505 (2019). https://doi.org/10.1109/HRI.2019.8673077

Wainer, J., Feil-Seifer, D.J., Shell, D.A., Mataric, M.J.: Embodiment and human-robot interaction: a task-based perspective. In: RO-MAN 2007 - The 16th IEEE International Symposium on Robot and Human Interactive Communication, pp. 872–877 (2007). https://doi.org/10.1109/ROMAN.2007.4415207

Wheeler, R.S.: Attitude change is not enough: disrupting deficit grading practices to disrupt dialect prejudice. Proc. Linguist. Soc. Am. 4(1), 10–12 (2019). https://doi.org/10.3765/plsa.v4i1.4505

Wlodkowski, R.J., Ginsberg, M.B.: Enhancing Adult Motivation to Learn: A Comprehensive Guide for Teaching All Adults. Wiley, Hoboken (2017)

Wullenkord, R., Fraune, M. R., Eyssel, F., Šabanović, S.: Getting in touch: how imagined, actual, and physical contact affect evaluations of robots. In: 2016 25th IEEE International Symposium on Robot and Human Interactive Communication (RO-MAN), pp. 980–985 (2016). https://doi.org/10.1109/ROMAN.2016.7745228

Xia, Y., LeTendre, G.: Robots for future classrooms: a cross-cultural validation study of "Negative Attitudes Toward Robots Scale" in the U.S. context. Int. J. Soc. Robot. 13(4), 703–714 (2020). https://doi.org/10.1007/s12369-020-00669-2

Effects of Social Robot's Face and Interface Design on Operation Efficiency and User Perceptions

Xiao-Yu Jia[✉] and Chien-Hsiung Chen

National Taiwan University of Science and Technology, No.43, Keelung Rd., Sec.4, Da'an District, Taipei City 10607, Taiwan
{D10810805,cchen}@mail.ntust.edu.tw

Abstract. Currently, humanoid service robots or social robots have been used in many places, such as hospitals, shopping malls, and hotels, etc. The robots are mainly divided into two forms: one is a form in which the head of the robot is separated from the interactive interface, and the other has only one integrated head and interactive user interface. Which of these two forms of robots is more efficient for users' operations, and which one gives people better perceptions, is worthy of our in-depth exploration. The purpose of this study was to adopt the method of combining eye tracking and evaluation scale to help investigate the influence of different display forms on the user's operation efficiency and perceptions pertinent to social robots. The generated results are as follows: (1) Both the appearance of the robot and the level of abstraction of the robot's face affect participants' perceptions of them to some extent. (2) The robot with abstract face was considered more humanlike and was much liked than the robot with concrete face. (3) It is generally believed that the separate form of the robot head and the user interface make the robot look more like a human and have a better impression. (4) Robots with separated head and operating interface were considered to have higher operability.

Keywords: Social robot · Robot face · User interface · Operation efficiency · Eye-tracking

1 Introduction

Exploring people's attitudes towards the appearance of social robots in a low-cost and efficient way, and enhancing the experience of human-robot interaction (HRI) have always been the topics of concern for some researchers. Currently, humanoid service robots or social robots have been used in many places, such as hospitals, shopping malls, and hotels, etc. The robots are mainly divided into two forms: one is a form in which the head of the robot is separated from the interactive interface (e.g., pepper [1]), and the other has only one integrated head and interactive interface. Which of these two forms of robots is more efficient for users' operations, and which one gives people better perceptions, is worthy of our in-depth exploration. In addition, there are also some studies showing that certain changes in the social robot's face, such as the degree of abstraction, also affect people's perceptions of the robot and the HRI experience to a certain extent. These issues all directly affect the efficiency and experience of HRI.

2 Related Work

2.1 The Experience of HRI

Social interactive robot (i.e., social robot) refers to "a robot in which social interaction plays a key role" [2]. It is a robot plus a social interface, and the social interface as a metaphor contains all social attributes. Observers perceive robots as social interaction partners through these social attributes [3].

In recent years, people from all walks of life have been paying more and more attention to HRI and social robots, and no longer only focus on technology research and development. More scholars focus on the human experience in the process of HRI. For social robots, interactive feedback should also be involved. Among them, the key to the success of social interaction robots is to establish a close and effective interaction between humans and robots, which usually involves many factors [2].

On the one hand, from the perspective of HRI, in robot design, one of the key issues affecting HRI is the appearance problem, which determines the first impression of human beings to robots. The other is the behavior of the robot in the interaction, which also implies social cues and other issues. The biological mechanism of a series of reactions of living organisms include human emotions, attitudes, and the process and results of this series of reactions and image evaluations.

2.2 Social Robot Face

The head of a robot is usually the main site of HRI [4]. If the robot has head-like features, the possibility of cooperation with it is greatly increased [5]. Much of the research on people's perception of robots is related to robot faces, and most of them are related to humanoid features or perceptions of robots [4, 6, 7].

For facial features, the main elements of the study included: eyes rendered (digitally) by rendering, authenticity and detail of facial features, present or absence of specific features. Some scholars express the social properties of robots through expressive eyes [8–10]. Scholars such as Hoffman et al. (2015) studied the deceptive behavior of participants by comparing robot and screen-based eye animations with real people. In addition, the realism and details of facial features have also attracted the attention of some scholars [11, 12].

However, at present, the types of specific use environments of robots that have been studied for HRI experience are still relatively small. There are few researchers on the suitable shape features of robots in different usage environments and the impact of changes in facial features on people's perceptions. These issues are worthy of further exploration.

3 Methods

The purpose of this study was to adopt the method of combining eye tracking (i.e., the SMI Remote Eye-tracking Device, RED 250mobile) and evaluation scale (i.e., adapted from the Godspeed questionnaire [13] and questionnaire of system usability scale (SUS) [14]) to help investigate the influence of different display forms on the user's operation efficiency and perceptions pertinent to social robots.

3.1 Participants

A total of 24 participants were invited by convenience sampling (12 males and 12 females) method. The number of participants with smart robot experience was 45.8%. In addition, the main age distribution of the participants was 19–30 years old (75%).

3.2 Materials

The experiment was conducted with a 2 × 2 mixed 2-way ANOVA design, the research variables were robot appearances (i.e., the head was separated from the operational interface, vs the integrated head and the operational interface) and the robot face (i.e., abstract face vs concrete face). The robot appearance was the within-subjects factor, the robot face was the between-subjects factor. The experimental prototypes were created as a flash animation displayed on a computer screen, which simulated the service scene of the robot through 3D modeling (i.e., the robot prototype was taken from the upper body of the robot Wangbao 5 [15]), and the participants needed to click on the corresponding operation with the mouse step by step to complete a simple task flow regarding the navigation in a shopping mall. The experimental program was written using E-prime 3.0. The presentation order of the stimuli was counterbalanced in advance to avoid the sequential effect. The experimental samples are shown in Fig. 1.

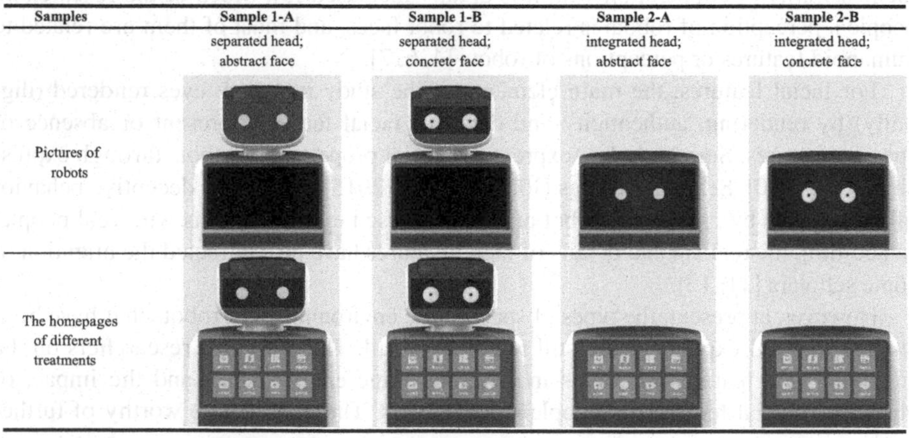

Samples	Sample 1-A	Sample 1-B	Sample 2-A	Sample 2-B
	separated head; abstract face	separated head; concrete face	integrated head; abstract face	integrated head; concrete face
Pictures of robots				
The homepages of different treatments				

Fig. 1. The descriptions of experimental samples

3.3 Procedure

The experimental process of this study was as follows:

Step1: Fill in the basic information. The participant needed to complete the basic information including gender, age and the experience with smart robots.

Step2: The task operation. The participant needed to independently complete a query task operation about navigating in a shopping mall according to the robot's instructions and the prompts on the screen.

Step3: Fill in the subjective scale and system usability scale (SUS). After the task was completed, the participant needed to fill in the corresponding questionnaires including the Godspeed questionnaire and SUS based on the task operation experience.

Step4: Calibration of the eye tracker. The participant needed to calibrate the eye-tracking device after sitting down in front of the screen in the fixed position.

Step5: Observe a set of robot pictures. Observe a set of robot pictures (a total of 7 pictures) that are presented immediately. These pictures include robot images of different treatments, and some pictures also include the homepage of the robot operation interface.

It should be noted that the eye-tracking device was fixed on the top of the screen in advance. From the beginning of the experiment to the end, the experimenter will not give any hints or interference on the participant's task operation until the experiment was completed [16]. The experimental process of Step 2 (the operational task) was shown in Fig. 2. The pictures of Step5 (Observe a set of robot pictures) were shown in Fig. 3.

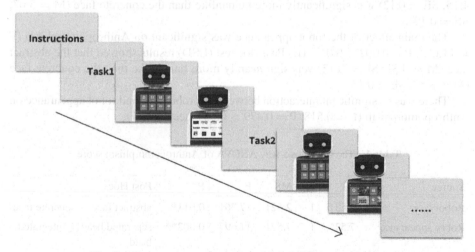

Fig. 2. The experimental process of Step2: The task operation

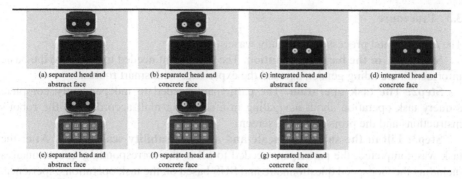

Fig. 3. Observe a set of robot pictures of Step5

4 Results

The collected data were analyzed using a mixed two-way analysis of variance (ANOVA) in SPSS with the robot appearance as the within-subjects factor, and the robot face as the between-subjects factor. The significant value α was set to 0.05.

4.1 The Godspeed Questionnaire Scores

The main effect of the robot face was significant on Anthropomorphism (F = 7.761, P = 0.011 < 0.05). The Post Hoc test (LSD) results showed that the abstract face (M = 4.15, SE = 0.12) was significantly more humanlike than the concrete face (M = 3.67, SE = 0.12).

The main effect of the robot appearance was significant on Anthropomorphism (F = 11.697, P = 0.002 < 0.01). The Post Hoc test (LSD) results showed that the abstract face (M = 4.31, SE = 0.13) was significantly more humanlike than the concrete face (M = 3.52, SE = 0.15).

There was no significant interaction between the robot face and robot appearance on Anthropomorphism (F = 0.518, P = 0.479 > 0.05) (see Table 1).

Table 1. The mixed two-way ANOVA of Anthropomorphism score

Source	SS	df	MS	F	P	Post Hoc
Robot face	2.521	1	2.521	7.761	0.011*	abstract face > concrete face
Robot appearance	7.521	1	7.521	11.697	0.002**	separated head > integrated head
Robot face × Robot appearance	0.333	1	0.333	0.518	0.479	

* Significantly different at $\alpha = 0.05$ level (* P < 0.05).
** Significantly different at $\alpha = 0.01$ level (**P < 0.01).

The main effect of the robot face (F = 0.365, P = 0.552 > 0.05) and robot appearance (F = 0.705, P = 0.410 > 0.05) were not significant on Animacy.

In addition, there was a significant interaction between the robot face and robot appearance on Animacy (F = 7.451, P = 0.012 < 0.05) (see Table 2). In combination with Fig. 4, it could be seen that the separated head with a concrete face (M = 4.13) was more animacy than that of the separated head with an abstract face (M = 3.46). On the contrary, the integrated head with an abstract face (M = 4.17) was more animacy than the integrated head with a concrete face (M = 3.75).

Table 2. The mixed two-way ANOVA of Animacy score

Source	SS	df	MS	F	P	Post Hoc
Robot face	0.188	1	0.188	0.365	0.552	
Robot appearance	0.333	1	0.333	0.705	0.410	
Robot face × Robot appearance	3.521	1	3.521	7.451	0.012*	

* Significantly different at $\alpha = 0.05$ level (* P < 0.05).
** Significantly different at $\alpha = 0.01$ level (**P < 0.01).

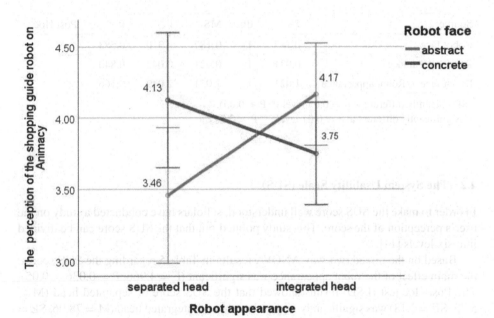

Fig. 4. The interaction of robot appearance and robot face on the perception of the robot on Animacy

The main effect of the robot face was significant on Likeability (F = 13.526, P = 0.001 < 0.01). The Post Hoc test (LSD) results showed that the abstract face (M = 4.65, SE = 0.14) was significantly more liked than the concrete face (M = 3.90, SE = 0.14).

There was no significant interaction between the robot face and robot appearance on Likeability (F = 0.473, P = 0.499 > 0.05) (see Table 3).

In addition, there was no significant difference on Perceived Intelligent (see Table 4).

Table 3. The mixed two-way ANOVA of Likeability score

Source	SS	df	MS	F	P	Post Hoc
Robot face	6.750	1	6.750	13.526	0.001**	abstract face > concrete face
Robot appearance	0.333	1	0.333	0.840	0.369	
Robot face × Robot appearance	0.187	1	0.187	0.473	0.499	

* Significantly different at $\alpha = 0.05$ level (* $P < 0.05$).
** Significantly different at $\alpha = 0.01$ level (**$P < 0.01$).

Table 4. The mixed two-way ANOVA of Perceived Intelligent score

Source	SS	df	MS	F	P	Post Hoc
Robot face	0.187	1	0.187	0.310	0.583	
Robot appearance	0.021	1	0.021	0.042	0.840	
Robot face × Robot appearance	1.021	1	1.021	2.049	0.166	

* Significantly different at $\alpha = 0.05$ level (* $P < 0.05$).
** Significantly different at $\alpha = 0.01$ level (**$P < 0.01$).

4.2 The System Usability Scale (SUS)

In order to make the SUS score well understood, scholars have conducted a study on the user's perception of the score. This study pointed out that the SUS score can be divided into six levels [14].

Based on the mixed two-way ANOVA results in Table 5 regarding the SUS scores, the main effect of the robot appearance was significant (F = 4.966, P = 0.036 < 0.05). The Post Hoc test (LSD) results showed that the SUS score of separated head (M = 5.73, SE = 2.18) was significantly higher than that of integrated head (M = 78.96, SE = 1.87). In addition, there was no significant interaction between robot face and the robot appearance on the SUS scores (F = 0.424, P = 0.522 > 0.05). Figure 5 showed the relationship between the SUS interval and the scores (see Table 6) of the four samples [14].

Table 5. The mixed two-way ANOVA of the System Usability Scale (SUS) scores

Source	SS	df	MS	F	P	Post Hoc
Robot face	15.755	1	15.755	0.181	0.675	
Robot appearance	550.130	1	550.130	4.966	0.036*	separated head > integrated head
Robot face × Robot appearance	47.005	1	47.005	0.424	0.522	

* Significantly different at $\alpha = 0.05$ level (* $P < 0.05$).
** Significantly different at $\alpha = 0.01$ level (**$P < 0.01$).

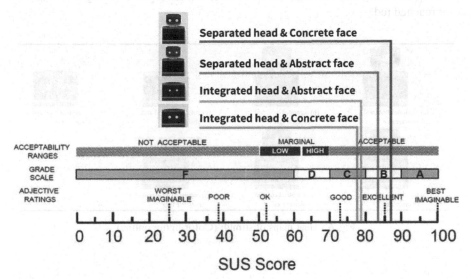

Fig. 5. The relationship between the interval of the System Usability Scale (SUS) and the scores of four samples

Table 6. Descriptive statistics of "shopping guide robot" on System Usability Scale (SUS) scores

	Sample 1-A separated head/abstract face	Sample 1-B separated head/concrete face	Sample 2-A integrated head/abstract face	Sample 2-B integrated head / abstract face
M	84.17	87.29	79.38	78.54
SD	10.35	11.00	9.12	9.20
N	12	12	12	12

* Significantly different at $\alpha = 0.05$ level (* $P < 0.05$).
** Significantly different at $\alpha = 0.01$ level (**$P < 0.01$).

4.3 The Eye-Tracking Data

Heat Maps. The eye tracking data analysis software can collect the fixation points of all participants in a certain group, and then superimpose them on the stimulus picture, and use the highlighted color to indicate the scanned position of the participants' gaze, from green to yellow and then to red. This indicates that a certain area is being watched more and more frequently. The gaze heat maps formed by the seven stimuli is shown in Fig. 6.

From this we could see that when the participants were interacting with the robot, their attention was also very focused. When the robot did not have a separate head, the participants mostly focused on the robot's operating interface; when the robot's operating interface and head were separated, the participants mostly focus on the robot's face and operating interface, and focus on the robot's head. The degree was higher, so that the color reached red.

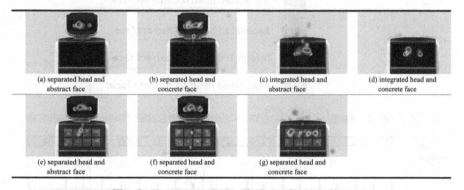

Fig. 6. Heat maps of stimuli (Color figure online)

Scan Paths. Scan paths help researchers understand the location of the areas on the stimulus material that attract the attention of the participants and the browsing sequence of the participants. As shown in Fig. 7, the scan paths reflect the path that the participants' eyes move on the screen. Longer fixations are represented by larger dots.

Figure 7 presents the 7 eye tracking paths of the stimulus materials while watching. Comparing the pictures, it could be seen that when the robot head and the operation interface information existed at the same time, the participants payed more attention and focus more on the area widely. When comparing the pictures of the robot head and the operation interface that existed at the same time, but the operation interface does not display information, it could be found that when the robot's head and the operation interface area overlapped. The participants' attention was the most concentrated, which was also what we expected. Nonetheless, the relevant differences were less pronounced for different face types.

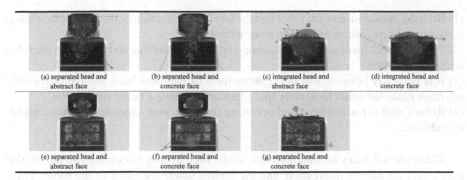

Fig. 7. Scan paths of stimuli

4.4 Discussions

In this study, we divided the common welcome robots on the market into two categories for exploration, and divided the degree of abstraction of the robot's face.

Firstly, needless to say, both the appearance of the robot and the level of abstraction of the robot's face affected participants' perceptions of them to some extent. For example, the abstract face was considered more humanlike than the concrete face. It seems that this result is not consistent with some studies, usually more concrete faces are perceived as more humanlike [6, 17, 18]. The reason for this result may be that the concrete eye is quite different from the real human being, and the eyes are the symbol of a living object even if they are abstract. In addition, participants also preferred abstract faces, probably because they looked more concise and kind.

Secondly, it seems that whether the robot's head is separated from the operation interface has little effect on the ease of use of the service robot, which is also consistent with our expected assumption: generally, the welcome robot in the shopping mall does not have many complicated functions, and most of them need to be designed simple and easy to use for people of all ages. In general, robots with separated head and operating interface are considered to have higher operability, and this result is also verified in the data results of eye tracking.

Thirdly, compared with the robot with the separated head and the operation interface, the robot with integrated head and the operation interface can attract the attention of the participants, but it is slightly less easy to operate. In fact, according to the service occasions and interface usage frequency of different social robots, the appearance of the robot will be different. This research study only focuses on the use experience of shopping mall robots, and there are more application scenarios, such as hospitals, banks or hotels, which are worthy of further exploration.

5 Conclusions and Future Implications

Based on the quantitative and qualitative research results, the following suggestions were proposed:

(1) Both the appearance of the robot and the level of abstraction of the robot's face affect participants' perceptions of them to some extent.

(2) The robot with abstract face was considered more humanlike and liked than the robot with concrete face.

(3) It is generally believed that the separate form of the robot head and the operational interface make the robot look more like a human and have a better impression.

(4) Robots with separated head and operating interface were considered to have higher operability.

There are still many limitations in this study, such as only discussing two factors that may affect the robot's impression, and the limited usage scenarios of the robot. These findings will serve as pre-experiments for subsequent experiments.

References

1. Aaltonen, I., Arvola, A., Heikkil., P., Lammi, H.: Hello pepper, may I tickle you? Children's and adults' responses to an entertainment robot at a shopping mall. In: ACM/IEEE International Conference on Human-Robot Interaction, pp. 53–54 (2017)
2. Fong, T., Nourbakhsh, I., Dautenhahn, K.: A survey of socially interactive robots. Robot. Auton. Syst. **42**(3–4), 143–166 (2003)
3. Hegel, F., Lohse, M., Wrede, B.: Effects of visual appearance on the attribution of applications in social robotics. In: RO-MAN 2009-The 18th IEEE International Symposium on Robot and Human Interactive Communication, pp. 64–71 (2009). https://doi.org/10.1109/RO-MAN. 2009.5326340
4. DiSalvo, C.F., Gemperle, F., Forlizzi, J., Kiesler, S.: All robots are not created equal: the design and perception of humanoid robot heads. In: Proceedings of the 4th Conference on Designing Interactive Systems: Processes, Practices, Methods, and Techniques, pp. 321–326 (2002)
5. McGinn, C.: Why do robots need a head? the role of social interfaces on service robots. Int. J. Soc. Robot. 1–15 (2019)
6. Mathur, M.B., Reichling, D.B.: Navigating a social world with robot partners: a quantitative cartography of the Uncanny Valley. Cognition **146**, 22–32 (2016)
7. Zhang, T., Kaber, D.B., Zhu, B., Swangnetr, M., Mosaly, P., Hodge, L.: Service robot feature design effects on user perceptions and emotional responses. Intel. Serv. Robot. **3**(2), 73–88 (2010)
8. Hoffman, G., et al.: Robot presence and human honesty: experimental evidence. In: 2015 10th ACM/IEEE International Conference on Human-Robot Interaction (HRI), pp. 181–188 (2015)
9. Tasaki, R., Kitazaki, M., Miura, J., Terashima, K.: Prototype design of medical round supporting robot "Terapio". In: 2015 IEEE International Conference on Robotics and Automation (ICRA), pp. 829–834. IEEE (2015). https://doi.org/10.1109/ICRA.2015.7139274
10. Björling, E.A., Rose, E.: Participatory research principles in human-centered design: engaging teens in the co-design of a social robot. Multimodal Technol. Interact. **3**(1), 8 (2019)
11. Kalegina, A., Schroeder, G., Allchin, A., Berlin, K., Cakmak, M.: Characterizing the design space of rendered robot faces. In: Proceedings of the 2018 ACM/IEEE International Conference on Human-Robot Interaction, pp. 96–104 (2018)
12. Wittig, S., Rätsch, M., Kloos, U.: Parameterized facial animation for socially interactive robots. In: Diefenbach, S., Henze, N., Pielot, M. (eds.) Mensch und Computer 2015 – Proceedings, pp. 355–358. De Gruyter Oldenbourg, Berlin (2015)

13. Bartneck, C., Kuli, D., Croft, E., Zoghbi, S.: Measurement instruments for the anthropomorphism, animacy, likeability, perceived intelligence, and perceived safety of robots. Int. J. Soc. Robot. **1**(1), 71–81 (2009)
14. Bangor, A., Kortum, P., Miller, J.: Determining what individual SUS scores mean: adding an adjective rating scale. J. Usability Stud. **4**(3), 114–123 (2009)
15. Cobos Commercial Robot Co., Ltd. (n.d.). Wang Bao 5-BENEBOT 5-A new generation of tool-based business service robots. http://www.ecovacs-c.com/product-series/interactive-service-robot/102.html
16. Lee, J., Ahn, J.H.: Attention to banner ads and their effectiveness: an eye-tracking approach. Int. J. Electron. Commer. **17**(1), 119–137 (2012)
17. Broadbent, E., et al.: Robots with display screens: a robot with a more humanlike face display is perceived to have more mind and a better personality. PloS one, **8**(8), e72589 (2013)
18. Mori, M., MacDorman, K.F., Kageki, N.: The uncanny valley [from the field]. IEEE Robot. Autom. Mag. **19**(2), 98–100 (2012). https://doi.org/10.1109/MRA.2012.2192811

Pilot Study for Myoelectric Control of a Supernumerary Robot During a Coordination Task

Sarah O'Meara[✉] [iD], Stephen Robinson, and Sanjay Joshi

University of California Davis, Davis, USA
someara@ucdavis.edu

Abstract. Robots are used in a wide variety of applications to augment the capability of humans. A relatively new category of assistive robots, supernumerary robots (SRs), create an additional, kinematically independent limb or appendage that may serve various functions. SR research has centered on device development and proof-of-concept but has generally not focused on the human interface and human-robot performance. In this pilot study, four subjects completed 80 cursor-to-target trials of a three-handed coordination task with a collaborative robot. The subjects used their two natural hands to control a cursor on a screen in 2-DOFs (degrees of freedom) and used a leg muscle signal to control the robotic hand. The robotic hand controlled the cursor in the third DOF. We calculated two metrics to assess coordination, the coordination score and the DOF activation. Subjects improved in the coordination score and DOF activation throughout the study duration. The subjects increased the percentage of trial time with 3-DOFs active and correspondingly decreased 1-DOF activation. The results indicated that subjects learned how to improve their coordination, while successfully completing trials and decreasing their trial completion time. The subjects tended to coordinate most of the time with their hands (41%) followed by all three limbs (19%). Future studies should focus on increasing the proportion of 3-DOF coordination for improved human-robot performance.

Keywords: Supernumerary robots · Human-machine interfaces · Myoelectric control

1 Introduction

Robots are used in a wide variety of applications including disaster response and minimally invasive surgery. In these cases, robots augment the capability of humans by extending their presence into an extreme or challenging environment. The research interest in human-robot collaboration has grown exponentially [1] and a related field has recently emerged: supernumerary robots (SRs). SRs are characterized by creating an additional, kinematically independent limb or appendage that may serve various functions. Of particular interest is SRs' potential to reduce risk and increase capability in challenging environments by providing a third, robotic arm for manipulation. The current state-of-the-art in SRs has focused on the development of the robot and less research

© The Author(s), under exclusive license to Springer Nature Switzerland AG 2022
M. Kurosu (Ed.): HCII 2022, LNCS 13303, pp. 518–536, 2022.
https://doi.org/10.1007/978-3-031-05409-9_38

has centered on the user interface and performance of the human-SR system. The experiments conducted with humans and SRs to complete a task have focused on specific use cases and tasks that do not provide as much detail on the human-robot interaction.

SRs are distinct from other assistive robots and comprise a relatively novel field of research. Exoskeletons augment the abilities of existing limbs, prosthetics restore functionality by replacing lost appendages, and SRs can create limbs that are kinematically independent from the user. SRs may manifest as arms [2–7], legs [8, 9], or fingers [10–15]. Current SRs have several potential use cases: body bracing [2, 8, 9], overhead tasks [3, 4], grasp assistance [11–13], and manipulation tasks [5–7] (a more detailed and potential usage taxonomy for wearable SR arms may be found in Ref. [16]). The research in this field has centered on device development and proof-of-concept but has generally not focused on the human interface and human-robot performance.

According to the classification framework proposed by Leigh et al. [17], human-robot systems that can be considered a single unit, may be classified by type of support and control methods. SR development has focused on indirect control, or "Pseudo-Mapping" and "Shared Control" according to Leigh's framework, by predicting the human's intent (for examples see Refs. [3, 4, 11]). In contrast to using prediction to identify intent, there has also been some work on direct control of SRs (i.e., "Direct Control"). For example, a supernumerary finger used a combination of hand gestures to control position and muscle signals (i.e., myoelectric control) to modulate the grip strength [10]. A subsequent version of the supernumerary finger incorporated buttons and haptic feedback [12]. Another SR, a supernumerary arm, was commanded by foot position and toe flexion to directly control 6-DOFs [6]. The selection of the control method, whether direct or indirect, may depend on the application including the role of the SR in the task. However, there has been little available guidance or knowledge regarding control methods and task allocation due to the novelty of the field. Therefore, this study aimed to focus on direct control for a primary task, which has not been well-studied in the field.

Direct control SRs that use Body-Machine Interfaces (BoMIs), such as gestures or muscle signals, need to use an existing part of the body, which may seem counter to the concept of SRs creating a limb. However, for tasks or applications where part of the body would not otherwise be used, it provides an opportunity to reallocate resources. Specifically, the lower limbs are available in seated tasks as demonstrated by Saraiji et al. [6] for the foot control of a 6-DOF SR. Furthermore, coordination between the hands and legs occurs in a variety of skilled tasks, such as the use of foot pedals by dentists and doctors. For example, in a virtual laparoscopic task at least one hand worked in coordination with the foot for 50% of the task time [18]. Similarly, instead of the foot controlling an instrument, the foot could also be represented as a hand. Abdi et al. compared two-handed and three-handed performance during a virtual task where subjects needed to catch falling objects [19]. The subjects controlled the third hand with their leg. The results showed that subjects missed fewer objects in the three-hand paradigm as task difficulty increased [19]. A similar study assessed coordination between the hands and legs for various virtual tasks and deemed the control strategy feasible for SRs [20]. However, the experiment did not include any robot simulation or hardware. Overall, the incorporation of foot control for SRs has precedent from other fields (refer to Ref. [21] for review of foot control in HCIs).

The purpose of this pilot study was to incorporate a direct control BoMI with a SR and assess the human's ability to coordinate between their hands and the lower limb while controlling the SR (the robotic, third hand). Subjects controlled the robotic, third hand through myoelectric control, where muscle activation was measured from the surface of the skin by a pair of electrodes, also known as surface electromyography (sEMG). The task was designed such that all three hands were needed to successfully complete the task. Simultaneous coordination of the hands was the goal communicated to the subjects, but it was possible to operate each hand independently. Instead of designing our own SR, we used a commercial, collaborative robot. We also did not constrain the SR to be physically attached to the human, since a wearable SR may not be necessary for every application. This study addressed current gaps in direct control interfaces and limb coordination for SR applications.

2 Materials and Methods

2.1 Subject Recruitment and Demographics

We designed a pilot experiment to investigate a three-handed, coordination task with two natural hands and a robotic, third hand. The protocol was approved by University of California Davis Institutional Review Board, and adult participants were recruited from the university. Exclusion criteria included history of neurological/neuromuscular disorders, limitations on arm and leg mobility, and failing coronavirus-specific screening. We chose to limit the age range of the participants to 18 through 39 years old based on the risk rates published by the Centers for Disease Control and Prevention [22]. Participants had to show proof of a negative coronavirus test and pass a coronavirus survey addressing symptoms and exposure risk on the day of their scheduled experiment session.

To further reduce the risk of coronavirus transmission, in addition to the coronavirus-specific screening, we remotely conducted the intake. At the start of the scheduled experiment session, the subject called the researcher to complete the coronavirus-specific screening. After passing the screening, the researcher reviewed the consent form with the subject; both the subject and researcher could view and sign the form online. Consented subjects then completed a pre-session survey to collect demographic information. The remainder of the experiment protocol occurred in-person at the research location. The in-person protocol consisted of experiment instructions, sEMG setup and calibration, a maximum voluntary contraction measurement, the task, a second maximum voluntary contraction measurement, and a post-session survey.

Four subjects consented to participate in this pilot experiment. The subjects ranged in age from 20 to 25 years with an equal participation of females and males. One subject identified their ethnicity as Hispanic, Latino/a, or Spanish and race as Asian. The remaining subjects were not of Hispanic, Latino/a, or Spanish ethnicity and identified their race as White. Origin and race survey questions followed the guidance document provided by the Food and Drug Administration [23]. All subjects self-reported a right hand dominance, and leg preference was determined using the revised Waterloo Footedness Questionnaire (WFQ-R) [24]. The leg preference was used for sEMG electrode placement, and three subjects reported a right leg preference. The remaining subject indicated a similar preference between left and right, but a recent injury resulted in the selection of the left leg. The subjects had some prior experience that may have made them amenable to the experiment's task. One subject had prior experience with myo-electric control, and all subjects played video games. Two subjects had significant prior experience with robots and the other two subjects had little to none, but all subjects answered that they thought they would be comfortable around robots.

2.2 Experiment Setup and System Architecture

The pilot experiment aimed to observe coordination between two natural hands and a robotic, third hand controlled by sEMG from the leg. We decided to not allow direct, physical interaction with this robot (UR5e, Universal Robots [25]), but used a computer-based task for indirect, physical interaction and direct myoelectric control and integration with the actual hardware. The overall experiment task software framework was created using AxoPy [26], which provides basic infrastructure to design and run myoelectric control experiments. Communication with the robot controller used the Universal Robots Real-Time Date Exchange (RTDE) interface [27] and leveraged the API created by the University of Southern Denmark (SDU) Robotics [28].

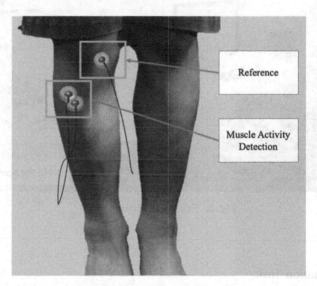

Fig. 1. Illustrative electrode placement on the tibialis anterior (image modified from [29])

The subjects completed a cursor-to-target task visualized on a desktop monitor. They used their natural hands to input keyboard commands to control the cursor in 2-DOFs and used their leg muscle to command the robotic hand position in the third DOF. The cursor position on the screen in the third DOF reflected the actual, scaled position of the robotic hand, or end effector. The ConMed 1620 Ag/AgCl center snap electrodes were placed approximately 2.5 cm apart on the tibialis anterior below the lateral tibial condyle to measure the muscle activation and a reference electrode was affixed to the kneecap (see Fig. 1). The electrodes were placed on the preferred leg as indicated by the WFQ-R. The sEMG signal acquisition followed [30] and was processed as described in [31], where the signal was sampled at 4096 Hz for 256-sample windows with a 4th order Butterworth filter (bandpass at 10 Hz and 500 Hz). The rms value for the window was normalized by each subject's calibration value and put in a moving average filter (length 0.5 s) to yield a processed signal update rate at 16 Hz. Commands and position data were exchanged between the experiment computer and robot controller at 16 Hz.

During the in-person portion of the experiment, the subjects sat at a desk in front of a desktop monitor. Subjects were instructed to adjust the chair height, so their feet rested comfortably on the floor and their thighs were approximately parallel to the floor. The robot was positioned within the field of view and off to the right of the desktop monitor. The subject and robot were separated by an adequate distance and stanchions were used as a physical barrier marking the keep out zone. The layout of the experiment room is shown in Fig. 2.

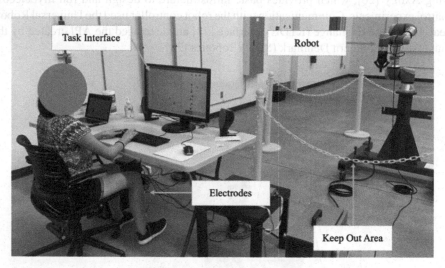

Fig. 2. Experiment room layout

2.3 Coordination Task

The subjects were informed during the experiment instructions that their task was to "move the cursor in three dimensions to select targets on a screen using three 'hands'" with the goal of simultaneous movement in 3-DOFs. The control method was deliberately chosen to require acquisition of a non-intuitive, complex control scheme to test the person's ability to acquire a new, complex motor skill. The development of an optimal control scheme could be the subject of future studies. In this pilot experiment, the subjects controlled the cursor motion using keyboard inputs with their hands and myoelectric control with their leg. Their left hands used keys *a* and *d* to move the cursor left and right along the x-axis, respectively. Each keypress increased or decreased the cursor speed in the x-direction meaning that a single press of key a would cause the cursor to continue moving left until either the cursor hit the task boundary and stopped, or a press of key d negated the leftward motion. The right hand manipulated the cursor motion along the z-axis, which was into and out of the screen. To show 3D motion in a 2D visualization, the cursor diameter decreased to show motion into the screen and the diameter increased for motion out of the screen. Key j decreased cursor diameter and key l increased the diameter. The cursor diameter was constrained from 0.15 to 2.45 times of the original diameter. The subjects' legs controlled robotic motion in the y-axis to move the cursor vertically. The subjects needed two commands, up and down, and communicated those commands by modulating their muscle activation. "Inputs" refer to muscle activations that exceeded a threshold; muscle activations below the threshold were considered "at rest." The first input selected the command and the second input resulted in forward motion for the duration that the processed sEMG signal input remained above the threshold, l_1. A short input (≤ 0.5 s) selected the "up" command and a long input (>0.5s) selected the "down" command. The robot moved at a constant velocity and therefore so did the cursor in the y-axis. The commands are summarized in Table 1.

Table 1. Summary of 3-DOF cursor commands

Axis	Direction	Command	Input method	Leg/Hand
x	Left	*a*	Keyboard	Left hand
	Right	*d*		
y	Up	*Short*	sEMG	Leg
	Down	*Long*		
z	In	*j*	Keyboard	Right hand
	Out	*l*		

The user interface included an information interface and a task interface for the cursor-to-target task (see Fig. 3). The information interface contained a set of status lights, the command key, and an sEMG signal bar. The status lights indicated in which DOFs the cursor was currently in motion by turning from gray to green. These lights could be helpful when the cursor moved at a low velocity, especially in the z axis, and provided a different visual representation of the subjects' goal, 3-DOF movement (i.e., keep all the status lights green). The subjects never had to memorize the cursor commands and could refer to the command key. The sEMG signal bar displayed their current processed signal value as an overlaid, dark gray bar. The light blue region and light pink region designated the rest area and active area, respectively.

In addition to the elements in the information interface, we used color feedback to provide additional information during the task. The cursor body had concurrent feedback to indicate the reception and interpretation of the sEMG signal. The cursor body changed from black to a dark gold when the sEMG signal crossed the threshold; the color would change to light blue if the first input time exceeded 0.5 s to indicate a long input. The cursor body remained the color of the selected command during the second input. This concurrent color feedback was the same scheme as the manual rotate method in our prior study [31]. The other two forms of color feedback applied to the target. To select the target, the cursor needed to be at approximately the same depth, which was represented by diameter. The cursor was considered at the same depth if difference in scale between the cursor and target diameters was within 0.10 units. In preliminary testing, we tried a fixed percentage of the target diameter, but the margins were too small for far targets and too large for near targets. Since it could be visually difficult to estimate the cursor depth, we used color feedback on the target body to indicate when the cursor and target were at approximately the same depth. The target was nominally light purple and turned green when the cursor was at depth. In addition to placing the cursor at the same depth as the target, the subjects needed to dwell on the target for 1 s to select it. The target turned orange when the cursor selected the target. If the cursor was not at the appropriate depth and overlapped with the target, the target would remain light purple. Table 2 contains information about the additional visual feedback elements.

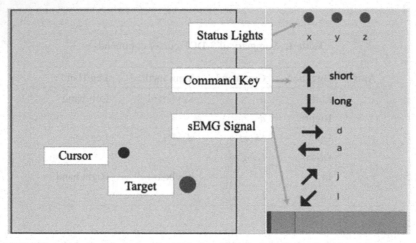

Fig. 3. The User Interface includes the Task Interface on the left-hand side and the Information Interface on the right-hand side.

The subjects completed 80 trials of the cursor-to-target task on the task interface. The task interface dimensions were normalized to have horizontal and vertical bounds of [−1,1] on a square, right-hand Cartesian coordinate system. At the beginning of each trial, the cursor started at the origin (i.e., center of the screen) with a diameter of 0.100 units. The cursor and target diameters were relative to the task interface dimensions. There were 16 unique target positions based on the target angles (45°, 135°, 225°, and 315°) and target diameters (0.025, 0.050, 0.150, 0.175) combinations, and all targets were positioned 0.80 units from the origin. A Block consisted of 4 trials and the subjects received a minimum 30 s break before starting the next Block; subjects could ask to rest longer. A set of four Blocks, or a Test, covered the 16 unique target positions in a pseudorandomized order. The five Tests each had the same pseudorandomized order of trials. The trials timed out after 30 s, which was based on preliminary testing. The total number of trials was determined by reviewing the results from our prior studies [31, 32], as well as our decision to reasonably minimize the duration of the in-person portion of the experiment due to coronavirus transmission concerns.

Table 2. Additional visual feedback during task

Object	Nominal color	Feedback color	Purpose
Cursor	Black	Dark gold	Indicates short input/up command
		Bright blue	Indicates long input/down command
Target	Light purple	Green	Cursor at target's depth
		Orange	Cursor selected target

3 Analysis

3.1 Coordination Metrics

To assess coordination between the hands and leg driving the robotic hand, we calculated a coordination score and DOF activation. The coordination score was calculated for each trial and was the weighted average of the time spent with 0-, 1-, 2-, and 3-DOFs activated. For each time step, points were added in proportion to the number of active DOFs. For example, if there were no DOFs active the time step would be assigned zero points. If any 1-DOF was active, then one point would be awarded. Each additional DOF earned another point. A final coordination score of 1 meant that on average 1-DOF was active during the trial. Larger coordination scores would indicate a more coordinated performance. The coordination score did not detail which DOFs were active, only the number of DOFs. The DOF activation metric provided a finer analysis of which DOFs were used and the relative percentage for each trial. The DOF activation metric measured the proportion of the trial time spent with 0-, 1-, 2-, and/or 3-DOFs activated. This metric was calculated for the overall comparison between all DOFs, as well as within 1-DOF and 2-DOFs. For the DOF activation within 1-DOF, the metric assessed the proportion of the trial time that the x, y-, and z- axes were activated. The 2-DOF activation metric measured the proportion of trial time for xy, xz, and yz activation. These metrics were calculated for all trials, regardless of success.

3.2 Task Metrics

Two task metrics were used to evaluate performance: percent of successful trials and completion time. The percent of successful trials was calculated as the number of successful trials divided by the total number of trials in a Test (16 trials). The completion time was only calculated for successful trials. Both metrics were averaged over each Test.

4 Results

The coordination metrics and task metrics were calculated for all trials regardless of success, except for completion time. Comparing performance during unsuccessful trials and successful trials may reveal useful insights, however, the number of unsuccessful trials decreased substantially starting in Test 3. Across subjects, there were 25 unsuccessful trials (40% of the total trials) in Test 1 and 9 unsuccessful trials (14% of the total trials) in Test 2. The remaining Tests had a total unsuccessful trial count of 8 trials. Therefore, it was difficult to make meaningful comparisons between successful and unsuccessful trials.

4.1 Coordination Metrics

The coordination score was calculated for each trial and averaged over all subjects per Test. As shown in Fig. 4, the coordination score increased each subsequent Test with a slight decrease in the last Test. The average coordination scores ($\mu \pm \sigma$) in order of Test were 1.61 ± 0.37, 1.76 ± 0.27, 1.86 ± 0.26, 1.96 ± 0.23, and 1.89 ± 0.25. The coordination scores ranged from 0.61 in Test 1 to 2.42 in Test 5. The individual subject scores (averaged over all their trials) ranged from 1.65 to 1.93. The subjects did have a variety of experiences that may have been helpful for this task, such as prior myoelectric control and video game experience. Interestingly, the one subject with prior myoelectric control experience did not have the highest average coordination score. Overall, the subjects appeared to perform similar to each other in terms of the coordination score. There did not appear to be noticeable changes in the coordination score per Test when the results were disaggregated by trial success, target angle, or target depth. The slight decrease in the coordination score from Test 4 to Test 5 did not appear to be attributed to muscle fatigue. Two subjects reported feeling some muscle fatigue in their feet, but their maximum voluntary contractions decreased by less than 12% from before the task to after the task and remained well above the threshold.

The coordination score improvements may be explained by increased 3-DOF activation and decreased 1-DOF activation, which was captured by the DOF activation metric (see Fig. 5). The largest changes occurred for 1-DOF and 3-DOF activation between Test 1 and Test 4. The 1-DOF activation decreased by 14 percentage points and 3-DOF activation increased by 16 percentage points, which may be explained as the subjects decreasing their 1-DOF control and learning to increase their 3-DOF control. In contrast, the 0-DOF and 2-DOF activation remained relatively constant between Tests 1 and 4 with a difference in percentage points of 3 and 1, respectively. At most, these differences in percentages for 0-DOF and 2-DOF activation account for less than 1 s of a trial. The changes across DOF activations from Test 4 to Test 5 translate to a time difference of less than 0.5 s. Therefore, the most meaningful changes in DOF activations occurred from Test 1 to Test 4 for the 1-DOF and 3-DOF activations. As with the coordination score, there did not appear to be noticeable changes in the coordination score per Test when the results were disaggregated by trial success, target angle, or target depth.

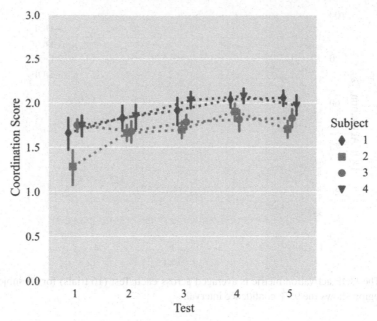

Fig. 4. The average coordination score for each Test (16 trials) is shown for individual subjects. Perfect 3-DOF coordination would achieve a score of 3.

In addition to the overall activation proportion between DOFs, it was also of interest to understand which axes were active within DOFs. As seen in Fig. 5, about half of the trial time was spent with 2-DOFs activated, and 1-DOF was activated between 16% and 30% of the trial time. Together the 1-DOF and 2-DOF activations accounted for most of the trial time. Within the 1-DOF activation during a trial, the activation tended to originate from one of the hands with keyboard inputs (see Fig. 6). It was relatively uncommon for 1-DOF activation with the leg, which occurred less than 10% of the time. For 2-DOF activation, the most likely pairing was for both natual hands together (xz-axes) for approximately 80% of the time (see Fig. 7). Coordination between the leg and left hand (xy-axes) occurred approximately 16% of time in 2-DOF activation, whereas the leg and right hand (xz-axes) coordination accounted for less than 4% of 2-DOF activation time. This analysis increased understanding of which axes were activated within a particular DOF activation case. However, it was also of interest to compare all combinations of DOFs and axes to determine an overall activation ranking. Each possible activation combination was ranked and percentage differences less than 1% were not considered different due to the small absolute time differences. The resulting 2-DOF activation order was both hands (xz, 41%), all three limbs (xyz, 19%), the left hand (x, 12%), and left hand-leg (xy)/right hand (z)/no activation all tied with each accounting for 8%. The right hand-leg (yz) and leg only (y) were 2% of the time each. These results indicated that subjects tended to coordinate their hands followed by all three limbs.

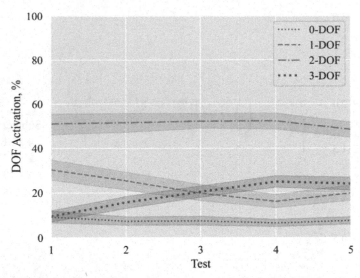

Fig. 5. The DOF activation metric is averaged across each Test (16 trials) for all subjects. The shaded region shows the 95% confidence interval.

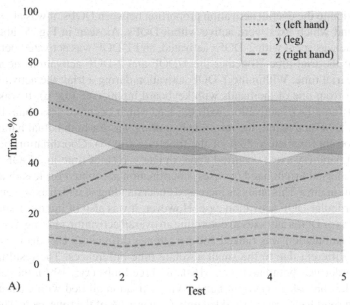

Fig. 6. The plots show the 1-DOF activation breakdown. The percentage of time is within 1-DOF activation time and not for the entire trial time. The shaded area shows the 95% confidence interval. The results are averaged over all trials within a Test (16 trials).

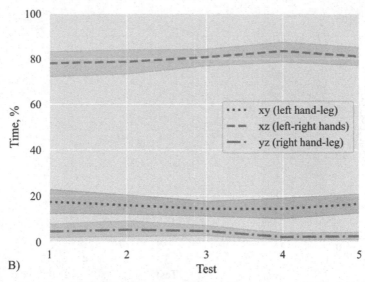

Fig. 7. The plots show the 2-DOF activation breakdown. The percentage of time is within 2-DOF activation time and not for the entire trial time. The shaded area shows the 95% confidence interval. The results are averaged over all trials within a Test (16 trials).

4.2 Task Metrics

The percent of successful trials was calculated for each Test and generally showed improvement throughout the experiment (see Fig. 8). By Test 3, all subjects successfully completed more than 90% of the trials, and there were no unsuccessful trials in Test 4. The trend followed the coordination score, where there was a small decrease in the percent of successful trials for Test 5. There appeared to be relatively large differences in this metric between subjects for Tests 1 and 2. One subject only successfully completed one trial in Test 1 and seven trials in Test 2. Another subject successfully completed seven trials in Test 1 and then successfully completed all trials in the remaining Tests. The early differences in percent of successful trials may provide evidence of individual learning rates, however, the number of subjects was too low to make any definitive conclusions. These results indicated that the number of trials was sufficient for learning how to complete the task.

The completion time continually decreased on average in each subsequent Test (see Fig. 9). The completion time was only calculated for successful trials, and trials had a maximum time of 30 s. In Test 1, the subjects used most of the allotted trial time with an average completion time of 21.98 ± 3.85 s ($\mu \pm \sigma$). The completion time decreased to less than half of the maximum trial time by Test 5 (11.84 ± 1.62 s). Although completion time looked to be leveling off, it was not clear if the completion time plateaued in Test 5, and it could be interesting to observe this metric over more trials. These results combined with the percentage of successful trials supported the reduced trial times compared to our prior study (60 s maximum trial time) [32].

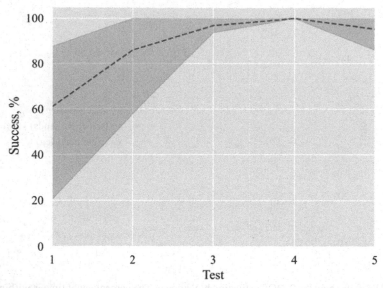

Fig. 8. The results for percentage of successful trials are averaged over the 16 trials within a Test. The shaded region indicates the 95% confidence interval.

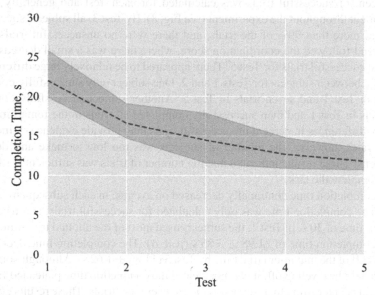

Fig. 9. The results for completion time are averaged over the 16 trials within a Test. The shaded area indicates the 95% confidence interval.

4.3 Additional Analysis

The coordination metrics and task metrics provided a high-level assessment of the average subject performance; however, it was of interest to examine trial data in more detail. After reviewing data from low- and high-performance trials, one case was selected to highlight some of the changes in subject cursor control. The data shown in Fig. 10 compares the normalized cursor velocities in each axis for the same target in Test 1 (Fig. 10A) and Test 5 (Fig. 10B). In the Test 1 trial, the subject moved the cursor primarily one axis at a time, except towards the end of the trial. The trial was unsuccessful and timed out with no inputs in the z-axis (i.e., depth/in and out motion). Directional corrections

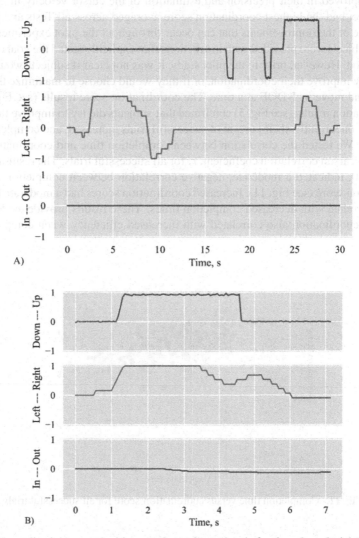

A)

B)

Fig. 10. Normalized cursor velocities are shown for each axis for the selected trial (diameter = 0.05, angle = 45°) in Test 1 (A) and Test 5 (B) for the same subject. The trial in Test 1 was not successful.

were made in both the x- and y- axes, as evidenced by the changing sign of the cursor velocities. In contrast, the trial data from Test 5 showed precisely timed inputs with minimal corrections. The subject correctly estimated the duration for the y-axis input, which was myoelectric control. The x-axis motion continued to the right once initiated with a gradual decrease and a minor correction to increase the velocity. The motion in the z-axis had the latest onset and smallest velocity but appeared to be sufficiently estimated to reach the target depth. The subject successfully completed the trial in 7.13 s. The subject may have been able to improve performance by holding the x-axis cursor velocity at the maximum for longer, ramping down the velocity quicker, and having an earlier onset for the z-axis cursor motion. Compared to the Test 1 trial data, it was evident that the subject improved in their precision and estimation of the cursor velocity in each axis. This subject had the highest coordination score averaged across all Tests and provided an example of the improvements that can occur throughout the pilot experiment.

The subjects were provided with instructions that explicitly stated the goal of 3-DOF coordination. However, prior to the pilot study, it was not clear if subjects would aim to continually improve their coordination, or if they would choose to maximize the cursor velocity and move in 1-DOF at a time. The coordination score results (see Fig. 4) and DOF activation results (see Fig. 5) confirmed that subjects did try to improve their coordination. Concurrently, their percent of successful trials increased, and completion time decreased. We tested the correlation between completion time and coordination score using the Pearson correlation coefficient, r, for all successful trials. The resulting value, $r = -0.50$, indicated a moderate, negative correlation between completion time and coordination score (see Fig. 11). Increased coordination scores had a moderate tendency to also correlate with decreased completion times. These results provide evidence that increased coordination also correlated with increased efficiency when completing the task.

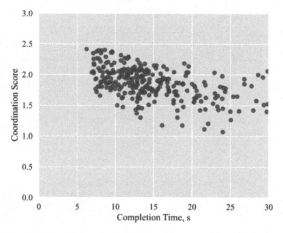

Fig. 11. Completion time versus coordination score for all successful trials

5   Discussion

The results from this pilot experiment showed increased coordination and task performance over its duration. The subjects were instructed to aim for 3-DOF coordination. The average coordination score in Test 4 and 5 was approximately a 2, which can be interpreted as an average of 2-DOF control during the trial. The goal was for subject to achieve 3-DOF coordination, and the highest coordination score was a 2.42 in Test 5. The average 3-DOF activation was 19% of the trial time. All subjects responded affirmatively when asked if they felt that "...you coordinated your hands and leg well." It may be beneficial in a future study to encourage subjects to increase their 3-DOF coordination. This encouragement could be achieved by showing the subjects their coordination score during or after each trial to give them a quantitative assessment of their performance. Another option would be to only allow cursor motion when all 3-DOFs are active as a training tool. This restriction could be removed during a subset of trials to evaluate their 3-DOF coordination retention.

The cursor and target both employed color feedback to provide additional information to the subjects during the task. Three of the subjects felt that the cursor color changes helped them confirm the command selection prior to cursor motion. The remaining subject said they largely ignored the color feedback and focused on resulting cursor motion. All subjects agreed that the target color feedback for depth aided them in aligning their cursor with the target. One subject further detailed that the target color feedback enabled them to time their actions. In contrast, the subjects minimally used the status lights and sEMG signal bar on the Information Interface. This information was not particularly surprising since it was expected that the subjects would allocate most of their visual attention to the Task Interface. However, the additional information was available as needed and the subjects did use the information occasionally to better understand myoelectric control (e.g., confirmation of crossing the threshold) and axes statuses.

This pilot experiment provided insights regarding the task design. The number of trials and trial duration was selected based on preliminary testing and the results from our prior studies [31, 32]. The results from the task metrics generally support these selections for the given task design. As discussed, it would be of interest to revise the training design to encourage increased 3-DOF coordination as compared to the modest improvements in coordination seen in this study. A task with direct, physical interaction may provide additional motivation and more obvious connection to the robot. Another change that should be considered in future studies is the muscle site. The tibialis anterior was originally selected due to its good signal quality and use in prior experiments (e.g., [33]). Subjects primarily flexed their foot or raised their toes to activate the muscle, and some reported fatigue in their foot. Overall, this study provided initial results and insights for myoelectric control of a collaborative robot during a computer-based task.

6   Conclusions

This pilot study expanded upon our previous work and demonstrated the sEMG system with a collaborative robot. The knowledge gained from previous studies helped us devise a task with a reasonable level of difficulty. Subjects appeared to follow the instructions and tried to coordinate their inputs, but the 3-DOF coordination remained relatively low. Different options have been discussed for encouraging increased 3-DOF coordination in future studies. The robot performed in a reliable and safe manner, which built confidence for future experiments with direct interaction. The metrics in this pilot experiment centered on coordination and task performance, and the other metrics we have previously used to address interaction factors like trust and cognitive workload should be incorporated in future studies. Although the robot did not physically interact with the subjects, the robot was integrated with the experiment software and established a basic infrastructure for future robotic myoelectric control experiments. Overall, this pilot experiment provided some interesting and encouraging results upon which to build more complex experiments in the future.

Acknowledgements. This material is based upon work supported by the National Science Foundation under Grant No. (1934792).

References

1. Ajoudani, A., Zanchettin, A.M., Ivaldi, S., Albu-Schäffer, A., Kosuge, K., Khatib, O.: Progress and prospects of the human–robot collaboration. Auton. Robot. **42**(5), 957–975 (2017). https://doi.org/10.1007/s10514-017-9677-2
2. Kurek, D.A., Asada, H.H.: The MantisBot: design and impedance control of supernumerary robotic limbs for near-ground work. In: 2017 IEEE International Conference on Robotics and Automation (ICRA), pp. 5942–5947. IEEE (2017)
3. Bonilla, B.L., Asada, H.H.: A robot on the shoulder: coordinated human-wearable robot control using coloured petri nets and partial least squares predictions. In: 2014 IEEE International Conference on Robotics and Automation (ICRA), pp. 119–125. IEEE (2014)
4. Shin, C.-Y., Bae, J., Hong, D.: Ceiling work scenario based hardware design and control algorithm of supernumerary robotic limbs. In: 2015 15th International Conference on Control, Automation and Systems (ICCAS), pp. 1228–1230. IEEE (2015)
5. Vatsal, V., Hoffman, G.: A wearable robotic forearm for human-robot collaboration. In: Companion of the 2018 ACM/IEEE International Conference on Human-Robot Interaction, pp. 329–330. ACM (2018)
6. Saraiji, M.Y., Sasaki, T., Kunze, K., Minamizawa, K., Inami, M.: MetaArms: body remapping using feet-controlled artificial arms. In: The 31st Annual ACM Symposium on User Interface Software and Technology - UIST 2018, pp. 65–74. ACM Press, Berlin, Germany (2018)
7. Llorens-Bonilla, B., Parietti, F., Asada, H.H.: Demonstration-based control of supernumerary robotic limbs. In: Presented at the RSJ International Conference on Intelligent Robots and Systems (IROS), 2012. IEEE (2012)
8. Parietti, F., Asada, H.: Supernumerary robotic limbs for human body support. IEEE Trans. Robot. **32**, 301–311 (2016). https://doi.org/10.1109/Tro.2016.2520486
9. Parietti, F., Chan, K., Asada, H.H.: Bracing the human body with supernumerary robotic limbs for physical assistance and load reduction. In: Presented at the 2014 IEEE International Conference on Robotics and Automation (ICRA) (2014)
10. Hussain, I., Spagnoletti, G., Salvietti, G., Prattichizzo, D.: An EMG interface for the control of motion and compliance of a supernumerary robotic finger. Front. Neurorobot. **10**, 18 (2016). https://doi.org/10.3389/fnbot.2016.00018

11. Wu, F.Y., Asada, H.H.: Implicit and intuitive grasp posture control for wearable robotic fingers: a data-driven method using partial least squares. IEEE Trans. Robot. **32**, 176–186 (2016). https://doi.org/10.1109/Tro.2015.2506731
12. Hussain, I., Meli, L., Pacchierotti, C., Prattichizzo, D.: A soft robotic supernumerary finger and a wearable cutaneous finger interface to compensate the missing grasping capabilities in chronic stroke patients. In: 2017 IEEE World Haptics Conference (WHC), pp. 183–188 (2017)
13. Tiziani, L., Hart, A., Cahoon, T., Wu, F.Y., Asada, H.H., Hammond, F.L.: Empirical characterization of modular variable stiffness inflatable structures for supernumerary grasp-assist devices. Int. J. Robot Res. **36**, 1391–1413 (2017). https://doi.org/10.1177/0278364917714062
14. Ariyanto, M., Ismail, R., Setiawan, J.D., Arifin, Z.: Development of low cost supernumerary robotic fingers as an assistive device. In: 2017 4th International Conference on Electrical Engineering, Computer Science and Informatics (EECSI), pp. 1–6. IEEE (2017)
15. Leigh, S., Maes, P.: Body integrated programmable joints interface. In: Proceedings of the 2016 CHI Conference on Human Factors in Computing Systems, pp. 6053–6057. ACM (2016)
16. Vatsal, V., Hoffman, G.: Wearing your arm on your sleeve: studying usage contexts for a wearable robotic forearm. In: 2017 26th IEEE International Symposium on Robot and Human Interactive Communication (RO-MAN), pp. 974–980. IEEE (2017)
17. Leigh, S.W., Agrawal, H., Maes, P.: Robotic symbionts interweaving human and machine actions. IEEE Pervas Comput. **17**, 34–43 (2018). https://doi.org/10.1109/Mprv.2018.022 511241
18. Abdi, E., Bouri, M., Burdet, E., Himidan, S., Bleuler, H.: Positioning the endoscope in laparoscopic surgery by foot: influential factors on surgeons' performance in virtual trainer. In: Engineering in Medicine and Biology Society (EMBC), 2017 39th Annual International Conference of the IEEE, pp. 3944–3948. IEEE (2017)
19. Abdi, E., Burdet, E., Bouri, M., Himidan, S., Bleuler, H.: In a demanding task, three-handed manipulation is preferred to two-handed manipulation. Sci. Rep. **6**, 21758 (2016). https://doi. org/10.1038/srep21758
20. Abdi, E., Burdet, E., Bouri, M., Bleuler, H.: Control of a supernumerary robotic hand by foot: an experimental study in virtual reality. PLoS ONE **10**, e0134501 (2015). https://doi.org/10. 1371/journal.pone.0134501
21. Velloso, E., Schmidt, D., Alexander, J., Gellersen, H., Bulling, A.: The feet in human-computer interaction: a survey of foot-based interaction. ACM Comput. Surv. **48**, 21 (2015). https:// doi.org/10.1145/2816455
22. CDC: Cases, Data, and Surveillance, https://www.cdc.gov/coronavirus/2019-ncov/covid-data/investigations-discovery/hospitalization-death-by-age.html
23. Office of the Commissioner: Collection of Race and Ethnicity Data in Clinical Trials, https://www.fda.gov/regulatory-information/search-fda-guidance-documents/collection-race-and-ethnicity-data-clinical-trials
24. Elias, L.J., Bryden, M.P., Bulman-Fleming, M.B.: Footedness is a better predictor than is handedness of emotional lateralization. Neuropsychologia **36**, 37–43 (1998). https://doi.org/ 10.1016/S0028-3932(97)00107-3
25. UR5 collaborative robot arm | Flexible and lightweight cobot, https://www.universal-robots. com/products/ur5-robot/
26. Lyons, K., Margolis, B.: AxoPy: a python library for implementing human-computer interface experiments. J. Open Source Softw. **4**, 1191 (2019)
27. Real-Time Data Exchange (RTDE) Guide - 22229, https://www.universal-robots.com/art icles/ur/interface-communication/real-time-data-exchange-rtde-guide/
28. SDU Robotics / ur_rtde. https://gitlab.com/sdurobotics/ur_rtde. Accessed 18 June 2021
29. Photo by Jordan Whitt on Unsplash. https://unsplash.com/photos/sobXgw6KfiQ. Accessed 30 July 2021

30. Lyons, K.R., Joshi, S.S.: Real-time evaluation of a myoelectric control method for high-level upper limb amputees based on homologous leg movements. In: 2016 38th Annual International Conference of the IEEE Engineering in Medicine and Biology Society (EMBC), pp. 6365–6368. IEEE (2016)

31. O'Meara, S.M., Shyr, M.C., Lyons, K.R., Joshi, S.S.: Comparing two different cursor control methods which use single-site surface electromyography. In: 2019 9th International IEEE/EMBS Conference on Neural Engineering (NER), pp. 1163–1166. IEEE (2019). https://doi.org/10.1109/ner.2019.8716903

32. O'Meara, S.M., Karasinski, J.A., Miller, C.L., Joshi, S.S., Robinson, S.K.: Effects of augmented feedback and motor learning adaptation on human–automation interaction factors. J. Aerospace Inf. Syst. 1–14 (2021). https://doi.org/10.2514/1.I010915

33. Lyons, K.R., Joshi, S.S., Joshi, S.S., Lyons, K.R.: Upper limb prosthesis control for high-level amputees via myoelectric recognition of leg gestures. IEEE Trans. Neural Syst. Rehabil. Eng. **26**, 1056–1066 (2018). https://doi.org/10.1109/TNSRE.2018.2807360

Comparison of Positive Feelings for CG Robots Between 2D Display and 3D HMD Using Heart Rate

Michiko Ohkura(✉) [ID], Narumon Jadram, and Tipporn Laohakangvalvit

Shibaura Institute of Technology, 3-7-5, Toyosu, Koto-ku, Tokyo 1358548, Japan
ohkura@sic.shibaura-it.ac.jp, {ma21067,
tipporn}@shibaura-it.ac.jp

Abstract. We have been conducting research focusing on positive feelings for a long time. The objective of this study is to compare the positive feelings caused by motions of CG robots between a 2D monitor used for 2D display and a head-mounted display (HMD) for 3D display. The target positive feelings are *excitement* and *relaxation*. Our evaluation employs not only a questionnaire but also the user's heart rate. The questionnaire results show the differences in preferences of robots between males and females. They also clarify the agreement between robot preference and the feeling of *excitement* when watching the motion of a robot, regardless of the display device used. The degree of *excitement* becomes stronger when the participant prefers the HMD over the 2D monitor.

Keywords: Positive feeling · Excitement · Relaxation · Head-mounted display · Heart rate

1 Introduction

The rapid progress of science and technology in the twentieth century has ushered in a materially affluent society. In particular, the dramatic development of information and communication technologies from the latter half of that century provided incredibly effective tools such as computers and networked environments. Against this backdrop, people in the twenty-first century tend to place more importance on spiritual wealth than material wealth, and they have modified their value systems from a physical-based to an information-based ones (e.g., [1]). Moreover, to break through the stagnation that had threatened Japanese manufacturing, the Japanese government selected Kansei (emotion or affection) as the fourth key product value, joining the values of function, reliability, and cost [2].

© The Author(s), under exclusive license to Springer Nature Switzerland AG 2022
M. Kurosu (Ed.): HCII 2022, LNCS 13303, pp. 537–547, 2022.
https://doi.org/10.1007/978-3-031-05409-9_39

To evaluate the affective value of such value-added products, subjective evaluation method such as questionnaires are commonly used. Questionnaires are well-known as established methodology for subjective evaluation, and they have various merits. At the same time, however, they also suffer from significant demerits:

- Linguistic ambiguity;
- Interfusion of experimenter and/or participant intention into the results; and
- Interruption of the system's stream of information input/output.

Solving these problems is crucial to evaluating the degree of interest and/or *excitement* generated by an industrial product or an interactive system, such as whether the system really is interesting, and to identifying the moment of *excitement*. Accordingly, evaluating the affective value of an industrial product or an interactive system using only such subjective evaluation methods as questionnaires is nearly impossible. We began our research [3] to objectively evaluate interactive systems by quantifying the relevant sensations using biological signals, which can supplement the use of questionnaires limited by the above disadvantages. This approach offers new advantages:

- Measurement by physical quantities;
- Avoiding the influence of the intentions of experimenter and participants; and
- Continuous measurement.

Much previous research has measured mental sensations using biological signals. Ohsuga et al. used biological signals to measure the negative sensations of mental stress or simulator sickness [4, 5]. On the other hand, Omori et al. measured ECG and EEG to evaluate autonomous and central nerve activities evoked by color stimuli, where they evaluated *relaxation* and *comfort* [6]. We previously used the alpha waves of EEG to estimate a participant's feelings of *relaxation* [7]. Compared with negative sensations, *relaxation* and *comfort* are considered positive sensations.

In our previous research, we first focused on a feeling called "*wakuwaku*," which is a Japanese word for a positive sensation evoked when someone feels something excited or captivated. The word most closely means thrilling or exhilarating in English. A *wakuwaku* feeling is also considered a positive sensation, as are *relaxation* and *comfort*. However, there is a big difference between those sensations: a *wakuwaku* feeling is considered dynamic, especially compared to the static sensations of *relaxation* and *comfort*. In Russell's circumplex model of affect [8] (Fig. 1), negative dynamic emotions such as stress are in the second quadrant, while positive static emotions such as *relaxation* and *comfort* are in the fourth quadrant. "*Wakuwaku*" feeling is in the first quadrant. In addition, our previous study showed the possibility of a single stimulus causing more than one emotion both in the 1st and 4th quadrants [9].

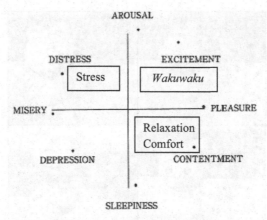

Fig. 1. Russell's circumplex model [8] and related feelings.

In the realm of human-machine interfaces, the 3D cyberworld becomes familiar very rapidly. We have been using VR spaces in affective evaluation for a long time, following earlier comparisons between VR space and real space [10, 11]. However, we have a few study [12] to compare the differences in effects on affective evaluation between 2D monitors and head-mounted displays (HMDs) which are now commonly used for 3D display.

Therefore, in this manuscript, we introduce the comparison results between a 2D monitor and an HMD as a 3D display device for the positive feelings caused by motions of CG robots. The target positive feelings are "*wakuwaku*" and *relaxation*, with the former in the 1st quadrant and the latter in the 4th quadrant of Fig. 1. In this work, we employ not only a questionnaire but also heart rate (HR) for evaluation.

Although "*wakuwaku*" is not quite the same as *excitement*, the latter term is used in the following descriptions to avoid confusion.

2 Experimental Method

2.1 Stimulus

The two CG robots shown in Figs. 2 and 3 were created as 3D models by Unity, for use in the activities of a remote collaboration project [13], but modified for this experiment. The modifications were removal of background furniture, elimination of voice audio, and automatic repetition of 20-s. motion.

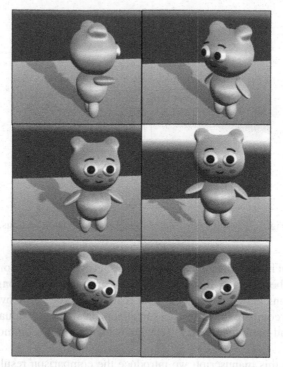

Fig. 2. Screenshots of motion of Pink Robot. (Color figure online)

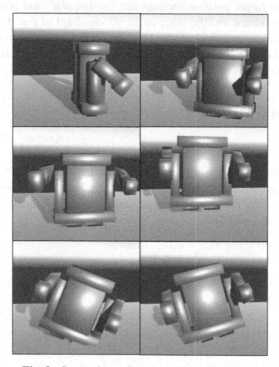

Fig. 3. Screenshots of motion of Metallic Robot.

2.2 Participants

Participants include three males and three females in their 20s and 30s. All of the participants are Asian.

2.3 Procedure

The procedure of the experiment is as follows:

1. Explanation of the experiment and obtaining consent.
2. Practice in heart rate measurement.
3. Sitting in front of a 2D monitor for 2D display.
4. Wearing an HMD for 3D display and closing eyes.
5. Opening eyes and watching the motion of one of the CG robots, as HR measurements are taken, for 30 s two times. The duration of the period when the eyes are closed is approx. 30 s. The total time of this watching process is approx. 2 min., with the detailed protocol shown in Fig. 4.

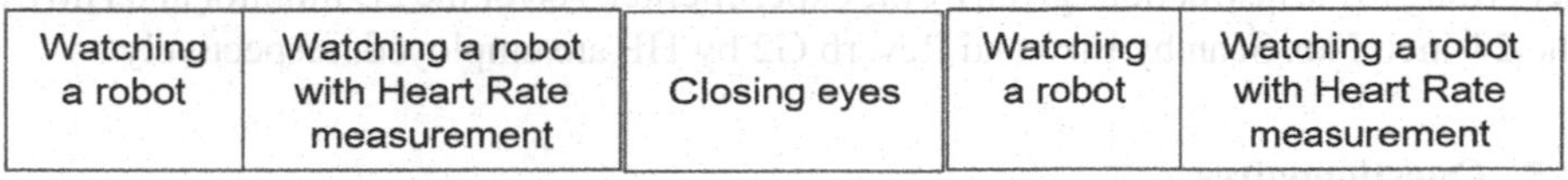

Watching a robot	Watching a robot with Heart Rate measurement	Closing eyes	Watching a robot	Watching a robot with Heart Rate measurement

Fig. 4. Protocol of a participant watching a robot.

6. Closing eyes.
7. Opening eyes and watching the motion of the other CG robot with HR measurement for 30 s two times.
8. Removal of HMD and answering the first questionnaire.
9. Closing eyes.
10. Opening eyes and watching the motion of one of the CG robots in the 2D monitor with HR measurement for 30 s twice.
11. Closing eyes.
12. Opening eyes and watching the motion of the other CG robot in the 2D monitor with HR measurement for 30 s two times.
13. Answering the second questionnaire.

Both the order of CG robots to be watched and the order of watching the robot in the 2D monitor or the HMD are counter-balanced as shown in Table 1.

Table 1. Participants and order of watching.

Participant number	Gender	First display: 2D/3D	First robot: Pink/Metallic
1	Male	3D	Metallic
2	Female	2D	Pink
3	Male	3D	Pink
4	Female	3D	Metallic
5	Male	2D	Pink
6	Female	2D	Metallic

2.4 Devices

ECG is measured and recorded by the Emay Portable ECG Monitor. This device can produce an ECG chart and the average HR during the measurement period set beforehand (30 s in this experiment). Participants use this device and measure their own heart rate according to the instructions given by the experimenter. As for the 2D monitor and HMD, the 24-inch Flex Scan by Eizo and Reverb G2 by HP are employed, respectively.

2.5 Questionnaires

Both the first and second questionnaires are prepared in Japanese. The first questionnaire consists of five question items as follows:

1. Which robot do you prefer and why?
2. How much excitement do you feel when watching the Pink Robot?
3. How much excitement do you feel when watching the Metallic Robot?
4. How much relaxation do you feel when watching the Pink Robot?
5. How much relaxation do you feel when watching the Metallic Robot?

The second questionnaire consists of 6 question items, which are the same items as the first one with the following additional question as the final item:

6. Which display device (2D or 3D) do you prefer and why?

We prepared two types of questionnaire sheets in which the order of robots were counter-balanced and then provided the appropriate sheet to each participant.

3　Experimental Results

3.1 Experiment

Examples of an experimental scene are shown in Fig. 5. The left figure shows that a participant is wearing an HMD and has a heart rate monitor. The right figure is a scene of watching a robot in the 2D monitor.

Fig. 5. Examples of experimental scenes.

3.2 Results of Questionnaire

The results of preference of robots (first question item) are as follows:

- Regardless of display device (2D/3D), all females preferred the Pink Robot. The reasons given are as follows:

- The face of the Pink Robot is kawaii.
- The facial features of the Pink Robot are friendlier.
- Its color looks softer.
- The Pink Robot is more animal-like.

- As for males, when watching the robots they preferred the Metallic Robot in both the HMD and the 2D monitor, except for one male who preferred the Pink Robot in the 2D monitor. The reason for their preference of the Metallic Robot are as follows:

- I prefer a metallic color and a robotic shape over the pink and round shape.
- I prefer the motion of the Metallic Robot over that of the other because the former is more active.
- I prefer a robot with no face.

For the results of the *excitement* felt in watching each robot, participants responded using terms such as "not at all," "a little bit," and "very." The results are as follows:

- Regardless of display device (2D/3D), all females felt much more excited about the Pink Robot than the Metallic Robot.

- Regardless of display device (2D/3D), all males felt more excited about the Metallic Robot than the Pink Robot except for one male who answered, when watching the robots in a 2D monitor, "not bad" for both robots.
- Some participants stated that their *excitement* for 3D is stronger than for 2D.

The results of feeling relaxed in watching the two robots are as follows:

- Regardless of display device (2D/3D), all females felt much more or more relaxed for the Pink Robot than the Metallic Robot.
- As for males, the answers were different as follows:

– One male felt more relaxed with the Metallic Robot than with the Pink Robot.
– One male felt a little bit relaxed with both robots for both display devices.
– One male, who had answered that his preference was the Pink Robot and that he felt "a little bit" excited for both robots in the 2D monitor, said he felt more relaxed with the Metallic Robot in the HMD but more relaxed with the Pink Robot in the 2D monitor.

As for the preference of display device, all females and one male preferred the HMD, while two males (Participant numbers 1 and 5) preferred the 2D monitor. Their reasons are as follows:

- I felt more reality in the HMD.
- I had a more immersive feeling in the HMD.
- I felt happy because the robots were nearer in the HMD
- Because I am not familiar with wearing an HMD, I felt at ease with the 2D monitor.
- An unrealistic situation is not suitable for an HMD.

3.3 Results of Heart Rate

As described in the experimental procedure (2.3), heart rate was measured twice for each session of watching, and the duration of each measurement was 30 s. Averaged HRs were calculated for each robot with each display device. However, since some HR values were identified as incorrect, we did not include those values in the average calculation. For participant number 6, all measurements resulted in failure. Due to the large individual differences in HR values, we calculated the total average for each participant except participant 6. The differences between averaged HR values for each session of watching and the total average are shown in Table 2.

From Table 2 and the previous questionnaire results, the following findings could be obtained:

- The HRs of two male participants who preferred the 2D monitor over the HMD (Participant numbers 1 and 5) were highest when watching the 2D Metallic Robot.
- The HR of one male who preferred the HMD (Participant number 3) was highest when watching the 3D Metallic Robot.

Table 2. Differences between averaged HR value and the total average value (BPM).

Participant number	2D Pink Robot	2D Metallic Robot	3D Pink Robot	3D Metallic Robot
1	−0.2	3.3	−0.2	−2.9
2	−0.5	0.0	1.5	−1.0
3	1.0	−3.9	−1.5	4.5
4	0.0	6.5	−2.5	−4.0
5	0.5	3.0	−4.0	0.5

- The HR of a female who felt very excited especially with the HMD (Participant number 2) was highest when watching the 3D Pink Robot and was lowest when watching the 3D Metallic Robot.
- The HR of a female (Participant number 4) was highest when watching the 2D Metallic Robot and lowest when watching the 3D Metallic Robot.

4 Discussion

Regardless of display device, in general, females preferred the Pink Robot and males preferred the Metallic Robot. One exception was an answer to watching via 2D monitor by one male who preferred the 2D monitor over the HMD. The participant answered that he felt more relaxed when watching the Pink Robot than the Metallic Robot in a 2D monitor. On the other hand, his HR was highest when watching the Metallic Robot in the 2D monitor. Therefore, the reason for this exception needs to be confirmed in future work.

Regardless of display device, females felt more excited about the Pink Robot than the Metallic Robot, while males felt more excited about the Metallic Robot except for one male when using the 2D monitor. This result is in agreement with the results of preference for robot. In addition, the *excitement* was stronger with the HMD than the 2D monitor in cases where the participant preferred the HMD over the 2D monitor. This result shows the possibility of using an HMD to increase the *excitement* of visual stimuli in cases where the user prefers an HMD.

Regardless of display device, females felt more relaxed with the Pink Robot than with the Metallic Robot. However, there are no differences between the HMD and the 2D monitor, even though all of them preferred the HMD. As for males, there is no relationship between the results of relaxed feeling and their preferences of display device.

From the results of preference of display device, it was found that the individual's familiarity with HMDs influences this preference, which might affect positive feelings. Although HMD can give an immersive feeling, it may also give a feeling of obstruction. After our long-time use of 3D screens/projectors and monitors with polarized eyeglasses as well as LCD-shuttered eyeglasses, we realize the importance of understanding the differences between our previous 3D display systems and HMDs.

The results of increased heart rate in males show agreement with their preferences of robot and display device. However, the results of only three participants are too few for drawing conclusions. More participants in new experiments are necessary for future work. In addition, in our previous studies [9, 14, 15], we employed different ECG measuring devices and obtained useful indexes calculated from ECG for affective evaluation. Employing those devices and calculating indexes other than HR also remain future work.

5   Conclusion

We have continued our research focused on positive feelings for a long time. The objective of this study is to compare the positive feelings evoked by the motions of CG robots between a 2D monitor for 2D display and an HMD for 3D display. The target positive feelings are *excitement* ("*wakuwaku*") and *relaxation*, with the former in the 1st quadrant and the latter in the 4th quadrant of Russell's circumplex model. For our evaluation, we employed not only questionnaire but also participants' heart rates.

The questionnaire results show the differences in preferences of robots between males and females. They also clarify the agreement between robot preference and the feeling of *excitement* when watching the motion of a robot, regardless of the display device used. The degree of *excitement* becomes stronger when the participant prefers the HMD over the 2D monitor. This result shows the possibility of using HMDs to increase the *excitement* of visual stimuli in cases where users prefer the HMD. However, the user's familiarity with HMDs influences the preference of display device, which might affect positive feelings. Although the results of heart rate in males show agreement with their preferences of robot and display device, we need more detailed experiments in future work.

Acknowledgements. Students from the Shibaura Institute of Technology are thanked for their participation in the experiments. This work was partially supported by a JSPS Grant-in-Aid for Scientific Research (20K12032).

References

1. Ohkura, M.: Interface for human-machine interaction. Trends Sci. **10**(8), 765–781 (2005)
2. Ministry of Economy, Trade and Industry. Kansei Value Creation, https://www.meti.go.jp/policy/mono/creative/kensei.html. Accessed 30 Jan 2021
3. Ohkura, M., Hamano, M., Watanabe, H., Aoto, T.: Measurement of "wakuwaku" feeling generated by interactive systems using biological signals. In: Proceedings of the Kansei Engineering and Emotion Research International Conference 2010 (KEER 2010), pp. 2293–2301. Paris (2010)
4. Hirao, N., et al.: Assessment of mental stress during a cooperative work using stress detection method triggered by physiological data. ITE Tech. Rep. **21**, 67–72 (1997)
5. Sakaguchi, T., et al.: Stress detection in a virtual ensemble using autonomic indices. In: Proceedings of the 59th National Convention of IPSJ, pp. 2–1–2–2 (1999)
6. Omori, M., Hashimoto, R., Kato, Y.: Relation between psychological and physiological responses on color stimulus. J. Color Sci. Assoc. Japan **26**(2), 50–63 (2002)

7. Ohkura, M., Oishi, M.: An alpha-wave-based motion control system for a mechanical pet. Kansei Eng. Int. **6**(2), 29–34 (2006)
8. Russell, J.: A circumplex model of affect. J. Pers. Soc. Psychol. **39**, 1161–1178 (1980)
9. Ohkura, M., Arashina, H., Tombe, T.: Evaluation of kawaii feelings caused by stuffed animals to reduce stress. In: Fukuda, S. (ed.) AHFE International Conference on Affective and Pleasurable Design 2019, AISC, vol. 952, pp. 213–223. Springer, Heidelberg (2020)
10. Ohkura, M., et al.: Comparison of the impression of the space between virtual environment and real environment. In: HCI International 2005, Las Vegas (2005)
11. Ohkura, M., et al.: Comparison of the impression of spaces in inclined projection display system. J. Japan Soc. Kansei Eng. **6**(2), 45–51 (2006)
12. Koinuma, Y., Ohkura, M.: Comparison of relaxation effect from watching images between 2D and head-mounted displays. In: Fukuda, S. (ed.) AHFE International Conference on Affective and Pleasurable Design 2018, AISC, vol. 774, pp. 269–276. Springer, Heidelberg (2019)
13. Ohkura, M., et al: Affective evaluation of virtual kawaii robotic gadgets using biological signals in a remote collaboration of American and Japanese students. In: Kurosu, M. (ed.) HCI International 2022 to appear
14. Tivatansakul, S., Ohkura, M.: Improvement of emotional healthcare system with stress detection from ECG signal. In: The 37th Annual International Conference of the IEEE Engineering in Medicine and Biology Society (EMBC2015), pp. 6792–6795, IEEE, NY (2015)
15. Ito, K., et al.: Evaluation of feelings of excitement caused by auditory stimulus in driving simulator using biosignals. In: Chung, W., Shin, C. (eds.) AHFE International Conference on Affective and Pleasurable Design 2016, AISC, vol. 483, pp. 231–240. Springer, Heidelberg (2017)

User Profile-Driven Large-Scale Multi-agent Learning from Demonstration in Federated Human-Robot Collaborative Environments

Georgios Th. Papadopoulos[1]([⊠]), Asterios Leonidis[1], Margherita Antona[1], and Constantine Stephanidis[1,2]

[1] Institute of Computer Science (ICS), Foundation for Research and Technology - Hellas (FORTH), 70013 Heraklion, Crete, Greece
{gepapado,leonidis,antona,cs}@ics.forth.gr
[2] Computer Science Department (CSD), University of Crete (UoC), 70013 Heraklion, Crete, Greece

Abstract. Learning from Demonstration (LfD) has been established as the dominant paradigm for efficiently transferring skills from human teachers to robots. In this context, the Federated Learning (FL) conceptualization has very recently been introduced for developing large-scale human-robot collaborative environments, targeting to robustly address, among others, the critical challenges of multi-agent learning and long-term autonomy. In the current work, the latter scheme is further extended and enhanced, by designing and integrating a novel user profile formulation for providing a fine-grained representation of the exhibited human behavior, adopting a Deep Learning (DL)-based formalism. In particular, a hierarchically organized set of key information sources is considered, including: a) User attributes (e.g. demographic, anthropomorphic, educational, etc.), b) User state (e.g. fatigue detection, stress detection, emotion recognition, etc.) and c) Psychophysiological measurements (e.g. gaze, electrodermal activity, heart rate, etc.) related data. Then, a combination of Long Short-Term Memory (LSTM) and stacked autoencoders, with appropriately defined neural network architectures, is employed for the modelling step. The overall designed scheme enables both short- and long-term analysis/interpretation of the human behavior (as observed during the feedback capturing sessions), so as to adaptively adjust the importance of the collected feedback samples when aggregating information originating from the same and different human teachers, respectively.

Keywords: User profile · Learning from demonstration · Human-robot interaction · Artificial intelligence · Federated learning

1 Introduction

Learning from Demonstration (LfD) constitutes the most dominant paradigm for robot programming through direct interaction with humans [1]. It relies on the fundamental

The work presented in this paper was supported by the ICS-FORTH internal RTD Programme 'Ambient Intelligence and Smart Environments'.

principle of robots acquiring new skills by learning to imitate a (human) teacher [27]. LfD has so far been successfully associated with multiple aspects of robotics technology, including human-robot interaction, machine learning, machine vision and motor control [10,29]. The main advantageous characteristics that have led to the widespread adoption of LfD in multiple and diverse application cases are [3]: a) It enables robot programming by non-expert users, b) It allows time-efficient learning, c) It enables adaptive robotic behaviors and d) It facilitates the robots to operate in complex and time-varying environments.

With respect to the different types of human demonstration means considered, LfD approaches generally fall into three main categories [27]:

- Kinesthetic teaching, where the human teacher provides demonstrations by physically moving the robot through the desired motions [6];
- Teleoperation, where an external input (e.g. joystick, graphical user interface or other means) is used to guide the robot [36];
- Passive observation, where the robot passively observes the exhibited user behavior for learning [20].

A critical factor for the success of any LfD scheme, while also in close relation with the particularities of the selected application case, concerns the adopted methodology for refining the robot learned policies. Different types of approaches have been introduced so far, including: a) Reinforcement learning, where a trial and error methodology is adopted to learn a policy to solve a given problem [34], b) Optimization, where the optimal solution is searched based on given criteria [7], c) Transfer learning, where knowledge of a task or a domain is used to enhance the learning procedure for another task [5], d) Apprenticeship learning, where the desired performance is modeled through the use of a set of demonstrated samples that serve as a template [33], e) Active learning, where the robot decides when to ask for an optimal response from a (human) expert to a given state and to use these active samples to improve its policy [15] and f) Structured predictions, where robotic actions are considered as a sequence of dependent predictions [8].

Although extensive research efforts have been devoted in the LfD field over the past years, crucial research challenges, namely multi-agent learning [13] and long-term autonomy [16], still remain to be reliably addressed. Achieving the latter will act as a tremendous facilitator for enabling the wide-spread use of robots in large-scale, open and complex environments; this is the typical case when considering e.g. industrial manufacturing scenarios. The above need to be also investigated in conjunction with typical challenges in Human-Robot Interaction (HRI) schemes, like developing appropriate user interfaces, variance in human performance, variability in knowledge across human subjects, learning from noisy/imprecise human input, learning from very large or very sparse datasets, incremental learning, etc.

The current work adopts the Federated Learning (FL) conceptualization that has very recently been introduced for designing large-scale LfD human-robot collaborative environments [25], aiming at providing reliable solutions, among others, to the current critical challenges of multi-agent learning and long-term autonomy. In particular, the cognitive architecture of [25] is further elaborated and enhanced, by designing and integrating a novel user profile formulation for estimating a fine-grained representation of the exhibited human behavior. The introduced user model follows the Deep Learning (DL)-based formalism; hence, rendering the overall approach end-to-end learnable. Specifically, a set of key information sources that are hierarchically organized is considered, including: a) User attributes concerning each human teacher's background (e.g. demographic, anthropomorphic, educational, etc.), b) User state information that encodes particular human behavioral characteristics (e.g. fatigue detection, stress detection, emotion recognition, etc.) and c) Psychophysiological measurements that convey critical details about the user's mental state, personality and idiosyncrasy (e.g. gaze, electrodermal activity, heart rate, etc.). Then, a combination of Long Short-Term Memory (LSTM) and stacked autoencoders, with appropriately defined neural network architectures, is employed for the modelling step and for producing a concrete user profile representation. The overall designed scheme supports both short- and long-term analysis/interpretation of the human behavior (as observed during the feedback capturing sessions), so as to adaptively modulate the importance of the collected feedback samples when aggregating information originating from the same and different human teachers, respectively.

The remainder of the paper is organized as follows: Sect. 2 describes challenges and open issues currently present in the LfD learning field. Additionally, Sect. 3 outlines the already introduced cognitive architecture for FL-based multi-agent human-robot collaborative learning. Moreover, Sect. 4 details the designed DL-based user profile modelling and knowledge aggregation approach. Finally, conclusions are drawn in Sect. 5.

2 Open Issues in LfD Learning

LfD has been shown to lead to significant advances in multiple and significantly diverse operational scenarios, involving the use of both manipulator [2,32] and mobile [21,24] robots. Regarding the targeted goal of the overall LfD procedure, this can be categorized to different levels of abstraction [27], including the learning of: a) Policies, i.e. the estimation of a function that generates the desired behavior, b) Cost and reward functions, where the ideal behavior is considered to stem out from the optimization of a hidden function, c) Plans, i.e. high level structured schemes, composed of several sub-tasks or primitive actions, and d) Multiple outcomes simultaneously, by jointly modeling complex behaviors at multiple levels of abstraction.

As already mentioned in Sect. 1, despite the extensive research efforts devoted by the LfD community, key technological challenges and open issues still remain to be robustly addressed, including, among others, the following ones [3,13,27,38]:

- To involve in a more robust way a broad number of teachers with different styles of and possibly conflicting demonstrations;
- To transfer skills across multiple agents, including multiple and diverse types of robots;
- To simultaneously learn multiple complex tasks, while storing and reusing prior knowledge at large scale;
- To robustly implement incremental learning schemes;
- To reinforce the generalization ability;
- To model compound tasks;

– To implement multi-agent imitation learning schemes;
– To operate in realistic, dynamic, time-varying and complex environments.

Towards providing a reliable solution to the above aspects, a novel cognitive architecture for multi-agent LfD robotic learning has recently been introduced [25], targeting to enable the efficient deployment of open, scalable and expandable robotic systems in large-scale and complex environments. In particular, the designed architecture capitalizes on the recent advances in the Artificial Intelligence (AI) (and especially the DL field), by establishing a FL-based framework for incarnating a multi-human multi-robot collaborative learning environment (as will be discussed in Sect. 3), going far beyond other literature approaches investigating relatively straight-forward implementations of FL schemes (without incorporating the human factor in the learning loop) in specific robotic tasks (e.g. autonomous navigation [19], motion planning [4], visual perception [37], etc.).

However, the conventional FL mechanism, which is a purely data-driven scheme and typically employs a simple 'Federated Averaging' operator for knowledge aggregation [22], lacks theoretical guarantees for convergence under realistic settings [17], i.e. when non-independent-and-identically-distributed (non-IID) data are available at the various network nodes. The latter assumption is highly likely to hold when considering human demonstration data (as required in the LfD scheme). In this context, the current work elaborates the multi-agent cognitive architecture conceptualization of [25], by introducing comprehensive DL-grounded user profile modelling and corresponding sophisticated knowledge aggregation strategies (explained in Sect. 4).

3   FL-based Multi-agent Human-Robot Collaborative Learning

3.1   Fundamental Conceptualization

According to [25], a multi-agent cognitive architecture for LfD learning is introduced that is grounded on the fundamental mechanism of the FL paradigm, while a high-level representation is provided in Fig. 1. In particular, a global AI model $\mathbf{W}$ (that bears the targeted robot policy to be learned), which is aimed to be collaboratively trained and shared among a network of human-robot pairs, is initially constructed using proxy data (stored either offline or at a central node). Model $\mathbf{W}$ materializes a cognitive process [26,31] underpinning the robotic task of interest, e.g. sensing, navigation, manipulation, control, human-robot interaction, etc. Subsequently, the model is made available to the network and downloaded by each node (i.e. every employed robot). Every node encapsulates a local database that is used to estimate improved updates of the global model parameters (e.g. using conventional Stochastic Gradient Descent (SGD) for the case of Neural Network (NN)-based AI modules), without making the local (federated) data available to the network (i.e. being a by-definition privacy-aware method). The computed local parameter updates (denoted $\Delta\mathbf{W}^l$ in Fig. 1) are asynchronously transmitted back to the central node (using encrypted communication), where an aggregation mechanism is responsible for combining them and periodically producing a new version of the global model. The overall process is iterative, i.e. continuously estimating

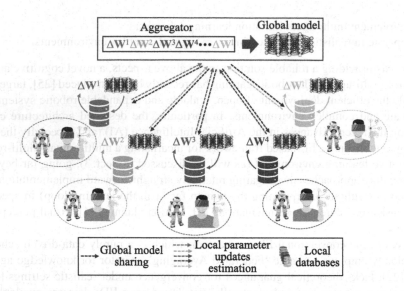

Fig. 1. High-level representation of the employed cognitive architecture for LfD learning.

improved versions of the global model. It needs to be highlighted that each local computational node can maintain a customized version of the global model, while using the locally stored data for fine-tuning purposes. Moreover, in the current work a single robot policy (unique global model **W**) is estimated for simplicity purposes, while the original version of the cognitive architecture of [25] considers the multi-task learning scenario.

3.2 Constituent Entities

The considered cognitive AI architecture is composed of the following real-world reference entities: a) The robotic platform and b) The human. In order to enable the perception and the collection of critical information about the surrounding environment and the exhibited human behavior, two comprehensive sets of sensing devices are considered; one that can be attached to the robot (denoted S^r) and one to the human (denoted S^h). In particular, the set of potentially supported types of sensors for each case, which can be significantly broad and also depends on the particular application scenario, are defined as follows:

$$S^r = \{s_i^r | i \in [1,I], i \in \mathbb{N}, I \in \mathbb{N}\}$$
$$= \{Vision, Light, Temperature, Chemical, Force,$$
$$Acoustic, Gas, Motion, Pressure, Position, ...\} \qquad (1)$$

$$S^h = \{s_k^h | k \in [1,K], k \in \mathbb{N}, K \in \mathbb{N}\}$$
$$= \{Gaze, Heart\ rate, Stress\ level, Motion,$$
$$Fatigue, Position, EEG, ...\} \qquad (2)$$

Regarding the robotic platform, this refers to the actual mechatronic equipment to be deployed. Depending on the specific operational scenario and the targeted robotic task (that may cover a large set of possible perception, cognition, motor and interaction functionalities), multiple types of robots can be used, supporting different requirements for mobility, positioning, manipulation, communication, size, payload, etc. The set of available types of robots is denoted:

$$R = \{r_j | j \in [1, J], j \in \mathbb{N}, J \in \mathbb{N}\}$$
$$= \{Arm, AGV, Humanoid, UAV, Vehicle, Industrial, ...\} \quad (3)$$

Taking into account the above-mentioned formalisms, a robotic platform P_l can be fully specified as follows:

$$P_l = \{S_l^r, R_l | S_l^r \subseteq S^r, R_l \subseteq R\}, l \in [1, L], \quad (4)$$

where L denotes the total number of robotic platforms present in the examined cognitive environment.

With respect to the human factor, although all types of LfD demonstration means methodologies (namely kinesthetic teaching, teleoperation and passive observation, as detailed in Sect. 1) are supported by the cognitive AI architecture, the adoption of a teleoperation-based approach is considered to exhibit significant advantageous characteristics. In particular, an intuitive and sophisticated teleoperation scheme is foreseen that is based on the combined used of Augmented Reality (AR) visualization mechanisms and eXplainable AI (XAI) technologies. Regarding the former, AR tools are employed in order to allow the human user to perform a physical inspection of the robot exhibited behaviors (and hence to identify malfunctions, hazardous situations, deviations from desired policies, etc.), while at the same time being constantly provided with key detailed insights about the AI processes being applied (e.g. the AI modules being used, their estimated outputs, how specific decisions are reached, etc.). Concerning XAI methods, such techniques are adopted in order to provide precise explanations/insights to the human operator regarding the deviation of the robot behavior from the desired one, i.e. enabling an in depth inspection of the robot behavior. It needs to be mentioned that the set of human operators involved in the designed cognitive architecture is denoted $H = \{h_m | m \in [1, M], m \in \mathbb{N}, M \in \mathbb{N}\}$.

3.3 Collective Cognitive AI Layer

A collective cognitive AI layer operates at the upper level of the designed architecture and its core functionality is based on the fundamental mechanism of the FL paradigm, as detailed in Sect. 3.1. The main building blocks of the cognitive AI layer, their formalism and detailed explanation of their functionalities are provided in the followings:
Network Nodes: Every robotic platform P_l corresponds to a network node of the defined architecture. Each P_l stores locally the generated data, which largely contain information collected from the set of sensors S_l^r incorporated by P_l.
Global AI Model: The goal of the overall framework is to collectively create a global AI model denoted $\mathbf{W} \leftarrow f_1(S^r, R)$, underpinning the implemented cognitive process present

in the examined environment, where $f_1(.)$ implies a generalized function or process that defines the exact NN-based materialization of model $\mathbf{W}$ while considering S^r and R as input parameters. However, each network node P_l can maintain a local/customized version of $\mathbf{W}$.

Learning Methodology: Regarding the specific methodology to be followed for refining the robot learned policies (i.e. for updating AI model $\mathbf{W}$), different options can be investigated (e.g. reinforcement learning, transfer learning, active learning, etc.), as discussed in Sect. 1. The most suitable selection depends on the particularities of the application domain and the examined $\mathbf{W}$.

Local Parameter Updates: Regardless of the particular learning methodology selected, each robotic platform P_l can estimate updates for model $\mathbf{W}$, using its locally stored data. More specifically, the following local parameter update mechanism is applied:

$$\mathbf{W}^{l,m} \leftarrow \mathbf{W}^{l,m} - lr^l \cdot \nabla \mathscr{L}(\mathbf{W}^{l,m}, \delta^l), \tag{5}$$

where $\mathbf{W}^{l,m}$ is the local/customized version of the global model $\mathbf{W}$ with respect to human teacher h_m, lr^l is the local learning rate, ∇ denotes the gradient of a function, $\mathscr{L}(.)$ represents the loss function defined for $\mathbf{W}$ and δ^l is the locally stored dataset. Consequently, the local parameter updates, which are iteratively estimated, to be sent to the central node (aggregator) are computed as follows:

$$\Delta \mathbf{W}^{l,m} = \mathbf{W}^{l,m} - \mathbf{W} \tag{6}$$

User Profiling: For efficiently initially interpreting and subsequently incorporating human feedback, in parallel with the $\mathbf{W}^{l,m}$ estimation process, an individual user profile $\mathbf{Q}^{l,m} \leftarrow f_2(\delta^l, S_m^h)$ is constructed for every human subject h_m at every node P_l. The latter is estimated using the appropriate sensorial data S_m^h to model the observed human behavior and a generalized function $f_2(.)$ that defines the exact (NN-based) implementation of the user profile while considering S_m^h as input parameters. Under the current conceptualization, DL-based approaches are considered for generating $\mathbf{Q}^{l,m}$, as in [9] and [18], aiming at combining increased modelling capabilities and easier integration to the designed FL-based framework.

Global Model Update: Having computed the local parameter updates $\Delta \mathbf{W}^{l,m}$ and the corresponding user profiles $\mathbf{Q}^{l,m}$ (using locally generated and processed data δ^l), these are sent to the central node (aggregator) so as to periodically produce updated versions of global model $\mathbf{W}$. According to the conventional FL mechanism, an updated version $\mathbf{W}'$ of $\mathbf{W}$ is generated on a regular basis, by applying a simple averaging operator, as follows:

$$\mathbf{W}' = \mathbf{W} + lr^g \cdot \Gamma \tag{7}$$

$$\Gamma = \frac{1}{\Lambda} \sum_{(l,m)} \Delta \mathbf{W}^{l,m}, \tag{8}$$

where lr^g denotes the global learning rate and Λ the total number of received $\Delta \mathbf{W}^{l,m}$ updates. For robustly confronting the observed variance in the behavior of the large number of involved human teachers h_m, the designed cognitive architecture (apart from possible sensorial data S_l^r pre-processing for invariance incorporation) encompasses the estimated user profiles $\mathbf{Q}^{l,m}$ in the global model update process, modifying (8) to the following general formalism:

$$\Gamma = \Phi(\{\mathbf{Q}^{l,m}\}, \{\Delta\mathbf{W}^{l,m}\}), \qquad (9)$$

where $\Phi(.)$ denotes a generalized function that combines the available $\mathbf{Q}^{l,m}$ and $\Delta\mathbf{W}^{l,m}$, estimated at every network node P_l. Depending on the particularities of the selected application domain (e.g. supported $\mathbf{W}$, S^r, S^h, R, etc.), the following main and purely data-driven materializations of $\Phi(.)$, which are capable of being combined, are considered in [25]: a) User weighting, where each human teacher h_m is modulated by a different weight factor based on a similarity metric from the global user model, b) Parameter weighting, which assigns varying weights to the parameters of $\mathbf{W}$, based on the degree of correlation among the parameters of $\mathbf{W}^{l,m}$ and $\mathbf{Q}^{l,m}$, and c) User clustering, which considers the generation of multiple instances $\mathbf{W}_\eta$ of the global model $\mathbf{W}$, in order to better capture the heterogeneity of data distributions across the different users h_m. In the remainder of this work the above-mentioned 'User weighting' conceptualization is considered and the focus is put on thoroughly defining an efficient $\mathbf{Q}^{l,m}$ formalism (Sect. 4), although 'Parameter weighting' and 'User clustering' (as well as any combination of the three alternatives) are equally applicable. In particular, the 'User weighting' approach adaptively adjusts the contribution of each human teacher h_m by a different weight factor based on his/her exhibited behavior, as follows:

$$\Gamma = \frac{1}{E} \sum_{(l,m)} \varepsilon(\mathbf{Q}^{l,m}) \cdot \Delta\mathbf{W}^{l,m}$$

$$\varepsilon(\mathbf{Q}^{l,m}) = 1/\|\mathbf{Q}^g - \mathbf{Q}^{l,m}\|$$

$$E = \sum_{(l,m)} \varepsilon(\mathbf{Q}^{l,m}), \qquad (10)$$

where $\varepsilon(\mathbf{Q}^{l,m})$ denotes the weight factor for each h_m at every P_l, $\mathbf{Q}^g$ the corresponding global user model (e.g. estimated through the same FL-based mechanism used for constructing $\mathbf{W}$) and $\|.\|$ a dissimilarity score metric (e.g. Euclidean distance between the parameters of the involved user models).

4 DL-based User Modelling and Knowledge Aggregation

Incorporating human feedback constitutes a fundamental part of the LfD approach and, consequently, of the employed cognitive architecture. However, the latter poses additional challenges to the problem formulation that need to be efficiently addressed (e.g. variance in human performance, variability in knowledge across human subjects, learning from noisy/imprecise human input, possible conflicts in provided human feedback information, handling of individuals with different idiosyncrasies, learning from very large or very sparse datasets, incremental learning, etc.). On the other hand, the strength of the utilized FL-based mechanism (detailed in Sect. 3) lies on incorporating a very large number Λ of samples and multiple iterative updates of $\mathbf{W}'$ that will likely lead to the convergence to well-performing and robust $\mathbf{W}$ models, while the network nodes P_l contributing in (8) may be sampled out of the available ones (usually in a random way). However, combining information ($\Delta \mathbf{W}^{l,m}$) related to different human subjects h_m (that presumably exhibit highly diverse and varying behavior) is in turn very likely to lead the FL process to be confined to a local maximum or even to a non-convergence of the FL procedure; hence, jeopardising the overall learning process. To this end, defining a detailed and robust user profile model $\mathbf{Q}^{l,m}$ is of vital importance for enabling: a) The accurate assessment and interpretation of the demonstrated behavior of each human teacher h_m and, subsequently, b) The appropriate adjustment of the importance of the provided human feedback from the same individual or across multiple ones, during the knowledge aggregation step.

In general, the purpose of defining user profile formalisms is to cover physical (e.g. human actions, physical capabilities, etc.), cognitive (e.g. intention, personality, etc.) and social (e.g. non-verbal cues, emotions, etc.) aspects, in order to model and efficiently interpret the exhibited human activity [28]. So far, the problem has been investigated and assessed from different disciplines and scientific perspectives, while methodologies that rely on the use of Machine Learning (ML) techniques and the integration of the generated models in broader computational/cognitive systems continuously receives increasing attention. One of the most popular examples of the latter category of methods constitutes the so called recommender systems (that aim to predict the preferences of each individual human user) [23, 35] and especially the so-called 'collaborative filtering' class [14]. However, the introduced profiles so far model relatively simple types of human behavior aspects (e.g. correlations of individual users and different information items [12]).

4.1 Considered Information Sources

Under the proposed conceptualization, a fine-grained multi-level DL-based computational approach is introduced for modelling user profile $\mathbf{Q}^{l,m}$, grounded on the efficient processing and sophisticated combination of various heterogeneous and diverse information streams. The overall goal is to meet the demanding requirements of the LfD setting for modelling the exhibited user behavior, focusing on the following two main pillars: a) Accurately interpreting the captured human behavior both in the short- and the long-term cases and b) Effectively handling the variance of cross-subject (and often conflicting) information and its efficient merging. For that purpose, the following (hierarchically organized) types of information sources are considered for generating $\mathbf{Q}^{l,m}$ (as also illustrated in Fig. 2):

- *User attributes*: These include valuable and explicitly defined information concerning each human teacher's h_m background, covering aspects like demographic (e.g. age, sex, race, origin, etc.), anthropomorphic (e.g. height, weight, possible disabilities, etc.), educational (e.g. level and types of education, etc.), work experience (e.g. duration, responsibilities/tasks, etc.), etc.;
- *User state*: This corresponds to particular modules/pipelines that (automatically) detect specific human behavior characteristics, e.g. fatigue detection, stress detection, emotion recognition, intention prediction, etc. For their extraction sensorial data types belonging to S^r and S^h are used;

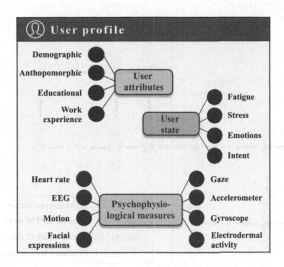

Fig. 2. Hierarchy of information sources for generating user profile $\mathbf{Q}^{l,m}$.

- *Psychophysiological measurements*: These comprise the actual raw sensorial data information streams captured (supporting data types of both S^r and S^h sets) and convey critical details about the user's mental state, personality and idiosyncrasy, e.g. heart rate, electroencephalogram (EEG), motion, facial expressions, gaze, accelerometer, gyroscope, electrodermal activity, etc.

It needs to be highlighted that the specific information sources (belonging to each of the above mentioned categories) to be considered depends on the particularities of the selected application case.

4.2 Processing of Collected Data

According to the formalism of the cognitive architecture for LfD learning defined in Sect. 3, each human teacher h_m can provide, in relation to a given robotic platform P_l, feedback information (denoted $\mu_v^{l,m}$) regarding the robot exhibited behavior, where v ($v \in [1, N], v \in \mathbb{N}, N \in \mathbb{N}$) indicates the index of the particular feedback session (denoted $\xi_v^{l,m}$) that consists of T_v time steps. The user attributes provided for human h_m, after being appropriately numerically encoded, are concatenated to form static feature vector $\mathbf{DE}^m$. On the other hand, the outputs of the specific feature detectors (that summarize the user's state) for human h_m at node P_l during session $\xi_v^{l,m}$, after also being appropriately numerically encoded (if needed), are similarly concatenated to produce static feature vector $\mathbf{DS}_v^{l,m}$. With respect to the corresponding psychophysiological measurements captured during session $\xi_v^{l,m}$, an individual multi-dimensional observation sequence $OS_{v,\rho}^{l,m}$ (of length T_v samples) is formed for every considered sensor type implied by index ρ. In order to estimate a static feature vector $\mathbf{DR}_{v,\rho}^{l,m}$ (out of each $OS_{v,\rho}^{l,m}$ sequence), a DL-based unsupervised feature representation learning methodology is considered. Specifically, an individual LSTM autoencoder, similar to the one described in [30] and

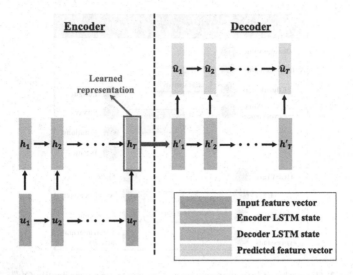

Fig. 3. Employed LSTM autoencoder for producing psychophysiological measurements representation $\mathbf{DR}_{v,\rho}^{l,m}$.

whose architecture is illustrated in Fig. 3, is introduced for each $OS_{v,\rho}^{l,m}$, since every $OS_{v,\rho}^{l,m}$ is in general related to a different sampling frequency and, hence, consists of a different number of samples. As can be seen in Fig. 3, the autoencoder consists of two LSTM models, namely an encoder and a decoder one. The encoder receives as input a series of feature vectors (i.e. $\mathbf{u}_1, \mathbf{u}_2, \ldots \mathbf{u}_T$) and updates at each time step its vectorial fixed-length internal state representation (i.e. $\mathbf{h}_1, \mathbf{h}_2, \ldots \mathbf{h}_T$), which models/encodes the input sequence until that time step. During the decoding phase, the second LSTM is initialized with internal state $\mathbf{h}'_1 \equiv \mathbf{h}_T$ and, through its fundamental sequential modelling mechanism, it recursively estimates new internal states (i.e. $\mathbf{h}'_1, \mathbf{h}'_2, \ldots \mathbf{h}'_T$) that correspondingly produce a respective series of prediction feature vectors (i.e. $\widehat{\mathbf{u}}_1, \widehat{\mathbf{u}}_2, \ldots \widehat{\mathbf{u}}_T$). The overall goal of the autoencoder is to adjust its internal parameters so that sequences $\mathbf{u}_1, \mathbf{u}_2, \ldots \mathbf{u}_T$ and $\widehat{\mathbf{u}}_1, \widehat{\mathbf{u}}_2, \ldots \widehat{\mathbf{u}}_T$ to be as similar as possible. Vector $\mathbf{h}_T$ that characterizes the overall input sequence $\mathbf{u}_1, \mathbf{u}_2, \ldots \mathbf{u}_T$ is considered to coincide with $\mathbf{DR}_{v,\rho}^{l,m}$ defined above.

4.3   Modeling of User Profile

The ultimate goal of designing a model of the human user profile $\mathbf{Q}^{l,m}$ (Sect. 3) is to provide a computational scheme that will simultaneously analyse, cross-correlate and eventually fuse the different heterogeneous information streams for producing a joint/compact representation that will efficiently encode/express the salient characteristics of each human teacher h_m (e.g. mental state, idiosyncrasy, preferences, etc.) in an implicit way. The latter is of paramount importance for interpreting the human behavior during the knowledge aggregation step, as will be discussed in Sect. 4.4.

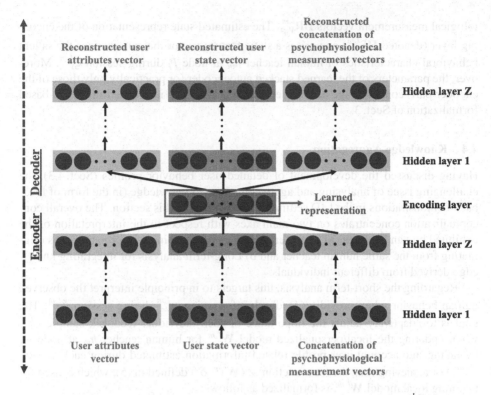

Fig. 4. Designed stacked autoencoder for generating user profile model $\mathbf{Q}^{l,m}$.

For creating a robust user profile, a DL-based hierarchical multi-stream unsupervised feature fusion approach is adopted. In particular, a multi-stream stacked autoencoder, similar to the one described in [11] and whose general architecture is illustrated in Fig. 4, is introduced. Each of the 3 defined autoencoder streams is in direct accordance to the information sources definition of Sect. 4.1. In particular, a stacked autoencoder is a neural network consisting of several layers of sparse autoencoders, where the output of each hidden layer is connected to the input of the successive hidden layer. The designed autoencoder considers a multi-stream architecture, which aims at initially capturing the correlations among the features of the same stream (while also leveraging knowledge from the other streams) and subsequently modelling the inter-dependencies among the different streams, as can been seen in Fig. 4. Similarly to the LSTM autoencoder (Sect. 4.2), the goal during the training process is for the input and output feature vectors to be as similar as possible. Moreover, the learned multi-modal representation (feature vector) of the middle/internal encoding layer compactly summarizes the salient attributes of the input feature vectors.

Regarding the actual user profile generation process, an individual stacked autoencoder is considered with respect to every $\mathbf{Q}^{l,m}$. The autoencoder receives as input (with respect to each associated feedback session $\xi_v^{l,m}$) the following feature vectors: a) User attributes vector $\mathbf{DE}^m$, b) User state vector $\mathbf{DS}_v^{l,m}$, and c) Concatenation of psychophysiological measurement vectors $\mathbf{DR}_{v,\rho}^{l,m}$. The estimated state representation of the encoding layer (denoted $\mathbf{HS}_v^{l,m}$) comprises a static feature vector that summarizes the salient behavioral characteristics of human teacher h_m at node P_l during session $\xi_v^{l,m}$. Moreover, the parameters of the learned stacked autoencoder (or practically only those of the encoder part) constitute the actual user profile model $\mathbf{Q}^{l,m}$ introduced in the FL-based formalization of Sect. 3.

4.4 Knowledge Aggregation

Having discussed the development of detailed user behavior profiles (Sect. 4.3), the challenging issue of analysing and aggregating human knowledge (in the form of feedback demonstrations in the LfD setting) is investigated in this section. The overall conceptualization concentrates on two main axes with respect to the interpretation of the exhibited human behavior: a) Short-term analysis for combining information cues originating from the same human teacher and b) Long-term analysis for integrating knowledge derived from different individuals.

Regarding the short-term analysis, this targets to in principle interpret the observed human behavior when providing feedback information $\mu_v^{l,m}$ during session $\xi_v^{l,m}$. The goal is to adaptively adjust the importance of each individual feedback sample $\mu_v^{l,m}$ when updating the local/personalized model $\mathbf{W}^{l,m}$ for human teacher h_m at node P_l, by taking into account user profile related information estimated during each session $\xi_v^{l,m}$. For achieving that, the loss function $\mathscr{L}(\mathbf{W}^{l,m}, \delta^l)$ defined in (5), which is used for updating local model $\mathbf{W}^{l,m}$, is formalized as follows:

$$\mathscr{L}(\mathbf{W}^{l,m}, \delta^l) = \frac{\sum_v \omega_v^{l,m} \cdot \mathscr{L}_v(\mu_v^{l,m}, \mathbf{W}^{l,m})}{\sum_v \omega_v^{l,m}}$$
$$\omega_v^{l,m} = 1/\|\mathbf{HS}_v^{l,m} - \overline{\mathbf{HS}}_v^{l,m}\|, \tag{11}$$

where $\mathscr{L}_v(\mu_v^{l,m}, \mathbf{W}^{l,m})$ is the loss factor for sample $\mu_v^{l,m}$, $\omega_v^{l,m}$ its associated weight factor, $\overline{\mathbf{HS}}_v^{l,m}$ the mean value of $\mathbf{HS}_v^{l,m}$ (calculated while considering all available $\mu_v^{l,m}$ samples) and $\|.\|$ a dissimilarity score metric (e.g. Euclidean distance). $\omega_v^{l,m}$ assigns varying importance to each $\mu_v^{l,m}$, contrary to the conventional practice of associating all $\mu_v^{l,m}$ samples with equal weight (i.e. $\omega_v^{l,m} = 1$). The motivation behind the latter choice lies on the fundamental consideration that observed human behaviors $\mathbf{HS}_v^{l,m}$ that deviate significantly from the expected personalized norm $\overline{\mathbf{HS}}_v^{l,m}$ (i.e. outliers) should receive decreased importance, since it is assumed that they are likely to be caused by undesirable user profile states (e.g. when in extreme situations of fatigue, stress, decreased attention, etc.).

With respect to the long-term analysis, the stacked autoencoder computational model $\mathbf{Q}^{l,m}$ described in Sect. 4.3 is used in the 'User weighting' scheme defined in (10), where $\mathbf{Q}^{l,m}$ that are similar to the respective global $\mathbf{Q}^g$ user profile receive increased impact. Similarly to the above, the explanation of the latter states that model updates $\Delta\mathbf{W}^{l,m}$ ((6)) should receive greater importance proportionally to the associated user profiles $Q^{l,m}$ being similar to the global norm or expected behavior Q^g. In other words, human teacher behaviors ($Q^{l,m}$) that deviate significantly from the global norm (Q^g) are considered to be due to frequent undesirable user profile states, which could very likely in turn jeopardize the convergence of the overall FL-based learning scheme; hence, decreasing their impact would facilitate and reinforce the robustness of the overall LfD learning environment. It needs to be highlighted that in the original work of [25] no specific materialization of $Q^{l,m}$ is provided.

5 Conclusions

In this paper, the recently introduced Federated Learning (FL)-based conceptualization for developing large-scale multi-agent Learning from Demonstration (LfD) human-robot collaborative environments was further elaborated and enhanced, by incorporating a novel Deep Learning (DL)-based user profile formulation for estimating a fine-grained representation of the exhibited human behavior. The overall integrated scheme supports both short- and long-term analysis/interpretation of the observed human teacher behavior, in order to adaptively adjust the importance of the collected feedback samples when aggregating information originating from the same and different human individuals, respectively. Future work includes the implementation and evaluation of the designed framework in real-world settings, the development of more sophisticated user profile models and the incorporation of more elaborate DL formalisms (e.g. (self-) attention schemes, transformer networks, etc.).

References

1. Argall, B.D., Chernova, S., Veloso, M., Browning, B.: A survey of robot learning from demonstration. Robot. Auton. Syst. **57**(5), 469–483 (2009)
2. Bhattacharjee, T., Lee, G., Song, H., Srinivasa, S.S.: Towards robotic feeding: role of haptics in fork-based food manipulation. IEEE Robot. Autom. Lett. **4**(2), 1485–1492 (2019)
3. Billard, A.G., Calinon, S., Dillmann, R.: Learning from humans. In: Siciliano, B., Khatib, O. (eds.) Springer Handbook of Robotics, pp. 1995–2014. Springer, Cham (2016). https://doi.org/10.1007/978-3-319-32552-1_74
4. Bretan, M., Oore, S., Sanan, S., Heck, L.: Robot learning by collaborative network training: a self-supervised method using ranking. In: Proceedings of the 18th International Conference on Autonomous Agents and MultiAgent Systems, pp. 1333–1340 (2019)
5. Brys, T., Harutyunyan, A., Taylor, M.E., Nowé, A.: Policy transfer using reward shaping. In: Proceedings of the 2015 International Conference on Autonomous Agents and Multiagent Systems, pp. 181–188 (2015)
6. Caccavale, R., Saveriano, M., Finzi, A., Lee, D.: Kinesthetic teaching and attentional supervision of structured tasks in human-robot interaction. Auton. Robots **43**(6), 1291–1307 (2019)
7. Cheng, R., Jin, Y.: A social learning particle swarm optimization algorithm for scalable optimization. Inf. Sci. **291**, 43–60 (2015)
8. Droniou, A., Ivaldi, S., Sigaud, O.: Learning a repertoire of actions with deep neural networks. In: 4th International Conference on Development and Learning and on Epigenetic Robotics, pp. 229–234. IEEE (2014)

9. Farnadi, G., Tang, J., De Cock, M., Moens, M.F.: User profiling through deep multimodal fusion. In: Proceedings of the Eleventh ACM International Conference on Web Search and Data Mining, pp. 171–179 (2018)
10. Furuta, D., Kutsuzawa, K., Sakaino, S., Tsuji, T.: Motion planning with success judgement model based on learning from demonstration. IEEE Access **8**, 73142–73150 (2020)
11. Gao, J., Li, P., Chen, Z., Zhang, J.: A survey on deep learning for multimodal data fusion. Neural Comput. **32**(5), 829–864 (2020)
12. He, X., Liao, L., Zhang, H., Nie, L., Hu, X., Chua, T.S.: Neural collaborative filtering. In: Proceedings of the 26th International Conference on World Wide Web, pp. 173–182 (2017)
13. Hussein, A., Gaber, M.M., Elyan, E., Jayne, C.: Imitation learning: a survey of learning methods. ACM Comput. Surv. (CSUR) **50**(2), 1–35 (2017)
14. Ji, D., Xiang, Z., Li, Y.: Dual relations network for collaborative filtering. IEEE Access **8**, 109747–109757 (2020)
15. Judah, K., Fern, A., Dietterich, T.G.: Active imitation learning via reduction to IID active learning. arXiv preprint arXiv:1210.4876 (2012)
16. Kunze, L., Hawes, N., Duckett, T., Hanheide, M., Krajník, T.: Artificial intelligence for long-term robot autonomy: a survey. IEEE Robot. Autom. Lett. **3**(4), 4023–4030 (2018)
17. Li, X., Huang, K., Yang, W., Wang, S., Zhang, Z.: On the convergence of FedAvg on non-IID data. arXiv preprint arXiv:1907.02189 (2019)
18. Liang, H.: Drprofiling: deep reinforcement user profiling for recommendations in heterogenous information networks. IEEE Trans. Knowl. Data Eng. (2020)
19. Liu, B., Wang, L., Liu, M.: Lifelong federated reinforcement learning: a learning architecture for navigation in cloud robotic systems. IEEE Robot. Autom. Lett. **4**(4), 4555–4562 (2019)
20. Liu, Y., Gupta, A., Abbeel, P., Levine, S.: Imitation from observation: learning to imitate behaviors from raw video via context translation. In: 2018 IEEE International Conference on Robotics and Automation (ICRA), pp. 1118–1125. IEEE (2018)
21. Loquercio, A., Maqueda, A.I., Del-Blanco, C.R., Scaramuzza, D.: DroNet: learning to fly by driving. IEEE Robot. Autom. Lett. **3**(2), 1088–1095 (2018)
22. McMahan, B., Moore, E., Ramage, D., Hampson, S., y Arcas, B.A.: Communication-efficient learning of deep networks from decentralized data. In: Artificial Intelligence and Statistics, pp. 1273–1282. PMLR (2017)
23. Mu, R.: A survey of recommender systems based on deep learning. IEEE Access **6**, 69009–69022 (2018)
24. Pan, Y., Cheng, C.A., Saigol, K., Lee, K., Yan, X., Theodorou, E., Boots, B.: Agile autonomous driving using end-to-end deep imitation learning. arXiv preprint arXiv:1709.07174 (2017)
25. Papadopoulos, G.T., Antona, M., Stephanidis, C.: Towards open and expandable cognitive AI architectures for large-scale multi-agent human-robot collaborative learning. arXiv preprint arXiv:2012.08174 (2020)
26. Papadopoulos, G.T., Daras, P.: Human action recognition using 3D reconstruction data. IEEE Trans. Circ. Syst. Video Technol. **28**(8), 1807–1823 (2016)
27. Ravichandar, H., Polydoros, A.S., Chernova, S., Billard, A.: Recent advances in robot learning from demonstration. Ann. Rev. Control Robot. Auton. Syst. **3**, 297–330 (2020)
28. Rossi, S., Ferland, F., Tapus, A.: User profiling and behavioral adaptation for HRI: a survey. Pattern Recogn. Lett. **99**, 3–12 (2017)
29. Seleem, I.A., El-Hussieny, H., Assal, S.F., Ishii, H.: Development and stability analysis of an imitation learning-based pose planning approach for multi-section continuum robot. IEEE Access, **8**, 99366–99379 (2020)
30. Srivastava, N., Mansimov, E., Salakhudinov, R.: Unsupervised learning of video representations using LSTMS. In: International Conference on Machine Learning, pp. 843–852. PMLR (2015)

31. Thermos, S., Papadopoulos, G.T., Daras, P., Potamianos, G.: Deep affordance-grounded sensorimotor object recognition. In: Proceedings of the IEEE Conference on Computer Vision and Pattern Recognition, pp. 6167–6175 (2017)
32. Vogt, D., Stepputtis, S., Grehl, S., Jung, B., Amor, H.B.: A system for learning continuous human-robot interactions from human-human demonstrations. In: 2017 IEEE International Conference on Robotics and Automation (ICRA), pp. 2882–2889. IEEE (2017)
33. Wulfmeier, M., Ondruska, P., Posner, I.: Maximum entropy deep inverse reinforcement learning. arXiv preprint arXiv:1507.04888 (2015)
34. Zhang, M., McCarthy, Z., Finn, C., Levine, S., Abbeel, P.: Learning deep neural network policies with continuous memory states. In: 2016 IEEE International Conference on Robotics and Automation (ICRA), pp. 520–527. IEEE (2016)
35. Zhang, S., Yao, L., Sun, A., Tay, Y.: Deep learning based recommender system: a survey and new perspectives. ACM Comput. Surv. (CSUR) 52(1), 1–38 (2019)
36. Zhang, T., et al.: Deep imitation learning for complex manipulation tasks from virtual reality teleoperation. In: 2018 IEEE International Conference on Robotics and Automation (ICRA), pp. 1–8. IEEE (2018)
37. Zhou, W., Li, Y., Chen, S., Ding, B.: Real-time data processing architecture for multi-robots based on differential federated learning. In: 2018 IEEE SmartWorld Congress, pp. 462–471. IEEE (2018)
38. Zhu, Z., Hu, H.: Robot learning from demonstration in robotic assembly: a survey. Robotics 7(2), 17 (2018)

Theory of Mind Assessment with Human-Human and Human-Robot Interactions

Trent Rabe[1]([✉]), Anisa Callis[2], Zhi Zheng[3], Jamison Heard[3], Reynold Bailey[3], and Cecilia Alm[3]

[1] University of Colorado, Boulder, USA
trent.rabe@colorado.edu
[2] Pennsylvania State University, State College, USA
[3] Rochester Institute of Technology, Rochester, USA

Abstract. Human-robot interaction has played an increasingly significant role in more recent research involving the Theory of Mind (ToM). As the use of robot facilitators increases, questions arise regarding the implications of their involvement in a research setting. This work addresses the effects of a humanoid robot facilitator in a ToM assessment. This paper analyzes subjects' performances on tasks meant to test ToM as those tasks are delivered by human or robot facilitators. Various modalities of data were collected: performance on ToM tasks, subjects' perceptions of the robot, results from a ToM survey, and response duration. This paper highlights the effects of human-robot interactions in ToM assessments, which ultimately leads to a discussion on the effectiveness of using robot facilitators in future human-subject research.

Keywords: Social robotics · Human-robotic interaction · Theory of Mind

1 Introduction

Humanoid robots are increasingly applied as Socially Assistive Robots (SARs), such as tutors, assessment/intervention facilitators, and companions [1]. Using SARs as facilitators has become more relevant, due to the potential for lower cost, reducing social stigma, and better accessibility. However, previous studies have indicated that information delivery is different between robots and humans, which raises concerns about the underlying bias when comparing human- with robot-facilitated experiments [2]. This prompts important questions surrounding the proliferation of SARs, including how effectively SARs can be used in human subjects research. This paper researches the effectiveness of humanoid robot facilitators using Theory of Mind studies. The *Theory of Mind (ToM)* is the ability to understand and reason about the mental state of another person, including one's emotions, beliefs, and intentions [3]. ToM has been extensively explored in human-robotic interaction research, but has typically focused on

© The Author(s), under exclusive license to Springer Nature Switzerland AG 2022
M. Kurosu (Ed.): HCII 2022, LNCS 13303, pp. 564–579, 2022.
https://doi.org/10.1007/978-3-031-05409-9_41

AI methods for providing a robot with ToM [4,5], instead of determining if a subject's ToM is impacted during robot interactions. There is also a lack of objective data in ToM research that relates the facilitator type (human vs. robot) to task performance. Understanding this multimodal data will provide valuable insight about the effectiveness of SARs as facilitators of ToM interactions.

This paper focuses on using a robot facilitator to deliver a ToM scenario in order to answer the following research questions: (1) Does performance change when ToM tasks are delivered by humans vs. robots? (2) How does participants' self-perceived ToM differ from their measured ToM? (3) How does participants' perception of the robot delivering a task change the participant's performance within the experiment? (4) How is the participants' response time affected by human or robot facilitators?

2   Related Work

Theory of Mind has been thoroughly researched over the past four decades after it was first introduced by Premack and Woodruff [3]. In more recent years, many ToM studies are focused on child development, specifically from ages 3 to 5 [6]. Wellman et al. [7] found that children under the age of 3 continuously failed the false-belief task due to their lack of conceptual understanding of the world. The same study found that children aged 4 and up were able to regularly pass false belief tasks they were given. Bernstein et al. [8] did find that in certain cases, middle and older aged adults have more errors on false belief tasks than children.

Theory of Mind has been extensively studied in children, but there has also been a few studies about Theory of Mind in adults. Much of this ToM research in adults has been geared towards understanding the declination of ToM capabilities over one's lifetime. There has been a debate on this topic which Pardini and Nichelli addressed in "Age-Related Decline in Mentalizing Skills Across Adult Life Span" [9]. In their work, they selected four groups of participants based on ages (range: 25–75) to complete ToM tasks. Their results "found that performance of the early middle-aged people was not significantly different from that of the young group, whereas both had better scores if compared with the other two groups. We also found that the old middle-aged group presented a deficit in this domain if compared with the two younger groups but was less impaired if compared with the elderly subjects." These results suggest that there is a peak in ToM capabilities in early to middle adulthood.

However, the debate continues as other studies come to the conclusion that ToM capabilities do deteriorate with age. In their study: "Social Understanding: How does it Fare with Advancing Years?" where they tested older adults ages (60–82 years old) and younger adults ages (20–46) Sullivan and Ruffman found that "The younger group performed significantly better than the older group on the theory of mind stories ... There was a trend for the younger group to do better on the control stories as well, although the effect failed to reach significance" [10].

The research presented in this paper analyzes ToM in early adulthood. According to previous research, the results found by this study are unlikely to be marred by developing or declining ToM in participants. This sort of change in the participants' abilities to understand others' mental states would pose issues if one participant were to be further along in the development process than another, indicating higher ToM scores, when in reality, they were just more mature in that regard. This is not an issue for the results of this paper as the subject pool was all in the young adult category from Pardini and Nichelli's work [9].

2.1   False-Belief Tasks

The Theory of Mind is commonly tested through false belief tasks, which were introduced by Wimmer and Perner in 1983 [11]. The first false-belief task was administered to children between three and nine years old; each given two pictures. The first picture showed a main character placing an object in 'x' place. The second picture allowed the children to witness the object being moved to 'y' place in the absence of the main character. The children were then asked where the main character would look for the object. This is a false-belief task because the child participants know where the object actually is while the main character in the story does not.

There are two types of false-belief tasks: first- and second-order. A first-order false-belief task measures "An individual's ability to comprehend false beliefs of others" [12]. A commonly used first order false belief task is called the "Smarties." A child is asked to predict what another child thinks is in the Smarties box. In reality, there is a pencil in the box [13]. A second-order false-belief tasks is "what an individual thinks about another person's thoughts" [12]. A commonly used second-order false-belief task is the Perner and Wimmer (1985) "ice-cream van story." Mary is the only character who knows the actual location of the ice cream truck and is asked to predict where John thinks the ice cream truck is located. John knows the former location of the truck but not the current location. Though Mary knows where the truck truly is, she must consider if what John knows is different from what she knows [11]. A variation of the original false belief task is the "Sally - Anne Task" [14]. This task expands the original task by using props to visually demonstrate the scenario, instead of showing story images. Most recent works are variations of this task, depicted in Fig. 6.

2.2   Theory of Mind Inventory

The Theory of Mind Inventory survey (ToMI:SR-A) is a 60 question survey designed to establish a ToM score for the test taker [15]. The results are described as 'self-assessed' as each participant provides answers to subjective questions about themselves. The answers are recorded on a 20-unit continuum similar to the traditional Likert-type scale. The subject is asked to rank how well they relate to each question on this scale. The answers are recorded for each question and averaged over all 60 questions, providing each subject a score of 0–20, with

Fig. 1. Photos that participants were shown in video tasks with human and robot facilitators. This is the "Sally-Anne" task. The object being moved is the toy plane. It is first moved into the basket, then it is moved twice with the absence of one of the characters. This gives enough movement of the object to ask the participants feasible questions for the false-belief tasks.

accuracy to one decimal place (e.g. 17.4). Neurotypical subjects with well developed ToM are expected to score at or above a 15 out of 20 on the ToMI:SR-A survey [15].

2.3   Testing Robot Theory of Mind Capabilities

Recently, there has been some ToM research involving robots. One study used robots as the facilitators in their scenarios [4], while other studies have used robots as subjects who are supposed to complete first-order false belief tasks [16–18]. Another study expanded the previous research by using robot subjects who are intended to complete higher-order false belief tasks [4].

While these previous studies use robots, few of them directly investigate the way that humans react to robot facilitators in terms of subject performance and perception of the robot facilitator. The previously mentioned studies also do not compare the performance differences between human and robot delivered tasks.

To the best of our knowledge, very little prior work has been done to identify the differences between human and robot facilitators on false-belief tasks. It has been suggested that robot facilitators could create less subject/facilitator bias when it comes to asking questions for false-belief tasks. One study found that when children were asked questions pertaining to a false-belief tasks, they answered incorrectly because they felt they were being questioned about their knowledge instead of being asked about the beliefs of the character in the story. Using a robot facilitator eliminated this feeling within the children participants [19]. There have, however, been some studies on how humans react to robot facilitators in scenarios and interactions outside of Theory of Mind [20]. The presented study analyzes audio data of subjects when answering questions from robot facilitators vs human facilitators, which allows researchers to directly observe the impact the robot facilitator has on subject performance.

The Godspeed Robot Perception Questionnaire assesses how people perceive the presence of humanoid robots in their environments using 5 overall categories: Anthropomorphism, Animacy, Likeability, Perceived Intelligence, and Perceived Safety [21]. One study had subjects interact with a lifelike humanoid robot and then complete the Godspeed Robot Perception Questionnaire. The results indicated that the more lifelike a robot was, the lower subject perceptions were. [20].

3   Methodology

False belief tasks are often used to assess an individual's ToM, where a participant is asked to identify a character's beliefs in a story when the participant knows those beliefs to be false [12]. The presented within-subjects experiment used such a task and manipulated facilitator types (human or robot).

3.1   Experiment Protocols

The research was approved by the Rochester Institute of Technology Institutional Review Board (ethics review). Various measures were built into the experiment to protect participant confidentiality and the experimental validity. All subjects completed an informed consent form prior to their participation. Subject and facilitator names were also changed before video recording began to help deidentify the data, due to the virtual nature of the experiment.

Thirty human subjects (mean age: 22.1 years; standard deviation: 4.0) completed four false-belief task scenarios. Each task was delivered virtually via Zoom by a recorded human or a NAO robot facilitator (see Fig. 2) and were accompanied by story-line pictures. After the story was told, the participants were asked questions about the characters' beliefs. The first two tasks were considered easy,

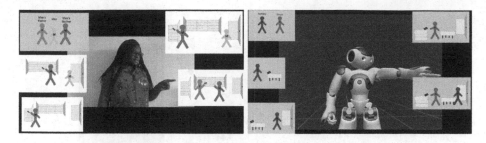

Fig. 2. Human and humanoid robot facilitators presenting false-belief scenarios to subjects who are tasked with identifying characters' beliefs in the story.

while the last two were considered difficult. The experiment manipulated the facilitator type (human or robot), where participants were randomly assigned a facilitator ordering. Each participant completed one easy and one hard task with a robot and the remaining tasks with a human. A standard ToM instrument survey [15] was administered prior to scenario completion to rate an individual's ToM. The participant's task performance (correctly answered questions), response duration times, and speech rate (number of words divided by response duration) were analyzed for each task. The subjects also rated their perceptions of the humanoid robot at the end using the Godspeed Questionnaire [21].

In each of the four tasks, pictures appeared on the screen as facilitators reached certain parts within the story. The images stayed on the screen for the duration for the task, including while the questions were being asked. This helps prevent the experiment from becoming memory based, as the participants are able to refer to the images so that they do not forget the order of the scenes in the story. The easy tasks were designed with two questions that were fairly straightforward for the subject to answer correctly. The harder tasks were designed with 5 questions that required the subject to think deeper about what they had heard in the video and how it compared to what they knew themselves.

3.2 NAO Robot Facilitator

The study used a virtual NAO robot. Figure 3 depicts Choregraphe, the graphical programming interface for the NAO. The drag and drop programming function was used to control the robots arm and head motions in order to have the NAO closely mimic the human facilitators' movements.

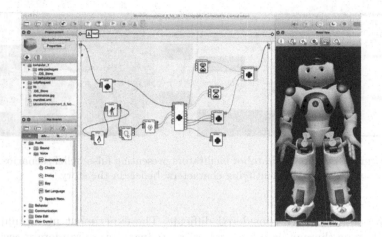

Fig. 3. Image of drag and drop program used to program the NAO.

4   Results

The first research question was: ***Does performance change when ToM tasks are delivered by humans vs. robots?*** This was addressed by comparing the number of correct answers each participant got on each robot facilitated task to the number of correct answers of each participant on the human facilitated task for each task. Comparing the number of correct answers a participant gave as the tasks were facilitated by a human or by a robot allowed for an analysis of changes in performance as the facilitator type changed. A Mann-Whitney U-test (see Table 1) found no significant difference for task performance between the robot and human facilitators for individual tasks. In addition, there was no significant difference between the percentage of correct answers for human- (median = 86%) and robot-facilitated tasks (median = 86%). These findings indicate that a robot-facilitated ToM study yields comparable task performance results to the same study using human facilitators.

Table 1. Mann-Whitney U-test results for robot vs. human.

Task	p-value	Median robot	Median human	w-value
1	0.39	1.5	2.0	227.0
2	0.65	2.0	2.0	221.0
3	0.80	5.0	5.0	226.0
4	0.92	4.0	4.0	229.5

Figure 4 shows the comparison between the number of correct answers on robot and human facilitated tasks for task 1. Comparing the performance on both types of facilitators allows the difference to be visible.

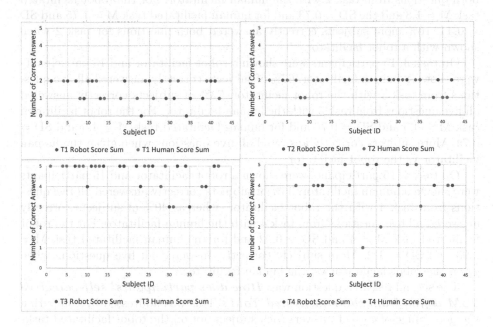

Fig. 4. Comparison of the number of correct answers per subject when the task was facilitated by a human vs. by a robot. Participants answered two questions on tasks 1 and 2 and five questions on tasks 3 and 4.

On task 1, 16 participants were shown a robot facilitator and 14 participants were shown a human facilitator. 50% of subjects correctly answered both questions from task 1 with the robot facilitator. 57% of subjects correctly answered both questions from task 1 with the human facilitator. For the robot facilitated task $M = 1.4$ and $SD = 0.74$ and for the human facilitated task $M = 1.57$ and $SD = 0.51$. Subjects scored, on average, higher on task 1 with human facilitators than with robot facilitators. This means that the participants were more likely to get one or even two questions correct for the first task when it was administered by a human. Although this preliminary data suggests that human facilitated tasks yield better results than robot facilitated tasks, this is likely not the case. A Mann-Whitney U-test was performed on this data and found that there was no difference between the type of facilitator (human vs. robot) and the scores on the task questions, as shown in Table 1.

On task 2, 14 participants were shown a robot facilitator and 16 participants were shown a human facilitator. 86% of subjects correctly answered both questions from task 2 with the robot facilitator. 75% of subjects correctly answered both questions from task 2 with the human facilitator. For the robot facilitated task M = 1.8 and the SD = 0.73 and for human facilitated task M = 1.75 and SD = 0.44. 16% more subjects correctly answered both questions for task 2 when shown with a robot facilitator.

On task 3, 15 participants were shown a robot facilitator and 15 participants were shown a human facilitator. 67% of subjects correctly answered all five questions from task 3 with the robot facilitator. 73% of subjects correctly answered all five questions from task 3 with the human facilitator. For the robot facilitated task M = 4.5 and SD = 0.76 and for human facilitated task M = 4.6 and SD = 0.74. More subjects correctly answered all five questions when given the human facilitator vs the robot facilitator.

On task 4, 15 participants were shown a robot facilitator and 15 participants were shown a human facilitator. 33% of subjects correctly answered all five questions from task 4 with the robot facilitator, whereas 40% of subjects correctly answered all five questions from task 4 with the human facilitator. For the robot facilitated task M = 4 and SD = 0.92 and for the human facilitated task M = 3.93 and SD = 1.2. More subjects correctly answered all five questions when given the robot facilitator vs. the human facilitator.

The second research question was: *How does participants' self-perceived ToM differ from their measured ToM?* This was addressed by comparing the percentage of correct answers each subject got on the robot facilitated tasks to their composite score on the Theory of Mind Self-Assessment. The same was also done to compare the percentage of correct answers each subject got on the human facilitated tasks to their composite score on the Theory of Mind Self-Assessment. This comparison was used because if a subject passed the false-belief task, that showed they were able to comprehend the mental state of another person. The more questions a subject gets correct, the more likely they are to have the Theory of Mind capabilities [22].

Figure 5 shows the comparison between the combined percentage of correct answers each subject got on the robot facilitated tasks vs. their composite score on the Theory of Mind Self Assessment. All participants were shown 2/4 task videos with robot facilitators. The Theory of Mind 60 question survey is a self-assessment. Therefore, there is always the risk of subject bias. Comparing that score to how well they do on the false-belief task will provide a more accurate prediction of a subject's Theory of Mind level.

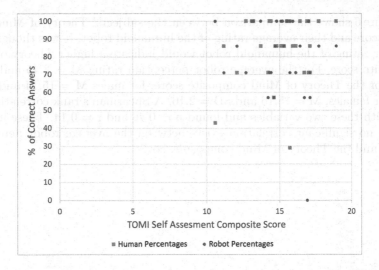

Fig. 5. Comparison of the percentage of correct answers per subject on two of four tasks with a robot facilitator, versus on two of four tasks with a human facilitator. The self-assessed composite score does not appear to have an effect on the percentage of correct answers and vice versa. The lowest percentage of correct answers (20%) does not correlate to the lowest composite score (11.19).

A Spearman's correlation test determined the relationship between task performance and the ToM inventory scores. No significant correlation was found for the robot-facilitated or human-facilitated sessions (see Table 2). These findings suggest that the use of a robot facilitator was comparable to a human facilitator.

Our third research question was: **How does participants' perception of the robot delivering a task change the participants' performance within the experiment?** This was addressed by comparing the subject composite score on the Theory of Mind Self-Assessment to the average rating they gave the humanoid robot based on the Godspeed Robot Perception Questionnaire. We hypothesized that how a subject viewed the humanoid robot in the experiment could affect their Theory of Mind performance in the given tasks. We also hypothesized that how a subject perceived the humanoid robot could positively or negative affect their performance on false-belief tasks given a robot facilitator.

Table 2. Spearman's rank correlation analysis comparing the percentage of correct answers on robot/human facilitated tasks with subjects' ToM Composite score.

Spearman values	Robot facilitated tasks vs. ToM composite score	Human facilitated tasks vs. ToM composite score
r - value	−0.12	0.12
p - value	0.53	0.51

Figure 6 shows the comparison between the subjects' Theory of Mind composite score and their average rating of the humanoid robot. It was thought that a higher rating of the humanoid robot would indicate a higher Theory of Mind composite score. For the average robot perception rating M = 3.45 and SD = 0.57. For the Theory of Mind composite score, for males M = 15.14 and SD = 1.86, for females, M = 15.16 and SD = 2.16. A Spearman's rank correlation was done with these two variables and found p = 0.46 and r = 0.14. These findings suggest no significant correlation exists between the average robot perception ratings and the Theory of Mind composite scores.

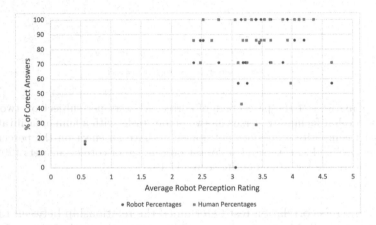

Fig. 6. Comparison between combined percentage of correct answers each subject got on the two out of four tasks they were shown which were robot facilitated and their average rating of the humanoid robot.

The self-assessed composite score does not appear to have an effect on the average robot perception rating and vice versa. The lowest robot rating of 2.36 does not correlate to the lowest composite score (11.19). 40% of subjects correctly answered all questions for robot facilitated videos. For the average robot perception rating, M = 3.45 and SD = 0.57. For percentage of correctly answered questions for robot facilitators M = 84.2 and SD = 16, These findings suggest no significant correlation between the average robot perception rating and the Theory of Mind composite score. The self-assessed composite score does not appear to have an effect on the percent of correct answers on robot facilitated tasks. The lowest percentage of correct answers on the robot facilitated tasks 57% does not correlate to the lowest composite score (2.36)

The fourth research question was: *How is participants' response time affected by human or robot facilitators?* By assigning timestamps to the beginning and end of each response, we were able to obtain the average response duration. A Mann-Whitney U-Test found no significant difference (w = 895, p = 0.77) between the participants' average response duration for robot (median = 18.35 s) and human (median = 19.30 s) facilitators. No significant correlation was found between the response duration and task performance for robot (r= −0.03, p = 0.82) and human (r= −0.01, p = 0.94) facilitators.

Figure 7 shows average response times for each task as they were delivered by a human or a robot. Over the span of four tasks, response time decreased. Average response times for task 1 were higher than those for task 2, etc. Originally, we thought that the response time for tasks 3 and 4 would be greater than response times for tasks 1 and 2 because they were designed to be more difficult, but this was not the case, likely due to the participants becoming acquainted with the process and thus answering quicker.

No significant difference was found (w = 971, p = 0.41) between the participants' speech rates for robot (median = 0.87 words/sec) and human facilitated tasks (median = 0.74 words/sec). There was also no significant correlation between speech rate and task performance for robot (r = −0.03 , p = 0.88) and human facilitated tasks (r = 0.12, p =0.53). These findings show comparable results between human- and robot-facilitated tasks.

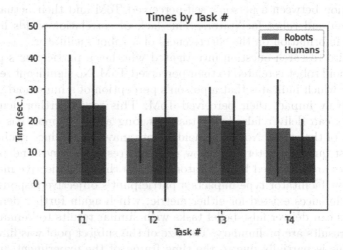

Fig. 7. The difference between response times on human and robot facilitated tasks. The black error bars are meant to illustrate the range of answers. One outlier was disregarded in the timestamp analysis as they had an average response time on task 2 of 104 s, which is over a minute longer than the mean.

5 Discussion

This study sought to investigate four research questions concerning a SAR facilitating first- and second-order ToM false-belief tasks. The first research question focused on determining if a NAO robot facilitator yields similar results to a human facilitator. Results showed that participant performances on the false-belief tasks were comparable between the two types of facilitators. This result suggests that robots can be effectively used as facilitators in future human subject research on ToM and potentially other similar research topics. Using robot facilitators can increase consistency among facilitation as robot facilitators are able to recite the same script in exactly the same manner between trials, unlike a human facilitator whose delivery may naturally vary. Recognition bias is also likely to decrease with the use of robot facilitators similar to the NAO robot because of its lack of human facial features [19]. Often, robot facilitators are easy to access and require less human work hours to set up than it would take for a human facilitator to actually run the experiment. While these robots are unlikely to replace human facilitators, they can still be used effectively to augment current approaches to human subject research.

Another important question is whether the participant's self-perceived ToM, as measured by means of a subjective questionnaire, differs from their measured ToM (performance on false-belief tasks) for robot and human facilitators. We expected that a significant correlation would exist for both facilitators; however, no significant correlation was found. This result indicates that there may be a disassociation between a person's self-perceived ToM and their actual ToM for both human and robot facilitators. This lack of correlation yields little to no additional information on the effectiveness of a robot facilitator.

The third research question investigated whether a participant's perception of a humanoid robot is related to their perceived ToM. No significant relationship was found, which indicates that a person's perception of a humanoid robot does not negatively impact their perceived ToM. This result further demonstrates that robots can deliver false-belief tasks as long as the human has a positive perception of the robot. Non-humanoid robots may not produce similar results.

The last question determined how question response times and participant speech rates are impacted by facilitator type, as the two objective metrics may indicate how facilitator type impacts a participant's objective response. No significant differences existed for either metric, which again further demonstrates that robots can deliver false-belief tasks with similar results to humans.

These results are preliminary. The size of the subject pool was limited to 30 people. This is partially due to the time frame of the experiment and limited resources for participant compensation. With more subjects, the results would be more precise. Future work should address this problem. Additionally, the average Theory of Mind composite score did not yield the expected results. According to the official Theory of Mind Instrument Documentation for the survey administered, there were some scores for both male and female participants that were below the cutoff score (2 male, 1 female for a cutoff of 13/20). The cutoff score is defined as the minimum score to be achieved such that the subject still possesses ToM. Three participants below the cut-off score may be attributed to the experiment's virtual design. Subjects tended to lose interest and pay less attention to the 60-question survey, which could be attributed to the virtual administration. An experimenter had to share their screen with the survey to the participant, who filled out their answers on a virtual form.

The results from the Godspeed Robot Perception Questionnaire were unexpected. None of the responses had an average below two out of five, which means that, on average, participants were not made uncomfortable by any aspect of the robot and its actions. Previous work suggests that when a human robot becomes more lifelike, people's perception rating of it will decrease. This is called the uncanny valley theory [20,23]. The concept suggests that as the appearance of the robot becomes more human they seem more familiar until a point when the response from an observer quickly drops from positive into strong revulsion. In many instances, things that are close to lifelike or closely mimic humans are expected to have human qualities but the robots are often not capable of this [24]. The robot in this experiment (NAO) is not lifelike enough to seem to mimic human reality. As a result, the subjects in this study did not have a negative reaction to the robot. If another robot had been used, it is likely that the participants would have reacted differently. Typically the NAO robot scores highly on the Godspeed Robot Perception Questionnaire [25,26].

Another reason why the ratings of the robot were high is the subjects' focal points. After completing the false-belief tasks, many subjects remarked that they had been so focused on following along with the videos that they paid less attention to the robot. This would change their conscious perception of the robot; though it may not have changed their responses or subconscious reactions. The balance of attention (looking at the robot vs. watching the videos) is something which should be addressed and mitigated in future work.

The NAO robot likely will not fully replace human researchers, but there is evidence supporting the effectiveness of its usage in augmenting human-subject studies. Participants reacted positively to the robot, and they performed comparably when false-belief tasks were delivered by human or robot facilitators. The robot-facilitated tasks did not yield longer response times or different speech rates. There was a significant difference in measured and surveyed ToM performances, but this did not correspond to the robot facilitator as subjects performed similarly on the ToMI survey regardless of the facilitator they were later shown. Overall, it is evident that robot facilitators yield the same results as human facilitators in human subject research on ToM.

6   Conclusion

This paper analyzed whether human subjects' performance on false belief tasks changed for human and robot facilitators. The research further examined how results from a standard ToM survey [15] correlated to true/false belief tasks performance. Additionally, speech data was analyzed to compare response duration and speech rates between human- and robot-facilitated tasks. Overall, no significant difference was found between the human and robot facilitator. The study's result supports the feasibility of using a robot facilitator for ToM tasks, which allows robots to be used more widely in related application scenarios, such as psychological/pedagogical tests and interventions.

Acknowledgement. This material is based upon work supported by the National Science Foundation under Award No. IIS-1851591. Any opinions, findings, and conclusions or recommendations expressed in this material are those of the authors and do not necessarily reflect the views of the National Science Foundation.

References

1. Tironi, A., Mainetti, R., Pezzera, M., Borghese, N.A.: An empathic virtual caregiver for assistance in exer-game-based rehabilitation therapies. In: 2019 IEEE 7th International Conference on Serious Games and Applications for Health (SeGAH), pp. 1–6. IEEE (2019)
2. Ko, S., et al.: The effects of robot appearances, voice types, and emotions on emotion perception accuracy and subjective perception on robots. In: Stephanidis, C., Kurosu, M., Degen, H., Reinerman-Jones, L. (eds.) HCII 2020. LNCS, vol. 12424, pp. 174–193. Springer, Cham (2020). https://doi.org/10.1007/978-3-030-60117-1_13
3. Premack, D., Woodruff, G.: Does the chimpanzee have a theory of mind? Behav. Brain Sci. **1**(4), 515–526 (1978)
4. Thellman, S., Silvervarg, A., Ziemke, T.: Some adults fail the false-belief task when the believer is a robot. In: Companion of the 2020 ACM/IEEE International Conference on Human-Robot Interaction, 479–481 (2020)
5. Dissing, L., Bolander, T.: Implementing theory of mind on a robot using dynamic epistemic logic. IJCA **I**, 1615–1621 (2020)
6. Cadinu, M.R., Kiesner, J.: Children's development of a theory of mind. Eur. J. Psychol. Educ. **15**(2), 93–111 (2000)
7. Wellman, H.M., Cross, D., Watson, J.: Meta-analysis of theory-of-mind development: the truth about false belief. Child Dev. **72**(3), 655–684 (2001)
8. Bernstein, D.M., Thornton, W.L., Sommerville, J.A.: Theory of mind through the ages: older and middle-aged adults exhibit more errors than do younger adults on a continuous false belief task. Exp. Aging Res. **37**(5), 481–502 (2011)
9. Pardini, M., Nichelli, P.: Age-related decline in mentalizing skills across adult life span. Exp. Aging Res. **35**, pp. 98–106 (2009)
10. Sullivan, S., Ruffman, T.: Social understanding: how does it fare with advancing years? Br. J. Psychol. **95**(1), 1–18 (2004)
11. Wimmer, H., Perner, J.: Beliefs about beliefs: representation and constraining function of wrong beliefs in young children's understanding of deception. Cognition **13**(1), 103–128 (1983)
12. Ward, T., et al.: False-belief task. In: Encyclopedia of Autism Spectrum Disorders, pp. 1249–1249 . Springer, New York (2013). https://doi.org/10.1007/978-1-4419-1698-3_91
13. Gopnik, A., Astington, J.W.: Children's understanding of representational change and its relation to the understanding of false belief and the appearance-reality distinction. Child Development, pp. 26–37 (1988)
14. Baron-Cohen, S., Leslie, A.M., Frith, U.: Does the autistic child have a "theory of mind"? Cognition **21**(1), 37–46 (1985)
15. Hutchins, T.L., Prelock, P.A., Lewis, L.: Technical Manual of the Theory of Mind Inventory: Self Report-Adult (ToMI:SR-A). Unpublished Manuscript. Available at theoryofmindinventory.com (2019)

16. Arkoudas, K., Bringsjord, S.: Toward formalizing common-sense psychology: an analysis of the false-belief task. In: Pacific Rim International Conference on Artificial Intelligence. Springer (2008) 17–29. https://doi.org/10.1007/978-3-540-89197-0_6

17. Breazeal, C., Gray, J., Berlin, M.: An embodied cognition approach to mindreading skills for socially intelligent robots. Int. J. Robot. Res. 28(5), 656–680 (2009)

18. Sindlar, M.P., Dastani, M.M., Dignum, F., Meyer, J.-J.C.: Mental state abduction of BDI-based agents. In: Baldoni, M., Son, T.C., van Riemsdijk, M.B., Winikoff, M. (eds.) DALT 2008. LNCS (LNAI), vol. 5397, pp. 161–178. Springer, Heidelberg (2009). https://doi.org/10.1007/978-3-540-93920-7_11

19. Baratgin, J., Dubois-Sage, M., Jacquet, B., Stilgenbauer, J.L., Jamet, F.: Pragmatics in the false-belief task: let the robot ask the question! Front. Psychol. 11, 3234 (2020)

20. Haring, K.S., Matsumoto, Y., Watanabe, K.: How do people perceive and trust a lifelike robot. In: Proceedings of the World Congress on Engineering and Computer Science, vol. 1, Citeseer (2013)

21. Bartneck, C., Kulić, D., Croft, E., Zoghbi, S.: Measurement instruments for the anthropomorphism, animacy, likeability, perceived intelligence, and perceived safety of robots. Int. J. Soc. Robot. 1(1), 71–81 (2009)

22. Campbell, D. et al.: Theory of mind. In: Encyclopedia of Autism Spectrum Disorders, pp. 3111–3115. Springer, New York (2013). https://doi.org/10.1007/978-1-4419-1698-3

23. Mori, M., MacDorman, K.F., Kageki, N.: The uncanny valley [from the field]. IEEE Robot. Autom. Mag. 19(2), 98–100 (2012)

24. Ho, C.C., MacDorman, K.F.: Revisiting the uncanny valley theory: Developing and validating an alternative to the Godspeed indices. Comput. Hum. Behav. 26(6), 1508–1518 (2010)

25. Lehmann, H., Rojik, A., Hoffmann, M.: Should a small robot have a small personal space? Investigating personal spatial zones and proxemic behavior in human-robot interaction (2020)

26. Thunberg, S.: Investigating the social influence of different humanoid robots. Undergraduate thesis, Linköping University (2017)

Evaluating Virtual and Local Pepper Presence in the Role of Communicator Interacting with Another Human Presenter at a Vocational Fair of Computer Sciences

Samantha Romero-Pérez[✉], Keyla Smith-Arias, Lizeth Corrales-Cortés,
Kryscia Ramírez-Benavides, Adrián Vega, and Ariel Mora

Universidad de Costa Rica, San José, Costa Rica
{samantha.romero,keyla.smith,lizeth.corrales,kryscia.ramirez,
adrian.vegavega,ariel.mora}@ucr.ac.cr

Abstract. This paper proposes the evaluation of the local and remote interaction of a Pepper Robot and a human presenter answering questions from high-school students at the Universidad de Costa Rica's vocational fair. The interactions were presented in two: 1) a group interacted locally in the same room 2) a group interacted remotely via online meeting. Within a sample of 18 Costa Rican high-school students, this study assessed criteria such as: perceived enjoyment, intention to use, perceived sociability, trust, intelligence, animacy, anthropomorphism, and sympathy, utilizing testing tools such as Unified Theory of Acceptance and Use of Technology (UTAUT) and Godspeed Questionnaire (GSQ). These instruments identified significant differences during the interaction in the perceived sociability and anthropomorphism in both scenarios. Suggesting different relevant information regarding the perception of the interaction with the robot and perception of the robot itself in both cases.

Keywords: Human-robot interaction · Remote interaction · HRI · UTAUT · GSQ

1 Introduction

Human-Robot Interaction (HRI) has received a great interest in the last decade. Focusing in studying the interaction between humans and robots in multiple environments, is a multidisciplinary field with contributions from HCI, Artificial Intelligence (AI), Natural Language Processing (NLP), design and social sciences [7]. This relatively new discipline has attracted much attention due to the increasing people's exposure to robots in their everyday lives [7,15].

As robots are expected to be available in multiple types of environments, social interactions with humans play an essential role where robots are expected

M. Kurosu (Ed.): HCII 2022, LNCS 13303, pp. 580–589, 2022.
https://doi.org/10.1007/978-3-031-05409-9_42

to demonstrate safe and reliable physical interaction, follow social norms and display socially acceptable behaviors.

Robots are often referred by researchers as artificial agents with capabilities of perception and action in the physical world as their workspace and their use became widespread in factories, but today they are more frequently found on most technologically advanced societies expanding their usability in critical domains such as rescue missions, military use, mine detection, scientific exploration, law enforcement, entertainment, hospital care, among others [9,12]. With service robotics tasks such as delivering hospital meals, mowing the lawn or vacuuming floors brought autonomous robots into environments shared with people [16], but the social aspect of these tasks is still minimal, where people are treated as obstacles to navigate around, rather than social beings to cooperate with.

Based on this basic interaction, there is an emerging need to create robotic systems that interact with people and other agents (robots) in their environment during more complex and common daily activities. Although the robot's limited capacity to interact with people, it is encouraging the development of robotic systems with increasingly realistic and socially sophisticated style.

At the Computer Sciences and Informatics School of the Universidad de Costa Rica HRI is one of the current research topics, using robots as personal assistants [13] or as presenters. An example of the latter is the usage of a Nao Robot [3] as a presenter alongside instructors answering questions from high-school students at the Universidad de Costa Rica's vocational fair, where the students could interacted and asked face-to-face with the robot. The Covid-19 pandemic caused a sudden shift at the Universidad de Costa Rica, where all mass face-to-face activities were transferred to online activities, including the vocational fair, opening an opportunity to use robots as another presenter on online meetings and research how its physical embodiment affects the perception on robot interaction instead of its physical presence [11].

The current study proposes the evaluation of the local and remote interaction of a Pepper Robot [4] and a human presenter answering questions from high-school students about the Bachelor career in Computer Sciences at the Universidad de Costa Rica's vocational fair. The interactions were presented in two groups:

1. A group physically interacting in the same room with the robot and presenter.
2. A group remotely interacting from their homes via Zoom meeting.

Based on User-Centered Design (UCD) [5,6,10] which proposes to focus technology design on how people use technologies rather than just the technology itself, the objectives of this study aims to (1) Evaluate variables such as intention to use, perceived enjoyment, perceived usefulness, (2) Evaluate variables such as animacy, anthropomorphism, intelligence and likeability, (3) Perception of the robot. To measure above variables in both scenarios we used UTAUT constructs and Godspeed Questionnaire.

2   Methods

2.1   Participants

The dataset consisted of 18 Costa-Rican high-school students: 10 in local interaction and 8 in remote interaction. The participants were recruited through advertisements on social media and divided based on their willingness to attend the session locally or remotely.

2.2   Instruments and Materials

Unified Theory of Acceptance and Use of Technology (UTAUT). UTAUT model [14] is a theoretical framework that was created to evaluate the acceptance and usage of technologies. It integrates elements of other theories such as the theory of reasoned action, motivation model, theory of social cognition, and innovation diffusion theory, among others.

Godspeed Questionnaire (GSQ). The GSQ [8] is a standardized instrument in the HRI field translated to multiple languages. It is supported by multicultural previous research. By using semiotic differential scales, the GSQ evaluates constructs such as anthropomorphism, animacy, likeability, and perceived intelligence.

Pepper Robot. The Pepper Robot is a social humanoid robot from SoftBank Robotics [4]. It is 120 cm tall with 20 degrees of freedom in limb movement, speech recognition and perception modules to recognize and interact with persons, sensors for multimodal interactions and autonomous navigation.

2.3   Sessions

Two sessions were made to complete the experiment: one locally at the Computer Sciences Facilities and another via online meeting on Zoom. For both sessions the same presenters were present. The Pepper Robot was programmed to answer autonomously to questions using the Conversation API of Pepper QiSDK [2]. For every answer, a set of movements from Pepper Movement Library [1] were executed to keep the participants engaged. The questions were taken from a Frequently Asked Questions bank that the Computer Sciences School has collected from previous vocational fairs.

Local Session. In this session the participants were in the same room as the robot and the presenters. First, the presenters began the session welcoming and greeting the participants. Then, introduced the Pepper Robot and explained its role on the session. Next, the Pepper Robot greeted the participants and introduced itself giving some backstory of its origins. After this, the presenters explained the structure for the questions from the participants: the participant gave some details about his question, if the questions could be answered by the robot the presenter invited the participant to ask directly to the robot, if could not, the presenter answered instead. Sometimes the robot did not understand the question asked by a participant, then the presenter repeated the question.

Remote Session. In this session the participants were connected to an online meeting via Zoom software. For this session, one of the presenters acted as the meeting host. Similar to the Local Session, first the presenters began the session with greetings for the participants, introduced and explained the role of the Pepper Robot, then Pepper Robot introduced itself and the presenters explained the structure for the questions from the participants. For this session the participants wrote their questions on the chat provided by Zoom and the presenter asked the question to the robot or answered himself. This decision was made to minimize speech recognition issues from the robot.

At the end of both sessions the participants were given a link to take the surveys of the instruments presented above.

3   Results

According to multiple one-way ANOVA analysis applied during UTAUT testing to the group, significant variance was identified only in the Perceived Sociability $F(1,17) = 4.74$, $p = 0.045$. No significant difference was identified in the Intention to Use $F(1,17) = 1.84$, $p = 0.194$, Perceived Enjoyment $F(1, 17) = 2.47$, $p = .136$, and Trust $F(1, 17) = 1.35$, $p = 0.262$ (Table 1 and 2).

Table 1. Test of Homogeneity of variances for UTAUT.

	Levene statistic	df1	df2	Sig.
Intention to use	2.09	1	16	.168
Perceived enjoyment	2.91	1	16	.107
Perceived sociability	.23	1	16	.637
Trust	.98	1	16	.337

Table 2. ANOVA analysis for UTAUT.

		Sum of squares	df1	Mean square	F	Sig.
Intention to use	Between groups	.63	1	.63	1.84	.194
	Within groups	5.43	16	.34		
	Total	6.06	17			
Perceived enjoyment	Between groups	1.05	1	1.05	2.47	.136
	Within groups	6.78	16	.42		
	Total	7.82	17			
Perceived sociability	Between groups	1.98	1	1.98	4.74	.045
	Within groups	6.67	16	.42		
	Total	8.64	17			
Trust	Between groups	.71	1	.71	1.35	.262
	Within groups	8.40	16	.53		
	Total	9.11	17			

Even though only Perceived Sociability presented a significant difference of the UTAUT Testing. The following table of the distributed means displays how the physical environment scored higher values in all the variables (Table 3).

Table 3. Distributed Means for UTAUT.

		N	Mean
Intention to use	Local	10	4.67
	Remote	8	4.29
	Total	18	4.50
Perceived enjoyment	Local	10	4.56
	Remote	8	4.08
	Total	18	4.34
Perceived sociability	Local	10	4.33
	Remote	8	3.67
	Total	18	4.04
Trust	Local	10	4.40
	Remote	8	4.00
	Total	18	4.22

Also, the multiple one-way ANOVA analysis applied during Godspeed testing to the group no significant difference was identified in the Animacy $F(1,17) = 1.03$, $p = 0.326$, Anthropomorphism $F(1, 17) = 0.22$, $p = 0.646$, Intelligence $F(1, 17) = 1.44$, $p = 0.248$, and Sympathy $F(1, 17) = 0.42$, $p = 0.524$ (Table 4).

Table 4. Test of Homogeneity of variances for GSQ.

	Levene statistic	df1	df2	Sig.
Animacy	.00	1	16	.993
Anthropomorphism	.53	1	16	.447
Intelligence	.14	1	16	.714
Sympathy	.15	1	16	.707

Table 5. ANOVA analysis for GSQ.

		Sum of squares	df1	Mean square	F	Sig.
Animacy	Between groups	.42	1	.42	1.03	.326
	Within groups	6.49	16	.41		
	Total	6.90	17			
Anthropomorphism	Between groups	.06	1	.06	.22	.646
	Within groups	4.68	16	.29		
	Total	4.74	17			
Intelligence	Between groups	.35	1	.35	1.44	.248
	Within groups	3.88	16	.24		
	Total	4.22	17			
Sympathy	Between groups	.07	1	.07	.42	.524
	Within groups	2.62	16	.16		
	Total	2.68	17			

Even though no significant differences were identified, the following table displays the means value for the Godspeed variables. On the opposite side than UTAUT higher values were identified in the Zoom virtual environment (Table 5 and 6).

About gender in the population sample composed by 14 males and 4 women. The only significant difference identified was during the Godspeed testing. In this test women (M = 3.30) qualified Anthropomorphism higher than males (M = 3.90), $F(1, 17) = 4.95$, $p = 0.41$ (Table 7 and 8).

Table 6. Distributed means for GSQ.

		N	Mean
Animacy	Local	10	3.72
	Remote	8	4.03
	Total	18	3.86
Anthropomorphism	Local	10	3.38
	Remote	8	3.50
	Total	18	3.43
Intelligence	Local	10	4.02
	Remote	8	4.30
	Total	18	4.14
Sympathy	Local	10	4.70
	Remote	8	4.57
	Total	18	4.64

Table 7. Test of Homogeneity of variances for GSQ.

	Levene statistic	df1	df2	Sig.
Animacy	.68	1	16	.422
Anthropomorphism	1.39	1	16	.256
Intelligence	.01	1	16	.933
Sympathy	.47	1	16	.501

Table 8. ANOVA analysis for GSQ.

		Sum of squares	df1	Mean square	F	Sig.
Animacy	Between groups	1.36	1	1.36	3.92	.065
	Within groups	5.54	16	.35		
	Total	6.90	17			
Anthropomorphism	Between groups	1.12	1	1.12	4.95	.041
	Within groups	3.62	16	.23		
	Total	4.74	17			
Intelligence	Between groups	.12	1	.12	.49	.496
	Within groups	4.10	16	.26		
	Total	4.22	17			
Sympathy	Between groups	.00	1	.00	.0	.976
	Within groups	2.68	16	.17		
	Total	2.68	17			

Finally, the activity evaluation of the activity presented significant differences in the physical and virtual environments in the accessibility of the presented information $F(1, 17) = 5.42$, $p = 0.033$ and the Robot Role Performance $F(1,$

17) $= 6.83$, $p = 0.019$. Not significant difference was identified in the Human Present-er Attitude $F(1, 17) = 0.67$, $p = 0.426$, performing better in during the physical presentations on all these variables (Table 9 and 10).

Table 9. Test of Homogeneity of variances for activity evaluation.

	Levene statistic	df1	df2	Sig.
Human presenter attitude	2.84	1	16	.111
Presented information	6.36	1	16	.023
Robot role performance	6.74	1	16	.020

Table 10. ANOVA analysis for activity evaluation.

		Sum of squares	df1	Mean square	F	Sig.
Human presenter attitude	Between groups	.10	1	.10	.67	.426
	Within groups	2.40	16	.15		
	Total	2.50	17			
Presented information	Between groups	4.67	1	4.67	5.42	.033
	Within groups	13.78	16	.86		
	Total	18.44	17			
Robot role performance	Between groups	1.88	1	1.88	6.83	.019
	Within groups	4.40	16	.28		
	Total	6.28	17			

4 Discussion

The significant difference identified by the UTAUT testing in the Perceived Sociability. Displays a better interactions with the robot during the physical interaction on site. This result is also consistent during the activity evaluation in the significant differences of the Information Accessibility and Robot Role Performance. Were this variables scored higher within the group on site. Suggesting that better interactions with robots are developed in physical interactions. Coinciding with the statements that physical presence affects in more favorable responses from participants than physical embodiment presented in the review by [11]. Reviewing other not statistically significant UTAUT results (Intention to Use, Perceived Enjoyment, and Trust) this arguments is also consistent.

A meaningful surprise on this research. Is the variables related to evaluate participants' perception about the robot in the Godspeed questionnaire. We must remember this test is more related to evaluate users perception of the robot itself not its interactions. During this test values scored higher in virtual group interaction evaluation. The values presented in the Godspeed Test are Animacy, Anthropomorphism, Intelligence, and Sympathy of the robot. These results might suggest than the characteristics of the virtual interaction helps the to improve the perception of the robot itself. A possible hypothesis could be that the characteristics and limitations of this virtual interaction in relation to a real life interaction helps to oversee or improve robots presence.

Further research supporting these results. It might required to more study with deeper evaluation tools of the bonding vs perception of the robots in these physical and virtual conditions. Studying if bonding with robots is easier during physical interaction like this sample suggest through the UTAUT evaluation. Also if the perception of the robot could be improved during interaction in virtual environments cause of the specific properties of this kind of interaction as the Godspeed might suggest. Also including a deeper analysis of the cause of these results. Exploring phenoms like the proximity effect in the development of emotional bonding and the Uncanny Valley Effect in the robots perception during interaction in virtual environments.

In this case the healthy global conditions push us forward to evaluate presence of robots in these different environments. But the simple evolution and facilities provide by the virtual environments justifies the need to advance in this context. Making a the virtual environments an everyday context required to better understand during human and robot interaction.

5   Conclusions

This research studied the impact of physical presence and physical embodiment in the local and virtual interaction of a Pepper Robot and a human presenter utilizing UTAUT constructs and Godspeed Questionnaire. The study shows that physical presence has a positive effect on robot and robot interaction. On the opposite side, robots perception itself presented a positive effect during virtual interaction. Further research is needed to support these findings. Evaluating if the same effects detected in the human interaction are detected in a human-robot interaction during this condition and the mediation of root factors such as the emotional bonding and perception capabilities. Also is needed to research how different conditions, such as remote interaction from participants via voice, view, augmented or virtual reality are samples that can affect the impact of presence and physical embodiment of the robot. The Covid-19 pandemic gives an opportunity to investigate human-robot interactions on remote environments helping to expand the current knowledge on this area and employ robots on new environments.

Acknowledgments. This work was supported by the CITIC-UCR (Centro de Investigaciones en Tecnologías de la Información y Comunicación) and by ECCI-UCR (Escuela de Ciencias de la Computación e Informática), grand No. 834-C0-02. Thanks to the User Interaction Group (USING) for supporting the research.

References

1. Animation browser/viewer | softbank robotics developer center, https://developer. softbankrobotics.com/pepper-qisdk/tools/animation-browser/viewer

2. Conversation | softbank robotics developer center, https://developer.softbankrobotics.com/pepper-qisdk/api/conversation
3. NAO the humanoid and programmable robot | SoftBank Robotics, https://www.softbankrobotics.com/emea/en/nao
4. Pepper the humanoid and programmable robot | SoftBank Robotics, https://www.softbankrobotics.com/emea/en/pepper
5. Usability engineering. Elsevier (1993). https://doi.org/10.1016/C2009-0-21512-1, https://linkinghub.elsevier.com/retrieve/pii/C20090215121
6. Affairs, A.S.F.P.: With measurable usability goals - we all score | usability. Gov, November 2013, https://www.usability.gov/get-involved/blog/2013/09/measurable-usability-goals.html
7. Bartneck, C., Okada, M.: Robotic user interfaces. In: Proceedings of the Human and Computer Conference (HC 2001), Aizu, pp. 130–140 (2001)
8. Bartneck, C., Kulić, D., Croft, E., Zoghbi, S.: Measurement instruments for the anthropomorphism, animacy, likeability, perceived intelligence, and perceived safety of robots. Int. J. Soc. Robot. **1**(1), 71–81 (2009) https://doi.org/10.1007/s12369-008-0001-3, http://link.springer.com/10.1007/s12369-008-0001-3
9. Dautenhahn, K.: Socially intelligent robots: dimensions of human-robot interaction. Philosophical Trans. Royal Soc. B: Biol. Sci. **362**(1480), 679–704 (2007) https://doi.org/10.1098/rstb.2006.2004, https://royalsocietypublishing.org/doi/10.1098/rstb.2006.2004
10. International Organization for Standardization: ISO 13407:1999, https://www.iso.org/cms/render/live/en/sites/isoorg/contents/data/standard/02/11/21197.html
11. Li, J.: The benefit of being physically present: a survey of experimental works comparing copresent robots, telepresent robots and virtual agents. Int. J. Hum. Comput. Stud. **77**, 23–37 (2015) https://doi.org/10.1016/j.ijhcs.2015.01.001, https://linkinghub.elsevier.com/retrieve/pii/S107158191500004X
12. Torta, E., Oberzaucher, J., Werner, F., Cuijpers, R.H., Juola, J.F.: Attitudes towards socially assistive robots in intelligent homes: results from laboratory studies and field trials. J. Hum. Robot Interact. **1**(2), 76–99 (2013). https://doi.org/10.5898/JHRI.1.2.Torta
13. Vega, A., Ramírez-Benavides, K., Guerrero, L.A., López, G.: Evaluating the NAO robot in the role of personal assistant: the effect of gender in robot performance evaluation. In: Multidisciplinary Digital Publishing Institute Proceedings, vol. 31, no. 1, p. 20, November 2019. https://doi.org/10.3390/proceedings2019031020, https://www.mdpi.com/2504-3900/31/1/20
14. Venkatesh, V., Morris, M.G., Davis, G.B., Davis, F.D.: User acceptance of information technology: toward a unified view. MIS Q. **27**(3), 425 (2003) https://doi.org/10.2307/30036540, https://www.jstor.org/stable/10.2307/30036540
15. Walters, M.L., et al.: Evaluating the robot personality and verbal behavior of domestic robots using video-based studies1. In: Household Service Robotics, pp. 467–486. Elsevier (2015). https://doi.org/10.1016/B978-0-12-800881-2.00021-9, https://linkinghub.elsevier.com/retrieve/pii/B9780128008812000219
16. Wilkes, D.M., Alford, A., Pack, R.T., Rogers, T., Peters, R.A., Kawamura, K.: Toward socially intelligent service robots. Appl. Artif. Intell. **12**(7–8), 729–766 (1998) https://doi.org/10.1080/088395198117604, http://www.tandfonline.com/doi/abs/10.1080/088395198117604

The Social Robot Expectation Gap Evaluation Framework

Julia Rosén[1](✉)(iD), Jessica Lindblom[1,2](iD), and Erik Billing[1](iD)

[1] Interaction Lab, University of Skövde, Box 408, 541 28 Skövde, Sweden
`julia.rosen@his.se`
[2] Department of Information Technology, Uppsala University, Box 337,
751 05 Uppsala, Sweden

Abstract. Social robots are designed in manners that encourage users to interact and communicate with them in socially appropriate ways, which implies that these robots should copy many social human behaviors to succeed in social settings. However, this approach has implications for what humans subsequently expect from these robots. There is a mismatch between expected capabilities and actual capabilities of social robots. Expectations of social robots are thus of high relevance for the field of Human-Robot Interaction (HRI). While there is recent interest of expectations in the HRI field there is no widely adapted or well formulated evaluation framework that offers a deeper understanding of how these expectations affect the success of the interaction. With basis in social psychology, user experience, and HRI, we have developed an evaluation framework for studying users' expectations of social robots. We have identified three main factors of expectations for assessing HRI: affect, cognitive processing, and behavior and performance. In our framework, we propose several data collection techniques and specific metrics for assessing these factors. The framework and its procedure enables analysis of the collected data via triangulation to identify problems and insights, which can grant us a richer understanding of the complex facets of expectations, including if the expectations were confirmed or disconfirmed in the interaction. Ultimately, by gaining a richer understanding of how expectations affect HRI, we can narrow the social robot expectation gap and create more successful interactions between humans and social robots in society.

Keywords: Human-robot interaction · Social robots · Evaluation framework · User experience · Expectations

1 Introduction

The ongoing increase of new interactive technologies in our daily lives results in growing expectations of these technologies from their intended users [15]. One such interactive technology is social robots, and their degree of participation in everyday activities in society are becoming more sophisticated [2,5,20]. Social

© The Author(s), under exclusive license to Springer Nature Switzerland AG 2022
M. Kurosu (Ed.): HCII 2022, LNCS 13303, pp. 590–610, 2022.
https://doi.org/10.1007/978-3-031-05409-9_43

robots have several characteristics that separate them from other kinds of more traditional technologies; they occupy space, act rather autonomously, and users have to respond to them "here and now." In addition, they are designed in a manner that encourage users to interact and communicate with them in socially appropriate ways. Given that social robots involve the intersection of a digital artifact and of agency as found in living creatures, social robots are often either positively experienced as fascinating and interesting or negatively experienced as frightening and scary [1]. Hence, social robots tend to blur the distinction between a thing and an agent, which results in several challenges for users regarding what to expect when interacting with social robots. To complicate the issue further, the majority of humans have either no first-hand experience or limited experience of interacting with social robots. Humans' main exposure to social robots are predominantly from movies and the media, which may result in misleading and inaccurate expectations of social robots [1, 6, 11, 31].

We argue, it is of utmost importance to gain a deeper understanding of the roles expectations play when users are interacting with robots as well as the impact of expectations on user experience (UX) before, during, and after the interaction. Some recent but limited research has studied humans' expectations of social robots [6, 11, 21, 23], but research conducted in the intersection of the UX, social robotics, and human-robot interaction (HRI) fields seems to be limited. Although there is an interest on this topic, there is no widely adapted or well formulated evaluation framework. Expectations are especially important to understand when they are disconfirmed as this can guide and inform the future design of social robots, which will ultimately lead to more successful interactions. We propose to narrow these knowledge gaps within HRI with inspiration from social psychology and UX. UX goes beyond usability and pragmatic factors to include hedonic factors, in which emotional and experiential aspects are emphasized enabling evaluation of users' expectations of social robots in a systematic way [8, 15]. In the present work, we provide an evaluation framework that considers the role of expectations when interacting with social robots. We will both describe key insights from the development of the evaluation framework and the proposed version of the evaluation framework, including the procedure for applying it when performing a minor empirical UX evaluation when interacting first-hand with a social robot [8, 20].

2 Background

2.1 Expectations of Social Robots: Related Work

The concept *expectation* is defined as believed probabilities of the future that sets the stage for the human belief system which guides our behavior, hopes, and intentions [29, 30]. As expectations relate to predictions of the future, expectations are often aligned with wishful thinking, and can thus result in disappointment and negative affect [29, 30]. Confirmed expectations occur when expectations and actual outcome is aligned; in contrast, disconfirmed expectations are when expectations and actual outcome is not aligned. Our work is inspired by the research done on *expectancy* in social psychology [29,30]; however, we will use the concept *expectation* which we view as similar when used in this context as expectations is another state of expectancy. Expectations play a crucial role in social interactions. In real-time interactions with other beings, expectations serve to orchestrate and predict possible actions. Expectations allow humans to co-exist and handle the complexity of the social world, and provide a way to decrease how complex the world is through stereotyping and norms. Stereotypes are expectations of groups or individuals that are exaggerated, biased, and overgeneralized [29]. Social robots are often stereotyped, commonly based on science fiction and limited actual interaction with social robots [3,34]. Not only do users who are intended to interact with social robots have expectations of social robots, but also the designers who create these robots have expectations while designing for these anticipated interactions.

Lohse [21] explicitly addressed the role of expectations in HRI, offering a starting point when introducing some assumptions on user expectations which needed to be studied and explored more systematically considering the influence of expectations on HRI research. She claimed that users' expectations can be inferred from data collected in actual HRI situations and analysis of the collected data can be advantageous by considering users' expectations as well as their views on the interaction situation. She pointed out that knowledge about users' expectations can support the design and development process of robots because expectations seem to be dependent on the robot's actual behavior, and as a result could be formed to improve the quality of the HRI. She also suggested that future work should not only consider research on users' expectations, but also to study robot's expectations, looking at both sides of the HRI coin. Finally, she questioned how expectations could be accurately measured. Since this publication, there has, to our knowledge, not been any attempts to develop a well formulated evaluation framework for expectations.

There has also been recent but limited research considering expectations of social robots. Manzi et al. [23] examined how the physical appearance and behaviors performed by the social robots affected the quality of interaction with humans. It was revealed that the participants' expectations were influenced by the interaction per se, and were surprisingly independent of the particular kind of social robot. Edwards et al. [6] examined how initial expectations and impressions may be modified and confirmed through short first-hand experience of communicating with a social robot based on HHI models of social interaction. Expectations were assessed by altered levels of (i) uncertainty, (ii) social attraction, and (iii) social presence. The results revealed that many participants reported feelings of affinity and connectedness, whereas a nearly identical encounter with a human experimenter resulted in opposite outcomes. The participants' modified expectations toward the robot may result in a so-called robot conformation, i.e., the human tendency to magnify the robot's confirmation responses and its limited ability to offer behavioral feedback contrasted to how humans act. Jokinen and Wilcock [14] studied expectations of social robots using the Expectations and Experience (EE) method. The EE model was used to investigate and analyze the quality of interaction, i.e., what the users experience in regard to what they desire or expect. The results confirm that expectations in general were rated higher than the actual experience, showing that a majority of the participants perceived a positive experience, and indicating that the participants perceived the interaction with the robot enjoyable and interesting. However, there are indications of a negative relationship between expectations of the robot's behavior and the extent to which the participants perceived that they were 'understood' by the robot. Interestingly, the authors note that the most experienced participants seemed to be the most critical ones. The authors concluded that insights from user evaluations of social robots should not be limited to increasing positive UX but could also be used to understand how to reduce the difference between the users' expectations and actual experiences. They argued that reducing expectations and experience mismatch is of major importance to cultivate long-term relations such as trust between social robots and their end-users.

Horstmann and Krämer [11] investigated which kinds of expectations humans have concerning social robots as well as the bases for forming these expectations. Their results indicate that humans' experiences of media regarding social robots lead to increased expectations of robots' abilities and capabilities, in turn successively enhancing humans' expectations of social robots. Moreover, humans' awareness and acquired knowledge of negatively perceived fictional social robots enlarges negative expectations of robots being threats to humans. Conversely, those humans who have more non-fiction knowledge about the capacities and limitations of robot technology show reduced levels of anxiety towards social robots. They pointed out that their findings are mostly based on subjective ratings and no first-hand encounters with social robots, which mainly revealed what their participants hypothesize what they should expect. They suggested that future work should examine what kinds of expectations and preconceptions humans hold towards robots, and in what ways these influence their behavior when interacting first-hand with a social robot. Later, Horstmann and Krämer [13] examined participants' expectations versus their actual behavior when interacting with the a social robot. The authors concluded that in general, during first-hand interaction with a social robot, the robot's perceived behavior is more influential for participants' evaluations of it than their formulated expectations. Hence, the main insight from their study, which also confirms prior research, indicates that the robot's behavior during the actual interaction is the key variable influencing how the participants evaluate the actual robot as well as the interaction quality with it. Moreover, Horstmann and Krämer [12] conducted an experiment aiming to examine how a negative expectancy violation caused by a social robot and its reward valence could demonstrate how desirable it is for the participants to interact with the social robot, and how this affected the evaluation of HRI quality after the interacting. The results indicate that when the robot negatively violated expectations, participants evaluated the robot competence, sociability, and interaction skills more negatively.

Moore [25] introduced the so-called "habitability gap", i.e., the perceived mismatch between the capabilities and expectations addressed by users and the actual features and intended benefits provided by social robots. Moore assumed that given the recent and rapid development of interactive technology, it should be expected that the capabilities of such digital artifacts would gradually develop, but there is a habitability gap in which UX drops when the robots' flexibility is enhanced. Schramm et al. [35] presented an initial conceptual framework for expectations of social robots, consisting of two aspects. The first aspect is the design (i.e., appearance and behavior) of the robot that "emits capability signals" [35, p. 439], which is divided into the life-likeness by the robot, the functional design of the robot (e.g., cameras means the robot is able to see), and how the robot is introduced. The second aspect is the mental model constructs of the robot held by the user, based on the design of robot, which are formed by the observation of the robot's mechanical (e.g., physical ability) and life-like capability (e.g., emotional system). The authors stressed how a simple robot behavior can lead to complex constructions of what to expect of the robot, thus creating a gap between expected and actual capabilities. Although the authors mentioned that they have started to develop measurement tools to evaluate and create a deeper understanding of expectations based on robot design, they did not present any measurements or evaluation framework. Hence, our framework complements the work done by the authors.

In summary, three main conclusions for future research can be drawn. First, there is a need to study users' expectations in actual HRI beyond the mere encounter with a social robot and to systematically study how users' expectations may be altered if their initial expectations are not confirmed (e.g., [6,11]). Second, the close relationship between expectations and UX provides a well-aligned approach to include the various time spans in UX. Third, there is a need to develop an evaluation framework that encompasses several main factors that systematically could be evaluated in actual HRI to better cope with mismatches of expected capabilities and actual capabilities of the robot.

2.2   Users' Experience and Expectations from a HRI Perspective

A relevant HRI angle is the intersection with the study of UX, which allows for a user-centered perspective, including studying users' expectations. Although this intersection of UX within HRI exists, and is getting more traction in the literature [2,17,31,36], it is often overlooked [2]. There are also overlaps between users' experience and users' expectations when interacting with technology [33]. User expectations could indicate the anticipated behavior, direct the focus of attention, serve as a source of reference for the actual UX and how it is interpreted, and subsequently has an impact on the users' overall perception of the technology [15]. As such, expectations can have a critical influence on the formation of the actual UX of the social robot. Research on expectations can reveal a deeper understanding of the central aspects of UX. One of the main components of UX, that is sometimes missing in HRI research, is the temporal aspect of an interaction [31].

A key aspect of UX occurs during the actual interaction with a system, but is not the only relevant UX aspect to consider [33]. Users are also affected by indirect experiences before their first encounter with an interactive system. Such indirect experiences are rooted in previous experiences and thoughts related to advertisements, presentations, and demonstrations of the system or related systems. Indirect experience may also include exposure to various media and movies, or other people's opinions. In the same way, users' indirect experiences may occur after the actual usage situation, such as when they are reflecting on previous usage and prior expectations, or through the impact from other users' assessment of the system which may retroactively alter the actual UX [33]. A key point in UX research is to study the temporal aspects of using a system which makes it highly relevant for expectations. Not only are expectations about future events, they are also dynamic and can change over time [29], making temporal aspects crucial in order to understand expectations. Roto et al. [33] identified four temporal aspects to consider in UX, including anticipated UX, momentary UX, episodic UX, and cumulative UX. These temporal aspects are dynamic and can vary depending on the situation. Anticipated UX refers to the period before an interaction, whether it is for the first time or repeated interaction. It is the imagined experience of future interaction. Momentary UX refers to the time span during the interaction of a system. Episodic UX refers to the appraisal of a particular episode after interaction with a system. Lastly, cumulative UX refers to opinions of a system as a whole, after interaction over time [33]. The temporal aspects are particularly relevant when it comes to expectations and subsequent interaction of a system, especially the interaction with social robots. The momentary use of social robots is typically the only temporal aspect studied in HRI research. Although not explicitly mentioned by Roto et al. [33], expectations are also important to consider, and can affect the interaction across all temporal aspects including before the interaction with the robot (anticipated use), during the interaction with the robot (momentary use), after the interaction with the robot (episodic use), and the interaction over time with the robot (cumulative use).

2.3   Olson's et al.'s Expectation Model

One of the psychological theories of expectations that Lohse [21] took a closer look at in relation to robots was the expectation process by Olson et al. [29]. We consider this model to be of major interest, and it serves as the foundation for our framework. However, we have made several adjustments to the original model. First, we modified its main focus on HHI to HRI. Second, we altered its social psychological perspective to a more user-centered one, applying concept commonly used within UX to better fit the purpose of our evaluation framework. In Fig. 1, we present this modified version of the expectation process model by Olson et al. [29, p. 231]. This model is adjusted to accommodate the interaction with social robots. There are also other models of expectations e.g., [24], though this model is, to our knowledge, one of the most comprehensive presentations of expectations, and is thus of major importance for our work.

As the model shows (Fig. 1), *direct experience, other*, and *beliefs* form expectations. Direct experience is the expectations built on first-hand experience.
Although not as common, some have their expectations built on actual first-hand
experience of robots. Direct experience is more common with robots already used
in society at large, such as vacuum cleaner robots or lawn mower robots. Expectations built on direct experience are typically held with greater certainty and
are a stronger predictor of future behavior [29]. *Other* refers to the expectations
built on indirect experience, including from other people (e.g., personal connections and from media) or from exposure to social robots in different ways. In
the original model, the "other" bubble refers to "other people", and is in the
present version expanded to include not only other people ("humans"), but also
social robots ("robots"). These two exist on a gradient scale as humans tend to
interpret social robots in an anthropomorphic manner [1]. This gradient does not
refer to how human-like a given social robots actually is, but rather how much
(by design or accident) a given social robot is expected to behave like humans,
i.e., the social robot may be perceived as a human-like creature, even if it is
not "human-like" in some objective way. *Beliefs* are sources of expectations that
can be inferred from other beliefs (e.g., "robots are intelligent in movies, thus
the robot I am interacting with is likely intelligent too"). Together with direct
experience and others, beliefs are built, thus are interrelated with each other.

Expectations can vary along four different dimensions: certainty, accessibility,
explicitness, and importance [29]. *Certainty* refers to the subjective estimated
probability of how likely it is that the outcome will occur. *Accessibility* refers
to how easy it is to activate and use a certain expectation. *Explicitness* refers
to what degree expectations are consciously generated. Some expectations are
implicitly assumed, usually related to the degree of certainty (e.g., "the sun will
rise in the morning"), whereas other expectations are consciously thought about
(e.g., how an interaction with a social robot will be like). *Importance* refers to the
expectation's significance, the higher the importance, the higher is the impact.

The rest of the model relates to the consequences of expectations [29]. These
factors can be divided into three categories: affective, cognitive, and behavioral.
Affective refers to emotional consequences, such as attitudes and anxiety. *Cognitive* refers to factors that has an effect on cognitive processes, such as interpretation and memory. *Behavioral* refers to consequences that causes choice of actions
due to the expectations, such as forming intentions to act, hypothesis testing, and
self-fulfilling prophesies. These factors occur when expectations are confirmed or
disconfirmed [29]. Confirmed expectations often lead to positive affects, are often
handled implicitly (and with ease), and results in expectations that are upheld
with greater certainty. In UX terms, confirmed expectations of the interaction
quality with social robots results in a positive UX. Confirmed expectations may
also, on rare instances, produce secondary affect (positive or negative), given
the inferences made after confirming the expectation. In contrast, disconfirmed
expectations often lead to negative affects and are handled explicitly as they are
surprising and need heavy cognitive processing in order to make sense of what
went wrong. Again in terms of UX, disconfirmed expectations of interacting with
social robots produces a negative UX. Sometimes there is a desire to retain (i.e.,

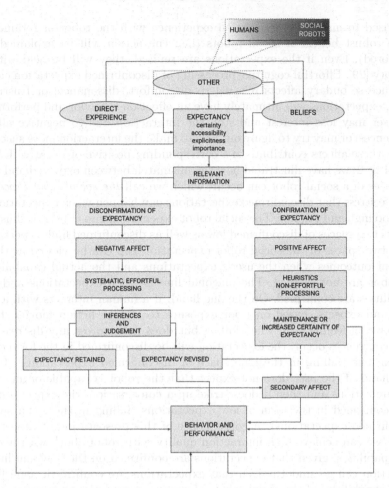

Fig. 1. A modified model of the expectation (expectancy) process by Olson et al. [29, p. 231]. The modified version is extended to include expectations of social robots.

uphold) the initial expectations and the event may be explained away. Other times there is a need to carefully consider what went wrong in order to revise the expectations for future instances. Future expectations of the instance are held with a higher level of uncertainty. Both confirmed and disconfirmed expectations may lead to altered behavior and performance [29].

When considering a social robot, a user may enter an interaction with high expectations of the robot's ability to interact socially. These beliefs may be built on the exposure to science fiction robots in the media. When the social robot is unable to uphold a complex interaction, the expectations are disconfirmed, resulting in negative affect, or negative UX, (e.g., disappointment) and effortful cognitive processing in order to rationalize what went wrong. This cognitive processing turns into inferences and judgment, and the expectations may either be revised to match the interaction experience with the robot or retained due to the robust beliefs of social robots (i.e., the action will be explained away or ignored). Even if the expectations are revised, they will be held with less certainty [29]. Effortful cognitive processing of disconfirmed expectation can also introduce secondary affects relating to discomfort, dissonance, or frustration. Lastly, expectations will ultimately have an effect on behavior and performance. The user may lose interest and stop the interaction due to negative affective experiences, or may try to figure out how to make the interaction more successful. Hence, these affects contribute to a corresponding positive or negative UX.

In Fig. 2, we have illustrated how the mismatch between expected and actual capacities of a social robot can occur, which we call *the social robot expectation gap*. We stress that disconfirmed expectations can happen when expectations are both too high and too low. The social robot expectation gap (Fig. 2) is illustrated with its two spaces of disconfirmed low as well as disconfirmed high expectations. These two spaces of the social robot expectation gap can be viewed as the two different outcomes when the user's expectations and the actual capabilities of the robot are not aligned. The diagonal line is when expectations and robot capabilities are confirmed. On the one hand, if a human interacts with a social robot and expects, based on prior exposure to science fiction movies, that it is capable of feeling pain when falling but does not express any distress when such occurrences occur, the expectation will be disconfirmed in the form of high expectations (falling in the blue space of disconfirmed expectations). On the other hand, if the user does not expect that the robot is capable of any verbal communications and then it does strike up a conversation, the expectation will be disconfirmed in the form of low expectations (falling in the green space of disconfirmed expectations). A consequence of this presentation of expectations is that we can achieve high interaction quality with robots both with high and low capabilities, given that expectations are confirmed on the diagonal line. An interaction can go smooth given that expectations are confirmed, regardless of actual capabilities of the social robot. Moreover, expectations are not static but dynamic across an interaction [33]. Therefore, this social robot expectation gap is also dynamic and may change before, during, and after the interaction.

Disconfirmed high expectations have been proposed previously by Kwon et al. [18], called the "expectation gap"; however, the authors do not account for disconfirmed low expectations. The figure presented (Fig. 2) here includes both too high and too low expectations of social robots. As mentioned previously, Moore [25] presented the "habitability gap" which is the perceived mismatch between the capabilities and expectations, and although this gap relates to the social robot expectation gap, it focuses on different aspects (e.g., flexibility and usability, voice-based systems) of interacting with new technology. Besides the obvious central theme of expectations, the social robot expectation gap, the expectation gap [18], and the habitability gap [25] demonstrate how the interaction is affected by human expectations of artifacts, in particular social robots in the case of this work. In addition, when expectations are low, there will be less interaction and thus the robot's capabilities will be less discovered, ultimately affecting the interaction quality. The social robot expectation gap serves, together with the model by Olson et al. [29], as the foundation for the design and development of the framework.

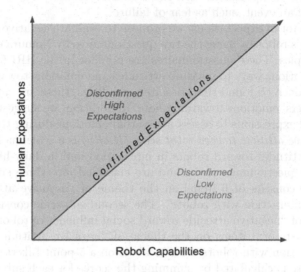

Fig. 2. The social robot expectation gap, with the two spaces of disconfirmed expectations that occurs when a robot's capabilities does not align with the expected capabilities.

3   Design and Development of the Framework

Drawing from the model by Olson et al. [29], we propose an evaluation framework for expectations in order to investigate the consequences of high and low expectations of social robots when a user interacts with a social robot, prior, during, and after the interaction. Based on the model (Fig. 1), we have identified three main factors in which expectations can be adequately evaluated: affect, cognitive processing, and behavior and performance. The data should be analyzed together in order to get a full picture of expectations; one metric alone may not be able to point at expectations, but together they are building blocks to extract information regarding expectations.

3.1   Affect

Affects are the factors that cause any sort of emotional reaction when expectations are either confirmed or disconfirmed. This is the first step after confirming or disconfirming expectations, following the Olson et al. model [29]. Attitudes is one such affect. Attitudes are defined as mental states that occur before the behavior, and are regarded in psychology research as one of the key elements for expectations [26,29]. Moreover, attitudes can be viewed as a user's belief of an object and its characteristics in relation to the user's perception of those characteristics. Anxiety is another affect, and expectations can both increase and decrease levels of anxiety. Expectations in themselves cannot cause anxiety, but certain contents of expectations can cause anxiety. Anxiety can be elicited as an anticipation of an event, such as fear of failure.

For this factor of expectations, we propose to evaluate negative attitudes and anxiety towards robot by using the two questionnaires by Nomura et al. [26] that cover these topics. These questionnaires are popular in the HRI field, and have been used in various ways to measure attitudes and emotions towards robots. de Graaf and Allouch [7] found that, despite some flaws, these are valid techniques to evaluate users' emotions towards robots. In addition, we suggest observations of users' facial expressions to assess non-verbal emotions during the interaction.

The negative attitude toward robot scale (NARS) is a scale made for measuring people's attitudes toward robots in interaction and in daily-life [26]. NARS consists of 14 questionnaire items and are classified into three sub-scales. The first sub-scale consists of 6 items on the theme of "negative attitude toward situations of interaction with robots". The second sub-scale consists of 5 items on the theme of "negative attitude toward social influence of robots". The third sub-scale consists of 3 items on the theme of "negative attitude toward emotions in interaction with robots". The scale is on a 5-point Likert scale, and the individual score is calculated by summing the scores for each sub-scale.

The robot anxiety scale (RAS) measures the altered behavior participants may have towards robots based on their anxiety towards robots. Nomura et al. [26,27] argued that negative attitudes may not lead to different behaviors toward robots. Anxiety is explained as emotions (anxiety or fear) that inhibit interaction with robots. RAS consists of 11 questionnaire items and are classified into three sub-scales. The first sub-scale consists of three items on the theme of "anxiety toward communication capability of robots" The second sub-scale consists of four items of the theme of "anxiety toward behavioral characteristics of robots" The third sub-scale consists of four items on the theme of "anxiety toward discourse with robots" The scale is on a 6-point Likert scale, and like NARS, the individual score is calculated by summing the scores for each sub-scale [26,27].

Facial Expressions is a complementary way to assess emotions by observation users' facial expressions during the interaction. The observations offer additional information of users' emotions during the interaction with the robot, compared to the questionnaires that are distributed after the interaction. Facial expressions provide non-verbal cues that may interpret the user's emotional states. Relevant facial expressions comprise, but are not limited to, anger, frustration, happiness, confusion, and surprise. Although there is an ongoing discussion on how reliable facial expression are for studying emotions [4], we have chosen to include this metric as these emotions should be interpreted as indicators together with the other metrics rather than inferred alone.

3.2 Cognitive Processing

Cognitive processing is the factor that causes any sort of cognitive strain, which is resource demanding for the users when expectations are either confirmed or disconfirmed [29,30]. Expectations are the basis of attention and have a direct influence on perception. When expectations are disconfirmed, attention is drawn to the event (due to the surprising outcome) and the event is consequently processed. This process happens because the information challenges current beliefs [30]. Moreover, expectations drive interpretations of that particular event. Users try to interpret perceptual events so they are aligned with their present expectations. This phenomenon is commonly recognized as stereotyping but has prolonged effects on how we perceive our surroundings even when we do not construct explicit stereotypes. For example, disconfirmed low expectations (c.f., Fig. 2) when the robot outperforms our expectations, is commonly treated by users as a fluke or luck [29]. Conversely, it is also likely that users may attribute disappointing performance from a social robot as a temporary fluke, stemming from disconfirmed high expectations. However, as pointed out by Olson et al. [29], disconfirmed expectations of behavior can also be attributed to deception. Thus, a social robot (or their designers) may be viewed as having ulterior motives, which can be related to trust in robots [22]. Cognitive processing affects memory, and disconfirmed expectations have been shown to cause better memory recall as more effortful cognitive processing occurs in these cases [9]. Recall is also related to how much effort the user puts on making sense of disconfirmed expectations. For this factor of expectations, we identified two aspects that can be tested during the interaction: memory recall and reaction time.

Memory recall can be used to measure cognitive processing. Expectations have an effect on memory [29,30], and with inspiration from Hashtroudi et al. [9], we propose to measure users' recall ability after the interactions with a social robot. Hashtroudi et al. [9] found that memory works better with disconfirmed expectations. The authors pointed out that irrelevant information has the lowest recall ability. Although the authors' research had a more complex experimental set-up, we propose a simple set-up where users are asked to write down what the remember from the interaction afterwards to gain insight into their cognitive processing. Tying the recall ability to NARS and RAS, we argue that is possible to investigate whether disconfirmed expectations may lead to better memory recall of the interaction with the robot. This is especially interesting if certain characteristics are ascribed to the robot that are related to greater fear of the robot. Thus, if the users view robots as having scary characteristics in the surveys, and this turns out to be disconfirmed, it is likely that the users remember more of the interaction. Alternatively, users with strongly held expectations which are then disconfirmed, may have created false memories that align with their expectations (e.g., stereotyping may lead to seeing certain behaviors that are false) [30]. Therefore, when collecting data through memory recall after the interactions, it is important to consider how the users' memory may be affected by their expectations. This effect has been formalized in the peak-end rule [16].

It is possible that users remember certain characteristics of the robot that are aligned with their view of the robot, although their behavior is similar. For this reason, we stress how triangulation can be used to understand the data further (e.g., users may score high on fear of robots via NARS, and also describe scary characteristics of the robot).

Reaction time can be used to measure cognitive processing, inspired by the study by Hashtroudi et al. [9]. Reaction time has been seen to be longer when dealing with demanding cognitive processing [9,29]. Reaction time, in our framework, refers to the reaction time for the users to interact with the robot's output, both verbal (e.g., conversation) and non-verbal (e.g., touch). Reaction time needs to be tailored for the robot and its capabilities. Studying whether reaction time has an effect on expectations can be of value in itself, but we also propose that we can tie memory recall and reaction time together, similar to the study by Hashtroudi et al. [9].

3.3 Behavior and Performance

Behavior and performance are the factors that cause changes in an user's deliberate actions. Expectations are the basis for basically any behavior because expectations drive our intentions and actions [29,30]. One specific kind of behavior that may be of relevance for assessing expectations is hypothesis testing. Because expectations involve believed probabilities users may test various hypotheses relating to the expected likelihood of various kinds of interactions. This tends to happen with expectations that do not have a 100% certainty and expectations that are explicit. Hypothesis testing is thus a behavior exhibited by a user when trying to make sense of an event. In UX, hypothesis testing can be characterized in terms of the seven stages of action model by Norman [20,28]. Similar to hypothesis testing, the seven stages of action model is about forming the intention to act by specifying and then executing a sequence of actions, followed by evaluating the outcome in relation to the intention.

For the evaluation of expectations of social robots, we have identified five behaviors and performance measures, which are presented below. Although behavior and performance have more aspects than the previous factors of expectations, they are all rather simple to measure as they are collected by the test leader. According to Nomura et al. [26], the results from NARS may not lead to behavioral changes which could mean that it wont be possible to measure NARS and the below behavioral changes together. We are not claiming fear of robots does not cause behavioral changes, but rather that this specific NARS scale may not catch subsequent behavior, according to the authors. NARS may have effect on the affect factor of expectations but not the behavior and performance factor. We propose, however, to look at the below measures alone and in relation to RAS. Moreover, it should be mentioned that reaction time does also fit the factor of behavior and performance, and we have chosen to present it under cognitive processing because it can be tied to memory recall as well. Therefore, reaction time can be used in this factor as well.

Gestures and body language done by the users can be used to measure behavior. Gestures and body language are forms of non-verbal behaviors [19]. Body language could be head nods by the user to confirm they understood the robot, or leaning away from the robot to show discomfort. Gesturing could include pointing as a way to communicate direction for the robot, or waving hands in front of the robot in attempts to get the robot's attention. For a given interaction, there could be many gestures and communicative body motions, and the aim is to observe any behavior that is noticeable and tie these to the expectation factors. Gestures and language could thus be compared to, for example, interruptions of interaction. Perhaps the user may wave their hands when interruptions occur as an attempt to get back on track.

Choice of conversation may be dependent on what kinds of expectations users have towards the social robot and can be used to measure behavior. By choice of conversation, we mean what users will choose to say to the robot during the interaction. Of course, if the robot communicates non-verbally this aspect is not relevant. However, since many social robots are able to uphold simple conversations, it is likely that users try to figure out what conversations are possible. This behavior relates therefore to the seven stages of action model by Norman [28]; that is, the users may try to figure out what kind of conversations are possible. If a user's expectations of a social robot is disconfirmed, it is possible that the user will spend more time trying new ways to discuss things with the robot, rather than having one single conversation. If a user's expectations of a social robot is confirmed, is possible the user will show an excited facial expression and uphold the same topic longer.

Repeating words refer to the number of repetitions the user makes during the interaction and can be used to measure performance. Yet again, the seven stages of action model [28] could be of relevance here. By repeating words, we mean if users need to repeat themselves to be understood by the robot. Perhaps the user chooses other similar words but different words as a way to test which words actually can be understood by the robot. This may be related to affect such as frustration with not being understood, or have an effect on cognitive processing. Therefore, this should be triangulated with the collected data from that section in order to form the expectations. The user may expect that the robot will be able to uphold complex conversations, and when this does not occur (i.e., disconfirmed expectations), the user shows a frustrated facial expression and repeats themselves several times. Subsequently, the user may try to correct (or revise) their expectations which causes behavioral changes. If the user expects certain conversation, and the robot is able to confirm this expectation, there might not be repeating of words and the interaction goes smooth.

Interruptions of interaction refer to the number of interruptions during the interaction and can be used to measure performance. Interruptions could be caused by the user when the interaction is not going as expected. Interruptions could also imply that the conversation is not flowing. It is possible that disconfirmed expectations may occur due to these interruptions. Is also possible that confirmed expectations may occur due to the user expecting a bad interaction. Interruptions may also be related to attempts to correct (revise) their expectations. Not only should the amount of interruptions be measured, but also under what circumstances they happen. Again, these could be tied to the other metrics in various ways, for example if choice of conversation changes after the interruptions and having better memory recall when interruptions occur.

Duration of interaction refer to the total time the interaction is taking place, and can be used to measure performance. As a rule of thumb, people behave in ways that are consistent with their expectations [29]. For example, people tend to choose tasks where they expect to be successful, and they will also put more effort and time into such tasks than ones they expect to fail [29]. The duration of the interaction, when applicable, could therefore be of relevance when users are interacting with the social robot; it is possible that users will interact longer with a robot if they expect to succeed in having a good interaction with the robot. Even more interesting would it be to compare duration of interaction in the first and second episodes of interaction. It is possible that users who had disconfirmed expectations of the interaction with the robot will have shorter duration of interaction in the second interaction episode as they know they will fail at having a successful interaction. This could be of interest in relation to the number of interruptions too. A lot of interruptions in the first interaction episode may lead to shorter duration of interaction in the second interaction episode since the user will expect these interruptions and will tend to avoid them in the second interaction. Perhaps scoring low on fear of robots may lead to longer duration of interaction as well.

4   Result

In this work, we have highlighted the importance of studying expectations in HRI. We have also started to specify how expectations could be studied and evaluated, and here we present the result: the Social Robot Expectation Gap Evaluation Framework. We base this framework on the model by Olson et al. [29] from the social psychology field, our Social Robot Expectation gap (Fig. 2) from the HRI field, and evaluation methods from the UX field [8,33]. This framework is intended for studying and evaluating expectations of social robots or other robots that act in a social manner in real interactions. The overall UX goal is to have expectations confirmed.

In this section we present the current version of our framework as illustrated in the matrix in Table 1. Included in this framework are UX goals and what metrics (data collection techniques) that are used to assess the three main factors. Each metric relates to either hedonic or pragmatic qualities [10]. Moreover, we present the proposed evaluation procedure (for further details on UX procedures, see [20].

Table 1. The three factors of expectations and the proposed metrics to study each when interacting with a social robot.

Expectation Factors	UX Goal	Metric	Details	Qualities
Affect	The user should expect to have neutral to positive emotions towards the robot	The Negative Attitude Toward Robot Scale (NARS)	A questionnaire measuring user's negative attitudes towards robots	Hedonic
		The Robot Anxiety Scale (RAS)	A questionnaire measuring user's anxiety towards robots	Hedonic
		Facial Expressions	Observing the kinds of facial expressions made by the user	Hedonic
Cognitive Processing	The user should experience effortless cognitive processing during the interaction	Memory Recall	Asking the user to write down what they remember of the interaction	Pragmatic
		Reaction Time	Measuring the time it takes for the user to react accordingly to the robot's output	Pragmatic
Behavior and Performance	The user should expect a pleasant and smooth interaction	Gestures and body language	Observing the kind of gestures and body language the user expresses	Hedonic
		Choice of Conversation	Observing the kinds of conversations the user tend to focus on during the interaction	Hedonic
	The user should expect to have ease of conversation	Repeating Words	Measuring the number of repetions the user makes during the interaction	Pragmatic
		Interruptions of Interaction	Measuring the amount of times, and what kind of, interruptions occur for the user during the interaction	Pragmatic
		Duration of Interaction	Measuring the total time spent in the interaction as well as the total time spent on each conversation for the user during the interaction	Pragmatic

4.1 Procedure

Phase 1: Identify the scenario. As a first step before carrying out the evaluation, one has to identify what kind of interaction to study, including identifying and creating scenarios between the human and the robot. We suggest two possible ways these scenarios can unfold, depending on what is being evaluated. First, the scenarios could be identical in order to compare them. If expectations are not confirmed in the first interaction, measuring changes in affect, cognitive processing, and behavior and performance is relevant as they would likely change. Another option is to have a scenario change in the second interaction, thus adding expectancy violation, similar to the study by Horstmann and Krämer [12]. Both these options offer different angles of studying and evaluating expectations of social robots. Once the scenario is chosen, baseline and max levels relating to the UX goals and metrics need to be set to fit the scenario [20]. We have chosen not to include baseline and max level in Table 1, as these need to be tailored to the actual scenario. This phase also includes recruiting participants, 5–8 is recommended for an empirical UX evaluation [20]. The different data collection techniques and metrics need to be prepared and tested in advance as well as informed consent to the participating users. The study needs to be in accordance with relevant ethical guidelines before being conducted [32].

Phase 2: Collect data. The proposed data collection techniques make it possible to collect complementary data for the factors of expectations (Table 1). In Fig. 3, we present a timeline of the step-wise procedure of this phase that aligns these aspects together. In particular, we highlight the temporal aspect of expectations, before, during, and after the interaction. We therefore urge the investigators to allow participants to repeat the same scenario at least twice or modify the second one to investigate and analyze how the temporal aspect affects the expectations of the interaction with the robot. The data collection phase is divided into the following steps 1) before the interaction, 2) during first interaction, 3) after first interaction, 4) during second interaction, and 5) after interaction (Fig. 3). The data is collected via questionnaires, observation (field notes or recordings), and interviews.

Before the first interaction, it is important to understand what kind of expectations participants may have of social robots. Therefore, we suggest a pre-questionnaire where previous experience with robots is asked for. Questions regarding what they expect of the robot in the interaction could also be of importance, in order to study participants' explicit expectations. We urge investigators to tailor the pre-questionnaire so it suits the scenario and the actual robot. It is important to avoid generating expectations through the pre-questionnaire process; we urge researchers to put extra care into this process when selecting questions. As the final step of the data collection phase, we suggest to collect data from doing a post-interview. Here, open-ended questions regarding their expectations and if they were confirmed are valuable for the overall analysis of the participants' expectations.

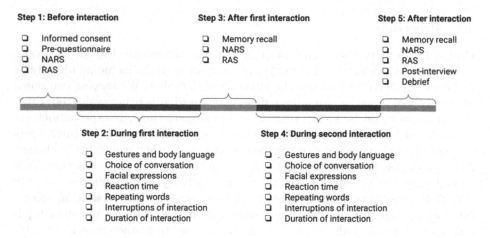

Fig. 3. The steps of phase 2: collect data

Phase 3: Analyzing the collected data. When the data collection has been carried out, the collected quantitative as well as qualitative data should be brought together and then analyzed, with a focus on identifying UX problems of coping with disconfirmed expectations. Triangulation is used to reach more reliable findings. Triangulation means that multiple data sources are used to compare and contrast the data in order to gain a deeper understanding of the obtained findings. Several findings that are pointing in the same direction imply that there is an identified UX problem that needs to be considered. The identified problems are then arranged into scope and severity. The scope can be either global or local, where global problems entail the interaction with the robot as a whole, and local problems only entail certain moment(s) of the interaction. The severity of problems provides insights of which kinds of re-design that should be prioritized or what aspects need to be studied in more depth. Degrees of severity is ranging from high to low, where higher degrees include severe mismatches between users' expectations and the actual interaction between a human and a robot. Lower degrees of severity include problems that have a minor negative effect on expectations in the HRI, as in situations when it is easy for the user to find an effortless workaround.

Phase 4: Reporting on findings and recommendations. A major outcome of the findings is to what extent the users had their expectations confirmed or disconfirmed, the underlying reasons for these findings, and where these are situated on the social robot expectation gap (Fig. 2), with the overall UX goal is to have users' expectations confirmed. The scope and severity dimensions provide some recommendations for how to reduce the disconfirmed expectations in the chosen scenario as well as some insights of how and why the participants altered or changed their expectations.

5   Discussion

With this work, we aim to contribute to the field of HRI by addressing and studying in further detail the role and relevance of expectations in HRI, including how to narrow the gap between expected capabilities and actual capabilities of social robots (i.e., the social robot expectation gap, Fig. 2) thus achieving confirmed expectations of an interaction with a social robot. By doing so, we have consequently addressed what role as well as impact expectations may play in HRI, especially for social robots in interactions with humans. The developed evaluation framework, which is based on prior research on expectations, and its procedure serves as the initial steps to contribute to the above aim. This framework takes inspiration from social psychology, UX, and HRI, and we stress the temporal aspect of expectations. That is, expectations are dynamic over time and can change before, during, and after the interaction. Our framework offers ways to assess expectations from the different factors (i.e., affect, cognitive processing, and behavior and performance), how they may change over time, and if the expectations are confirmed or disconfirmed. We envision the framework to be tailored and adapted to the specific situation that is being studied. Therefore, as these metrics are extensive, it can be scaled down to a few selected metrics that are suitable for the chosen situation. Triangulation should be used for the analysis of these metrics to reach more reliable findings

Future work includes applying the framework in practice and collect empirical data, which has been hindered due to the current covid-19 pandemic situation. By conducting an empirical evaluation based on the framework, its potential could be validated and relevant improvements could be made on the current version of the framework. Additional implications of the framework is that the obtained findings based on severity and scope could offer significant insights for future more experimental studies on certain aspects of humans' expectations of interacting with social robots. In the long run, this work will contribute to the inclusion of social robots in society.

References

1. Alač, M.: Social robots: things or agents? AI Soc. **31**(4), 519–535 (2015). https://doi.org/10.1007/s00146-015-0631-6
2. Alenljung, B., Lindblom, J., Andreasson, R., Ziemke, T.: User experience in social human-robot interaction. In: Rapid Automation: Concepts, Methodologies, Tools, and Applications, pp. 1468–1490. IGI Global (2019)
3. Alves-Oliveira, P., Ribeiro, T., Petisca, S., Di Tullio, E., Melo, F., Paiva, A.: An empathic robotic tutor for school classrooms. In: International Conference on Social Robotics. pp. 21–30. Springer (2015). https://doi.org/10.1007/978-3-319-25554-5_3
4. Barrett, L., Adolphs, R., Marsella, S., Martinez, A., Pollak, S.: Emotional expressions reconsidered. Psychol. Sci. Pub. Interest **20**(1), 1–68 (2019)
5. Dautenhahn, K.: Methodology themes of human-robot interaction. Int. J. Adv. Rob. Syst. **4**(1), 15 (2007)
6. Edwards, A., Edwards, C., Westerman, D., Spence, P.: Initial expectations, interactions, and beyond with social robots. Comput. Hum. Behav. **90**, 308–314 (2019)
7. de Graaf, M.M., Allouch, S.B.: The relation between people's attitude and anxiety towards robots in human-robot interaction. In: 2013 IEEE RO-MAN, pp. 632–637. IEEE (2013)
8. Hartson, H., Pyla, P.: The UX Book. Morgan Kaufmann, Burlington (2018)
9. Hashtroudi, S., Parker, E.S., DeLisi, L.E., Wyatt, R.J., Mutter, S.A.: Intact retention in acute alcohol amnesia. J. Exp. Psychol. Learn. Mem. Cogn. **10**(1), 156 (1984)
10. Hassenzahl, M., Tractinsky, N.: User experience - a research agenda. Behav. Inf. Technol. **25**(2), 91–97 (2006)
11. Horstmann, A., Krämer, N.: Great expectations? Relation of previous experiences with social robots in real life or in the media and expectancies based on qualitative and quantitative assessment. Front. Psychol. **10**, 939 (2019)
12. Horstmann, A., Krämer, N.: When a robot violates expectations. In: Companion of the 2020 ACM/IEEE International Conference on Human-Robot Interaction, pp. 254–256 (2020)
13. Horstmann, A.C., Krämer, N.C.: Expectations vs. actual behavior of a social robot. Plos One **15**(8), e0238133 (2020)
14. Jokinen, K., Wilcock, G.: Expectations and first experience with a social robot. In: Proceedings of the 5th International Conference on Human Agent Interaction, pp. 511–515 (2017)
15. Kaasinen, E., Kymäläinen, T., Niemelä, M., Olsson, T., Kanerva, M., Ikonen, V.: A user-centric view of intelligent environments. Computers **2**(1), 1–33 (2013)
16. Kahneman, D., Fredrickson, B.L., Schreiber, C.A., Redelmeier, D.A.: When more pain is preferred to less. Psychol. Sci. **4**(6), 401–405 (1993)
17. Khan, S., Germak, C.: Reframing HRI design opportunities for social robots. Fut. Internet **10**(10), 101 (2018)
18. Kwon, M., Jung, M., Knepper, R.: Human expectations of social robots. In: 2016 11th ACM/IEEE International Conference on Human-Robot Interaction (HRI), pp. 463–464. IEEE (2016)

19. Lindblom, J.: Embodied social cognition. Cognitive systems monographs (COS-MOS). Springer International Publishing Switzerland (2015). https://doi.org/10.1007/978-3-319-20315-7_3
20. Lindblom, J., Alenljung, B.: The anemone: theoretical foundations for UX evaluation of action and intention recognition in human-robot interaction. Sensors **20**(15), 4284 (2020)
21. Lohse, M.: The role of expectations in HRI. New Frontiers in Human-Robot Interaction, pp. 35–56 (2009)
22. Malle, B., Fischer, K., Young, J., Moon, A., Collins, E.: Trust and the discrepancy between expectations and actual capabilities. In: Zhang, D., Wei, B. (eds.) Human-Robot Interaction: Control, Analysis, and Design, chap. 1, pp. 1–23. Cambridge Scholars Publishing (2020)
23. Manzi, F., Massaro, D., Di Lernia, D., Maggioni, M.A., Riva, G., Marchetti, A.: Robots are not all the same. Cyberpsychol. Behav. Soc. Netw. **24**(5), 307–314 (2021)
24. Meister, M.: When is a robot really social? An outline of the robot sociologicus. Sci. Technol. Innov. Stud. **10**(1), 107–134 (2014)
25. Moore, R.K.: Is spoken language all-or-nothing? Implications for future speech-based human-machine interaction. In: Dialogues with Social Robots, pp. 281–291. Springer (2017). https://doi.org/10.1007/978-981-10-2585-3_22
26. Nomura, T., Kanda, T., Suzuki, T., Kato, K.: Psychology in human-robot communication. In: RO-MAN 2004. 13th IEEE International Workshop on Robot and Human Interactive Communication (IEEE Catalog No. 04TH8759), pp. 35–40. IEEE (2004)
27. Nomura, T., Suzuki, T., Kanda, T., Kato, K.: Measurement of anxiety toward robots. In: ROMAN 2006-The 15th IEEE International Symposium on Robot and Human Interactive Communication, pp. 372–377. IEEE (2006)
28. Norman, D.: The Design of Everyday Things. Basic Books, New York (2013)
29. Olson, J., Roese, N., Zanna, M.: Expectancies, pp. 211–238. Guilford Press (1996)
30. Roese, N., Sherman, J.: Expectancy. In: Kruglanski, A.W., Higgins, E.T. (eds.) Social Psychology: Handbook of Basic Principles. The Guilford Press, New York (2007)
31. Rosén, J.: Expectations in human robot interaction. In: Neuroergonomics and Cognitive Engineering: Proceedings of the International Conference on Applied Human Factors and Ergonomics, pp. 98–105. Springer (2021). https://doi.org/10.1007/978-3-030-80285-1_12
32. Rosén, J., Lindblom, J., Billing, E.: Reporting of ethical conduct in human-robot interaction research. In: Zallio, M., Raymundo Ibañez, C., Hernandez, J.H. (eds.) AHFE 2021. LNNS, vol. 268, pp. 87–94. Springer, Cham (2021). https://doi.org/10.1007/978-3-030-79997-7_11
33. Roto, V., Law, E., Vermeeren, A., Hoonhout, J.: User experience white paper - bringing clarity to the concept of user experience. In: Dagstuhl Seminar on Demarcating user Experience (2011)
34. Sandoval, E., Mubin, O., Obaid, M.: Human robot interaction and fiction. In: International Conference on Social Robotics. pp. 54–63. Springer (2014). https://doi.org/10.1007/978-3-319-11973-1_6

35. Schramm, L.T., Dufault, D., Young, J.E.: Warning: this robot is not what it seems! exploring expectation discrepancy resulting from robot design. In: Companion of the 2020 ACM/IEEE International Conference on Human-Robot Interaction, pp. 439–441 (2020)
36. Tonkin, M., Vitale, J., Herse, S., Williams, M., Judge, W., Wang, X.: Design methodology for the UX of HRI. In: Proceedings of the 2018 ACM/IEEE International Conference on Human-Robot Interaction, pp. 407–415 (2018)

Modeling Approach and Avoidance Behavior with Social Considerations for Others in Public Situations

Takafumi Sakamoto[✉] and Yugo Takeuchi

Shizuoka University, Hamamatsu, Shizuoka 4328011, Japan
sakamoto@sapientia.inf.shizuoka.ac.jp, takeuchi@inf.shizuoka.ac.jp
http://www.cog.cs.inf.shizuoka.ac.jp

Abstract. At the beginning of verbal interaction, a dialogue's premise must be shared by demonstrating a talking behavior to another and then talking easily to him/her. In particular, when talking to an unspecified person in a public scene, the other person's internal state must be estimated concerning the dialogue and an action chosen based on that other person's state. However, when a communication robot is installed in a public scene, it often passively waits for others to approach it because such approaching and avoiding behaviors that take into account the others in a scene have not been designed. In this study, we develop a computational model (CA model) that can estimate another person's internal state based on the changes in the body arrangement in relation to the other person and generate behaviors that express consideration of him/her.

Keywords: Social consideration · Interaction · Estimation · Human-robot interaction

1 Introduction

If autonomous robots are to establish and maintain relationships with others, they need to interact with them in a manner that adheres to the social protocols of human society. For example, in public situations, when strangers are passing through the same space, the movement direction, its speed, and the gaze direction are controlled to avoid excessive interaction [1]. If a robot implements such interaction dynamics and behaves according to the model, human society will more likely welcome it as an acceptable entity.

Many studies have focused on the approach behavior of robots to initiate communication with people and avoidance behavior to prevent collisions and avoid discomfort [2,3]. In addition, methods have been proposed in which a robot

This research had been granted by MEXT/JSPS Grant-in-Aid for Scientific Research on Innovative Areas: 20H05559.

can predict or classify human behavior in public situations and choose and approach an appropriate conversation partner [4,5]. Some studies have focused on the predictability of others, for example, generating predictable avoidance trajectories [6] or examining the effect of a robot's motor noise on the acceptance of its approach [7]. These researches are navigating the robot along an appropriate route and adaptively coordinating a human's movements with those of the robot instead of estimating the human's internal conditions and considering how the robot should behave. People, however, have internal conditions that exhibit preferential reactions to their external environment and the behavior of others. They can choose their actions based on their internal conditions. This property is called autonomy, and people represent typical autonomous beings or agents. Not only people but almost all agents possess internal conditions with which they interact with the outside world.

Therefore, when agents interact with each other or with agents, there is generally an approach that depends on the agent's internal condition. For example, if the target is a person, the agent should avoid doing anything the person does not want because such an action may cause discomfort in the target. In other words, if we intend to interact with a person or an agent based on social considerations, we need to ensure that the interaction includes the process of recognizing the internal conditions of that person or agent, i.e., the other person.

Thus, we proposed a cognitive model (CA model) for generating approach and avoidance behaviors in communication-starting situations based on the internal states of a person and an interaction partner and verified it using computer simulations [8]. In addition, by estimating the interaction partner's internal condition, we discussed the variables required for constructing a cognitive model of interaction, including behavior that considers the convenience of the interaction partner.

In this study, we extend our previous CA model and conduct an interaction experiment between a human and an agent by action planning based on the CA model of an agent that acts based on consideration for others. We conducted interaction experiments in a VR environment as a preliminary step.

2   Interaction with Consideration for Others Based on the CA Model

2.1   Definitions

Generally, considering others involves a state and attitude of supporting them as much as possible and respecting their intentions and actions. On the other hand, the cognitive aspect of interaction can be defined as adjusting one's internal condition in response to the internal condition of others (especially their desires) and an estimated value of their behavior. Therefore, to quantitatively describe interactions between agents (people) that involve consideration for others, we must define the variables and functions shown in Fig. 1. In particular, the behavior of an agent that involves consideration for others can be expressed through a function that estimates the value of another's internal condition and a function that adjusts the relative value of its internal condition based on the estimated value (bold line in Fig. 1).

Based on this processing structure, we consider a model that generates behavior that considers another person at the beginning of an interaction through a function that minimizes the difference between the estimated level of that person's desire and our level of desire. At the same time, this model expresses a level of consideration for others through a quantitative parameter that expresses how little this difference declines relatively.

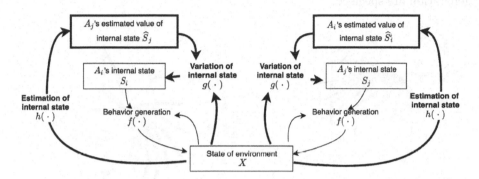

Fig. 1. Functions and variables required to describe interactions with consideration for others

A model of interaction based on approach and avoidance behaviors in a communication-initiation scene between two agents is described in the following. For the internal conditions, the action generations, and the estimation of the internal conditions, only a summary is given when there is overlap with our previous research [8].

2.2   Internal Condition and Behavior Generation

We use the model of our previous study [8] for the action-generation function of agents according to the value of the assumed internal condition. In this model, the physical interaction between agents A_1 and A_2 is represented by the temporal changes in environment $\mathbf{x}_{12} = \{r_{12}, \theta_{12}, \theta_{21}\}$. Note that r_{12} represents the distance between A_1–A_2, and θ_{12} and θ_{21} represent the absolute value of the relative angle from A_1 and A_2.

An agent's internal condition represents variables that facilitate or inhibit its behavior. Here we address two variables of the internal condition in the communication-starting scene: the preference (**Control**) for involvement from oneself to another agent and the preference (**Acceptance**) for involvement from the other agent to oneself. The internal condition of $\mathbf{A}_1$ with respect to $\mathbf{A}_2$ is denoted by $\mathbf{S}_{1\rightarrow2} = (c_1, a_1)$ and the internal condition of $\mathbf{A}_2$ by $\mathbf{S}_{2\rightarrow1} = (c_2, a_2)$.

Each action of an agent is represented by a temporal change in $\mathbf{x}_{12}$. The action of A_1, $\Delta_1\mathbf{x}_{12}$, is represented by the following equation with function f of behavior generation:

$$\Delta_1\mathbf{x}_{12} = f\left(\mathbf{x}_{12}, \mathbf{s}_{1\rightarrow2}; \phi_1\right). \tag{1}$$

However, value ϕ_1 represents an action property, such as the maximum movement speed. $\mathbf{s}_{1\rightarrow2}$ represents the value of the internal condition of A_1, and $\mathbf{s}_{1\rightarrow2} = (c_1, a_1) \in [-1, 1]^2$.

Based on these variables, Fig. 2 shows the approach and avoidance behaviors that are only generated when the internal condition and function f for behavior generation are specified.

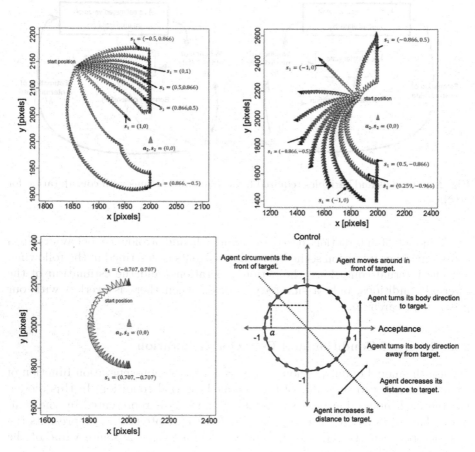

Fig. 2. Examples of approach and avoidance actions generated according to internal state values [8]

2.3   Estimation Function of Internal Condition

In generating behaviors that have consideration, the internal conditions of other agents must be estimated. Here they are estimated by applying the function of behavior generation in Eq. (1).

When A_1 infers the internal condition of A_2 from behavior $\Delta_2 \mathbf{x}_{12}$, $\mathbf{x}_{12}$ is an observable variable. ϕ_2 must be inferred. But since it is a variable that represents behavioral characteristics, we assume that it can be roughly inferred by observing the behavior. Then the estimated value of $\mathbf{s}_{2 \to 1}$ by A_1, $\hat{\mathbf{s}}_{2 \to 1}$, can be expressed by the following equation using function hh:

$$\hat{\mathbf{s}}_2^{(t)} = h\left(x_{12}, \Delta_2 \mathbf{x}_{12}, \hat{\phi}_2\right)$$

$$= \underset{\hat{\mathbf{s}}}{\mathrm{argmax}}\left(L\left(\Delta_2\mathbf{x}_{12}; \hat{\phi}_2\right)\right). \tag{2}$$

However, $L(\cdot)$ is defined as follows:

$$L(\cdot) = 1 - l\left(f(x, \hat{s}) - \Delta_2\mathbf{x}_{12}; \hat{\phi}_2\right). \tag{3}$$

l represents a function that normalizes the difference between the behaviors that can be generated by f and $\Delta_2\mathbf{x}_{12}$, where $0 \leq l(\cdot) \leq 1$. This definition estimates the internal condition that can generate the action that is most similar to $\Delta_2\mathbf{x}_{12}$. In this case, since $\mathbf{s}_{2 \to 1}$ is a two-dimensional variable, the solution can be approximated by a grid search.

2.4   Function Representing the Change in the Internal Condition

The change in the internal condition is expressed with function g. When dealing only with changes in the internal condition based on behavioral outcomes, the change in the internal condition of A_1, $\Delta\mathbf{s}_{1 \to 2}$, is represented by the following equation:

$$\Delta\mathbf{s}_{1 \to 2} = g(\mathbf{x}_{12}, \mathbf{s}_{1 \to 2}; \psi_1). \tag{4}$$

Here ψ_1 represents such cognitive properties as the speed of the change of the internal condition of A_1. As in our previous study, to represent the internal state's change when A_1 is concerned with A_2, we extend function g:

$$\Delta\mathbf{s}_{1 \to 2} = g(\mathbf{x}_{12}, \mathbf{s}_{1 \to 2}, \hat{\mathbf{s}}_{2 \to 1}; \psi_1) \tag{5}$$

This procedure determines the level of consideration the agent will give to the other agent, depending on the values specified for function g and parameter ψ.

2.5   Parameters for Consideration of Others

In this study, consideration for others is represented by the value of one parameter, ψ. Since two preferences, which are internal condition variables, represent the differences in the direction of the preference for involvement from one agent

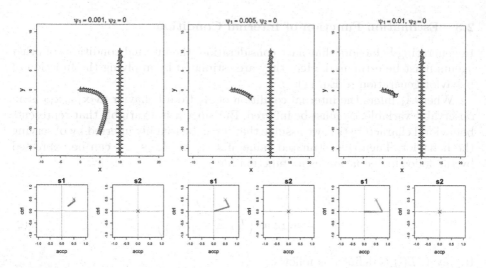

Fig. 3. Examples of behaviors when other agent does not respond

to another, it follows that the value of **Control** in one agent corresponds to the value of **Acceptance** in the other. In other words, if the **Control** value of one agent and the **Acceptance** value of another agent are identical, their preferences will be satisfied. Therefore, we define function g of the internal condition change to feedback the gap between the **Control** and **Acceptance** values. The change in the internal condition of A_1 is represented by the following equations:

$$\Delta c_1 = -\psi_1(\hat{a}_2 - c_1) \tag{6}$$

$$\Delta a_1 = -\psi_1(\hat{c}_2 - a_1) \tag{7}$$

In this case, parameter ψ_1 represents the amount by which A_1 changes its internal condition in consideration of A_2. When ψ_1 is positive, A_1 exhibits behavior that is considerate of A_2. The larger the value of ψ_1 is, the faster the internal condition of A_1 will be adjusted. On the other hand, there is a case where ψ_1 takes a negative value. If this case occurs, the action will ignore the preferences of the other agent, which is the opposite of consideration.

2.6   Simulation

We generate an agent's trajectory to examine how the interaction might differ depending on the value of the parameter that represents consideration. Assuming a situation where agent A_1 tries to talk to agent A_2, we set the value of consideration parameter ψ_1 in three ways: 0.001, 0.005, and 0.01. Since this is a scene where A_1 is trying to talk to A_2, the initial value of the internal condition of A_1 is set to $\{c_1^{(0)}, a_1^{(0)}\} = \{0.5, 0.5\}$. When the value of the internal condition for A_2 is smaller than a certain value for A_1 ($|s_2| < 0.3$), A_2 moves at a certain speed toward the destination.

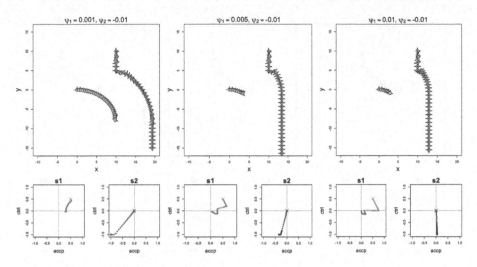

Fig. 4. Examples of behaviors when other agent reacts with a denial

The trajectory of A_2 is shown in Fig. 3 when it is unconcerned with A_1 and the initial value of the internal condition is set to $\{c_2^{(0)}, a_2^{(0)}\} = \{0, 0\}$. Note that the upper part of Fig. 3 shows the changes in the position and the body direction of A_1 and A_2, and the lower part shows the changes in the internal state. The trajectories in Fig. 3 correspond to ψ_1 values of 0.001, 0.005, and 0.01 from the left, and the larger the value of ψ_1 is, the more quickly A_1 stops chasing A_2.

The desired behavior when A_2 shows a rejection reaction to the approach of A_1 can be generated by setting ψ_2 to a negative value. Figure 4 shows the trajectory of the interaction generated when ψ_2 is set to -0.01. The value of the internal condition of A_2 changes in a negative direction during the approach of A_1 (lower right side of Fig. 4). As a result, the trajectory of A_2 is such that it takes a distance away from A_1. Comparing the trajectories for each value of ψ_1, the larger it is, the more quickly A_1 interrupts its approach to A_2, and the smaller the amount is by which A_2 avoids A_1. This situation suggests that the value of ψ_1 can be applied to express the degree of consideration of A_1.

Figure 5 shows the trajectory of the interaction when A_2 wants to communicate with A_1 and the initial value of the internal condition of A_2 is set to $\{c_2^{(0)}, a_2^{(0)}\} = \{0.5, 0.5\}$. In this case, the trajectories do not differ due to the difference in the value of ψ_1 because the preferences of A_1 and A_2 are identical.

3   Interaction Experiments in VR Environment

In this section, we experimentally verified how our model's parameters, which generate considerate behavior and affect the interaction between a human and an agent, implemented the model described in the previous section. The experiment was conducted in a VR environment, where a virtual robot, which appears to

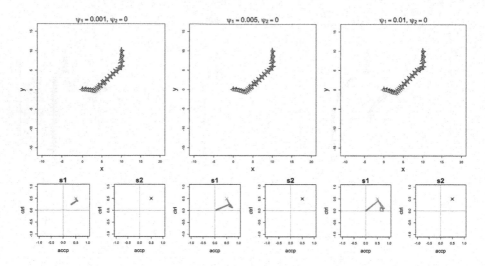

Fig. 5. Examples of behavior when another agent approaches

move in the VR environment, is used as an agent to analyze the human responses to human interactions.

3.1 Experiment Environment

Figure 6 shows an overview of our experimental environment, which was conducted in a VR environment built with Unity. The participants wore a Head Mounted Display (HMD, Oculus Rift) to see the visual information in the VR environment. They also wore shoes to which sensors were attached and moved and changed direction in the VR environment on a treadmill (KATWALK C).

We placed poles at six locations in the field of the VR environment and positioned the robot in the center (Fig. 7). The poles function as the target positions for the experimental tasks. The virtual robot's appearance is comprised of a combination of abstractly shaped objects to reduce the information given by its appearance. For example, its body part is a rectangle, its head is a cylinder, and part of its head is colored black to indicate its body direction (Fig. 6). The robot generates behaviors based on the model described above in the previous section according to the experimental conditions.

3.2 Experimental Task

The participants approached the designated pole or the object (target) held by the virtual robot out of the six poles in the field. The color of the pole or object changed to red to indicate where they should approach. We explained to our participants that "the robot cannot determine the color of the target and knows nothing about its given task." We also told them that "the robot is currently handing off the objects it is holding."

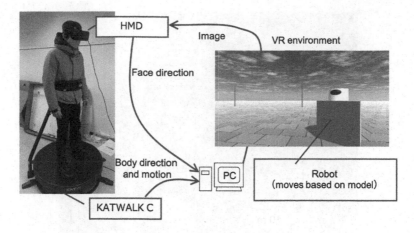

Fig. 6. Experiment environment

First, to get used to the KATWALK C in the VR environment, the participants moved between poles several times in the VR environment while wearing a HMD. After they basically became accustomed to walking in the VR environment, they practiced moving between poles five times while the virtual robot remained stationary and finally approached an object held by the virtual robot. At this point, if the participant has sufficiently approached the target, a bell rings, and a subsequent position is indicated to which the participant should proceed. The pole's location is determined randomly among the three poles located on the opposite side of the current pole.

Subsequently, an interaction is started between a human and a virtual robot that operates based on the described model. The participants are instructed to go to the target 10 times and move to the object held by the robot on the fourth and ninth trials and to the pole for the remaining eight trials. After removing their HMDs and getting off the KATWALK C, they filled out a questionnaire. Then, according to the situation, trials and questionnaires are conducted for the robot with different parameter values (maximum of three trials and questionnaires). We explained that our research ethics policy allowed them to stop participating in the experiment at any time.

3.3   Measurement and Analysis

The virtual robot's parameter values are 0.001, 0.005, or 0.01 with which it generated behaviors that express consideration for human behavior based on the CA model. These results are analyzed by including the participants' behaviors in the experiment when the virtual robot is stationary during the practice trials.

In this experiment, if a pole is directed to a place to which the participant should move, it is defined as a condition where the participant wants to avoid interaction with the virtual robot. If the participant is not affected by the virtual robot's movement, he/she can proceed directly to the target location. Conversely,

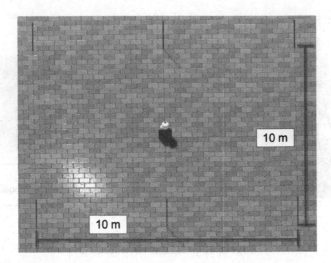

Fig. 7. Experiment's virtual space

the component of the direction vector, which is perpendicular to the target's orientation (in this case, the pole), is an indicator of a movement that evades the virtual robot. Hence, the circumferential component of Fig. 8 is adopted as the evaluation index for the movements of participants when the pole is designated as the target.

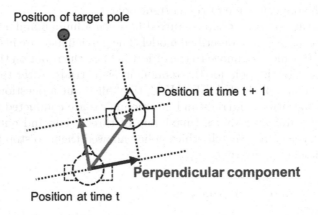

Fig. 8. Vertical component of movement vector used to assess amount of virtual robot's avoidance

On the other hand, if the object held by the virtual robot is a target that the participant should approach, then the participant wants to engage with the virtual robot. In this case, the virtual robot infers the participant's internal condition and approaches the participant by itself, thereby removing any necessity that the participant must move. Hence, the amount of the participant's movement is employed as an evaluation index to indicate that the participant wants to approach the virtual robot when it is holding the target.

Our experiment had five participants, each of whom conducted one to three trials depending on the situation.

3.4 Results and Considerations

Figure 9 shows the amount of movement by the participants to avoid the virtual robot when they moved toward the pole in each experimental condition. Psi in Fig. 9 represents a parameter that generates a movement with consideration by the virtual robot in the trial, and the horizontal axis of each graph represents the number of times the movement (target designation) was made in the trial (the 1st to 3th, 5th to 8th, and 10th times are the movements when the pole is the target point). The horizontal axis of each graph represents the number of moves (target designation) in the trial. In addition, STOP represents the practice trials, which are the index's baseline because the virtual robot was stationary in them, although the number of moves in the practice trial ranged from 1 to 5. The straight line on the graph represents the regression line, and the gray area represents the 95% confidence interval.

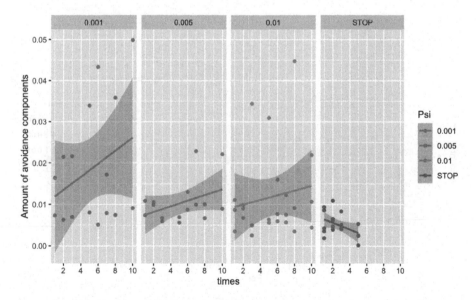

Fig. 9. The amount of movement that the participant avoids the robot when approaching the pole (where Psi is the value of the parameter that represents the robot's consideration and "STOP" represents a practice trial).

In the leftmost graph of Fig. 9, when the value of the parameter was 0.001 for representing a movement by the virtual robot with consideration, the straight line goes up and to the right, indicating that the behavior of the participants to avoid the virtual robot increased as they repeatedly moved in the virtual field. The second and third graphs from the left in Fig. 9 show the trials where the parameters were set to 0.005 and 0.01 for generating movements with consideration. Compared to the practice trials in the rightmost graph, the tendency to increase was smaller than in the 0.001 cases. If this value increased, the participants moved circuitously toward the target location. Therefore, when the value of the parameter was small (0.001) for the virtual robot to generate considerate movements toward the participant, it could not make sufficiently considerate movements that reflect the participant's internal state and behavior based on it.

Figure 10 shows the total amount of movement (distance traveled) when the participant goes toward the object held by the virtual robot. In the practice trials, the virtual robot is stationary, so the amount of movement at this time is the baseline. As shown in Fig. 10, the amount of movements of the experimental participants was small regardless of the parameter values for the virtual robot to generate considerate movements: 0.001, 0.005, or 0.01. When the participant was required to approach the virtual robot, it correctly inferred the participant's internal condition and appropriately approached by itself.

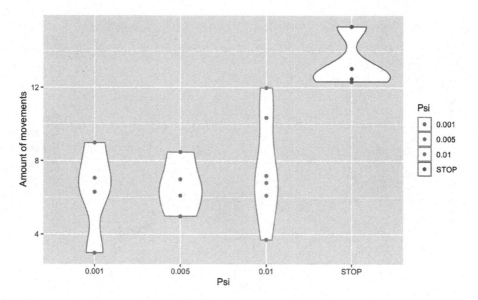

Fig. 10. Amount of participant movements when approaching robot: Psi denotes value of parameter that represents robot's consideration, and STOP represents a practice trial.

These results indicate that when people do not intend to interact with the virtual robot, the amount of behavior with which they avoid the virtual robot changes depending on the parameter's value that generates considerate movements for humans. However, when the human does plan to approach the virtual robot, there was no effect on the parameter's value that indicates the considerate response of the virtual robot to the human's behavior. These results resemble those verified by our simulation, suggesting that the CA model proposed and extended in this study has validity as a model for describing considerate and polite behavior.

However, at this present stage, due to the limited number of participants in our experiment, we cannot verify that sufficient analysis has been conducted. In addition, since this experiment was conducted in a VR environment, we must conduct real-world experiments using actual robots and field experiments in a more natural environment in the future.

4   Conclusion

This paper describes the implementation and evaluation of a mechanism that extends the CA model for generating both approach and avoidance behaviors in communication-initiation situations and generates behaviors based on consideration for others by estimating and referring to internal conditions and behaviors. Through experiments conducted in a VR environment, we verified the influence of parameters for generating behaviors with consideration for others on the structure of interactions between humans and virtual robots. Our experiment's results suggest that when the value of the parameter for generating behaviors with consideration for others by the extended CA model was minor (0.001), the participants' avoidance of the virtual robot increased. Conversely, when the parameter value was of a specific size (0.005 or 0.01), the tendency suppressed avoidance behaviors. Thus, the extended CA model proposed in this study has validity as a model for generating behavior with consideration for another agent.

References

1. Goffman, E.: Behavior in Public Place. Free Press, New York (1963)
2. Krusea, T., Kumar, A.P., Alami, R., Kirsch, A.: Human-aware robot navigation: a survey. Robot. Autonom. Syst. **61**(12), 1726–1743 (2013)
3. Rios-Martinez, J., Spalanzani, A., Laugier, C.: From proxemics theory to socially-aware navigation: a survey. Int. J. Soc. Robot. **7**(2), 137–153 (2015)
4. Kanda, T., Glas, D.F., Shiomi, M., Hagita, N.: Abstracting people's trajectories for social robots to proactively approach customers. IEEE Trans. Robot. **25**(6), 1382–1396 (2009)
5. Satake, S., Kanda, T., Glas, D.F., Imai, M., Ishiguro, H., Hagita, N.: A robot that approaches pedestrians. IEEE Trans. Robot. **29**(2), 508–524 (2012)
6. Mavrogiannis, C.I., Thomason, W.B., Knepper, R.A.: Social momentum: a framework for legible navigation in dynamic multi-agent environments. In: Proceedings of the 2018 ACM/IEEE International Conference on Human-Robot Interaction, pp. 361–369 (2018)

7. Joosse, M., Lohse, M., Berkel, N.V., Sardar, A., Evers, V.: Making appearances: how robots should approach people. ACM Trans. Hum.-Rob. Interact. (THRI) **10**(1), 1–24 (2021)
8. Sakamoto, T., Takeuchi, Y.: Simulation of spatial behavior based on an agent model in human-agent initial interaction. In: Proceedings of the 6th International Conference on Human-Agent Interaction, pp. 310–317 (2018)

BlocksBot: Towards an Empathic Robot Offering Multi-modal Emotion Detection Based on a Distributed Hybrid System

Agnese Salutari[1,2]([✉]), Laura Tarantino[2]([✉]), and Giovanni De Gasperis[2]([✉])

[1] Reiss Romoli s.r.l., Via Enrico Berlinguer 3, 67100 L'Aquila, Italy
agnese.salutari@ssgrr.com
[2] Università degli Studi dell'Aquila, Via Vetoio 1, 67100 L'Aquila, Italy
{laura.tarantino,giovanni.degasperis}@univaq.it

Abstract. Studies show that people expectations on robots and their behavior are similar to those regarding living objects, and that users ascribe robots with human attributes, qualities, and capabilities even when the robot is not conceived for social interaction. Actually, the increasing availability of sensors able to capture situational data makes it possible to achieve adaptive systems able to dynamically take into account users' and context information with unprecedented precision, thus showing some degree of empathy and emotional intelligence. Modern robots can use their sensors, like cameras and microphones, not only for their more traditional goals, but also for classifying human emotional states in order to emulate an empathic behavior, and to put the users at ease and tempt them in continuing the interaction. They can offer a human-like communication occurring over different verbal and non-verbal communication channels. Anyhow, since multimodal emotion detection is a complex technique requiring a proper combination of all the deriving data, handling it can be very demanding, and maybe impossible to achieve for many machines because of hardware limitations or simply for an unaffordable battery power consumption, with an ultimate effect on usability, which can degrade up to an unacceptable degree. In this paper we discuss how these problems have been faced within the framework of the BlocksBot project and how its Hybrid Distributed approach allows to overcome such limitations.

Keywords: Human-Robot Interaction · Empathy · Multimodal emotion detection · Performances

1 Introduction

The diffusion of robots in application domains like entertainment, teaching, assistance for children and elderly, autistic, and handicapped persons is making the interaction between people and robots increasingly socially-situated and multi-faceted [13, 21]. Actually, it is recognized that emotional levels of interaction affect users' acceptance of any kind of technology or artifact [1, 14]. Anyhow, if the lack of "empathy" can be considered acceptable by users in many kinds of traditional computers applications, the

M. Kurosu (Ed.): HCII 2022, LNCS 13303, pp. 625–638, 2022.
https://doi.org/10.1007/978-3-031-05409-9_45

same does not hold when moving towards applications and devices acting as personal assistants or companions, like (possibly anthropomorphic) robots, from which one does expect some kind of "emotional intelligence" [15, 18]: people naturally tend to treat robots similarly to how they would treat living objects, and ascribe them with life-like qualities, such as names and personalities, even when the robot is not explicitly designed for social interaction [11, 21].

The idea of humans and robots having internal mental models of one another has long been suggested (e.g., [19, 20]), soliciting research aimed at making robots able to understand users' behavior and intentions, and to estimate their emotional state. The more and more increasing availability of sensors able to capture situational data (like cams and microphones) allows designers and researchers to conceive adaptive applications able to dynamically take into account users' and context information with unprecedented precision, thus providing applications with some degree of "empathy". The design of social robots looks for developing natural interfaces for a multimodal affective interaction in which users can communicate their emotional state to the robot using several diverse input channels as in human communication (see, e.g., [2, 8, 10, 16, 17]).

Actually, as discussed in [12], the main Human-Robot Interaction (HRI) problem is "to understand and shape the interactions between one or more humans and one or more robots". Desirable human-robot interaction can be achieved by designing technological solutions based on the evaluation of the capabilities of both humans and robots.

On the human side, interactions are mostly focused on the exchange of information, which can occur over different communication channels. When people talk to each other, they not only express themselves in terms of speech, but they continuously show their feelings and mood by facial expressions, voice characteristics, pose, proximity and many other indirect ways. A modern and satisfying human-robot interaction should hence take into account all these mechanisms, and robots should use their sensors, like cameras and microphones, not only for their more traditional goals, but also for detecting as many as possible of these aspects about the users, thus achieving a multimodal emotion detection. It would be essential for a robot to classify human emotional state in order to emulate an empathic behavior, to put the users at ease and tempt them in continuing the interaction.

On the robot side, anyhow, multi-modal emotion detection is a very complex task that implies the correct detection of emotions from many different channels, like voice tone and pose, and the proper combination of all the deriving data. Managing all these tasks is computationally expensive and might be impossible to face for many machines because of hardware limitations or simply for an unaffordable battery power consumption. Moreover, robots are actually very heterogeneous, depending on their context, the usage they are designed for, and their productors, and for this reason we cannot take processing capabilities or other software/hardware features for granted when developing models and techniques of general applicability.

Summarizing, if, on the one hand, new challenges are spreading out in HRI research aimed at making noticeable User Experience improvements by taking into account human untold needs, and creating human-like robots that can interact with people and communicate in the most appropriate way, reality can be a bit different: what can developers do with their nice humanoid robot if it spends something like half its CPU just to stay up on its own legs without falling, while it is neither walking? Actually, the link between system performance evaluation and usability evaluation was already emphasized [6, 7] as well as the idea of dynamically configuring the "interaction experience" according to system performances [6].

In this paper we discuss how these challenges have been faced within the BlocksBot project, aimed at developing a social empathic robot overcoming these limitations by a Hybrid Distributed approach combining Multi-Agent System (MAS) programming with the more traditional Object Oriented Programming (OOP) and Event Driven Programming (EDP).

The remainder of the paper is organized as follows: Sect. 2 presents the BlocksBot communication model and the BlocksBot abstract architecture model, Sect. 3 illustrates the main technological choices, Sect. 4 illustrates how BlocksBot models and technological choices translate into a hybrid architecture, and Sect. 5 discusses how all these design choices allow to guarantee a desirable user experience; finally, in Sect. 6 conclusions are drawn.

2 Underlying Models of BlocksBot

Human communication exploits both verbal and non-verbal channels involving a complex combination of sensory information based on audition, vision, olfaction/taste, tactility. Since such multiple channels in human-human interaction can be recognized as proposed by the literature in theory of communication, in previous studies our research group proposed a *communication model* based on a set of pillars in the context of interaction between human and an empathic robot [3, 4]:

- Verbal dimensions:

    - speech,
    - text

- Non-verbal dimensions:

    - prosody (i.e., voice management): pitch, length, rate, intonation, loudness, tempo
    - paralanguage: gasp, sigh, throat-clear, mhm, etc.
    - kinesics (i.e., body language): facial expression, oculesics (gaze, eye contact and movement), gestures, odors, tactility and skin response /haptics, color, humidity)
    - proxemics (i.e., space management)
    - chronemics (i.e., time management)

In association with the communication model, we proposed also a *design methodology* mirroring it. The basic idea is to model the perception in a robot as a set of subsystems that can build an abstract representation starting from data fluxes coming from sensors [5], relying on conventional data mining and data fusion techniques or deep learning neural networks for vision, like image classifiers or object detectors. The proposed architectural model requires that sub-system's controllers go beyond a basic reactive behavior and be implemented as agents that communicate to each other according to a multi-modal hierarchy by means of asynchronous events. As illustrated in Fig. 1, each significant pillar in the communication model has an agent role assigned to it that has to be coordinated with the others. The agents communicate according to the hierarchy of the dimensions of the communication model.

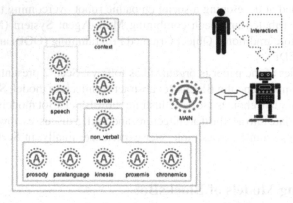

Fig. 1. Multi-agent system organization to implement an emphatic human-robot interaction.

3   The HW/SW Platform

The proposed design methodology has been applied to the BlocksBot project, to be tested in a simplified scenario currently including the following modal channels:

- Voice intonation
- Facial expression
- Body pose

For the BlocksBot project, we used Nao5, a humanoid robot created by SoftBank Robotics (see Fig. 2). Nao has become a standard in education and research, thanks to it open and fully programmable platform, and is also used as an assistant by companies and healthcare centers to welcome, inform and entertain visitors, resulting appropriate for BlocksBot purpose. It is provided with an ATOM Z530 1.6 GHz CPU and 1 GB RAM. Its body is characterized by 25 degrees of freedom, which enable him to move and adapt to his environment. It is equipped with four directional microphones and speakers to interact with users and two 2D cameras to recognize shapes, objects and even people.

In its current implementation the BlocksBot aim is to detect users' emotions by analyzing facial expressions, poses, and voice, based on images and audio records. Image and audio processing are complex tasks that are usually managed by Neural Networks. Since a good Neural Net needs a big amount of data as a dataset to perform training, leaning on services that provide pre-trained and very efficient Neural Networks can be a convenient choice, when applicable. So, we compared off-the-shelf solutions to identify the best combination of services (see Tables 1, 2 and 3).

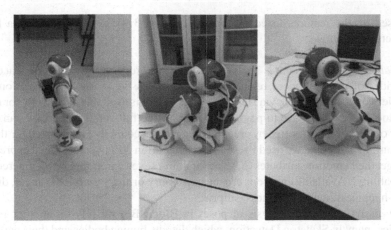

Fig. 2. The NAO robot.

Table 1. Off-the-shelf solutions for the detection of *facial expressions*.

Solution	Characteristics	Cost
Amazon Rekognition	It can detect nine emotions	No free version
Emotiva	It can detect six emotions	No free version
Face + +	It can detect seven emotion It can detect also pose	Free version available
Morphcast	It can detect seven emotions	No free version
Viso.ai	It can detect five emotions	No free version

Table 2. Off-the-shelf solutions for the detection of *gestures (pose)*.

Solution	Cost
Face + +	Free version available
Google ML Kit Pose Detection	Free version available
Nuitrack	No free version
Skeleton Tracking	No free version

Table 3. Off-the-shelf solutions for *voice analysis*.

Solution	Cost
Emphat	Limit for free usage
Vokaturi	Free version available

Based on the features listed in Tables 1, 2 and 3 we decided to build a hybrid architecture as follows:

- *Facial expressions.* For the analysis of facial expressions, we rely on Face++, a provider of many services related to image processing. Face++ is based on Neural Networks, it is callable via HTTP requests, and it is available as an SDK for offline use too. Developers have to pay for SDK or online full version, but they can try all their online services for free by creating their own account (we have opted for this last option). In particular, we used Face++ Face Detection API to detect facial expressions and get their emotion attributes (a Json containing seven emotions and their percentage probability). Available emotions are the customary primary emotions: anger, disgust, fear, happiness, neutral, sadness, surprise.
- *Pose analysis.* For the analysis of poses in BlocksBot we rely on another Face++ service, namely Skeleton Detection, which detects human bodies and their parts (like head, shoulders, and so on), returning their coordinates. In this case, Face++ doesn't provide emotion probabilities. In the current implementation we get an attitude value by detecting distance between hands: when hands are close to each other a person has an introverted attitude, otherwise he/she has an extroverted attitude. It is necessary to observe, anyway, that Face Detection API is more reliable than Skeleton Detection.
- *Voice analysis.* For voice analysis we chose the free version of Vokaturi, which can analyze speech emotions and it is independent of the language of the speaker. Vokaturi is available as an SDK and can be easily integrated into existing software applications. Its full versions, VokaturiPlus and VokaturiPro, can recognize seven emotions (neutral, happiness, sadness, anger, fear, disgust, boredom) and have an accuracy of 76.1%. The free opensource version, Open-Vokaturi, can recognize five emotions (neutral, happiness, sadness, anger, fear) and has an accuracy of 66.5%. Like as Face++ services, Vokaturi detected emotions are accompanied by their probabilities.

4   The Resulting BlocksBot Architecture

4.1   Overview

Based on the models presented in Sect. 2 and on the technological choices discussed in Sect. 3, the current implementation of BlocksBot is a hybrid system combining Multi-Agent System (MAS) programming with the more traditional Object-Oriented Programming (OOP) and Event Driven Programming (EDP). The system includes two different sets of agents:

- The first group is made of 4 agents responsible for the emotion detection: *FacialEmotionsAgent, PoseEmotionsAgent* and *VocalEmotionsAgent* have to analyze images and audio recordings in order to detect emotions while *DecisionMakerAgent* is in charge for combining their results in order to decide which is the most probable emotion.
- The second group is made of 3 agents running on the real robot: *AudioManager* and *VideoManager* capture images and audio recordings, while *ReactionNaoBotManager* has to perform the proper reaction to the current emotion.

Furthermore, there is one special *Runner* agent that have to start and stop all the other agents in order to have clean start and exit for the parallel daemon processes.

Figure 3 illustrates the BlocksBot architecture and the used technologies. In particular:

- Ovals represent BlocksBot agents
- Redis is the MAS message broker/shared memory
- Face++ is used as an online service
- Vokaturi is embedded as an SDK.
- Arrows represent different data flows, by color and direction:

    - *VideoManager* stores on Redis its captured images data (green output arrow)
    - *AudioManager* stores on Redis its audio recordings data (blue output arrow)
    - *FacialEmotionsAgent* and *PoseEmotionsAgent* both take from Redis captured images data (green input arrow) and put their result (purple output arrow)
    - *VocalEmotionsAgent* takes from Redis audio recordings data (blue input arrow) and puts its result (purple output arrow)

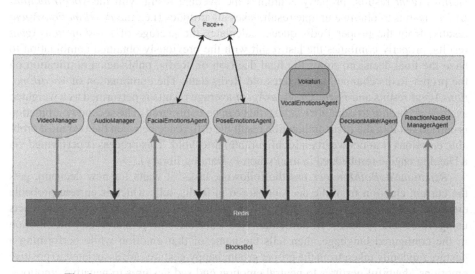

Fig. 3. The MAS-based architecture of the current version of BlocksBot

Interested readers can find additional details on agents' behavior and communication in Sect. 4.2 and simulation results in Sect. 4.3, while for a discussion on the effect of the architectural choices on performances and usability we refer to Sect. 5.

4.2   A Closer Look to the Agents and Their Cooperation

FacialEmotionsAgent and *PoseEmotionsAgent* have the following tasks: they wait for new image notifications, get each new image from Redis, analyze the new image by using Face++ proper services, put analysis results in the proper format, store resulting data on Redis. The velocity of these two agents depends on the Internet and on Face++ servers. Usually, they can process around three images in a second.

VocalEmotionsAgent has the following tasks: it waits for new audio recording notifications, gets each new audio from Redis, analyzes the new audio recording by using the Vokaturi library, puts analysis results in the proper format, stores resulting data on Redis, and publishes a notification on the proper Redis channel when a new vocal emotion result is stored on Redis. *VocalEmotionsAgent* is the slowest one to give its result, because it has to wait until a new audio recording is available; actually, capturing an image is much faster than recording the voice, so the vocal emotion result is usually the last of all and, for this reason, *VocalEmotionsAgents* is the one in charge of notifying when it is done processing.

DecisionMakerAgent has the following tasks: it waits until *VocalEmotionsAgent* is done processing, retrieves *VocalEmotionsAgent* result from Redis, takes all the *FacialEmotionsAgent* results from the proper Redis queue, calculates the average of the *FacialEmotionsAgent* results, properly combines the average result with the *VocalEmotionsAgent* results to obtain a unique result, takes all attitudes (i.e., the *PoseEmotionsAgent* results) from the proper Redis queue, calculates the average of *PoseEmotionsAgent* results, properly combines the last result with the previously obtained combination to have the final decision, stores the final decision on Redis, publishes a notification on the proper Redis channel, and deletes old Redis data. The combination of *VocalEmotionsAgent* results and *FacialEmotionsAgent* average results is performed as a weighted average according to reliability factors that can be configured. The second combination is carried out if in the first combination result the difference between the two most probable emotions is under a certain (configurable) threshold. This process is performed via a Datalog engine (embedded in the Python PyDatalog library).

ReactionNaoBotManager has the following tasks: it waits for new decision, gets the current emotion from the decision stored in Redis, tells which is current probable emotion, and properly reacts to that emotion. In the current implementation Nao reacts using voice and gestures. In particular, Nao translates the probable current emotion in the configured language, then tells the name of that emotion while performing a gesture randomly taken from the proper group: happy gestures are associated to positive emotions, doubtful gestures to neutral emotion end sad gestures to negative emotions. The gesture-emotion associations are defined in the system configuration and can be easily changed (e.g., to be adapted to specific application domains).

As to the overall cooperation of BlocksBot agents, Fig. 4 illustrates the BlocksBot Enterprise Integration Patterns Diagram, while Fig. 5 depicts a simplified version of the BlocksBot Sequence Diagram.

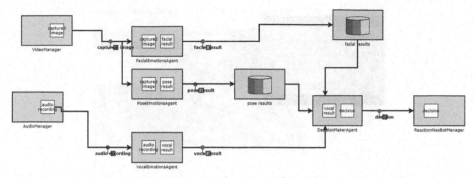

Fig. 4. The BlocksBot enterprise integration patterns diagram.

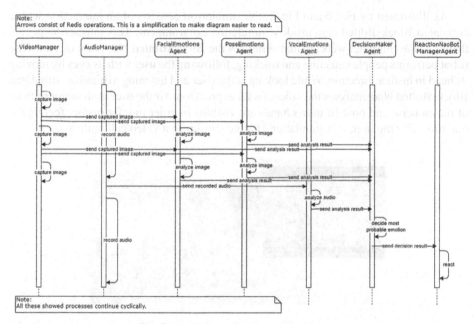

Fig. 5. The BlocksBot sequence diagram.

4.3 Human-Nao Interaction in a Simulated Environment

Within BlocksBot, we provided also a simulation environment for seeing the project in action needing only a computer with a microphone, a webcam and CoppeliaSim simulator (www.coppeliarobotics.com) installed on it. Two BlocksBot agents manage CoppeliaSim simulation, capturing images with the webcam and recording audio, and a *Runners* agent (as for the real Nao) starts and stops all the other agents in order to have clean start and exit for the parallel daemon processes (Fig. 6).

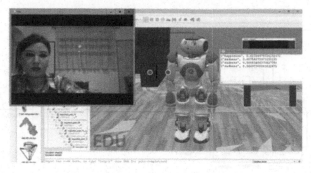

Fig. 6. Simulated BlocksBotted Nao looking and listening at the user.

As illustrated by Fig. 6 and Fig. 7, the simulation consists of an interaction with a simulated BlocksBotted Nao inside a simulation environment. This interaction occurs thanks to the computer webcam that simulates the BlocksBotted Nao point of view. The robot performs people detection and tracking, following the user with its eyes by moving its head in his/her direction. While looking at the user and listening to him/her, simulated BlocksBotted Nao analyses the voice, facial expressions (if the user is showing in front of the camera) and pose (if user's hands are visible) in order to infer his/her feelings in real time. For the user, this simulation is quite similar to a video call with Nao.

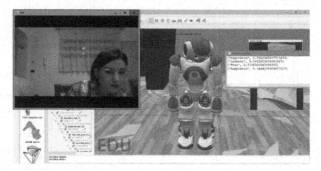

Fig. 7. Simulated BlocksBotted Nao follows the user with its eyes while detecting her emotions.

5   Discussion

It is interesting to discuss the implementation choice with respect to our initial goal of achieving performances able to guarantee the usability objectives, in terms of efficacy, efficiency and users' satisfaction.

5.1   Advantages of the Hybrid Distributed Approach

As previously illustrated, BlocksBot divides the code into agents, each one in charge of managing a different task. The technology used by each agent can vary based on the goal it has to achieve. Different agents, in fact, can easily communicate via a common message broker, independently of their technologies. As a consequence, the system is scalable, so that new agents can be added without any problem and the system can be easily integrated in pre-existing environments. Therefore, the system is easily extendable to include additional emotional channels and associated dedicated agents. Furthermore, the distributed approach offers the following advantages:

- It makes it possible to distribute the computational charge over many machines, allowing even less powerful robots to provide the most user experience possible.
- It favors the formalization of BlocksBot adaptation approach.

5.2 BlocksBot Adaptation Approach

In [6], we introduced an interaction design approach based on a dynamic configuration of the "interaction experience" according to system performances. The designer should (1) reason in terms of specification of goals, properties, and constraints (to be considered as "adaptation targets") and (2) conceive a system with choice of behavior, capable of preserving both its mission and the capacity of user involvement also in cases of dynamic changes (in our case, system performance downgrading risks), possibly degrading grace-fully to meet end users' requirements and expectations in a manner which is as good as possible under the circumstances. Notice that with graceful degradation we do not mean a system performance degradation but rather a possible end-user goal relaxation, within a process as transparent as possible to the final user.

In the case of BlocksBot, the expected functionalities can be ranked from the most essential to the most advanced one, to specify the criteria for the end-user goal relaxation, with the constraints that some degree of Nao interaction must be always guaranteed. Our hierarchical ranking of system tasks is fixed as follows in ascending order of importance:

1. *People detection* and *tracking*, which represent the minimal requirement (i.e., Nao must always react even if it cannot recognize the current user's emotion), handled by *VideoManager*.
2. *Vocal analysis* for voice emotion recognition is performed by *VocalEmotionsAgent* (based on Vokaturi SDK).
3. *Image analysis* for:

   - Pose emotion recognition by *PoseEmotionsAgent*
   - Facial emotion recognition by *FacialEmotionsAgent*

In our BlocksBotted Nao, we installed the *VocalEmotionsAgent* onboard and the other ones distributed on other machines. As a consequence:

- If *FacialEmotionsAgent* is not available, BlocksBotted Nao can still use the information coming from *PoseEmotionsAgent* and *VocalEmotionsAgent* and can behave as usual by looking at the user and appearing empathic. Its result would be less precise, but the user wouldn't even notice a disservice.

- If *FacialEmotionsAgent* and *PoseEmotionsAgent* agents are both down, BlocksBotted Nao can still use vocal analysis information and can behave as usual by looking at the user and appearing empathic. Its result would be even less precise than the previous case, but the user wouldn't notice a disservice.

The choice of installing *VocalEmotionsAgent* onboard guarantees that, actually, case 1 (minimal requirement) is never reached and empathy is always guaranteed, Anyhow, if we had installed the *VocalEmotionsAgent* on another machine which becomes unavailable too, though BlocksBotted Nao could not detect emotions from any channel, it would still perform people detection and tracking (minimal requirement). The user would notice the lack of empathy while the Internet connection is lost, realizing to be observed without emotional feedback. Basic features would be guaranteed anyway, so BlocksBotted Nao would not be considered as broken or completely useless, even in this worst scenario.

6 Conclusions and Future Work

In this paper, we discussed some features of the BlocksBot project, aimed at realizing an emphatic robot to be applied in human-robot social interaction applications. In particular, we are interested here in discussing architectural and technological choices that impact also on the final usability of the system, for guaranteeing a satisfying human-robot interaction.

The final objective is an engaging user experience, comprising the robot ability of understanding users' unexpressed needs and taking into account their emotions for properly communicating with them. The designer challenge is to overcome the difficulties that many robots face in supporting such complex features in combinations with their basic ones, like standing on their own legs without falling or moving towards the room while avoiding obstacles. We discussed our solution within the BlocksBot project and our framework/architecture relying on our set of robotics tools, for developing multimodal empathic robots without impacting the machines' resources thanks to our hybrid approach distributing agents (and hence the computational charge) over many machines, thus allowing even less powerful robots to provide the most user experience possible (the current version of BlocksBot code is available at the following link: https://github. com/agnsal/BlocksBot).

As to future work, we plan to include additional emotional modes and, consequently, to extend our algorithm for emotion combinations, and to make it even more robust. Another objective is to model in more detail BlocksBotted Nao reactions. Currently, our BlocksBotted Nao can express empathic reactions by its voice only: it says the name of the last detected user's emotion with joy in case of positive emotions, doubt in case of his/her neutral state, or displease in case of a user's negative emotion. In future, BlocksBotted Nao could respond with movements for better showing its reactions and maybe try to use its emotional feedbacks to make the user feel better, for example by properly using proximity, coming near to the user when he/she is in a sociable mood and maintaining distance when he/she seems to prefer a less sociable interaction.

Acknowledgment. This work is partially supported by Reiss Romoli S.R.L.

References

1. Breazeal, C.L.: Toward sociable robots. Robot Autonom Syst. **42**(3–4), 167–175 (2003)
2. Burgos, F.C., Manso, L.J., Trujillo, P.N.: A novel multimodal emotion recognition approach for affective human robot interaction. In: Proceedings of Workshop on Multimodal Semantics for Robotic Systems (MuSRobS) IEEE/RSJ International Conference on Intelligent Robots and Systems (2015)
3. Costantini, S., De Gasperis, G., Migliarini, P.: Multi-agent system engineering for emphatic human-robot interaction. In: 2019 IEEE Second International Conference on Artificial Intelligence and Knowledge Engineering (AIKE). pp. 36–42 (2019)
4. Costantini, S., De Gasperis, G., Migliarini, P, Salutari, A.: Proposal of a empathic multi-agent robot design based on theory of mind. In: Proceedings of cAESAR 2020, 1st Workshop on Workshop on Adapted intEraction with SociAl Robots (2020)
5. Costantini, S., DeGasperis, G., Pitoni, V., Salutari, A.: DALI: a multi agent system framework for the web, cognitive robotic and complex event processing. In: Proceedings of Joint 18th Italian Conference on Theoretical Computer Science and the 32nd Italian Conference on Computational Logic, ICTCS 2017 and CILC 2017, vol. 1949, pp. 286–300, (2017).
6. Di Mascio, T., Tarantino, L., De Gasperis, G.: If usability evaluation and software performance evaluation shook their hands: a perspective. In: Abrahamsson, Pekka, Corral, Luis, Oivo, Markku, Russo, Barbara (eds.) PROFES 2015. LNCS, vol. 9459, pp. 479–489. Springer, Cham (2015). https://doi.org/10.1007/978-3-319-26844-6_35
7. Di Mascio, T., Tarantino, L., Vittorini, P., Caputo, M.: Design choices: affected by user feedback? affected by system performances? Lessons learned from the TERENCE project. In: Proceedings of 10th Biannual Conference on Italian SIGCHI Chapter (CHItaly2013). ACM New York (2013)
8. D'mello, S.K., Kory, J.: A review and meta-analysis of multimodal affect detection systems. ACM Comput. Surv. **47**(3), 1–36 (2015)
9. Ekman, P.: Universal facial expressions of emotion. California Mental Health Res. Digest **8**(4), 151–158 (1970)
10. Fernaeus, Y., Ljungblad, S., Jacobsson, M., Taylor, A.: Where third wave HCI meets HRI: report from a workshop on user-centred design of robots. In: 2009 4th ACM/IEEE International Conference on Human-Robot Interaction (HRI), pp. 293–294 (2009)
11. Forlizzi, J., DiSalvo, C.: Service robots in the domestic environment: a study of the roomba vacuum in the home. In: Proceedings of the 1st ACM SIGCHI/SIGART Conference on Human-Robot Interaction. HRI 2006, New York, pp. 258–256. ACM (2006)
12. Goodrich, M.A., Schultz, A.C.: Human-robot interaction: a survey. Found. Trends Hum.-Comput. Interact. **1**(3), 203–275 (2007)
13. Kiesler, S., Hinds, P.: Introduction to this special issue on human-robot interaction. Human Comput Interact **19**(1/2), 1–8 (2004)
14. Norman, D.A.: Emotional Design: Why We Love (or hate) Everyday Things. Basic Books, New York (2004)
15. Picard, R.: Toward computers that recognize and respond to user emotion. IBM Syst. J. **39**(3&4), 705–719 (2000)
16. Politou, E., Alepis, E., Patsakis, C.: A survey on mobile affective computing. Comput. Sci. Rev. **25**, 79–100 (2017)
17. Poria, S., Cambria, E., Bajpai, R., Hussain, A.: A review of affective computing: From unimodal analysis to multimodal fusion. Inf. Fus. **37**, 98–125 (2017)
18. Salovey, P., Mayer, J.D.: Emotional intelligence. Imagination, Cognit. Person. **9**(3), 185–211 (2000)

19. Sheridan, T.B.: Human–robot interaction: status and challenges. Hum. Factors **58**(4), 525–532 (2016)
20. Sheridan, T.B., Verplank, W.L.: Human and computer control of undersea teleoperators. Man-Machine Systems Laboratory report, Massachusetts Institute of Technology, Cambridge (1978)
21. Young, J., et al.: Evaluating human-robot interaction: focusing on the holistic interaction experience. I. J. Social Robotics **3**, 53–67 (2011)

User-Centered Robots for Municipal Services: What Do Customers and Service Experts Expect from Robots in Municipal Institutions?

Carolin Straßmann[1,2](✉) ⓘ, Sabrina C. Eimler[1,2]ⓘ, Isabel Peltzer[1,2],
Julia Hermann[1,2]ⓘ, Aysegül Dogangün[1,2]ⓘ, and Simone Roth[1,3]ⓘ

[1] Hochschule Ruhr West University of Applied Sciences, Bottrop, Mülheim, Germany
{carolin.strassmann,sabrina.eimler,julia.hermann,ayseguel.doganguen,
simone.roth}@hs-ruhrwest.de
[2] Institute of Computer Science, Research Institute of Positive Computing,
Bottrop, Germany
[3] Institute of Business Administration, Mülheim an der Ruhr, Germany
https://www.hochschule-ruhr-west.de/

Abstract. The present work uses a user-centered design approach to investigate potential design requirements and user scenarios of social robots in municipal services. Qualitative interviews paired with two interactive workshops compared the expectations of potential costumers with those of administration experts of municipalities. The results indicate mainly similar expectations of the robot's design and functionality, but revealed different perspectives: Customers thought more about specific design characteristics (e.g. the robots body temperature), while administration experts reflected more on service aspects (e.g. adapting the needs of different customers and especially people in need of support or the robustness of the system). Moreover, precise user scenarios that integrate the different ideas and preferences are presented. These can help researchers and practitioners to extract design requirements and application scenarios that are considered by the different stakeholders.

Keywords: Social robots · Municipal service · User-centered design · Mixed-methods

1 Introduction

As part of accelerating digitization processes, robots are likely to play an essential part in future society. Since autonomous and embodied robots often attract the attention of people in public spaces, customer service can highly benefit from the application of robots (Bartneck et al. 2019) [1]. Multiple studies already investigated the application of robots in customer services and public places ([2,3,5,6]). For municipal institutions, service robots are able to close the service gap that emerges from the shortage of skilled workers due to demographic

ⓒ The Author(s), under exclusive license to Springer Nature Switzerland AG 2022
M. Kurosu (Ed.): HCII 2022, LNCS 13303, pp. 639–655, 2022.
https://doi.org/10.1007/978-3-031-05409-9_46

change. Moreover, they might have capabilities to deliver a more user-oriented service (e.g. translation and communication in multiple languages to fulfill the needs of heterogeneous customers). However, recent field studies in public spaces demonstrated that citizens have problems with adopting and accepting service robots: only five percent of the visitors of a Danish city administration center interacted with the robot Pepper [2]. In line with this, new robotic systems with a wide range of functions enter the market on a regular basis, but fail to establish themselves long term (cf. the recent news that production of the Pepper robot has been stopped). This is often not due to a lack of basic functionality or poor design, but rather the absence of established deployment processes considering human diversity in the overall application system. Accordingly, this research paper focuses on a participatory design process for the application of social robots in municipalities. To apply service robots successfully and sustainably, the devices and their aspired applications need to match the preferences and expectations of the users as well as the employees working in the municipal institutions. In order to find meaningful and human-centered uses, the thoughts and feelings of different potential stakeholders have to be considered. However, this is challenging if the preferences of different stakeholder groups (customers and employees) deviate. Since no prior research compared the preferences of different stakeholder groups in regard to service robots in municipal institutions this work contributes insights to the following research questions:

- RQ 1: What are citizens' preferences and expectancies regarding the application of social robots in their municipal institutions?
- RQ 2: What are municipal employees' preferences and expectancies regarding the application of social robots in their work environment?
- RQ 3: How do the preferences and expectancies of customers and service employees align?

To investigate the above-mentioned research questions a qualitative mixed methods approach (semi-structured interviews combined with interactive workshops) was used, which assessed users' and employees' expectations regarding the robot's appearance, behavior, tasks and functions. Figure 1 illustrates the methodological procedure. The practical contribution of this research are stakeholder-centered user scenarios integrating the expectations of different stakeholder groups. From these scenarios researchers and practitioners can derive requirements to embed social robots in municipal institutions.

2   Qualitative Interviews with User Group

As a start, qualitative interviews with potential users were conducted with the goal of revealing their expectations and feelings regarding social robots in municipalities and capturing their habits and routines during visits of municipal institutions. The results were used to create different personas representing a diverse user group in the further scenario building process.

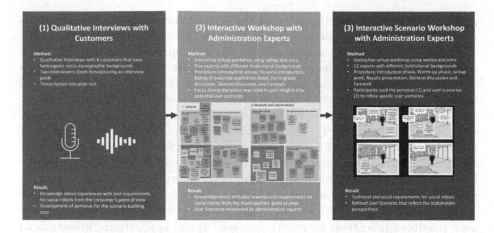

Fig. 1. Overview about the used mixed method approach.

2.1 Sample, Methods and Procedure

Using a qualitative approach, general thoughts and attitudes of potential users regarding the application of social robots in municipal facilities were collected. Eight interviews, were conducted by two female interviewers, covering a variety of diversity facets in terms of age, gender and occupation. 2 males and 6 females with an age range between 18 and 71 years and a mostly higher education level (2 A-level; 5 university degree; 1 lower secondary school degree) participated. 3 participants were employees, 3 were students, 1 person was unemployed and 1 person was a pensioner. While most of the participants live in a large city, 2 people came from a small town. All participants were German native speakers.

To guarantee that all participants give answers to the same questions, an interview guideline was used. Nevertheless, the interviewers adapted the order and exact wording to the participants' answers and needs (e.g. adapt the complexity of the wording or gave more detailed explanation when needed). In the beginning of the interview, the participants provided informed consent and the interviewer explained the project goal. After this short introduction, participants' experiences with the service of the municipalities was queried ("Which municipal facilities do you use?", "In what frequency? Where have you experienced good/bad service?", "How would you describe good/bad service?", "Which aspects in the municipal service require improvements?"). Since these questions are not of special interest to answer the given research questions, they are not included in the present data analysis. However, they were used to create personas used in the final scenario workshop (see Fig. 3). After that, participants outlined their prior experiences with robots ("What experience have you already had with robots?", "What do you imagine social robots to be?", "Are you already familiar with social robots?"), and were asked how they imagine the application of robots in municipal service institutions ("Do you have an idea where a social robot could support municipal facilities?", "How could a robot help you with problems in municipal facilities?"). In the end, the interviewer collected demographic variables of the participants and thanked them for their participation.

To analyze the data, a coding scheme was developed based on the interview guideline as well as on the participants' statements (deductive and inductive data analysis [4]). Since the goal was to compare the expectations of general users with those of application experts (that were assessed in a subsequent workshop), the coding scheme was adapted to the focus group and interactive workshop (see Chapter 3 and 4). The final coding scheme contained 4 main and 24 sub-categories (see Table 1). Although there was no focus on the desired robot appearance, participants stated several preferences with regard to their expectations of the robot's outer design features (category 1). In addition, participants described how they assume the robot to behave and which design features are important to them with regard to the robot's behavior (category 2). Moreover, possible applications for robots (category 3) and applications, where robots should not be used (category 4), were mentioned.

Table 1. Overview of the final coding scheme for interview and focus group analysis

Main category	Sub-category
1. Appearances variables	Human-likeness
	Robot's feature specification
	Temperature
	Target-group specific design
2. Behavioral variables	Friendly behavior
	Human-like communication
	Pleasant voice
	Emotionless
	Adaptability to customers
	Durability
	Interaction modality
	Different communication channels
	Should learn from experience
3. Application areas and robot's functions	Navigation
	Using different languages/Translation
	Reception
	Administrative tasks
	Information
	Receive complaints from customers
	Support of people with disabilities
4. Areas without robot application	Personal interaction with employees
	Non-tech sawy people
	Areas not under city administration

2.2 Results

The categorization was used to sort and analyze participants' statements. Accordingly, the statements are described along the four main categories in the following chapters. Subcategories are indicated by italics.

Appearance Variables. With regard to the robots' *human-likeness* participants mentioned both extremes of human-likeness: while some participants want the robot "to be as human as possible", others rejected this idea: "I think it would be odd if they looked like humans. I don't know, I don't need that, then I would choose a human." Participants further mentioned different expectations regarding the *robot's feature specifications*. One statement demonstrates that human beauty ideals are also applied to humanoid robots: "Most of the time, people like to have symmetrical facial features and they want beautiful hair too." Others wish for round body features in the robot, since this is perceived as harmless: "Somehow they have something harmless, they are round, round head, so not a square head, but round head." Moreover, the robot's height was mentioned to have an impact on its acceptance : "So maybe I would be a little scared if there was such a huge thing standing in front of me. I don't know, you shouldn't make them taller than 1.75." Based on prior experiences, one participant wished that the robot's body *temperature* gets adjusted, since they "didn't like [...] the coldness of the materials."

Behavioral Variables. Participants stated that a *friendly behavior* is needed for the application of robots: "So not very aggressive, but slowly flowing, friendly, probably." Like for the outer appearance participants disagree upon the *human-likeness of the communication*. On the one hand, participants preferred a human-like voice that they are used to from conversational agents, since this leads to higher identification: "Siri or other smartphone robots. She has a human-like voice, so I think it's easier to identify with" On the other hand, others did not like the fact that robots pretend to be humans by using a human-like behavior: "I think you shouldn't try to make robots [...] like humans, because they aren't" In addition to that, participants see the benefits of a *pleasant voice*: "The voice has to be pleasant. " However, one person also stated that the robot should be *emotionless*: "But I don't need it to, uh, to go the emotional route, I think that's stupid." Moreover, participants stated different expectations about the *interaction modality* of the robot. Given the future application in public, participants liked to have the choice about how the robot interacts with them: "I would like to have the choice of whether he can talk to me or whether that could possibly happen in a different way." Other participants liked to have verbal communication ("So that you can talk to them or give them commands."), but only if they have already addressed the robot ("He should only respond if spoken to."). By saying "Maybe a robot that somehow also interacts through colors or signals." participants indicated that *communication through different communication channels* is suggested to be beneficial. Participants were in disagreement whether the robot should be *mobile* in the municipal administration services or not. And that this "[...] depends on where he's standing. If he was in the entrance area, he should be able to walk." However, others were worried about the navigation function, since they do not want the robot to follow them: "It's already enough for me if people follow me around, haha, please not robots too."

Areas of Application and Robot's Functions. One mentioned task of the robot was the *translation and the usage of different languages*: "For this very reason, I believe that when different nationalities come together or different languages are spoken, such a robot is incredibly helpful." A majority of people placed robots at a *reception* ("Yeah, I'd probably put him at reception.") so that it can give *information* to the customers ("These typical things: Which room do I have to go to? Do I have to draw a number now? And so on and so forth. I definitely see a robot there."). In addition to the information giving robot e.g. at receptions, participants stated that robots could help with *administrative tasks* or even do them for the customers: "That all these bureaucratic management things can be left to a robot." In accordance to this rather unpopular task, one participant mentioned that robots could take *customer complaints*, so that the customers anger does not reach the human employees: "Oh, yes, people also have problems and then have to get rid of their frustration and instead of complaining to the city employees, the robot can take all the anger on itself."

Areas without Robot Application. The majority of the participants agreed that robots should not replace the *personal interaction with employees* and that they would have a bad conscience if humans were to lose their jobs (even if humans are not satisfied with their job): "So if I were to say that the dissatisfied people would then no longer be able to work and their work would be done by robots, I don't think I could reconcile that with my conscience." Accordingly, participants "wouldn't include the personal conversation" in the functionalities and tasks of a robot.

2.3 Interview Outcome: Personas

On the basis of the interviews, four different personas were described , that reflect and combine different expectations, habits and socio-demographic variables of potential users. The personas differed in age, gender, education level, mother tongue and place of residence (urban vs. rural). Additionally, each persona (see Fig. 2) was equipped with a specific habit related to municipal institutions and attitudes towards social robots in municipalities (expressed by quotes that are adapted from the interviewees statements).

3 Interactive Workshop with Service Experts

To complement the user interviews with the perspectives of application experts that aim to provide and implement robots in their work environment, an interactive expert workshop was carried out. The main goal of this workshop was to

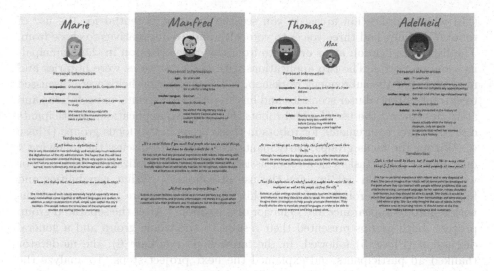

Fig. 2. Personas derived from the interviews.

investigate the expectations and feelings of employees that would use robots in their working routine and find out whether they have different ideas of the implementation of social robots in municipalities than the potential clients. Moreover, we derived different user scenarios from the workshops' results which represent tasks and situations in which social robots could potentially assist in the future.

3.1 Sample, Methods and Procedure

Five experts (3 male and 2 female) that work in the same municipality in the Ruhr area (Western Germany) participated in this workshop. Their fields of expertise include the following: (a) Department of Digitization and "Smart City", (b) all administration and customer related processes in the library, (c) media education modules for different user groups and (d) development and maintenance of an online service portal.

The workshop was moderated and guided by four researchers. Due to the Covid-19 pandemic we conducted the interactive workshop online using Cisco Webex . In addition to the Webex meeting, the collaborative whiteboard Miro was used to sort and capture the thoughts and discussion statements of the participants. The workshop contained 6 phases: (Phase 1) Introduction phase, (Phase 2) Personal introduction, (Phase 3) Rating of potential application fields, (Phase 4) Focus group discussion, (Phase 5) General discussion, and (Phase 6) Farewell. After a short welcoming phase, participants gave informed consent, received an introduction of the overall project goals (Phase 1) and the participants and experimenter introduced themselves (Phase 2). The main workshop part contained a short warm-up phase (Phase 3) in which the participants were asked to indicate for which application field they would value the usage of robots

("In which application areas do you see the greatest potential for the use of robots?"). They had three voices to vote with and 16 alternatives to chose from. The listed application areas originate from the categorization in the municipality's online portal. The two applications with the most votes were libraries and museums. For the subsequent workshop, these application fields were discussed to extract potential user scenarios and investigate participants' expectations and attitudes toward the use of social robots. For the two applications, participants discussed the requirements for robots in these areas in two focus groups (Phase 4). Within the focus groups, participants were asked to discuss the following 4 questions: "What tasks can a robot assist with in this application field?", "For which tasks do you not imagine the use of robots?", "What capabilities and functions does the robot perform in this area?", "What are your expectations with regard to appearance and behavior of the robot?" After the separated group process, both groups presented their results to the whole group and a general discussion (Phase 5) followed. In the farewell part (Phase 6), the moderator thanked all participants and explained the next project steps. To analyze the workshop data, the same coding scheme as the one used for the interview analysis was applied (see Table 1).

3.2   Results

Rating of Potential Application Fields. Since each participant had the chance to give 3 votes, over all 15 votes are possible for the following 16 different application fields: The two applications with the most votes are libraries (n = 4) and museums (n = 2). Job center, foreigner department, vehicle registration and driving license authority, youth welfare office, service center, health office, adult education center, park as well as schools and day-care center received one vote each. No participant voted for the registry office, department for social and habitation issues, public order office, tax office and town hall. Since no application area stands out with a high number of votes and the votes were pretty equally spread, this could indicate that robots are usable for nearly all application fields in the municipal service. For the subsequent workshop, the application fields library and museum were discussed. As only 15 votes in total were possible, the above listed votes do only represent a prioritization and do not mean that application fields with no votes could not benefit from the usage of social robots.

Appearance Variables. Just as the interviewees, participants of the focus groups differed in their preference for the robot's *human-likeness*. Some stated that a humanoid robot like Pepper would work well ("Pepper that looks at you, that for example works for me."), but at the same time they wished that the robot "still has to be recognizable as a robot". In contrast to the interviewees, participants of the focus group did not express expectations about *robot's feature specifications* or *temperature*. However, participants stated that the appearance of the robot needs to match the *needs of the target-group*: "suitable to the target group: different for children than for the elderly". Relating to this, it was stated that the "robot adapts to humans and not the other way around".

Behavioral Variables. Similar to the interviewees, participants desire *friendly behavior* and a *pleasant voice*. Moreover, they were more sure than the interviewees that the *communication has to be human-like* and wished for "a human touch". Participants also mentioned that the robot should *communicate through different communication channels*. But while the interviewees refereed to modalities, like light and sound, participants stated more human-like communication channels and desired for nonverbal behavior: "We have agreed on verbal communication, supported by non-verbal communication." Unlike the interviewees, the workshop participants did not mention any preferences with regard to the robot's *interaction modality* and *mobility* or if they expect the robot to be *emotionless*. However, the administration experts focused more on technical features of the robot that the interviewees did not mention. They were worried about the *durability* of the robot and stated that "he should be robust against application errors". Moreover, they desired a *learning system* that "should be able to learn from experiences". In addition to that, participants desire an *adaptability to customers'* needs: "That I can say 'I need the font larger.' or 'Please speak louder.'"

Areas of Application and Robot's Functions. The administration experts mostly agreed with the imagined functions of the customers regarding *translation functions*, using robots at the *reception*, for *information* purposes and executing *administrative tasks*. While one interviewee liked the idea that robots take *customer complaints*, the experts did not want the customers to be left alone with the robot for problems and complaints: "So you don't have the feeling that you can only speak to a machine." In addition, participants stated that a *navigation* function is useful: "That he can help guide you. That he can drive around and you can follow him around." Moreover, participants saw the potential of robots *assisting people in need of support* : "That he is there to support you and you don't have the feeling that you have to ask for help.".

Areas without Robot Application. Like the customers, participants agreed that the *personal interaction with employees* is still necessary and that robots can only assist but not replace the human employees: "Human contact must also be available." In addition, the application of robots is not possible in municipal institutions for *areas that are not under city administration* e.g. bistros in museums: "We quickly discarded that because it is rented out externally and there are external providers working there." Moreover, participants were worried about *people with low technology affinity*: "People who don't know how to use the technology, you still need people for that."

3.3 Workshop Outcome: User Scenarios

In addition to the analysis of the employees' preferences and expectations of social robots in municipalities, we looked at the potential user scenarios that arose during the workshop. Based on these results, we constructed eight different scenarios describing use cases of robots in municipal institutions mentioned by the workshop participants:

- 1: Imagine you are new in town and go to the public library for the first time. You run to the reception desk to register as a new customer.
- 2: You are in the mood for a new book, but you are not sure which one to borrow and you are overwhelmed by what is available.
- 3: Imagine you go to the public library with your child. You go to the fantasy section. Your child walks into the children's section, picks out a book, and waits to be read to.
- 4: You are in the museum and want to book a guided tour in your native language. You wonder when the next guided tour is bookable for you.
- 5: You would like to borrow your city's anniversary publication, but you do not know where this department is located. The employees are nowhere to be seen.
- 6: Imagine you are in a new museum. It is very large, with many different areas and you do not know your way around. You are looking for the current exhibition on the historical history of the city.
- 7: You visit the Natural History Museum together with your child and stand in front of an exhibit. You and your child would like to learn more about the exhibit.
- 8: There is another special exhibition in the municipal museum, for which you need an additional ticket. You want to buy this ticket at the entrance of the special exhibition.

The next step was a refinement of the user scenarios and collection of specific requirements for social robots within the different user scenarios. In accordance with these insights and specific requirements, researchers and institutions are able to choose the robots that suit the application and stakeholder needs the most. This helps to integrate social robots better in the socio-technological system of the institutions and forms a foundation for a sustainable application and use. The refinement was done in a second interactive expert workshop with the goal of exctracting more detailed user scenarios.

4 Interactive Scenario Refinement Workshop with Different Municipalities

To combine the results of the first interactive workshop with service experts with the results of the user interviews and to derive application scenarios for social robots in municipal facilities, a second interactive workshop was organized. The results of the interviews and the first workshop directly flowed into the structure and method of the workshop, since the described personas and user scenarios were used.

4.1   Sample, Methods and Procedure

In total, 12 experts that work in different municipalities in the Ruhr area participated in the second workshop. The workshop was again moderated and guided by four researchers and held online using Cisco Webex in combination with a collaborative Miro board. The workshop contained 6 phases: (Phase 1) Introduction phase, (Phase 2) Warm-up phase, (Phase 3) Group work, (Phase 4) Results presentation, (Phase 5) General discussion and (Phase 7) Farewell. After a short introduction given by the experimenters (Phase 1), the participants were asked to showcase in which city they were working on a map and what their field of expertise was (Phase 2). The listed working areas included (a) digitization (n = 5), libraries (n = 3), cultural institutions (n = 0) and others (n = 1). The main workshop part involved group work (Phase 3), where participants discussed the user scenarios in accordance to the personas. The participants were divided into 3 groups consisting of 4 to 5 people including one moderator from the research team per group. Based on the user interviews and the first workshop with the service experts, each group was given one persona and two brief scenarios. Please see Fig. 3 for the given combinations of personas and scenarios. Since the overall goal of this workshop was to specify and refine the user scenarios, participants were asked to build a story board of the interaction between the user (given persona) and the robot. On the Miro board participants found a film strip and several items (differently shaped robots, persons, speech and thought-bubbles and sticky-notes to capture their thoughts and ideas for the given interaction (see Fig. 3). By filling in this filmstrip and shaping a specific situation, participants further discussed their expectancies and preferences of how the robot should look and behave. This was guided by the moderators from the research team in order to assess participants' thoughts holistically. After the separated group process, each group presented their discussion results to the whole group and a general discussion (Phase 5) followed. In the farewell part (Phase 6), the experimenters thanked the participants and explained the next project steps.

4.2   Results

Appearance Variables. Just as the interviewees and the participants of the focus group, participants of this workshop differed in their preference for the robot's *human-likeness*. Some stated that they would like the robot to be more human-like ("I would say more human like") while some preferred "a tiny robot which would fit into a handbag and doesn't look human at all". Like the participants of the focus group, none had any expectations about the robot's *feature specifications* or *temperature*. However, participants of this workshop also stated that the appearance of the robot needs to match the *needs of the target-group* ("There have to be adjustments for children or a mixed audience."). Moreover, they relied on the given expertise of the human-robot-interaction researchers, since they expressed that there certainly will be scientific knowledge about how a robot should be designed in accordance with specific target-groups. Overall,

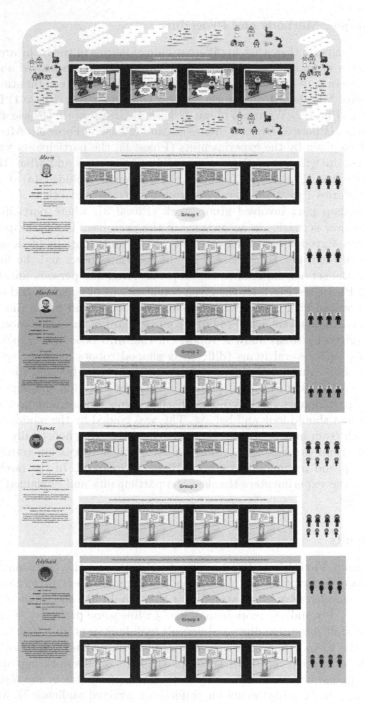

Fig. 3. Template of the Miro board, in which participants refined their ideas of the user scenarios. Each group discussed two used scenarios from the first workshop in relation to one of the four personas.

they preferred a friendly appearance like Pepper: "Friendly appearance. That's what Pepper also has." Regarding this, participants stated that "round features made them look friendly".

Behavioral Variables. Similar to the interviewees and the participants of the focus group, participants preferred a *friendly behavior* and *calm pleasant voice*. Regarding this, they stated that users should be able to choose different voices ("They should also be able to choose if they want to have a deep male voice."). While talking about libraries, a participant desired the *adaptability to customers* and suggested "setting up user-oriented accounts". Participants also stated that the robot should communicate through different *communication channels*: "You have to strive for an audio-visual mix." Regarding the interaction between user and robot the participants differed in their preference. While some preferred the robot "to actively address the user", others wanted the robot to wait until spoken to ("You have to walk up to him to interact with him."). Regarding the *robot's mobility* they all stated that the robot should be able to move around these large places: "The museum is spacious, so the robot has to be mobile." Similar to the participants of the focus group, they desired a *learning system* that "should be able to learn from interaction and communication".

Areas of Application and Robot's Functions. The experts mostly agreed with the imagined functions of the customers and the focus group regarding *translation functions*, using robots at the *reception*, for information purposes and to executing *administrative tasks*. Unlike the participants of the focus group, participants of this workshop stated that the robot should be able to *navigate* customers around the museum and function as a moderator regarding the exhibits ("Which leads the two through the museum, but the exhibits themselves provide other means of communication or information."). While participants of the focus group saw the potential that robots could *support and help people with disabilities*, the experts in this workshop did not state that. However, they preferred the robot "to monitor the health status of the elderly".

Areas without Robot Application. In comparison to the interviewees and the participants of the focus group, the experts of this workshop did not state any areas where they thought a robot application would be impossible. This might be due to the fact that participants of this workshop discussed more concrete user scenarios, which have already been created by the assumptions of experts in the application field.

4.3   Refined User Scenarios

Besides the above coded statements that reflect participants expectations, we extracted their imagined interaction between the customers and the robot. In order to do so, the created filmstrips (see Fig. 4) and related group presentations were structured and two detailed user scenarios haven been written:

Fig. 4. Original results from the group-discussions contributed by the municipalities' experts on the collaborative Miro board. The workshop language was German.

Scenario 1: "Marie (28 years old) moved from China to Dortmund for her studies a year ago. She visited the library regularly in her home country. Now she also wants to be registered in the Dortmund City Library. When she enters the library, she sees a robot at the reception. Since she is very open to new technology, she approaches him directly (arrival phase). He greets her by saying: 'Welcome to the Dortmund City Library. How can I help you? You are welcome to ask me questions.' in German (first contact). Marie has been living in Germany for only a year and is still very unsure about communicating in German. That's why she answers the robot in a mix of English, German and Chinese: 'Do you speak English? Wo finde ich Deutschkurse? ('Where can I find German courses?' in German) Wǒ zài nǎlǐ kěyǐ zhǎodào yǒuguān réngōng zhìnéng de shūjí? ('Where can I find books about artificial intelligence?' in Chinese)?' Thanks to its multilingual function, he understands Marie without any problems and shows her the way to the books she wants on the tablet. 'Shall I accompany you to the shelves?' he asks here in Chinese. Marie politely declines and sets off to find the books. After finding them, she goes back to the robot to borrow them (loyalty phase). 'Do you have a library card already?' he asks in Chinese, since he has recognized Marie. Since it is Marie's first visit to the library, she does not have a library card yet. 'That's not a problem. Creating a library card is very easy and quick.' Marie then enters her personal details on the robot's screen and selects PayPal as her payment method. The robot then prints out her new library card directly. "To borrow the books, please hold your library card in front of the scanner until you hear the beep." Marie holds her library card in front of the scanner. "Thank you. Now please hold your books in front of the scanner one after the other until you hear the beep." Marie then holds her books in front of the scanner one after the other. "Thank you. Your books are on loan until July 28, 2021. Is there anything else I can do for you?" Marie declines (completion of the task), says goodbye and goes home satisfied.

Scenario 2: "Thomas (41 years old) regularly goes to the Duisburg City Library with his son Max (7 years old). He has heard that the library is now using various robots and is curious, but at the same time skeptical as to whether they are sufficiently developed to be able to provide real assistance. Thomas has made an appointment in advance via the library's homepage with one of the reading robots that Max had chosen (arrival). These robots are specially designed for children: they are at children's eye level, friendly and colorful in the form of a rag doll. When they enter the library, one of the reading robots comes straight up to them and speaks to the son in a child-friendly voice and language: 'Hello Max, it's nice to have you here and that we're spending time together today.' (first contact). 'Hello Robbie, I'm looking forward to it.' Max replies. 'Let's go and choose a book, I have an idea what you might like.' says Robbie to Max. He already knows which books Max has read so far and, based on these, he selects a book to read. Together, the two go to the children's corner, where there is also a human supervisor who monitors the children's interaction with the robots. Thomas then says goodbye and goes to the department with the cookbooks. He is always in touch with Robbie via app and is notified if something should happen. After an interesting afternoon (completed tasks) in the library, Thomas and Max say goodbye to Robbie and arrange the next reading date at home (loyalty)."

5 Final Discussion

In times where smart cities and digitized municipalities are the main focus of most governments, have a high potential to enhance city administrations and municipal institutions. In this work we used a qualitative approach to detect the expectancies of customers and administration experts and to aim for a user-and-employee-centered application of robots. In our approach we combined qualitative interviews with potential customers of municipal institutions and two interactive workshops with administration experts from different municipalities. The results have been coded along four main categories: robot appearance, robot behavior, areas of application and robot's function and areas without possible robot application.

While the interviewees were more focused on the appearance of the robot and its social behavior (RQ 1), the participants in the workshops supplemented more technical (e.g. robustness or self-learning system) as well as ethical and service-oriented components (e.g. adapting to the users' needs, accessibility for several groups)(RQ 2). Interviewees mentioned thoughts that have been coded with 5 sub-categories, which have not been used in the workshops: the robot's feature specifications, temperature of the robot, an emotionless behavior of the robot and different interaction modalities (speech, text or graphical user interface). These statements and sub-categories mainly represent the perspective the interviewees had on the robot and the interaction with it. They envisioned themselves using the robot and therefore thought about more specific things like touching it (which comes along with the robot's body temperature) or using it in front of other customers (which requires an interaction modality that can also guarantee privacy).

In return, administration experts in the workshops brought up 7 subcategories that differ from the customers' statements in the interviews: targetgroup specific design, adaptability to customers, robustness of the robot, learning system, assistance of people in need of support and that robots can not be applied in areas that are not under city administration as well as for people with low technological affinity. Here, the administration experts were more aware of service and application-oriented components. Their perspective was more holistic and less concentrated onto design details. Participants in the workshops were mainly leaders of municipal institutions, they are decision makers deciding about the application of robots in municipalities. However, they are probably not the ones, who will work with the robots on a daily basis. This is reflected by the perspective they contributed within the workshops. Therefore, future research needs to focus even more on the individuals that will do the daily work and interact with the robots on an employee level.

The results overall demonstrated that customers and administrative experts have mostly similar imaginations on how robots should be designed and applied (RQ 3). In 10 sub-categories customers (based on the interviews) and administration experts (based on both workshops) mentioned similar aspects: human-likeness of the robot, friendly behavior, human-like communication, pleasant voice, using multiple communication styles (verbal and nonverbal), using robots for translation, at the reception, for information and administrative task and that robots should not replace the personal interaction with employees. Customers and administration experts both mentioned the robot's mobility, but disagreed how this should look like. While people in the interviews stated that the robot should not follow them and move around, the experts in the workshop imagined the robot to guide people and move around in the municipal institutions. Besides this exception, all expectancies and preferences related to the robots' design and application are well compatible and often match existing research findings. For example, the debate about the robot's human-likeness and perceived anthropomorphism, is also reflected by state-of-the-art research. A meta-analysis indicates relevant moderators, such as the field of application, the task relevance or exposure of the robot [7]. In addition, preferences with regard to appearance are target-group related [8], which has also been discussed by the workshop participants.

The results demonstrate that both stakeholder groups have different perspectives, but overall envision similar design and application features. However, the theoretical implications for robot design characteristics are rather limited, since most of the mentioned characteristics have already been discussed in the research community. The workshop participants highlighted this even in their statements. During the discussion they strongly referred to the researchers and asked for existing scientific knowledge. Accordingly, they did not state their individual preferences and feelings (as they might not know how they would design the robot), but relied on experts. This might be an illustration of weakness of the user-centered approach, especially in areas where users only have scarce or no experience at all with the system that is to be designed. The administration experts gave their responsibility and the potential to decide about the future of their work environment to researchers that are not familiar with the intended application scenarios. When robots are embedded into work environments, researchers and practitioners need to carefully empower the stakeholders to make their own informed decisions. This requires methods enabling users to understand potential functionalities of existing systems and state of the art research outcomes in the field of human-robot-interaction. This could give them the feeling of self-efficacy and knowledge to take such design and application decisions. Future steps in the presented project are methods that enable stakeholders even more, e.g. integrate citizen scientists into the design process or build transparency about the current state-of-the-art using interactive science communication events.

Acknowledgements. The presented work was supported by the RuhrBotS project (16SV8589) funded by the Federal Ministry of Education and Research Germany. The authors thank all participants of the interviews and workshops as well as institutions under city administration making this research possible. Additional thanks go to Pasquale Hinrichs, Anna-Marie Schweizer, Lara Oldach und Noémi Tschiesche for comments on the manuscript. Moreover, we thank Elias Thiele for his assistance with the transcripts and coding. Presentation of this work is funded by the initiative for quality improvement in teaching of the Institute of Computer Science.

References

1. Bartneck, C., Belpaeme, T., Eyssel, F., Kanda, T., Keijsers, M., Šabanovic, S.: Mensch-roboter-interaktion. Hanser, Eine Einführung, München (2020)
2. Hansen, S.T., Hansen, K.D.: What's a robot doing in the citizen service centre? In: Companion of the 2021 ACM/IEEE International Conference on Human-Robot Interaction, pp. 677–679 (2021)
3. Kaipainen, K., Ahtinen, A., Hiltunen, A.: Nice surprise, more present than a machine: experiences evoked by a social robot for guidance and edutainment at a city service point. In: Proceedings of the 22nd International Academic Mindtrek Conference, pp. 163–171 (2018)
4. Mey, G., Mruck, K.: Handbuch qualitative Forschung in der Psychologie. Springer (2010). https://doi.org/10.1007/978-3-531-92052-8
5. Mubin, O., Kharub, I., Khan, A.: Pepper in the library" students' first impressions. In: Extended Abstracts of the 2020 CHI Conference on Human Factors in Computing Systems, pp. 1–9 (2020)
6. Pitsch, K., Kuzuoka, H., Suzuki, Y., Sussenbach, L., Luff, P., Heath, C.: "The first five seconds": contingent stepwise entry into an interaction as a means to secure sustained engagement in HRI. In: RO-MAN 2009-The 18th IEEE International Symposium on Robot and Human Interactive Communication, pp. 985–991. IEEE (2009)
7. Roesler, E., Manzey, D., Onnasch, L.: A meta-analysis on the effectiveness of anthropomorphism in human-robot interaction. Sci. Robot. 6(58), eabj5425 (2021)
8. Straßmann, C., Krämer, N.C.: A two-study approach to explore the effect of user characteristics on users' perception and evaluation of a virtual assistant's appearance. Multimodal Technol. Interact. 2(4), 66 (2018)

Designing Social Interactions for Learning Personalized Knowledge in Service Robots

Shengchen Zhang and Xiaohua Sun[✉]

College of Design and Innovation, Tongji University, Shanghai, China
{shengchenzhang,xsun}@tongji.edu.cn

Abstract. Service robots are required to effectively gather and utilize personalized knowledge in a working environment, especially through social interaction with their users. Existing works have shown the significant influence of interaction design on the efficiency, accuracy, and user experience of learning interactions. Designing social interaction for learning personalized knowledge poses new challenges for HRI designers, which signifies a need for designerly knowledge in the form of tools, methods, and effective patterns. In this paper, we present a toolkit to help the design of social interaction with service robots for the learning of personalized knowledge, by informing designers of key challenges and potentially applicable patterns to help ideation. We discuss five key challenges for interactively learning personalized knowledge based on existing literature, and propose ten interaction design patterns that can be employed to help the ideation. We then present a preliminary evaluation of the toolkit through workshop sessions with HRI designers. Questionnaires and semi-structured interviews were used to gather feedback from the participants. The results show the ability of the toolkit for aiding ideation and its potential for flexible ways of use, and point towards future directions to improve and expand the toolkit.

Keywords: Social human-robot interaction · Design heuristics · Design toolkit · Robot knowledge

1 Introduction

As services robots are increasingly deployed into the real world, they are envisioned to complete complex tasks based on high-level goals and interact with users in an easily-understandable way [11]. Moreover, emphasis is put on the ability to adapt to user traits and preferences in order to provide better collaboration, personalized service, and robust interactions [21]. This requires robots to effectively gather and utilize personalized knowledge about the user and related objects, places, and events in the robot's working environment [9, 23]. Such knowledge is specific to the robot's environment and cannot be observed before deployment. Therefore, many researchers have proposed methods for robots to

M. Kurosu (Ed.): HCII 2022, LNCS 13303, pp. 656–671, 2022.
https://doi.org/10.1007/978-3-031-05409-9_47

learn the knowledge through the detection of human activity, social cues, and many more [21], and by interacting with humans to acquire the knowledge that is needed [6]. To this end, many methods of knowledge acquisition using social interaction have been proposed as well, such as learning the preferred way of executing a task through dialogue [17], or interactively clarifying an unknown reference to an item [18]. Current research has also explored the effect of different manners of interaction on robot learning. It has been shown that the design of a robot's questions can significantly impact the quality of data gathered [20], and different interaction modes can affect user perception of the robot as well as learning accuracy [2].

However, less emphasis is put on the "designerly" aspects, especially tools and methods to aid the design of personalized knowledge learning interactions under concrete service scenarios. It will be especially challenging for professional interaction designers and engineers that create and implement robot services for specific working environments and tasks. They are tasked with designing interactions that are grounded in the service context, can handle complex situations in real service scenarios, and often for repeated or long-term interaction. This requires the design to account for practical issues such as user attitude towards a learning robot and the effects that the learning interaction may have on user response and data quality. While existing works each provided general guidance, HRI designers can greatly benefit from a curated set of patterns and tools to help the identification of potential challenges and the ideation of suitable interaction design.

In this paper, we present a toolkit to help the design of social interaction with a service robots for the learning of personalized knowledge. We identify five key challenges for interactively learning personalized knowledge based on existing literature, and discuss the constraints and opportunities they impose on the design of the learning interaction. We then propose ten interaction design patterns that can be employed to help the ideation of social interaction for service robots to learn the personalized knowledge of users. The challenges and patterns are presented as a design toolkit in the form of cards. The toolkit is evaluated by organizing workshop sessions, in which HRI researchers and participants with HRI design experience used our tools to improve an existing interaction flow of a service robot. We conducted semi-structured interviews after each workshop session with a focus to evaluate the tool's *ease of understanding*, *informativeness*, *usefulness*, and *ease of incorporating into existing designs*, as well as to collect suggestions of improvement from our participants.

Our contributions are as follows:

- We identified five challenges for HRI designers when designing social interactions for learning personalized knowledge under a concrete service context.
- We proposed ten interaction design patterns to address these challenges that support the ideation and design of social HRI.
- We developed a design toolkit based on the challenges and patterns, and presented an evaluation of the toolkit through workshop sessions with HRI designers.

2 Related Works

2.1 Tools and Patterns for HRI Design

Löwgren [16] identified heuristics, design tools and methods, and patterns as some of the important types of intermediate-level knowledge in the field of human-computer interaction. Lupetti et al. [15] argued similarly for HRI, pointing out the importance of designerly knowledge in HRI, and calling for investigations into the conceptual implication of HRI research artifacts.

Much research into HRI design has taken the form of collections of concepts, ideas, or patterns. Alves-Oliveira et al. [1] developed a collection of metaphors for the roles of a robot to provide aid in examining new human-robot relationships. Kang et al. developed a toolkit in the form of cards to help design social human-robot interaction. Kahn et al. [10] introduced the concept of design patterns, and proposed eight HRI patterns that can be employed to enhance robot sociality. Sauppé and Mutlu [22] derived interaction patterns from human-human dyadic interaction and developed a prototyping tool to aid the application of these patterns in HRI design. Our previous work [23] on designing robot interfaces to communicate its knowledge has also taken the form of a collection of patterns.

In line with previous works, this paper adds to the designerly HRI literature by presenting a toolkit containing interaction patterns for learning personalized knowledge.

2.2 Robot Learning Through Social Interaction

Learning through social interaction has been proposed as a way to utilize the knowledge of humans to improve robot capabilities. Many works examined the design and effects of socially-guided learning in service robots. Lockerd and Breazeal [13] proposed the concept of socially-guided machine learning—learning tasks and skills from end-users through social interaction. Many works proposed effective methods for learning through social interaction. Chao et al. [4] developed a system that involves human teachers through active learning. Gervasio et al. [8] proposed a method to automatically learns question-asking strategies.

Researchers have also studied the effect of different interaction modes on learning efficiency. Rosenthal et al. [20] studied how the design of a robot's questions influences the quality of data gathered. Cakmak et al. [2] showed how different interaction modes can affect user perception of the robot as well as learning accuracy. Cakmak and Thomaz [3] also showed the varying efficiency of different question-asking modes.

Existing research has shown that learning through social interaction could be an effective method to account for complex tasks in service scenarios, and pointed out that the manner of interaction has a significant impact on learning accuracy, efficiency, and user perception. Our toolkit is prompted by these insights to help HRI designers take into account these factors.

2.3   Personalized Knowledge in Service Robots

It has been recognized that personalized knowledge can help enable adaptive robotic services. Olivares-Alarcos et al. provided an overview of using ontology to represent and utilize knowledge in robots [19]. Our previous work [23] further identified the types of knowledge related to specific service situations for service robots, including objects, environment, users, actions, and context.

Many methods have been proposed to learn personalized knowledge interactively. Rossi et al. [21] provided a survey of methods for user profiling, which includes interactive methods to learn user-related knowledge. Previous research has also developed designing interfaces to help domain experts directly view and manipulate the knowledge graph in a robot in order to understand and operate it [12]. Researchers looked into developing a set of human-friendly vocabulary to build robot ontology [5], which has the potential to help communicate robot behaviors in interactive knowledge learning.

Our work is informed by the challenges and types of knowledge learning tasks identified by current research. Existing cases also provide material for analysis that helps produce the patterns in our toolkit.

3   Design Toolkit

The proposed toolkit consists of two set of cards: *challenges* and *patterns*, as shown in Fig. 1 and 2. The content of the cards are detailed in the sections that follow, along with a discussion of the curated literature and cases that informed its inclusion.

Fig. 1. The *challenges* cards. Each card consists of a title naming the challenge, and a short description providing the reasoning and issues.

The *challenges* set consists of five cards that describe the issues that needs to be taken into consideration when designing HRI that utilize or are aimed at learning personalized knowledge. These challenges stem from the intrinsic properties of personalized knowledge (*Open World*), the users of the service robot (*User Acceptance* and *Multiple Parties*), as well as the design task itself (*Question Effectiveness* and *Data Quality*).

The *patterns* set consists of ten cards containing potentially applicable patterns that serves as prompts for ideation. Each of the cards corresponds to a

Fig. 2. The *patterns* cards. Each card consists of a title and a short prompt in the form of a question, followed by a example of applying the patterns under a concrete service scenario. The cards are color-coded to depict their connection to the challenges.

certain challenge in the *challenges* set, indicating the challenge it could be user to address.

3.1   Open World

The first challenge stems from the property of personalized knowledge. In contrast with commonsense knowledge, personalized knowledge could often be incomplete or outdated. When making use of personalized knowledge, it should not be assumed to be complete and error-free. For example, the robot should not assume that employees unknown to it do not belong in the office, and objects whose location is unknown could still be present in the current space. This poses a unique challenge for HRI designers to bear in mind when designing interactions that utilize or aim to learn personalized knowledge. The lack of knowledge could be the result of various possibilities, which should be addressed differently to achieve a natural and fluent user experience. Two design patterns are proposed to address this challenge: *just ask* and *socially-assisted robotics*.

Just Ask. This pattern is directly prompted by works related to active learning through social interaction, where robots ask verbal questions to learn perception and task skills [2,3]. The designer is prompted to add an interaction step to directly query the user when there could be a lack of personalized knowledge. An example of this solution could be that when encountering an unidentifiable user, rather than assuming it is a first-time encounter, the robot could apologize for not recognizing the user, and then ask for their identity.

Socially-Assisted Robotics. The name is a twist on the name of the field socially-assistive robotics, which develops social robots to assist humans. The core idea of this pattern, in contrast, is to enable users to help the robot through social interaction. This pattern is inspired by relevant discussions in HRI around robots as citizens within the society. Lupetti and Giaccardi [14] proposed a concept named "the handleable robot", where they address the issue of navigating complex outdoor intersections by turning to the robot's shared membership in the community and asking for help from nearby pedestrians. The designer is prompted to take advantage of the fact that users could be considered domain experts on personalized knowledge, and design a mechanism to let other users provide the missing information or help the robot.

3.2   User Acceptance

The second challenge stems from the attitude of the users. In the context of a service robot, the experience and acceptance of the user are considered vital to the quality of the service. This has led to two issues that require balancing from the designer.

The first issue concerns utility, specifically utility to the robot versus utility to the user. For a service robot, it is usually expected to provide a certain utility to the user. However, the utility of personalized knowledge learning is mainly to the robot, and may only enhance the service quality of the robot in the long run, which might not be obvious to especially non-expert users. This could make the user reluctant to participate in teaching the robot. Moreover, in long-term interaction, repetitive asking could significantly impact user experience. This challenges HRI designers to produce more engaging learning interactions, or try to make the utility of robot learning more obvious.

The second issue concerns automation versus user control. Chao et al. investigated the user's attitude towards an active learning robot and found that "balance of control between the robot and the human is a parameter to tune carefully when designing an interaction", as the completely robot-initiated active learning could deprive the user's sense of control in the learning process [4]. This challenges HRI designer to devise more flexible learning interactions that enable the user to shape the robot learning process. Two design patterns are proposed to address this challenge: *back-up plans* and *it's a feature!*

Back-Up Plans. Fong et al. [7] showed that users may disengage the robot when it repeatedly asks the same question. In response, they suggested that contextual dialogue management could be a solution. In this card, the designer is prompted to consider whether a question is asked differently according to context. An example would be that the robot can record the times it has asked a question to a user. When a question has to be asked a second time, the robot could express awareness of the situation, such as by apologizing for repeated asking.

It's a Feature!. This pattern is in direct response to the issue of utility to the user. The designer is prompted to try turning a learning interaction into something that could also provide utility to the user. The example given is that at environments like offices and classrooms, new users are introduced periodically. While learning faces by interacting with new users one-by-one would be inefficient and provide little utility to the users, a robot could be designed to contain an ice-breaking function, where the robot can help lead an ice-breaking session between the newcomers. During the interaction, the robot can learn the correspondence between names and faces along with the users.

3.3 Multiple Parties

Another challenge posed by users is the presence of multiple interacting parties. There might be multiple users with different intentions trying to interact with the robot at the same time. This, in turn, could lead to mismatches between training data and labels, or cause interruptions in user demonstrations. To address this problem, HRI designers will need to devise effective interaction strategies to manage the situation and recover from unexpected interruptions.

Isolation. A strategy that people often use in group settings is to isolate the person of interest through cues like posture and objects. For example, in group activities and speeches, it is often that the speaker stands up, or holds objects that signify their position. The designer is prompted to let the robot guide the person of interest to do something significantly different than others. The robot could encourage such behavior, in order to separate the speaker from the rest by a distinct posture or human-object relationship.

3.4 Question Effectiveness

The task of designing social interactions for robot learning itself poses challenges to HRI designers as well. The first challenge posed is the effectiveness of asking questions. A direct and common way for robots to learn from users is by asking questions. However, Rosenthal et al. [20] found that if the questions are ill-posed, they may result in erroneous or useless responses. They also found that users might not fully understand the intention of the learning robot due to a lack of context. This highlights the importance of designing effective questions. The following patterns are mainly derived from strategies that are shown effective by Rosenthal et al. [20].

To Err Is Human. The naming suggests that by properly communicating potentially erroneous results to users, the robot could handle errors in recognition more gracefully ("human-ly"). The robot's recognition results are not always accurate, and providing recognition results can help users identify errors and give corrections. For example, when approaching a user, the robot could proactively show the name of the user that is detected, or show the absence of a name in a clear manner.

Describe Uncertainty. The robot could use multiple modalities to describe its uncertainty when asking questions to a user. Describing the uncertainty of the results may help users to recognize potential problems, and may improve the accuracy of their feedback. For example, when referring to an object, person, or location to a user, the robot can use descriptive expressions to convey its confidence, such as "I'm sure that...", "I guess that...", or "it should be..." This could also be color-coded to represent uncertainty.

Provide Context. The robot could use multiple modalities to explain the current context to the user when asking a question. The responses provided by users are not necessarily accurate, and providing more contextual information may help users to provide more accurate responses. For example, when describing an object to the user, the robot can show relevant information such as its last seen location, photos of the object, or similar objects.

3.5   Data Quality

The second challenge posed by the task of designing social interactions for learning is the quality of gathered data. First of all, the quantity of data that can be gathered through interaction is limited. It would be best to gather high-quality data, such as with clear image features and proper labels. This requires guidance on the robot's part, especially for non-expert users. Second, it is necessary to take into account inaccuracies in the robot's perception. Wizard-of-Oz user studies are common in the field of HRI, which does not account for inaccuracies. To achieve more robust interaction, the design should include interaction flows to recover from such errors. Two design patterns are proposed to address this challenge: *hands-on* and *waiting for windfalls*.

Hands-On. It is commonplace in commercial products that a tutorial is presented to the user to guide data collection. An example would be Apple's Face ID, where an interactive animation is used to help users provide a higher quality facial model. The designer is invited to consider whether the robot can guide the user into doing something that better helps the robot learn, and design interactions to guide the user into performing the appropriate actions. For example, the robot could correct the way the user is holding an object, or guide the user into a specific posture.

Waiting for Windfalls. In larger working environments, interaction with users might be scarce due to a low chance of encounter, further making collecting high-quality training data a challenge. The designer is prompted to let the robot utilize its idle time to go and wait for encounters at the most possible location. For example, for an office robot, it could ask for the charging station to be located at the break room, where many people would go and is suitable for social chit-chat.

4   Evaluation of the Design Toolkit

The proposed design tool is evaluated by organizing workshop sessions, in which HRI researchers and participants with HRI design experience used our tools to improve an existing interaction flow of a service robot. We conducted semi-structured interviews after each workshop session with a focus to evaluate the tool's *ease of understanding*, *informativeness*, and *ease of incorporating into existing designs*, as well as to collect suggestions of improvement from our participants.

4.1   Participants

Four HRI designers (F = 1, M = 3) unrelated to this research were recruited for the workshop sessions. The participants filled in a questionnaire on their knowledge background and past experience, where they were asked to rate their familiarity with the topics of robotics and relevant technology, HRI theory and technology, and HRI design. The scale ranged from "no knowledge", "acquainted with the topic", "familiar with the topic", and "professional/expert knowledge". Participants are also asked whether they had experience on designing HRI in general, and in particular designing HRI for a specific service scenario.

All participants reported varying knowledge in the three topics. In terms of robotics and relevant technology, two participants reported to be "acquainted with the topic", one reported as "familiar", and one of them "professional/expert level knowledge". In terms of HRI theory and technology, two of the participants reported "acquainted with the topic", one "familiar", and one "professional/expert". In terms of HRI design, two of the participants rated their knowledge as "acquainted with the topic", and two rated "familiar". One participant reported no experience in designing HRI. For the other three participants who had experience, two had designed HRI for a specific service context, among whom one had professional experience.

4.2   Procedure

The workshop sessions were conducted online using FigJam,[1] an collaborative whiteboard application. Participants took part in the workshop individually. The

---

[1] https://www.figma.com/figjam/.

workshop begins with an introduction to the general theme and procedures. Participants were then shown two videos of different robot receptionists performing greeting and guidance service in an office environment,[2] in order to establish context.

Participants went through two introductory steps, introducing the types of learning tasks, and the challenges of personalized knowledge learning. At each step the facilitator introduces the concepts with a visual aid, followed by guiding the participants through a warm-up exercise, where they brainstorm examples of the concepts just discussed, to familiarize the participants with their usage. For the design toolkit, the facilitator gave an overview of the cards, and introduced one of the cards in detail as an example. The participants are then given time to read all of the cards, and facilitator answered their questions as needed.

After the introduction, the participants are given a task two improve an existing greet and guidance HRI, extracted from the two demo videos the participants saw at the beginning. They are provided with a interaction flowchart depicting the design, and instructed to complete the tasks in two steps. In the first step, participants went through the HRI process, trying to identify potential challenges related to personalized knowledge learning.

Finally, participants filled in a questionnaire asking them to evaluate the informativeness, ease of understanding, usefulness, and ease of applying into existing HRI designs. The questions are listed in Fig. 3. Similar questions were then discussed in an semi-structured interview that follows.

4.3   Results

The questionnaire results were plotted and shown in Fig. 3. Overall, participants unanimously agree that the toolkit helped enhance their understanding of the HRI design issues related to personalized knowledge learning, and that the cards are presented in a manner that is easy to understand. Participants generally agree that the cards can be useful in improving the quality of HRI design (mean = 4.75, sd = 0.5), and that the patterns presented can be relatively easily incorporated into existing HRI designs (mean = 1.25, sd = 0.5).

The interview recordings (67 min in total) were transcribed and analyzed through thematic analysis by iterative coding using ATLAS.ti.[3] During the first iteration, quotations were extracted for any comments, suggestions, reasoning, and expression of judgement. The quotations were open-coded, and the codes were grouped according to themes. In the end, three major themes were identified, the details and implication of which will be discussed in the following section.

---

[2] The videos are available at https://www.youtube.com/watch?v=diid3b25CbM and https://www.youtube.com/watch?v=LT4G161ImqE. An archived version is also available at the project repository https://github.com/tongji-cdi/design-learning-hri.

[3] https://atlasti.com/.

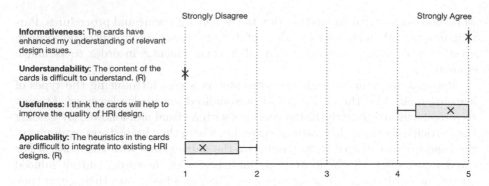

Fig. 3. Questionnaire results. Questions labeled (R) are asked in a reversed manner to improve reliability.

5 Discussion

Our interview with participants provided a more in-depth look into the effects, pitfalls, and future potential of the toolkit. We summarize and discuss notable themes that resulted from our thematic analysis below.

5.1 Aiding Ideation

Participants reported how the toolkit helped their ideation process in the task. In terms of the *challenges* cards, participants noted that the challenges presented in the toolkit helped them gain understanding of the design task and discover potential problems. P3 remarked that it helped to gain a deeper understanding of the problem. P4 (who claimed expert knowledge on robotics and related technologies) commented that although he had been aware of most of the challenges individually, seeing them together in the toolkit is still very helpful. P1 described the challenges as a "checklist" that could help systematically check for potential problems in an HRI design. This suggests that the toolkit helps provide a more structured way of approaching the design task.

In terms of the *patterns* cards, participants expressed varying levels of satisfaction. Most participants described situations where the ideas in the patterns are new to them, and helped them generate solutions in the workshop. P1 noted the value of *socially-assisted robotics* in real world scenarios is not only functional, but also emotional, by referring to past experience in designing HRI for delivery robots.

> "(In the case of a door malfunction) the robot would ask a nearby pedestrian, 'can you help me close my door?' ... People are happy to help. When we conducted interviews, people would say they helped the robot. It made them feel more trusting towards the robot." (P1)

P4 thinks that the example given in *isolation* and *describe uncertainty* provided new ideas outside of technical solutions.

"(In my past solutions) the robot used multi-modal information to try to recognize the users. But I think making this into a game to confirm identity is a very good way as well. ... I did not consider how to communicate it to users when encountering uncertainty. I think it is a good way and opens up many possibilities." (P4)

However, participants also noted cases where the toolkit was ineffective in aiding ideation. P2 mentioned that it felt restrictive that *isolation* was the only pattern in *multiple parties*, and expressed reluctance to use patterns in one category to address another challenge, even in cases he thought that they were applicable. He attributed the reluctance to a strong sense of categorization due to the visual design of the cards.

Overall, comments from the participants suggest that the toolkit was effective in aiding ideation from three aspects. First, the toolkit informs HRI designers of potential challenges and solutions, therefore enhancing their understanding of the design task. Second, by enumerating challenges in HRI design for personalized knowledge learning, the toolkit provides a structured way of discovering potential flaws in a design. Third, patterns in the toolkit highlights potential "designerly" solutions outside of technical ones, and may help broaden the search space for a most suitable solution under given service scenarios.

The comments also highlight problems with the current toolkit. First, the number of patterns may be lacking, so that it restricts the ideation of designers. Second, the visual design could be improved so that it remains informative of the connection between challenges and patterns, but also does not enforce a correspondence.

5.2   Ways of Using the Toolkit

During the workshop process, in addition to the general two-step process instructed by the facilitator, participants demonstrated creative ways of using the toolkit.

First of all, multiple participants used patterns across categories. P1 saw the challenges as inspirations, and used it to check for problems in the HRI design, while believing that the connection between challenges and patterns are unimportant. P4 held similar views, additionally pointing out that multiple challenges can arise in the same interaction step in the design, and highlighting the need for new patterns.

"(Reception robot meeting new people) is a case of *open world* and *multiple parties* combined... What are the patterns to deal with two challenges at once? ... I think this is a problem of '1 + 1 > 2.' " (P4)

Participants also combined multiple patterns. In the case above, P4 proposed to combine *socially-assisted robotics* and *isolation*, engaging new users one by one while sending messages to office members for information and clarification at the same time.

Another interesting observation, made by P2, is that some challenges has pairs of "direct" methods and "indirect" methods as patterns. P2 then used this intuition to help generate ideas for dealing with other challenges.

"*Open world* and *user acceptance* each had two patterns. One of them is more direct (in the way of asking), and the other is more indirect. After I realized this, when I look at other problems, I would also think whether there are direct or indirect ways of addressing this challenge." (P2)

To summarize, comments in this theme highlights the potential for elements in the toolkit to restructure and recombine. This indicates that both the challenges and patterns supports a certain degree of flexibility in the way of use, which we think is desirable for a design toolkit. Meanwhile, this also highlights a need of further structuring of the patterns, and doing so may enable designers to expand the patterns during the design process as well.

5.3 Future Directions

Participants also suggested future directions as to how to improve the design toolkit. Some participants pointed out that some patterns appeared commonplace. P1 noted that *just ask* seemed to be the default solution and need not be included. P2 and P3 held similar opinions towards *multiple choices*. P3 also highlighted similarities between *hands-on* and existing solutions in fingerprint and face data collection, but thinks that it may still need to be included in the toolkit.

The need for better wording is also mentioned multiple times. P1 expressed confusion about the name "open world" and why it is a challenge, citing that intuitively all reasoning of humans are open-world. P2 considers the prompts in the *patterns* cards too abstract, yet the examples that follow are too concrete. P2 suggests adding a "intermediate-level description", such as a description of the general interaction process of a pattern. When asked which part he focused on the most during the task, P2 said he mostly focused on reading the examples given on the cards. Meanwhile, P3 commented that the prompts are helpful for verifying whether he correctly understood the pattern, and the examples were mostly used to help understanding the core idea. P3 said he spent half of the time reading the prompts.

P2 also stressed the need for real-world testing. P1 echoed this point by providing detailed accounts of unanticipated ways of interacting with a delivery robot observed in her field studies. These comments highlight a need for implementing the patterns under concrete scenarios and studying the extent of their effects.

In combination with the themes discussed above, several future directions for the design toolkit can be identified. First, the design and wording of existing cards can be improved, in terms of using more understandable wording, providing additional explanation of the patterns, and removing unnecessary emphasis on the categorization of patterns. Second, the design patterns could be refined by removing commonplace practices and include more cases from both the literature and existing artifacts. Third, future research could look into constructing a framework to systematically categorize and generate the patterns. Finally, HRI designers should be invited to contribute to the toolkit by presenting artifacts, developing patterns, as well as implementing and testing existing patterns.

6   Conclusion

This paper presented a toolkit aimed to help the design of social human-robot interactions for learning personalized knowledge. Our preliminary evaluation shows its ability for aiding ideation and the potential for flexible ways of use. However, we note that the development and evaluation of a design toolkit are never-ending, and require application in the real world. Our future work lies in the continued refinement of the toolkit through analysis of emerging artifacts, especially patterns embedded within commercial robot products and concrete HRI scenarios. Future research should also look into constructing a framework to systematically categorize and help generate these patterns. Finally, HRI designers should be invited and enabled to contribute to the toolkit by presenting artifacts, developing toolkit content, as well as implementing and testing existing ones.

References

1. Alves-Oliveira, P., et al.: Collection of Metaphors for Human-Robot Interaction, pp. 1366–1379. Association for Computing Machinery, New York, NY, USA (2021). https://doi.org/10.1145/3461778.3462060
2. Cakmak, M., Chao, C., Thomaz, A.L.: Designing interactions for robot active learners. IEEE Trans. Autonom. Mental Dev. **2**(2), 108–118 (2010)
3. Cakmak, M., Thomaz, A.L.: Designing robot learners that ask good questions. In: Proceedings of the Seventh Annual ACM/IEEE International Conference on Human-Robot Interaction - HRI 2012, p. 17. ACM Press, Boston, Massachusetts, USA (2012). https://doi.org/10.1145/2157689.2157693,http://dl.acm.org/citation.cfm?doid=2157689.2157693
4. Chao, C., Cakmak, M., Thomaz, A.L.: Transparent active learning for robots. In: 2010 5th ACM/IEEE International Conference on Human-Robot Interaction (HRI), pp. 317–324. IEEE, Osaka, Japan, March 2010. https://doi.org/10.1109/HRI.2010.5453178, http://ieeexplore.ieee.org/document/5453178/
5. Diprose, J.P., Plimmer, B., MacDonald, B.A., Hosking, J.G.: How People Naturally Describe Robot Behaviour, New Zealand, p. 9 (2012)
6. Fang, R., Doering, M., Chai, J.Y.: Embodied collaborative referring expression generation in situated human-robot interaction. In: Proceedings of the Tenth Annual ACM/IEEE International Conference on Human-Robot Interaction, pp. 271–278 (2015)
7. Fong, T., Thorpe, C., Baur, C.: Robot, asker of questions. Robot. Autonom. Syst. **42**(3), 235–243 (2003). https://doi.org/10.1016/S0921-8890(02)00378-0, https://www.sciencedirect.com/science/article/pii/S0921889002003780, socially Interactive Robots

8. Gervasio, M., Yeh, E., Myers, K.: Learning to ask the right questions to help a learner learn. In: Proceedings of the 15th International Conference on Intelligent User Interfaces - IUI 2011, p. 135. ACM Press, Palo Alto, CA, USA (2011). https://doi.org/10.1145/1943403.1943425, http://portal.acm.org/citation.cfm?doid=1943403.1943425

9. Javia, B., Cimiano, P.: A knowledge-based architecture supporting declarative action representation for manipulation of everyday objects. In: Proceedings of the 3rd Workshop on Model-Driven Robot Software Engineering, pp. 40–46 (2016)

10. Kahn, P.H., et al.: Design patterns for sociality in human-robot interaction. In: Proceedings of the 3rd ACM/IEEE International Conference on Human Robot Interaction, pp. 97–104. HRI 2008. Association for Computing Machinery, New York, NY, USA (2008). https://doi.org/10.1145/1349822.1349836

11. Kattepur, A.: RoboPlanner: autonomous robotic action planning via knowledge graph queries. In: Proceedings of the 34th ACM/SIGAPP Symposium on Applied Computing, pp. 953–956 (2019)

12. Lemaignan, S., Warnier, M., Sisbot, E.A., Clodic, A., Alami, R.: Artificial cognition for social human-robot interaction: an implementation. Artif. Intell. **247**, 45–69 (2017). https://doi.org/10.1016/j.artint.2016.07.002, https://www.sciencedirect.com/science/article/pii/S0004370216300790

13. Lockerd, A., Breazeal, C.: Tutelage and socially guided robot learning. In: 2004 IEEE/RSJ International Conference on Intelligent Robots and Systems (IROS) (IEEE Cat. No. 04CH37566), vol. 4, pp. 3475–3480. IEEE, Sendai, Japan (2004). https://doi.org/10.1109/IROS.2004.1389954, http://ieeexplore.ieee.org/document/1389954/

14. Lupetti, M., Bendor, R., Giaccardi, E.: Robot citizenship: a design perspective. In: Colombo, S., Alonso, M.B., Lim, Y., Chen, L., Djajadiningrat, T. (eds.) Design and Semantics of Form and Movement, pp. 87–95 (2019). green Open Access added to TU Delft Institutional Repository 'You share, we take care!' - Taverne project https://www.openaccess.nl/en/you-share-we-take-care. Otherwise as indicated in the copyright section: the publisher is the copyright holder of this work and the author uses the Dutch legislation to make this work public.; DeSforM 2019: Beyond Intelligence; Conference date: 09-10-2019 Through 09-10-2019

15. Lupetti, M.L., Zaga, C., Cila, N.: Designerly Ways of knowing in HRI: broadening the scope of design-oriented HRI through the concept of intermediate-level knowledge. In: Proceedings of the 2021 ACM/IEEE International Conference on Human-Robot Interaction, pp. 389–398. ACM, Boulder CO USA, March 2021. https://doi.org/10.1145/3434073.3444668, https://dl.acm.org/doi/10.1145/3434073.3444668

16. Löwgren, J.: Annotated portfolios and other forms of intermediate-level knowledge. Interactions **20**(1), 30–34 (2013)

17. Munzer, T., Toussaint, M., Lopes, M.: Preference learning on the execution of collaborative human-robot tasks. In: 2017 IEEE International Conference on Robotics and Automation (ICRA), pp. 879–885. IEEE, Singapore, Singapore, May 2017. https://doi.org/10.1109/ICRA.2017.7989108, http://ieeexplore.ieee.org/document/7989108/

18. Muthugala, M.A.V.J., Jayasekara, A.G.B.P.: MIRob: an intelligent service robot that learns from interactive discussions while handling uncertain information in user instructions. In: 2016 Moratuwa Engineering Research Conference (MERCon), pp. 397–402. IEEE, Moratuwa, April 2016. https://doi.org/10.1109/MERCon.2016.7480174, https://ieeexplore.ieee.org/document/7480174/

19. Olivares-Alarcos, A., et al.: A review and comparison of ontology-based approaches to robot autonomy. Knowl. Eng. Rev. **34**, e29 (2019). https://doi.org/10.1017/S0269888919000237
20. Rosenthal, S., Dey, A.K., Veloso, M.: How robots' questions affect the accuracy of the human responses. In: RO-MAN 2009 - The 18th IEEE International Symposium on Robot and Human Interactive Communication, pp. 1137–1142. IEEE, Toyama, Japan, September 2009. https://doi.org/10.1109/ROMAN.2009.5326291, http://ieeexplore.ieee.org/document/5326291/
21. Rossi, S., Ferland, F., Tapus, A.: User profiling and behavioral adaptation for HRI: a survey. Patt. Recogn. Lett. **99**, 3–12 (2017). https://doi.org/10.1016/j.patrec.2017.06.002, https://www.sciencedirect.com/science/article/pii/S0167865517301976, user Profiling and Behavior Adaptation for Human-Robot Interaction
22. Sauppé, A., Mutlu, B.: Design patterns for exploring and prototyping human-robot interactions. In: Proceedings of the 32nd Annual ACM Conference on Human Factors in Computing Systems - CHI 2014, pp. 1439–1448. ACM Press, Toronto, Ontario, Canada (2014). https://doi.org/10.1145/2556288.2557057, http://dl.acm.org/citation.cfm?doid=2556288.2557057
23. Zhang, S., Wang, Z., Chen, C., Dai, Y., Ye, L., Sun, X.: Patterns for representing knowledge graphs to communicate situational knowledge of service robots. In: Proceedings of the 2021 CHI Conference on Human Factors in Computing Systems. CHI 2021. Association for Computing Machinery, New York, NY, USA (2021). https://doi.org/10.1145/3411764.3445767

Author Index